Oracle9*i* Instant PL/SQL Scripts

Kevin Loney, Megh Thakkar, and Rachel Carmichael

Osborne **McGraw-Hill**

New York   Chicago   San Francisco
Lisbon   London   Madrid   Mexico City   Milan
New Delhi   San Juan   Seoul   Singapore   Sydney   Toronto

Osborne/**McGraw-Hill**
2600 Tenth Street
Berkeley, California 94710
U.S.A.

To arrange bulk purchase discounts for sales promotions, premiums, or fund-raisers, please contact Osborne/**McGraw-Hill** at the above address. For information on translations or book distributors outside the U.S.A., please see the International Contact Information page immediately following the index of this book.

Oracle9i Instant PL/SQL Scripts

1234567890 CUS CUS 01987654321

Book p/n 0-07-213219-1 and CD p/n 0-07-213220-5
parts of
ISBN 0-07-213218-3

Publisher
  Brandon A. Nordin

Vice President & Associate Publisher
  Scott Rogers

Associate Acquisitions Editor
  Lisa McClain

Senior Project Editor
  Pamela Woolf

Technical Editor
  Mitch Flatland

Copy Editor
  Lisa Theobald

Proofreader
  Sossity Smith

Indexer
  Valerie Perry

Computer Designers
  Tabitha M. Cagan, Elizabeth Jang,
  Jim Kussow, Lauren McCarthy

Illustrators
  Michael Mueller, Lyssa Wald

Cover Series Design
  Damore Johann Design Inc.

Series Design
  Peter Hancik, Roberta Steele

This book was composed with Corel VENTURA™ Publisher.

Contents at a Glance

The following chapters are on the accompanying CD:

8 Database Management

9 Managing Java in the Database

A PL/SQL, Dynamic PL/SQL, and Procedures

Contents

The following chapters are on the accompanying CD:

8 Database Management

9 Managing Java in the Database

A PL/SQL, Dynamic PL/SQL, and Procedures

Acknowledgments

A number of people have helped me directly or indirectly in reaching my goals in life. Writing a book such as this not only provides me with a lot of personal satisfaction but also gives me an opportunity to thank the various people who have contributed to my accomplishments.

Thanks to Michael Jordan, for being such a great source of inspiration, his determination both on the basketball court and off the court in real life has provided me with invaluable strength at various critical stages throughout my career.

I would like to thank my coauthors Kevin Loney and Rachel Carmichael for their contribution to the book and making valuable suggestions.

A very special thanks to my wife, Komal and my son, Varun, for their patience during this long period of extra stress. Words can't express how much I appreciate their love and understanding. Thanks to my brothers, Krishnaraj, Jayraj and Ramraj for their support.

Thanks to John Symington and Tracy Dunkelberger for their encouragement.

Thanks to the readers of my past books for reading my work and providing useful comments and suggestions. I have tried to incorporate most of these tips and suggestions in the book.

Thanks to people like Eyal Aronoff, Mark Gurry, Jonathan Lewis, Rich Niemiec, Marlene Theriault, Steven Feuerstein, and many others in the Oracle community who have shared their knowledge with me.

Thanks to the wonderful group at Osborne/McGraw-Hill: Mitchell Flatland for his reviews and valuable suggestions, Pamela Woolf, Lisa Theobald, Paulina Pobocha, Jessica Wilson and Ross Doll for converting my drafts into readable prose, and everyone else on the team for working hard with very tight deadlines, and especially Lisa McClain for pulling it all together.

Introduction

Oracle professionals responsible for managing and developing Oracle systems face a number of issues on a daily basis, for example, ensuring that the performance of the system is acceptable, system is available for users, response time is adequate, database objects are sized properly and have room for growth, resources are optimally utilized, database structures are documented as well as have well-tested backups to quickly recover from a system failure. Most Oracle professionals have a "bag of tools" they have collected from a number of sources and use these on an on-going basis to accomplish their tasks. However, requirements and demands placed on the system increase and more and more time is spent by the DBAs and developers in writing and maintaining the scripts that they have written for diagnosing the problems instead of focusing on resolving the issues. Similarly, changes are made on the fly to Oracle systems to fix an urgent problem and soon these "minor" changes are forgotten because of lack of documentation. Eventually the management of such Oracle systems becomes a nightmare even for the seasoned DBAs, and a pose a special challenge to an Oracle DBA that has just started managing these not-so-well documented systems.

This book contains a comprehensive collection of SQL and PL/SQL scripts, organized into chapters by function. The scripts provided are intended to be useful to professionals of varying levels of expertise who are responsible for the administration, management, and development of Oracle systems. Oracle DBAs as well as developers will benefit from the information discussed in this book. Within each chapter, you will see scripts you can use to manage your data or the database structures affected by your data. All the major versions of Oracle in use—Oracle7.x through Oracle9i—are covered by the scripts. Each script is fully documented, and sample results are shown. After reviewing a sample script, you should be able to

◆ Understand how the script works

◆ Customize the script with confidence

◆ Act properly on the script's results

The scripts in this book come from a variety of sources: some originated within Oracle support, some came from the authors' personal scripts archives, and many were written specifically for this book. Because of the detailed annotations provided for each script, this book is more than just a manual accompanying a library of scripts on a CD-ROM; it is a set of examples of coding styles and data retrieval that have wide-ranging application within your Oracle systems. Thus, the utility of the scripts is twofold: in their content and in their style.

The book is organized as follows:

- **Chapter 1, Oracle9i—Specific Scripts**   Shows you scripts written specifically to deal with the most important new features introduced in Oracle9i such as non-standard block sizes and undo space management

- **Chapter 2, Scripts for Managing Performance**   Shows you scripts dealing with database performance management issues

- **Chapter 3, Transaction Management**   Shows you scripts dealing with transaction management activities such as locking, rollback, and redo issues

- **Chapter 4, Data Management**   Sshows you scripts dealing with object dependencies and data management

- **Chapter 5, Object Management**   Shows you scripts dealing with the management of various types of database objects as well as the management of jobs

- **Chapter 6, Space Management**   Shows you scripts dealing with space management issues in the database

- **Chapter 7, User Management**   Show you scripts dealing with the management of users and roles

- **Chapter 8, Database Management**   Show you scripts that can be used to regenerate tablespaces and databases. *This chapter is only available on the CD-ROM.*

- **Chapter 9, Managing Java in the Database**   Shows you scripts that can be used to manage Java classes, sources, resources as well as the Java Virtual Machine of Oracle. *This chapter is only available on the CD-ROM.*

- **Appendix A, PL/SQL, Dynamic PL/SQL, and Procedures**   Contains descriptions of PL/SQL, stored procedures, dynamic PL/SQL as well as the new native PL/SQL compilation feature of Oracle9i. *This appendix is only available on the CD-ROM.*

You should use the annotations to understand the scripts in this archive. The better you understand the scripts, their structure, and their output, the more useful they will be.

Oracle9*i*—
Specific Scripts

db_props.sql

sp_params.sql

stored_settings.sql

undo_stats.sql

db_cache_advice.sql

non_std_blksize.sql

racle9i provides a number of new features, such as the use of server parameter files, undo tablespaces, native PL/SQL compilation, and non-standard block sizes. The scripts that appear in this chapter address features that are specific to Oracle9i. A number of these scripts provide information about how your Oracle9i database makes use of Oracle's new features.

The major scripts covered in this chapter are shown in Table 1-1.

NOTE

Other scripts used in this book can be used for Oracle 9i as well as Oracle7.x and Oracle8.x.

Database Properties

In Oracle9i, you can assign a default temporary tablespace for the database, which allows database users access to a default temporary tablespace other than the SYSTEM tablespace. Similarly, the database export views may be of a version different from Oracle9i. These and many such database properties can be viewed by querying the DATABASE_PROPERTIES data dictionary view.

Script	Description
db_props.sql	Determine the database properties in effect
sp_params.sql	Determine the parameters set by the use of a server parameter file
stored_settings.sql	Determine how native PL/SQL compilation is used
undo_stats.sql	Show the undo tablespace statistics
db_cache_advice.sql	Obtain advice regarding the use of database buffer cache size
non_std_blksize.sql	Obtain information about non-standard block sizes in use

TABLE 1-1.   Major Scripts in This Chapter

Determine the Database Properties in Effect

The following script can be used to display the database properties in effect:

db_props.sql

```
REM
REM db_props.sql
REM This script can be used for Oracle9.x and above
REM This script shows the various database properties
REM
set echo off feedback off pagesize 50 term off linesize 80
column Property_Name format a20
column Property_Value format a40
column Description format a80
spool db_props.txt
select Property_Name,
       Property_Value,
       Description
from database_properties;
spool off
set feedback 6 pagesize 24 term on
clear columns
```

Sample output of executing the script db_props.sql is shown here:

```
PROPERTY_NAME            PROPERTY_VALUE
------------------       -----------------------------------------
DESCRIPTION
-----------------------------------------------------------------
DICT.BASE                2
dictionary base tables version #

DEFAULT_TEMP_TABLESP TEMP
ACE
Name of default temporary tablespace

DBTIMEZONE               -04:00
DB time zone

NLS_LANGUAGE             AMERICAN
Language
```

NLS_TERRITORY   AMERICA
Territory

NLS_CURRENCY $
Local currency

NLS_ISO_CURRENCY   AMERICA
ISO currency

NLS_NUMERIC_CHARACTE   .,
RS
Numeric characters

NLS_CHARACTERSET   US7ASCII
Character set

NLS_CALENDAR   GREGORIAN
Calendar system

NLS_DATE_FORMAT   DD-MON-RR
Date format

NLS_DATE_LANGUAGE   AMERICAN
Date language

NLS_SORT   BINARY
Linguistic definition

NLS_TIME_FORMAT   HH.MI.SSXFF AM
Time format

NLS_TIMESTAMP_FORMAT DD-MON-RR HH.MI.SSXFF AM
Time stamp format

NLS_TIME_TZ_FORMAT   HH.MI.SSXFF AM TZR
Time with timezone format

NLS_TIMESTAMP_TZ_FOR DD-MON-RR HH.MI.SSXFF AM TZR
MAT
Timestamp with timezone format

NLS_DUAL_CURRENCY $
Dual currency symbol

```
NLS_COMP                BINARY
NLS comparison

NLS_LENGTH_SEMANTICS BYTE
NLS length semantics

NLS_NCHAR_CONV_EXCP  FALSE
NLS conversion exception

NLS_NCHAR_CHARACTERS UTF8
ET
NCHAR Character set

NLS_RDBMS_VERSION    9.0.1.0.0
RDBMS version for NLS parameters

GLOBAL_DB_NAME       HY901.OZ.QUEST.COM
Global database name

EXPORT_VIEWS_VERSION 8
Export views revision #
```

Server Parameter File (spfile)

The *server parameter file* (also referred to as *stored parameter file*) is a new feature in Oracle9i that can be used in a Real Application Clusters (RAC) environment for auto-tuning an Oracle9i database. (The auto-tuning feature of Oracle9i is discussed in more detail in Chapter 2.) The server parameter file allows you to store a binary copy of your initialization parameter file, which allows you to make permanent dynamic changes to parameters within the database while changing certain parameters in memory only.

PROGRAMMER'S NOTE   *In an Oracle RAC environment, a server parameter file can be shared between instances.*

Determine Parameters in the spfile

sp_params.sql

The **Alter System** command can be used to change spfile parameters. It is also possible to specify the scope of parameters to determine whether to change a parameter in memory, in your spfile, or in both. In addition, you can also define the Oracle instance *system ID* (SID) to change instance specific parameters.

For example, the following code specifies that the job_queue_processes parameter should be set to 60 in memory as well as in the spfile. The specified change applies to the Oracle SID O910.

```
SQL> alter system set job_queue_processes=60 scope=both sid=O910;
```

The parameter job_queue_processes can be reset back to its default setting as follows:

```
SQL> alter system reset job_queue_processes scope=both sid=O910;
```

The following script displays the parameters in the spfile:

```
REM
REM sp_params.sql
REM This script can be used for Oracle9.x and above
REM This script shows the parameters of the spfile
REM
set echo off feedback off pagesize 50 term off linesize 80
column SID format a20
column Name heading "Parameter Name" format a20
column Value heading "Parameter Value" format a80
column Update_Comment heading "Comments for last update" format a80
spool sp_params.txt
select SID,
       Name,
       Value,
       Update_Comment
from v$spparameter
where Isspecified = 'TRUE';
spool off
set feedback 6 pagesize 24 term on
clear columns
```

Sample output of executing the script sp_params.sql is shown here:

```
SID                     Parameter Name
-------------------- --------------------
Parameter Value
-----------------------------------------------------------------
Comments for last update
-----------------------------------------------------------------
*                       processes
150
```

```
*                       timed_statistics
TRUE


*                       shared_pool_size
104857600


*                       large_pool_size
1048576


*                       java_pool_size
104857600


*                       resource_manager_plan
SYSTEM_PLAN


*                       control_files
/oradata1/0910/control01.ctl


*                       control_files
/oradata2/0910/control02.ctl


*                       control_files
/oradata3/0910/control03.ctl


*                       db_block_size
8192


*                       db_cache_size
52428800


*                       compatible
9.0.0
```

```
*                       fast_start_mttr_target
300


*                       undo_management
AUTO


*                       undo_tablespace
UNDOTBS


*                       remote_login_passwor
                        dfile
EXCLUSIVE


*                       db_domain
oz.meghmc.com


*                       instance_name
0910


*                       dispatchers
(PROTOCOL=TCP)(SER=MODOSE)


*                       dispatchers
(PROTOCOL=TCP)(PRE=oracle.aurora.server.GiopServer)


*                       dispatchers
(PROTOCOL=TCP)(PRE=oracle.aurora.server.SGiopServer)

*                       background_dump_dest
/oraadmin/0910/bdump


*                       user_dump_dest
/oraadmin/0910/udump
```

```
*                    core_dump_dest
/oraadmin/0910/cdump


*                    sort_area_size
524288


*                    db_name
0910


*                    open_cursors
300
```

Native Compilation of PL/SQL Program Units

In Oracle versions prior to Oracle9i, all PL/SQL stored program units are compiled to p-code (pseudocode); the resulting p-code is stored in the database and interpreted at runtime. This results in portable solutions, but the performance is not necessarily great, because interpreted languages are usually slower than natively compiled languages. Oracle9i provides the ability to compile PL/SQL code natively into shared libraries. When the PL/SQL program unit is invoked at runtime, the corresponding shared libraries are loaded and executed.

Native compilation of PL/SQL program units, if properly configured, is transparent to both the user compiling a PL/SQL program unit and to the end user invoking that PL/SQL program unit.

PROGRAMMER'S NOTE *For native compilation to work, a C compiler must be installed on the same host, because Oracle9i generates C code corresponding to the PL/SQL, code and then compiles and links the resulting C code into shared libraries using the compiler and linker for that platform.*

A number of initialization parameters are used with native PL/SQL compilation:

♦ **plsql_compiler_flags** Determines whether PL/SQL code is natively compiled or interpreted. You can also specify whether to include debug information. Possible values are Interpreted, Native, Debug, and Non_debug. The default values are Interpreted and "Non_debug. This parameter can be set at both the system level (using the **ALTER SYSTEM** command) and session level (using the **ALTER SESSION** command).

PROGRAMMER'S NOTE *Debugging of natively compiled PL/SQL code is not yet supported in Oracle9i.*

◆ **plsql_native_make_file_name**   Specifies the full path to the makefile used to create the shared libraries that contain the natively compiled PL/SQL code. This parameter can be set only at the system level. If the plsql_compiler_flags parameter is set to NATIVE, this parameter must be used. Set this parameter to the full pathname of the makefile provided with Oracle9i. On UNIX, the makefile provided with Oracle9i is called spnc_makefile.mk and resides in $ORACLE_HOME/plsql.

◆ **plsql_native_make_utility**   Specifies the full path of the make utility that is used to process the makefile specified via plsql_native_make_file_name. This parameter can be set only at the system level. If the plsql_compiler_flags parameter is set to NATIVE, this parameter must be used.

◆ **plsql_native_library_dir**   Specifies the directory name used to store the shared libraries that contain the natively compiled PL/SQL code. This parameter can be set only at the system level. If the plsql_compiler_flags parameter is set to NATIVE, this parameter must be used. The "oracle" user must have write permissions on this directory.

◆ **plsql_native_c_copiler**   Specifies the full pathname to the C compiler used to compile the C code that corresponds to the PL/SQL program unit being compiled. This parameter can be set only at the system level.

◆ **plsql_native_linker**   Specifies the full pathname to the linker used to link the objects generated from the C code and generate the shared libraries. This parameter can be set only at the system level.

◆ **plsql_native_library_subdir_count**   Specifies the number of subdirectories to be created in the directory specified by the plsql_native_library_dir parameter. The default value is 0. It is recommended that this parameter be set if the number of PL/SQL program units to be natively compiled exceeds 10,000. Not setting this parameter appropriately can result in performance problems with certain file operations.

PROGRAMMER'S NOTE   *Parameters related to native PL/SQL compilation can be set in the init.ora file, and if a stored parameter file (spfile) exists, any **alter system** command executed to set these parameters will persist the changes to the spfile and will be retained even if the instance is restarted.*

Determine Compilation Settings of Stored PL/SQL Units

stored_settings.sql   When you use natively compiled PL/SQL code, you may want to verify whether the appropriate parameters have been set. You can determine the current settings via the **show parameters plsql** command in SQL*Plus or by querying the v$parameter table directly. The following script will tell you whether or not a PL/SQL program unit was created as natively compiled:

```
REM
REM stored_settings.sql
REM This script can be used for Oracle9.x and above
REM This script lists information about
REM    persistent parameter settings for stored PL/SQL units
REM
set echo off feedback off pagesize 50 term on
set linesize 80 verify off
accept own prompt "Enter Owner: "
accept objname prompt "Enter Object Name: "
set term off
spool stored_settings.txt
select Owner,
       Object_Name,
       Object_Type,
       Param_Name,
       Param_Value
from DBA_STORED_SETTINGS
where Owner like UPPER('&&own')
and   Object_Name like UPPER('&&objname')
order by Owner, Object_Name, Object_Type, Param_Name;
spool off
set feedback 6 pagesize 24 term on verify on
undefine own
undefine objname
```

Sample output of executing the script stored_settings.sql is shown here:

```
OWNER                            OBJECT_NAME                     OBJECT_TYPE
-------------------------------- ------------------------------- -------------
PARAM_NAME
----------------------------------
PARAM_VALUE
---------------------------------------------------------------------------

MEGH                             MT_IW_CHANGE_NAME_TABLE         PROCEDURE
nls_length_semantics
BYTE

MEGH                             MT_IW_CHANGE_NAME_TABLE         PROCEDURE
plsql_compiler_flags
INTERPRETED,NON_DEBUG
```

MEGH nls_length_semantics BYTE	MT_IW_CHECK_ORA_SPACE_PKG	PACKAGE
MEGH plsql_compiler_flags INTERPRETED,NON_DEBUG	MT_IW_CHECK_ORA_SPACE_PKG	PACKAGE
MEGH nls_length_semantics BYTE	MT_IW_CHECK_ORA_SPACE_PKG	PACKAGE BODY
MEGH plsql_compiler_flags INTERPRETED,NON_DEBUG	MT_IW_CHECK_ORA_SPACE_PKG	PACKAGE BODY
MEGH nls_length_semantics BYTE	MT_IW_DROP_SEQ	PROCEDURE
MEGH plsql_compiler_flags INTERPRETED,NON_DEBUG	MT_IW_DROP_SEQ	PROCEDURE
MEGH nls_length_semantics BYTE	MT_IW_DROP_TABLE	PROCEDURE
MEGH plsql_compiler_flags INTERPRETED,NON_DEBUG	MT_IW_DROP_TABLE	PROCEDURE

As in earlier versions of Oracle, if change occurs in an object that some natively compiled PL/SQL program unit depends on, the PL/SQL module is invalidated. The next time the same PL/SQL program unit is executed, an attempt is made to revalidate/recompile the module. This recompilation occurs using the stored settings in the USER/ALL/DBA_STORED_SETTINGS data dictionary views. However, it should be noted that any time a PL/SQL module is explicitly compiled via **create or replace** or **alter...compile** command, the current setting for the session is used.

PROGRAMMER'S NOTE   *Natively compiled PL/SQL program units are dependent on their implementation shared libraries, but the database is unable to track such dependencies because the libraries reside on the file system and can be manipulated using operating-system commands. Also, shared libraries corresponding to a PL/SQL program unit are not automatically deleted when the program unit is dropped.*

Managing Undo Space

In versions prior to Oracle9i, the undo space is managed with the help of rollback segments. Oracle9i databases are capable of managing their own undo (rollback) space. Database administrators don't have to worry about planning and tuning the number and size of rollback segments or determine a strategy of assigning transactions to appropriate rollback segments. In addition, Oracle9i allows administrators to allocate their undo space in a single undo tablespace. This self managing of undo space allows Oracle to take care of issues such as undo block contention, consistent read retention, and utilization of undo space, so the database administrator doesn't have to spend a considerable amount of time working through these issues.

It should be noted, however, that you can still make use of rollback segments to manage undo space in an Oracle9i database. The UNDO_MANAGEMENT initialization parameter determines the method of managing undo space in use. If you use the rollback segment method for undo space management, you are using a *rollback segment undo (RBU) scheme,* and if you use the undo tablespace method for managing undo space, you are using the *system-management undo (SMU) scheme.*

The following initialization parameters control the management of undo space in an Oracle9i database:

- ◆ **UNDO_MANAGEMENT**   If set to auto, SMU scheme is in effect; if set to manual, RMU scheme is in effect. The default for Oracle9i is auto.

- ◆ **UNDO_TABLESPACE**   This dynamically changeable parameter specifies the undo tablespace to use in an SMU-managed Oracle9i database. When UNDO_MANAGEMENT is set to auto and the instance is started, the undo tablespace specified by UNDO_TABLESPACE is used. This undo tablespace should already have been created. If this parameter is omitted, the first available undo tablespace in the database is chosen; if none is available the SYSTEM rollback segment is used.

- ◆ **UNDO_RETENTION**   This dynamically changeable parameter specifies the length of time to retain undo. The default is 5 minutes.

- ◆ **UNDO_SUPRESS_ERROR**   This dynamically changeable parameter specifies whether or not error messages are to be generated if RMU SQL statements are issued while running the database in the SMU-mode. The default value of false indicates that error messages are not to be suppressed.

- ◆ **ROLLBACK_SEGMENTS**   When operating in the RMU mode, this parameter specifies the rollback segments to acquire at startup.

- ◆ **TRANSACTIONS**   When operating in the RMU mode, this parameter specifies the maximum number of concurrent transactions.

◆ **TRANSACTIONS_PER_ROLLBACK_SEGMENT**   When operating in the RMU mode, this parameter specifies the maximum number of concurrent transactions that each rollback segment is expected to handle.

◆ **MAX_ROLLBACK_SEGMENTS**   When operating in the RMU mode, this parameter specifies the maximum number of rollback segments that can be online for this instance.

undostats.sql

Determine Undo Space Consumption

The V$UNDOSTAT view can be used to monitor the effects of transaction execution on undo space in the current instance.

The following script shows how to obtain statistics about undo space consumption in the instance:

```
REM
REM undo_stats.sql
REM This script can be used for Oracle9.x and above
REM
set echo off feedback off pagesize 50 term off linesize 80
spool undo_stats.txt
select TO_CHAR(MIN(Begin_Time),'DD-MON-YYYY HH24:MI:SS')
                                "Begin Time",
        TO_CHAR(MAX(End_Time),'DD-MON-YYYY HH24:MI:SS')
                                "End Time",
        SUM(Undoblks)        "Total Undo Blocks Used",
        SUM(Txncount)        "Total Num Trans Exec",
        MAX(Maxquerylen)     "Longest Query(in secs)",
        MAX(Maxconcurrency)  "Highest Concurrent Trans Count",
        SUM(Ssolderrcnt),
        SUM(Nospaceerrcnt)
from V$UNDOSTAT;
spool off
set feedback 6 pagesize 24 term on
```

Sample output of running the script is shown here:

```
Begin Time             End Time               Total Undo Blocks Used
-------------------    -------------------    ----------------------
Total Num Trans Exec Longest Query(in secs) Highest Concurrent Trans Count
-------------------  ---------------------- ------------------------------
SUM(SSOLDERRCNT) SUM(NOSPACEERRCNT)
---------------- ------------------
11-JUL-2001 12:01:57 11-JUL-2001 12:28:12                       20
                  30                   11                            4
            0                    0
```

Obtaining Advice About Database Cache Size

In Oracle9i, the DB_CACHE_ADVICE parameter can be set to enable the prediction of the physical reads for database buffer cache of various sizes. DB_CACHE_ADVICE can have the following values:

- **OFF**   This is the default value. The OFF setting disables the generation of advice and also memory for advisory is not allocated.

- **READY**   This setting turns off the generation of advisory information but the memory allocated for the advisory is retained.

- **ON**   This setting enables advisory information to be generated. If you attempt to set the parameter to the ON state when it is already OFF, an error is generated. However, if the parameter is in the READY state and you set it to ON, the view V$DB_CACHE_ADVICE is reset and statistics are gathered to this newly refreshed view.

Predicting the Physical Read Factor

db_cache_advice.sql

Once the DB_CACHE_ADVICE parameter is set to ON, the V$DB_CACHE_ADVICE view can be queried to determine the *physical read factor* for various buffer cache sizes. The physical read factor is defined as follows:

```
Physical read factor=num_estimated_reads/num_actual_reads
```

The V$DB_CACHE_ADVICE view contains rows that predict the number of physical reads for the cache size corresponding to each row. The following script, when executed, will display the contents of the V$DB_CACHE_ADVICE view:

```
REM
REM db_cache_advice.sql
REM This script can be used for Oracle9.x and above
REM
column Id heading "Buffer Pool ID"
column Name heading "Buffer Pool Name"
set echo off feedback off pagesize 50 term off linesize 80
spool db_cache_advice.txt
select *
from V$DB_CACHE_ADVICE;
spool off
set feedback 6 pagesize 24 term on
clear columns
```

Sample output of executing the script is shown here:

```
Buffer Pool ID Buffer Pool Name      BLOCK_SIZE ADV SIZE_FOR_ESTIMATE
-------------- -------------------- ---------- --- ----------------
BUFFERS_FOR_ESTIMATE ESTD_PHYSICAL_READ_FACTOR ESTD_PHYSICAL_READS
-------------------- ------------------------- -------------------
             3 DEFAULT                    8192 ON            6.2031
                 794               3.4316                      1723

             3 DEFAULT                    8192 ON           12.4063
                1588               1.5979                       802

             3 DEFAULT                    8192 ON           18.6094
                2382               1.1023                       553

             3 DEFAULT                    8192 ON           24.8125
                3176                    1                       502

             3 DEFAULT                    8192 ON           31.0156
                3970                    1                       502

             3 DEFAULT                    8192 ON           37.2188
                4764                    1                       502

             3 DEFAULT                    8192 ON           43.4219
                5558                    1                       502

             3 DEFAULT                    8192 ON            49.625
                6352                    1                       502

             3 DEFAULT                    8192 ON           55.8281
                7146                    1                       502

             3 DEFAULT                    8192 ON           62.0313
                7940                    1                       502

             3 DEFAULT                    8192 ON           68.2344
                8734                    1                       502

             3 DEFAULT                    8192 ON           74.4375
                9528                    1                       502

             3 DEFAULT                    8192 ON           80.6406
               10322                    1                       502

             3 DEFAULT                    8192 ON           86.8438
               11116                    1                       502

             3 DEFAULT                    8192 ON           93.0469
```

11910	1	502
3 DEFAULT	8192 ON	99.25
12704	1	502
3 DEFAULT	8192 ON	105.4531
13498	1	502
3 DEFAULT	8192 ON	111.6563
14292	1	502
3 DEFAULT	8192 ON	117.8594
15086	1	502
3 DEFAULT	8192 ON	124.0625
15880	1	502

Working With Nonstandard Block Sizes

The DB_BLOCK_SIZE initialization parameter specifies the standard block size for the database. This block size is used in the SYSTEM tablespace and by default in other tablespaces. Oracle9i supports up to five additional non-standard block sizes. If a DB_BLOCK_SIZE is not specified, the default data block size is operating-system specific. The database block size cannot be changed after database creation; therefore, you should choose it properly. The standard database block size (as specified by DB_BLOCK_SIZE) should be chosen by using several considerations:

◆ Choose the most commonly used block size as the database block size.

◆ Choose the database block size to be a multiple of the operating system's block size.

◆ Understand the nature of transactions run against the database. Larger block sizes can help in decision support systems (DSS) and provide greater efficiency in disk and memory I/O.

It is possible that the nature of your applications is such that the "one size fits all" approach might not work for you. Oracle9i allows you to create tablespaces of nonstandard block sizes by using the **create tablespace** command and specifying the BLOCKSIZE clause. These non-standard block sizes can have any power of two values between 2K and 32K. It should be noted, however, that some platform-specific restrictions may prevent the use of certain sizes on some platforms. The use of multiple block sizes is particularly useful if you plan to transport tablespaces from one application environment to another.

Determine Non-Standard Block Sizes in Use

non_std_blksize.sql

To make use of multiple block sizes, you must configure sub-caches within the buffer cache area of the SGA for all of the non-standard block sizes that you plan to use. To use multiple block sizes in the database, the DB_CACHE_SIZE and at least one of DB_*n*K_CACHE_SIZE parameters must be set.

PROGRAMMER'S NOTE   *The performance of the buffer cache is determined by its size. Large buffer cache sizes generally reduce the number of disk reads and writes, but if set to a very large value, the cache may take up too much memory, resulting in paging and swapping.*

The DB_CACHE_SIZE specifies the size of the cache for a standard block size buffer (the standard block size itself is specified by DB_BLOCK_SIZE). The size and numbers of non-standard block size buffers is specified by the following dynamic parameters. Each parameter specifies the size of the buffer cache of the corresponding block size.

- ◆ DB_2K_CACHE_SIZE
- ◆ DB_4K_CACHE_SIZE
- ◆ DB_8K_CACHE_SIZE
- ◆ DB_16K_CACHE_SIZE
- ◆ DB_32K_CACHE_SIZE

PROGRAMMER'S NOTE   *The MAX_SGA_SIZE initialization parameter specifies the maximum size of the System Global Area (SGA) for the lifetime of the instance. Oracle9i allows you to change dynamically the initialization parameters affecting the size of the buffer caches, shared pool, and large pool but only to the extent that the sum of these sizes combined with the size of the other SGA components (fixed SGA, variable SGA, and redo log buffers) doesn't exceed the size specified by MAX_SGA_SIZE.*

The following script shows the tablespaces that are making use of non-standard block sizes:

```
REM
REM non_std_blksize.sql
REM This script can be used for Oracle9.x and above
REM
set echo off feedback off pagesize 50 term off linesize 80
spool non_std_blksize.txt
select Tablespace_Name,
       Block_Size
from DBA_TABLESPACES
where Block_Size != (select Value
                     from v$parameter
```

```
                 where name = 'db_block_size');
spool off
set newpage 1 verify on feedback 6 pagesize 24
set linesize 80 heading on
```

Sample output of running the script is shown here:

```
TABLESPACE_NAME                    BLOCK_SIZE
------------------------------- ----------
DRSYS                                  8192
EXAMPLE                                8192
INDX                                  16384
MY_PRODS                               8192
PROJ                                   8192
TOOLS                                 16384
USERS                                  8192
```

Scripts for Managing Performance

sgasize.sql	objlst_buf_7.sql	enq_res.sql
hitr7.sql	objlst_buf_80.sql	fts_larg.sql
hitr7_th.sql	objlst_buf_81.sql	disksort.sql
hitr8.sql	hitrpool.sql	pqo_stat.sql
hitr8_th.sql	pool_str.sql	redocopy.sql
missr8.sql	poolustt.sql	mts_stat.sql
missr8_th.sql	sh_hutil.sql	dbwrstat.sql
hitr_usr.sql	litersql.sql	fileio.sql
buff_usg_7.sql	shp_age.sql	params.sql
buff_usg_80.sql	obj_spac7.sql	gen_stat.sql
cr_vbufp81.sql	obj_spac8.sql	explain.sql
buff_usg_81.sql	largpool_util.sql	sql_to_explain.sql
buff_cnt7.sql	log_bufs.sql	explain_enh7.sql
buff_cnt8.sql	multblck.sql	explain_enh8.sql

Y our tuning efforts should start from the application architecture and design phase itself, rather than waiting until a problem occurs in your production system. During the application design, table design and index usage should be considered to help you determine the best application design for your purposes as well as to help you determine the I/O distribution on the available drives. As the application usage and characteristics become clearer, you should focus on tuning the queries using a reasonable set of data. Once you have a reasonably tuned application, you should then focus on the database parameters and tune the memory structures, as discussed in this chapter.

To tune an application, you must understand how the application's environment works. Ask yourself the following questions: Is the application making the best use of the available shared memory areas in the System Global Area (SGA)? Is the shared SQL area large enough? How much of the SGA is unused? After you verify that the environment is functioning properly as a well-performing system, you can focus on tuning individual queries that are experiencing performance problems.

In this chapter, you will see scripts that allow you to verify the performance of the application. Many of the queries focus on the usage of specific shared memory areas, allowing you to pinpoint potential environmental causes of performance problems. At the end of this chapter, you will see how to generate *explain plans* that can help you evaluate the performance of specific queries.

The major scripts presented in this chapter are shown in Table 2-1.

Script	Description
sgasize.sql	Overall SGA size
hitr7.sql	Data block buffer hit ratio (Oracle7.x)
hitr7_th.sql	Data block buffer hit ratio, with threshold (Oracle7.x)
hitr8.sql	Data block buffer hit ratio (Oracle8.x)
hitr8_th.sql	Data block buffer hit ratio, with threshold (Oracle8.x)
missr8.sql	Data block buffer miss ratio (Oracle8.x)
missr8_th.sql	Data block buffer miss ratio, with threshold (Oracle8.x)
hitr_usr.sql	Data block buffer hit ratio, by user
buff_usg_7.sql	Buffer usage within the SGA (Oracle7.x)
buff_usg_80.sql	Buffer usage within the SGA (Oracle8.0.x)
cr_vbufp_81.sql	Create view v$buffer_pool_v81 that will be used by buff_usg_81.sql
buff_usg_81.sql	Buffer usage within the SGA (Oracle8.1.x)

TABLE 2-1.   Performance Scripts Used in This Chapter

Script	Description
buff_cnt7.sql	Number of buffers in the buffer cache (Oracle7.x)
buff_cnt8.sql	Number of buffers in each pool of the buffer cache (Oracle8.x)
objlst_buf_7.sql	List of objects in the buffer cache (Oracle7.x)
objlst_buf_80.sql	List of objects in each pool of the buffer cache (Oracle8.0.x)
objlst_buf_81.sql	List of objects in each pool of the buffer cache (Oracle8.1.x)
hitrpool.sql	Shared SQL area hit ratio
pool_str.sql	Shared SQL area structures
poolustt.sql	Shared SQL area user statistics
sh_hutil.sql	SQL statements using large amounts of shared memory
litersql.sql	SQL statements that can benefit with the use of bind variables
shp_age.sql	SQL statements causing shared pool age-outs
obj_spac7.sql	Estimate space usage by shared SQL objects (Oracle7.x)
obj_spac8.sql	Estimate space usage by shared SQL objects (Oracle8.x)
largpool_util.sql	Large pool utilization (Oracle8.x)
log_bufs.sql	Log buffers size
multblck.sql	Multiblock read count setting
enq_res.sql	Enqueue resources setting
fts_larg.sql	Full table scans of large tables
disksort.sql	In-memory vs. disk sorts
pqo_stat.sql	Check parallel query server processes status
redocopy.sql	Check for contention on redo copy latches
mts_stat.sql	Multithreaded server statistics
dbwrstat.sql	Database writer/wait statistics
fileio.sql	Datafile I/O distribution
params.sql	Show parameter settings
gen_stat.sql	General statistics
explain.sql	Show explain plan for a query
sql_to_explain.sql	File containing the SQL statement whose explain plan is to be generated
explain_enh7.sql	Enhanced explain plan for a query (Oracle7.x)
explain_enh8.sql	Enhanced explain plan for a query (Oracle8.x)

TABLE 2-1. Performance Scripts Used in This Chapter *(continued)*

When tuning an application, you should be aware of the growth rates for the objects used by the application. If the application's tables grow quickly—or if some of its tables grow far more quickly than the rest of its tables—you will need to schedule regular performance tuning checks, using the diagnostic and utility scripts provided in this chapter.

In evaluating the performance of the database environment, the scripts in this chapter examine the following:

♦ The SGA, including the data block buffers, the shared SQL area, the redo log buffers, and latches

♦ The use of large table scans and temporary segments

♦ The use of the multithreaded server (MTS)

♦ The parallel query server process usage

♦ The distribution of I/O among datafiles

After you have evaluated your environment with the scripts provided in this chapter, you will be able to test the impact of any environmental changes you make. For example, if you change the size of the sort area, you could check to see whether the percentage of sorts performed in memory has increased following the change. The impact of all environmental changes on the database and on the server and operating system should be monitored.

PROGRAMMER'S NOTE   *Except where indicated, the scripts can be run from any user account with DBA privileges.*

Looking Inside the SGA

The database structure with the greatest performance impact is the SGA. The SGA allows multiple users to share data within memory, avoiding the need to access data physically from disks repeatedly. As the Oracle RDBMS products and options grow in complexity, the types of objects shared via the SGA increase in number. For example, the SGA may share data blocks, rollback segment blocks, SQL statements, and multithreaded server information.

Determine the SGA Size

sgasize.sql

If the SGA is well tuned for your application, the database's memory usage may be eliminated as a cause of potential performance problems.

You can query V$SGA to see the size of the SGA, as shown in the following listing.

```
REM sgasize.sql
REM    SGA Size
REM
select *
  from V$SGA;
```

Sample output from V$SGA, shown in the following listing, shows the size of the different areas within the SGA:

```
NAME                          VALUE
--------------------  --------------
Fixed Size                    38904
Variable Size              10313056
Database Buffers           10240000
Redo Buffers                  16384
```

As shown in the V$SGA query output, the database has 10,240,000 bytes dedicated to its database block buffer cache (the "Database Buffers" line). The redo log buffer cache (the "Redo Buffers" line) is 16,384 bytes in size. The shared SQL area is the chief component of the "Variable Size" of the SGA, which accounts for 10,313,056 bytes in the example.

The SGA sizing information is also available from within Server Manager. In the following example, the **svrmgrl** command is used to access the line mode interface of Server Manager. The **show sga** command retrieves data from V$SGA, and adds a "Total" line to show the total memory area required by the SGA:

```
svrmgrl
SVRMGR> connect internal
SVRMGR> show sga
Total System Global Area      20608344 bytes
Fixed Size                       38904 bytes
Variable Size                 10313056 bytes
Database Buffers              10240000 bytes
Redo Buffers                     16384 bytes
```

It should be noted that as of Oracle9i, the "connect internal" command and the server manager utility are deprecated and you should instead use the "show sga" command with the sql*plus utility while connected using the SYS account as SYSDBA. An example is shown here:

```
c:>sqlplus "sys/sys_password@mt900.world as sysdba"
SQL> show sga
```

```
Total System Global Area   118259984 bytes
Fixed Size                     278800 bytes
Variable Size                75497472 bytes
Database Buffers             41943040 bytes
Redo Buffers                   540672 bytes
```

In general, increasing the size of the SGA will improve the performance of your database environment. The size of the SGA is usually 2 percent of the size of the total allocated datafile space for the database. The hit ratio calculations shown in the next section will allow you to measure the performance impact as you increase the size of the SGA. However, the SGA should not be so large that it causes swapping and paging to occur at the operating system level. The queries of the shared SQL area shown later in this chapter will help you identify whether unused space within the SGA can be made available to the operating system.

hitr7.sql
hitr7_th.sql
hitr8.sql
hitr8_th.sql
missr8.sql
missr8_th.sql

The Hit Ratio and the Miss Rate

The data block buffer cache of the SGA stores blocks of data as users issue requests. The blocks of data stay in memory so that future requests for the same data by any user can be resolved without requiring access to the datafile containing the data. The data block buffer cache is limited in size, so a least recently used (LRU) algorithm manages the contents of the cache. When more space is needed within the data block buffer cache, the LRU blocks are removed from the cache and replaced with the new blocks. If the data block buffer cache is too small, requests for data blocks will result in a low *hit ratio*—the percentage of time a data block request is satisfied by data already in the data block buffer cache. A low hit ratio indicates that your database is not using the data block buffer cache effectively, and performance will suffer.

The cache hit ratio is a derived statistic, and the most common formula for the buffer cache for Oracle7/8 is

```
Hitratio = 100* (1 - ((physical_reads)/(consistent_gets +
db_block_gets)))
```

However, in Oracle 7.3.4 and Oracle8 and later, the definition of the "physical reads" statistic changed to include direct block reads as well as reads to get data into the buffer cache. As a result, the preceding formula gives only a lower bound for the hit ratio on these releases. For Oracle8i/9i, a better formula is this:

```
Hitratio = 100*(1-(((physical_reads)-(physical_reads_direct +
physical_reads_direct(LOB))/(session_logical_reads)))
```

Alternatively, for Oracle8i and above, you can query the V$BUFFER_POOL_STATISTICS view and use the following hit ratio formula. This technique is used in the query hitr8.sql.

```
Hitratio = 100* (1 - ((physical_reads)/(consistent_gets + db_block_gets)))
```

If you know the hit ratio for the data block buffer cache, you can estimate the adequacy of the data block buffer cache's size for the application. The threshold values indicating acceptable performance vary by type of application:

◆ For OLTP (online transaction processing) applications, in which many users execute small transactions, the hit ratio should be at least 98 percent. The target hit ratio is artificially high because it is inflated by the database activity associated with index-based accesses common to OLTP applications.

◆ For batch applications, in which few users execute large transactions, the hit ratio should be at least 89 percent.

If the hit ratio is below your target values, you should examine the database environment to determine whether the size of the data block buffer cache should be increased. After changing the size of the database block buffer cache, you should test the impact of the change on the hit ratio.

The following queries allow you to measure the hit ratio for the data block buffer cache, either alone or against a threshold value. For Oracle7.x, the queries reference the V$SYSSTAT, while for Oracle8.x, the queries reference the V$BUFFER_POOL_STATISTICS dynamic performance statistics table. Because the statistics in V$SYSSTAT and V$BUFFER_POOL_STATISTICS are cumulative, the results will show the cumulative hit ratio since the database was last started. Since the data block buffer cache is initially empty at database startup, the first queries will require physical data accesses, thereby initially lowering the cache's hit ratio. Although system startup will have an effect on the data block buffer cache hit ratio, the effect is usually negligible over time.

PROGRAMMER'S NOTE *Don't try to tune unless the database has been exercised under standard load for at least four hours.*

```
REM hitr7.sql
REM
REM  Data Block Buffer Cache Hit Ratio
REM
REM  This script is useful for Oracle7.x only
REM  For Oracle8.x onwards, use the script hitr8.sql
REM
REM  target minimum: 89%.   (98% for OLTP applications.)
REM
col BUFFER_POOL_NAME format A20
select
    'DEFAULT' BUFFER_POOL_NAME,
    SUM(DECODE(Name, 'consistent gets',Value,0)) Consistent,
    SUM(DECODE(Name, 'db block gets',Value,0)) Dbblockgets,
```

```
SUM(DECODE(Name, 'physical reads',Value,0)) Physrds,
ROUND(((SUM(DECODE(Name, 'consistent gets', Value, 0))+
  SUM(DECODE(Name, 'db block gets', Value, 0)) -
  SUM(DECODE(Name, 'physical reads', Value, 0)) )/
 (SUM(DECODE(Name, 'consistent gets',Value,0))+
  SUM(DECODE(Name, 'db block gets', Value, 0)))) *100,2)
      HitRatio
 from V$SYSSTAT;
```

The query in this listing determines the data block buffer cache hit ratio for Oracle7.x by selecting three values from V$SYSSTAT. The statistics for consistent gets and db block gets, added together, give the total number of logical reads (requests for rows or blocks) for the database. The physical reads statistic reflects the number of times the database had to perform a physical read of a datafile to satisfy the logical read request. If the data is already in the data block buffer cache, no physical read is required.

The first four columns selected by the query are the buffer_pool_name, consistent gets, db block gets, and physical reads statistics from V$SYSSTAT:

```
select
   'DEFAULT' BUFFER_POOL_NAME,
   SUM(DECODE(Name, 'consistent gets',Value,0)) Consistent,
   SUM(DECODE(Name, 'db block gets',Value,0)) Dbblockgets,
   SUM(DECODE(Name, 'physical reads',Value,0)) Physrds,
```

The hit ratio is determined by subtracting the number of physical reads from the number of logical reads, and dividing the difference by the number of logical reads. To determine the hit ratio, the statistics for the consistent gets and db block gets are added together and then compared to the physical reads statistic. The result is rounded to two decimal places via the **ROUND** function:

```
ROUND(((SUM(DECODE(Name, 'consistent gets', Value, 0))+
 SUM(DECODE(Name, 'db block gets', Value, 0)) -
 SUM(DECODE(Name, 'physical reads', Value, 0)) )/
 (SUM(DECODE(Name, 'consistent gets',Value,0))+
  SUM(DECODE(Name, 'db block gets', Value, 0)))) *100,2)
      HitRatio
```

The higher the hit ratio, the greater the number of logical reads resolved by data already in memory. The following listing shows sample output from the hit ratio query for an OLTP application.

CONSISTENT	DBBLOCKGETS	PHYSRDS	HITRATIO
1208863	1179	8826	99.27

As shown in the output listing, the database has performed more than 1.2 million logical reads. The logical reads required only 8,826 physical reads in order to be satisfied. Since this is a cumulative hit ratio, it reflects the physical reads needed since the database was first started. The hit ratio, 99.27, is above the target hit ratio of 98 percent used for OLTP applications, so it is not necessary to increase the size of the data block buffer cache.

Objects are accessed in different ways and with different frequency, and therefore their cache behavior may vary. In Oracle7.x, you can use only the DEFAULT pool. In Oracle8.0 and later, it is possible to use multiple buffer pools by setting the BUFFER_POOL_KEEP and/or BUFFER_POOL_RECYCLE init.ora parameters.

When using the BUFFER_POOL parameters, you may want to modify DB_BLOCK_BUFFERS and DB_BLOCK_LRU_LATCHES because the KEEP and RECYCLE pool get their buffers from the DB_BLOCK_BUFFERS and DB_BLOCK_LRU_LATCHES parameters. Specification for the BUFFER_POOL_KEEP and the BUFFER_POOL_RECYCLE parameters is done as follows (examples are shown later):

```
'<number of buffers for the pool>,<number of lru latches for the pool>'
```

Therefore, objects can be placed in three types of pools: KEEP, RECYCLE, and DEFAULT.

- ◆ **KEEP** The KEEP buffer pool is good to pin frequently accessed objects. This pool is sized by the BUFFER_POOL_KEEP parameter.

- ◆ **RECYCLE** The RECYCLE buffer pool is good for large objects that you want flushed out of memory quickly as soon as a query or transaction is complete. This is faster than the normal LRU algorithm. This pool is sized by the BUFFER_POOL_RECYCLE parameter.

- ◆ **DEFAULT** The DEFAULT pool works under the LRU algorithm for aging out blocks. An object that is not assigned to the KEEP or RECYCLE buffer pool will default to this pool. The size of this pool is affected by the settings of DB_BLOCK_BUFFERS, BUFFER_POOL_KEEP, and BUFFER_POOL_RECYCLE parameters such that

  ```
  DB_BLOCK_BUFFERS = (Size of DEFAULT pool +
                       Size of KEEP pool +
                       Size of RECYCLE pool)
  ```

For example, consider the following settings:

DB_BLOCK_BUFFERS = 1000
DB_BLOCK_LRU_LATCHES = 8
BUFFER_POOL_KEEP = '100,2'
BUFFER_POOL_RECYCLE = '50,1'

Then the following is the result:

- ◆ KEEP pool has 100 buffers and 2 LRU latch
- ◆ RECYCLE pool has 50 buffers and 1 LRU latch
- ◆ DEFAULT pool has 850 buffers and 5 LRU latches

You should try to use at least 50 blocks per LRU latch.

Prior to Oracle8i, the LRU algorithm is used for all the pools to allocate and release space, but beginning with Oracle8i, the undocumented parameters _db_percent_hot_default, _db_percent_hot_keep, and _db_percent_hot_recycle are used to split the pool into "hot" and "cold" regions, and newly read blocks go at the top of the cold region and not to the top/MRU end of the buffer.

PROGRAMMER'S NOTE   *If the parameters BUFFER_POOL_KEEP and BUFFER_POOL_RECYCLE are not set, the respective pool (KEEP and RECYCLE) will not exist.*

You can assign an object to a buffer pool when it is created or by altering it, for example,

```
Create table mytable(
Col1 varchar2(10),
Col2 varchar2(2))
Tablespace users
Storage (buffer_pool keep);
```

Blocks for an object without an explicitly set buffer pool will go into the DEFAULT buffer pool. When an object is altered to change its buffer pool, all blocks of the altered segment that are currently in a buffer pool remain as they were before the ALTER statement but newly loaded blocks and any blocks that have aged out are reloaded into the new buffer pool specified.

Beginning with Oracle8.x, the hit rate for each pool can be calculated using the statistics shown in the V$BUFFER_POOL_STATISTICS view. The next query performs calculations to determine the buffer cache hit ratio for the various buffer pools in an Oracle8.x database.

PROGRAMMER'S NOTE   *Prior to Oracle8.1.6, the V$BUFFER_POOL_STATISTICS view is created using the CATPERF.SQL script located in $ORACLE_HOME/rdbms/admin directory connected as user SYS, but it is a standard view in Oracle8.1.6 and later.*

```
REM hitr8.sql
REM
REM  Data Block Buffer Cache Hit Ratio
REM
REM  This script is useful for Oracle8.x onwards only
```

```
REM   For Oracle7.x, use the script hitr7.sql
REM
REM For Oracle 8.1.7, the V$BUFFER_POOL_STATISTICS view shows 0 for
REM   consistent_gets and db_block_gets (Oracle bug# 1491213)
REM   and therefore this query is useless in that release.
REM
REM   target minimum: 89%.   (98% for OLTP applications.)
REM
col BUFFER_POOL_NAME format A20
select
   name BUFFER_POOL_NAME,
   consistent_gets Consistent,
   db_block_gets Dbblockgets,
   physical_reads Physrds,
   ROUND(100*(1 -
         (physical_reads/(consistent_gets + db_block_gets))),2)
      HitRatio
   from v$buffer_pool_statistics
         where (consistent_gets + db_block_gets) != 0;
```

PROGRAMMER'S NOTE   *For Oracle 8.1.7, the V$BUFFER_POOL_STATISTICS view shows 0 for consistent_gets and db_block_gets (Oracle bug# 1491213), and therefore the queries hitr8.sql and hitr8_th.sql are useless in that release.*

You can use the number of logical reads to compare the relative activity level of the database at different times. For example, you could monitor changes in the number of logical reads after increasing the number of users or adding a new module to an application.

Data block buffer cache hit ratios below your target value occur for two reasons: either the cache is too small or the application's queries do not take advantage of indexes. You can increase the size of the data block buffer cache by increasing the value of the DB_BLOCK_BUFFERS parameter in the database's init.ora file and performing an instance shutdown/restart. The DB_BLOCK_BUFFERS parameter is expressed in term of database blocks, so if you change the database block size (the DB_BLOCK_SIZE parameter) during a database rebuild, you will need to change the DB_BLOCK_BUFFERS parameter. For example, if you increase the DB_BLOCK_SIZE from 2,048 to 4,096, your data block buffer cache will double in size unless you halve the DB_BLOCK_BUFFERS parameter.

If your data block buffer cache hit ratio is below your target value, you should first try to increase the size of the cache. If increasing the size of the data block buffer cache has no impact on the hit ratio, you should examine the longest running queries to determine whether they have been properly optimized.

The data block buffer cache hit ratio query can be modified to return a record only if the hit ratio is below a specified threshold. In the following listing, a variable

(&*threshold*) is used; the user will be prompted to enter a value for the threshold. If the hit ratio is below the threshold, a record will be returned. If the hit ratio is above the threshold, no record will be returned.

```
REM   hitr7_thr.sql
REM
REM   Data Block Buffer Cache Hit Ratio, with Threshold
REM
REM   This script is useful for Oracle7.x only
REM   For Oracle8.x onwards, use the script hitr8_th.sql
REM
REM
set verify off
col BUFFER_POOL_NAME format A20
select
   'DEFAULT' BUFFER_POOL_NAME,
   SUM(DECODE(Name, 'consistent gets',Value,0)) Consistent,
   SUM(DECODE(Name, 'db block gets',Value,0)) Dbblockgets,
   SUM(DECODE(Name, 'physical reads',Value,0)) Physrds,
   ROUND((((SUM(DECODE(Name, 'consistent gets', Value, 0))+
    SUM(DECODE(Name, 'db block gets', Value, 0)) -
    SUM(DECODE(Name, 'physical reads', Value, 0)) )/
    (SUM(DECODE(Name, 'consistent gets',Value,0))+
     SUM(DECODE(Name, 'db block gets', Value, 0)))) *100,2)
       HitRatio
  from V$SYSSTAT
having ROUND((((SUM(DECODE(Name, 'consistent gets', Value, 0))+
   SUM(DECODE(Name, 'db block gets', Value, 0)) -
   SUM(DECODE(Name, 'physical reads', Value, 0)) )/
    (SUM(DECODE(Name, 'consistent gets',Value,0))+
     SUM(DECODE(Name, 'db block gets', Value, 0)))) *100,2)
        < &threshold;
```

To add the threshold check to the hit ratio query, the following clause was added to the query:

```
having ROUND((((SUM(DECODE(Name, 'consistent gets', Value, 0))+
   SUM(DECODE(Name, 'db block gets', Value, 0)) -
   SUM(DECODE(Name, 'physical reads', Value, 0)) )/
    (SUM(DECODE(Name, 'consistent gets',Value,0))+
     SUM(DECODE(Name, 'db block gets', Value, 0)))) *100,2)
        < &threshold;
```

The **having** clause in the preceding query calculates the hit ratio via the same calculation used in the previous queries and compares that result to the user-specified value (*&threshold*).

The following query returns similar results for an Oracle8.x database:

```
REM hitr8_th.sql
REM
REM  Data Block Buffer Cache Hit Ratio - with threshold
REM
REM  This script is useful for Oracle8.x onwards only
REM  For Oracle7.x, use the script hitr7.sql
REM
REM For Oracle 8.1.7, the V$BUFFER_POOL_STATISTICS view shows 0 for
REM  consistent_gets and db_block_gets (Oracle bug# 1491213)
REM  and therefore this query is useless in that release.
REM
REM  target minimum: 89%.   (98% for OLTP applications.)
REM
col BUFFER_POOL_NAME format A20
set verify off

select
   name BUFFER_POOL_NAME,
   consistent_gets Consistent,
   db_block_gets Dbblockgets,
   physical_reads Physrds,
   ROUND(100*(1 -
          (physical_reads/(consistent_gets + db_block_gets))),2)
      HitRatio
  from v$buffer_pool_statistics
  where (consistent_gets + db_block_gets) != 0 and
         ROUND(100*(1 -
           (physical_reads/(consistent_gets + db_block_gets))),2) <
                                                &threshold;
```

It should be noted that a hit ratio that is close to 100 percent does not necessarily mean that the application is good, because it is possible to get an excellent hit ratio that is artificially high by using an unselective (or skewed) index in a heavily used SQL statement while the overall performance is very poor. As a result, the hit ratio should not be used as the best measure of performance.

You may have assumed that if the cache hit rate is 90 percent, the cache miss rate is 10 percent—i.e., 100 percent minus the cache hit rate. But this is not true. Oracle actually performs direct reads for certain operations such as parallel scans (or even serial scans in Oracle8.1.x using the _serial_direct_reads parameter) and reads from temporary tablespaces. During direct reads, blocks are read directly into private buffers in the PGA (Program Global Area) rather than into the database buffer cache in the SGA (Shared Global Area). As a result, during direct reads, blocks are not searched for in the cache before being read and therefore no cache hits occur. In addition, the blocks are not cached, but are instead discarded after use, so there are no subsequent cache hits. It should be noted, however, that direct reads actually improve the cache hit rate, because the cache is not loaded with blocks that are generally accessed infrequently and also the load on the buffer cache latches are minimized, resulting in improved concurrency.

The previous discussion of direct reads indicates that the cache miss rate is a more important factor to consider than the hit rate during buffer cache sizing. Generally, the miss rate should not be greater than 1 percent. Unfortunately, in Oracle7.x, it is not possible in a reliable manner to calculate the buffer cache miss rate because Oracle7 does not provide statistics that enable you to distinguish between direct reads and cache misses. In Oracle8.x, however, the physical reads reported against each buffer pool (via V$BUFFER_POOL_STATISTICS) are exclusive of direct reads. They are not, however, exclusive of the mutiblock reads associated with serial full table and index scans.

The following queries show the miss rate calculations for Oracle8.x and later directly by accessing the X$ tables, as measured independently or against a threshold:

```
REM  missr8.sql
REM  Buffer cache miss rate
REM  For Oracle8.x and higher
REM  This script fails in Oracle 8.1.7 and
REM          Oracle9.x due to bug# 1491213
REM
column Miss_Rate format 999.99
select
 b.bp_name  "BUFFER POOL",
 decode(sum(a.pread), 0, ' THIS POOL IS NOT USED',
 to_char(100 * sum(a.pread) /decode(sum(a.dbbget + a.conget), 0, 1, sum(a.dbbget +
a.conget)),
      '9990.00') || '%')  Miss_Rate
from
  sys.x_$kcbwds a,
  sys.x_$kcbwbpd b
where
  a.inst_id = userenv('Instance') and
  b.inst_id = userenv('Instance') and
  a.set_id >= b.bp_lo_sid and
  a.set_id <= b.bp_hi_sid and
  b.bp_size != 0
group by
  b.bp_name;
```

In this query, the X$ tables sys.x_$kcbwds and sys.x_$kcbwbpd are queried to read the amount of physical reads, consistent gets, and db block gets for each buffer pool. The miss rate is determined by dividing the physical reads by the logical reads (consistent gets + db block gets):

```
decode(sum(a.pread), 0, ' THIS POOL IS NOT USED',
 to_char(100 * sum(a.pread) /decode(sum(a.dbbget + a.conget), 0, 1, sum(a.dbbget +
a.conget)),
      '9990.00') || '%')  Miss_Rate
```

During the determination of the statistics for physical and logical reads, the where clause is used to choose the proper instance

```
a.inst_id = userenv('Instance') and
b.inst_id = userenv('Instance') and
```

and the proper set_ids:

```
a.set_id >= b.bp_lo_sid and
a.set_id <= b.bp_hi_sid and
```

Another clause is used to ensure that the buffer pools that are not used are filtered out from the result:

```
b.bp_size != 0
```

The result set is grouped by the name of the buffer pool:

```
group by
  b.bp_name;
```

The following query shows the buffer pools for which the miss rate exceeds a user-specified threshold:

```
REM  missr8_th.sql
REM  Buffer cache miss rate - with Threshold
REM  For Oracle8.x and higher
REM  This script fails in Oracle 8.1.7 due to bug# 1491213
REM
column Miss_Rate format 999.99
set verify off
select
 b.bp_name  "BUFFER POOL",
 decode(sum(a.pread), 0, ' THIS POOL IS NOT USED',
 to_char(100 * sum(a.pread) /decode(sum(a.dbbget + a.conget), 0, 1, sum(a.dbbget +
a.conget)),
      '9990.00') || '%')  Miss_Rate
from
  sys.x_$kcbwds a,
  sys.x_$kcbwbpd b
```

```
where
  a.inst_id = userenv('Instance') and
  b.inst_id = userenv('Instance') and
  a.set_id >= b.bp_lo_sid and
  a.set_id <= b.bp_hi_sid and
  b.bp_size != 0
group by
  b.bp_name
having
 to_char(100 * sum(a.pread) /
  decode(sum(a.dbbget + a.conget), 0, 1, sum(a.dbbget + a.conget)),
      '9990.00') > &threshold;
```

When evaluating a below-threshold hit ratio, it is often useful to determine the hit ratio for each current user's data requests. In the next section, you will see how to calculate the hit ratio for users who are currently logged into the database.

Hit Ratio by User

htr_usr.sql

To identify which users are having the greatest negative or positive impact on the overall hit ratio, you can query V$SESS_IO. The query output will show the hit ratio per user as well as the number of logical and physical reads per user. The number of logical reads per user allows you to judge quickly which users are the most active users in the database. If the overall hit ratio is below your target value, you should look for very active users who have hit ratios below your target value.

PROGRAMMER'S NOTE   *The following query will show hit ratio information only for users who are currently logged in to the database. If a user is no longer logged in to the database, the user's session will have no entry in V$SESS_IO, and therefore will not be reported via this query.*

```
REM hitr_usr.sql
REM   Hit Ratio by User
REM
column HitRatio format 999.99
select Username,
       Consistent_Gets,
       Block_Gets,
       Physical_Reads,
       100*(Consistent_Gets+Block_Gets-Physical_Reads)/
           (Consistent_Gets+Block_Gets) HitRatio
  from V$SESSION, V$SESS_IO
 where V$SESSION.SID = V$SESS_IO.SID
   and (Consistent_Gets+Block_Gets)>0
   and Username is not null;
```

This query selects data from V$SESSION and V$SESS_IO. V$SESS_IO contains columns named Consistent_Gets, Block_Gets, and Physical_Reads, making this query of hit ratio information simpler than the query in the previous section.

The user's hit ratio is calculated in the same manner used to calculate the overall hit ratio. The number of physical reads is subtracted from the number of logical reads (Consistent_Gets+Block_Gets) and the difference is divided by the number of logical reads:

```
100*(Consistent_Gets+Block_Gets-Physical_Reads)/
        (Consistent_Gets+Block_Gets) HitRatio
```

PROGRAMMER'S NOTE   *For Oracle8i and later, use the modified hit ratio calculation described earlier in the section on hit ratios. Again, it looks like this:*

```
Hitratio = 100*(1-(((physical_reads)-(physical_reads_direct +
    physical_reads_direct(LOB))/(session_logical_reads)))
```

Two limiting conditions are placed on records returned by the hit ratio query. The first condition eliminates from the result set all users who have not performed any logical reads. This limiting condition prevents the result set from containing many entries for users who are not contributing to the overall database hit ratio.

```
and (Consistent_Gets+Block_Gets)>0
```

The second limiting condition eliminates from the result set any user who has a Null value for Username. This limiting condition prevents the Oracle server background processes from being listed in the query's result set.

```
and Username is not null;
```

The following listing shows sample output from the query for an OLTP application.

USERNAME	CONSISTENT_GETS	BLOCK_GETS	PHYSICAL_READS	HITRATIO
SYSTEM	214	8	9	95.95
APPL_MAINT	1232681	66	4669	99.62
OPS$APPL_1	28	8	0	100.00
APPL1_MAINT2	5687	4	53	99.07
APPL1_MAINT2	29677	20	49	99.84

The results shown here are consistent with the overall system hit ratio calculated in the previous section. Every user—except for SYSTEM—has a hit ratio that exceeds the target 98 percent. The user with the highest number of physical reads also has the highest number of logical reads and a high hit ratio.

If your users can perform ad hoc queries against your application, you may see hit ratio by user output that resembles the following listing:

USERNAME	CONSISTENT_GETS	BLOCK_GETS	PHYSICAL_READS	HITRATIO
SYSTEM	214	8	9	95.95
APPL_MAINT	1232681	66	4669	99.62
OPS$APPL_1	28	8	0	100.00
APPL1_MAINT2	5687	4	53	99.07
APPL1_MAINT2	29677	20	49	99.84
USER_ADHOC	200000	50	100000	50.01

In the revised listing, the user named USER_ADHOC has a hit ratio well below the target hit ratio for the database. The high number of physical reads accessed by this user will adversely affect the overall data block buffer cache hit ratio. This query output allows you to determine which users are causing the greatest negative impact on your data block buffer cache hit ratio. In this example, you should work with the USER_ADHOC user to determine which queries are causing the observed system usage. It is likely that the user is not using indexes during the query, either because of the query syntax or because of the lack of an available index. Having isolated the problem, you can then begin to address it specifically, while the rest of the database environment is left unchanged.

You could use a threshold value to limit the query set only to those sessions whose hit ratios fall below your target value, but that may not give you an accurate picture of your database. If you eliminate sessions based on their hit ratio, you may not see sessions that account for the majority of the logical and physical reads in the database (and therefore that have the greatest impact on the overall hit ratio).

Buffer Usage Within the SGA

buff_usg_7.sql
buff_usg_80.sql
cr_vbufpv81.sql
buff_usg_81.sql
buff_cnt7.sql
buff_cnt8.sql
objlst_buf_7.sql
objlst_buf_80.sql
objlst_buf_81.sql

The data block buffer cache is used to share different types of blocks. For example, when a table is read by a user, the table's blocks are stored in the data block buffer cache. However, blocks read by full table scans go to the LRU list and are rapidly paged out.

If the table is accessed via an index, the relevant index blocks are also read into the data block buffer cache. If the table's records are changed, the rollback segment's blocks are stored in the data block buffer cache as well, so that other queries using the data can reconstruct the data as it existed prior to the start of the transaction.

At any time, the data block buffer cache contains several different types of blocks. If you know the number of each type of block currently stored in the data block buffer cache, you can measure the impact of increasing the size of the cache. You can also use this information to measure the impact of large transactions (with their associated rollback segment blocks) on the data block buffer cache.

The following queries list each type of buffer stored in the data block buffer cache, based on data in the SYS.X$BH table. The queries should be run while logged in to the database as the SYS user. Prior to Oracle9.x, you can also use Server Manager and 'connect internal.' Only four classes of blocks—Data, Sort, Header, and Rollback—are reported via these queries.

```
REM  buff_usg_7.sql
REM  Number of each type of buffer in the SGA
REM  This script is useful for Oracle7.x only
REM
column Class format A10
select DECODE(GREATEST(Class,10),10,
         DECODE(Class,1,'Data',2,'Sort',4,'Header',
         TO_CHAR(Class)),'Rollback') Class,
         SUM(DECODE(BITAND(Flag,1),1,0,1)) NotDirty,
         SUM(DECODE(BITAND(Flag,1),1,1,0)) Dirty,
         SUM(Dirty_Queue) OnDirtyQ, count(*) Total
  from X$BH
 where Class in (1,2,4,10)
 group by DECODE(GREATEST(Class,10),10,
      DECODE(Class,1,'Data',2,'Sort',4,'Header',
      TO_CHAR(Class)),'Rollback')
/
```

The following listing shows the query output for a small database. Of the four classes checked by the query, three are present in the data block buffer cache. No Sort blocks (associated with sorting operations) are present in the data block buffer cache in the example database, and 54 header blocks (such as table header blocks and rollback segment header blocks) and 10 rollback segment data blocks are present.

CLASS	NOTDIRTY	DIRTY	ONDIRTYQ	TOTAL
Data	1209	6	0	1215
Header	54	0	0	54
Rollback	10	0	0	10

In the preceding output, notice references to blocks that are "not dirty," "dirty," and "on the dirty queue." A *dirty block* is a block that has changed since being read into memory. Thus, of the 1215 data blocks in memory, 6 of them are dirty. The *dirty queue* is a list of dirty blocks to be written to the datafiles. If not enough DBWR (database writer process) I/O slave processes are in use in your database, you will see non-zero values for the dirty queue count throughout the application's usage. You can then increase the number of DBWR I/O slave processes by setting or changing the DB_WRITERS (ORACLE7) or DBWR_IO_SLAVES (ORACLE8) init.ora parameter and stopping and restarting your database. In addition, you should also check that the operating system (O/S) you are running on supports IO_SLAVES and whether the O/S supports synchronous or asynchronous operations.

The following query shows how to determine the types of buffers for the various types of buffer pools in an Oracle8.0.x database:

```
REM  buff_usg_80.sql
REM  Number of each type of buffer in the SGA
REM  This script is useful for Oracle8.0.x only
REM
column Class format A10
column BUFFER_POOL format A12
select 'DEFAULT' "BUFFER_POOL", DECODE(GREATEST(Class,10),10,
            DECODE(Class,1,'Data',2,'Sort',4,'Header',
            TO_CHAR(Class)),'Rollback') Class,
            SUM(DECODE(BITAND(Flag,1),1,0,1)) NotDirty,
            SUM(DECODE(BITAND(Flag,1),1,1,0)) Dirty,
            SUM(Dirty_Queue) OnDirtyQ, count(*) Total
   from X$BH
  where Class in (1,2,4,10) and
        buf# >= (SELECT lo_bnum
                   FROM v$buffer_pool
                   WHERE name = 'DEFAULT'
                   AND buffers > 0) and
        buf# <= (SELECT hi_bnum
                   FROM v$buffer_pool
                   WHERE name = 'DEFAULT'
                   AND buffers > 0)
   group by 'DEFAULT', DECODE(GREATEST(Class,10),10,
        DECODE(Class,1,'Data',2,'Sort',4,'Header',
        TO_CHAR(Class)),'Rollback')
UNION ALL
select 'KEEP' "BUFFER_POOL", DECODE(GREATEST(Class,10),10,
            DECODE(Class,1,'Data',2,'Sort',4,'Header',
            TO_CHAR(Class)),'Rollback') Class,
            SUM(DECODE(BITAND(Flag,1),1,0,1)) NotDirty,
            SUM(DECODE(BITAND(Flag,1),1,1,0)) Dirty,
            SUM(Dirty_Queue) OnDirtyQ, count(*) Total
   from X$BH
  where Class in (1,2,4,10) and
        buf# >= (SELECT lo_bnum
                   FROM v$buffer_pool
                   WHERE name = 'KEEP'
                   AND buffers > 0) and
```

```
        buf# <= (SELECT hi_bnum
                 FROM v$buffer_pool
                 WHERE name = 'KEEP'
                 AND buffers > 0)
group by 'KEEP', DECODE(GREATEST(Class,10),10,
     DECODE(Class,1,'Data',2,'Sort',4,'Header',
     TO_CHAR(Class)),'Rollback')
UNION ALL
select 'RECYCLE' "BUFFER_POOL", DECODE(GREATEST(Class,10),10,
        DECODE(Class,1,'Data',2,'Sort',4,'Header',
        TO_CHAR(Class)),'Rollback') Class,
        SUM(DECODE(BITAND(Flag,1),1,0,1)) NotDirty,
        SUM(DECODE(BITAND(Flag,1),1,1,0)) Dirty,
        SUM(Dirty_Queue) OnDirtyQ, count(*) Total
  from X$BH
where Class in (1,2,4,10) and
      buf# >= (SELECT lo_bnum
               FROM v$buffer_pool
               WHERE name = 'RECYCLE'
               AND buffers > 0) and
      buf# <= (SELECT hi_bnum
               FROM v$buffer_pool
               WHERE name = 'RECYCLE'
               AND buffers > 0)
group by 'RECYCLE', DECODE(GREATEST(Class,10),10,
     DECODE(Class,1,'Data',2,'Sort',4,'Header',
     TO_CHAR(Class)),'Rollback');
```

The preceding query is similar to the query for Oracle7.x, except here it determines the types of buffers for each buffer pool and performs a UNION ALL of the individual results. UNION ALL is used instead of UNION because the results from the independent queries don't overlap and the use of UNION ALL will improve performance. For each of the buffer pool, the v$buffer_pool view is used to determine the low and high buffer number for that pool—for example, this one for the KEEP pool:

```
    buf# >= (SELECT lo_bnum
             FROM v$buffer_pool
             WHERE name = 'KEEP'
             AND buffers > 0) and
      buf# <= (SELECT hi_bnum
               FROM v$buffer_pool
               WHERE name = 'KEEP'
               AND buffers > 0)
```

In Oracle8.1.x, the lo_bnum and the hi_bnum columns have been removed from the v$buffer_pool view and therefore that view can't be used as is. The following query cr_vbuf_81.sql can be used to create a modified view v$buffer_pool_v81 that can then be used to determine the low and high buffer numbers for each buffer pool instead of using the v$buffer_pool view:

```
REM cr_vbuf_8i.sql
REM Create a modified view "v$buffer_pool_v81" that shows
REM the low and high buffer number for each type of buffer pool.
REM
create or replace view v$buffer_pool_v81 as
select name,
       min(START_BUF#) lo_bnum,
       max(END_BUF#) hi_bnum,
       max(END_BUF#) - min(START_BUF#) buffers
from v$buffer_pool v, x$kcbwds s
where (LO_SETID = SET_ID or HI_SETID = SET_ID) and buffers > 0
group by name
/
```

The following query is the same as the query buff_usg_80.sql except that it uses v$buffer_pool_v81 view instead of the view v$buffer_pool:

```
REM  buff_usg_81.sql
REM  Number of each type of buffer in the SGA
REM  This script is useful for Oracle8.1.x only
REM
column Class format A10
column BUFFER_POOL format A12
select 'DEFAULT' "BUFFER_POOL", DECODE(GREATEST(Class,10),10,
          DECODE(Class,1,'Data',2,'Sort',4,'Header',
          TO_CHAR(Class)),'Rollback') Class,
          SUM(DECODE(BITAND(Flag,1),1,0,1)) NotDirty,
          SUM(DECODE(BITAND(Flag,1),1,1,0)) Dirty,
          SUM(Dirty_Queue) OnDirtyQ, count(*) Total
   from X$BH
  where Class in (1,2,4,10) and
        buf# >= (SELECT lo_bnum
                 FROM v$buffer_pool_v81
                 WHERE name = 'DEFAULT'
                 AND buffers > 0) and
        buf# <= (SELECT hi_bnum
                 FROM v$buffer_pool_v81
                 WHERE name = 'DEFAULT'
                 AND buffers > 0)
```

```
   group by 'DEFAULT', DECODE(GREATEST(Class,10),10,
       DECODE(Class,1,'Data',2,'Sort',4,'Header',
       TO_CHAR(Class)),'Rollback')
UNION ALL
select 'KEEP' "BUFFER_POOL", DECODE(GREATEST(Class,10),10,
          DECODE(Class,1,'Data',2,'Sort',4,'Header',
          TO_CHAR(Class)),'Rollback') Class,
          SUM(DECODE(BITAND(Flag,1),1,0,1)) NotDirty,
          SUM(DECODE(BITAND(Flag,1),1,1,0)) Dirty,
          SUM(Dirty_Queue) OnDirtyQ, count(*) Total
  from X$BH
 where Class in (1,2,4,10) and
       buf# >= (SELECT lo_bnum
               FROM v$buffer_pool_v81
               WHERE name = 'KEEP'
               AND buffers > 0) and
       buf# <= (SELECT hi_bnum
               FROM v$buffer_pool_v81
               WHERE name = 'KEEP'
               AND buffers > 0)
   group by 'KEEP', DECODE(GREATEST(Class,10),10,
       DECODE(Class,1,'Data',2,'Sort',4,'Header',
       TO_CHAR(Class)),'Rollback')
UNION ALL
select 'RECYCLE' "BUFFER_POOL", DECODE(GREATEST(Class,10),10,
          DECODE(Class,1,'Data',2,'Sort',4,'Header',
          TO_CHAR(Class)),'Rollback') Class,
          SUM(DECODE(BITAND(Flag,1),1,0,1)) NotDirty,
          SUM(DECODE(BITAND(Flag,1),1,1,0)) Dirty,
          SUM(Dirty_Queue) OnDirtyQ, count(*) Total
  from X$BH
 where Class in (1,2,4,10) and
       buf# >= (SELECT lo_bnum
               FROM v$buffer_pool_v81
               WHERE name = 'RECYCLE'
               AND buffers > 0) and
       buf# <= (SELECT hi_bnum
               FROM v$buffer_pool_v81
               WHERE name = 'RECYCLE'
               AND buffers > 0)
   group by 'RECYCLE', DECODE(GREATEST(Class,10),10,
       DECODE(Class,1,'Data',2,'Sort',4,'Header',
       TO_CHAR(Class)),'Rollback');
```

The following queries show the total number of buffers in each type of buffer pool. For Oracle7.x, the v$parameter view is used, while for Oracle8.x, the v$buffer_pool view is used:

```
REM   buff_cnt7.sql
REM   Number of buffers in the Default buffer pool
REM   This script is useful for Oracle7.x only
REM
column "NAME" format A10
column "BUFFERS" format A10
SELECT 'DEFAULT' "NAME", value "BUFFERS"
FROM v$parameter
WHERE name = 'db_block_buffers';


REM   buff_cnt8.sql
REM   Number of buffers in each buffer pool
REM   This script is useful for Oracle8.x only
REM
SELECT name, buffers
FROM v$buffer_pool
WHERE name is not null;
```

At times, you may want to determine the list of objects that have been placed in the various buffer pools. This information can help you in determining whether you need to consider, for example

◆   Moving certain objects from the DEFAULT pool to the KEEP pool or the RECYCLE pool.

◆   Moving large objects to the large pool (the large pool is discussed later in this chapter).

Earlier in the chapter, we discussed how the various types of buffer pools can be used. The following script shows how to determine the objects in the various buffer pools.

```
REM   objlst_buf_7.sql
REM   Determine the list of objects in each buffer pool
REM   This script is useful for Oracle7.x only
REM This script shows objects that have more than 500 blocks
REM
column Class format A10
column Buffer_Pool format A12

select to_char(Sysdate,'HH24:MI:SS') "TIME",
```

```
      count(Addr) "#BLOCKS",
      Segment_Name,
      Tablespace_Name
from X$BH a, DBA_EXTENTS b
where a.Dbafil=b.File_Id and
      a.Dbablk >= b.Block_Id and
      a.Dbablk <= (b.Block_Id + b.Blocks - 1) and
      a.State != 0
group by Segment_Name, Tablespace_Name
having count(Addr) > 500
order by 2 desc
/
```

The preceding query shows the objects, the tablespace they belong to, and the number of blocks for each object at a particular time.

```
select to_char(Sysdate,'HH24:MI:SS') "TIME",
       count(Addr) "#BLOCKS",
       Segment_Name,
       Tablespace_Name
```

The result set is limited to show only those objects that have more than 500 blocks:

```
having count(Addr) > 500
```

Further, the result set is sorted by the size of objects in descending order:

```
order by 2 desc
```

The following queries, objlst_buf_80.sql and objlst_buf_81.sql, show the list of objects in each buffer pool. As before, the query objlst_buf_81.sql makes use of the modified view v$buffer_pool_v81 instead of v$buffer_pool to determine the low and high buffer numbers of the various buffer pools:

```
REM   objlst_buf_80.sql
REM   Determine the list of objects in each buffer pool
REM   This script is useful for Oracle8.0.x only
REM
column Class format A10
column Buffer_Pool format A12

select 'DEFAULT' "BUFFER_POOL", o.Name, count(Buf#) BLOCKS
from SYS.OBJ$ o, X$BH x
where o.Dataobj# = x.Obj   and
      x.State != 0 and
      o.Owner# != 0 and
      Buf# >= (select Lo_Bnum
```

```
                        from V$BUFFER_POOL
                    where Name = 'DEFAULT' and
                            Buffers > 0) and
          Buf# <= (select Hi_Bnum
                    from V$BUFFER_POOL
                    where Name = 'DEFAULT' and
                            Buffers > 0)
group by 'DEFAULT', o.name
union all
select 'KEEP' "BUFFER_POOL", o.Name, count(Buf#) BLOCKS
from SYS.OBJ$ o, X$BH x
where o.Dataobj# = x.Obj   and
      x.State != 0 and
      o.Owner# != 0 and
      Buf# >= (select Lo_Bnum
                from V$BUFFER_POOL
                where Name = 'KEEP' and
                        Buffers > 0) and
      Buf# <= (select Hi_Bnum
                from V$BUFFER_POOL
                where Name = 'KEEP' and
                        Buffers > 0)
group by 'KEEP', o.name
union all
select 'RECYCLE' "BUFFER_POOL", o.Name, count(Buf#) BLOCKS
from SYS.OBJ$ o, X$BH x
where o.Dataobj# = x.Obj   and
      x.State != 0 and
      o.Owner# != 0 and
      Buf# >= (select Lo_Bnum
                from V$BUFFER_POOL
                where Name = 'RECYCLE' and
                        Buffers > 0) and
      Buf# <= (select Hi_Bnum
                from V$BUFFER_POOL
                where Name = 'RECYCLE' and
                        Buffers > 0)
group by 'RECYCLE', o.name;

REM  objlst_buf_81.sql
REM  Determine the list of objects in each buffer pool
REM  This script is useful for Oracle8.1.x only
REM
```

```
column Class format A10
column BUFFER_POOL format A12

select 'DEFAULT' "BUFFER_POOL", o.Name, count(Buf#) BLOCKS
from SYS.OBJ$ o, X$BH x
where o.Dataobj# = x.Obj  and
      x.State != 0 and
      o.Owner# != 0 and
      Buf# >= (select Lo_Bnum
               from V$BUFFER_POOL_V81
               where Name = 'DEFAULT' and
                     Buffers > 0) and
      Buf# <= (select Hi_Bnum
               from V$BUFFER_POOL_V81
               where Name = 'DEFAULT' and
                     Buffers > 0)
group by 'DEFAULT', o.Name
union all
select 'KEEP' "BUFFER_POOL", o.Name, count(Buf#) BLOCKS
from SYS.OBJ$ o, X$BH x
where o.Dataobj# = x.Obj  and
      x.State != 0 and
      o.Owner# != 0 and
      Buf# >= (select Lo_Bnum
               from V$BUFFER_POOL_V81
               where Name = 'KEEP' and
                     Buffers > 0) and
      Buf# <= (select Hi_Bnum
               from V$BUFFER_POOL_V81
               where Name = 'KEEP' and
                     Buffers > 0)
group by 'KEEP', o.Name
union all
select 'RECYCLE' "BUFFER_POOL", o.Name, count(Buf#) BLOCKS
from SYS.OBJ$ o, X$BH x
where o.Dataobj# = x.Obj  and
      x.State != 0 and
      o.Owner# != 0 and
      Buf# >= (select Lo_Bnum
               from V$BUFFER_POOL_V81
               where Name = 'RECYCLE' and
                     Buffers > 0) and
```

```
        Buf# <= (select Hi_Bnum
                 from V$BUFFER_POOL_V81
                 where Name = 'RECYCLE' and
                       Buffers > 0)
group by 'RECYCLE', o.Name;
```

Shared SQL Area Hit Ratio

hitrpool.sql

The shared SQL area stores several different caches in memory. The shared structures include the library cache (which caches information about database objects such as stored procedures and views) and the cursor cache that caches SQL statements. In a multithreaded server (MTS) configuration, the shared SQL area is used to store session-specific information, such as the context area and the sort area. You need to verify that the shared SQL area is being accessed in an effective manner, with a high hit ratio for accesses to its entries.

The shared SQL area can consume a large amount of memory. In applications that make use of stored procedures or the MTS, the shared SQL area may be larger than the data block buffer cache. The demand on the shared SQL area is directly dependent on the breadth of your application. OLTP applications require more shared memory than batch-oriented applications, because there are more users executing more distinct transactions with OLTP. Aggravating the memory requirements for the shared SQL area is the implementation of stored procedures, packages, triggers, and even views in the shared memory.

In this section and the sections that follow, you will see scripts that help you determine whether your shared SQL area is being used effectively. You can use the scripts in these sections to determine the size of the memory area used by individual objects as well as the proper sizing of the shared SQL area.

In the following script, the shared SQL area hit ratio is calculated; like the database block buffer cache, the shared SQL area is fixed in size and is managed by an LRU algorithm. The shared SQL area hit ratio reflects the number of times a statement is parsed and stored in memory (*pinned*), compared to the number of times the statement has been aged out of memory and must be reparsed (*reloaded*). If the shared SQL area is not large enough, previously parsed statements will have to be continually reloaded. If the shared SQL area is large enough, the shared SQL area hit ratio, as calculated by the following script, will continually be greater than 99 percent. The script also calculates the *miss ratio*, which is the percentage of time a statement had to be reloaded into the shared SQL area.

```
REM  hitrpool.sql

REM Shared SQL Area Hit Ratio
REM  Target:  Hit Ratio > 99 percent.
REM
column Miss_Ratio format 999.99
```

```
column Hit_Ratio format 999.99
select
   SUM(Pins) Execs,
   SUM(Reloads) Cache_Misses,
   DECODE(SUM(Pins),0,0,(SUM(Reloads)/SUM(Pins))*100)
      Miss_Ratio,
   DECODE(SUM(Pins),0,0,((SUM(Pins)-SUM(Reloads))/SUM(Pins))*100)
      Hit_Ratio
from V$LIBRARYCACHE;
```

Sample output from the shared SQL area hit ratio query is shown in the following listing. The Execs column shows the number of times a SQL statement was executed. The Cache_Misses column shows the number of times a needed statement was no longer in the shared SQL area.

```
    EXECS CACHE_MISSES MISS_RATIO HIT_RATIO
--------- ------------ ---------- ---------
     8436           10        .12     99.88
```

The Execs column value is based on the Pins column value in the V$LIBRARYCACHE dynamic performance view. The Cache_Misses value is taken from the Reloads column of V$LIBRARYCACHE. The Pins and Reloads columns are used to generate the shared SQL area hit ratio:

```
DECODE(SUM(Pins),0,0,((SUM(Pins)-SUM(Reloads))/SUM(Pins))*100)
      Hit_Ratio
```

To calculate the hit ratio, the number of pins is first checked. If there have been 0 pins, the shared SQL area hit ratio is 0. Next, the number of reloads is subtracted from the number of pins, and the difference is divided by the number of pins. The result is the hit ratio for the shared SQL area.

In the sample data shown in the prior listing, the shared SQL area hit ratio was 99.88. If the shared SQL area hit ratio is below 99 percent (or the Miss_Ratio value exceeds 1.0), you should increase the size of the shared SQL area. The size of the shared SQL area is controlled via the SHARED_POOL_SIZE parameter in the init.ora file. Changes to the SHARED_POOL_SIZE value (expressed in bytes) in the init.ora file take effect when the database is shut down and restarted. After changing the shared SQL area size, check the new hit ratio. When increasing SHARED_POOL_SIZE, make sure the increase in SGA size does not cause swapping or paging to occur at the operating system level.

PROGRAMMER'S NOTE *The shared SQL area uses the LRU algorithm to manage the statements within the library cache. The most recently used statements are placed at the bottom of the LRU list and are kept the longest within the shared SQL area. To improve the performance of the shared SQL area, you can pin frequently used packages in the library cache. A pinned package is immediately placed at the bottom of the LRU list, thus staying longer within the shared SQL area.*

Shared Pool Structures

pool_str.sql

Just as you can query the database for information about the internals of the SGA, you can query it for information about the structures within the shared SQL area. The script in this section will show information on the total allocated and used space within the shared SQL area, as well as the number of statements currently stored in the library cache.

In this example, a different programming style is introduced. The data needed by the script is stored in many different tables and views. To present the data in a unified fashion, data is read via multiple queries. As data is retrieved from a query, the value returned is stored in a variable via the **new_value** option of the SQL*Plus **column** command. Once all the variables have been assigned values, a final query is executed to present the results in a unified fashion.

Following the script, you will see a sample data listing followed by an annotated walk-through of the script.

```
REM pool_str.sql
REM  Shared Pool Structures
REM
set pagesize 60 heading off termout off echo off verify off
ttitle off
REM
REM  The results from each query are assigned to
REM   variables via the new_value column option.
REM
col val1 new_val x_sp_size noprint
select Value val1
  from V$PARAMETER
 where Name='shared_pool_size'
/

col val2 new_val x_sp_used noprint
select SUM(Sharable_Mem+Persistent_Mem+Runtime_Mem) val2
  from V$SQLAREA
/

col val3 new_val x_sp_used_shr noprint
col val4 new_val x_sp_used_per noprint
col val5 new_val x_sp_used_run noprint
col val6 new_val x_sp_no_stmts noprint
select SUM(Sharable_Mem) val3,
       SUM(Persistent_Mem) val4,
       SUM(Runtime_Mem) val5,
       COUNT(*) val6
```

```
   from V$SQLAREA
/

col val7 new_val x_sp_no_obj noprint
select COUNT(*) val7
  from V$DB_OBJECT_CACHE
/

col val8 new_val x_sp_avail noprint
select &x_sp_size-&x_sp_used val8
  from DUAL
/

col val9 new_val x_sp_no_pins noprint
select COUNT(*) val9
  from V$SESSION A, V$SQLTEXT B
 where A.SQL_Address||A.SQL_Hash_Value = B.Address||B.Hash_Value
/

col val10 new_val x_sp_sz_pins noprint
select SUM(Sharable_Mem+Persistent_Mem+Runtime_Mem) val10
  from V$SESSION A,
       V$SQLTEXT B,
       V$SQLAREA C
 where A.SQL_Address||A.SQL_Hash_Value =
         B.Address||B.Hash_Value
   and B.Address||B.Hash_Value = C.Address||C.Hash_Value
/

set termout on
ttitle -
  center  'Shared Pool Library Cache Information' skip 2

select  'Size                            : '
  ||&x_sp_size sp_size,
       'Used (total)                    : '
  ||&x_sp_used,
       '        sharable                : '
  ||&x_sp_used_shr sp_used_shr,
       '        persistent              : '
  ||&x_sp_used_per sp_used_per,
       '        runtime                 : '
  ||&x_sp_used_run sp_used_run,
       'Available                       : '
```

```
   ||&x_sp_avail sp_avail,
          'Number of SQL statements                        : '
   ||&x_sp_no_stmts sp_no_stmts,
          'Number of programmatic constructs               : '
   ||&x_sp_no_obj sp_no_obj,
         'Pinned statements                                : '
   ||&x_sp_no_pins sp_no_pins,
          'Pinned statements size                          : '
   ||&x_sp_sz_pins sp_sz_pins
  from DUAL
/
ttitle off
set pagesize 24 heading on termout on echo off verify on
set feedback 6 linesize 80
undefine x_sp_size
undefine x_sp_used
undefine x_sp_used_shr
undefine x_sp_used_per
undefine x_sp_used_run
undefine x_sp_avail
undefine x_sp_no_stmts
undefine x_sp_no_obj
undefine x_sp_no_pins
undefine x_sp_sz_pins
```

Sample output from the script is shown in the following listing, followed by output interpretation and an annotated walk-through of the script.

```
            Shared Pool Library Cache Information


Size                                      : 8000000
Used (total)                              : 6022354
     sharable                             : 4465514
     persistent                           : 221624
     runtime                              : 1335216
Available                                 : 1977646
Number of SQL statements                  : 253
Number of programmatic constructs         : 211
Pinned statements                         : 9
Pinned statements size                    : 400628
```

The script output shows that for the example database, the shared SQL area is 8,000,000 bytes in size (as set via the SHARED_POOL_SIZE parameter in the init.ora file). Of that area, 1,977,646 bytes are available and the rest is used. Of the 253 SQL statements that have been parsed into the shared SQL area, 9 statements have been pinned.

ANNOTATIONS

The shared SQL area structures script uses a unique method of assigning variables and generating a unified presentation of the disconnected data. Because of its structure, the script is easy to customize and enhance.

The first section of the script establishes the system settings needed by the script. The **set verify off** command is critical, since it suppresses the writing of "before" and "after" value information each time a variable is assigned a value. The **set termout off echo off** command will suppress the display of the intermediate queries that generate the variable values. You should also turn **ttitle off** at this point, or else the report title will be displayed for each query that is executed.

```
REM   Shared Pool Structures
REM
set pagesize 60 heading off termout off echo off verify off
ttitle off
REM
```

In the next section, the first query is executed and its variable is assigned. In the first query, the V$PARAMETER view is queried for the Value setting for the SHARED_POOL_SIZE init.ora parameter. In the query, the Value column is given an alias of Val1. Because of the **column** command that precedes the query, the value of Val1 is assigned to the variable named *X_SP_SIZE*. The *X_SP_SIZE* variable will be used in the final query of the script.

```
REM
REM   The results from each query are assigned to
REM    variables via the new_value column option.
REM
col val1 new_val x_sp_size noprint
select Value val1
  from V$PARAMETER
 where Name='shared_pool_size'
/
```

In the next part of the script, the same technique is used to store data from the V$SQLAREA view in the *X_SP_USED* variable.

```
col val2 new_val x_sp_used noprint
select SUM(Sharable_Mem+Persistent_Mem+Runtime_Mem) val2
  from V$SQLAREA
/
```

The next part of the script, shown in the following listing, provides greater detail about the memory usage in the shared SQL area. Four variables are assigned, for use in the final query.

```
col val3 new_val x_sp_used_shr noprint
col val4 new_val x_sp_used_per noprint
col val5 new_val x_sp_used_run noprint
col val6 new_val x_sp_no_stmts noprint
select SUM(Sharable_Mem) val3,
       SUM(Persistent_Mem) val4,
       SUM(Runtime_Mem) val5,
       COUNT(*) val6
  from V$SQLAREA
/
```

In the next listing, the number of objects in the shared SQL area is queried from V$DB_OBJECT_CACHE. As with the previous queries, the result is stored in a variable for future use. The variable columns are marked as **noprint** via the **column** command so that no results from intermediate queries will be displayed to the user; only the final query's results will be displayed to the user.

```
col val7 new_val x_sp_no_obj noprint
select COUNT(*) val7
  from V$DB_OBJECT_CACHE
/
```

In the next section, a variable is assigned based on the difference between two previously defined variable values. The SYS.DUAL table (a one-row, one-column table) is used to generate the output. The difference between the two variables will be calculated, and the result will be assigned to a new variable, *X_SP_AVAIL*.

```
col val8 new_val x_sp_avail noprint
select &x_sp_size-&x_sp_used val8
  from DUAL
/
```

In the next section, the number of pinned objects is determined by querying V$SESSION, V$SQLTEXT, and V$SQLAREA.

```
col val9 new_val x_sp_no_pins noprint
select COUNT(*) val9
  from V$SESSION A, V$SQLTEXT B
 where A.SQL_Address||A.SQL_Hash_Value = B.Address||B.Hash_Value
/
```

```
col val10 new_val x_sp_sz_pins noprint
select SUM(Sharable_Mem+Persistent_Mem+Runtime_Mem) val12
  from V$SESSION A,
       V$SQLTEXT B,
       V$SQLAREA C
 where A.SQL_Address||A.SQL_Hash_Value =
         B.Address||B.Hash_Value
   and B.Address||B.Hash_Value = C.Address||C.Hash_Value
/
```

At this point in the script processing, all of the variables have had values assigned to them. The final query selects text strings from DUAL, followed by the variables. In the output, the values of the variables will be shown, as seen in the sample output listing repeated following the final query.

Before the final query is executed, the **set termout on** and **ttitle** commands are executed so that data will be displayed and the report will be properly titled.

```
set termout on
ttitle -
  center  'Shared Pool Library Cache Information' skip 2

select  'Size                                  : '
  ||&x_sp_size sp_size,
        'Used (total)                          : '
  ||&x_sp_used,
        '        sharable                      : '
  ||&x_sp_used_shr sp_used_shr,
        '        persistent                    : '
  ||&x_sp_used_per sp_used_per,
        '        runtime                       : '
  ||&x_sp_used_run sp_used_run,
        'Available                             : '
  ||&x_sp_avail sp_avail,
        'Number of SQL statements              : '
  ||&x_sp_no_stmts sp_no_stmts,
        'Number of programmatic constructs     : '
  ||&x_sp_no_obj sp_no_obj,
        'Pinned statements                     : '
  ||&x_sp_no_pins sp_no_pins,
        'Pinned statements size                : '
  ||&x_sp_sz_pins sp_sz_pins
  from DUAL
/
```

The sample output does not show the result of any of the interim queries. It shows a single, unified set of data generated by queries of many different views and tables. Because it involves so many queries, it may take longer for this script to complete than a script containing only one query.

```
            Shared Pool Library Cache Information


Size                                         : 8000000
Used (total)                                 : 6022354
        sharable                             : 4465514
        persistent                           : 221624
        runtime                              : 1335216
Available                                    : 1977646
Number of SQL statements                     : 253
Number of programmatic constructs             : 211
Pinned statements                             : 9
Pinned statements size                       : 400628
```

If the Available value is small or shrinks over time, increase the SHARED_POOL_SIZE init.ora parameter and stop and restart the database.

Shared SQL Area User Statistics

poolustt.sql

In the previous sections, you have seen how to measure how well the shared SQL area is being used (via its hit ratio) and how many statements are stored in the shared SQL area. In addition to that information, you can also determine the number of times statements have been executed and the number of users per statement. This additional information may be useful in measuring the impact of changes to the size of your shared SQL area. For example, you can monitor changes in the number of users per statement as the shared SQL area increases, showing measurable benefit from the increase in the available area.

The output of the following script contains three main sections: the data block buffer cache hit ratio, the shared SQL area hit ratio, and the user information for the shared SQL area. Although the hit ratios were shown in previous sections, they are repeated here to provide context to the user statistics.

The script is a set of queries, using the variable assignment technique described in the "Shared Pool Structures" section earlier in this chapter. The script will be shown in its entirety, followed by sample output and an annotated walk-through.

```
REM poolustt.sql
REM  Shared SQL area user statistics
REM
clear columns
set pagesize 60 heading off termout off echo off verify off
```

```
ttitle off
REM
col val1 new_val lib noprint
select 100*(1-(SUM(Reloads)/SUM(Pins))) val1
  from V$LIBRARYCACHE
/

col val2 new_val dict noprint
select 100*(1-(SUM(Getmisses)/SUM(Gets))) val2
  from V$ROWCACHE
/

col val3 new_val phys_reads noprint
select Value val3
  from V$SYSSTAT
 where Name = 'physical reads'
/

col val4 new_val log1_reads noprint
select Value val4
  from V$SYSSTAT
 where Name = 'db block gets'
/

col val5 new_val log2_reads noprint
select Value val5
  from V$SYSSTAT
 where Name = 'consistent gets'
/

col val6 new_val chr noprint
select 100*(1-(&phys_reads / (&log1_reads + &log2_reads))) val6
  from DUAL
/

col val7 new_val avg_users_cursor noprint
col val8 new_val avg_stmts_exe    noprint
select SUM(Users_Opening)/COUNT(*) val7,
       SUM(Executions)/COUNT(*)    val8
  from V$SQLAREA
/

set termout on
set heading off
```

```
ttitle -
  center  'SGA Cache Hit Ratios' skip 2

select  'Data Block Buffer Hit Ratio : '||&chr db_hit_ratio,
        '  Shared SQL Pool                          ',
        '  Dictionary Hit Ratio      : '||&dict dict_hit,
        '  Shared SQL Buffers (Library Cache)           ',
        '    Cache Hit Ratio         : '||&lib lib_hit,
        '    Avg. Users/Stmt         : '||
             &avg_users_cursor||'              ',
        '    Avg. Executes/Stmt      : '||
             &avg_stmts_exe||'              '
  from DUAL
/
clear columns
undefine chr
undefine dict
undefine lib
undefine avg_users_cursor
undefine avg_stmts_exe
undefine phys_reads
undefine log1_reads
undefine log2_reads
set pagesize 24 heading on termout on verify on
ttitle off
```

Sample output from the script is shown in the following listing.

```
                    SGA Cache Hit Ratios

Data Block Buffer Hit Ratio : 99.6101479
  Shared SQL Pool
  Dictionary Hit Ratio      : 98.5751095
  Shared SQL Buffers (Library Cache)
    Cache Hit Ratio         : 99.906068
    Avg. Users/Stmt         : .010791367
    Avg. Executes/Stmt      : 10.7230216
```

The sample output shows the data block buffer cache hit ratio, followed by the hit ratios for the dictionary cache and library cache portions of the shared SQL area. The average number of users per statement shows that an average user executes 100 statements. Each statement is executed an average of 10.7 times.

The *dictionary cache* stores information about the objects used by queries. For example, a query of a table requires the data dictionary information for the table, its indexes, its columns, and any relevant table-level or column-level privileges.

The data dictionary information required by the query is stored in the dictionary cache portion of the shared SQL area. You cannot size the dictionary cache; it is automatically created as part of the shared SQL area. If the dictionary cache hit ratio is below 98 percent, you should check the library cache hit ratio to determine whether you need to increase the size of the shared SQL area. In the example database, the library cache hit ratio is very high (99.9 percent), so you do not need to increase the size of the shared SQL area.

ANNOTATIONS

The shared SQL area user statistics script uses the variable assignment technique described in the "Shared Pool Structures" section earlier in this chapter. In the header of the script, the script's settings are established. The **set verify off** command is used to suppress information displays each time a variable has a value assigned to it. The **set termout off echo off** command suppresses the display of the interim queries.

```
REM   Shared SQL area user statistics
REM
clear columns
set pagesize 60 heading off termout off echo off verify off
ttitle off
REM
```

In the next section of the report, a series of queries is executed. As the queries are executed, the **new_value** option of the **column** command is used to assign the retrieved value to a variable. The **noprint** option of the **column** command prevents the data from being displayed to the user at this point; no data is displayed until the final report is generated.

The first two queries generate the library cache hit ratio and the dictionary cache hit ratio.

```
col val1 new_val lib noprint
select 100*(1-(SUM(Reloads)/SUM(Pins))) val1
  from V$LIBRARYCACHE
/

col val2 new_val dict noprint
select 100*(1-(SUM(Getmisses)/SUM(Gets))) val2
  from V$ROWCACHE
/
```

The next series of queries is used to determine the data block buffer cache hit ratio. The logical reads statistics (consistent gets and db block gets) and physical reads statistics are used to calculate the overall data block buffer cache hit ratio.

This series of queries is an alternative to the single-query method shown in "The Hit Ratio and the Miss Rate" earlier in this chapter.

```
col val3 new_val phys_reads noprint
select Value val3
  from V$SYSSTAT
 where Name = 'physical reads'
/

col val4 new_val log1_reads noprint
select Value val4
  from V$SYSSTAT
 where Name = 'db block gets'
/

col val5 new_val log2_reads noprint
select Value val5
  from V$SYSSTAT
 where Name = 'consistent gets'   -
/

col val6 new_val chr noprint
select 100*(1-(&phys_reads / (&log1_reads + &log2_reads))) val6
  from DUAL
/
```

The final series of queries compares the number of users and executions to the number of statements in the V$SQLAREA view. The result will show the average number of users per statement and executions per statement.

```
col val7 new_val avg_users_cursor noprint
col val8 new_val avg_stmts_exe    noprint
select SUM(Users_Opening)/COUNT(*)  val7,
       SUM(Executions)/COUNT(*)     val8
  from V$SQLAREA
/
```

Once all of the variables have had values assigned to them via the queries, the final query of the script selects the variables' values and formats them into a unified output.

```
set termout on
set heading off
ttitle -
```

```
center  'SGA Cache Hit Ratios' skip 2

select  'Data Block Buffer Hit Ratio : '||&chr db_hit_ratio,
        '  Shared SQL Pool                        ',
        '  Dictionary Hit Ratio       : '||&dict dict_hit,
        '  Shared SQL Buffers (Library Cache)             ',
        '    Cache Hit Ratio          : '||&lib lib_hit,
        '    Avg. Users/Stmt        : '||
            &avg_users_cursor||'           ',
        '    Avg. Executes/Stmt     : '||
            &avg_stmts_exe||'           '
   from DUAL
/
```

The output from the script is shown in the following listing. You can customize the report by adding or removing queries. For each new query, assign its output a unique column name and use the **new_value** option of the **column** command to assign the result to a variable. Once the value has been assigned to a variable, you can use the variable in the unified report.

```
                    SGA Cache Hit Ratios

Data Block Buffer Hit Ratio : 99.6101479
   Shared SQL Pool
   Dictionary Hit Ratio       : 98.5751095
   Shared SQL Buffers (Library Cache)
      Cache Hit Ratio          : 99.906068
      Avg. Users/Stmt        : .010791367
      Avg. Executes/Stmt     : 10.7230216
```

obj_spac7.sql
obj_spac8.sql

Estimate Space Usage by Shared SQL Objects

In addition to determining the hit ratios of the SGA's caches, you can measure how much of the shared pool is currently in use. The next script measures the amount of space used by objects within the shared SQL area and estimates the space required by the multithreaded server processes.

The script gathers data from many different views via a set of queries. In previous examples, the query results were read into SQL*Plus variables and later reported via unified queries. In this script, PL/SQL is used to manage the variables. The queries are executed within a PL/SQL block and the query results are stored in PL/SQL variables. At the end of the script, the values are displayed via the DBMS_OUTPUT package.

The script is shown next, followed by sample output and an annotated walk-through of the script. Obj_spac7.sql is applicable only for Oracle7.x, while obj_spac8.sql shown later is applicable for Oracle8.x and above.

```
REM   obj_spac7.sql
REM   Space Usage for shared SQL objects
REM If running MTS uncomment the mts calculation and output
REM commands.
REM
REM  This script is useful for Oracle7.x only
REMset echo off
set termout on
set serveroutput on;

declare
        object_mem number;
        shared_sql number;
        cursor_mem number;
        mts_mem number;
        used_pool_size number;
        free_mem number;
        pool_size varchar2(512);
begin

-- Stored objects (packages, views)
select SUM(Sharable_Mem) into object_mem
  from V$DB_OBJECT_CACHE;

-- Shared SQL
-- need to have additional memory if dynamic SQL used
select SUM(Sharable_Mem) into shared_sql
  from V$SQLAREA;

-- User Cursor Usage -- run this during peak usage.
--   assumes 250 bytes per open cursor, for each concurrent user.
select SUM(250*Users_Opening) into cursor_mem
  from V$SQLAREA;

-- For a test system -- get usage for one user, multiply by # users

-- select (250 * Value) bytes_per_user
-- from V$SESSTAT S, V$STATNAME N
-- where S.Statistic# = N.Statistic#
-- and N.Name = 'opened cursors current'
```

```
-- and S.SID = 25;   -- where 25 is the sid of the process

-- MTS memory needed to hold session information for
--      shared server users
-- This query computes a total for all currently logged on users
-- (run during peak period). Alternatively calculate for a single

--   user and multiply by # users.
select SUM(Value) into mts_mem
  from V$SESSTAT S, V$STATNAME N
 where S.Statistic#=N.Statistic#
   and N.Name='session uga memory max';

-- Free (unused) memory in the SGA: gives an indication of how much
-- memory is being wasted out of the total allocated.
select Bytes into free_mem
  from V$SGASTAT
 where Name = 'free memory';

-- For non-MTS add up object, shared sql, cursors and 20% overhead.
used_pool_size := ROUND(1.2*(object_mem+shared_sql+cursor_mem));

-- For MTS mts contribution needs to be included (comment out
-- previous line)
-- used_pool_size  :=
-- ROUND(1.2*(object_mem+shared_sql+cursor_mem+mts_mem));
select Value into pool_size
  from V$PARAMETER
 where Name='shared_pool_size';

-- Display results
DBMS_OUTPUT.PUT_LINE ('Object mem:    '||
                      TO_CHAR (object_mem) || ' bytes');
DBMS_OUTPUT.PUT_LINE ('Shared SQL:    '||
                      TO_CHAR (shared_sql) || ' bytes');
DBMS_OUTPUT.PUT_LINE ('Cursors:       '||
                      TO_CHAR (cursor_mem) || ' bytes');
-- DBMS_OUTPUT.PUT_LINE ('MTS session:   '||
--                       TO_CHAR (mts_mem) || ' bytes');
DBMS_OUTPUT.PUT_LINE ('Free memory:   '||
                      TO_CHAR (free_mem) || ' bytes ' ||
                '('   || TO_CHAR(ROUND(free_mem/1024/1024,2)) ||
                      'MB)');
DBMS_OUTPUT.PUT_LINE ('Shared pool utilization (total):  '||
```

```
TO_CHAR(used_pool_size) || ' bytes ' || '(' ||
TO_CHAR(round(used_pool_size/1024/1024,2)) || 'MB)');
DBMS_OUTPUT.PUT_LINE ('Shared pool allocation (actual):  '||
                                            pool_size

                    ||' bytes ' || '(' ||
                    TO_CHAR(ROUND(pool_size/1024/1024,2))
                    ||'MB)');
DBMS_OUTPUT.PUT_LINE ('Percentage Utilized:  '||to_char
(ROUND(used_pool_size/pool_size*100)) || '%');
end;
/
```

Sample output from the query (with the MTS data displayed) is shown in the following listing. If you do not enable the MTS query output (see the "Annotations" section, next), the "MTS session" line will not be displayed in the output.

```
Object mem:     610546 bytes
Shared SQL:     2951830 bytes
Cursors:        1250 bytes
MTS session:    611376 bytes
Free memory:    1209000 bytes (1.15MB)
Shared pool utilization (total):  5010002 bytes (4.78MB)
Shared pool allocation (actual):  8000000 bytes (7.63MB)
Percentage Utilized:  63%

PL/SQL procedure successfully completed.
```

The query output shows that for this database, only 63 percent of the shared SQL area is utilized. The MTS session information is second in size only to the library cache (the "Shared SQL" value). In systems that make extensive use of the MTS, the memory area required by the MTS session information may exceed the size of the library cache.

ANNOTATIONS

By default, several sections of the script are not executed. You should customize the script to reflect your database's structure and usage, as described in the following comments. To see the most relevant output, the script should be run during a time of peak usage in the database; the views it queries are sensitive to the number of active users in the database at the time the script is executed.

In the first section of the script, the variables used to hold the query results are defined. The variables will be referenced twice more in the script: when they are populated via queries and when their values are displayed at the end of the script.

```
declare
        object_mem number;
        shared_sql number;
        cursor_mem number;
        mts_mem number;
        used_pool_size number;
        free_mem number;
        pool_size varchar2(512);
```

In the next section of the script, the PL/SQL block starts and the first query is executed.

```
begin

-- Stored objects (packages, views)
select SUM(Sharable_Mem) into object_mem
  from V$DB_OBJECT_CACHE;
```

The result of the preceding query is assigned to the *object_mem* variable via the query's **into** clause. The *object_mem* variable stores the amount of memory used by objects in the shared SQL area's library cache. In the next query, the memory required by shared SQL is calculated. If dynamic SQL is used in your application, the amount of space used by shared SQL may increase dramatically.

```
-- Shared SQL
-- need to have additional memory if dynamic SQL used
   select SUM(Sharable_Mem) into shared_sql
   from V$SQLAREA;
```

The next section of the script attempts to estimate the memory area used by cursors. The query assumes that an average cursor requires 250 bytes. If you run the query during peak usage of the application, you will be able to see the maximum amount of space required by the cursors.

The commented-out query in this section allows you to estimate the cursor usage more accurately, but the query should not be run as part of this script. The query determines the number of cursors opened by a particular user, and it uses that number to estimate the space usage, in bytes, of the cursors used by that user. You can then estimate the total cursor memory used for all of your users. Run this query on a test system, using the V$SESSTAT.SID for a typical user process.

```
User Cursor Usage -- run this during peak usage.
--   assumes 250 bytes per open cursor, for each concurrent user.
select SUM(250*Users_Opening) into cursor_mem
  from V$SQLAREA;
```

```
-- For a test system -- get usage for one user, multiply by # users
-- select (250 * Value) bytes_per_user
-- from V$SESSTAT S, V$STATNAME N
-- where S.Statistic# = N.Statistic#
-- and N.Name = 'opened cursors current'
-- and S.SID = 25;  -- where 25 is the sid of the process
```

In the next section of the script, the MTS memory statistics are queried to determine the amount of memory used to hold MTS user session information.

```
-- MTS memory needed to hold session information
--         for shared server users
-- This query computes a total for all currently logged on users
-- (run during peak period).
-- Alternatively calculate for a single user
-- and multiply by # users.
select SUM(Value) into mts_mem
   from V$SESSTAT S, V$STATNAME N
 where S.Statistic#=N.Statistic#
    and N.Name='session uga memory max';
```

In the next query in the script, the V$SGASTAT view is queried to determine the amount of unused memory within the SGA. Because the SGA is allocated when the database is started, unused ("free") memory is wasted—no other applications can use that memory, and the database is not using it. If you persistently see large portions of your SGA marked as free memory, you should examine whether the memory can be better used for your application. For example, you may want to reclaim space from the shared SQL area and make that memory available to the data block buffer cache or log buffer cache. Alternatively, you may decide to reduce the size of your SGA, allowing user processes to access more memory directly. If you manipulate the size of your SGA, you should run this script periodically to verify the used and unused space measures for the database.

```
Free (unused) memory in the SGA: gives an indication of how much
-- memory is being wasted out of the total allocated.
select Bytes into free_mem
   from V$SGASTAT
 where Name = 'free memory';
```

The next section of the script needs to be modified, depending on whether or not you are using MTS. If you are using MTS, the first assignment of a value to the *used_pool_size* variable should be commented out by adding two dashes (--) to the front of the line, and the comment marks should be removed from the second assignment of the variable.

For databases using MTS, this section of the script should read as follows:

```
-- For non-MTS add up object, shared sql, cursors and 20% overhead.
-- used_pool_size := ROUND(1.2*(object_mem+shared_sql+cursor_mem));
-- For MTS mts contribution needs to be included (comment out
-- previous line)
used_pool_size :=
        ROUND(1.2*(object_mem+shared_sql+cursor_mem+mts_mem));
select Value into pool_size
  from V$PARAMETER
 where Name='shared_pool_size';
```

For databases that are not using MTS, this section of the script should be modified, as shown in the following listing. For both the MTS and non-MTS calculation, 20 percent overhead is added to the memory requirements estimates. The 20 percent overhead estimate may be high for systems with a small number of users and may result in report output showing that you are using more memory than you have allocated.

```
-- For non-MTS add up object, shared sql, cursors and 20% overhead.
used_pool_size := ROUND(1.2*(object_mem+shared_sql+cursor_mem));

-- For MTS mts contribution needs to be included (comment out
-- previous line)
-- used_pool_size :=
-- ROUND(1.2*(object_mem+shared_sql+cursor_mem+mts_mem));
select Value into pool_size from V$PARAMETER
 where Name='shared_pool_size';
```

Now that all the variable assignments are complete, the report output is generated via the DBMS_OUTPUT package. Each line is created via the PUT_LINE procedure of the DBMS_OUTPUT package, and the PL/SQL block is ended.

One of the output lines is commented out. If you are using MTS, you should remove the comment marks that precede the output showing the MTS session output.

```
-- Display results
DBMS_OUTPUT.PUT_LINE ('Object mem:     '||TO_CHAR (object_mem) || ' bytes');
DBMS_OUTPUT.PUT_LINE ('Shared SQL:     '||TO_CHAR (shared_sql) || ' bytes');
DBMS_OUTPUT.PUT_LINE ('Cursors:        '||TO_CHAR (cursor_mem) || ' bytes');
-- DBMS_OUTPUT.PUT_LINE ('MTS session:    '||TO_CHAR (mts_mem) || ' bytes');
DBMS_OUTPUT.PUT_LINE ('Free memory:    '||TO_CHAR (free_mem) || ' bytes ' ||
'('    || TO_CHAR(ROUND(free_mem/1024/1024,2)) || 'MB)');
DBMS_OUTPUT.PUT_LINE ('Shared pool utilization (total):  '||
TO_CHAR(used_pool_size) || ' bytes ' || '(' ||
TO_CHAR(ROUND(used_pool_size/1024/1024,2)) || 'MB)');
DBMS_OUTPUT.PUT_LINE ('Shared pool allocation (actual):  '|| pool_size
```

```
||' bytes ' || '(' || TO_CHAR(ROUND(pool_size/1024/1024,2)) || 'MB)');
DBMS_OUTPUT.PUT_LINE ('Percentage Utilized:  '||TO_CHAR
(ROUND(used_pool_size/pool_size*100)) || '%');
end;
/
```

If you modify the size of your SGA, you should use this script to determine whether the amount of free space within the SGA changes. If your Percentage Utilized value reaches 100 percent, you should check the data block buffer cache hit ratio and the library cache hit ratio to determine which could benefit the most from increased available memory.

The following query shows the calculation of space utilization for the shared SQL objects in an Oracle8.x database:

```
REM   obj_spac8.sql
REM   Space Usage for shared SQL objects
REM If running MTS uncomment the mts calculation and output
REM commands.
REM
REM   This script is useful for Oracle8.x and above
REM
set echo off
set termout on
set serveroutput on;

declare
        object_mem number;
        shared_sql number;
        cursor_mem number;
        mts_mem number;
        used_pool_size number;
        free_mem number;
        pool_size varchar2(512);
begin

-- Stored objects (packages, views)
select SUM(Sharable_Mem) into object_mem
  from V$DB_OBJECT_CACHE;

-- Shared SQL -- need to have additional memory if dynamic SQL used
select SUM(Sharable_Mem) into shared_sql
  from V$SQLAREA;

-- User Cursor Usage -- run this during peak usage.
--   assumes 250 bytes per open cursor, for each concurrent user.
select SUM(250*Users_Opening) into cursor_mem
  from V$SQLAREA;

-- For a test system -- get usage for one user, multiply by # users
```

```
-- select (250 * Value) bytes_per_user
-- from V$SESSTAT S, V$STATNAME N
-- where S.Statistic# = N.Statistic#
-- and N.Name = 'opened cursors current'
-- and S.SID = 25;   -- where 25 is the sid of the process

-- MTS memory needed to hold session information
--          for shared server users
-- This query computes a total for all currently logged on users
-- (run  during peak period). Alternatively calculate for a single user
and  multiply by # users.
select SUM(Value) into mts_mem
  from V$SESSTAT S, V$STATNAME N
 where S.Statistic#=N.Statistic#
   and N.Name='session uga memory max';

-- Free (unused) memory in the SGA:
-- gives an indication of how much memory
-- is being wasted out of the total allocated.
select Bytes into free_mem
  from V$SGASTAT
 where pool = 'shared pool' and
       Name = 'free memory';

-- For non-MTS add up object, shared sql, cursors and 20% overhead.
used_pool_size := ROUND(1.2*(object_mem+shared_sql+cursor_mem));

-- For MTS mts contribution needs to be included (comment out previous line)
-- used_pool_size := ROUND(1.2*(object_mem+shared_sql+cursor_mem+mts_mem));
select Value into pool_size
  from V$PARAMETER
 where Name='shared_pool_size';

-- Display results
DBMS_OUTPUT.PUT_LINE ('Object mem:     '||TO_CHAR (object_mem) || ' bytes');
DBMS_OUTPUT.PUT_LINE ('Shared SQL:    '||TO_CHAR (shared_sql) || ' bytes');
DBMS_OUTPUT.PUT_LINE ('Cursors:       '||TO_CHAR (cursor_mem) || ' bytes');
-- DBMS_OUTPUT.PUT_LINE ('MTS session:    '||TO_CHAR (mts_mem) || ' bytes');
DBMS_OUTPUT.PUT_LINE ('Free memory:    '||TO_CHAR (free_mem) || ' bytes ' ||
 '('   || TO_CHAR(ROUND(free_mem/1024/1024,2)) || 'MB)');
DBMS_OUTPUT.PUT_LINE ('Shared pool utilization (total):  '||
TO_CHAR(used_pool_size) || ' bytes ' || '(' ||
TO_CHAR(round(used_pool_size/1024/1024,2)) || 'MB)');
DBMS_OUTPUT.PUT_LINE ('Shared pool allocation (actual):  '|| pool_size
||' bytes ' || '(' || TO_CHAR(ROUND(pool_size/1024/1024,2)) || 'MB)');
DBMS_OUTPUT.PUT_LINE ('Percentage Utilized:  '||to_char
(ROUND(used_pool_size/pool_size*100)) || '%');
end;
/
```

The output from the proceeding block of code looks like this:

```
Object mem:     21667998 bytes
Shared SQL:     12238601 bytes
Cursors:        1000 bytes
Free memory:    47887780 bytes (45.67MB)
Shared pool utilization (total):   40689119 bytes (38.8MB)
Shared pool allocation (actual):   58720256 bytes (56MB)
Percentage Utilized:   69%


PL/SQL procedure successfully completed.
```

The preceding query is similar to the query for Oracle7.x except that it considers the possibility of using "large pool" in Oracle8.x and focuses on space calculation of just the shared pool:

```
select Bytes into free_mem
  from V$SGASTAT
 where pool = 'shared pool' and
       Name = 'free memory';
```

SQL Statements that Use Shared Memory Improperly

sh_hutil.sql
litersql.sql
shp_age.sql

The following queries can be used to determine the SQL statements that use shared pool memory improperly. This should show whether any literal statements or multiple versions of a statement could benefit from the use of bind variables.

```
REM   sh_hutil.sql
REM   Identify statements that use large amounts of shared pool memory
REM   Generally the threshold should be 10% of the shared pool size in bytes
REM
set verify off
SELECT substr(sql_text,1,60) "Statement",
       count(*),
       sum(sharable_mem) "Sharable Memory",
       sum(users_opening) "Users Opening",
       sum(executions) "Executions"
FROM v$sql
GROUP BY substr(sql_text,1,60)
HAVING sum(sharable_mem) > &threshold;
```

The preceding query accesses the V$SQL view to determine SQL statements that use large amount of shared pool memory. A threshold (that is usually 10 percent of the shared pool size) can be used to filter out from the result set those SQL statements that don't use large amounts of shared memory. The SQL statements identified by the preceding query should be checked to determine whether they can benefit from the use of bind variables. The **substr** function is used to extract the first 60 characters of the SQL statements.

```
SELECT substr(sql_text,1,60) "Statement",
```

Similarly, the following query shows SQL statements that use literals and can add to any latch contention that may exist.

```
REM   litersql.sql
REM   This script shows SQL in the SGA
REM           where there are a large number of similar statements.
REM   The literal statements identified should be considered as candidates
REM           for converting to use bind variables.
REM   The values 60, 5 and 20 in the following query are examples and
REM       identify different SQL statements whose
REM       (1) first 60 characters are the same,
REM       (2) have been executed a few times (less than 5) and
REM       (3) there are at least 20 occurences in the shared pool
REM
REM
SELECT substr(sql_text,1,60) "SQL",
       count(*),
       sum(executions) "TOTAL EXECUTIONS"
FROM   v$sqlarea
WHERE  executions < 5
GROUP BY substr(sql_text,1,60)
HAVING count(*) > 20
ORDER BY 2;
```

The following query identifies SQL statements that cause shared pool memory to age-out and hence may be contributing to a large number of reloads of other statements.

```
REM   shp_age.sql
REM   Identify allocations that cause share pool
REM       memory to be "aged" out
REM
SELECT *
FROM x$ksmlru
WHERE ksmlrnum > 0;
```

Large Pool Utilization

largpool_util.sql

In Oracle8.x and later you can configure the *large pool*. The large pool is an area of the SGA that can be used for certain special operations. Only certain types and sizes of memory can be allocated in this pool. Memory needed for the large pool is not taken from the shared pool but directly from the SGA, and hence it can contribute to the amount of memory needed by Oracle to start up. The large pool is used for the following:

- Buffering for sequential file I/O
- Message buffers used by parallel executions
- Disk I/O buffers used during backup
- User Global Area (UGA) of sessions connected using MTS

By default, the large pool is not allocated and must be explicitly configured using the following init.ora parameters:

- LARGE_POOL_SIZE   Specifies the size of the large pool
- LARGE_POOL_MIN_ALLOC   Specifies the minimum size chunk of memory that can be allocated to the large pool

It is important that you set the large pool size, because if it is left unset and the large pool is required by either parallel query or backup I/O slaves, Oracle will compute a value automatically. This can occur when any of the following is set:

- PARALLEL_AUTOMATIC_TUNING
- PARALLEL_MIN_SERVERS
- DBWR_IO_SLAVES

The default computation is based on several parameters and can result in a size that may be too large to be allocated or may cause performance problems. The following parameters are used in the automatic computation of the large pool size:

- PARALLEL_MAX_SERVERS
- PARALLEL_SERVER_INSTANCES
- MTS_DISPATCHERS
- PARALLEL_THREADS_PER_CPU
- DBWR_IO_SLAVES

The large pool is protected by the shared pool latch that manages its memory allocation. Each session is responsible for allocating and releasing its memory in the large pool, because there is no LRU mechanism in place in the large pool and, therefore, chunks of memory allocated in the large pool never age out.

When the large pool is not configured (as in Oracle7) and MTS is configured, the sessions entire UGA is allocated in the shared pool. On the other hand, when the large pool is configured, a new MTS session allocates a small amount of memory (known as the *fixed UGA*) in the shared pool and the rest of the session memory (UGA) is allocated in the large pool.

The following query shows the large pool utilization:

```
REM   largpool_util.sql
REM   Determine the utilization of the Large Pool
REM   This script is useful for Oracle8.x and higher
REM
set echo off
set termout on
set serveroutput on

declare
        large_pool_size number;
        free_mem number;
        used_pool_size number;
begin

select value into large_pool_size
from v$parameter
where name = 'large_pool_size';

select Bytes into free_mem
  from V$SGASTAT
 where pool = 'large pool' and
       Name = 'free memory';

used_pool_size := large_pool_size - free_mem;


-- Display results
DBMS_OUTPUT.PUT_LINE ('Large Pool Size:    '||
 TO_CHAR (large_pool_size) || ' bytes' ||
 '('    || TO_CHAR(ROUND(large_pool_size/1024/1024,2)) || 'MB)');

DBMS_OUTPUT.PUT_LINE ('Free memory:        '||
 TO_CHAR (free_mem) || ' bytes ' ||
 '('    || TO_CHAR(ROUND(free_mem/1024/1024,2)) || 'MB)');

DBMS_OUTPUT.PUT_LINE ('Large pool utilization (total):  '||
```

```
   TO_CHAR(used_pool_size) || ' bytes ' ||
'(' || TO_CHAR(round(used_pool_size/1024/1024,2)) || 'MB)');

DBMS_OUTPUT.PUT_LINE ('Percentage Utilized:  '||to_char
(ROUND(used_pool_size/large_pool_size*100)) || '%');
end;
/
```

An example of the output obtained by running the preceding script follows

```
Large Pool Size:    5728640 bytes(5.46MB)
Free memory:        5615800 bytes (5.36MB)
Large pool utilization (total):  112840 bytes (.11MB)
Percentage Utilized:  2%

PL/SQL procedure successfully completed.
```

If the large pool utilization is high, you should consider increasing its size; otherwise you may soon see error ORA-4031 when new allocations won't be possible (as allocated memory doesn't automatically age-out).

Log Buffer Cache Size

The *log buffer cache* is the portion of the SGA used to store records of transactions before the transaction information is written to the online redo log files. The size of the log buffer cache is set (in bytes) via the LOG_BUFFER parameter in the database's init.ora file.

Records are written from the log buffer cache to the online redo log files on a timed basis. Every few seconds, the log writer (LGWR) background process reads the data from the log buffer cache and writes the data to the online redo log files. If the log buffer is not large enough to hold the data from the ongoing transactions, the transactions will be delayed by the wait for space in the log buffer cache. Because the log buffer cache entries provide a chronological history of the transactions in the database, an LRU algorithm cannot be used to manage the cache. If the log buffer cache is full, incoming transactions must wait.

You can determine the number of waits for log buffer cache space by querying V$SYSSTAT. You should compare the number of waits to the size of the log buffer cache, as shown in the following example:

```
REM log_bufs.sql
REM  Log Buffer Size - check for redo log space requests
REM
column log_buffer_size format A20
select A.Value  Log_Buffer_Size,
       B.Value  Log_Buffer_Space_Waits
```

```
     from V$PARAMETER A,  V$SYSSTAT B
   where A.Name = 'log_buffer'
     and B.Name = 'redo log space requests';
```

Sample output from the preceding query is shown here:

```
LOG_BUFFER_SIZE          LOG_BUFFER_SPACE_WAITS
--------------------     ----------------------
327680                                       33
```

The output shows that for the sample database, the log buffer is 327,680 bytes in size. There were 33 waits for space in the log buffer cache. It is difficult to eliminate log buffer space waits completely; you should monitor your database activity to establish a threshold value for log buffer cache space waits.

The following version of the script adds a threshold value check to the query. When the script is executed, the user will be prompted for a threshold value for the redo log space requests. A record will be returned only if the number of redo log space requests exceeds the threshold value.

```
REM  Log Buffer Size - with threshold
REM
column log_buffer_size format A20
select A.Value  Log_Buffer_Size,
       B.Value  Log_Buffer_Space_Waits
  from V$PARAMETER A, V$SYSSTAT B
 where A.Name = 'log_buffer'
   and B.Name = 'redo log space requests'
   and B.Value > &threshold;
```

Multiblock Read Setting

When a table is scanned via a TABLE ACCESS FULL operation, multiple blocks are read during each read from the table. The number of blocks read at a time is determined by the setting of the DB_FILE_MULTIBLOCK_READ_COUNT parameter in the database's init.ora file. Multiblock reads affect only full table scans; table accesses by RowID and index accesses are not affected.

When they are read into the data block buffer cache, the blocks read via a full table scan are automatically marked as the least recently used blocks in the cache (unless the table is marked as a "cache" table, or if the table is five or fewer blocks in size). Thus, as the table is scanned, the blocks read via the full table scan occupy little space within the SGA. The space occupied by the full table scan blocks is equal to the product of the database block size and the multiblock read count setting.

For example, if the database block size is 4KB, and DB_FILE_MULTIBLOCK_READ_COUNT is set to 8, 32KB (eight 4KB blocks) is read during each database read, and 32KB within the data block buffer cache is used by the scan. When data from the second read arrives at the data block buffer cache, the blocks read via the first read are removed from the cache and replaced with the blocks from the second read. Thus, although you may be performing a large full table scan, the majority of your data block buffer cache is unaffected; only 32KB of the data block buffer cache is used. The rest of the data block buffer cache will not be overwritten by the data read via the full table scan, and the ability to share commonly used data among users via the data block buffer cache will not be impacted.

multblck.sql

Proper setting of DB_FILE_MULTIBLOCK_READ_COUNT

Setting your DB_FILE_MULTIBLOCK_READ_COUNT parameter to a higher value will improve the performance of the full table scan, because more data will be read during each read of the table. However, increasing the multiblock read count parameter will increase the impact of full table scans on the data block buffer cache—the temporary holding area for the table scan blocks will grow in size. Thus, setting the DB_FILE_MULTIBLOCK_READ_COUNT parameter involves balancing the performance of the full table scans against the use of the rest of the data block buffer cache.

If your application is an OLTP application, with many users executing small transactions, you should try to minimize the impact of full table scans on the database. If your application is a batch application with few users executing large transactions, you may increase the multiblock read count to improve the table scan performance without negatively impacting the application as a whole.

In general, you should set the multiblock read count parameter so that a single physical read takes advantage of the buffer used by the operating system during a physical read. For example, if the operating system's read buffer is 64KB in size, you should start with a multiblock read count that enables 64KB to be buffered per read. That is, if your database block size is 4KB, your DB_FILE_MULTIBLOCK_READ_COUNT parameter should be set to 16.

The query in the following listing queries V$PARAMETER to determine the current settings for the database block size and the multiblock read count value. The two parameter values are multiplied to determine the amount of data read during each multiblock read. You should compare the output of this query to the size of your operating system's read buffer and the overall space available in the data block buffer cache to determine the adequacy of the setting.

```
REM multblck.sql

REM Multiblock Read Count check
REM
select to_number(v1.Value)*to_number(v2.Value)
```

```
    Batch_Read_Size
  from V$PARAMETER V1, V$PARAMETER V2
 where V1.Name = 'db_block_size'
   and V2.Name = 'db_file_multiblock_read_count'
/
```

Sample output from the preceding query is shown in the following listing.

```
BATCH_READ_SIZE
---------------
          65536
```

The batch read size in the listing is expressed in bytes. 65,536 bytes is 64KB, which is the size of the operating system's read buffer in the test system.

Enqueue Resources

An *enqueue resource* is needed for every table that is locked by the database lock manager. You need to have enough enqueue resources—as set via the ENQUEUE_RESOURCES parameter in your database's init.ora file—to support the locking requirements of your application. The number of locks on a table is irrelevant; the number of tables locked determines the number of enqueue resources required.

Check Enqueue Resources Against Enqueue Waits

enq_res.sql

If your application is an OLTP application with many small tables, you will need to increase the default ENQUEUE_RESOURCES setting to avoid waiting for resources to become available. Enqueue waits are reported via the V$SYSSTAT dynamic performance view. In the query in the next listing, the ENQUEUE_RESOURCES setting (from V$PARAMETER) is compared to the number of enqueue waits (from V$SYSSTAT).

PROGRAMMER'S NOTE *Enqueue waits can be affected by free lists, free list groups and MAX TRANS for table creation.*

```
REM enq_res.sql

REM  Enqueue_resources - check against enqueue waits
REM
column Enqueue_Resources format A20
select A.Value Enqueue_Resources,
```

```
        B.Value Enqueue_Waits
   from V$PARAMETER A, V$SYSSTAT B
  where A.Name = 'enqueue_resources'
    and B.Name = 'enqueue waits';
```

Sample output from the query is shown here:

```
ENQUEUE_RESOURCES      ENQUEUE_WAITS
-------------------    -------------
520                                0
```

For the test application, 520 enqueue resources were established, with no subsequent enqueue waits. You may therefore choose to decrease the number of enqueue resources allocated to the database. If you decrease the number of available enqueue resources, you should monitor the database for an associated rise in the number of enqueue waits.

ANNOTATIONS

You may want to add to the query a threshold value as a limiting condition for the number of enqueue waits. Enqueue waits are common, and you can monitor your applications to determine a typical number of waits for your application. If the number of waits exceeds this threshold, the following query will return a record; if the number of waits is below the threshold, no rows will be returned by the query.

```
REM   Enqueue_resources - with threshold
REM
column Enqueue_Resources format A20
select A.Value Enqueue_Resources,
       B.Value Enqueue_Waits
  from V$PARAMETER A, V$SYSSTAT B
 where A.Name = 'enqueue_resources'
   and B.Name = 'enqueue waits'
   and B.Value > &threshold;
```

Full Table Scans of Large Tables

Full table scans usually indicate that either no indexes are available for the table being queried or the query is written in a manner that prevents the use of indexes. Full table scans of small tables may be efficient data access methods, since the database may be able to read the full table into memory quickly. Full table scans of large tables typically perform worse than comparable index-based accesses of large tables. A large table is one that is larger than five database blocks in size.

PROGRAMMER'S NOTE *In Oracle7, the Parallel Query Option (PQO) cannot parallelize index scans; therefore, you may have written queries deliberately using full table scans to exploit the PQO. If you use the PQO extensively in Oracle7, you will have a high percentage of full table scans of large tables. Beginning with Oracle8, the PQO can parallelize index scans. If you have previously modified your queries to use full table scans to parallelize them, you should investigate the use of parallelized index scans instead.*

Determine Full Table Scans of Large Tables

fts_larg.sql

The following query determines the percentage of full table scans that are performed on large tables. If you have many table scans of large tables, you should evaluate the queries being executed within your application.

```
REM fts_larg.sql
REM  Full table scans of large tables
REM
select A.Value  Large_Table_Scans,
       B.Value  Small_Table_Scans,
       ROUND(100*A.Value/
       DECODE((A.Value+B.Value),0,1,(A.Value+B.Value)),2)
          Pct_Large_Scans
  from V$SYSSTAT A, V$SYSSTAT B
 where A.Name = 'table scans (long tables)'
   and B.Name = 'table scans (short tables)';
```

Sample output from the query is shown in the following listing.

```
LARGE_TABLE_SCANS SMALL_TABLE_SCANS PCT_LARGE_SCANS
----------------- ----------------- ---------------
              292              5067            5.45
```

The sample output shows that scans of large tables make up over 5 percent of all table scans. Table scans of small tables appear to be frequently used (more than 5,000 times) in the test application.

ANNOTATIONS

You should monitor your databases to determine the acceptable percentage of large full table scans for your applications. If large tables account for more than 20 percent of your full table scans, you will typically have a data block buffer cache hit ratio that falls below your target hit ratio. If large tables account for more than 10 percent of your full table scans, you should closely examine the queries and processes within your application to determine whether queries need to be rewritten or indexes need to be added.

The following query will prompt you for a threshold value for the percentage of full table scans caused by large tables. If the percentage of full table scans that is caused by large tables exceeds the threshold, a record will be returned by the query. If the percentage of table scans caused by large tables is below the threshold, no record will be returned from the query.

```
REM   Full table scans of large tables - with threshold
REM
REM   Can use a threshold value (e.g., 10 for 10 percent)
REM
select A.Value Large_Table_Scans,
       B.Value Small_Table_Scans,
       ROUND(100*A.Value/
       DECODE((A.Value+B.Value),0,1,(A.Value+B.Value)),2)
          Pct_Large_Scans
  from V$SYSSTAT A, V$SYSSTAT B
 where A.Name = 'table scans (long tables)'
   and B.Name = 'table scans (short tables)'
   and ROUND(100*A.Value/
       DECODE((A.Value+B.Value),0,1,(A.Value+B.Value)),2)
          >> &threshold;
```

If you use the PQO extensively, the threshold-based version of this query will not be as useful for you, because you may be forcing full table scans of large tables to occur.

Sort Area

Sorting operations—such as index creations or **order by** clauses within queries—require temporary work areas within the database. If possible, the sorting is performed entirely within memory. If not enough memory is available to support the sort's space requirements, a temporary segment is allocated and the sort uses disk space.

Managing the sort area requires balancing two competing objectives. First, you should minimize the amount of sort data written to disk, since writing and reading from disk is much slower than writing and reading from memory. The more sort data you write to disk (via temporary segments), the worse the query may perform. Second, available physical memory is limited, so you don't want to use all of the available memory for sort space. Your objective should be to allocate enough sort area in memory so that most sorts initiated by OLTP users complete within memory, while sorts initiated by long-running batch users employ temporary segments.

The available sort area in memory is set via the SORT_AREA_SIZE parameter in your database's init.ora file. The SORT_AREA_RETAINED_SIZE should be set to a value at or below that of SORT_AREA_SIZE; a low retained size lets users release memory from the sort area after the sort completes.

Determine In-Memory versus Disk Sorts

disksort.sql

In the following query, the number of sorts performed in memory is compared to the number of sorts performed via temporary segments. Both statistics are retrieved from V$SYSSTAT, a dynamic performance view that maintains cumulative totals for these statistics.

```
REM disksort.sql

REM  In-memory vs disk sorts
REM
select A.Value Disk_Sorts,
       B.Value Memory_Sorts,
       ROUND(100*A.Value/
       DECODE((A.Value+B.Value),0,1,(A.Value+B.Value)),2)
          Pct_Disk_Sorts
  from V$SYSSTAT A, V$SYSSTAT B
 where A.Name = 'sorts (disk)'
   and B.Name = 'sorts (memory)';
```

Sample output from the query is shown in the following listing.

```
DISK_SORTS MEMORY_SORTS PCT_DISK_SORTS
---------- ------------ --------------
        91        81771            .11
```

The output shows that disk sorts have almost never been used since the database was last started. The very low percentage of disk sorts is typical for OLTP applications with a high value for SORT_AREA_SIZE. Since the percentage of sorts performed on disk is so low, you may consider reducing SORT_AREA_SIZE and dedicating the saved memory area to the shared SQL area or the data block buffer cache.

ANNOTATIONS

You can establish a threshold percentage of disk sorts to serve as a limiting condition for the query. If the percentage of sorts performed on disk exceeds the threshold, a record will be returned; if it is below the threshold, no record will be returned. The threshold version of the disk sort percentage query is shown in the following listing.

```
REM   In-memory vs disk sorts - with threshold
REM
REM   Specify a threshold percentage, such as 10 for
REM   10 percent disk sorts.
REM
select A.Value Disk_Sorts,
       B.Value Memory_Sorts,
       ROUND(100*A.Value/
       DECODE((A.Value+B.Value),0,1,(A.Value+B.Value)),2)
           Pct_Disk_Sorts
  from V$SYSSTAT A, V$SYSSTAT B
 where A.Name = 'sorts (disk)'
   and B.Name = 'sorts (memory)'
   and ROUND(100*A.Value/
      DECODE((A.Value+B.Value),0,1,(A.Value+B.Value)),2)
            > &threshold;
```

If you are performing more than 10 percent of your sorts on disk, you should either increase the SORT_AREA_SIZE or evaluate your processes to determine whether you can eliminate unnecessary sorts. For example, you may be able to replace a **union** operator (which performs a SORT UNIQUE after merging rows from two queries) with a **union all** operator (which does not eliminate duplicates prior to merging the queries' output). The **union** and **union all** operators return different sets of records (**union** eliminates duplicates; **union all** does not), so they are not always interchangeable; however, this is one example of the kind of change that can help reduce sorting requirements.

A high number of sorting operations may indicate a high number of joins performed via the MERGE JOIN operation (which first executes a SORT JOIN on each table in the join). A MERGE JOIN may be used if indexes cannot be used for the join conditions of the query. If indexes can be used, a NESTED LOOPS join may be used instead—eliminating the need for sort area either in memory or on disk.

Parallel Query Server Processes

To effectively use the PQO, you need to manage the pool of parallel query server processes available to the database. The number of parallel query server processes started when the database is started is determined by setting the PARALLEL_MIN_SERVERS parameter in the database's init.ora file. If you set the minimum number of parallel query server processes too high, you will waste system resources. If you set the minimum number of parallel query server processes too low, you will force the database continually to start new parallel query server processes to support the processing requirements.

The maximum number of parallel query server processes that can run simultaneously in your database is determined by the setting of the PARALLEL_MAX_SERVERS parameter in the database's init.ora file. If you set the maximum number of parallel query server processes too high, you will be wasting system resources. If you set the maximum number of parallel query server processes too low for your application, you will reduce the degree to which the application's queries can be parallelized.

pqo_stat.sql

Determine Effectiveness of Parallel Query Setting

Activity involving the parallel query server processes can be seen via queries of V$PQ_SYSSTAT. The queries in this section compare the number of parallel query server processes in use (from V$PQ_SYSSTAT) with the PARALLEL_MIN_SERVERS and PARALLEL_MAX_SERVERS settings.

The first query, shown in the following listing, checks to determine whether PARALLEL_MIN_ SERVERS is set too high. The query of V$PQ_SYSSTAT requires you to perform an **RTRIM** function on the Statistic description column; although it is a VARCHAR2 column, it is right-padded with blanks to be 30 characters wide.

```
REM pqo_stat.sql

REM  Are parallel query server processes unused?
REM
column Parallel_Min_Servers format 999999999
select TO_NUMBER(A.Value) Parallel_Min_Servers,
       B.Value Servers_Busy
  from V$PARAMETER A, V$PQ_SYSSTAT B
 where A.Name = 'parallel_min_servers'
   and RTRIM(B.Statistic) = 'Servers Busy';
```

Sample output for the first query is shown in the following listing. According to the output, the minimum number of parallel query server processes started for the database is 20. Of those 20, only 16 are currently in use. If the current usage is typical of the application, the PARALLEL_MIN_SERVERS parameter may be lowered to 16 without causing the database to dynamically start new parallel query server processes.

```
PARALLEL_MIN_SERVERS SERVERS_BUSY
-------------------- ------------
                  20           16
```

In general, you should set PARALLEL_MIN_SERVERS to a low value and bear the performance penalty of starting and stopping parallel query server processes.

If the minimum number of parallel query server processes is high, unused processes will remain on your server—and may not release the memory they acquired during their processing. As a result, the server may become flooded with unused processes holding memory that no other users can address.

The second query of the set checks to see whether any parallel query server processes have been started since the database was started and the initial parallel query server processes were created. The 'Servers Started' statistic in V$PQ_SYSSTAT is cumulative, and thus reflects activity that occurred before the current users logged in to the database.

```
REM  Have any servers been started?
REM
Select Statistic, Value Servers_Started
From V$PQ_SYSSTAT
Where RTRIM(Statistic) = 'Servers Started';
```

Sample output from the second query of the set is shown in the following listing. The query output shows that 472 parallel query server processes have been started since the database was started. Thus, although the current number of busy parallel query server processes is below the initial number of parallel query server processes created (from the first query's output), at previous times the number of parallel query server processes required exceeded the PARALLEL_MIN_SERVERS setting. When more than the minimum number of parallel query server processes was required by the database, more servers were started—and the 'Servers Started' statistic was incremented, as reflected in the following listing.

```
STATISTIC                          SERVERS_STARTED
------------------------------     ---------------
Servers Started                                472
```

The third query of the set, shown in the following listing, compares the highest number of busy parallel query server processes to the PARALLEL_MAX_SERVERS setting in your database's init.ora file. If the highest number of parallel query server processes ever in use is within 10 percent of the maximum number of parallel query server processes, you may need to consider increasing the PARALLEL_MAX_SERVERS setting. This query refers to the 'Servers Highwater' statistic in V$PQ_SYSSTAT.

```
REM Is Parallel_Max_Servers high enough for current usage?
REM
column Parallel_Max_Servers format 999999999
select TO_NUMBER(A.Value) Parallel_Max_Servers,
       B.Value Servers_HW
  from V$PARAMETER A, V$PQ_SYSSTAT B
 where A.Name = 'parallel_max_servers'
   and RTRIM(B.Statistic) = 'Servers Highwater';
```

Sample output from the third parallel query server process query is shown in the following listing.

```
PARALLEL_MAX_SERVERS    SERVERS_HW
--------------------    ------------
                 160           120
```

As shown in the query output, the highest number of busy parallel query server processes since the database started is 120. The maximum number of parallel query server processes is set to 160. If the current usage of the test database is typical of the application's database activity, you may be able to decrease the PARALLEL_MAX_SERVERS setting without adversely affecting the application's performance. Decreasing PARALLEL_MAX_SERVERS reduces the potential parallelism of database activities during heavy application usage.

Effectiveness of Redo Copy Latches

The *redo allocation latch* serializes the writing of entries to the log buffer cache of the SGA. The redo allocation latch allocates space in the log buffer cache for each transaction's entry. If transactions are small, or if there is only one CPU on the server, the redo allocation latch also copies the transaction data into the log buffer cache.

If multiple CPUs are available, you can create multiple *redo copy latches*. The redo copy latches will copy transaction data into the log buffer cache, freeing the redo allocation latch from performing this task. You can create multiple redo copy latches (usually up to two times the number of available CPUs). The number of redo copy latches created is set via the LOG_SIMULTANEOUS_COPIES parameter in your database's init.ora file.

If LOG_SIMULTANEOUS_COPIES is set to a non-zero value, the redo allocation latch will check the size of the transaction entry and compare it against otherinit.ora settings. If the size of the transaction entry is smaller than the value of the LOG_SMALL_ENTRY_MAX_SIZE init.ora parameter, the copy of the transaction entry into the log buffer cache is performed by the redo allocation latch. If the size of the transaction entry exceeds LOG_SMALL_ENTRY_MAX_SIZE, the transaction entry is copied into the log buffer cache by a redo copy latch.

redocopy.sql

Contention for Redo Copy Latches

The following query determines the miss ratio and the "immediate" miss ratio for redo copy latches. If either miss ratio is greater than 1 percent, you should increase the number of redo copy latches (set LOG_SIMULTANEOUS_COPIES > 0) and decrease the value of the LOG_SMALL_ENTRY_MAX_SIZE parameter.

```
REM redocopy.sql

REM  Latch contention check
REM
select SUBSTR(V$LATCH.Name,1,30) Name,
       (Misses/(Gets+.001))*100 Miss_Ratio,
       (Immediate_Misses/(Immediate_Gets+.001))*100
          Immediate_Miss_Ratio
  from V$LATCH, V$LATCHNAME
where V$LATCH.Latch# = V$LATCHNAME.Latch#
  and V$LATCH.Name = 'redo copy';
```

Sample output from the preceding query is shown here:

```
NAME                           MISS_RATIO IMMEDIATE_MISS_RATIO
------------------------------ ---------- --------------------
redo copy                      49.9750125           .001483911
```

The query output shows that the redo copy latch has a miss ratio of almost 50 percent. The performance of transactions within the database could be improved (if multiple CPUs are available) by increasing the number of redo copy latches enabled within the database.

Effectiveness of Multithreaded Server

The MTS allows multiple users to share common dispatcher (user process manager) and server (database request manager) processes, thereby reducing the memory requirements per user process. At instance startup, init.ora parameters are used to determine the number of dispatchers and servers started. If more dispatchers or servers are needed by the user processes, the database will start more, up to the maximum number specified via the init.ora parameters. If the maximum number of dispatchers or servers is too low, user requests will be forced to wait and the perceived performance of the application will suffer.

mts_stat.sql

MultiThreaded Server Statistics

The MTS_SERVERS parameter in the database's init.ora file specifies the number of server processes to start when the database starts. As more servers are needed, they are added until the number of servers reaches the setting of the MTS_MAX_SERVERS init.ora parameter.

The query shown in the following listing will show the average wait, in hundredths of a second, in the request queue. If the average wait is greater than one second, you should increase the MTS_MAX_SERVERS setting, thereby increasing the number of available servers.

```
REM mts_stat.sql

REM    Is MTS_MAX_SERVERS high enough?
REM
select DECODE( Totalq, 0, 'No Requests',
       ROUND(Wait/Totalq,2) || ' hundredths of seconds')
        Avg_Wait_Per_Request_Queue
  from V$QUEUE
 where Type = 'COMMON';
```

Sample output for the preceding query is shown in the following listing.

```
AVG_WAIT_PER_REQUEST_QUEUE
-----------------------------------------------------------------
.25 hundredths of seconds
```

Because the average wait in the request queue is less than one second, there is no need to increase the MTS_MAX_SERVERS setting in the test database.

The MTS_DISPATCHERS parameter in the database's init.ora file specifies the number of dispatcher processes to start when the database starts. As more dispatchers are needed, they are added until the number of dispatchers reaches the setting of the MTS_MAX_DISPATCHERS init.ora parameter.

The query shown in the following listing will show the average wait, in hundredths of a second, in the response queue. If the average wait is greater than one second, you should increase the MTS_MAX_DISPATCHERS setting, thereby increasing the number of available dispatchers.

```
REM   Average wait per response queue
REM
select DECODE(SUM(Totalq), 0, 'No Responses',
       ROUND(SUM(Wait)/SUM(Totalq),2) || ' hundredths of seconds')
            Avg_Wait_Per_Response_Queue
  from V$QUEUE Q, V$DISPATCHER D
 where Q.Type = 'DISPATCHER'
   and Q.Paddr = D.Paddr;
```

Sample output for the preceding query is shown here:

```
AVG_WAIT_PER_RESPONSE_QUEUE
-----------------------------------------------------------------
.04 hundredths of seconds
```

Because the average wait in the response queue is less than one second, there is no need to increase MTS_MAX_DISPATCHERS in the test database.

Effectiveness of Database Writer Process

The DBWR process writes changed blocks from the data block buffer cache to the datafiles. If the database has a heavy transaction load, the DBWR process may not always be able to keep up with the pace of changes in the data block buffer cache. When the DBWR process fails to write the changed data promptly, a *data block wait* is recorded. The cumulative number of data block waits that have occurred since the database was started is recorded in the V$WAITSTAT dynamic performance view.

Compare DBWR to Data Block Waits

dbwrstat.sql

The following query will show the number of DBWR processes in the database as defined by the DB_WRITERS (for Oracle7) or DB_WRITER_PROCESSES (Oracle8) parameter in the database's init.ora file and the cumulative number of data block waits. The script looks for both parameters—only one of them will be found in V$PARAMETER, so the query will work in both Oracle7 and Oracle8. You will rarely have a value of 0 for data block waits.

```
REM dbwrstat.sql

REM Check for data block waits
REM
column DB_Writers format A20
select A.Value   DB_Writers,
       B.Count   Data_Block_Waits
  from V$PARAMETER A, V$WAITSTAT B
 where (A.Name = 'db_writers' or A.Name = 'db_writer_processes')
   and B.Class = 'data block';
```

You should monitor your applications to determine the typical acceptable value for data block waits in your databases. You can then establish a threshold—for example, 10,000 data block waits for an OLTP application—and increase the number of DBWR processes or I/O slaves when the number of data block waits exceeds the threshold. Since the number of data block waits is cumulative, you should be sure to measure the number of waits at a set point in time following database startup.

Sample output for the data block wait query is shown here:

```
DB_WRITERS               DATA_BLOCK_WAITS
--------------------     ----------------
2                                   98414
```

The query output shows that two DBWR processes are active for the test database (the default is for only one DBWR process to be used).

To interpret the data block waits statistic, you need to be familiar with the application and the timing of the query. Applications that have many users executing many concurrent transactions will by their nature have a higher number of data block waits. Also, since the data block waits statistic is cumulative, you need to know how long it has been since the database was last started.

As of Oracle8.x, you can use the parameter DB_WRITER_PROCESSES for systems that modify data heavily. It specifies the initial number of database writer processes for that instance. It should be noted, however, that if you use the parameter DBWR_IO_SLAVES, Oracle uses only one database writer process, regardless of the setting for the DB_WRITER_PROCESSES parameter. The DBWR_IO_SLAVES parameter is relevant only on systems with one database writer process. It can be used to specify the number of I/O server processes used by the database writer process. By default, the DBWR_IO_SLAVES parameter is 0 and the I/O server processes are not used.

ANNOTATIONS

You should monitor the data block waits in your database over time and determine the typical pattern of DBWR processing for your application. You can then select a threshold to use when evaluating the data block waits statistic.

You can add a threshold to the query by adding the following limiting condition:

```
and B.Count > &threshold
```

When the revised query is executed, a record will be returned only if the number of data block waits exceeds the threshold value you specify.

In some performance guides, the number of DBWR processes to create is tied to the number of available disks in the database. Instead of using the disk-based method for setting the number of DBWR processes, monitor the data block waits as described in this section.

Beyond the SGA

The SGA is directly involved in almost every effort to tune queries and applications. Once your SGA is properly tuned, you can look beyond the SGA to other aspects of the database that affect performance. In this section, you will see how to

- ◆ Analyze the I/O against datafiles
- ◆ Query overall system usage statistics
- ◆ View current parameter settings along with undocumented parameters
- ◆ Generate explain plans
- ◆ Use the utlbstat/utlestat scripts to supplement the scripts in this chapter

Datafile I/O Distribution

You may encounter performance problems with your application if the I/O performed by the application is not properly distributed across files, disks, and hardware controllers. The queries in this section will help you determine which files are the most actively accessed within your database. Once you know which files are the most frequently accessed, you can tune the accesses to those files.

Tuning accesses to files may involve the following:

◆ **Moving objects into separate tablespaces**   For example, you may want to move frequently used tables into their own tablespaces, apart from smaller static tables. Isolating active tables in this manner makes it easier to move them onto less actively used hardware devices.

◆ **Striping extents across files**   You can structure a table's space allocation to force it to create extents in different files, thereby distributing the table's I/O load across multiple files.

◆ **Striping files across disks**   You can use the operating system to spread a single file across multiple disks (using mirroring or RAID technology). By involving multiple disks in the resolution of the I/O request, the burden on any single disk is reduced and a potential I/O bottleneck is avoided.

When tuning I/O, you need to be aware of the most frequently accessed files and the manner in which the database is using them. In the following query, the V$FILESTAT view is joined to the V$DATAFILE view; the result will show the total I/O by datafile. The I/O is expressed in terms of database blocks read and written.

```
REM fileio.sql

REM  Datafile I/O distribution, across all datafiles
REM
column File_Name format A39
select DF.Name File_Name,
       FS.Phyblkrd Blocks_Read,
       FS.Phyblkwrt Blocks_Written,
       FS.Phyblkrd+FS.Phyblkwrt Total_IOs
  from V$FILESTAT FS, V$DATAFILE DF
 where DF.File#=FS.File#
 order by FS.Phyblkrd+FS.Phyblkwrt desc;
```

Sample output for the datafile I/O distribution query is shown in the following listing.

FILE_NAME	BLOCKS_READ	BLOCKS_WRITTEN	TOTAL_IOS
/db01/oracle/APP1/sys01.dbf	70601	83	70684
/db10/oracle/APP1/apptab01.dbf	35642	70	35712
/db10/oracle/APP1/apptab02.dbf	8481	4	8485
/db07/oracle/APP1/users01.dbf	7640	0	7640
/db13/oracle/APP1/tools01.dbf	7052	0	7052
/db07/oracle/APP1/temp01.dbf	0	418	418
/db10/oracle/APP1/rbs01.dbf	55	89	144
/db01/oracle/APP1/users02.dbf	132	0	132
/db01/oracle/APP1/appindx02.dbf	83	0	83
/db06/oracle/APP1/apptest.dbf	64	0	64
/db01/oracle/APP1/users03.dbf	60	0	60
/db01/oracle/APP1/appindx04.dbf	22	1	23
/db01/oracle/APP1/appindx03.dbf	17	0	17
/db01/oracle/APP1/appindx01.dbf	14	1	15

```
14 rows selected.
```

In the preceding listing, the datafiles are listed in descending order of total I/O activity. The "read" and "write" I/Os are shown as well, so you can identify the type of activity prevalent in each file's access pattern. In this example, the datafile for the SYSTEM tablespace accounts for most of the I/O activity, followed by the data tablespace for the application (the "apptab" datafiles). The application is read-intensive, with many more reads than writes. Although it is read-intensive, there have been very few accesses to the index tablespace for the application (the "appindx" datafiles). Based on this information, you should check the hit ratio for the database to determine whether you need to investigate the queries used and index structures available. You may also want to separate the datafiles for the APPTAB tablespace onto separate devices (both are presently on /db10, as is the rollback segment tablespace's datafile).

ANNOTATIONS

You can modify the full datafile I/O distribution query to show only those datafiles that account for more than a given percentage of the total I/O performed in the database. You can select a threshold percentage—for example, 10 percent—and only the datafiles that account for at least that percentage of the database I/O will be shown.

In the following listing, the datafile I/O distribution query is shown with a threshold variable. When the query is executed, you will be prompted for the percentage to use as the threshold (such as 10 for 10 percent).

```
REM  Datafile I/O distribution - with threshold.
REM
REM  You will be prompted for a threshold percentage,
```

```
REM   such as 10 to check for any file that accounts for
REM   at least 10 percent of the I/O in the database.
REM
set verify off
column File_Name format A39
select DF.Name File_Name,
       FS.Phyblkrd Blocks_Read,
       FS.Phyblkwrt Blocks_Written,
       FS.Phyblkrd+FS.Phyblkwrt Total_Ios
  from V$FILESTAT FS, V$DATAFILE DF
 where DF.File#=FS.File#
   and (FS.Phyblkrd+FS.Phyblkwrt) >
       (select (&threshold/100)*sum (FS.Phyblkrd+FS.Phyblkwrt)
          from V$FILESTAT FS, V$DATAFILE DF
         where DF.File#=FS.File#)
 order by FS.Phyblkrd+FS.Phyblkwrt desc;
```

Sample output for the datafile I/O distribution query with a threshold is shown in the following listing.

```
Enter value for threshold: 10
```

FILE_NAME	BLOCKS_READ	BLOCKS_WRITTEN	TOTAL_IOS
/db01/oracle/APP1/sys01.dbf	70601	83	70684
/db10/oracle/APP1/apptab01.dbf	35642	70	35712

The threshold-based datafile I/O query output allows you quickly to identify the most frequently accessed files. Because it does not show all of the files, it does not show any other files on those devices. For example, in the test database, only one of the APPTAB tablespace's datafiles is listed in the output of the threshold-based query; there is no indication that a second datafile for the same tablespace is stored on the same device. Therefore, you should use the threshold-based report to identify candidates for I/O bottlenecks, and use the full report to see the distribution of datafile I/O across all datafiles and disks.

params.sql

Parameter Settings

The database initialization parameters may be stored in several different operating system files and, as of Oracle7.3, may be altered after the database has been started. Certain parameters can be changed either at the session level (via the **alter session** command) or at the database level (via the **alter system** command). If you change parameter settings at the session level, the settings remain in effect for the duration of your session. If you change parameter settings at the database level, the new settings stay in effect even after you shut down and restart the database—the new settings override the init.ora parameter settings! You should therefore check the database settings against the init.ora settings on a regular basis and update the init.ora settings as needed.

Because parameters can dynamically change, you cannot always rely on the database's init.ora file to show the most recent settings for the instance parameters. Instead, you should query the V$PARAMETER dynamic performance view directly, as shown in the following listing.

```
REM params.sql


REM   Current parameter settings, from V$PARAMETER
REM
column Name format A50
column Value format A28
select Name,
       Value
   from V$PARAMETER;
```

ANNOTATIONS

The V$PARAMETER view contains columns you can use to determine which parameters can be dynamically modified at the session and database levels. If a parameter can be altered at the session level, the IsSes_Modifiable column in V$PARAMETER will have a value of TRUE. If a parameter can be altered at the database level, the IsSys_Modifiable column in V$PARAMETER will have a value of IMMEDIATE.

The query in the following listing shows the parameters that you can dynamically change at session or database level.

```
REM   Dynamic parameter settings, from V$PARAMETER
REM
column Name format A50
column IsSes_Modifiable format A5
column IsSys_Modifiable format A10
select Name,
       IsSes_Modifiable,
       IsSys_Modifiable
  from V$PARAMETER
 where IsSes_Modifiable = 'TRUE'
    or IsSys_Modifiable = 'IMMEDIATE';
```

Sample output showing dynamically changeable parameters (in an ORACLE9i database) is shown in the following listing.

```
NAME                            ISSES ISSYS_MOD
------------------------------- ----- ---------
tracefile_identifier            TRUE  FALSE
timed_statistics                TRUE  IMMEDIATE
timed_os_statistics             TRUE  IMMEDIATE
nls_language                    TRUE  FALSE
nls_territory                   TRUE  FALSE
nls_sort                        TRUE  FALSE
nls_date_language               TRUE  FALSE
nls_date_format                 TRUE  FALSE
nls_currency                    TRUE  FALSE
nls_numeric_characters          TRUE  FALSE
nls_iso_currency                TRUE  FALSE


NAME                            ISSES ISSYS_MOD
------------------------------- ----- ---------
nls_calendar                    TRUE  FALSE
nls_time_format                 TRUE  FALSE
nls_timestamp_format            TRUE  FALSE
nls_time_tz_format              TRUE  FALSE
nls_timestamp_tz_format         TRUE  FALSE
nls_dual_currency               TRUE  FALSE
nls_comp                        TRUE  FALSE
log_archive_dest_1              TRUE  IMMEDIATE
log_archive_dest_2              TRUE  IMMEDIATE
log_archive_dest_3              TRUE  IMMEDIATE
log_archive_dest_4              TRUE  IMMEDIATE


NAME                            ISSES ISSYS_MOD
------------------------------- ----- ---------
log_archive_dest_5              TRUE  IMMEDIATE
log_archive_dest_6              TRUE  IMMEDIATE
log_archive_dest_7              TRUE  IMMEDIATE
log_archive_dest_8              TRUE  IMMEDIATE
log_archive_dest_9              TRUE  IMMEDIATE
log_archive_dest_10             TRUE  IMMEDIATE
log_archive_dest_state_1        TRUE  IMMEDIATE
log_archive_dest_state_2        TRUE  IMMEDIATE
log_archive_dest_state_3        TRUE  IMMEDIATE
log_archive_dest_state_4        TRUE  IMMEDIATE
log_archive_dest_state_5        TRUE  IMMEDIATE
```

```
NAME                              ISSES ISSYS_MOD
-------------------------------   ----- ---------
log_archive_dest_state_6          TRUE  IMMEDIATE
log_archive_dest_state_7          TRUE  IMMEDIATE
log_archive_dest_state_8          TRUE  IMMEDIATE
log_archive_dest_state_9          TRUE  IMMEDIATE
log_archive_dest_state_10         TRUE  IMMEDIATE
log_archive_min_succeed_dest      TRUE  IMMEDIATE
db_file_multiblock_read_count     TRUE  IMMEDIATE
db_create_file_dest               TRUE  IMMEDIATE
db_create_online_log_dest_1       TRUE  IMMEDIATE
db_create_online_log_dest_2       TRUE  IMMEDIATE
db_create_online_log_dest_3       TRUE  IMMEDIATE


NAME                              ISSES ISSYS_MOD
-------------------------------   ----- ---------
db_create_online_log_dest_4       TRUE  IMMEDIATE
db_create_online_log_dest_5       TRUE  IMMEDIATE
undo_suppress_errors              TRUE  IMMEDIATE
db_block_checking                 TRUE  IMMEDIATE
global_names                      TRUE  IMMEDIATE
session_cached_cursors            TRUE  FALSE
remote_dependencies_mode          TRUE  IMMEDIATE
plsql_v2_compatibility            TRUE  IMMEDIATE
plsql_compiler_flags              TRUE  IMMEDIATE
parallel_min_percent              TRUE  FALSE
cursor_sharing                    TRUE  IMMEDIATE


NAME                              ISSES ISSYS_MOD
-------------------------------   ----- ---------
parallel_instance_group           TRUE  IMMEDIATE
hash_join_enabled                 TRUE  FALSE
hash_area_size                    TRUE  FALSE
max_dump_file_size                TRUE  IMMEDIATE
oracle_trace_enable               TRUE  IMMEDIATE
object_cache_optimal_size         TRUE  DEFERRED
object_cache_max_size_percent     TRUE  DEFERRED
sort_area_size                    TRUE  DEFERRED
sort_area_retained_size           TRUE  DEFERRED
optimizer_mode                    TRUE  FALSE
partition_view_enabled            TRUE  FALSE
```

```
NAME                              ISSES  ISSYS_MOD
-------------------------------   -----  ---------
star_transformation_enabled       TRUE   FALSE
parallel_broadcast_enabled        TRUE   FALSE
optimizer_max_permutations        TRUE   FALSE
optimizer_index_cost_adj          TRUE   FALSE
optimizer_index_caching           TRUE   FALSE
query_rewrite_enabled             TRUE   IMMEDIATE
query_rewrite_integrity           TRUE   IMMEDIATE
sql_version                       TRUE   FALSE
workarea_size_policy              TRUE   IMMEDIATE

75 rows selected.
```

PROGRAMMER'S NOTE   *The parameters that can be dynamically modified at the session and database level may change between database versions.*

While V$PARAMETER shows the parameter settings for the documented parameters, you can set additional parameters. Usually, these parameters are either left over from previous versions of the RDBMS or will be documented as supported parameters in later versions of the RDBMS. In almost all cases, the first letter of a parameter is an underscore (_). The parameters can have their values specified via your database's init.ora file. For example, Oracle Financials users should use the parameter setting

```
_optimizer_undo_changes = TRUE
```

in their init.ora file to dynamically undo changes to the way the Oracle optimizer interprets correlated subqueries in RDBMS versions after Oracle release 6.0.31.

The query shown in the next listing must be run as the SYS user. The query will list all of the parameters starting with an underscore that are recognized by the database.

PROGRAMMER'S NOTE   *The undocumented parameters are subject to change without notice as database versions change.*

```
REM  Undocumented parameters - subject to change!
REM
col Ksppinm format a28 head 'Parameter' justify c trunc
col Ksppdesc format a40 head 'Description' justify c trunc
  select Ksppinm,
         Ksppdesc
    frcm X$KSPPI
   where Ksppinm like '\_%' escape '\'
order by Ksppinm;
```

The **where** clause of this query searches for strings beginning with an underscore (_). In ORACLE, the underscore is a single-character wildcard. If your **where** clause had read

```
where Ksppinm like '\_%'
```

every row whose Ksppinm value contained at least one character would have passed that **where** clause criteria. Instead, you can use the **escape** clause of the **like** operator. The **escape** clause tells the database that the character that follows it (in this example, a backslash) is a special character. In the **like** clause, the character following the backslash (the underscore) will be interpreted literally, as an underscore instead of a wildcard. Thus, this **where** clause

```
where Ksppinm like '\_%' escape '\'
```

is interpreted by the database as limiting the output to those records whose Ksppinm values begin with an underscore.

PROGRAMMER'S NOTE *Before modifying one of the undocumented parameters, check with Oracle Support to find out alternatives to the modification you are making, and whether the change is supported.*

gen_stat.sql

General Statistics

You can query V$SYSSTAT and V$SGASTAT to see general statistics regarding the database's activity. The queries earlier in this chapter referred to specific rows in V$SYSSTAT and V$SGASTAT. The queries in the following listing will show all statistics available via those dynamic performance views.

```
REM gen_stat.sql

REM   Query of general statistics
REM
select *
  from V$SYSSTAT;

select *
  from V$SGASTAT;
```

In the section dealing with the management of the pool of available parallel query server processes earlier in this chapter, specific rows of the V$PQ_SYSSTAT dynamic performance view were queried. You can see all of the statistics concerning the PQO by executing this query:

```
REM   General statistics concerning parallelism
REM
select *
  from V$PQ_SYSSTAT;
```

The statistics available via V$PQ_SYSSTAT are shown here:

```
select Statistic
   from V$PQ_SYSSTAT;


STATISTIC
------------------------------
Servers Busy
Servers Idle
Servers Highwater
Server Sessions
Servers Started
Servers Shutdown
Servers Cleaned Up
Queries Initiated
DFO Trees
Local Msgs Sent
Distr Msgs Sent
Local Msgs Recv'd
Distr Msgs Recv'd
```

The length of each Statistic value is 30 characters. Although the column is a VARCHAR2 column, each value is padded with spaces. To query V$PQ_SYSSTAT for a particular Statistic value, you should use the **RTRIM** function to strip the trailing blanks, as shown in the following listing.

```
Select Statistic,
        Value
From V$PQ_SYSSTAT
Where RTRIM(Statistic) = 'Servers Busy';
```

explain.sql
sql_to_explain.sql
explain_enh7.sql
explain_enh8.sql

Generating Explain Plans

You can determine the path that Oracle will choose for a query's execution (known as the *execution path* or the *explain plan*) without running the query. To determine the execution path, you must use the **explain plan** command in Oracle. This command will evaluate the steps in the execution path for a query and will place one row for each step into a table named PLAN_TABLE. The records in PLAN_TABLE will describe the operations used at each step of the query execution and the relationships between the execution path steps. If you are using the cost-based optimizer (CBO), the explain plan will show the relative "cost" of each step in the execution path.

To use **explain plan**, you first need to create a PLAN_TABLE table in the schema that you will be using (usually, the schema that owns the tables used by the query).

Oracle provides a script to create the PLAN_TABLE; named utlxplan.sql, it is usually stored in the /rdbms/admin subdirectory under the Oracle software home directory. Run the utlxplan.sql script from within SQL*Plus, as shown in the following example of a UNIX user creating PLAN_TABLE.

```
@@$ORACLE_HOME/rdbms/admin/utlxplan
```

```
Table created.
```

If the utlxplan.sql script fails to create the table, you lack one of the following:

- ◆ The CREATE TABLE privilege
- ◆ Adequate free space within your default tablespace
- ◆ Any more space within your space quota for your default tablespace

PROGRAMMER'S NOTE *The utlxplan.sql script may change between Oracle versions and sometimes between minor releases. You should drop PLAN_TABLE and run this script every time you upgrade your Oracle version to guarantee that you will see all available execution path information.*

Once PLAN_TABLE has been created in your schema, you can begin to determine the execution paths of selected queries. To determine the execution path of a query, prefix the query with the SQL shown in the following listing.

```
explain plan
set Statement_ID = 'TEST'
for
```

To make the tuning process simpler, always use the same Statement_ID value, and delete the records for each execution path before using the **explain plan** command a second time.

An example of execution of the **explain plan** command is shown in the following listing. The query shown in the listing will not be run during the command; only its execution path steps will be generated, and they will be inserted as records in PLAN_TABLE.

```
explain plan
set Statement_ID = 'TEST'
for
select Name, Lodging, BirthDate
  from WORKER
 where Lodging = 'ROSE HILL'
   and Name like 'J%';
```

```
Explained.
```

The records have now been inserted into PLAN_TABLE. You can query the PLAN_TABLE using the following query. The results of this query will show the operations performed at each step and the parent-child relationships between the execution path steps.

```
REM explain.sql

REM  Standard query of PLAN_TABLE
REM
select LPAD(' ',2*Level)||Operation||' '||Options
             ||' '||Object_Name    Q_Plan
  from PLAN_TABLE
 where Statement_ID = 'TEST'
connect by prior ID = Parent_ID and Statement_ID = 'TEST'
   start with ID=1;
```

The query shown in the preceding listing uses the **connect by** operator to evaluate the hierarchy of steps in the query's execution path. The query in the listing assumes the Statement_ID field has been set to 'TEST'. The execution path steps will be displayed in the column given the Q_Plan alias.

If the WORKER table in the prior example had two single-column, nonunique indexes on its Lodging and Name columns, the Q_Plan value—the execution path—may resemble the output shown in the next listing.

PROGRAMMER'S NOTE   *The actual execution path chosen by the optimizer will vary depending on the distribution of values within the table and the selectivity of the indexes.*

```
Q_PLAN
-------------------------------------------------------------
TABLE ACCESS WORKER BY ROWID
  AND-EQUAL
    INDEX RANGE SCAN WORKER$NAME
    INDEX RANGE SCAN WORKER$LODGING
```

The AND-EQUAL operation combines the results of the two index scans (on the WORKER$NAME and WORKER$LODGING indexes).

If you are using the CBO, you can query PLAN_TABLE to determine the relative cost of the query. The relative cost of the query is stored in the Position column of PLAN_TABLE, in the row with an ID value of 0. The query shown in the following listing will show the cost of the query whose explain plan has just been generated.

```
REM  Show relative cost of a query's execution path
REM
select Position  Cost
  from PLAN_TABLE
```

```
where ID = 0
  and Statement_ID = 'TEST';
```

The relative cost of a query cannot be compared to the cost of any other query; it is useful only when estimating the performance impact of modifications to the query.

ANNOTATIONS

As of Oracle7.3, you can generate the explain plan automatically for every transaction you execute within SQL*Plus. The **set autotrace on** command will cause each query, after being executed, to display both its execution path and high-level trace information about the processing involved in resolving the query. The explain plan generated via **set autotrace on** will show the cost associated with each step of the query, the number of rows returned from each step of the query, and any parallelism used during the query's execution.

PROGRAMMER'S NOTE

*To use **set autotrace on**, you must have first created the PLAN_TABLE table within your account and you must have access to the dynamic performance views. If you do not have DBA authority, you can access the dynamic performance views if you have been granted the PLUSTRACE role. The PLUSTRACE role is not created in the database by default; a script provided by Oracle (usually called plustrce.sql) to create the role is typically located in the /sqlplus/admin subdirectory under the Oracle software home directory. Once the script has been run by a DBA, you can be granted the PLUSTRACE role and you will then be able to use the **set autotrace on** command.*

When using the **set autotrace on** command, you do not set a Statement_ID, and you do not have to manage the records within the PLAN_TABLE. To disable the autotrace feature, use the **set autotrace off** command.

To use the autotrace capability, turn it on for your SQL*Plus session, execute your queries, and then turn it off, as shown here:

```
set autotrace on

select… from …
<records displayed>
<explain plan displayed>
<parallelism displayed>
<statistics for the query displayed>

set autotrace off
```

If you use the **set autotrace on** command, you will not see the explain plan for your queries until after the queries complete. The **explain plan** command, on the other hand, shows the execution paths without running the queries first. Therefore, if the performance of a query is unknown, use the **explain plan** command to analyze the query before running it. If you are fairly certain that the performance of a query is acceptable, use **set autotrace on** to verify its execution path.

The following queries show an enhanced version of the explain plan output that is similar to the results shown in the autotracing facility.

```
REM   explain_enh7.sql
REM
REM   Enhanced Explain Plan query for Oracle7.x only
REM   The SQL statement to be explained is placed
REM     in the file sql_to_explain.sql (ended by a ;)
REM This script displays the audit id and displays the explain plan
REM

set pagesize 36
set linesize 120
set verify off

column plan         format A120 heading "Plan"
column id           format 999  heading "Id"
column parent_id    format 999  heading "Parent_ID"
column position     format 999 heading "Position"
column object_instance  format 999   heading "Object Instance"
column state_id new_value statement_identifier

select userenv('sessionid') state_id from dual;

explain plan
set statement_id = '&statement_identifier'
for
@sql_to_explain.sql

set feedback off

select
      id,
      parent_id,
       position,
      object_instance,
      rpad(' ',2*level) ||
      operation || ' ' ||
      decode(optimizer,null,null,
             '(' || lower(optimizer) || ') '
      )  ||
      object_type || ' ' ||
      object_owner || ' ' ||
      object_name || ' ' ||
      decode(options,null,null,'('||lower(options)||') ') ||
      other_tag || ' ' ||
      decode(cost,null,null,
             'Cost (' || cost || ',' || cardinality || ',' || bytes || ')'
      )     plan
```

```
from
      plan_table
connect by
      prior id = parent_id and statement_id = '&statement_identifier'
start with
      id = 0 and statement_id = '&statement_identifier'
order by
      id;
```

The preceding query uses the 'sessionid' as the statement identifier to distinguish the plan generated for this statement from other plans in the PLAN_TABLE. The particular code section is shown here:

```
column state_id new_value statement_identifier

select userenv('sessionid') state_id from dual;

explain plan
set statement_id = '&statement_identifier'
for
```

The SQL statement to be explained is placed in the file sql_to_explain.sql and ended by a semicolon. The explain plan is generated for that statement and the plan_table is queried to display the plan generated.

Sample output of running the script explain_enh7.sql against the query "select * from scott.dept" (in an Oracle7.3.4 database) is shown here:

```
STATE_ID
----------
     98505


Explained.


  Id Parent_ID Position Object Instance
 ---- --------- -------- ----------------
Plan
-----------------------------------------------------------------------
   0·                    1
   SELECT STATEMENT (choose)      Cost (1,4,104)

   1         0        1              1
     TABLE ACCESS (analyzed)  SCOTT DEPT (full)  Cost (1,4,104)
```

The following query shows the enhanced explain plan for an Oracle8.x database. The main difference between the enhanced explain plans for Oracle7 and Oracle8 is that the enhanced explain plan for Oracle8 considers the partitioning feature of objects.

```
REM   explain_enh8.sql
REM
REM   Enhanced Explain Plan query for Oracle8.x only
REM   The SQL statement to be explained is placed
REM      in the file sql_to_explain.sql (ended by a ;)
REM This script displays the audit id and displays the explain plan
REM
REM   The main difference between this script and
REM        explain_enh7.sql is that
REM        this script also considers partitioning
REM

set pagesize 36
set linesize 120
set verify off

column plan        format A120 heading "Plan"
column id          format 999  heading "Id"
column parent_id   format 999  heading "Parent_ID"
column position     format 999 heading "Position"
column object_instance  format 999  heading "Object Instance"
column state_id new_value statement_identifier

select userenv('sessionid') state_id from dual;

explain plan
set statement_id = '&statement_identifier'
for
@sql_to_explain.sql

set feedback off

select
     id,
     parent_id,
     position,
     object_instance,
     rpad(' ',2*level) ||
     operation || ' ' ||
     decode(optimizer,null,null,
            '(' || lower(optimizer) || ') '
     ) ||
     object_type || ' ' ||
     object_owner || ' ' ||
      object_name || ' ' ||
```

```
      decode(options,null,null,'('||lower(options)||') ') ||
      decode(search_columns, null,null,
            '(Columns ' || search_columns || ' '
      )  ||
      other_tag || ' ' ||
      decode(partition_id,null,null,
        'Pt id: ' || partition_id || ' '
      )  ||
      decode(partition_start,null,null,
            'Pt Range: ' || partition_start || ' - ' ||
            partition_stop || ' '
      ) ||
      decode(cost,null,null,
            'Cost (' || cost || ',' || cardinality || ',' || bytes || ')'
      )
      plan
from
      plan_table
connect by
      prior id = parent_id and statement_id = '&statement_identifier'
start with
      id = 0 and statement_id = '&statement_identifier'
order by
      id;
```

Sample output of running the script explain_enh8.sql against the query select * from system.mtest_part (in an Oracle8.1.6 database) is shown next. The table system.mtest_part used in the example is a partitioned table:

```
STATE_ID
----------
    229864



Explained.



  Id Parent_ID Position Object Instance
 ---- --------- -------- ---------------
Plan
 -------------------------------------------------------------------
  0                    1
  SELECT STATEMENT (choose)     Cost (1,82,3034)

  1         0          1                    1
    TABLE ACCESS   SYSTEM MTEST_PART (full)
            Pt id: 1 Pt Range: 1 - 1 Cost (1,82,3034)
```

Using utlbstat/utlestat

Two scripts—utlbstat.sql and utlestat.sql—are the current versions of two original Oracle tuning scripts called bstat.sql and estat.sql, which were included with Oracle version 5. The utlbstat.sql and utlestat.sql scripts allow you to determine the differences in statistics between two points in time. When you run the utlbstat.sql script, a number of tables are created and the tables are populated with the initial (beginning) Statistics values. When you run the utlestat.sql script at a later point in time, a second set of tables is populated and a report is generated showing the changes in the statistics for the period tested.

The output report generated by utlestat.sql script gives you an overview of the database performance, but it does not focus on specific problems to the degree that the scripts in this chapter do. The chief benefit of the utlbstat/utlestat scripts is that they reflect the statistics during a set period of time and do not reflect statistical changes due to database startup. The utlbstat/utlestat scripts also let you determine the differences in the database usage by the OLTP and batch portions of your application. For example, if your application is used by OLTP users during the day and batch users at night, you could run utlbstat/utlestat to measure the statistics twice—once to reflect the OLTP usage and a second time to reflect the batch usage.

Most systems do not have an equal mix of OLTP and batch usage. Therefore, you can bypass using utlbstat/utlestat and use the scripts provided in this chapter in their place. Because many of Oracle's statistics are cumulative, the database startup activity will contribute to the overall statistics and may suppress performance-related statistics such as the hit ratio. For OLTP applications in particular, the impact of database startup on performance-related statistics is a small concern. The nature of index-intensive queries leads to a high hit ratio even if the data block buffer cache is initially empty.

You can minimize the impact of database startup on the hit ratio for the shared SQL area by pinning commonly used packages in the shared SQL area when the database is started.

Because you can minimize the impact database startup activities have on the overall cumulative statistics, you should use the scripts provided in this chapter to evaluate your database environment. For best results, run the scripts during a time of high activity, at least one day of normal usage following the most recent database startup. If you need to monitor the database activity during a time of unusual activity—such as during a stress test—you should either use the utlbstat/utlestat scripts or shut down and restart the database (to rezero the system statistics) prior to the start of the test, and use the scripts provided in this chapter to identify potential problem areas.

Statspack

As of Oracle8.1.6, you can make use of the statspack package that is provided by Oracle. Statspack is a set of SQL, PL/SQL and SQL*Plus scripts that allows you to collect, automate, store, and view performance data about your database. The installation script automatically creates a user—PERFSTAT—that owns all the objects needed by this package. The PERFSTAT user is granted limited query-only privileges on the V$views. The main difference between statspack and the utlbstat/utlestat tuning scripts is that statspack collects more information and it also allows you to store the performance statistics data permanently in the Oracle tables. The stored data can later be loaded for reporting and analysis tasks. The data collected via statspack can also be analyzed using the report provided. This report includes several important features, including the following:

◆ An "instance health and load" summary page

◆ High resource SQL statements page

◆ Traditional wait event

◆ Initialization parameters

PROGRAMMER'S NOTE *Prior to executing the statspack procedures, set the parameter TIMED_STATISTICS to TRUE. This will allow statspack to collect important timing information.*

The simplest way to take a statspack snapshot is to log in to SQL*Plus as the PERFSTAT user and execute the procedure statspack.snap:

```
SQL>connect perfstat/perfstat
SQL> execute statspack.snap;
```

When executed, the statspack.snap procedure will store the current values for the performance statistics in the statspack tables. The procedure can be used as a baseline snapshot for comparison with another snapshot taken later.

PROGRAMMER'S NOTE *A statspack snapshot must be taken on each instance so that you can compare the various snapshots. Also, a snapshot taken on one instance can be compared to another snapshot taken on the same instance only.*

Several parameters can be passed to the statspack procedures—statspack.snap and statspack.modify_statspack_parameter—as shown in Table 2-2.

Parameter Name	Usage
i_snap_level	Specify the snapshot level
i_ucomment	Specify the comment to be stored with the snapshot
i_executions_th	Specify the SQL threshold: the number of times the statement was executed
i_disk_reads_th	Specify the SQL threshold: the number of disk reads made by the statement
i_parse_calls_th	Specify the SQL threshold: the number of parse calls made by the statement
i_buffer_gets_th	Specify the SQL threshold: the number of buffer gets made by the statement
i_session_id	Session ID of the Oracle session whose session granular statistics are to be captured
i_modify_parameter	Specify whether the parameters specified are to be saved for future snapshots

TABLE 2-2.   Parameters Passed to the Statspack Procedures

After snapshots are taken, you can generate a performance report. The SQL script that generates the report is statsrep.sql (for Oracle8.1.6) and spreport.sql (for Oracle8.1.7 and Oracle9i) and is located in the $ORACLE_HOME/rdbms/admin directory. Statsrep.sql or spreport.sql should be run while being accessed by the PERFSTAT user. When running statsrep.sql or spreport.sql, you will be prompted to provide the following parameters:

◆   Beginning snapshot ID

◆   Ending snapshot ID

◆   Name of the report text file to be created

Autotuning with SPFILE.ORA

Oracle9i Real Application Clusters (and even single-instance Oracle9i databases) allow you to record parameter settings for your database in a server initialization parameter file that resides on a server. The installation process can be used to create this file (called SPFILE.ORA by default). The SPFILE.ORA records both global and instance-specific parameter settings. Using SPFILE.ORA allows Oracle9i to perform self-tuning of the database by automatically modifying parameter settings in SPFILE.ORA. SPFILE.ORA is a binary file and should not be edited directly; instead, the parameter settings should be changed using Oracle Enterprise Manager (OEM) or *ALTER SYSTEM SET* SQL statements.

PROGRAMMER'S NOTE *Oracle9i Real Application Clusters has three types of parameters: parameters that can have any valid value for any instance; parameters that must have identical settings for all instances; and parameters that must have unique settings for each instance.*

With Oracle9i, even though you can use the traditional client-side parameter file (initSID.ora), Oracle Corporation recommends that you administer parameters using SPFILE.ORA; otherwise, parameter changes made by Oracle as a result of self-tuning are lost after shutdown. Oracle searches for your initialization parameter file by examining directories in the following order:

1. $ORACLE_HOME/dbs/spfile$ORACLE_SID.ora

2. $ORACLE_HOME/dbs/spfile.ora

3. $ORACLE_HOME/dbs/init$ORACLE_SID.ora

Oracle9i allows you to use one or more client-side parameter files to manage parameter settings in Oracle9i Real Application Clusters as well as in Oracle9i single-instance database servers. By default, if PFILE is not specified in your STARTUP command, Oracle uses a server-side (SPFILE.ORA) parameter file.

PROGRAMMER'S NOTE *If client-side parameter files are used, self-tuning parameter changes made by Oracle are lost after shutdown.*

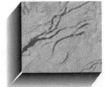

Transaction Management

Every transaction within the database uses a set of internal database objects to record and manage it. If the database objects supporting the transaction are not properly sized or tuned, the transaction may fail, perform poorly, or wait forever for a needed lock. In this chapter, you'll see scripts you can use for manipulating the objects involved in managing transactions.

The major scripts presented in this chapter are shown in Table 3-1.

The first section of the chapter features scripts for managing rollback segments. These scripts allow you to determine which user is using a particular rollback segment, how the rollback segment's space is being managed, and how large you should make your rollback segments. You will also see how to measure the amount of rollback space required by a transaction.

In the second section, you will see scripts related to locking. The scripts allow you to see which sessions are currently holding locks or waiting for locks to be released. You'll

Script	Description
mon_rol.sql	Monitor the number of rollback segments needed
mon_rsiz.sql	Monitor the size of rollback segments
mon_rext.sql	Monitor the rollback segment extent size
rol_users.sql	Monitor who is using which rollback segment
transsiz.sql	Monitor the size of rollback segment entries per transaction
traninfo.sql	Obtain transaction information such as Oracle user, OS user, transaction start time, command executed, rollback segment used
sho_dead_7.sql	Show the sessions involved in deadlocks (Oracle7.x only)
sho_dead_8.sql	Show the sessions involved in deadlocks (Oracle8.x and above)
termwait.sql	Generate the session termination commands for sessions waiting for locks
termhold.sql	Generate the session termination commands for sessions holding requested locks
lockdtab_7.sql	Show the tables being locked by deadlocked transactions (Oracle7.x only)
lockdtab_8.sql	Show the tables being locked by deadlocked transactions (Oracle8.x and above)
lock_sql_7.sql	Show the SQL associated with deadlocked transactions (Oracle7.x only)
lock_sql_8.sql	Show the SQL associated with deadlocked transactions (Oracle8.x and above)
switches.sql	Show the log switch history of the online redo log files

TABLE 3-1.   Management Scripts Used in This Chapter

also see the objects being locked, the text of the SQL used in the locking transactions, and the scripts needed to kill the sessions holding or waiting for the locks.

The final section discusses how to determine whether your online redo log files are properly sized. The combination of environmental diagnostics (properly sized online redo log files and rollback segments) and utilities (to detect the SQL text of locks and generate session kill scripts) provided in this chapter allows you to create a database environment that supports your transactions—while providing ad hoc management capabilities as well.

Rollback Segments

Rollback segments store the "before" image of data—the data as it existed prior to the beginning of a transaction. When managing rollback segments, you need to manage their number to provide enough rollback segments in your database to support all of the concurrent transactions, and their space allocations to provide enough space to accommodate rollbacks. If you provide too few rollback segments, new transactions attempting to write data to the segments will be forced to wait temporarily. You can use the scripts in this section to monitor the rollback header waits and determine whether you have enough rollback segments in your database.

If the rollback segments are too small, transactions may fail. If a large transaction requires more space than the rollback segment has already allocated, the rollback segment will extend into the free space remaining in the tablespace. If the rollback segment requires more space than is available in the tablespace, the transaction causing the rollback segment to extend will fail. You can monitor the number of times the rollback segments had to extend to support the database transaction load.

If the extents within the rollback segment are too small, the transaction will "wrap" from one extent to another within the rollback segment. Ideally, a transaction's rollback segment entry will fit entirely within one extent of the rollback segment, thereby minimizing the performance and internal space management issues associated with wraps. You can monitor the number of times the rollback segment entries wrap from one extent to another within the rollback segment.

In the following section, you will see scripts that can be used to diagnose problems with the rollback segment's number and space allocation. You'll see how to determine which users are currently using which rollback segments and how to predict the rollback segment usage for a transaction.

mon_rol.sql

Monitor the Number of Rollback Segments

A single rollback segment can contain data from many different transactions. As each transaction begins to allocate space within a rollback segment, the transaction must first create an entry in the rollback segment's header. If many users are executing many small transactions (as is common in an online transaction processing application), transactions may have to wait to access the rollback segment header.

To avoid rollback segment header waits, you should create more rollback segments. If the transactions do not reference a specific rollback segment, the transactions should be evenly divided among the available rollback segments. For example, if four rollback segments are available for users (excluding the SYSTEM rollback segment), the first 12 transactions may be distributed as shown in Table 3-2.

If the number of rollback segments changes, the number of transactions supported per rollback segment will change. In Table 3-2, four rollback segments supported 12 transactions—3 transactions per rollback segment. If you reduce the number of available rollback segments from four to three, the number of transactions supported per rollback segment in the prior example will increase from 3 to 4.

The size of the transactions is not considered when the transactions are assigned to rollback segments, so if you have large transactions, you should use the **set transaction use rollback segment** command to force a transaction to use a specific rollback segment. Regardless of the size of the transactions, you need to verify that you have enough rollback segments to support the number of transactions without incurring rollback segment header waits. In the following script, the V$WAITSTAT and V$ROLLSTAT views are queried. The V$ROLLSTAT dynamic performance view records statistics about rollback segments and in this script is used to determine how many rollback segments are available. The Count statistic of V$WAITSTAT is queried for the rollback segment header waits ('undo header') statistic value.

```
REM    Do you have enough rollback segments?
REM
select COUNT(V$ROLLSTAT.USN)   Num_Rollbacks,
       V$WAITSTAT.Count        Rollback_Header_Waits
from V$WAITSTAT, V$ROLLSTAT
where V$ROLLSTAT.Status = 'ONLINE'
  and V$WAITSTAT.Class = 'undo header'
group by V$WAITSTAT.Count;
```

Sample output from the preceding script is shown here:

```
NUM_ROLLBACKS ROLLBACK_HEADER_WAITS
------------- ---------------------
            3                     6
```

The script will generate a single line of output that shows the number of online rollback segments (in this example, 3), and the number of rollback header waits (6) that have occurred since the database was last opened. You will seldom see a value of 0 rollback segment header waits.

Transaction Number	Rollback Segment
1	R1
2	R2
3	R3
4	R4
5	R1
6	R2
7	R3
8	R4
9	R1
10	R2
11	R3
12	R4

TABLE 3-2. Sample Distribution of Rollback Segments

ANNOTATIONS

You should monitor your applications to determine an acceptable number of rollback segment header waits per application. For batch applications, you should see few rollback segment header waits; for OLTP (online transaction processing) applications, the number of rollback segment header waits will depend on the number of concurrent transactions. Once you have determined the acceptable number of rollback segment header waits for your application, you can add a threshold value to the query by adding the following limiting condition:

```
and V$WAITSTAT.Count > &threshold
```

The full text of the revised query is shown here:

```
REM    Rollback segments count check - with threshold
REM
select COUNT(V$ROLLSTAT.USN)   Num_Rollbacks,
       V$WAITSTAT.Count        Rollback_Header_Waits
from V$WAITSTAT, V$ROLLSTAT
where V$ROLLSTAT.Status = 'ONLINE'
  and V$WAITSTAT.Class = 'undo header'
  and V$WAITSTAT.Count > &threshold
group by V$WAITSTAT.Count;
```

When the revised query is executed, you will be prompted for the threshold number of rollback segment header waits. If the number of waits is less than the threshold, no record will be returned by the query.

The query in the preceding listing does not join the two views in its **where** clause. The V$WAITSTAT view is restricted by limiting conditions so it will return only one row.

mon_rsiz.sql

Monitor Rollback Segment Size

All transactions, regardless of their size, compete for the same rollback segments. Unless you specifically use the **set transaction use rollback segment** command *after every commit*, you have no control over which rollback segment will be used during your transaction. If you use the **set transaction use rollback segment** command to support a large transaction, you should create a rollback segment that is specially sized for the transaction. If you do not use the **set transaction use rollback segment** command, a rollback segment will be assigned to your transaction in a round-robin fashion. Since most rollback segment assignments for transactions are random, you should use a standard size for all of your rollback segments (except for those that specifically support large transactions).

A single rollback segment can store the data from multiple transactions. Any of the entries within the rollback segment can force the rollback segment to extend; thus, a rollback segment extension may be caused by many concurrent small transactions rather than a single large transaction.

To control the extension of rollback segments, you can set an *optimal* size for the rollback segment. Use the *optimal* parameter of the **storage** clause to set the value when executing the **create rollback segment** or **alter rollback segment** command. The value of the rollback segment's *optimal* parameter setting, like other rollback segment statistics, can be queried via the V$ROLLSTAT dynamic performance view. The V$ROLLSTAT view records cumulative statistics regarding all rollback segment usage since the database was last started.

If you have set an *optimal* size for your rollback segments, rollback segments that have extended beyond their *optimal* size can actually "shrink." The *optimal* size should be set to minimize the number of extensions and shrinks required for the rollback segment to support the size and volume of transactions.

In the following script, V$ROLLSTAT is queried along with V$ROLLNAME. The V$ROLLNAME view shows the names of the online rollback segments; in V$ROLLSTAT, the rollback segments are identified only by their USN (Undo Segment Number) value. The query in the following listing will list the *optimal* size, number of shrinks, average size per shrink, and number of extensions per rollback segment.

```
REM   Rollback Segment Extensions
REM
column Name format A20
```

```
select Name, OptSize, Shrinks, AveShrink, Extends
from V$ROLLSTAT, V$ROLLNAME
where V$ROLLSTAT.USN=V$ROLLNAME.USN;
```

Sample output for the V$ROLLSTAT query is shown in the following listing.

```
NAME                        OPTSIZE     SHRINKS   AVESHRINK     EXTENDS
--------------------     ----------  ----------  ----------   ----------
SYSTEM                                        0           0            0
R01                       10485760            4    41943040           32
R02                       10485760            2    44564480           17
```

As shown in the listing, there are three active rollback segments in the database. The SYSTEM rollback segment is used for data dictionary transactions. Users' transactions are assigned to either the R01 or R02 rollback segment. Each of the user rollback segments has an *optimal* size of 10MB (10,485,760 bytes). Each user rollback segment has extended beyond its *optimal* value and has been forced to shrink back to its *optimal* size.

The rollback segments have shrunk by an average of almost 40MB each time they have shrunk. Thus, the R01 and R02 rollback segments are not properly sized for the transactions they are supporting. They are frequently extending (49 times since the last database startup) and extend, on average, to five times their *optimal* size. If a rollback segment has to constantly extend beyond its *optimal* setting and then shrink back to its *optimal* setting, it is performing a great deal of unnecessary space management work. To reduce the number of rollback segment extensions, you should modify the rollback segments' *optimal* settings, increasing them to at least 40MB. After modifying the rollback segments' storage settings, you can periodically re-execute the script to determine the impact of the changes.

ANNOTATIONS

When a rollback segment extends beyond its *optimal* setting the first time, the rollback segment will not shrink. The second time the rollback segment extends beyond its *optimal* setting, the rollback segment will shrink—provided the second transaction forced the rollback segment to allocate a new extent. Setting a value for the *optimal* parameter will not prevent all space management issues, but it can help limit the space management issues associated with rollback segments.

Because of the manner in which rollback segments extend and shrink, the number of "Extends" in the preceding script's output should always exceed the number of "Shrinks". For example, if the rollback segment started with a size less than its *optimal* setting, acquiring new extents would increment the "Extends" statistic value but no "Shrink" would be necessary. Once a rollback exceeds its *optimal* setting in size, it shrinks only at the end of a transaction—and that transaction may have forced multiple extensions.

Beginning with Oracle7.2, you can use the **alter rollback segment** command to shrink rollback segments to a size of your choosing. The rollback segments will still have a minimum of two extents. If you do not specify a shrink size, the rollback segment will shrink to its *optimal* size. In the following listing, the R01 rollback segment is shrunk back to its *optimal* size.

```
alter rollback segment R01 shrink;
```

mon_rext.sql

Monitor Rollback Segment Extent Size

To simplify the management of multiple rollback segment entries within a rollback segment, you should size the rollback segment so that each of its extents is large enough to support a typical transaction.

When a transaction's rollback segment entry cannot be stored within a single extent, the entry wraps into a second extent within the rollback segment. The extents within a rollback segment are assigned cyclically, so a rollback segment entry can wrap from the last extent of the rollback segment to its first extent—provided an active rollback segment entry is not already in the first extent. If an active rollback segment entry is already present in the first extent, the rollback segment will extend.

You can query the V$ROLLSTAT dynamic performance view to see the number of wraps that have occurred in each rollback segment since the last time the database was started. If no wraps have occurred in the rollback segment, its extents are properly sized for the transactions it supports. If there is a non-zero value for the number of wraps, you should re-create the rollback segments with larger extent sizes.

```
REM    Rollback Segment Wraps Check
REM
column Name format A20
select Name, OptSize, Shrinks, AveShrink, Wraps, Extends
from V$ROLLSTAT, V$ROLLNAME
where V$ROLLSTAT.USN=V$ROLLNAME.USN;
```

Like the query for rollback segment extension, this script queries statistics from V$ROLLSTAT along with the rollback segment names from V$ROLLNAME. Sample output from this query is shown here:

NAME	OPTSIZE	SHRINKS	AVESHRINK	WRAPS	EXTENDS
SYSTEM		0	0	0	0
R01	10485760	4	41943040	41	32
R02	10485760	2	44564480	26	17

The sample query output shows that 67 wraps have occurred since the last time the database was started. Given the number of extensions that have occurred, the number of wraps is not surprising (since extensions usually require wraps). The extensions indicate that the rollback segments are handling larger transactions than they were designed for; and if the entire rollback segment cannot handle a transaction's rollback information, a single extent will not be able to hold it either. Thus, rollback segments that extend will frequently have high numbers of wraps.

A second set of sample output is shown in the following listing. This output is slightly modified from the preceding output—there are no extensions, but there are wraps.

NAME	OPTSIZE	SHRINKS	AVESHRINK	WRAPS	EXTENDS
SYSTEM		0	0	0	0
R01	10485760	0	0	41	0
R02	10485760	0	0	26	0

If there are wraps but no extensions, as shown in this listing, the rollback segment has the proper *optimal* setting, but its extent sizes are too small. That is, the rollback segment is large enough to support its transactions without extending; however, the transaction entries require multiple extents within the rollback segment. If you have wraps with no extensions, you should re-create your rollback segments using the same *optimal* setting but larger extent sizes.

rol_usrs.sql

Monitor Who Is Using Which Rollback Segment

While monitoring user activity, you can determine which users are currently writing data to the online rollback segments. You can use this information to track users' transactions and isolate the cause of rollback segment extensions. For example, you could monitor the rollback segments periodically to determine which users' transactions are repeatedly shown using the same rollback segment—and thus run the longest.

The script shown in the following listing uses the V$LOCK dynamic performance view to relate V$SESSION (user sessions) to V$ROLLNAME (rollback segment names).

```
REM  Users in rollback segments
REM
column rr heading 'RB Segment' format a18
column us heading 'Username' format a15
column os heading 'OS User' format a10
column te heading 'Terminal' format a10
select R.Name rr,
       NVL(S.Username,'no transaction') us,
       S.Osuser os,
       S.Terminal te
  from V$LOCK L, V$SESSION S, V$ROLLNAME R
 where L.Sid = S.Sid(+)
   and TRUNC(L.Id1/65536) = R.USN
   and L.Type = 'TX'
   and L.Lmode = 6
order by R.Name
/
```

Sample output for this query is shown in the following listing.

```
RB Segment           Username           OS User     Terminal
------------------   ----------------   ----------  ----------
R01                  APPL1_BAT          georgehj    ttypc
R02                  APPL1_BAT          detmerst    ttypb
```

This query output shows that two separate operating system users—GEORGEHJ and DETMERST—have active transactions in the database's rollback segments. The GEORGEHJ user is the only user writing to the R01 rollback segment, and DETMERST is writing to the R02 rollback segment. Both operating system users are using the same database account (APPL1_BAT).

ANNOTATIONS

This query script uses locking information to identify rollback segment activity. A 'TX' lock is a transaction lock on a table; it indicates that the transaction has locked at least one row of the table. The Id1 value is used to determine to which rollback segment the transaction is writing. A locking mode of 6 indicates an exclusive lock. The limiting conditions related to locking in the query are shown in the following listing.

```
  and TRUNC(L.Id1/65536) = R.USN
 and L.Type = 'TX'
 and L.Lmode = 6
```

You can expand the query to include additional session-related information from V$SESSION. You could also display rollback segment statistics from V$ROLLSTAT, since the script refers to V$ROLLNAME and there is a one-to-one relationship between V$ROLLSTAT and V$ROLLNAME. For example, you could add V$ROLLSTAT to the **from** clause, like so

```
from V$LOCK L, V$SESSION S, V$ROLLNAME R, V$ROLLSTAT RS
```

and add a limiting condition to join V$ROLLSTAT to V$ROLLNAME in the **where** clause:

```
and RS.USN = R.USN
```

The statistics available in V$ROLLSTAT include the *optimal* size of the rollback segment (the OptSize column) and the number of extensions (the Extends column).

PROGRAMMER'S NOTE   *As of Oracle9.x, you can make use of undo tablespaces to manage your undo information. Undo tablespaces are used solely for storing undo information. Other types of segments, such as tables or indexes, are not allowed to be created in the undo tablespace. Each database can contain zero or more undo tablespaces. Refer to Chapter 1 for a full description of undo tablespaces and their usage.*

transsiz.sql
traninfo.sql

Obtain Transaction Information and Monitor the Size of Rollback Entries Per Transaction

The Oracle RDBMS maintains statistics that record the cumulative activity against each rollback segment. If you can isolate a transaction so that it is the only transaction occurring in a specific rollback segment at a given time, you can determine exactly how much rollback segment space the transaction requires.

The V$ROLLSTAT dynamic performance view maintains a Writes statistic that reflects the number of bytes written to each rollback segment. The query in the following listing will display the number of writes per rollback segment. Each rollback segment is identified by its USN.

```
select USN,
       Writes
  from V$ROLLSTAT;
```

Sample output from the preceding query is shown in the following listing.

```
       USN      WRITES
---------- ----------
         0        1060
         2      191530
         3      279052
```

This output shows three online rollback segments. The rollback segment with the USN value of 0 is the SYSTEM rollback segment. If you run this query repeatedly and the Writes value remains unchanged, you can verify that no activity is occurring in the database.

In the following listing, a sample update is executed against the EMPLOYEE table:

```
update EMPLOYEE
   set State_Code = 1
 where Emplid =1;
```

```
1 row updated.
```

Following the **update**, query V$ROLLSTAT again, as shown here:

```
select USN,
       Writes
  from V$ROLLSTAT;
```

The output of the V$ROLLSTAT query reflects the rollback segment activity generated by the **update**, as shown here:

```
       USN      WRITES
---------- ----------
        0        1060
        2      191530
        3      279556
```

The number of Writes in rollback segment 3 have increased from 279,052 to 279,556. Thus, the transaction generated 504 bytes of data in its rollback segment entry. A subsequent **commit** does not increase the number of bytes written to the rollback segments.

To use this technique effectively, you must be able to isolate the transaction to be tested at a time when no other transactions are occurring. For example, if another transaction had taken place at the same time, it would have altered the statistics that were queried. For this reason, you should avoid storing the "before" and "after" statistics values in a table—since inserting the rows into a table generates a transaction in the database, which in turn generates rollback segment activity!

The following script, traninfo.sql, can be used to obtain general information about transactions, such as the start time of the transaction, rollback segment used, command being executed, transaction status, the Oracle user and OS user who are performing the transaction, and so on:

```
REM transact_info.sql
REM This script can be used
REM     to obtain information about transactions
SELECT a.sid ,
       a.serial# ,
       a.username "Oracle User",
       d.name "Command",
       a.status "Session Status",
       a.osuser "OS User",
       b.status "Transaction Status",
       b.start_time "Transaction Start Time",
       c.name "Rollback Segment Used"
  FROM v$session a,
       v$transaction b,
       v$rollname c,
       audit_actions d
 WHERE a.command = d.action
   AND a.taddr = b.addr (+)
   AND b.xidusn = c.usn;
```

Traninfo.sql obtains the transaction information by querying V$SESSION, V$TRANSACTION, V$ROLLNAME, and AUDIT_ACTIONS dictionary views.

Locking

When users share access to database tables, they may prevent each other from completing transactions because of the manner in which their table locks are managed. A user who locks a table—or a single record during an **update**—may prevent other transactions from acquiring the locks those transactions need to complete. As a result, the transactions enter into a *wait* state. Once a transaction has entered a wait state, it must either acquire the lock it is waiting for, which requires that the lock holder either complete or be manually terminated; or it must cancel its transaction, thus canceling its need for the lock.

If multiple transactions are held in wait states, it is possible for the locks to be unresolvable. For example, if transaction A cannot complete until it acquires a lock used by transaction B, and transaction B cannot complete until it acquires a lock used by transaction A, neither transaction can complete—they are in a *deadlock* state, and neither can complete unless the other is terminated. In the scripts in this section, you will see how to determine which transactions are in wait or deadlock states. You can use the scripts provided here to generate the SQL commands needed to kill either the waiting transactions or the lock-holding transactions. You will also see scripts that show the SQL commands being executed by the locking transactions and the tables they are accessing. Throughout this section, the focus is on diagnosis and resolution of situations in which a requested lock has not immediately been obtained by a transaction.

Show Sessions Involved in Lock Waits

sho_dead_7.sql
sho_dead_8.sql

The following scripts (sho_dead_7.sql and sho_dead_8.sql) will show all sessions that are waiting for locks, as well as the sessions that are holding the locks in question. The script sho_dead_7.sql should be used only for Oracle7.x. Sho_dead_7.sql combines information from V$SESSION, which shows session-specific information such as Username, and V$LOCK, which shows data regarding the status of locks in the database. The script uses the **DECODE** function to interpret the lock states. Following the script, you will see sample output and an annotated walk-through of the script.

```
REM   sho_dead_7.sql
REM   Show deadlocks
REM   This script should be used for Oracle7.x only
REM
set feedback on
column Username format   A15
column Sid       format   9990      heading SID
column Type      format   A4
column LKmode    format   990       heading 'HELD'
column LRequest  format   990       heading 'REQ'
column Id1       format   9999990
```

```
column Id2        format  9999990
break on Id1 skip 1 dup
select SN.Username,
       M.Sid,
       M.Type,
       DECODE(M.Lmode, 0, 'None',
                       1, 'Null',
                       2, 'Row Share',
                       3, 'Row Excl.',
                       4, 'Share',
                       5, 'S/Row Excl.',
                       6, 'Exclusive',
              M.Lmode, LTRIM(TO_CHAR(M.Lmode,'990'))) LKmode,
       DECODE(M.Request, 0, 'None',
                         1, 'Null',
                         2, 'Row Share',
                         3, 'Row Excl.',
                         4, 'Share',
                         5, 'S/Row Excl.',
                         6, 'Exclusive',
              M.Request, LTRIM(TO_CHAR(M.Request,
                                '990'))) LRequest,
       M.Id1, M.Id2
  from V$SESSION SN, V$LOCK M
 where (SN.Sid = M.Sid
        and M.Request != 0)
    or (SN.Sid = M.Sid
        and M.Request = 0 and M.Lmode != 4
        and (M.Id1, M.Id2) in
          (select S.Id1, S.Id2
             from V$LOCK S
            where S.Request != 0
              and S.Id1 = M.Id1
              and S.Id2 = M.Id2)  )
order by M.Id1, M.Id2, LRequest;

clear breaks
clear columns
```

In Oracle8.x, a number of bugs on V$LOCK causes the fetches from V$LOCK to go in an indefinite loop and, as a result, the sho_dead_7.sql hangs if used with Oracle8.x. For Oracle8.x and above, then, you should use the following script, sho_dead_8.sql, which uses the data dictionary view GV$LOCK instead of the V$LOCK view.

```
REM   sho_dead_8.sql
REM   Show deadlocks
REM   This script should be used for Oracle8.x and above
REM
set feedback on
column Username format  A15
column Sid      format  9990     heading SID
column Type     format  A4
column LKmode   format  990      heading 'HELD'
column LRequest format  990      heading 'REQ'
column Id1      format  9999990
column Id2      format  9999990
break on Id1 skip 1 dup
select SN.Username,
       M.Sid,
       M.Type,
       DECODE(M.Lmode, 0, 'None',
                       1, 'Null',
                       2, 'Row Share',
                       3, 'Row Excl.',
                       4, 'Share',
                       5, 'S/Row Excl.',
                       6, 'Exclusive',
              M.Lmode, LTRIM(TO_CHAR(M.Lmode,'990'))) LKmode,
       DECODE(M.Request, 0, 'None',
                         1, 'Null',
                         2, 'Row Share',
                         3, 'Row Excl.',
                         4, 'Share',
                         5, 'S/Row Excl.',
                         6, 'Exclusive',
              M.Request, LTRIM(TO_CHAR(M.Request,
                                 '990'))) LRequest,
       M.Id1, M.Id2
  from V$SESSION SN, GV$LOCK M
 where (SN.Sid = M.Sid
        and M.Request != 0)
    or (SN.Sid = M.Sid
        and M.Request = 0 and M.Lmode != 4
        and (M.Id1, M.Id2) in
          (select S.Id1, S.Id2
             from GV$LOCK S
            where S.Request != 0
              and S.Id1 = M.Id1
```

```
                    and S.Id2 = M.Id2)   )
order by M.Id1, M.Id2, LRequest;

clear breaks
clear columns
```

Sample output from the lock detection script is shown here:

```
USERNAME          SID TYPE HELD           REQ            ID1      ID2
------------- ----- ---- ------------- ----------- -------- --------
OPS$GEORGE        8 TX   Exclusive     None          655398    19328
OPS$BERTHA        7 TX   None          Exclusive     655398    19328
```

The script output shows that session 7, with an Oracle username of OPS$BERTHA, is waiting for a lock. The OPS$BERTHA user has requested an exclusive lock (the "REQ" column) that is held by the OPS$GEORGE user (the "HELD" column). To resolve the situation, you must either kill one of the transactions or wait for OPS$GEORGE's transaction to complete.

If the lock is held at the table level, the "ID2" column value will usually be left blank. Since the "ID2" column has a value, the lock contention is most likely due to a row-level lock—two users attempting to **update** the same row at the same time.

ANNOTATIONS

The first part of the script defines the **column** and **break** settings to be used for the report:

```
set feedback on
column Username format   A15
column Sid       format  9990      heading SID
column Type      format  A4
column LKmode    format  990       heading 'HELD'
column LRequest  format  990       heading 'REQ'
column Id1       format  9999990
column Id2       format  9999990
break on Id1 skip 1 dup
```

The first part of the query selects the username, the session's SID value, and the type of lock. Because of the limiting conditions used in the query, the types of locks displayed are limited; you will see only lock waiters and holders:

```
select SN.Username,
       M.Sid,
       M.Type,
```

The next section of the query decodes the information in the Lmode column of the V$LOCK dynamic performance view. The Lmode column describes the lock mode for the locks currently held by the session.

```
DECODE(M.Lmode, 0, 'None',
                1, 'Null',
                2, 'Row Share',
                3, 'Row Excl.',
                4, 'Share',
                5, 'S/Row Excl.',
                6, 'Exclusive',
           Lmode, LTRIM(TO_CHAR(Lmode,'990'))) LKmode,
```

The next section of the query shows the lock mode for the locks requested, but not held, by the session:

```
DECODE(M.Request, 0, 'None',
                  1, 'Null',
                  2, 'Row Share',
                  3, 'Row Excl.',
                  4, 'Share',
                  5, 'S/Row Excl.',
                  6, 'Exclusive',
            Request, LTRIM(TO_CHAR(M.Request,
                         '990'))) LRequest,
```

The last columns selected by the query show the Id1 and Id2 values for the resource against which a lock is requested:

```
    M.Id1, M.Id2
from V$SESSION SN, GV$LOCK M
```

The limiting conditions for the query are in two sections. The first section selects all of the waiters—all those sessions for whom the Request value in V$LOCK is a non-zero value. Once the requested lock is held, the Request value changes to 0.

```
where (SN.Sid = M.Sid
       and M.Request != 0)
```

The second section of limiting conditions queries V$LOCK to determine the holder of locks that other sessions are requesting. The Id1 and Id2 columns are used by the query to determine which sessions are holding locks that other sessions need.

```
   or (SN.Sid = M.Sid
       and M.Request = 0 and M.Lmode != 4
       and (M.Id1, M.Id2) in
       (select S.Id1, S.Id2
```

```
        from GV$LOCK S
       where S.Request != 0
         and S.Id1 = M.Id1
         and S.Id2 = M.Id2)   )
order by M.Id1, M.Id2, LRequest;


clear breaks
clear columns
```

The sample output is shown in the following listing. The record for OPS$BERTHA was generated via the first section in the limiting conditions—the Request value is non-zero and is decoded to a value of "Exclusive". The OPS$GEORGE entry was generated via the second section in the limiting conditions—it is holding the lock requested by the OPS$BERTHA user.

USERNAME	SID	TYPE	HELD	REQ	ID1	ID2
OPS$GEORGE	8	TX	Exclusive	None	655398	19328
OPS$BERTHA	7	TX	None	Exclusive	655398	19328

In the following sections, you will see how to display the SQL used by the locked transactions and how to generate the commands needed to kill all the waiters or all the lock holders automatically.

termwait.sql

Generate Commands to Terminate Waiting Sessions

You can terminate a session via the **alter system kill session** command. To execute an **alter system** command, you must have been granted either the DBA role or the ALTER SYSTEM system privilege. To kill the session, you must know the session ID and serial number. The session ID and serial number can be queried from the V$SESSION dynamic performance view; you can join V$SESSION to V$LOCK to retrieve the session ID and serial number for only those sessions that are waiting to obtain locks.

During the resolution of lock wait scenarios, you may need to kill the waiting sessions. For example, a user who encounters a deadlock may start a second session, which encounters the same deadlock. The number of transactions locked in this fashion may grow rapidly, and the waiting transactions may be interdependent. In such a situation, the only way to untangle the locked sessions may be to kill the sessions selectively.

The following listing generates a SQL script that you can run to kill waiting sessions. It does not execute the script that it generates, and you should check the accuracy of the generated script prior to executing it. The SQL script is generated by selecting the SQL commands as literal character strings, combined with the session ID and serial number variables.

```
REM   termwait.sql
REM   Generate SQL commands to kill waiting sessions
REM
set newpage 0 pagesize 0 feedback off
select 'alter system kill session '||''''
          ||M.Sid||','||SN.Serial#||''''||'; /*'
          ||SN.Username||'*/'
   from V$SESSION SN, V$LOCK M
  where (SN.Sid = M.Sid and M.Request != 0)
  order by M.Sid

spool kill_waits.sql/
spool off
set newpage 1 pagesize 24 feedback 6
```

Sample output, which is written to the kill_waits.sql script, is shown in the following listing.

```
alter system kill session '7,924'; /* OPS$BERTHA */
```

The OPS$BERTHA session, with a session ID of 7 and a serial number of 924, was shown in the previous section of this chapter to be waiting for a lock. The **alter system** command shown here, when executed, will terminate the OPS$BERTHA session. The session username at the end of the command is not necessary for the completion of the command; it is provided solely for your reference when validating the script prior to its execution.

ANNOTATIONS

Within the script, the SQL command is built by selecting literal characters and database values. First, the **alter system kill session** text is selected as a literal string of characters:

```
select 'alter system kill session '
```

Next, a single quote is selected. To have a single quote written to the output, you need to use two single quotes in succession—and these must be placed within two single quotes. Thus, to write a single quote to the output file following the **alter system kill session** text, select four successive single quotes, like so:

```
select 'alter system kill session '||''''
```

The session ID (Sid) and serial number (Serial#) are next selected, since those values are required by the command. Note the ',' in the string that forces the comma that separates the two values in the output.

Following those values, a closing single quote is created, along with the semicolon to execute the command and the comment at the end of the command. The generation of this information for the command is shown here:

```
            ||M.Sid||','||SN.Serial#||''''||'; /*'
            ||SN.Username||'*/'
  from V$SESSION SN, V$LOCK M
```

The final part of the query uses the criteria from the previous section to detect sessions waiting for locks. If the Request column of the V$LOCK dynamic performance view contains a non-zero value, the session is waiting for a lock and will be selected by this query.

Following the **order by** clause, the query is not immediately executed. Instead, an output file is opened via the **spool** command and then the query is executed. The query output will be written to the output file and the file will then be closed.

PROGRAMMER'S NOTE *A blank line must precede the **spool** command, or the database will assume that the **spool** command is part of the query. Alternatively, you can place the spool command before the SQL statement as shown here:*

```
REM   termwait.sql
REM   Generate SQL commands to kill waiting sessions
REM
spool kill_waits.sql

set newpage 0 pagesize 0 feedback off
select 'alter system kill session '||''''
            ||M.Sid||','||SN.Serial#||''''||'; /*'
            ||SN.Username||'*/'
  from V$SESSION SN, V$LOCK M
 where (SN.Sid = M.Sid and M.Request != 0)
 order by M.Sid
spool off
set newpage 1 pagesize 24 feedback 6
where (SN.Sid = M.Sid and M.Request != 0)
 order by M.Sid

spool kill_waits.sql
/
spool off
```

After the query is executed, the environment should be returned to its original state:

```
set newpage 1 pagesize 24 feedback 6
```

Generate Commands to Terminate Sessions Holding Locks

termhold.sql

You can terminate a session via the **alter system kill session** command. To kill the session, you must know the session ID and serial number. The session ID and serial number can be queried from the V$SESSION dynamic performance view; you can join V$SESSION to V$LOCK to retrieve the session ID and serial number for only those sessions that are presently holding locks that other sessions are waiting to acquire.

During the resolution of lock wait scenarios, you may need to kill the sessions that are holding locks. For example, in a deadlock scenario, two sessions hold locks that prevent each other's transactions from completing. To resolve the deadlock, you will need to terminate at least one of the sessions involved in the deadlock.

The following listing generates a SQL script that you can run to terminate sessions that are presently holding locks that other sessions are waiting to acquire. It does not execute the script that it generates, and you should check the accuracy of the generated script prior to executing it. The SQL script is generated by selecting the SQL commands as literal character strings, combined with the session ID and serial number variables.

```
REM   termhold.sql
REM   Generate SQL commands to kill waiting sessions
REM
set newpage 0 pagesize 0
select 'alter system kill session '||''''
       ||M.Sid||','||SN.Serial#||''''||'; /*'
       ||SN.Username||'*/'
  from V$SESSION SN, V$LOCK M
 where SN.Sid = M.Sid
       and M.Request = 0 and Lmode != 4
       and (id1, id2) in
         (select S.Id1, S.Id2
            from V$LOCK S
           where Request != 0
             and S.Id1 = M.Id1
             and S.Id2 = M.Id2)
  order by M.Sid

spool kill_holds.sql
/
```

```
spool off
set newpage 1 pagesize 24 feedback 6
```

Sample output from the script is shown in the following listing. When the script is run, the output is written to the kill_holds.sql file.

```
alter system kill session '8,3098'; /* OPS$GEORGE */
```

The kill_holds.sql script, when executed, will kill the OPS$GEORGE session identified as holding a lock in the previous sections of this chapter. The only sessions listed in the file will be those that are holding locks that other sessions are waiting to acquire. If a session is holding no locks that other sessions are waiting to acquire, that session will not be returned by the query.

ANNOTATIONS

Within the script, the SQL command is built by selecting literal characters and database values. The construction of the SQL command is identical to the method described in the previous section on automatically generating the session termination commands for sessions waiting for locks. The only difference between the preceding script and the script in this section is the **where** clause.

For this script, you want to return only records that are holding locks (those with a Request value of 0) for which other sessions are waiting. The ID values of the V$LOCK dynamic performance view are used to determine which sessions are holding requested resources. The **where** clause for the script is shown in the following listing:

```
where SN.Sid = M.Sid
      and M.Request = 0 and Lmode != 4
      and (Id1, Id2) in
       (select S.Id1, S.Id2
          from V$LOCK S
        where Request != 0
           and S.Id1 = M.Id1
           and S.Id2 = M.Id2)
```

Note that no semicolon is used at the end of the query because the query should not be executed until after the output file has been created via the **spool** command. A blank line must precede the **spool** command, or the database will assume that the **spool** command is part of the query. Alternatively, you can place the spool command before the SQL statement as shown here:

```
REM  termhold.sql
REM  Generate SQL commands to kill sessions holding locks
REM
set newpage 0 pagesize 0 feedback off
spool kill_holds.sql
```

```
select 'alter system kill session '||''''
        ||M.Sid||','||SN.Serial#||''''||'; /*'
        ||SN.Username||'*/'
  from V$SESSION SN, V$LOCK M
 where SN.Sid = M.Sid
          and M.Request = 0 and M.Lmode != 4
          and (M.Id1, M.Id2) in
            (select S.Id1, S.Id2
                from V$LOCK S
              where S.Request != 0
                and S.Id1 = M.Id1
                and S.Id2 = M.Id2)
   order by M.Sid
/
spool off
set newpage 1 pagesize 24 feedback 6
set newpage 1 pagesize 24 feedback 6
```

lockdtab_7.sql
lockdtab_8.sql

Show the Tables Being Locked

You can query the V$ACCESS table to see the names of the objects that are currently locked. The V$ACCESS information can be added to the deadlock queries shown earlier in this chapter: sho_dead_7.sql and sho_dead_8.sql. The resulting queries lockdtab_7.sql (for Oracle7.x only) and lockdtab_8.sql (Oracle8.x and above) are shown in the following listings. In the following listings, the Owner and Object columns are selected from V$ACCESS; because of the limiting conditions on the query, you will see only those sessions currently waiting for locks or holding locks that another session is attempting to acquire. The following listing shows lockdtab_7.sql:

```
REM   lockdtab_7.sql
REM   Show tables being locked
REM   This script should be used for Oracle7.x only
REM
set feedback on
column Username format  A15
column Sid       format  9990      heading SID
column Type      format  A4
column LKmode     format  990      heading 'HELD'
column LRequest  format  990      heading 'REQ'
column Id1       format  9999990
column Id2       format  9999990
column Owner     format  A20
column Object    format  A32
break on Id1 skip 1 dup
```

```
select SN.Username,
       M.Sid,
       M.Type,
       A.Owner,
       A.Object,
       DECODE(M.Lmode, 0, 'None',
                       1, 'Null',
                       2, 'Row Share',
                       3, 'Row Excl.',
                       4, 'Share',
                       5, 'S/Row Excl.',
                       6, 'Exclusive',
               M.Lmode, LTRIM(TO_CHAR(M.Lmode,'990'))) LKmode,
       DECODE(M.Request, 0, 'None',
                         1, 'Null',
                         2, 'Row Share',
                         3, 'Row Excl.',
                         4, 'Share',
                         5, 'S/Row Excl.',
                         6, 'Exclusive',
               M.Request, LTRIM(TO_CHAR(M.Request,
                                    '990'))) LRequest,
         M.Id1, M.Id2
  from V$SESSION SN, V$LOCK M, V$ACCESS A
 where SN.Sid = A.Sid and A.Owner <> 'SYS'
   and ((SN.Sid = M.Sid
           and M.Request != 0)
      or (SN.Sid = M.Sid
           and M.Request = 0 and M.Lmode != 4
           and (M.Id1, M.Id2) in
             (select S.Id1, S.Id2
                from V$LOCK S
               where S.Request != 0
                 and S.Id1 = M.Id1
                 and S.Id2 = M.Id2)  ) )
 order by Id1, Id2, LRequest;

clear breaks
clear columns
```

The following listing shows lockdtab_8.sql:

```
REM   lockdtab_8.sql
REM   Show tables being locked
```

```
REM   This script should be used for Oracle8.x and above
REM
set feedback on
column Username format   A15
column Sid       format   9990      heading SID
column Type      format   A4
column LKmode    format   990       heading 'HELD'
column LRequest  format   990       heading 'REQ'
column Id1       format   9999990
column Id2       format   9999990
column Owner     format   A20
column Object    format   A32
break on Id1 skip 1 dup
select SN.Username,
       M.Sid,
       M.Type,
       A.Owner,
       A.Object,
       DECODE(M.Lmode, 0, 'None',
                       1, 'Null',
                       2, 'Row Share',
                       3, 'Row Excl.',
                       4, 'Share',
                       5, 'S/Row Excl.',
                       6, 'Exclusive',
               M.Lmode, LTRIM(TO_CHAR(M.Lmode,'990'))) LKmode,
       DECODE(M.Request, 0, 'None',
                       1, 'Null',
                       2, 'Row Share',
                       3, 'Row Excl.',
                       4, 'Share',
                       5, 'S/Row Excl.',
                       6, 'Exclusive',
               M.Request, LTRIM(TO_CHAR(M.Request,
                                  '990'))) LRequest,
       M.Id1, M.Id2
 from V$SESSION SN, GV$LOCK M, V$ACCESS A
where SN.Sid = A.Sid and A.Owner <> 'SYS'
  and ((SN.Sid = M.Sid
        and M.Request != 0)
     or (SN.Sid = M.Sid
        and M.Request = 0 and M.Lmode != 4
```

```
            and (M.Id1, M.Id2) in
             (select S.Id1, S.Id2
                from GV$LOCK S
               where S.Request != 0
                 and S.Id1 = M.Id1
                 and S.Id2 = M.Id2)  ) )
order by Id1, Id2, LRequest;

clear breaks
clear columns
```

Sample output for the preceding script is shown here:

```
USERNAME            SID TYPE OWNER                   OBJECT
---------------     ----- ---- --------------------- ----------------
HELD          REQ                  ID1      ID2
-----------   -----------    -------- --------
OPS$GEORGE           8 TX    APPOWNER                EMPLOYEE
Exclusive     None                 655398   19328

OPS$BERTHA           7 TX    APPOWNER                EMPLOYEE
None          Exclusive            655398   19328
```

The query output shows that the OPS$GEORGE account has a lock on a row of
the APPOWNER.EMPLOYEE table. (Due to the width of the output, each row of
output spans two lines.) For the OPS$GEORGE user, the SID value is 8, the table
being locked is APPOWNER.EMPLOYEE, an Exclusive lock is held, and no lock
is requested. For the OPS$BERTHA user, the same object is desired, but the Held
column value is None—showing that the OPS$BERTHA user still does not hold
the requested lock.

ANNOTATIONS

To show the tables being locked, the V$ACCESS dynamic performance view was
added to the script. The changes involved adding V$ACCESS to the **from** clause,

```
from V$SESSION SN, GV$LOCK M, V$ACCESS A
```

adding its columns to the **column** formatting commands,

```
column Owner     format   A20
column Object    format   A32
```

adding its columns to the **select** list,

```
select SN.Username,
       M.Sid,
       M.Type,
```

```
A.Owner,
A.Object,
DECODE(M.Lmode,  0,  'None',
                 1,  'Null',
                 2,  'Row Share',
                 3,  'Row Excl.',
                 4,  'Share',
                 5,  'S/Row Excl.',
                 6,  'Exclusive',
        M.Lmode,  LTRIM(TO_CHAR(M.Lmode,'990')))  LKmode,
DECODE(M.Request,  0,  'None',
                   1,  'Null',
                   2,  'Row Share',
                   3,  'Row Excl.',
                   4,  'Share',
                   5,  'S/Row Excl.',
                   6,  'Exclusive',
        M.Request,  LTRIM(TO_CHAR(M.Request,
                            '990')))  LRequest,
    M.Id1, M.Id2
```

and modifying the **where** clause:

```
where SN.Sid = A.Sid and A.Owner <> 'SYS'
```

To preserve the logic of the remainder of the **where** clause, a set of parentheses was placed around the two limiting conditions used in the query. The clause

```
A.Owner <> 'SYS'
```

is necessary because V$ACCESS shows all locks in the database—including the locks that the database obtains against the tables owned by SYS. If you do not exclude the SYS-owned tables from the query, the output will show all of the recursive data dictionary locks currently held by the sessions in question—making it difficult to find the records you care about among the records in the output.

Show the SQL Associated with Locks

lock_sql_7.sql
lock_sql_8.sql

You can build on the scripts used in the preceding sections of this chapter. For example, since you know the session information for the sessions that are waiting for or holding locks, you can determine the SQL text associated with each lock that is associated with a wait or deadlock state.

The scripts shown in the following listings, lock_sql_7.sql (for Oracle7.x only) and lock_sql_8.sql (for Oracle8.x and above), query the V$SQLTEXT dynamic performance view for the SQL text for sessions. The sessions to be displayed are determined by their lock status—they are either waiting for locks or holding locks that other sessions are waiting to acquire. The following listing shows lock_sql_7.sql:

```
REM  lock_sql_7.sql
REM  Show SQL text associated with locked sessions
REM  This script should be used for Oracle7.x only
REM
column username format  A15
column sid       format  9990      heading SID
column type      format  A4
column LKmode     format  990       heading HELD
column LRequest  format  990       heading REQ
column id1        format  9999990
column id2        format  9999990
break on Sid
select SN.Username,
       M.Sid,
       SN.Serial#,
       M.Type,
       DECODE(M.Lmode, 0, 'None',
                       1, 'Null',
                       2, 'Row Share',
                       3, 'Row Excl.',
                       4, 'Share',
                       5, 'S/Row Excl.',
                       6, 'Exclusive',
              M.Lmode, LTRIM(TO_CHAR(M.Lmode,'990'))) LKmode,
       DECODE(M.Request, 0, 'None',
                         1, 'Null',
                         2, 'Row Share',
                         3, 'Row Excl.',
                         4, 'Share',
                         5, 'S/Row Excl.',
                         6, 'Exclusive',
              M.Request, LTRIM(TO_CHAR(M.Request,
                                     '990'))) LRequest,
       M.Id1,
       M.Id2,
       T.Sql_Text sql
  from V$SESSION SN, V$LOCK M , V$SQLTEXT T
 where T.Address = SN.Sql_Address
   and T.Hash_Value = SN.Sql_Hash_Value
   and ( (SN.Sid = M.Sid
          and M.Request != 0)
     or (SN.Sid = M.Sid
          and M.Request = 0 and M.Lmode != 4
          and (M.Id1, M.Id2) in
            (select S.Id1, S.Id2
               from V$LOCK S
```

```
            where S.Request != 0
              and S.Id1 = M.Id1
              and S.Id2 = M.Id2)  ) )
order by SN.Username, SN.Sid, T.Piece;

clear breaks
clear columns
```

For Oracle8.x, a number of bugs on the V$SQLTEXT data dictionary view exist due to an index missing on the view, and as a result the joins that make use of ADDRESS and HASH_VALUE columns cause the query to hang. The script lock_sql_8.sql can be used for Oracle8.x and above:

```
REM   lock_sql_8.sql
REM   Show SQL text associated with locked sessions
REM   This script should be used for Oracle8.x and above
REM
column username format   A15
column sid         format   9990       heading SID
column type        format   A4
column LKmode      format   990         heading HELD
column LRequest    format   990         heading REQ
column id1         format   9999990
column id2         format   9999990
break on Sid
select /* rule*/
       SN.Username,
       M.Sid,
       SN.Serial#,
       M.Type,
       DECODE(M.Lmode, 0, 'None',
                       1, 'Null',
                       2, 'Row Share',
                       3, 'Row Excl.',
                       4, 'Share',
                       5, 'S/Row Excl.',
                       6, 'Exclusive',
              M.Lmode, LTRIM(TO_CHAR(M.Lmode,'990'))) LKmode,
       DECODE(M.Request, 0, 'None',
                         1, 'Null',
                         2, 'Row Share',
                         3, 'Row Excl.',
                         4, 'Share',
                         5, 'S/Row Excl.',
                         6, 'Exclusive',
              M.Request, LTRIM(TO_CHAR(M.Request,
                              '990'))) LRequest,
       M.Id1,
       M.Id2,
```

```
         T.Sql_Text sql
  from V$SESSION SN, GV$LOCK M , V$SQLTEXT T
 where T.Address = SN.Sql_Address
   and T.Hash_Value+0 = SN.Sql_Hash_Value
   and ( (SN.Sid = M.Sid
          and M.Request != 0)
    or (SN.Sid = M.Sid
          and M.Request = 0 and M.Lmode != 4
          and (M.Id1, M.Id2) in
            (select S.Id1, S.Id2
               from GV$LOCK S
              where S.Request != 0
                and S.Id1 = M.Id1
                and S.Id2 = M.Id2)  ) )
 order by SN.Username, SN.Sid, T.Piece;


 clear breaks
 clear columns
```

Lock_sql_8.sql modifies the query sho_dead_8.sql (which resolves V$LOCK-related bugs) by using the RULE hint for the optimizer and also eliminating the use of the problem index on the HASH_VALUE column of the V$SQLTEXT data dictionary view by adding a 0 to the HASH_VALUE column.

```
where T.Address = SN.Sql_Address
   and T.Hash_Value+0 = SN.Sql_Hash_Value
```

Sample output for the preceding script is shown here:

```
USERNAME       SID     SERIAL# TYPE HELD        REQ            ID1       ID2
-------------- ------- ------- ---- ----------- ----------- --------- --------
SQL
------------------------------------------------------------------
OPS$BERTHA      7        924 TX   None        Exclusive     655398    19328
update employee set dept_code = 1 where emplid = 1

OPS$GEORGE      8       3098 TX   Exclusive   None          655398    19328
update employee set dept_code = 1, job_code = 10, state_code = 2

OPS$GEORGE              3098 TX   Exclusive   None          655398    19328
, start_date = sysdate where emplid = 1
```

The output in the preceding listing shows the SQL commands being executed by both the locking transaction (OPS$GEORGE, with a SID value of 8) and the waiting transaction (OPS$BERTHA, SID 7). The locking information from the previous sections of this chapter is repeated here so there will be no question regarding which session is holding the lock and which is waiting for the lock. Since the OPS$GEORGE user is not waiting for any locks (the Req value is None), that user is holding a lock that another user—OPS$BERTHA—is waiting to acquire.

The text of SQL commands in the V$SQLTEXT dynamic performance view spans multiple records. As seen in the preceding output listing, two records are returned for the OPS$GEORGE user—but there is only one command! Each text segment in V$SQLTEXT is limited to 64 characters; thus, to determine the command issued by OPS$GEORGE, you need to combine the multiple records selected from V$SQLTEXT.

The command issued by the OPS$GEORGE user was

```
update employee
   set dept_code = 1,
       job_code = 10,
       state_code = 2,
       start_date = sysdate
 where emplid = 1;
```

When this command was executed, a row-level lock was acquired on the EMPLOYEE row with an Emplid value of 1. After this command was executed, and prior to the **commit** of the updated record, the OPS$BERTHA user executed the following command:

```
update employee
   set dept_code = 1
 where emplid = 1;
```

Because the EMPLOYEE record associated with an Emplid value of 1 was already locked for update by the OPS$GEORGE user, the OPS$BERTHA user's **update** command failed to immediately obtain the lock it required.

Deadlocks and waits for locks typically arise in the following situations:

◆ **The application locks more records than necessary, or sooner than necessary**   For example, if the application locks all records **for update** when the records are first selected, your users may acquire locks they never use.

◆ **Users initiate multiple sessions, and lock themselves**   If a client-server user's client process terminates abnormally, the database may not immediately detect that the related server session should be terminated. If the server session remains active, all of the locks held by the server session remain in effect—and the user, on reconnecting, will be unable to lock the records he or she was previously locking.

◆ **Multiple users own the same business process**   In the example shown in this section, two users were updating the EMPLOYEE table. Whenever multiple users own the same business process (in this case, updating the EMPLOYEE table information for employees with a Dept_Code value of 1), lock waits or deadlocks are possible. The more you separate business process ownership among users, the more you reduce the chances for lock wait situations.

A fourth possible cause of lock wait situations applies mainly to databases using a pre–Oracle7.1.5 version of the Oracle RDBMS. In those versions, you needed to be sure to index foreign key columns to avoid unnecessary table locks during updates. A script that can be used to detect this problem is provided in Chapter 4.

ANNOTATIONS

The scripts lock_sql_7.sql and lock_sql_8.sql described in this section join V$SQLTEXT to V$SESSION based on two values—an address and a SQL hash value. The **where** clause used to join V$SQLTEXT (aliased as "T") and V$SESSION (aliased as "SN") is shown in the following listing (for lock_sql_7.sql):

```
where T.Address = SN.Sql_Address
  and T.Hash_Value = SN.Sql_Hash_Value
```

For lock_sql_8.sql, the index on the HASH_VALUE column of V$SQL_TEXT is avoided by adding a 0 to the HASH_VALUE column while doing a join:

```
where T.Address = SN.Sql_Address
  and T.Hash_Value+0 = SN.Sql_Hash_Value
```

When displaying the records from V$SQLTEXT, you need to order them by the Piece column (a numeric identifier for each piece of text in a SQL command), which is not selected via the query. The **order by** clause for the query, shown in the following listing, will list the records by username, session ID, and text piece number.

```
order by SN.Username, SN.Sid, T.Piece;
```

If you do not order by Piece, the text strings will not be displayed in an order that allows you to read the combined SQL easily.

switches.sql

Online Redo Logs

When you create an Oracle database, you specify the number of online redo log files available to the database. The online redo log files should be sized to support the volume of transactions within the database.

Since the online redo log files record the transactions within a database, the space requirements of the online redo log files depend on the transaction activity within the database. When an online redo log file fills, a *log switch* occurs. In an OLTP system, you should have enough online redo log files so that a log switch will occur not more than every 20 to 30 minutes. If log switches occur more often than that, the maintenance of the online redo log files may impact the overall performance of the transactions. For a high availability database, where minimal or no loss of data is acceptable, you may wish to sacrifice some performance for more frequent log switches.

To view how often log switches occur in your system, you can query V$LOG_HISTORY, which records the time of each log switch in the database for the most recent 100 log switches. You can determine the cumulative time for the last 100 log switches by selecting the minimum Time value from V$LOG_HISTORY. The difference between the current system time and the minimum Time value will be the cumulative time required for the last 100 log switches in days, as selected by the query shown here:

```
REM   switches.sql
REM   Online Redo Log File switch rate
REM   Prior to Oracle8.x, the 'FIRST_TIME' column in V$LOG_HISTORY
REM       was called 'TIME' and
REM       therefore for Oracle7.x, 'TIME' should be used
REM
ttitle 'Frequency of log switches'
REM
select max(first_time) - min(first_time) Days_For_Last_100_Switches
from v$log_history
where rownum < 100;
ttitle off
```

When running this script under some versions of Oracle8, you will need to change the **from** clause to

```
from V_$LOG_HISTORY;
```

since a synonym for V$LOG_HISTORY is not always created. Sample output for the preceding query is shown in the following listing.

```
Frequency of log switches

DAYS_FOR_LAST_100_SWITCHES
--------------------------
                13.1193866
```

PROGRAMMER'S NOTE   *The preceding query assumes that at least 100 log switches have occurred since the database was created. To verify this, you can execute the following command:*

```
select count(*) from V$LOG_HISTORY;
```

If the count from V$LOG_HISTORY is less than 100, the query's results will show the number of days between the first log switch and today.

The output shows that for the sample database, 100 log switches have occurred in just over 13 days—an average of around 8 log switches per day. On average, a log switch occurs every three hours.

The preceding query will show whether your online redo log files are too small. But how do you know whether you have enough online redo log files? As a general rule, you should create extra online redo log files when creating the database—for example, use six online redo log files instead of the default of three. Having additional online redo log files has a small impact on your database's space requirements, but it may help you avoid performance problems during transaction-intensive database activity.

If your database is running in ARCHIVELOG mode, the contents of an online redo log file must be written to the archive log directory before the online redo log file can be reused. If you have too few online redo log files, the database may need to reuse an online redo log file before it has been fully archived. If that occurs, you will see messages in your database's alert log that resemble the following listing (with warning messages shown as regular, not bold, text):

```
Mon Feb 13 19:05:21
Thread 1 advanced to log sequence 941
  Current log# 2 seq# 941 mem# 0: /db04/oracle/APP1/log2a.rdo
Mon Feb 13 19:06:14
Thread 1 cannot allocate new log, sequence 942
Checkpoint not complete
Current log# 2 seq# 941 mem# 0: /db04/oracle/APP1/log2a.rdo
Thread 1 advanced to log sequence 942
  Current log# 3 seq# 942 mem# 0: /db03/oracle/APP1/log3a.rdo
Mon Feb 13 19:07:05
```

In this example, the database was not able to complete a log switch because the online redo log file was still being archived. The transaction must wait until the space is freed within the online redo log file, resulting in a performance penalty for the application. The more online redo log files that exist, the greater the transaction volume required to fill all of the online redo log files—and thus, the individual online redo log files are more seldom used, making the warning shown in the this listing rarer.

ANNOTATIONS

In addition to seeing the cumulative time required for the last 100 log switches, you can use the V$LOG_HISTORY dynamic performance view to see trends in the transaction rate within the database. Usually, the rate of transactions varies throughout the day, influenced by the running of batch transactions and the number of concurrent online users.

PROGRAMMER'S NOTE   *You can also look in the alert log to check frequency trends and rate of switching.*

The query shown in the following listing will display all 100 of the records from V$LOG_HISTORY. The records will be listed from the most recent log switch to the earliest.

```
alter session set nls_date_format='MM/DD/YY HH24:MI:SS';
REM
select SysDate - MIN(TO_DATE(First_Time,'MM/DD/YY HH24:MI:SS'))
        Days_For_Last_100_Switches
  from V$LOG_HISTORY;
```

The log switch timing information is also printed in the alert log. When running this script under some versions of Oracle8, you will need to change the **from** clause to

```
from V_$LOG_HISTORY;
```

because a synonym for V$LOG_HISTORY is not always created.

Querying V$LOG_HISTORY for the times of each log switch may illustrate a need for larger online redo log files, even if the cumulative statistics do not show that. For example, the cumulative statistics may show that five days were needed for the last 100 log switches. But if two of those days fell over the weekend, and the log switches were concentrated around short periods of high usage, you may need to increase the size of the logs to relieve the high usage periods of the performance impact of many log switches.

If you have the appropriate number of properly sized online redo log files, the online redo log files should not affect your transaction performance. You can use the scripts provided earlier in this chapter to make sure your rollback segments are properly sized. The lock information scripts will help you manage situations in which multiple users contend for access to the same resources. If you create a stable transaction environment and use the ad hoc management scripts provided in this chapter, you can effectively manage the transactions within your database.

Data Management

I f you are not careful, the management of your data structures can become a burden on your database administrators and developers. In this chapter, you will see scripts that simplify the management of your data objects. For example, the diagnostic scripts in this chapter will verify that your data structures have been created properly and that all dependencies among objects will be displayed. You can use the utilities presented in this chapter to break large **delete**s into smaller transactions dynamically and generate random numbers within the database.

The major scripts presented in this chapter are shown in Table 4-1

Diagnostic Scripts

You can use the diagnostic scripts in this section to determine the effectiveness of your implementation of constraints and dependencies among your database objects.

Script	Description
depends.sql	Evaluate object dependencies
usr_fkys.sql	Identify foreign key columns
usr_pkys.sql	Identify primary key columns
no_pks.sql	Identify tables lacking primary keys
pk_indexes.sql	Associate primary keys with the corresponding indexes they use
obj_chng.sql	Identify tables that changed yesterday
usr_cons.sql	List all constraints owned by a user
fk_index.sql	Ensure foreign keys are indexed
rows_fil.sql	Evaluate distribution of a table's rows per datafile
del_comt.sql	Force **commit**s during a **delete** operation
hextodec.sql	Convert a Hexadecimal value to a Decimal value
bus_days.sql	Calculate the number of business days between two dates
random.sql	Generate a random number
dbmsrandom.sql	Use the DBMS_RANDOM package provided by Oracle for random number generation

TABLE 4-1.   Major Scripts in This Chapter

depends.sql

Object Dependencies

Objects are not usually created in isolation. Views depend on the underlying tables, tables have foreign key constraints to other tables, and packages and procedures depend on the views and tables. To manage the dependencies among your objects and ensure that changes to the parent object do not invalidate the dependent objects, you need to be aware of these relationships. You can use an Oracle-provided procedure to determine the dependencies among your objects. The procedure, called DEPTREE_FILL, is created via a file called utldtree.sql. The utldtree.sql file is usually located in the /rdbms/admin subdirectory under the Oracle software home directory.

In addition to using DEPTREE_FILL, you can query the data dictionary views DBA_DEPENDENCIES and USER_DEPENDENCIES to extract object dependency information. Querying the DBA_DEPENDENCIES data dictionary view will show you only the first level of dependencies for an object; it will not show you additional levels of dependency. For example, if a package uses a view, querying DBA_DEPENDENCIES will list the package as dependent on the view; however, the tables on which the view is dependent will not be displayed. To see the additional levels of dependency via the DBA_DEPENDENCIES data dictionary view, you will need to query the data dictionary repeatedly, substituting the dependent object from the prior query to find all levels of dependencies.

The following example shows the usage of the Oracle-provided package.

PROGRAMMER'S NOTE *You must have the CREATE PROCEDURE privilege to create the DEPTREE_FILL package.*

1. Create the DEPTREE_FILL procedure in your schema by running the Oracle-provided script in the utldtree.sql file:

```
@@utldtree
```

2. Execute the DEPTREE_FILL procedure. There are three parameters for the procedure:

   ◆ The type of object

   ◆ The name of the schema owner for the object

   ◆ The name of the object whose dependencies will be evaluated

   A sample execution of the DEPTREE_FILL procedure (for a table named DEPTREE_TEMPTAB, which is created by the utldtree.sql script) is shown in the following listing:

```
execute DEPTREE_FILL ('table','qc_user','deptree_temptab');

PL/SQL procedure successfully completed.
```

3. The DEPTREE_FILL procedure **insert**s records into a table named DEPTREE. After you have executed DEPTREE_FILL, you can select the dependency data from DEPTREE, as shown in the following listing:

```
rem depends.sql

col Nested_Level format 99 heading 'LV'

col Schema format A20

select Nested_Level,

        Type,

        Schema,

        Name

   from DEPTREE

   order by Seq#;

clear columns
```

The output of the query is shown here:

```
LV TYPE          SCHEMA                NAME
-- -----------   --------------------  --------------------------
 0 TABLE         QC_USER               DEPTREE_TEMPTAB
 1 PROCEDURE     QC_USER               DEPTREE_FILL
 1 VIEW          QC_USER               DEPTREE
 2 VIEW          QC_USER               IDEPTREE
```

The output shows that the base object for this analysis (the level 0 object) is DEPTREE_TEMPTAB, a table. That object has two dependencies—the DEPTREE_FILL procedure and the DEPTREE view. The IDEPTREE view is another level down the dependency tree, but it is not immediately clear from this query output on which of the level 1 objects IDEPTREE is dependent.

Oracle provides an alternative, more easily read output listing that shows the relationships among the multiple levels of dependent objects. You can query the IDEPTREE view to see the formatted form of the dependency information:

```
select * from IDEPTREE;

DEPENDENCIES
----------------------------------------------
TABLE QC_USER.DEPTREE_TEMPTAB
   PROCEDURE QC_USER.DEPTREE_FILL
   VIEW QC_USER.DEPTREE
      VIEW QC_USER.IDEPTREE
```

The output shows that the IDEPTREE view is dependent on the DEPTREE view.
The output uses indenting to indicate the level of each dependency.

ANNOTATIONS

Before querying DEPTREE and IDEPTREE, you must execute the DEPTREE_FILL
procedure, filling the DEPTREE_TEMPTAB table with information to be extracted.
You do not have to be the owner of the object to execute this procedure for the
object; however, if you do not have permission on one of the underlying dependent
objects, a row of **NULL** values will be returned.

   After the dependency records have been **insert**ed into the DEPTREE_TEMPTAB
table, you can query them via the DEPTREE and IDEPTREE views. The simplest
method for displaying the dependency data is to use the IDEPTREE view:

```
select * from IDEPTREE;
```

   An alternative to using DEPTREE_FILL is to query the data dictionary view
DBA_DEPENDENCIES, as shown here:

```
set term on echo on heading on linesize 80

col Type format a12

col Referenced_Type format a12 heading 'REF TYPE'

col Referenced_Owner format a20 heading 'REF OWNER'

col Name format a20

col Referenced_Name format a20 heading 'REF NAME'
```

```
select Name,

       Type,

       Referenced_Owner,

       Referenced_Name,

       Referenced_Type

  from DBA_DEPENDENCIES

 where Referenced_Name ='DEPTREE_TEMPTAB'

   and Referenced_Owner='QC_USER';

clear columns
```

The output for the query for the DEPTREE_TEMPTAB dependencies is shown here:

```
NAME                     TYPE           REF OWNER
REF NAME                 REF TYPE
-------------------- ------------- --------------------
-------------------- ----------
DEPTREE_FILL             PROCEDURE      QC_USER
DEPTREE_TEMPTAB          TABLE
DEPTREE                  VIEW           QC_USER
DEPTREE_TEMPTAB          TABLE
```

The major disadvantage to using the DBA_DEPENDENCIES data dictionary view is that only a single level of dependency is shown. To get the same results as the prior example using DEPTREE_FILL, the query will have to be run three more times, substituting DEPTREE_FILL, DEPTREE, and IDEPTREE for Referenced_Name in place of DEPTREE_TEMPTAB in the example **where** clause. Alternatively, the **'start with...connect by'** hierarchical query clause can be used.

usr_fkys.sql

Foreign Key Columns

Within Oracle, you can define foreign keys that refer to primary keys or unique constraints. The enforcement of referential integrity within the database can make it difficult to change tables that are referenced by other tables. If you attempt to alter a table that is referenced by foreign keys elsewhere, you will receive the following message:

```
ORA-02266: unique/primary keys in table referenced
           by enabled foreign keys
```

Unfortunately, this message doesn't reveal either the name of the constraint or the name of the table referencing the parent table. To resolve the situation, you need to know information about the referential integrity clauses that caused the error message to be displayed. The following script will list, by parent table, all foreign key constraints, the child table, and the columns the constraint is on:

```
Rem usr_fkys.sql

set pagesize 60 linesize 132 colsep ' '

col Parent_Table format a25

col Child_Table format a25

col Column_Name format a25

break on Parent_Table on Child_Table skip 1

set term on echo on heading on feedback off


select B.Table_Name Parent_Table,

       A.Table_Name Child_Table,

       C.Column_Name

  from USER_CONSTRAINTS A,

       USER_CONSTRAINTS B,

       USER_CONS_COLUMNS C

 where A.R_Constraint_Name = B.Constraint_Name

   and A.Constraint_Type='R'

   and (B.Constraint_Type ='P' or B.Constraint_Type = 'U')

   and A.Constraint_Name=C.Constraint_Name
```

```
    and A.Table_Name=C.Table_Name

  order by B.Table_Name, A.Table_Name, C.Position

/
clear columns
clear breaks
set pagesize 24 linesize 80 feedback 6
```

Sample output for the query is shown here:

```
PARENT_TABLE
CHILD_TABLE                 COLUMN_NAME
------------------------
------------------------ ------------------------
ORDERS
ORDER_DETAILS                ORDER_NO
                             ORDER_DATE


INVOICE_DETAILS              ORDER_NO
                             ORDER_DATE
```

The query output shows that two tables with two foreign keys refer to the primary key of the ORDERS table. Both the ORDER_DETAILS table and the INVOICE_DETAILS table refer to the primary key of the ORDERS table. The columns of the foreign keys, in order, are Order_No and Order_Date.

ANNOTATIONS

The script joins the USER_CONSTRAINTS data dictionary view to itself to find the parent and child tables. The script then uses the child constraint name to extract the foreign key columns from the USER_CONS_COLUMNS data dictionary view.

In general, you should document your database from within the database itself. You can use the usr_cons.sql script, along with the script in the next section, to maintain accurate and current documentation.

usr_pkys.sql

Primary Key Columns

Creating a primary key on a table creates a unique, non-nullable index for that table. The following script will document the existing primary keys, by selected user:

```
REM  usr_pkys.sql
set term on echo off heading on verify off feedback on
set colsep '' pagesize 60
col Column_Name heading 'Primary Key columns' format a40
```

```
break on Table_Name

select A.Table_Name,
       B.Column_Name
  from DBA_CONSTRAINTS A,
       DBA_CONS_COLUMNS B
 where A.Constraint_Type='P'
   and A.Constraint_Name=B.Constraint_Name
   and A.Owner=UPPER('&usernm')
   and B.Owner=A.Owner
 order by A.Table_Name, B.Position
/
clear breaks
clear columns
set echo on verify on feedback 6
undefine usernm
```

When you execute this query, you will be prompted for a value for the *usernm*
value—the username for which the primary keys will be displayed. Sample output
for the preceding query is shown here:

```
TABLE_NAME                          PRIMARY KEY COLUMNS
--------------------------          -------------------------------
ORDERS                              ORDER_NO
                                    ORDER_DATE
```

The query output shows that the primary key for the ORDERS table has two
columns: Order_No and Order_Date.

no_pks.sql

Tables Without Primary Keys

You can use the script in the preceding section to list all the primary keys within your
schema. You can modify that script to show the tables in your schema for which no
primary keys have been defined. You may then determine the proper primary keys
for the tables.

```
REM   no_pks.sql
set term on echo off heading on verify off feedback on
set colsep '' pagesize 60
col Table_Name heading 'Tables in current schema without PKs'
                       format a40

break on Table_Name

select Table_Name
```

```
 from USER_TABLES
where not exists
    (select 1 from USER_CONSTRAINTS
      where USER_CONSTRAINTS.Table_Name = USER_TABLES.Table_Name
        and USER_CONSTRAINTS.Constraint_Type='P');
set echo on verify on feedback 6 pagesize 24
clear columns
```

This script will return the name of any table that does not have a constraint whose constraint type is 'P' (for primary key). You should investigate whether there are primary keys that should be defined for such tables.

NOTE

In Oracle8i and Oracle9i, it is possible to create a unique or primary key constraint using a NonUnique Index.

Associate Primary Keys with the Corresponding Indexes

pk_indexes.sql

When you create a primary key, it automatically creates a new unique index or uses an already existing index on the columns that comprise the primary key. It is possible for several primary keys to share the same index. During object maintenance, a DBA or a developer may need to find out exactly which indexes are being used by primary keys and/or associate primary keys to the actual indexes that they use. The following script creates a view that can be used to associate primary keys to the corresponding indexes that they use. Once the view pk_indexes is created, you can grant privileges on the view to anyone without the person having direct privileges on the underlying SYS-owned objects.

```
REM pk_indexes.sql
REM This script creates a view that can be used to reconcile
REM      a primary key to the index it uses.
REM
REM The following script can be used as is for Oracle8.x and above.
REM For Oracle7.x, TYPE should be used instead of TYPE#
REM                as the column of the sys.cdef$ table
REM
REM
set term on echo on feedback on
create or replace view pk_indexes as
select e.name owner,
       c.name table_name,
       b.name constraint_name,
       d.name index_name
 from sys.cdef$ a,
```

```
       sys.con$ b,
       sys.obj$ c,
       sys.obj$ d,
       sys.user$ e
where  a.type#=2 and
       a.con# = b.con# and
       a.obj# = c.obj# and
       a.enabled = d.obj# and
       b.owner# = e.user#;
```

PROGRAMMER'S NOTE   *In the script pk_indexes.sql, for Oracle7.x, TYPE should be used instead of TYPE# as the column of the sys.cdef$ table. In other words, the where clause should be:*

```
where a.type=2 and
      a.con# = b.con# and
      a.obj# = c.obj# and
      a.enabled = d.obj# and
      b.owner# = e.user#
```

Which Objects Changed Yesterday?

obj_chng.sql

In addition to monitoring the relationships among your database objects, you may also choose to monitor when the objects change. For example, if another user alters a table that you depend on, you should be informed prior to the change being made. However, if you are not informed prior to the change, you can query the data dictionary for the record of the change after it has taken place. The script in this section will return a list of the tables that have been changed during the past day. If you run the following script daily, you will always be informed of the changes that occur in your database.

```
REM obj_chng.sql
set term on echo on feedback off heading on

set pagesize 60 colsep ' '

col Owner format a20

col Object_Name format a30

col Ddltime format a20

break on Owner


select Owner,
```

```
       Object_Name,

       Timestamp  Ddltime

  from DBA_OBJECTS

 where Object_Type ='TABLE'

   and  SysDate - TO_DATE(TimeStamp,'YYYY-MM-DD:HH24:MI:SS') < 1

 order by Owner, Object_Name

/
clear breaks
clear columns
set feedback 6
```

Sample output from the preceding query is shown here:

```
OWNER                        OBJECT_NAME
DDLTIME
----------------------    --------------------------------
------------------
PROD_USER                    AUTH
1998-04-11:12:01:02
PROD_USER                    AUTH_CODES
1998-04-11:10:02:34
PROD_USER                    CLIENTS
1998-04-11:09:51:39
TEST_USER                    LOCK_MANAGER
1998-04-11:11:39:12
QCA                          ACCOUNT
1998-04-11:11:31:30
```

The query output shows that five tables have changed within the past day. The
where clause of the script specifically queries for changes made to tables:

```
where Object_Type ='TABLE'
```

so only tables are shown in the query output.

ANNOTATIONS

This script uses the data dictionary view DBA_OBJECTS to monitor changes. The
Timestamp column of that view is used rather than the Last_DDL_Time because

the Timestamp column reflects only changes to the object's structure while Last_DDL_Time will also reflect index or view creation and **grant**s issued on that object.

The Timestamp column in the DBA_OBJECTS view is a VARCHAR2 column and must be converted to date format (via the **TO_DATE** function) for the query to succeed.

All Constraints Defined for a User's Tables

usr_cons.sql

As you manage your tables, you will often need to know the constraints that have been created on the tables. For example, you may need to know the foreign keys that exist prior to dropping a table that the foreign keys reference.

Oracle has simplified the commands used to manage tables and their constraints. For example, you can drop a primary key constraint without knowing the name of the constraint, and you can drop the associated foreign keys at the same time. To drop the primary key constraint on a table named DEPARTMENT, you can issue the following **alter table** command:

```
alter table DEPARTMENT drop primary key;
```

If there are foreign keys that reference the DEPARTMENT table's primary key, you must use the **cascade** clause of the **alter table** command, as shown here:

```
alter table DEPARTMENT drop primary key cascade;
```

In these examples, the names of the constraints were not specified. However, you may need to know the names of the constraints if you wish to disable or enable specific constraints or if you are trying to understand the relationships among the tables that constitute an application schema. The following script will report all constraints for the tables in the current user's schema:

```
REM  usr_cons.sql
ttitle center 'User Constraints' skip 2

column Ctabname format a15 heading 'Table Name' trunc

column Cname     format a15 heading 'Constraint Name' trunc

column Cdecode   format a15 heading 'Type' trunc

column On_Col    format a15 heading 'On column' trunc

column Cstatus   format a4  heading 'Status' trunc

break on Ctabname
```

```
select UC1.Table_Name Ctabname,

       UC1.Constraint_Name Cname,

       UCC1.Column_Name On_Col,

       DECODE(Constraint_Type,'C','Check',

                              'P','Prim Key',

                              'U','Unique',

                              'R','Foreign Key',

                              'V','With Chck Opt',

                              'O','With ReadOnly') Cdecode,

       Status Cstatus

  from USER_CONSTRAINTS UC1, USER_CONS_COLUMNS UCC1

 where UC1.Constraint_Name = UCC1.Constraint_Name(+)

   and UC1.Owner = UCC1.Owner

 order by UC1.Table_Name ;
ttitle off
clear breaks
clear columns
```

Sample output for the preceding script is shown in the following listing.

```
                        User Constraints
```

Table Name	Constraint Name	On column	Type	Stat
BANK CODE	SYS_C0039844	BANK_COD	Check	ENAB
	SYS_C0039845	SYS_NAM	Check	ENAB
	SYS_C0039846	CUTOFF_TM	Check	ENAB
BRANCH	SYS_C0039847	PTY_ID	Check	ENAB
	SYS_C0039848	PTY_TYP	Check	ENAB
	SYS_C0039849	BR_TYP	Check	ENAB
	SYS_C0039850	ISO_CTRY_COD	Check	ENAB
CARDHOLDER	PK_CH_ACCT	ACCT_NUM	Prim Key	ENAB
	SYS_C0046222	ACCT_NUM	Check	ENAB
DAL_OWNER	PK_DAL_OWNER	DALNAME	Prim Key	ENAB

DAL_USER	FK_DAL_OWNER	DALNAME	Foreign Key	ENAB
TRANSACTION	PK_TRANSACTION	TRAN_NO	Prim Key	ENAB
	SYS_C0046225	TRAN_TYP	Check	ENAB
	SYS_C0046226	VERSION_NO	Check	ENAB

The status value of "ENAB" indicates that the constraints are enabled.

ANNOTATIONS

The script in this section shows all of the constraints owned by a single user. In general, constraints on a table should be created by the owner of the table. You may grant other users the ability to create constraints (and indexes) on your tables, but the more complex your constraint ownership, the more complex the management of your constraints will be. If possible, create all constraints under the same user for which the table was created.

fk_index.sql

Make Sure Foreign Key Columns Are Indexed

When you create a primary key on a table, Oracle automatically creates an index on the primary key columns. When you create a foreign key, however, Oracle does not automatically index the foreign key columns.

For example, if you have a table named DEPARTMENT with a primary key of Department_Number, Oracle will create a unique index on the Department_Number column. If you then create a table called EMPLOYEE with a Department_Number column that references the DEPARTMENT.Department_Number column via a foreign key, Oracle will not create an index on the EMPLOYEE.Department_Number column. You will need to create the index on the EMPLOYEE.Department_Number column manually.

Indexing foreign keys gives the Oracle optimizer more options to use when resolving joins. Foreign key columns are frequently used during joins, so indexing them allows the optimizer to consider index-based access paths when resolving the join condition. In early versions of Oracle7, the foreign key columns had to be indexed to avoid table-locking problems. Although the locking problems have been resolved, you should still index your foreign keys to improve your tuning options and your query performance.

The script in this section (fk_index.sql) checks a user's foreign keys for the following conditions. If either of those conditions is not met, the script will report the correct order of columns to index.

◆ All foreign key columns have indexes.

◆ If the foreign key has multiple columns, the columns in the index are in the same order as the foreign key columns.

The script is shown in the following listing. Sample output is shown following the script listing. Annotations follow the sample output listing.

```
REM   fk_index.sql
set echo off

drop table CK_LOG;
create table CK_LOG (
LineNum NUMBER,
LineMsg VARCHAR2(2000));

declare
T_Constraint_Type        USER_CONSTRAINTS.Constraint_Type%TYPE;
T_Constraint_Name        USER_CONSTRAINTS.Constraint_Name%TYPE;
T_Table_Name             USER_CONSTRAINTS.Table_Name%TYPE;
T_R_Constraint_Name      USER_CONSTRAINTS.R_Constraint_Name%TYPE;
TT_Constraint_Name       USER_CONS_COLUMNS.Constraint_Name%TYPE;
TT_Table_Name            USER_CONS_COLUMNS.Table_Name%TYPE;
TT_Column_Name           USER_CONS_COLUMNS.Column_Name%TYPE;
TT_Position              USER_CONS_COLUMNS.Position%TYPE;
TT_Dummy                 NUMBER;
TT_DummyChar             VARCHAR2(2000);
L_Cons_Found_Flag        VARCHAR2(1);
Err_Table_Name           USER_CONSTRAINTS.Table_Name%TYPE;
Err_Column_Name          USER_CONS_COLUMNS.Column_Name%TYPE;
Err_Position             USER_CONS_COLUMNS.Position%TYPE;
TLineNum                 NUMBER;
cursor UserTabs is
  select Table_Name
    from USER_TABLES
   order by Table_Name;
cursor TableCons is
  select Constraint_Type,
         Constraint_Name,
         R_Constraint_Name
    from USER_CONSTRAINTS
   where Owner = User
     and Table_Name = T_Table_Name
     and Constraint_Type  = 'R'
   order by Table_Name, Constraint_Name;
cursor ConColumns is
  select Constraint_Name,
         Table_Name,
         Column_Name,
         Position
    from USER_CONS_COLUMNS
   where Owner = User
     and Constraint_Name = T_Constraint_Name
   order by Position;
```

```
cursor IndexColumns is
  select Table_Name,
         Column_Name,
         Position
    from USER_CONS_COLUMNS
   where Owner = User
     and Constraint_Name = T_Constraint_Name
   order by Position;
DebugLevel     NUMBER := 99; -- >>> 99 = dump all info`
DebugFlag      VARCHAR(1) := 'N'; -- Turn Debugging off
T_Error_Found  VARCHAR(1);

begin
  tLineNum := 1000;
  open UserTabs;
  LOOP
    Fetch UserTabs into t_TABLE_NAME;
    T_Error_Found := 'N';
    exit when UserTabs%NOTFOUND;
-- Log current table
    TLineNum := TLineNum + 1;
    insert into CK_LOG ( LineNum, LineMsg ) values
      (TLineNum, NULL );
    TLineNum := tLineNum + 1;       '
    insert into CK_LOG ( LineNum, LineMsg ) values
      (TLineNum, 'Checking Table '||T_Table_Name);
    L_Cons_Found_Flag := 'N';
    open TableCons;
    LOOP
      FETCH TableCons into T_Constraint_Type,
                           T_Constraint_Name,
                           T_R_Constraint_Name;
      exit when TableCons%NOTFOUND;
      if ( DebugFlag = 'Y' and DebugLevel >= 99 )
      then
        begin
          TLineNum := TLineNum + 1;
          insert into CK_LOG ( LineNum, LineMsg ) values
            (TLineNum, 'Found CONSTRAINT_NAME = '|| T_Constraint_Name);
          TLineNum := tLineNum + 1;
          insert into CK_LOG ( LineNum, LineMsg ) values
            (tLineNum, 'Found CONSTRAINT_TYPE = '|| T_Constraint_Type);
          TLineNum := TLineNum + 1;
          insert into CK_LOG ( LineNum, LineMsg ) values
            (tLineNum, 'Found R_CONSTRAINT_NAME = '|| T_R_Constraint_Name);
          commit;
        end;
      end if;
      open ConColumns;
```

```
LOOP
FETCH ConColumns INTO
                  TT_Constraint_Name,
                  TT_Table_Name,
                  TT_Column_Name,
                  TT_Position;
exit when ConColumns%NOTFOUND;
if ( DebugFlag = 'Y' and DebugLevel >= 99 )
then
  begin
    TLineNum := TLineNum + 1;
    insert into CK_LOG ( LineNum, LineMsg ) values
      (TLineNum, NULL );
    tLineNum := tLineNum + 1;
    insert into CK_LOG ( LineNum, LineMsg ) values
      (TLineNum, 'Found CONSTRAINT_NAME = '|| TT_Constraint_Name);
    TLineNum := TLineNum + 1;
    insert into ck_log ( LineNum, LineMsg ) values
      (TLineNum, 'Found TABLE_NAME = '|| TT_Table_Name);
    TLineNum := TLineNum + 1;
    insert into CK_LOG ( LineNum, LineMsg ) values
      (TLineNum, 'Found COLUMN_NAME = '|| TT_Column_Name);
    TLineNum := TLineNum + 1;
    insert into CK_LOG ( LineNum, LineMsg ) values
      (TLineNum, 'Found POSITION = '|| TT_Position);
  commit;
  end;
end if;
begin
  select 1 into TT_Dummy
    from USER_IND_COLUMNS
   where Table_Name =  TT_Table_Name
     and Column_Name = TT_Column_Name
     and Column_Position = TT_Position;
  if ( DebugFlag = 'Y' and DebugLevel >= 99 )
  then
      begin
      tLineNum := tLineNum + 1;
      insert into CK_LOG ( LineNum, LineMsg ) values
      ( TLineNum, 'Row Has matching Index' );
      end;
  end if;
exception
when TOO_MANY_ROWS then
if ( DebugFlag = 'Y' and DebugLevel >= 99 ) then
    begin
      TLineNum := TLineNum + 1;
      insert into CK_LOG ( LineNum, LineMsg ) values
        (tLineNum, 'Row Has matching Index' );
```

```
        end;
      end if;
    when NO_DATA_FOUND then
      if ( DebugFlag = 'Y' and DebugLevel >= 99 )
      then
        begin
          TLineNum := TLineNum + 1;
          insert into CK_LOG ( LineNum, LineMsg ) values
            (TLineNum, 'NO MATCH FOUND' );
        commit;
        end;
      end if;
    T_Error_Found := 'Y';
    select distinct Table_Name
      into TT_DummyChar
      from USER_CONS_COLUMNS
     where Owner = User
       and Constraint_Name = T_R_Constraint_Name;
    TLineNum := TLineNum + 1;
    insert into CK_LOG ( LineNum, LineMsg ) values
      ( tLineNum, 'Table '||TT_DummyChar||' is missing an FK index. ');
    commit;
      TLineNum := TLineNum + 1;
      insert into ck_log ( LineNum, LineMsg ) values
        (tLineNum,'Create an index on the following columns: ');
      open IndexColumns ;
      LOOP
        FETCH IndexColumns into Err_Table_Name,
                                Err_Column_Name,
                                Err_Position;
        exit when IndexColumns%NOTFOUND;
        TLineNum := TLineNum + 1;
        insert into CK_LOG ( LineNum, LineMsg ) values
          (TLineNum,'Column = '||Err_Column_Name||' ('||Err_Position||')');
      end loop;
      close IndexColumns;
    end;
  end loop;
  commit;
close ConColumns;
end loop;
if ( t_Error_Found = 'N' )
then
  begin
    TLineNum := TLineNum + 1;
    insert into CK_LOG ( LineNum, LineMsg ) values
      (TLineNum,'No foreign key errors found');
  end;
end if;
```

```
  commit;
  close TableCons;
end loop;
commit;
close UserTabs;
end;
/
select LineMsg
from CK_LOG
order by LineNum;
```

Here's the sample output from the query of the CK_LOG table:

```
LINEMSG
----------------------------------------------------

Checking Table ACCOUNT
No foreign key errors found

Checking Table BONUS
No foreign key errors found

Checking Table CK_LOG
No foreign key errors found

Checking Table DEPT
No foreign key errors found

Checking Table EMP
Table DEPT is missing an FK index.
Create an index on the following columns:
Column = DEPTNO (1)

Checking Table HPE_ADJ_OUTPUT_QTY
No foreign key errors found

Checking Table IC_MOVEMENTS
No foreign key errors found

Checking Table RECEIPT
No foreign key errors found

Checking Table SALGRADE
No foreign key errors found
```

```
Checking Table SHIPMENT_TABLE
No foreign key errors found

Checking Table TEST
No foreign key errors found
35 rows selected.
```

Based on the output of the query, you should create four new indexes. The first index should be on the DeptNo column of the EMPLOYEE table. You should create the second index on the Mgr column of the EMPLOYEE table. The third index should be a concatenated index on the Item_Cat and Item_Bus_Unit columns of the ITEMS table. You should create the fourth index on the CustID column of the ORD table.

Once you create those indexes, your foreign key columns will be properly indexed. If you change any table relationships at a later date, you can re-execute this diagnostic script and any missing foreign key indexes will be reported by the script.

ANNOTATIONS

You can run the script in this section manually by repeatedly executing SQL statements. The benefit of this script is the manner in which it uses PL/SQL to navigate through the result sets of multiple queries. The first cursor generates a list of the user's tables. For each table, the next cursor generates a list of all of the foreign key constraints on the table (those constraints that have a Constraint_Type value of 'R'). For each of those constraints, the columns of the constraint are queried by the third cursor. The constraint columns are then compared to the columns of the user's indexes.

Rows will be returned by this query only if the user has index(es) whose column definitions and positions do not match the foreign key constraints. This script uses the PL/SQL NO_DATA_FOUND error flag to capture this condition:

```
when NO_DATA_FOUND then

    if ( DebugFlag = 'Y' and DebugLevel >= 99 )

    then

      begin

        TLineNum := TLineNum + 1;

        insert into CK_LOG ( LineNum, LineMsg ) values

        (TLineNum, 'NO MATCH FOUND' );
```

```
        commit;

        end;

    end if;
```

You can use the *DebugLevel* variable shown here as a tool to assist in your debugging of long scripts. For example, you can set the *DebugLevel* within a loop and check its value after the loop completes to make sure the processing is occurring in the manner you intend.

You can write a script that generates the missing foreign key index information by querying USER_CONS_COLUMNS, USER_CONSTRAINTS, USER_TABLES, and USER_IND_COLUMNS directly, as shown in the following query.

```
ttitle 'FK columns requiring indexes'
select UCC.Table_Name,
       UCC.Column_Name,
       UCC.Position
  from USER_CONS_COLUMNS UCC,
       USER_CONSTRAINTS UC,
       USER_TABLES UT
 where UT.Table_Name = UC.Table_Name
   and UC.Constraint_Type = 'R'
   and UC.Constraint_Name = UCC.Constraint_Name
   and not exists
      (select 1
         from USER_IND_COLUMNS UIC
        where UCC.Table_Name = UIC.Table_Name
          and UCC.Column_Name = UIC.Column_Name
          and UCC.Position = UIC.Column_Position)
 order by Table_Name, Position;
ttitle off
```

The script in this listing will return a list of the columns that require indexes. You should note the column position within the constraint (the Position value) so the index will contain the columns in the proper order.

```
                    FK columns requiring indexes
```

TABLE_NAME	COLUMN_NAME	POSITION
EMPLOYEE	DEPTNO	1
EMPLOYEE	MGR	1
ITEMS	ITEM_CAT	1
ITEMS	ITEM_BUS_UNIT	2
ORD	CUST_ID	1

rows_fil.sql

Rows Per File (Striping Effectiveness of a Table)

You can query Oracle directly to determine how your data is distributed among the datafiles of a tablespace. If your table's data is all stored in a single datafile, you are more likely to encounter I/O bottlenecks during times of high activity for the table. If the data is distributed among multiple files, you are less likely to encounter I/O bottlenecks during table accesses.

Because the RowID values contain information about the physical location of rows, you can query RowIDs to determine how well a table's data is distributed among multiple datafiles assigned to the table's tablespace. In the following listing, the Oracle8 DBMS_ROWID package is used to extract file ID information about each row. The **ROWID_TO_RESTRICTED** function has two parameters: the extended RowID value and the type of conversion. Use *0* for the conversion type value, as shown in the following listing.

```
REM   rows_fil.sql
REM   Use the following script for Oracle8.x and above
REM   For Oracle7.x,
REM     Remove the usage of the DBMS_ROWID.ROWID_TO_RESTRICITED function
REM         and simply use the "Rowid" of the rows,
REM         for example, SUBSTR(rowid,15,4) gives the "File ID"
REM
REM
set verify off feedback off term on
col "File ID" format a16
col "Num of data rows" format 9999999999999999999
select SUBSTR(DBMS_ROWID.ROWID_TO_RESTRICTED(Rowid,0),15,4) "File ID",
       COUNT(*) "Num of data rows"
from &&table
group by SUBSTR(DBMS_ROWID.ROWID_TO_RESTRICTED(Rowid,0),15,4); undefine table
set verify on feedback6
```

The result of the query will be the count of rows in the table for each datafile in the tablespace. This method relies on the structure of the Oracle7 (restricted) RowID—the values in digits 15 through 18 are the hexadecimal version of the file number.

A simpler approach may be to use the **ROWID_RELATIVE_FNO** function of the DBMS_ROWID package. The **ROWID_RELATIVE_FNO** function returns the relative file number direction from the RowID values. In the following listing, **ROWID_RELATIVE_FNO** returns the number of rows per relative file number (in decimal) of the file in which the row is stored.

```
select SUBSTR(DBMS_ROWID.ROWID_TO_RESTRICTED(Rowid,0),15,4) "File ID",
       COUNT(*) "Num of data rows"
from &&table
group by SUBSTR(DBMS_ROWID.ROWID_TO_RESTRICTED(Rowid,0),15,4);
```

You can verify the relative file number by querying the file information from DBA_DATA_FILES. When querying with the new relative file numbers, use the decimal version of the RELATIVE_FNO value. The following example shows the DBA_DATA_FILES entry for the rows queried in the preceding listing:

```
select File_Name, File_ID

  from DBA_DATA_FILES

 where Relative_FNO = 80;


FILE_NAME                                          FILE_ID

------------------------------------------- ----------

/db02/oracle/CC1/users01.dbf                            5
```

The File_ID value of 5 represents the *absolute* file number for the data file; 80 is the *relative* file number.

ANNOTATIONS

The rows_fil.sql script shown in this example uses the Oracle8 DBMS_ROWID package to convert RowID values into the "restricted" format. The restricted format of the Oracle8 RowID is the same as the format for Oracle7 RowIDs. Therefore, if you need to run the script against an Oracle7 database, you must remove the reference to the DBMS_ROWID package, as shown in the following listing:

```
select SUBSTR(Rowid,15,4),

       COUNT(*)

from &&table

group by SUBSTR(Rowid,15,4);
```

The query output will be the file number, in hexadecimal, along with the number of rows stored in the file.

Utilities

The scripts in this section create procedures and functions within your database. You can use these procedures and functions to manage your transactions, to manipulate data values, and to generate new data (such as a random number) in your database. Because these scripts create procedures and functions in your database, you must have the CREATE PROCEDURE system privilege to execute them.

DELETE_COMMIT Procedure

del_comt.sql

When you **delete** a large number of records, you may exceed the amount of rollback space available for a single transaction. If you exceed the rollback segment space available, your **delete** transaction will fail. Therefore, you may need to make the size of the **delete** transaction smaller, or you may configure your database so you can use the **truncate** command in place of the **delete** command.

The **truncate** command deletes all of the records in the table, but it does so without using any rollback segment space. By default, the table's non-initial extents are de-allocated during a truncation.

PROGRAMMER'S NOTE   *You cannot roll back a **truncate** command.*

The **truncate** command is not always a suitable alternative to the **delete** command. For example, you may not be able to support deleting all the records from a table. If you want to **delete** only half the records in a large table, you will need to find a way to make the transaction smaller. You can use the partitioning capabilities introduced in Oracle8 to improve your ability to **delete** larger numbers of records in a transaction, since you can **truncate** a partition. As an example, if you create a table with two partitions, you can **truncate** one of the partitions without affecting the other partition. Therefore, if your partitions are defined based on criteria commonly used for mass deletions, you can greatly improve your ability to manage large deletions.

However, you may not be able to use partitions, or the key columns used for partitioning may be different than those used for mass deletions. Consider a table called PROBLEM_REPORT that is used to store records of all of the calls to a helpdesk. Periodically, you will need to archive old records out of the PROBLEM_REPORT table (based on the values of its Report_Date column). For example, you may issue a command to **delete** all records from the PROBLEM_REPORT table if the records are more than one year old:

```
delete from PROBLEM_REPORT

where Report_Date < (sysdate-365);
```

If your rollback segments are not large enough to support that transaction, the **delete** command will fail.

To divide a single **delete** transaction into multiple smaller transactions, use the procedure created by the del_comt.sql script shown in the following listing. You will see examples of its use following the script listing. When you execute the DELETE_COMMIT procedure, you pass in as variables the **delete** command and the number of records after which a **commit** should be executed. For example, if you execute DELETE_COMMIT and use 500 as the **commit** variable, a **commit** will be executed after every 500 records have been deleted. The DELETE_COMMIT procedure uses dynamic SQL to accomplish this task.

```
REM  del_comt.sql
create or replace procedure DELETE_COMMIT
( P_Statement             in VARCHAR2,
  P_Commit_Batch_Size   in NUMBER default 10000)
is
        CID                     INTEGER;
        Changed_Statement       VARCHAR2(2000);
        Finished                BOOLEAN;
        Nofrows                 INTEGER;
        Lrowid                  ROWID;
        Rowcnt                  INTEGER;
        Errpsn                  INTEGER;
        Sqlfcd                  INTEGER;
        Errc                    INTEGER;
        Errm                    VARCHAR2(2000);
begin
        /* If the actual statement contains a WHERE clause, then append a
           rownum < n clause after that using AND, else use WHERE
           rownum < n clause */
        if ( UPPER(P_Statement) like '% WHERE %') then
                Changed_Statement := P_Statement||' AND rownum < '
                ||TO_CHAR(P_Commit_Batch_Size + 1);
        else
                Changed_Statement := P_Statement||' WHERE rownum < '
                ||TO_CHAR(P_Commit_Batch_Size + 1);
        end if;
        begin
  CID := DBMS_SQL.OPEN_CURSOR; -- Open a cursor for the task
                DBMS_SQL.PARSE(CID,Changed_Statement, DBMS_SQL.NATIVE);
                        -- parse the cursor.
                Rowcnt := DBMS_SQL.LAST_ROW_COUNT;
                        -- store for some future reporting
        exception
           when others then
                   Errpsn := DBMS_SQL.LAST_ERROR_POSITION;
                        -- gives the error position in the changed sql
                        -- delete statement if anything happens
                   Sqlfcd := DBMS_SQL.LAST_SQL_FUNCTION_CODE;
                        -- function code can be found in the OCI manual
                   Lrowid := DBMS_SQL.LAST_ROW_ID;
                        -- store all these values for error
                        -- reporting. However all these are
                        -- really useful in a stand-alone
                        -- proc execution for DBMS_OUTPUT
```

```
                        -- to be successful, not possible
                        -- when called from a form or
                        -- front-end tool.
                Errc := SQLCODE;
                Errm := SQLERRM;
                DBMS_OUTPUT.PUT_LINE('Error '||TO_CHAR(Errc)||
                        ' Posn '||TO_CHAR(Errpsn)||
                        ' SQL fCode '||TO_CHAR(Sqlfcd)||
                        ' rowid '||ROWIDTOCHAR(Lrowid));
                RAISE_APPLICATION_ERROR(-20000,Errm);
                        -- this will ensure the display of at least
                        -- the error message if something happens,
                        -- even in a frontend tool.
end;
Finished := FALSE;
while not (Finished)
loop -- keep on executing the cursor
        -- till there is no more to process.
        begin
          Nofrows := DBMS_SQL.EXECUTE(CID);
          Rowcnt := DBMS_SQL.LAST_ROW_COUNT;
        exception
                when others then
                   Errpsn := DBMS_SQL.LAST_ERROR_POSITION;
                   Sqlfcd := DBMS_SQL.LAST_SQL_FUNCTION_CODE;
                   Lrowid := DBMS_SQL.LAST_ROW_ID;
                   Errc   := SQLCODE;
                   Errm   := SQLERRM;
                DBMS_OUTPUT.PUT_LINE('Error '||TO_CHAR(Errc)||
                        ' Posn '||TO_CHAR(Errpsn)||
                        ' SQL fCode '||TO_CHAR(Sqlfcd)||
                        ' rowid '||ROWIDTOCHAR(Lrowid));
                RAISE_APPLICATION_ERROR(-20000,Errm);
        end;
        if Nofrows = 0 then
                Finished := TRUE;
        else
         Finished := FALSE;
        end if;
        commit;
end loop;
begin
        DBMS_SQL.CLOSE_CURSOR(CID);
                -- close the cursor for a clean finish
exception
        when others then
                Errpsn := DBMS_SQL.LAST_ERROR_POSITION;
                Sqlfcd := DBMS_SQL.LAST_SQL_FUNCTION_CODE;
                Lrowid := DBMS_SQL.LAST_ROW_ID;
```

```
             Errc    := SQLCODE;
             Errm    := SQLERRM;
      DBMS_OUTPUT.PUT_LINE('Error '||TO_CHAR(Errc)||
             ' Posn '||TO_CHAR(Errpsn)||
             ' SQL fCode '||TO_CHAR(Sqlfcd)||
             ' rowid '||ROWIDTOCHAR(Lrowid));
      RAISE_APPLICATION_ERROR(-20000,Errm);
   end;
end;
/
```

Once you have created the DELETE_COMMIT procedure, you can use it to force **commit**s to occur during your **delete**s. For example, the **delete** shown earlier in this section is as follows:

```
delete from PROBLEM_REPORT

where Report_Date < (sysdate-365);
```

You can execute this via a call of the DELETE_COMMIT procedure. The first parameter passed to the procedure is the SQL statement to execute; the second parameter is the number of records to be **commit**ted at a time. The following listing shows the DELETE_COMMIT execution for this sample **delete**.

```
execute DELETE_COMMIT('delete from PROBLEM_REPORT
                   where Report_Date < (sysdate-365)', 500);
```

As shown in the example, you must enclose the **delete** command in single quotes. If your **delete** command contains single quotes (for example, surrounding a character string value), you must substitute two single quotes for each single quote in your command. For example, if your **delete** command is

```
delete from PROBLEM_REPORT where Department = 'IT';
```

the matching execution of DELETE_COMMIT will be

```
execute DELETE_COMMIT('delete from PROBLEM_REPORT
                   where Dept= ''IT''', 500);
```

In the DELETE_COMMIT execution, the entire **delete** command is enclosed within single quotes, and each single quote surrounding a character string is changed to a set of two single quotes.

PROGRAMMER'S NOTE *Do not put a semicolon within the text of the SQL statement you pass to DELETE_COMMIT.*

ANNOTATIONS

The DELETE_COMMIT procedure works by modifying the **delete** command you give it. When you pass DELETE_COMMIT a **delete** command, the procedure uses the **commit** batch size parameter to modify the SQL to include a **where** clause using the RowNum pseudo-column to limit the number of records affected. For example, in the previous section, the following command was shown:

```
execute DELETE_COMMIT('delete from PROBLEM_REPORT
                where Dept= ''IT''', 500);
```

When processed by DELETE_COMMIT, this command will be changed to this:

```
delete from PROBLEM_REPORT

where Dept='IT'

and rownum < 501;
```

The **rownum < 501** clause tells Oracle to **delete** only the first 500 rows it finds that match the criteria in the **where** clause. Once these records have been deleted, the exact same **delete** command is executed repeatedly until no rows that match the **where** clause criteria remain in the table.

There are several potential issues with this approach:

◆ **Consistency**   When you execute a single **delete** command, Oracle guarantees that your data will be consistent throughout the transaction. When you use DELETE_COMMIT, you are executing multiple transactions, and there is no guarantee of data consistency. You should therefore execute this script at a time when you can guarantee that no other users are accessing the table. Since DELETE_COMMIT is usually used as part of a batch maintenance operation, there should not be any online users of the table during the maintenance period.

◆ **Performance**   You *must* index the columns used in the **where** clause. For example, if you use the Department_Number column in the **where** clause and the Department_Number column is not indexed, Oracle will perform a full scan of the PROBLEM_REPORT table. Since the DELETE_COMMIT procedure repeatedly executes your **delete** command, you will be performing full table scans repeatedly, with a potential effect on the performance of your database. If you create an index on the Department_Number column (even if only for this **delete** operation), your deletions will perform dramatically faster.

PROGRAMMER'S NOTE *To optimize the space usage within your indexes, you should rebuild indexes on any table that has had mass deletions. If you create an index that is intended solely to improve the performance of your deletions, you may drop that index following the completion of the **delete**.*

If your **delete** command does not have a **where** clause, you should investigate the possibility of using the **truncate** command in its place. If you are unable to use the **truncate** command, you can use DELETE_COMMIT to divide the **delete** command into smaller **delete** commands. If you do not have a **where** clause in your **delete** command, DELETE_COMMIT will append a **where rownum <** clause to your command instead of an **and rownum <** clause, as shown in the following listing.

```
if ( UPPER(P_Statement) like '% WHERE %') then

        Changed_Statement := P_Statement||' AND rownum < '
  ||TO_CHAR(P_Commit_Batch_Size + 1);


    else
        Changed_Statement := P_Statement||' WHERE rownum < '
  ||TO_CHAR(P_Commit_Batch_Size + 1);

    end if;
```

Once the changed statement has been created, dynamic SQL is used to execute it. First, a cursor is opened and the statement is parsed:

```
CID := DBMS_SQL.OPEN_CURSOR; -- Open a cursor for the task

DBMS_SQL.PARSE(CID,Changed_Statement, DBMS_SQL.NATIVE);
```

Next, a binary variable named *Finished* is set to FALSE, and a While loop is used to coordinate the execution of the modified **delete** command:

```
Finished := FALSE;
while not (Finished)

loop -- keep on executing the cursor till there is no more to

    -- process.

    begin

        Nofrows := DBMS_SQL.EXECUTE(CID);

        Rowcnt := DBMS_SQL.LAST_ROW_COUNT;
```

After each execution, the deleted batch of rows is **commit**ted:

```
commit;
```

```
end loop;
```

You can theoretically use DELETE_COMMIT to support transactions other than **delete**, but that is not its intended use. Because DELETE_COMMIT generates multiple transactions, the data processed by each transaction is not guaranteed to be consistent with the data used by any other transaction. As a result, DELETE_COMMIT is most applicable to processing **delete**s; it should not be used to process **update**s or **insert**s that depend on consistency of data throughout the entire data set processed.

Hexadecimal to Decimal Conversion

hextodec.sql

Oracle provides a function called **HEX_TO_RAW** that converts a hexadecimal value to a RAW datatype value. However, there is no function provided that converts hexadecimal values to decimal values. Database administrators and application developers may occasionally need to convert a hexadecimal value to a decimal value; the script in this section accomplishes that task.

The following listing creates a stored function in the database. As a result, you can call this function within all of your SQL commands. To create the function, you must have the CREATE PROCEDURE system privilege.

```
REM  hextodec.sql
create function HEXTODEC (Hexnum in CHAR)
   RETURN NUMBER IS
           X                NUMBER;
           Digits           NUMBER;
           Result           NUMBER := 0;
           Current_Digit    CHAR(1);
           Current_Digit_Dec NUMBER;
begin
     Digits := LENGTH(Hexnum);
     for X in 1..Digits loop
         Current_Digit := UPPER(SUBSTR(Hexnum, X, 1));
         if Current_Digit in ('A','B','C','D','E','F') then
            Current_Digit_Dec := ASCII(Current_Digit) - ASCII('A') + 10;
         else
            Current_Digit_Dec := TO_NUMBER(Current_Digit);
         end if;
         Result := (Result * 16) + Current_Digit_Dec;
     end loop;
return Result;
end;
/
```

The **HEXTODEC** function has a single input variable—the hexadecimal value to be converted to a decimal value. Since you can execute functions within your SQL commands, you can use the **HEXTODEC** function in the same places you use functions such as **LENGTH** and **UPPER**. The following listing shows an example of the use of the **HEXTODEC** function:

```
select HEXTODEC('A3')

  from DUAL;
```

ANNOTATIONS

When evaluating a hexadecimal value, the **HEXTODEC** function examines each digit of the value separately. The function first determines the number of digits in the value,

```
Digits := LENGTH(Hexnum);
```

and then executes a For loop to evaluate each digit in turn:

```
for X in 1..Digits loop
```

Within the loop, each digit is examined to determine whether it contains a letter value ('A' through 'F' hexadecimal signify 10 through 15 in decimal). If a letter is found, the ASCII function is used to determine the proper value for the digit. The ASCII value for 'A' is subtracted from the ASCII value for the digit, and 10 is added to the difference. For example, if the digit is 'C', the ASCII value for 'A' is subtracted from the ASCII value for 'C', leaving a difference of 2; 10 is then added to the difference, for a value of 12.

```
if Current_Digit in ('A','B','C','D','E','F') then

  Current_Digit_Dec := ASCII(Current_Digit) - ASCII('A') + 10;

else

  Current_Digit_Dec := TO_NUMBER(Current_Digit);

end if;
```

Once the digit has been converted to a numeric value, the value is added to the *Result* variable. If there is already a *Result* value, then the previous value is multiplied by 16 before adding in the new value:

```
Result := (Result * 16) + Current_Digit_Dec;
```

In the example shown earlier, the hexadecimal value was A3. In evaluating that value, the **HEXTODEC** function first evaluates the 'A' digit. The 'A' digit is assigned the value of 10 during the first execution of the loop within **HEXTODEC**, and the *Result* variable is assigned a value of 10. The second pass through the loop evaluates the '3' digit. Because '3' is a number, there is no need to convert it before processing it. The previous value of the *Result* variable (10) is multiplied by 16 prior to adding the second digit to the *Result*. The function then returns 163 as the result of the hexadecimal to decimal conversion.

bus_days.sql

Count the Number of Business Days Between Two Given Dates

Within Oracle, you can determine the number of days between two dates by subtracting one date from the other. However, you may need more specific information about the time lapse between the dates. In this section, you will see how to eliminate weekends and holidays from the calculation of the difference between two dates.

The **COUNT_BUSINESS_DAYS** function, shown in the following listing, counts the number of weekdays between two given dates. The function has two input parameters: a start date and an end date. The end date will be counted as one of the business days, unless it is a weekend date.

```
REM   bus_days.sql
create function COUNT_BUSINESS_DAYS
    (Start_Date in DATE, End_Date in DATE)
return NUMBER is
    CurrDate      DATE := Start_Date;
    TheDay        VARCHAR2(10);     /* day of the week for CurrDate */
    CountBusiness   NUMBER := 0; /* counter for business days */
Begin
    if end_date - start_date <= 0 then
        return (0);
    end if;
    loop
          /* go to the next day */
        CurrDate := TO_DATE(CurrDate+1);
          /* finished if End_Date is reached */
        exit when CurrDate > End_Date;
          /* what day of the week is it? */
        TheDay := TO_CHAR(CurrDate,'fmDay');
          /* count it only if it is a weekday */
        if TheDay <> 'Saturday' and TheDay <> 'Sunday' then
            CountBusiness := CountBusiness + 1;
```

```
      end if;
   end loop;
return (CountBusiness);
end;
/
```

You can execute the **COUNT_BUSINESS_DAYS** function created by the preceding script within a SQL statement, as shown in the following example.

```
select COUNT_BUSINESS_DAYS('01-JUL-98','08-JUL-98') Bus_Days

  from DUAL;


    Bus Days

 ------------

        5
```

The function's output reveals that there are five business days between the two given dates.

ANNOTATIONS

Because the script consists of only one loop, it is easy to modify. For example, if you want to maintain a list of corporate holidays in a table within your database, you can use that list of values as part of your **COUNT_BUSINESS_DAYS** function. The ability to modify the script is important, since if a day other than a Saturday or Sunday is a non-business day for your company, you should not count that day toward the total number of business days between two dates.

For example, you could create a table named HOLIDAY:

```
create table HOLIDAY

(Hol_Date  DATE);
```

You can modify the **COUNT_BUSINESS_DAYS** function to query HOLIDAY as the function evaluates each date. The following script is a modified version of the function shown earlier; the script will work only if you have first created a table named HOLIDAY, as shown.

```
create function NUM_BUSINESS_DAYS
   (Start_Date in DATE, End_Date in DATE)
return NUMBER is
   CurrDate    DATE := Start_Date;
```

```
   TheDay        VARCHAR2(10);    /* day of the week for CurrDate */
   CountBusiness    NUMBER := 0; /* counter for business days */
   Hol_Check    NUMBER := 0;     /* for holiday check */
begin
   if end_date - start_date < 0 then return (0);
   end if;
   loop
      Hol_Check := 0;
         /* go to the next day */
      CurrDate := TO_DATE(CurrDate+1);
         /* finished if End_Date is reached */
      exit when CurrDate > End_Date;
         /* what day of the week is it? */
      TheDay := TO_CHAR(CurrDate,'fmDay');
         /* count it only if it is a weekday */
      if TheDay <> 'Saturday' and TheDay <> 'Sunday' then
         /* check to see if CurrDate is a holiday */
            select COUNT(*) into Hol_Check
              from HOLIDAY
            where Hol_Date = TO_DATE(CurrDate);
         if Hol_Check <> 1 then
            CountBusiness := CountBusiness + 1;
         end if;
end if;
   end loop;
return (CountBusiness);
end;
/
```

The modifications to the script are shown in bold in the preceding listing. The modification adds an additional check to the *CurrDate* evaluation. If the *CurrDate* value matches a date in the HOLIDAY column, the *CountBusiness* variable is not incremented. The value to be returned by the function is incremented only if the days are neither weekends nor holidays.

random.sql
dbmsrandom.sql

Generate Random Numbers

You may occasionally need the ability to generate random numbers in the database. The script provided in this section will generate a random number. To simplify the script, the following assumptions have been made:

◆ The numbers generated will all be non-negative integers.

◆ The numbers generated will all be less than 1,000,000.

◆ A new value will be generated each second.

◆ Two successive generated numbers will be independent of each other.

◆ If two different users execute the function at exactly the same time, they will receive different values from the function.

Given the first two criteria, the output values are not limitless; they are, however, returned in a random order.

In the following listing, the script that is used to create a function is named **RANDOM**. The **RANDOM** function has a single input parameter (since it is a function), but that value is not used by the function. The function uses two "seed" values: the user's session ID value and the current time. Those two values are manipulated by the function to produce a random number between 0 and 1,000,000; that number serves as the seed value for the rest of the processing.

```
REM   random.sql
create or replace function RANDOM
    (Dummy in VARCHAR2)
return NUMBER is
    Seed1           NUMBER;
    Seed2           NUMBER;
    SeedProduct     NUMBER;
    NatLog          NUMBER;
    DecNatLog       NUMBER;
    RandomValTemp   NUMBER;
    X               NUMBER;
    ReverseVal      NUMBER;
    NatLogFinal     NUMBER;
    DecNatLogFinal  NUMBER;
    RandomValFinal  NUMBER;
begin
    select USERENV('SESSIONID')
      into Seed1 from DUAL;
    select TO_NUMBER(TO_CHAR(SysDate,'SSSSS'))
      into Seed2 from DUAL;
    SeedProduct := Seed1*Seed2;
    NatLog := LN(SeedProduct);
    DecNatLog := NatLog - TRUNC(NatLog);
    RandomValTemp := TRUNC(1000000*DecNatLog);
    ReverseVal := NULL;
    for x in 1..6 loop
      ReverseVal := ReverseVal||SUBSTR(RandomValTemp,(7-X),1);
    end loop;
    NatLogFinal := LN(ReverseVal);
```

```
    DecNatLogFinal := NatLogFinal - TRUNC(NatLogFinal);
    RandomValFinal := TRUNC(1000000*DecNatLogFinal);
return (RandomValFinal);
end;
/
```

Sample execution of the **RANDOM** function is shown in the following listing. The results shown in the listing were achieved by executing the **RANDOM** function once per second.

```
set heading off
select RANDOM('x') from DUAL;
     93872
/
    500579
/
    720950
/
    500488
/

    252993
/
    101697
/

    614443
/
```

The numbers are generated in a random order. You can modify the range of possible values and the manner in which the numbers are generated, as described in the "Annotations" section. You can also automate the creation of many random numbers via a procedure, which is also documented in the "Annotations" section.

ANNOTATIONS

The script that creates the **RANDOM** function performs a combination of several Oracle functions. The intent of those functions is to generate a new number that will be substantially different than the next number generated. The two "seed" values used are the user's session ID and the number of seconds that have elapsed in the current day.

The script obtains the user's session ID via the **USERENV** function:

```
select USERENV('SESSIONID')
  into Seed1 from DUAL;
```

A sample value for the session ID is shown here:

```
select USERENV('SESSIONID') from DUAL;
USERENV('SESSIONID')
--------------------
                1797
```

A user's session ID value does not change during a session. Each session has a distinct session ID, so two users who execute the **RANDOM** function at the same time will have different seed values for their random number generation.

The second seed value for the function is the number of seconds since midnight in the current day. If you execute the function twice in the same second, you will get the same output twice, since the two executions will use identical seed values.

```
select TO_NUMBER(TO_CHAR(SysDate,'SSSSS'))

    into Seed2 from DUAL;
```

The 'SSSSS' date format of the **TO_CHAR** function returns the number of seconds since midnight. If you execute the **RANDOM** function twice in the same second, the same value will be assigned to the *Seed2* variable. If two separate sessions execute **RANDOM** at the same time, they will use the same value for *Seed2* but will have different values for *Seed1*.

PROGRAMMER'S NOTE   *There are 86,400 seconds in a day, so this function generates a maximum of 86,400 unique values for each session. See the procedure-based version of this function at the end of this chapter for additional randomization techniques.*

Once the two variables' values have been assigned, they are multiplied to generate a new value:

```
SeedProduct := Seed1*Seed2;
```

Next, take the natural (base *e*) logarithm of that number. The purpose of this step is to generate a set of digits that is not directly related to the original seed values.

```
NatLog := LN(SeedProduct);
```

The next step in the process is to trim off all but the decimal portion of the natural logarithm value. Since the **TRUNC** of the *NatLog* variable returns the integer portion of the variable's value, subtracting **TRUNC**(*NatLog*) from *NatLog* returns the decimal portion of the value.

```
DecNatLog := NatLog - TRUNC(NatLog);
```

Given the decimal value, the next step selects the first six digits and converts them into a new integer value.

```
RandomValTemp := TRUNC(1000000*DecNatLog);
```

At this point, a new number has been generated, but repeated execution of the **RANDOM** function will generate RandomValTemp values that are close together. For example, the values may be 355110, then 355135, and then 355156. Because the seed values are all close together, the natural logarithms of those values are close together. However, you can use these new values to generate numbers that are significantly different. To change them, reverse them. Change 355110 to 011553, change 355135 to 531553, and change 355156 to 651553.

The code in the following listing performs the reversal of the digits. A For loop is created, and the **SUBSTR** function selects one digit at a time. The first time through the loop, the variable *X* has a value of 1, so the **SUBSTR** function starts at position 6 (7-1). The second time through the loop, the **SUBSTR** function starts at position 5 (7-2). The result is the reversal of the digits in the value. Prior to starting the loop, the *ReverseVal* variable is initialized.

```
ReverseVal := NULL;

for x in 1..6 loop

    ReverseVal := ReverseVal||SUBSTR(RandomValTemp,(7-X),1);

end loop;
```

Given these reversed values, you can now manipulate them the way the seed variables' products were manipulated earlier in the function. Take the natural log of the reversed number, and use the first six digits after the decimal as your new value. That value is the random number that is returned.

```
NatLogFinal := LN(ReverseVal);
DecNatLogFinal := NatLogFinal - TRUNC(NatLogFinal);
RandomValFinal := TRUNC(1000000*DecNatLogFinal);
return (RandomValFinal);
```

PROGRAMMER'S NOTE   *A set of random numbers may contain duplicates. The order of the values should be random. The generated values are not guaranteed to be statistically randomized.*

To increase the maximum generated value, you will need to increase the following:

♦   The value that the *DecNatLog* variable is multiplied by.

♦   The maximum value for the variable *X* in the loop control command to reflect the number of digits.

♦   The value used to establish the start position for the **SUBSTR** function during the digit reversal process.

♦   The value that the *DecNatLogFinal* variable is multiplied by.

For example, to increase the maximum generated value to 1,000,000,000, you must

1. Increase the value that the *DecNatLog* variable is multiplied by to 1000000000 to capture nine digits.

2. Change the **for** command to **for X in** 1..9 **loop** to reflect the nine digits of the value.

3. Change the **SUBSTR** command to use 10-X instead of 7-X to reflect the nine digits reversed.

4. Increase the value that the *DecNatLogFinal* variable is multiplied by to 1000000000 to capture nine digits.

You can convert the function into a procedure to programmatically insert a large number of random values into a table. In so doing, you should add a third seed value into the number generation. Determine the number of values you want to generate, and create a loop that executes a variable number of times. Since the procedure will execute the loop multiple times per second, you must use a loop counter variable to generate distinct seed values.

To store the generated values, you must first create a table. During the execution of the procedure, the generated values will be inserted into the following table:

```
create table RANDOMNESS

(RandomVal  NUMBER);
```

The procedure version of the **RANDOM** function (called RANDOM_P) is shown in the following listing. The significant changes are shown without bold.

```
create or replace procedure RANDOM_P
    (MaxCount in NUMBER)
  is
Counter              NUMBER;
    Seed1            NUMBER;
    Seed2            NUMBER;
    SeedProduct      NUMBER;
    NatLog           NUMBER;
    DecNatLog        NUMBER;
    RandomValTemp    NUMBER;
    X                NUMBER;
    ReverseVal       NUMBER;
    NatLogFinal      NUMBER;
    DecNatLogFinal   NUMBER;
    RandomValFinal   NUMBER;
begin
```

```
    select USERENV('SESSIONID')
        into Seed1 from DUAL;
  for Counter in 1..MaxCount loop
    select TO_NUMBER(TO_CHAR(SysDate,'SSSSS'))
        into Seed2 from DUAL;
    SeedProduct := Seed1*Seed2*Counter;
    NatLog := LN(SeedProduct);
    DecNatLog := NatLog - TRUNC(NatLog);
    RandomValTemp := TRUNC(1000000*DecNatLog);
    ReverseVal := NULL;
    for x in 1..6 loop
      ReverseVal := ReverseVal||SUBSTR(RandomValTemp,(7-X),1);
    end loop;
    NatLogFinal := LN(ReverseVal);
    DecNatLogFinal := NatLogFinal - TRUNC(NatLogFinal);
    RandomValFinal := TRUNC(1000000*DecNatLogFinal);
    insert into RANDOMNESS values (RandomValFinal);
end loop;
commit;
end;
/
```

The procedure accepts a value into a variable named *MaxCount*. A *Counter* variable is then incremented from 1 to the *MaxCount* value. For each value of the *Counter* variable, the *Counter* value is multiplied by the two other seed values (as shown in the following listing) to determine the number evaluated by the natural logarithm function prior to the digit reversal process.

```
SeedProduct := Seed1*Seed2*Counter;
```

When the program **insert**s multiple records per second, each execution of the loop uses a different value for the *SeedProduct* variable.

The following listing shows the generation of 100,000 random numbers inserted into the RANDOMNESS table.

```
execute RANDOM_P(100000);
```

When you execute the RANDOM_P procedure, you will likely find that the generated numbers are not all unique. Randomness and uniqueness are different concepts. If you need to generate unique numbers, you should use sequences instead of this random number generation procedure.

In this random value generation program, the generated values were all non-negative integer values. You can easily modify the program to include negative numbers. For example, you could subtract 500,000 from each of the final generated values, so the range of values would then be from –500,000 to 499,999. If you want to generate character strings, you can translate each digit of a number into a character after the number has been generated. The result will be a series of random character strings.

During the execution of the RANDOM_P procedure, all of the values were inserted into the RANDOMNESS table via a single **insert** transaction. If the size of the transaction causes errors due to rollback segment space requirements, there are two alternatives to consider. First, you can execute the procedure multiple times instead of one time. For example, instead of executing

```
execute RANDOM_P(100000);
```

you could instead generate 20,000 values at a time:

```
execute RANDOM_P(20000);
```

```
execute RANDOM_P(20000);
```

```
execute RANDOM_P(20000);
```

```
execute RANDOM_P(20000);
```

```
execute RANDOM_P(20000);
```

Each execution will use different seed values than the others, since the seed value generated by the time of day will be different for each (unless they are run simultaneously). If you execute the RANDOM_P procedure multiple times, you should schedule the executions to run one after another.

A second way of reducing the rollback segment requirements for the random number **insert**s requires modifying the procedure. Move the **commit** command inside the loop that generates the numbers. Each new number will be **commit**ted as soon as it is **insert**ed. The following listing shows the program block portion of the RANDOM_P procedure, with the moved command order shown in regular, not bold, text:

```
begin
   select USERENV('SESSIONID')
       into Seed1 from DUAL;
   for Counter in 1..MaxCount loop
     select TO_NUMBER(TO_CHAR(SysDate,'SSSSS'))
       into Seed2 from DUAL;
     SeedProduct := Seed1*Seed2*Counter;
     NatLog := LN(SeedProduct);
     DecNatLog := NatLog - TRUNC(NatLog);
     RandomValTemp := TRUNC(1000000*DecNatLog);
     ReverseVal := NULL;
     for x in 1..6 loop
       ReverseVal := ReverseVal||SUBSTR(RandomValTemp,(7-X),1);
```

```
      end loop;
      NatLogFinal := LN(ReverseVal);
      DecNatLogFinal := NatLogFinal - TRUNC(NatLogFinal);
      RandomValFinal := TRUNC(1000000*DecNatLogFinal);
      insert into RANDOMNESS values (RandomValFinal);
      commit;
   end loop;
end;
```

The modified version of the RANDOM_P procedure **commit**s each row as it is **insert**ed. Although this modification resolves the rollback segment problem, it introduces a new potential problem: if your execution is interrupted, you will not have the full set of random numbers required. If that occurs, you can query the RANDOMNESS table to determine how many values have been generated and then reexecute the RANDOM_P procedure to generate enough random values to meet your needs.

Instead of writing your own random number generation function, as of Oracle8.x, you can make use of the DBMS_RANDOM package and its routines to generate random numbers for you. The DBMS_RANDOM package provides a built-in random number generator that calls Oracle's internal random number generator; as a result it is faster than the generators written in PL/SQL. The generator provided by DBMS_RANDOM package produces eight-digit integers and is a simple interface to the random number generator. You should make use of the DBMS_CRYPTO_TOOLKIT package for more sophisticated generators.

Prior to calling the random number generator, the DBMS_RANDOM package must be initialized; if the initialization routine is not called the package raises an exception. The DBMS_RANDOM package is created by the dbmsrand.sql script that is located in $ORACLE_HOME/rdbms/admin directory. A public synonym is created for the package and EXECUTE privilege on the package is granted to PUBLIC. The dbmsrand.sql script is automatically called by the catoctk.sql script, which contains the code needed to use the PL/SQL cryptographics toolkit interface.

DBMS_RANDOM package contains the following routines:

- **INITIALIZE procedure**   The procedure initializes the random number generated with a seed value. Before using the DBMS_RANDOM package for random number generation, you must run this procedure to initialize the seed with at least five digits to ensure randomness.

- **RANDOM function**   This function should be called to generate the random number.

- **SEED procedure**   After the first initialization, the seed value can be changed using this procedure.

- **TERMINATE procedure**   After you have finished using the random number generator, this procedure should be called to release the memory.

If you get errors (ORA-06550, PLS-00201, ORA-04068, ORA-04063, ORA-6508, and/or ORA-06512) while initializing the DBMS_RANDOM package, you should connect as the SYS account and execute the following scripts located in $ORACLE_HOME/rdbms/admin:

◆ Dbmsoctk.sql

◆ Prvtoctk.sql

◆ Dbmsrand.sql

The following script, dbmsrandom.sql, shows an example of how the DBMS_RANDOM routines can be used to generate random numbers:

```
REM  dbmsrandom.sql
create or replace procedure gen_rand(ranvalues in number)
is
counter number;
rv number;
begin
 dbms_random.initialize(12345);
 for counter in 1..ranvalues
 loop
   rv := dbms_random.random;
   dbms_output.put_line(rv);
  end loop;
  dbms_random.terminate;
end;
/
```

When the script is executed, it creates a procedure called gen_rand. The number of random values desired is passed as a parameter to the gen_rand procedure. The following description demonstrates the creation and execution of the gen_rand procedure.

As described earlier, before using the random number generator of the DBMS_RANDOM package, call the **INITIALIZE** function and provide a seed value. The procedure gen_rand initializes the random number generator with a seed value of 12345:

```
dbms_random.initialize(12345);
```

Depending on the number of random values desired, the procedure loops that many times, calls the RANDOM procedure, and displays the random value generated.

```
for counter in 1..ranvalues
 loop
   rv := dbms_random.random;
```

```
  dbms_output.put_line(rv);
 end loop;
```

The following example shows the creation of the gen_rand procedure by executing the dbmsrandom.sql script and then executing the gen_rand procedure to generate 20 random values.

```
SQL> @dbmsrandom.sql
 13  /

Procedure created.

SQL> set term on
SQL> set serveroutput on
SQL> exec gen_rand(20);
-1817329670
-610488908
1775775349
-1974231734
-861483099
1044932800
1916512750
808190358
-1880806196
-1406274277
378824720
183054383
1930552618
459007094
474503982
-1502999260
-373369630
-1874648073
687956613
891670144


PL/SQL procedure successfully completed.
```

Object Management

Managing the objects within your database can be an overwhelming process. How do you determine which objects are invalid and need recompilation? Can you tell what jobs are in the job queue and when they will next execute? Do you have up-to-date documentation on each object within the database, its structure and storage? In this chapter, you will see scripts that help you to manage the objects in your database. You can use the diagnostic scripts to document your tables and jobs, and you can use the utility scripts to create a series of scripts to regenerate and document the database structure.

The major scripts presented in this chapter are shown in Table 5-1.

Script	Description
tab_desc.sql	Fully describes a table—storage, indexes, column, and constraint information
list_sub.sql	Lists submitted jobs in the job queue and their execution information
list_run.sql	Lists currently executing jobs in the job queue and their execution information
invalobj.sql	Lists all invalid objects in the database and generates a script to recompile them
desc_adt.sql	Shows the full column description of tables that use abstract datatypes (Oracle8.0.x and above)
desc_ad3.sql	Shows the full column description of tables that use abstract datatypes—multilevel (Oracle8.0.x and above)
pinsize.sql	Lists packages that are candidates for pinning in the SGA
revalobj.sql	Generates compilation commands to revalidate invalid objects
gen_tbl_7.sql	Generates a script to re-create a table and its constraints (Oracle7.x only)
gen_tbl_80.sql	Generates a script to re-create a table and its constraints (Oracle8.0.x only)
gen_tbl_81.sql	Generates a script to re-create a table and its constraints (Oracle8.1.x only)
gen_tbl_9.sql	Generates a script to re-create a table and its constraints (Oracle9.x only)
part_dis.sql	Shows the distribution of values across a table's partitions
gen_indx_7.sql	Generates a script to re-create indexes for a given table (Oracle7.x only)
gen_indx_80.sql	Generates a script to re-create indexes for a given table (Oracle8.0.x only)
gen_indx_81n9.sql	Generates a script to re-create indexes for a given table (Oracle8.1.x and above)

TABLE 5-1.   Major Scripts Presented in This Chapter

Script	Description
part_idi.sql	Shows the distribution of values across an index's partitions
gen_trig_7n80.sql	Generates a script to re-create triggers for a given table (Oracle7.x and Oracle8.0.x only)
gen_trig_81n9.sql	Generates a script to re-create triggers for a given table (Oracle8.1.x and above)
gen_view_7.sql	Generates a script to re-create a view (Oracle7.x only)
gen_view_8.sql	Generates a script to re-create a view (Oracle8.x only)
gen_view_9.sql	Generates a script to re-create a view (Oracle9.x only)
gen_syn.sql	Generates a script to re-create synonyms for an object
gen_proc.sql	Generates a script to re-create a procedure
gen_func.sql	Generates a script to re-create a function
gen_pkg.sql	Generates a script to re-create a package
gen_lib.sql	Generates a script to re-create a library
gen_seq.sql	Generates a script to re-create a sequence
gen_dblnk_7.sql	Generates a script to re-create database links (Oracle7.x only)
gen_dblnk_8n9.sql	Generates a script to re-create database links (Oracle8.x and above)
gen_snap_7.sql	Generates a script to re-create snapshots (Oracle7.x only)
gen_snap_80.sql	Generates a script to re-create snapshots (Oracle8.0.x only)
gen_mview_81n9.sql	Generates a script to re-create materialized views (Oracle8.1.x and above)
gen_snap_log_7.sql	Generates a script to re-create snapshot logs (Oracle7.x only)
gen_snap_log_80.sql	Generates a script to re-create snapshot logs (Oracle8.0.x only)
gen_mview_log_81.sql	Generates a script to re-create materialized views logs (Oracle8.1.x only)
gen_mview_log_9.sql	Generates a script to re-create materialized views logs (Oracle9.x only)
gen_type.sql	Generates the code necessary to re-create existing abstract datatypes (Oracle8.0.x and above)
gen_grnt_7n8.sql	Generates a script to re-create grants for a given table (Oracle7.x and Oracle8.x only)
gen_grnt_9.sql	Generates a script to re-create grants for a given table (Oracle9.x only)

TABLE 5-1.   Major Scripts Presented in This Chapter *(continued)*

All the scripts in this chapter should be run from an account that has DBA privileges or that has been granted the select privilege on all the DBA_ views.

PROGRAMMER'S NOTE   *Many of the scripts in this chapter assume that object names and owners are all case-insensitive. The scripts can be easily modified by using the **UPPER** function to convert the object names and/or owner to all uppercase.*

Diagnostics

You can use the scripts in this section to report on the state of various objects within your database. The diagnostic scripts in this section include reports on the status of jobs in the job queue and lists of the invalid objects within the database.

tab_desc.sql

Fully Describe a Table

While we all start out with the good intentions of keeping documentation on database tables up to date, the reality is that updating documentation is rarely a priority. Table changes are made on the fly to meet production needs, indexes are added to speed performance, and constraints are added (or dropped) for expediency's sake when coding.

This script will generate up-to-date documentation on the selected table, including storage parameters, column descriptions and defaults, indexes on the table, and all constraint data.

```
REM tab_desc.sql
set echo off term on
accept table_name prompt "Enter the name of the Table: "
accept tab_owner prompt "Enter table owner: "
set heading on newpage 0
ttitle 'Table Description - Space Definition'
spool tab_desc.log

btitle off
column Nline newline
set pagesize 54
set linesize 78
set heading off embedded off verify off
accept report_comment char prompt 'Enter a comment to identify system: '
set term off
select 'Date -  '||TO_CHAR(sysdate,'Day Ddth Month YYYY HH24:MI:SS'),
       'At            - '||'&&report_comment' nline,
       'Username      - '||User  nline
   from SYS.DUAL
/

prompt
```

```
set embedded on heading on

column Ts format a30
column Ta format a30
column Clu format a30
column Pcf format 99999999999990
column Pcu format 99999999999990
column Int format 99,999,999,990
column Mat format 99,999,999,990
column Inx format 99,999,999,990
column Nxt format 99,999,999,990
column Mix format 99,999,999,990
column Max format 99,999,999,990
column Pci format 99999999999990
column Num format 99,999,999,990
column Blo format 99,999,999,990
column Emp format 99,999,999,990
column Avg format 99,999,999,990
column Cha format 99,999,999,990
column Rln format 99,999,999,990
column Hdg format a30 newline
set heading off
select 'Table Name' Hdg,              Table_Name           Ta,
       'Tablespace Name' Hdg,         Tablespace_Name      Ts,
       'Cluster Name' Hdg,            Cluster_Name         Clu,
       '% Free' Hdg,                  Pct_Free             Pcf,
       '% Used' Hdg,                  Pct_Used             Pcu,
       'Ini Trans' Hdg,              Ini_Trans            Int,
       'Max Trans' Hdg,              Max_Trans            Mat,
       'Initial Extent (K)' Hdg,     Initial_Extent/1024  Inx,
       'Next Extent (K)' Hdg,        Next_Extent/1024     Nxt,
       'Min Extents' Hdg,            Min_Extents          Mix,
       'Max Extents' Hdg,            Max_Extents          Max,
       '% Increase' Hdg,             Pct_Increase         Pci,
       'Number of Rows' Hdg,         Num_Rows             Num,
       'Number of Blocks' Hdg,       Blocks               Blo,
       'Number of Empty Blocks' Hdg, Empty_Blocks         Emp,
       'Average Space' Hdg,          Avg_Space            Avg,
       'Chain Count' Hdg,            Chain_Cnt            Cha,
       'Average Row Length' Hdg,     Avg_Row_len          Rln
  from DBA_TABLES
 where Table_Name=UPPER('&&table_name')
   and Owner=UPPER('&&tab_owner')
/
```

```
set heading on
set embedded off
column Cn format a30 heading 'Column Name'
column Fo format a15 heading 'Type'
column Nu format a8 heading 'Null'
column Nds format 99,999,999 heading 'No Distinct'
column Dfl format 9999 heading 'Dflt Len'
column Dfv format a40 heading 'Default Value'
ttitle 'Table Description - Column Definition'select Column_Name Cn,
       Data_Type ||
       DECODE(Data_Type,
              'NUMBER',
                  '('||TO_CHAR(Data_Precision)||
                      DECODE(Data_Scale,0,'',','||
                      TO_CHAR(Data_Scale))||')',
              'VARCHAR2',
                  '('||TO_CHAR(Data_Length)||')',
              'CHAR',
                  '('||TO_CHAR(Data_Length)||')',
              'DATE','',
              'LONG','',
              'Error') Fo,
       DECODE(Nullable,'Y','','NOT NULL') Nu,
       Num_Distinct Nds,
       Default_Length Dfl,
       Data_Default Dfv
  from DBA_TAB_COLUMNS
 where Table_Name=UPPER('&&table_name')
   and Owner=UPPER('&&tab_owner')
 order by Column_ID
/
ttitle off
prompt
prompt TABLE CONSTRAINTS
prompt
set heading on
column Cn format a30 heading 'Primary Constraint'
column Cln format a45 heading 'Table.Column Name'
column Ct format a7 heading 'Type'
column St format a7 heading 'Status'
column Ro format a30 heading 'Ref Owner|Constraint Name'
column Se format a70 heading 'Criteria ' newline
break on Cn on St
set embedded on
```

```
prompt Primary Key
prompt
select CNS.Constraint_Name Cn,
       CNS.Table_Name||'.'||CLS.Column_Name Cln,
       INITCAP(CNS.Status) St
  from DBA_CONSTRAINTS CNS,
       DBA_CONS_COLUMNS CLS
 where CNS.Table_Name=UPPER('&&table_name')
   and CNS.Owner=UPPER('&&tab_owner')
   and CNS.Constraint_Type='P'
   and CNS.Constraint_Name=CLS.Constraint_Name
 order by CLS.Position
/
prompt Unique Key
prompt
column Cn format a30 heading 'Unique Key'
select CNS.Constraint_Name Cn,
       CNS.Table_Name||'.'||CLS.Column_Name Cln,
       INITCAP(CNS.Status) St
  from DBA_CONSTRAINTS CNS,
       DBA_CONS_COLUMNS CLS
 where CNS.Table_Name=UPPER('&&table_name')
   and CNS.Owner=UPPER('&&tab_owner')
   and CNS.Constraint_Type='U'
   and CNS.Constraint_Name=CLS.Constraint_Name
 order by CLS.Position
/
prompt Foreign Keys
prompt
column Cln format a38 heading 'Foreign Key' newline
column Clfn format a38 heading 'Parent Key'
column Cn format a40 heading 'Foreign Constraint'
break on Cn on St skip 1
select CNS.Constraint_Name Cn,
       INITCAP(CNS.Status) St,
       CLS.Table_Name||'.'||CLS.Column_Name Cln,
       CLF.Owner||'.'||CLF.Table_Name||'.'||CLF.Column_Name Clfn
  from DBA_CONSTRAINTS CNS,
       DBA_CONS_COLUMNS CLF,
       DBA_CONS_COLUMNS CLS
 where CNS.Table_Name=UPPER('&&table_name')
   and CNS.Owner=UPPER('&&tab_owner')
   and CNS.Constraint_Type='R'
   and CNS.Constraint_Name=CLS.Constraint_Name
```

```
      and CLF.Constraint_Name = CNS.R_Constraint_Name
      and CLF.Owner = CNS.Owner
      and CLF.Position = CLS.Position
  order by CNS.Constraint_Name, CLS.Position
/
prompt Check Constraints
prompt
column Cn format a40 heading 'Check Constraint'
column Se format a75 heading 'Criteria'set arraysize 1
set long 32000
select Constraint_Name Cn,
       INITCAP(Status) St,
       Search_Condition Se
  from DBA_CONSTRAINTS
 where Table_Name=UPPER('&&table_name')
   and Owner=UPPER('&&tab_owner')
   and Constraint_Type='C'
/
prompt View Constraints
column Cn format a40 heading 'View Constraint'
select Constraint_Name Cn,
       INITCAP(Status) St,
       Search_Condition Se
  from DBA_CONSTRAINTS
 where Table_Name=UPPER('&&table_name')
   and Owner=UPPER('&&tab_owner')
   and Constraint_Type='V'
/
spool off
set arraysize 30
set newpage 1 verify on feedback 6 pagesize 24 linesize 80
set heading on embedded off term on arraysize 15 long 80
undefine table_name
undefine tab_owner
undefine report_comment
ttitle off
btitle off
clear columns
```

Sample output for the tab_desc.sql script run against an Oracle9i database is shown in the following listing. The first part of the output shows the table's storage information, followed by its column definitions and constraints.

```
Enter a comment to identify system: or9i
Fri Jun 29                                             page  1
```

Table Description - Space Definition

```
Date -  Friday     29th June     2001 20:43:29
At            -  or9i
Username      -  MEGH
```

```
Table Name                 APP_REFERRALS
Tablespace Name            TOOLS
Cluster Name
% Free                              10
% Used                              40
Ini Trans                            1
Max Trans                          255
Initial Extent (K)                  10
Next Extent (K)                     10
Min Extents                          1
Max Extents                        121
% Increase                          50
Number of Rows                      36
Number of Blocks                     1
Number of Empty Blocks               8
Average Space                      714
Chain Count                          0
Average Row Length                  33
```

```
Fri Jun 29                                          page  1
            Table Description - Column Definition
```

Column Name	Type	Null	No Distinct	Dflt Len
---------------------------	-------------	--------	-----------	--------
Default Value				

CODE	VARCHAR2(3)	NOT NULL		857
REFR_TYPE	VARCHAR2(3)	NOT NULL		1
DESCRIPTION	VARCHAR2(25)	NOT NULL		784
USR_CRTD	VARCHAR2(30)	NOT NULL		1
DT_CRTD	DATE	NOT NULL		9

```
STATUS                    VARCHAR2(3)                          0


USR_MDFD                  VARCHAR2(30)                         2


DT_MDFD                   DATE                                 7


REFR_CODE                 VARCHAR2(3)                          0


DISCOUNT                  NUMBER(8,2)                         17


DISCOUNT_TYPE             CHAR(1)                              3



11 rows selected.


TABLE CONSTRAINTS

Primary Key

Primary Constraint         Table.Column Name
-----------------------    ---------------------------------------------
Status
-------
REFR_PK                    APP_REFERRALS.CODE
Enabled


Unique Key


no rows selected

Foreign Keys

Foreign Constraint                 Status
-------------------------------    -------
Foreign Key                        Parent Key
-------------------------------    -------------------------------------
REFR_REFR_FK                       Enabled
APP_REFERRALS.REFR_CODE            APP.APP_REFERRALS.CODE
```

```
Check Constraints

Check Constraint                         Status
---------------------------------------- -------
Criteria
-----------------------------------------------------------------------
SYS_C002237                              Enabled
CODE IS NOT NULL


SYS_C002238                              Enabled
REFR_TYPE IS NOT NULL


SYS_C002239                              Enabled
DESCRIPTION IS NOT NULL


SYS_C002240                              Enabled
USR_CRTD IS NOT NULL


SYS_C002241                              Enabled
DT_CRTD IS NOT NULL



View Constraints

no rows selected
```

ANNOTATIONS

The first section of the script does the initial setup, prompting for the table name and table owner for later use via the **accept** command, which, unlike simply using the variable with the '&' or '&&' in a SQL statement, allows you to define the datatype of the variable (the **char** in the **accept report_comment** command) and to define your own prompt for the variable. In addition, the **ttitle** statement is used to define the report heading, and the **newpage** option of the **set** command is used to tell Oracle not to print any white space above the title. Defining the column Nline as **newline** forces a carriage return before the column is displayed.

```
set echo off term on
accept table_name prompt "Enter the name of the Table: "
accept tab_owner prompt "Enter table owner: "
set heading on newpage 0
```

```
ttitle 'Table Description - Space Definition'
spool tab_desc.log

btitle off
column Nline newline
set pagesize 54
set linesize 78
set heading off embedded off verify off
accept report_comment char prompt 'Enter a comment to identify system: '
set term off
select 'Date -   '||TO_CHAR(sysdate,'Day Ddth Month YYYY HH24:MI:SS'),
       'At        - '||'&&report_comment' nline,
       'Username  - '||User  nline
  from SYS.DUAL
/

prompt
set embedded on heading on
```

The SQL*Plus **set** command has a variety of variables that can be defined for reporting purposes. The **embedded** option controls where on a page the report will begin. By setting **embedded** to **off** initially, the report is forced to the top of the new page. Turning it back **on** after the **select** from DUAL means that the remainder of the report will print immediately following the results of that **select**.

The **select** statement includes the pseudo-column User, which returns the name of the current user. The User value is displayed as well to indicate which userid ran the script.

Formatting the numeric columns with a "0" at the end of the format string, as shown in the following listing, forces the display of a zero rather than a blank if the column value is zero. The pseudo-column Hdg is defined with the **newline** option to force a carriage return before the column is displayed and is used for the text strings. This formatting, combined with the **set heading off** statement, is a simple way to make a report line display vertically rather than horizontally for a **select** that will return a single row.

```
column Ts format a30
column Ta format a30
column Clu format a30
column Pcf format 99999999999990
column Pcu format 99999999999990
column Int format 99,999,999,990
column Mat format 99,999,999,990
column Inx format 99,999,999,990
column Nxt format 99,999,999,990
```

```
column Mix format 99,999,999,990
column Max format 99,999,999,990
column Pci format 99999999999990
column Num format 99,999,999,990
column Blo format 99,999,999,990
column Emp format 99,999,999,990
column Avg format 99,999,999,990
column Cha format 99,999,999,990
column Rln format 99,999,999,990
column Hdg format a30 newline
set heading off
select 'Table Name' Hdg,              Table_Name          Ta,
       'Tablespace Name' Hdg,         Tablespace_Name     Ts,
       'Cluster Name' Hdg,            Cluster_Name        Clu,
       '% Free' Hdg,                  Pct_Free            Pcf,
       '% Used' Hdg,                  Pct_Used            Pcu,
       'Ini Trans' Hdg,              Ini_Trans           Int,
       'Max Trans' Hdg,              Max_Trans           Mat,
       'Initial Extent (K)' Hdg,     Initial_Extent/1024 Inx,
       'Next Extent (K)' Hdg,        Next_Extent/1024    Nxt,
       'Min Extents' Hdg,            Min_Extents         Mix,
       'Max Extents' Hdg,            Max_Extents         Max,
       '% Increase' Hdg,             Pct_Increase        Pci,
       'Number of Rows' Hdg,         Num_Rows            Num,
       'Number of Blocks' Hdg,       Blocks              Blo,
       'Number of Empty Blocks' Hdg, Empty_Blocks        Emp,
       'Average Space' Hdg,          Avg_Space           Avg,
       'Chain Count' Hdg,            Chain_Cnt           Cha,
       'Average Row Length' Hdg,     Avg_Row_len         Rln
  from DBA_TABLES
 where Table_Name=UPPER('&&table_name')
   and Owner=UPPER('&&tab_owner')
/
```

Sample output for the storage section of the report is shown here:

```
Table Name                      APP_REFERRALS
Tablespace Name                 USER_DATA
Cluster Name
% Free                                        10
% Used                                        40
Ini Trans                                      1
Max Trans                                    255
Initial Extent (K)                            72
```

Next Extent (K)	1,024
Min Extents	1
Max Extents	500
% Increase	0
Number of Rows	857
Number of Blocks	9
Number of Empty Blocks	0
Average Space	2,901
Chain Count	0
Average Row Length	53

The table is not a clustered table and was defined using the standard Oracle defaults for **pctfree**, **pctused**, **initrans**, **maxtrans**, and **minextents**. The maximum extents value for this table has been increased to 500 extents. As of Oracle7.3, tables can be created with an unlimited value for **maxextents**. The initial extent is 72KB and the next extent is 1MB. Because the number of blocks the table is currently using is only 9, the table has not extended and the database block size must be 8KB. There are no empty blocks in the table, so unless the table is a static table or one with low activity, it will most likely have to extend soon. The average space value is the average available free space in the table. Since the chain count is 0, there are no chained rows.

The next section of the script displays the column information for the table:

```
set heading on
set embedded off
column Cn format a30 heading 'Column Name'
column Fo format a15 heading 'Type'
column Nu format a8 heading 'Null'
column Nds format 99,999,999 heading 'No Distinct'
column Dfl format 9999 heading 'Dflt Len'
column Dfv format a40 heading 'Default Value'
ttitle 'Table Description - Column Definition'
select Column_Name Cn,
       Data_Type ||
       DECODE(Data_Type,
              'NUMBER',
                  '('||TO_CHAR(Data_Precision)||
                      DECODE(Data_Scale,0,'',',')||
                      TO_CHAR(Data_Scale))||')',
              'VARCHAR2',
                  '('||TO_CHAR(Data_Length)||')',
              'CHAR',
                  '('||TO_CHAR(Data_Length)||')',
              'DATE','',
              'LONG','',
              'Error') Fo,
```

```
         DECODE(Nullable,'Y','','NOT NULL') Nu,
         Num_Distinct Nds,
         Default_Length Dfl,
         Data_Default Dfv
  from DBA_TAB_COLUMNS
 where Table_Name=UPPER('&&table_name')
   and Owner=UPPER('&&tab_owner')
 order by Column_ID
/
```

The **DECODE** function causes different formatting to be displayed depending on the value of the Data_Type column checked in the **DECODE**. The value of the Data_Type column determines whether the **select** statement will then look at the Data_Precision and Data_Scale columns (for a Data_Type of NUMBER), the Data_Length column (for a Data_Type of VARCHAR2 or CHAR) or no other column (for a Data_Type of DATE or LONG).

The **DECODE** function includes a "search/result" pair as well as a default value in case the expression being checked does not meet any of the explicitly defined search criteria. In this statement, the **DECODE** function is used first to search for matches on the Data_Type column values, with a non-match on the search defaulting to the string. It is used again within the initial **DECODE** to determine whether the NUMBER datatype has been defined with decimal places (a non-zero Data_Scale column); if it has, the **DECODE** will format it properly.

DECODE is used again to display either NOT NULL or blank spaces, depending on the value of the Nullable column.

The Num_Distinct column lists the number of distinct values in this column. The Default_Length and Data_Default columns refer to any default values defined for the column. In the following example output, the table has columns with datatypes of VARCHAR2, CHAR, DATE, and NUMBER. Although the first five columns are NOT NULL, the column with the most distinct values is the Code column, and this is most likely the primary key column for the table.

```
Fri Jun 29                                                  page  1
                  Table Description - Column Definition

Column Name                     Type          Null     No Distinct Dflt Len
----------------------------- ------------- -------- ----------- --------
Default Value
----------------------------------------------
CODE                            VARCHAR2(3)   NOT NULL            857


REFR_TYPE                       VARCHAR2(3)   NOT NULL              1


DESCRIPTION                     VARCHAR2(25)  NOT NULL            784
```

USR_CRTD	VARCHAR2(30)	NOT NULL	1
DT_CRTD	DATE	NOT NULL	9
STATUS	VARCHAR2(3)		0
USR_MDFD	VARCHAR2(30)		2
DT_MDFD	DATE		7
REFR_CODE	VARCHAR2(3)		0
DISCOUNT	NUMBER(8,2)		17
DISCOUNT_TYPE	CHAR(1)		3

```
11 rows selected.
```

The next section of the script displays information on the constraints defined on the table. Five types of constraints can be defined on a table: primary key, unique key, foreign key, check, and view. If you do not explicitly name the constraint, Oracle will generate the name, using the format 'SYS_C#####'. You should use meaningful names and name all constraints to avoid confusion and make it easier to see the relationships between tables.

```
ttitle off
prompt
prompt TABLE CONSTRAINTS
prompt
set heading on
column Cn format a30 heading 'Primary Constraint'
column Cln format a45 heading 'Table.Column Name'
column Ct format a7 heading 'Type'
column St format a7 heading 'Status'
column Ro format a30 heading 'Ref Owner|Constraint Name'
column Se format a70 heading 'Criteria ' newline
break on Cn on St
set embedded on
```

```
prompt Primary Key
prompt
select CNS.Constraint_Name Cn,
       CNS.Table_Name||'.'||CLS.Column_Name Cln,
       INITCAP(CNS.Status) St
  from DBA_CONSTRAINTS CNS,
       DBA_CONS_COLUMNS CLS
 where CNS.Table_Name=UPPER('&&table_name')
   and CNS.Owner=UPPER('&&tab_owner')
   and CNS.Constraint_Type='P'
   and CNS.Constraint_Name=CLS.Constraint_Name
 order by CLS.Position
/
```

This section lists the information on the primary key constraint on the table. A table can have one and only one primary key, although the key, like an index key, can consist of several concatenated columns, as long as this combination will point to one and only one row of the table. Primary key columns may not contain nulls.

The primary key constraint will have a constraint type of 'P.' The **INITCAP** function is used for formatting the output of the Status column of DBA_CONSTRAINTS for readability by capitalizing the first letter of each word. The status of the constraint can be either "enabled" or "disabled" (enforced or ignored on input, respectively). The **order by** clause will list the primary key columns in the order in which the key is created.

```
TABLE CONSTRAINTS

Primary Key

Primary Constraint                 Table.Column Name
-------------------------          ------------------------------------
Status
--------
REFR_PK                            APP_REFERRALS.CODE
Enabled
```

In this example, the primary key is a single column and the constraint is enforced on the table.

The next section of the script checks for unique constraints. You can define multiple unique keys on a table, and their columns may contain nulls.

```
prompt Unique Key
prompt
column Cn format a30 heading 'Unique Key'
select CNS.Constraint_Name Cn,
```

```
        CNS.Table_Name||'.'||CLS.Column_Name Cln,
        INITCAP(CNS.Status) St
   from DBA_CONSTRAINTS CNS,
        DBA_CONS_COLUMNS CLS
  where CNS.Table_Name=UPPER('&&table_name')
    and CNS.Owner=UPPER('&&tab_owner')
    and CNS.Constraint_Type='U'
    and CNS.Constraint_Name=CLS.Constraint_Name
  order by CLS.Position
/
```

You cannot create a unique key on the same columns as the primary key. Adding a unique constraint on a table will also create a unique index on the constraint's columns. Creating a unique index for the table will *not* add the unique constraint to the table. Sample output for the unique constraint check on the APP_REFERRALS table is shown here:

```
Unique Key


no rows selected
```

In this example, there are no additional unique key constraints. The next section of the script checks for the existence of foreign key constraints on the table.

Foreign key constraints enforce integrity relationships between tables in the same database. A foreign key constraint may be defined on either the primary key or unique key of a table (parent table). You can define a foreign key with the **on delete cascade** clause, which will allow deletions in the parent table if child records exist and will automatically delete the dependent rows in the child table. By default, deletions are not allowed on the parent table if dependent rows are defined by the foreign key.

Extracting the foreign key relationships from the data dictionary is slightly more complex than extracting the primary key. In addition to knowing the name of the foreign key constraint and column(s) for the table being listed, you must know the owner, table name, and column name(s) of the table being referenced. To retrieve the information, the DBA_CONS_COLUMNS view is joined twice into the query to extract the foreign key columns (CLS alias) and to extract the information on the primary key being referenced (CLF alias). The name of the primary key constraint being referenced by the foreign key is contained in the R_Constraint_Name column of DBA_CONSTRAINTS.

```
prompt Foreign Keys
prompt
column Cln format a38 heading 'Foreign Key' newline
column Clfn format a38 heading 'Parent Key'
column Cn format a40 heading 'Foreign Constraint'
```

```
break on Cn on St skip 1
select CNS.Constraint_Name Cn,
       INITCAP(CNS.Status) St,
       CLS.Table_Name||'.'||CLS.Column_Name Cln,
       CLF.Owner||'.'||CLF.Table_Name||'.'||CLF.Column_Name Clfn
  from DBA_CONSTRAINTS CNS,
       DBA_CONS_COLUMNS CLF,
       DBA_CONS_COLUMNS CLS
 where CNS.Table_Name=UPPER('&&table_name')
   and CNS.Owner=UPPER('&&tab_owner')
   and CNS.Constraint_Type='R'
   and CNS.Constraint_Name=CLS.Constraint_Name
   and CLF.Constraint_Name = CNS.R_Constraint_Name
   and CLF.Owner = CNS.Owner
   and CLF.Position = CLS.Position
 order by CNS.Constraint_Name, CLS.Position
/
```

Sample output for the foreign key portion of the tab_desc.sql script is shown in the following listing:

```
Foreign Keys

Foreign Constraint                          Status
----------------------------------------    ------
Foreign Key                                 Parent Key
----------------------------                ----------------------------
REFR_REFR_FK                                Enabled
APP_REFERRALS.REFR_CODE                     APP.APP_REFERRALS.CODE
```

This constraint is self-referring, pointing back to the primary key of its own table. That is, the Refr_Code in the APP_REFERRALS table is a foreign key to the Code column in the same table.

Since foreign key columns are usually used as part of a join between the primary key table and the foreign key table in SQL statements, you should create an index on the columns of the foreign key to speed performance.

PROGRAMMER'S NOTE *See Chapter 4 for a script that determines which foreign keys are not properly indexed.*

The next portion of the tab_desc.sql script examines the table's Check constraints.

```
prompt Check Constraints
prompt
column Cn format a40 heading 'Check Constraint'
column Se format a75 heading 'Criteria'
set arraysize 1
```

```
set long 32000
select Constraint_Name Cn,
       INITCAP(Status) St,
       Search_Condition Se
  from DBA_CONSTRAINTS
 where Table_Name=UPPER('&&table_name')
   and Owner=UPPER('&&tab_owner')
   and Constraint_Type='C'
/
```

Check constraints are used to explicitly define a condition that the column must meet for the insert or update to succeed. If you create the column as NOT NULL, Oracle will create a constraint for you. You can define multiple Check constraints on a column, but Oracle will not check that they are mutually exclusive. You cannot check the values in columns in other tables when creating a Check constraint, but you can refer to columns in the same table and row.

Sample output for the Check constraint portion of the tab_desc.sql script is shown in the following listing:

```
Check Constraints

Check Constraint                         Status
---------------------------------------- -------
Criteria
-----------------------------------------------------------------
SYS_C002237                              Enabled
CODE IS NOT NULL


SYS_C002238                              Enabled
REFR_TYPE IS NOT NULL


SYS_C002239                              Enabled
DESCRIPTION IS NOT NULL


SYS_C002240                              Enabled
USR_CRTD IS NOT NULL


SYS_C002241                              Enabled
DT_CRTD IS NOT NULL
```

The only Check constraints on this table are the NOT NULL constraints, with system-generated constraint names. The constraints are enabled, so **insert**s and **update**s to this table must have values for these columns.

The next portion of the script evaluates View constraints:

```
prompt View Constraints
column Cn format a40 heading 'View Constraint'
select Constraint_Name Cn,
       INITCAP(Status) St,
       Search_Condition Se
  from DBA_CONSTRAINTS
 where Table_Name=UPPER('&&table_name')
   and Owner=UPPER('&&tab_owner')
   and Constraint_Type='V'
/
spool off
```

View constraints are created when a view is created on the table using the **with check option** clause. A View constraint ensures that **insert**s and **update**s performed through the view must result in rows that the view query can **select**. The constraint will be created on the view itself, not on the underlying table.

This listing shows the sample output for the View constraints query for the APP_REFERRALS table.

```
View Constraints


no rows selected
```

Finally the environment is reset back to its original state:

```
set arraysize 30
set newpage 1 verify on feedback 6 pagesize 24
set linesize 80 heading on embedded on
```

List Submitted Jobs

list_sub.sql

Which of your users has jobs running in your database and when are they scheduled to run? Are the scheduled jobs actually executing or are they broken? Oracle supports the concept of job queues within the database, allowing users to schedule and execute batch jobs. The following script will display all jobs submitted to the queue, along with the information on who submitted the job, when the job will execute, and the status of the last execution.

```
REM list_sub.sql
set echo off term off pagesize 60
```

```
spool list_sub.log

ttitle -
  center  'List Submitted Jobs' skip 2
col Jid  format 9999  heading 'Id'
col Subu format a10   heading 'Submitter'      trunc
col Secd format a10   heading 'Security'       trunc
col Proc format a20   heading 'Job'            word_wrapped
col Lsd  format a5    heading 'Last|Ok|Date'
col Lst  format a5    heading 'Last|Ok|Time'
col Nrd  format a5    heading 'Next|Run|Date'
col Nrt  format a5    heading 'Next|Run|Time'
col Fail format 999   heading 'Errs'
col Ok   format a2    heading 'Ok'

select Job  Jid,
       Log_User Subu,
       Priv_User Secd,
       What Proc,
       TO_CHAR(Last_Date,'MM/DD') Lsd,
       SUBSTR(Last_Sec,1,5) Lst,
       TO_CHAR(Next_Date,'MM/DD') Nrd,
       SUBSTR(Next_Sec,1,5) Nrt,
       Failures Fail,
       DECODE(Broken,'Y','N','Y') Ok
  from DBA_JOBS
/
spool off
set newpage 1 verify on feedback 6 pagesize 24 linesize 80
set heading on embedded off
clear columns
ttitle off
```

Sample output for the list_sub.sql script is shown in the following listing, which shows that five separate jobs have been submitted, all by the APPDBA user.

```
                           List Submitted Jobs
                            Last  Last  Next  Next
                            Ok    Ok    Run   Run
    Id Submitter Security Job        Date  Time  Date  Time  Errs Ok
 ----- ---------- -------- ---------------- ----- ----- ----- ----- ---- --
   353 APPDBA     APPDBA   table_analyze('APP',       06/06 13:23      1 Y
                           'APP_TELEPHONES');

   294 APPDBA     APPDBA   table_analyze('APP',       06/06 13:23      1 Y
                           'APP_GIFT_CERTIFICAT
                           ES');
```

```
256 APPDBA      APPDBA     table_analyze('APP',         06/06 13:23   1 Y
                                      'APP_CUSTOMERS');

247 APPDBA      APPDBA     table_analyze('APP',         06/06 12:08     Y
                                      'APP_CREDIT_CARDS');

220 APPDBA      APPDBA     table_analyze('APP',         06/06 12:08     Y
                                      'APP_ADDRESSES');
```

ANNOTATIONS

You can use the job queue to schedule user-defined routines (procedures) and run them from the background process at times and intervals that you define, and under the same environment and user privileges and access as they were submitted. To run jobs in the database, the init.ora parameters JOB_QUEUE_PROCESSES and JOB_QUEUE_INTERVAL must be set. JOB_QUEUE_PROCESSES defines the number of background processes that will be started to run the jobs in the job queues. At the operating system level, these processes are created as **ora_snp#_<>**, where **#** begins with *0*. JOB_QUEUE_INTERVAL defines the sleep time for the processes between checking the job queue for jobs to run. You can use the job queue to schedule database maintenance jobs at times of low user activity. Jobs are submitted to and manipulated in the job queue using the Oracle-provided package **DBMS_JOB**.

The first portion of the list_sub.sql script defines the column characteristics for displaying output:

```
set echo off term off pagesize 60
spool list_sub.log

ttitle -
   center  'List Submitted Jobs' skip 2
col Jid  format 9999   heading 'Id'
col Subu format a10    heading 'Submitter'        trunc
col Secd format a10    heading 'Security'         trunc
col Proc format a20    heading 'Job'              word_wrapped
col Lsd  format a5     heading 'Last|Ok|Date'
col Lst  format a5     heading 'Last|Ok|Time'
col Nrd  format a5     heading 'Next|Run|Date'
col Nrt  format a5     heading 'Next|Run|Time'
col Fail format 999    heading 'Errs'
col Ok   format a2     heading 'Ok'
```

The **column** command has several uses in addition to that of formatting the column output. The **heading** parameter will replace the default heading of the column name with the specified heading. You can use a pipe symbol (|) in the heading definition to create a multiple-line column heading. The **trunc** parameter, used for CHAR,

VARCHAR2, LONG, and DATE strings, will truncate the string after the specified format has been displayed, rather than wrap the column value over several lines. The **word_wrapped** parameter will wrap the output string within the defined column boundaries, in this case 20 characters, and will left-justify each line.

```
select Job  Jid,
       Log_User Subu,
       Priv_User Secd,
       What Proc,
       TO_CHAR(Last_Date,'MM/DD') Lsd,
       SUBSTR(Last_Sec,1,5) Lst,
       TO_CHAR(Next_Date,'MM/DD') Nrd,
       SUBSTR(Next_Sec,1,5) Nrt,
       Failures Fail,
       DECODE(Broken,'Y','N','Y') Ok
  from DBA_JOBS
/
spool off
```

The Job column, given the alias Jid, is the unique job number assigned to the submitted job. This number is not reused and will retain its value if the database is exported and imported. Log_User is the user who submitted the job, Priv_User is the user whose default privileges will be used to run the job, and the What column value is the PL/SQL block that will be executed when the job runs. Last_Date is the last date that the job successfully executed, Last_Sec the time of the last successful execution. Next_Date and Next_Sec are the date and time, respectively, that the job is next scheduled to run. The Failures column value is the number of times the job was started and failed since the last time it was successfully executed. The Broken column indicates whether or not the system should try to execute the job. If 16 unsuccessful attempts are made to execute the job, it will be flagged as broken. The following script reverses the value of Broken via the **DECODE** command, to display a *Y* rather than an *N* if the job is executable:

```
                              List Submitted Jobs
                              Last  Last  Next  Next
                              Ok    Ok    Run   Run
   Id Submitter  Security Job          Date  Time  Date  Time  Errs Ok
----- ---------- -------- ---------------- ----- ----- ----- ----- ---- --
  353 APPDBA     APPDBA   table_analyze('APP',       06/06 13:23    1 Y
                          'APP_TELEPHONES');

  294 APPDBA     APPDBA   table_analyze('APP',       06/06 13:23    1 Y
                          'APP_GIFT_CERTIFICAT
                          ES');
```

```
    256 APPDBA      APPDBA     table_analyze('APP',          06/06 13:23    1 Y
                               'APP_CUSTOMERS');

    247 APPDBA      APPDBA     table_analyze('APP',          06/06 12:08      Y
                               'APP_CREDIT_CARDS');

    220 APPDBA      APPDBA     table_analyze('APP',          06/06 12:08      Y
                               'APP_ADDRESSES');
```

The sample output shows that five jobs are waiting in the queue. Of the five, three have encountered errors once when running. All five were submitted by the same user, and each will execute the same stored procedure with different input parameters.

List Running Jobs

list_run.sql

The script in the previous section lists jobs submitted to the job queue. The list_run.sql script, shown in the following listing, shows jobs that are currently running and displays the last time they were successfully run as well as the time that the current execution began.

```
REM list_run.sql
set echo off term off pagesize 60
spool list_run.log

ttitle -
  center  'List Running Jobs' skip 2
col Jid  format 9999  heading 'Id'
col Subu format a10   heading 'Submitter'      trunc
col Secd format a10   heading 'Security'       trunc
col Proc format a20   heading 'Job'            word_wrapped
col Lsd  format a5    heading 'Last|Ok|Date'
col Lst  format a5    heading 'Last|Ok|Time'
col Trd  format a5    heading 'This|Run|Date'
col Trt  format a5    heading 'This|Run|Time'
col Fail format 999   heading 'Errs'

select R.Job  Jid,
       J.Log_User Subu,
       J.Priv_User Secd,
       J.What Proc,
       TO_CHAR(R.Last_Date,'MM/DD') Lsd,
       SUBSTR(R.Last_Sec,1,5) Lst,
```

```
        TO_CHAR(R.This_Date,'MM/DD') Trd,
        SUBSTR(R.This_Sec,1,5) Trt,
        R.Failures Fail
  from DBA_JOBS_RUNNING R, DBA_JOBS J
 where R.Job = J.Job
/
spool off
set newpage 1 verify on feedback 6 pagesize 24 linesize 80
set heading on embedded off term on
clear columns
ttitle off
```

Sample output of the list_run.sql script is shown in the following listing.

```
                              List Running Jobs

                                 Last  Last  This  This
                                 Ok    Ok    Run   Run
   Id Submitter  Security Job    Date  Time  Date  Time  Errs
   ----- ---------- -------- ------------------ ----- ----- ----- ----- ----
   86 APPDBA     APPDBA   table_analyze('APP',       06/06 01:17     1
                          'APP_ADDRESSES');
```

ANNOTATIONS

This script is similar to the list_sub.sql script, with the exception that this script displays only jobs that are currently executing in the job queues. The maximum number of jobs that can execute at any one time is determined by the init.ora parameter JOB_QUEUE_PROCESSES. If you have a large number of jobs that need to be run at the same time, JOB_QUEUE_PROCESSES should be set to a high number. Remember that each job queue that is created has an operating system process associated with it.

The **select** portion of the script, shown in the next listing, joins the DBA_JOBS view, which contains a list of all jobs in the job queues, with the DBA_JOBS_RUNNING view, which contains information on the currently executing jobs. The Last_Date and Last_Sec columns refer to the date and time of the last successful execution of this job; if they are blank, the job has never been successfully run. The This_Date and This_Sec columns contain the date and time that the job started executing. The Failures column value is the number of times Oracle attempted to execute the job.

Jobs can fail for a number of reasons: the table they reference may be locked, the procedure they execute may have become invalid and cannot be revalidated, or the owner of the procedure may not have the privileges needed to execute the procedure successfully. Oracle will attempt to execute the job 16 times before marking it "broken."

```
select R.Job  Jid,
       J.Log_User Subu,
       J.Priv_User Secd,
```

```
        J.What Proc,
        TO_CHAR(R.Last_Date,'MM/DD') Lsd,
        SUBSTR(R.Last_Sec,1,5) Lst,
        TO_CHAR(R.This_Date,'MM/DD') Trd,
        SUBSTR(R.This_Sec,1,5) Trt,
        R.Failures Fail
   from DBA_JOBS_RUNNING R, DBA_JOBS J
  where R.Job = J.Job
/
```

For the sample database, the output in the following listing shows that only one job is currently running in the job queue. Oracle is attempting to execute the job for the second time (Errs column has a value of 1); the first attempt was unsuccessful.

```
List Running Jobs


                                        Last  Last  This  This
                                        Ok    Ok    Run   Run
    Id Submitter  Security Job          Date  Time  Date  Time  Errs
 ----- ---------- -------- ------------------ ----- ----- ----- ----- ----
    86 APPDBA     APPDBA   table_analyze('APP',     06/06 01:17    1
                           'APP_ADDRESSES');
```

invalobj.sql

List Invalid Objects

Which objects in your database are invalid and need recompilation? Changes to a table will invalidate views, procedures, and packages that depend on that table. Oracle does not tell you which objects are forced to be invalid when other objects change. The next time an invalid view, procedure, or package is executed, Oracle will recompile it and performance may be affected by the runtime compilation. You can avoid the performance degradation by scheduling checks and recompilation of invalid objects for low-usage times.

You can use the following script, invalobj.sql, to identify invalid objects and combine this script with the revalobj.sql script in the "Utilities" section of this chapter to recompile these objects, scheduling them through the Oracle job queues to run at low-usage times.

```
REM invalobj.sql
set echo off verify off term off feedback off
spool invalobj.log

ttitle -
  center  'Verify Stored Procedures' skip 2

col Oown  format a10 heading 'Owner'       word_wrapped
col Oname format a30 heading 'Object Name' trunc
```

```
col Otype format a12 heading 'Object Type' trunc
col Prob  format a13 heading 'Problem'       trunc
break on oown skip 1 on otype

select A.Owner Oown,
       A.Object_Name Oname,
       A.Object_Type Otype,
       'Miss Pkg Body' Prob
  from DBA_OBJECTS A
 where A.Object_Type = 'PACKAGE'
   and A.Owner not in ('SYS','SYSTEM')
   and not exists
         (select 'x'
            from DBA_OBJECTS B
           where B.Object_Name = A.Object_Name
             and B.Owner = A.Owner
             and B.Object_Type = 'PACKAGE BODY')
union
select Owner Oown,
       Object_Name Oname,
       Object_Type Otype,
       'Invalid Obj' Prob
  from DBA_OBJECTS
 where Object_Type in
     ('PROCEDURE','PACKAGE','FUNCTION',
'TRIGGER','PACKAGE BODY','VIEW')
   and Owner not in ('SYS','SYSTEM')
   and Status != 'VALID'
 order by 1,4,3,2
/
spool off
set newpage 1 verify on feedback 6 pagesize 24 linesize 80
set heading on embedded off term on
ttitle off
clear breaks
clear columns
```

Sample output for the preceding script is shown in this listing:

```
                        Verify Stored Procedures

Owner      Object Name                        Object Type  Problem
---------- --------------------------------- ------------ ------------
APP        APP_A_MSG1_PRIORITY_FUNC           FUNCTION     Invalid Obj
```

```
           APP_MAST1_PRIORITY_FUNC                      Invalid Obj
           APP_INSERT_CUSTOMER         PACKAGE BODY Invalid Obj
           PKG_EXPRESS_SAVE                            Invalid Obj
           PKG_ORDER_SAVE                              Invalid Obj
           P_INT_ORDER_PROCESS         PROCEDURE    Invalid Obj
           REMOVE_CUSTOMER                             Invalid Obj
           REMOVE_EMPLOYEE                             Invalid Obj
           PDT_PRE_INS_DBT             TRIGGER      Invalid Obj
           PMN_PRE_INS_DBT                             Invalid Obj
           TEC_PRE_INS_DBT                             Invalid Obj

TRAIN      PKG_ORDER_SAVE             PACKAGE      Miss Pkg Body
           FINAL                      VIEW         Invalid Obj
```

The output shows that a number of database objects are currently marked as "invalid" because of missing package bodies or changes in dependent objects.

ANNOTATIONS

The script contains two **select** statements, with their output joined by the **union** clause. This query structure allows the script to combine two different types of information, missing package bodies and invalid objects, into a single report and group the output by owner.

The first query in the **union** checks for missing package bodies by selecting for objects with a type of 'PACKAGE' (the package specification) from DBA_OBJECTS and then sub-selecting for the existence of a matching object with a type of 'PACKAGE BODY'. The **not exists** clause in the **where** clause of the **select** does not need an actual value returned; the check is just to determine whether the matching package body exists. If the package body exists, the **not exists** fails and the package will not be included in the output of this half of the **union** select.

```
select A.Owner Oown,
       A.Object_Name Oname,
       A.Object_Type Otype,
       'Miss Pkg Body' Prob
  from DBA_OBJECTS A
 where A.Object_Type = 'PACKAGE'
   and A.Owner not in ('SYS','SYSTEM')
   and not exists
        (select 'x'
           from DBA_OBJECTS B
          where B.Object_Name = A.Object_Name
            and B.Owner = A.Owner
            and B.Object_Type = 'PACKAGE BODY')
```

The second half of the **union** selects for invalid objects. Neither query includes objects owned by either SYS or SYSTEM.

```
union
select Owner Oown,
       Object_Name Oname,
       Object_Type Otype,
       'Invalid Obj' Prob
  from DBA_OBJECTS
  where Object_Type in
      ('PROCEDURE','PACKAGE','FUNCTION','TRIGGER',
'PACKAGE BODY','VIEW')
    and Owner not in ('SYS','SYSTEM')
    and Status != 'VALID'
```

You should not use the SYSTEM user for application objects. If you believe there are problems with objects owned by either SYS or SYSTEM, you can change the queries to look for objects owned specifically by these users:

```
and Owner in ('SYS','SYSTEM')
```

If you do get a report of invalid objects or missing package bodies for SYS or SYSTEM, contact Oracle Support before attempting to correct the problem on your own.

Because the queries are **union**ed together, you must obey the formatting rules for **union**s. In each query, the columns must be of the same datatype. The datatypes and column names for the **union** query are determined by the datatypes of the first query in the **union**. You don't need to specify column names for the columns in any but the first query of the **union**.

```
 order by 1,4,3,2
/
spool off
```

This **order by** clause uses the column's ordinal positions. Prior to Oracle7.1, you had to use ordinal positions in your **order by** clauses if you used an expression (such as in this script, since it selects text strings instead of column values). As of Oracle7.1, you can use the **as** clause to name a selected expression, and you can use that name in your **order by** clauses. You therefore do not need to use ordinal values in your **order by** clauses—unless you are using a **union**. If you use a **union** clause in your queries, you should use the ordinal positions of the columns in your **order by** clause. The use of ordinal positions in **order by** clauses for **union** queries is advisable because you may select different columns in each part of the query; as long as they have the same datatype, the query will succeed.

Sample output for the invalobj.sql script is shown here:

```
                              Verify Stored Procedures


Owner       Object Name                        Object Type  Problem
----------  --------------------------------   ------------ ------------
APP         APP_A_MSG1_PRIORITY_FUNC           FUNCTION     Invalid Obj
            APP_MAST1_PRIORITY_FUNC                         Invalid Obj
            APP_INSERT_CUSTOMER                PACKAGE BODY Invalid Obj
            PKG_EXPRESS_SAVE                                Invalid Obj
            PKG_ORDER_SAVE                                  Invalid Obj
            P_INT_ORDER_PROCESS                PROCEDURE    Invalid Obj
            REMOVE_CUSTOMER                                 Invalid Obj
            REMOVE_EMPLOYEE                                 Invalid Obj
            PDT_PRE_INS_DBT                    TRIGGER      Invalid Obj
            PMN_PRE_INS_DBT                                 Invalid Obj
            TEC_PRE_INS_DBT                                 Invalid Obj


TRAIN       PKG_ORDER_SAVE                     PACKAGE      Miss Pkg Body
            FINAL                              VIEW         Invalid Obj
```

In this database, two users have problems with their objects. The first, APP, has a number of invalid objects. The functions and procedures that are invalid are independent objects that are not contained within a package body. It is not possible for only a portion of a package body to become invalid—if a change to the database affects one function or procedure within the package body, the entire package body is invalidated. A package specification can become valid, while the underlying package body can become invalid. Package invalidation can occur if the package specification remains the same and the package body is changed incorrectly, or if an underlying table or view is changed.

The second user has one invalid view and is missing the package body for the package PKG_ORDER_SAVE. This error will occur if the package specification is written and created and the body has not yet been created.

desc_adt.sql
desc_ad3.sql

Describe Tables That Use Abstract Datatypes

The more you use abstract datatypes, the more complicated your **describe** commands become. If you create abstract datatypes that rely on other abstract datatypes, your ability to see the full description of a table will be adversely affected unless you write utility scripts to retrieve the full hierarchy of the abstract datatypes. In this section, you will see a script, desc_adt.sql, that describes tables with one or more abstract datatypes. To illustrate the problem that the script solves, the initial portion of this section creates a sample table based on multiple datatypes.

For the examples in this section, a new datatype will be created: AUTHOR_TY. The AUTHOR_TY script has two attributes about an author: Name and Date_of_Birth. The command in the following listing creates the AUTHOR_TY datatype:

```
create or replace type AUTHOR_TY as object
(Name            VARCHAR2(50),
 Date_of_Birth   DATE);
```

Next, a second datatype, ARTICLE_TY, is created. The ARTICLE_TY datatype relies on the AUTHOR_TY datatype. Each article has an Author (as defined by the AUTHOR_TY datatype), a Title, a Year_Published, and a Publication. The SQL command shown in the following listing creates the ARTICLE_TY datatype:

```
create or replace type ARTICLE_TY as object
(Author          AUTHOR_TY,
 Title           VARCHAR2(100),
 Year_Published  NUMBER(4),
 Publication     VARCHAR2(100));
```

The following listing uses the ARTICLE_TY datatype to create a table named COMPILATION_ARTICLES. The COMPILATION_ARTICLES table will have one record for each article published as part of a special compilation.

```
create table COMPILATION_ARTICLES
(Sequence_Number   NUMBER(4),
 Article           ARTICLE_TY);
```

What columns can you select from the COMPILATION_ARTICLES table? Since the Article column uses the ARTICLE_TY datatype, you can select the following columns:

◆ Sequence_Number

◆ Article

◆ Article.Author

◆ Article.Title

◆ Article.Year_Published

◆ Article.Publication

Because Article.Author uses the AUTHOR_TY datatype, you can also select these columns:

◆ Article.Author.Name

◆ Article.Author.Date_of_Birth

Thus, there are eight different columns you can select from the COMPILATION_ ARTICLES table. However, the **describe** command does not show these columns:

```
describe COMPILATION_ARTICLES
```

```
Name                                Null?     Type
-------------------------------- --------- ----
SEQUENCE_NUMBER                               NUMBER
ARTICLE                                       ARTICLE_TY
```

The **describe** command shows only the first two columns—the attributes of the Article column (and the attributes of the datatypes nested within it) are not shown.

PROGRAMMER'S NOTE *In Oracle8.0.3, the **describe** command does not show the actual datatype; it shows a value of "NAMED TYPE" instead. To see the real datatype in Oracle8.0.3, you need to query USER_TAB_COLUMNS.*

The following script, desc_adt.sql, creates a view called DBA_DESCRIBE. You can query the DBA_DESCRIBE view to see a listing of all columns that you can select from a table using abstract datatypes. The desc_adt.sql script will show the full details for any table whose datatypes use no more than two levels of nesting; the annotations show how to expand this script to support even greater levels of nesting.

```
REM desc_adt.sql
 create or replace view SYS.DBA_DESCRIBE
      (Owner, Table_Name,
       Column_Name, Data_Type, Data_Type_Mod,
       Data_Type_Owner, Data_Length, Data_Precision,
       Data_Scale, Column_Id, Character_Set_Name )
    as
select Owner, Table_Name,
       Column_Name, Data_Type, Data_Type_Mod,
       Data_Type_Owner, Data_Length, Data_Precision,
       Data_Scale, Column_Id, Character_Set_Name
  from DBA_TAB_COLUMNS
 union all
select B.Owner, B.Table_Name,
       '  '||B.Column_Name||'.'||A.Attr_Name, A.Attr_Type_Name,
       A.Attr_Type_Mod, A.Attr_Type_Owner, A.Length,
       A.Precision, A.Scale, B.Column_ID,
       A.Character_Set_Name
  from DBA_TYPE_ATTRS A, DBA_TAB_COLUMNS B
 where B.Data_Type = A.Type_Name
```

```
      and B.Data_Type_Owner = A.Owner
  union all
select C.Owner, C.Table_Name,
         '    '||C.Column_Name||'.'||B.Attr_Name||'.'||A.Attr_Name,
         A.Attr_Type_Name, A.Attr_Type_Mod,
         A.Attr_Type_Owner, A.Length, A.Precision,
         A.Scale, C.Column_ID, A.Character_Set_Name
   from DBA_TYPE_ATTRS A, DBA_TYPE_ATTRS B, DBA_TAB_COLUMNS C
  where C.Data_Type = B.Type_Name
    and C.Data_Type_Owner = B.Owner
    and A.Type_Name = B.Attr_Type_Name
    and A.Owner = B.Attr_Type_Owner;
```

Sample output from the DBA_DESCRIBE view is shown in the following listing:

```
column Column_Name format A40
column Data_Type format A25
select Column_Name, Data_Type
  from DBA_DESCRIBE
 where Table_Name = 'COMPILATION_ARTICLES';
clear columns
```

COLUMN_NAME	DATA_TYPE
SEQUENCE_NUMBER	NUMBER
ARTICLE	ARTICLE_TY
ARTICLE.AUTHOR	AUTHOR_TY
ARTICLE.TITLE	VARCHAR2
ARTICLE.YEAR_PUBLISHED	NUMBER
ARTICLE.PUBLICATION	VARCHAR2
ARTICLE.AUTHOR.NAME	VARCHAR2
ARTICLE.AUTHOR.DATE_OF_BIRTH	DATE

```
8 rows selected.
```

The DBA_DESCRIBE output shows the eight possible columns you can select from the COMPILATION_ARTICLES table. Attributes of abstract datatypes are preceded by sets of blanks to indicate that they are datatype attributes.

ANNOTATIONS

You can expand the desc_adt.sql script to handle a third level of datatype nesting by adding an additional query to the **union** query that provides the basis for the DBA_DESCRIBE view. The following query will retrieve the attribute data for a datatype that is nested three levels deep (for instance, if AUTHOR_TY relied on an abstract datatype):

```
select D.Owner, D.Table_Name,  '     '||
        D.Column_Name||'.'||C.Attr_Name||'.'||B.Attr_Name
 ||'.'||A.ATTR_NAME,
        A.Attr_Type_Name, A.Attr_Type_Mod,
        A.Attr_Type_Owner, A.Length, A.Precision, A.Scale,
 D.Column_ID, A.Character_Set_Name
   from DBA_TYPE_ATTRS A, DBA_TYPE_ATTRS B, DBA_TYPE_ATTRS C,
 DBA_TAB_COLUMNS D
  where D.Data_Type = C.Type_Name
    and D.Data_Type_Owner = C.Owner
    and A.Type_Name = B.Attr_Type_Name
    and A.Owner = B.Attr_Type_Owner
    and B.Type_Name = C.Attr_Type_Name
    and B.Owner = C.Attr_Type_Owner;
```

In the combined version of the desc_adt.sql script, this new query is **union**ed to the rest of the view definition script, as shown in the following listing (this query is also available in the script desc_ad3.sql that is available on the CD-ROM with this book):

```
REM desc_ad3.sql
REM desc_adt.sql, modified to include a third level of nesting.
REM
create or replace view SYS.DBA_DESCRIBE
        (Owner, Table_Name,
         Column_Name, Data_Type, Data_Type_Mod,
         Data_Type_Owner, Data_Length, Data_Precision,
         Data_Scale, Column_Id, Character_Set_Name )
     as
select Owner, Table_Name,
        Column_Name, Data_Type, Data_Type_Mod,
        Data_Type_Owner, Data_Length, Data_Precision,
        Data_Scale, Column_Id, Character_Set_Name
   from DBA_TAB_COLUMNS
  union all
select B.Owner, B.Table_Name,
        '   '||B.Column_Name||'.'||A.Attr_Name, A.Attr_Type_Name,
        A.Attr_Type_Mod, A.Attr_Type_Owner, A.Length,
        A.Precision, A.Scale, B.Column_ID,
        A.Character_Set_Name
   from DBA_TYPE_ATTRS A, DBA_TAB_COLUMNS B
  where B.Data_Type = A.Type_Name
    and B.Data_Type_Owner = A.Owner
  union all
select C.Owner, C.Table_Name,
        '    '||C.Column_Name||'.'||B.Attr_Name||'.'||A.Attr_Name,
```

```
      A.Attr_Type_Name, A.Attr_Type_Mod,
      A.Attr_Type_Owner, A.Length, A.Precision,
      A.Scale, C.Column_ID, A.Character_Set_Name
  from DBA_TYPE_ATTRS A, DBA_TYPE_ATTRS B, DBA_TAB_COLUMNS C
 where C.Data_Type = B.Type_Name
   and C.Data_Type_Owner = B.Owner
   and A.Type_Name = B.Attr_Type_Name
   and A.Owner = B.Attr_Type_Owner
 union all
select D.Owner, D.Table_Name,      '        '||
      D.Column_Name||'.'||C.Attr_Name||'.'||B.Attr_Name
||'.'||A.ATTR_NAME,
      A.Attr_Type_Name, A.Attr_Type_Mod,
      A.Attr_Type_Owner, A.Length, A.Precision, A.Scale,
D.Column_ID,
      A.Character_Set_Name
  from DBA_TYPE_ATTRS A, DBA_TYPE_ATTRS B, DBA_TYPE_ATTRS C,
DBA_TAB_COLUMNS D
 where D.Data_Type = C.Type_Name
   and D.Data_Type_Owner = C.Owner
   and A.Type_Name = B.Attr_Type_Name
   and A.Owner = B.Attr_Type_Owner
   and B.Type_Name = C.Attr_Type_Name
   and B.Owner = C.Attr_Type_Owner;
```

The first portion of the desc_adt.sql script, shown in the following listing, defines the columns for the DBA_DESCRIBE view:

```
create or replace view SYS.DBA_DESCRIBE
      (Owner, Table_Name,
       Column_Name, Data_Type, Data_Type_Mod,
       Data_Type_Owner, Data_Length, Data_Precision,
       Data_Scale, Column_Id, Character_Set_Name )
    as
```

The next portion of the DBA_DESCRIBE view is the base query for the view. The first portion of the **union**ed query, shown in the following listing, retrieves the names of the table's columns from the DBA_TAB_COLUMNS data dictionary view.

```
select Owner, Table_Name,
       Column_Name, Data_Type, Data_Type_Mod,
       Data_Type_Owner, Data_Length, Data_Precision,
       Data_Scale, Column_Id, Character_Set_Name
  from DBA_TAB_COLUMNS
 union all
```

The second part of the **union**ed query for the view retrieves the data for the table's abstract datatypes. The query joins the DBA_TAB_COLUMNS data dictionary view to the DBA_TYPE_ATTRS view.

```
select B.Owner, B.Table_Name,
       '  '||B.Column_Name||'.'||A.Attr_Name, A.Attr_Type_Name,
       A.Attr_Type_Mod, A.Attr_Type_Owner, A.Length,
       A.Precision, A.Scale, B.Column_ID,
       A.Character_Set_Name
  from DBA_TYPE_ATTRS A, DBA_TAB_COLUMNS B
 where B.Data_Type = A.Type_Name
   and B.Data_Type_Owner = A.Owner
union all
```

The third part of the **union**ed query, shown in the next listing, generates the data for the next level of abstraction (when abstract datatypes rely on other abstract datatypes). In this query, the DBA_TAB_COLUMNS view joins to the DBA_TYPE_ATTRS view, and DBA_TYPE_ATTRS joins to itself.

Within DBA_TYPE_ATTRS, Oracle tracks the relationships between different abstract datatypes. Thus, DBA_TYPE_ATTRS has a Type_Name column and a Attr_Type_Name column. Consider the example of the COMPILATION_ARTICLES table and its use of the ARTICLE_TY datatype. In the preceding part of the **union**ed query, the first join between DBA_TAB_COLUMNS and DBA_TYPE_ATTRS returns the name of the column, Article.Author, with a datatype of AUTHOR_TY. In that instance, AUTHOR_TY is the value in the Attr_Type_Name column. To go one step further down the hierarchy of datatypes, you need to select from a second instance of DBA_TYPE_ATTRS—this time, where the Type_Name column is equal to AUTHOR_TY, the Attr_Type_Name value returned from the first join.

The next query accomplishes this join. DBA_TAB_COLUMNS, given the alias C, joins to DBA_TYPE_ATTRS (B), and DBA_TYPE_ATTRS (B) then joins to DBA_TYPE_ATTRS (A) to retrieve the second-level data for the attributes. In the **select**, the second line references three columns, which are, in order, C, B, and A. When expanding the desc_adt.sql script, you will need to maintain the order of values selected.

```
select C.Owner, C.Table_Name,
       '    '||C.Column_Name||'.'||B.Attr_Name||'.'||A.Attr_Name,
       A.Attr_Type_Name, A.Attr_Type_Mod,
       A.Attr_Type_Owner, A.Length, A.Precision,
       A.Scale, C.Column_ID, A.Character_Set_Name
  from DBA_TYPE_ATTRS A, DBA_TYPE_ATTRS B, DBA_TAB_COLUMNS C
 where C.Data_Type = B.Type_Name
   and C.Data_Type_Owner = B.Owner
   and A.Type_Name = B.Attr_Type_Name
   and A.Owner = B.Attr_Type_Owner
union all
```

The next part of the **union**ed query is not part of the standard desc_adt.sql script, but is provided to demonstrate the way in which the script can be easily extended. In this query, a third instance of DBA_TYPE_ATTRS is added to the **from** clause. DBA_TAB_COLUMNS is given the alias of D and the three instances of DBA_TYPE_ATTRS are given the aliases A, B, and C.

PROGRAMMER'S NOTE   *The more complicated you make the base query for the DBA_DESCRIBE view, the greater the impact you will have on its performance. The underlying data dictionary tables are not optimized for this query.*

```
select D.Owner, D.Table_Name,     '         '||
        D.Column_Name||'.'||C.Attr_Name||'.'||B.Attr_Name
||'.'||A.Attr_Name,
        A.Attr_Type_Name, A.Attr_Type_Mod,
        A.Attr_Type_Owner, A.Length, A.Precision, A.Scale,
D.Column_ID,
        A.Character_Set_Name
  from DBA_TYPE_ATTRS A, DBA_TYPE_ATTRS B, DBA_TYPE_ATTRS C,
DBA_TAB_COLUMNS D
 where D.Data_Type = C.Type_Name
   and D.Data_Type_Owner = C.Owner
   and B.Type_Name = C.Attr_Type_Name
   and B.Owner = C.Attr_Type_Owner
   and A.Type_Name = B.Attr_Type_Name
   and A.Owner = B.Attr_Type_Owner
;
```

The modifications to this script are as follows:

◆ Adding another call to DBA_TYPE_ATTRS in the **from** clause.

◆ Modifying the table aliases so that DBA_TAB_COLUMNS is D and DBA_TYPE_ATTRS is now A, B, and C.

◆ In the first line of the query, selecting the columns from D (DBA_TAB_COLUMNS).

◆ In the second line of the query, changing the string being selected. The first value should be from DBA_TAB_COLUMNS, and the rest should be from the three instances of DBA_TYPE_ATTRS, in order from D to C to B to A.

◆ In the fifth line of the query, selecting the Column_ID value from D (DBA_TAB_COLUMNS).

◆ In the **where** clause, joining D to C, C to B, and B to A.

Based on these steps, you can generate the query needed to select a fourth level of hierarchy of datatypes from the data dictionary. However, each new part of the **union**ed query affects the performance of the DBA_DESCRIBE view. Even if you do not have any datatypes nested three levels deep, you incur the performance penalty of that part of the **union**ed query each time you **select** from DBA_DESCRIBE.

Unfortunately, you can't use **connect by** to simplify the query. You cannot use **connect by** in conjunction with joins, so you can't select data about columns (from the underlying COL$ table) and attributes (from the ATTR$ table) while using **connect by**.

Utilities

The scripts in this section can be used to generate scripts to re-create or document existing objects in the database, to recompile invalid objects to avoid runtime recompilation, and to determine which packages to pin into memory.

Running the Oracle Import utility with **"show=y rows=n"** on a full database export will generate a log file with all the commands necessary to re-create database objects. However, this file is not very readable, is poorly organized for documentation purposes, and is not executable without extensive editing. The scripts in this section will generate readable, executable scripts to regenerate or document objects within the database.

pinsize.sql

Pinning Packages

PL/SQL objects, when used, are stored in the library cache of the shared SQL area within the SGA. If a package has already been loaded into memory by a user, other users will experience improved performance when executing that package. Thus, keeping a package "pinned" in memory decreases the response time to the user during package executions.

To improve the ability to keep large PL/SQL objects pinned in the library cache, you should load them into the SGA as soon as the database is opened. Pinning packages immediately after startup increases the likelihood that a contiguous section of memory will be available in which to store the package. You can use the DBMS_SHARED_POOL package to pin PL/SQL objects in the SGA.

You should pin the largest packages first. To determine the proper order, you can use the script shown in the following listing. It uses the DBA_OBJECT_SIZE view to list the order in which the objects should be pinned.

```
REM pinsize.sql
set term off echo off pagesize 60
col Owner format a15
col Name  format a35
col Type  format a12
```

```
col Total_Bytes format 999,999,999
spool pinsize.log
select Owner,
       Name,
       Type,
       Source_Size+Code_Size+Parsed_Size+Error_Size  Total_Bytes
  from DBA_OBJECT_SIZE
 where Type = 'PACKAGE BODY'
   and Owner not in ('SYS','SYSTEM')
 order by Total_Bytes desc
/
spool off
set newpage 1 verify on feedback 6 pagesize 24 linesize 80
set heading on embedded off term on
clear columns
```

Sample output for the pinsize.sql script is shown in this listing.

OWNER	NAME	TYPE	TOTAL_BYTES
APP	PKG_ORDER_SAVE1	PACKAGE BODY	83,171
APP	PKG_ORDER_SAVE2	PACKAGE BODY	60,767
APP	APP_NEW_CUSTOMER_PKG	PACKAGE BODY	33,210
APP	APP_EMP_WEEKLY_UPDATE_PKG	PACKAGE BODY	32,819
APP	APP_EMP_PAYROLL_PKG	PACKAGE BODY	31,175
APP	PKG_EXPRESS_SAVE	PACKAGE BODY	25,813
APP	APP_CC_PKG	PACKAGE BODY	18,377
APP	APP_EMP_SCHEDULE_PKG	PACKAGE BODY	16,995
APP	APP_TIME_CONVERSIONS_PKG	PACKAGE BODY	8,220
APP	APP_INSERT_CUSTOMER	PACKAGE BODY	7,497
APP	APP_PRINT_PKG	PACKAGE BODY	6,405
SCOTT	DEMOKIT	PACKAGE BODY	5,964
APP	APP_PRODUCTS_PKG	PACKAGE BODY	4,753
APP	APP_EMPLOYEE_PKG	PACKAGE BODY	2,555

The output shows the packages that can be stored in memory, with the largest packages listed first.

ANNOTATIONS

When a package is loaded into memory, it is not just the parsed version of the code that is loaded. To get an accurate determination of how much space the package will take, you must sum the Source_Size (plain text version), Code_Size (source minus comments and extraneous spaces), Parsed_Size (size of the parsed form of the object), and Error_Size (size of the error messages). This calculation is shown in the following portion of the pinsize.sql script:

```
select Owner,
       Name,
       Type,
       Source_Size+Code_Size+Parsed_Size+Error_Size   Total_Bytes
  from DBA_OBJECT_SIZE
 where Type = 'PACKAGE BODY'
   and Owner not in ('SYS','SYSTEM')
 order by Total_Bytes desc
/
```

Not every large package should be pinned. Packages that are used frequently are good candidates for pinning; packages that are used rarely should not be pinned. Several large packages in the sample data are shown in the following listing. If the packages are used rarely, or used only during low-activity times, they do not have to be pinned. Packages should not be pinned merely because they are large.

OWNER	NAME	TYPE	TOTAL_BYTES
APP	PKG_ORDER_SAVE1	PACKAGE BODY	83,171
APP	PKG_ORDER_SAVE2	PACKAGE BODY	60,767
APP	APP_NEW_CUSTOMER_PKG	PACKAGE BODY	33,210
APP	APP_EMP_WEEKLY_UPDATE_PKG	PACKAGE BODY	32,819
APP	APP_EMP_PAYROLL_PKG	PACKAGE BODY	31,175
APP	PKG_EXPRESS_SAVE	PACKAGE BODY	25,813
APP	APP_CC_PKG	PACKAGE BODY	18,377
APP	APP_EMP_SCHEDULE_PKG	PACKAGE BODY	16,995
APP	APP_TIME_CONVERSIONS_PKG	PACKAGE BODY	8,220
APP	APP_INSERT_CUSTOMER	PACKAGE BODY	7,497
APP	APP_PRINT_PKG	PACKAGE BODY	6,405
SCOTT	DEMOKIT	PACKAGE BODY	5,964
APP	APP_PRODUCTS_PKG	PACKAGE BODY	4,753
APP	APP_EMPLOYEE_PKG	PACKAGE BODY	2,555

Once you have decided which packages to pin in memory, you can use DBMS_ SHARED_POOL to pin them. To use DBMS_SHARED_POOL, you first need to reference the objects that you want to pin in memory. To load a package in memory, you can reference a dummy procedure defined in the package or you can recompile the package. The core set of packages provided by Oracle does not need to be referenced or recompiled before pinning and will be loaded the first time it is executed. You can pin a cursor by executing its SQL statement.

Once the object has been referenced, you can execute the DBMS_SHARED_
POOL.KEEP procedure to pin the object. The KEEP procedure of DBMS_SHARED_
POOL, as shown in the following listing, takes as its input parameters the name of
the object and the type of object ('P' for packages, 'C' for cursors; the default is 'P').

```
alter package APP.PKG_ORDER_SAVE1 compile;
execute DBMS_SHARED_POOL.KEEP('APP.PKG_ORDER_SAVE1','P');
```

This listing illustrates the two-step process involved in pinning packages in memory:
The package is first referenced (via the compilation step) and is then marked for keeping.

To allow a pinned object to be removed from the SGA via the normal Least Recently
Used algorithm for cache management, use the UNKEEP procedure of the DBMS_
SHARED_POOL package. As shown in the following listing, the UNKEEP procedure
takes the same parameters the KEEP procedure took—the object name and the object
type (the default is 'P' for packages).

```
execute DBMS_SHARED_POOL.UNKEEP('APP.PKG_ORDER_SAVE1');
```

UNKEEP is usually not needed, but you can use it to manage your memory
allocations within the SGA if you do not have a lot of system memory available.
Pinning your most-used packages in memory immediately after startup will
improve your chances of acquiring contiguous space for them within the SGA.

revalobj.sql

Revalidating Objects

In the "Diagnostics" section, you saw the invalobj.sql script, which lists all the
invalid objects in the database. The script in this section, revalobj.sql, will generate a
script to recompile those invalid objects. This script can then be scheduled to run
during low-
peak database activity, to avoid the possible performance degradation of runtime
compilation.

If you recompile a procedure successfully, the procedure becomes valid. If
recompiling the procedure results in compilation errors, Oracle returns an error
and the procedure remains invalid.

To generate a script to recompile and revalidate the invalid objects, use the
following script:

```
REM revalobj.sql
ttitle off
set pagesize 0 feedback off verify off heading off
set term off echo off
spool revaldte.sql
select 'alter '||
          DECODE(Object_Type,'PACKAGE BODY','PACKAGE',Object_Type)||
          ' '||Owner ||'.'|| Object_Name ||' compile '||
```

```
         DECODE(Object_Type,'PACKAGE BODY','BODY',null)||';'
  from DBA_OBJECTS
 where Object_Type in
         ('PROCEDURE','PACKAGE','FUNCTION','TRIGGER',
              'VIEW','PACKAGE BODY')
   and Owner not in ('SYS','SYSTEM')
   and Status != 'VALID'
 order by Owner, Object_Type, Object_Name
/
spool off
set newpage 1 verify on feedback 6 pagesize 24 linesize 80
set heading on embedded off term on
```

The script will generate a script similar to this:

```
alter FUNCTION APP.APP_A_MSG1_PRIORITY_FUNC compile;
alter FUNCTION APP.APP_MAST1_PRIORITY_FUNC compile;
alter PACKAGE APP.APP_INSERT_CUSTOMER compile BODY;
alter PACKAGE APP.PKG_EXPRESS_SAVE compile BODY;
alter PACKAGE APP.PKG_ORDER_SAVE compile BODY;
alter PROCEDURE APP.P_INT_ORDER_PROCESS compile;
alter PROCEDURE APP.REMOVE_CUSTOMER compile;
alter PROCEDURE APP.REMOVE_EMPLOYEE compile;
alter TRIGGER APP.PDT_PRE_INS_DBT compile;
alter TRIGGER APP.PMN_PRE_INS_DBT compile;
alter TRIGGER APP.TEC_PRE_INS_DBT compile;
alter VIEW TRAIN.FINAL compile;
```

You can then execute the generated script to compile your invalid objects.

PROGRAMMER'S NOTE *The script generated by running revalobj.sql does not take into account object dependencies and assumes that compilation order does not matter.*

ANNOTATIONS

The revalobj.sql script generates a script to be executed, so its formatting eliminates the display of extraneous text. The output formatting for the script is shown here:

```
ttitle off
set pagesize 0 feedback off verify off heading off
set term off echo off
spool revaldte.sql
```

Setting **pagesize** to 0 will remove all page breaks and headings from the output listing. You should always **set pagesize 0** when you are running SQL to generate SQL.

```
Select 'alter '||
        DECODE(Object_Type,'PACKAGE BODY','PACKAGE',Object_Type)||
        ' '||Owner ||'.'|| Object_Name ||' compile '||
        DECODE(Object_Type,'PACKAGE BODY','BODY',null)||';'
   from DBA_OBJECTS
  where Object_Type in
        ('PROCEDURE','PACKAGE','FUNCTION','TRIGGER',
             'VIEW','PACKAGE BODY')
    and Owner not in ('SYS','SYSTEM')
    and Status != 'VALID'
  order by Owner, Object_Type, Object_Name
/
spool off
```

The syntax of the **alter** statement for recompilation is slightly different for package bodies than it is for all other types of objects. For most objects, the statement includes the object type after the **alter** command. For package bodies, the object type is **package**, and the word *body* must be included after the word *compile*. To do this in a single **select** statement, the **DECODE** function is used twice on the Object_Type column—the first time to replace the column value 'PACKAGE BODY' with the word 'PACKAGE' and the second time to append the word 'BODY' if the column value is 'PACKAGE BODY.'

Objects owned by SYS or SYSTEM should not be automatically recompiled if they are invalid. Invalid objects owned by SYS or SYSTEM could indicate a problem within the database and you should check with Oracle Support before attempting to fix it.

To automate the recompilation, add this line to the end of the revalobj.sql script:

```
start  revaldte.sql
```

gen_tbl_7.sql
gen_tbl_80.sql
gen_tbl_81.sql
gen_tbl_9.sql
part_dis.sql

Generate Tables

You must know what your tables actually look like and what constraints you have imposed on them to ensure that your application will work the way you want it to. While the tab_desc.sql script in the Diagnostics section of this chapter will document a table and its indexes and constraints, it does not generate executable SQL to re-create the table. As you move a table from one database to another, or change the table within the database, you may find it difficult to save off and re-create the table and its constraints manually. The scripts in this section, gen_tbl_*.sql, will generate a script to re-create a table and its constraints. The scripts gen_tbl_7.sql, gen_tbl_80.sql, gen_tbl_81.sql, and gen_tbl_9.sql can be used for Oracle7.x, Oracle8.0.x, Oracle8.1.x, and Oracle9.x, respectively, as they deal with the special features introduced in the particular Oracle version.

The full gen_tbl_9.sql script is shown in the following listing. This script is long; its method of generating the **create table** command for a table is described in the "Annotations" section that follows.

PROGRAMMER'S NOTE   *The gen_tbl_*.sql scripts do not cover object tables.*

```
REM
REM gen_tbl_9.sql
REM This script can be used for Oracle9.x only
REM This script does not cover object tables
REM
set echo off term on verify off feedback off pagesize 0 heading off
select 'Creating table build script...' from DUAL;

accept table_name prompt "Enter the name of the Table: "
accept tab_owner prompt "Enter table owner: "
set term off


drop table TAB_TEMP;

create table TAB_TEMP (
        Lineno NUMBER,
        Id_Owner VARCHAR2(30),
        Id_Name VARCHAR2(30),
        Text VARCHAR2(2000))
/

declare
    cursor TAB_CURSOR is
        select Owner,
                Table_Name,
                Tablespace_Name,
                Pct_Free,
                Pct_Used,
                Ini_Trans,
                Max_Trans,
                Initial_Extent,
                Next_Extent,
                Min_Extents,
                Max_Extents,
                Pct_Increase,
                Freelists,
                Freelist_Groups,
                Degree,
                Instances,
                Cache,
                Buffer_Pool,
                Partitioned,
                Iot_Type,
                Temporary,
                Duration,
                Logging,
```

```
                    Row_Movement,
                    Monitoring
              from DBA_TABLES
             where Owner = UPPER('&&tab_owner')
               and Table_Name like UPPER('&&table_name')
             order by Table_Name;

   cursor COL_CURSOR (C_Owner    VARCHAR2,
                      C_Tabname VARCHAR2) is
         select Column_Name,
                Data_Type,
                Data_Length,
                Data_Precision,
                Data_Scale,
                Nullable,
                Default_Length,
                Data_Default
           from DBA_TAB_COLUMNS
          where Owner      = C_Owner
            and Table_Name = C_Tabname
          order by Column_ID;

   cursor PART_COL_CURSOR (P_Owner    VARCHAR2,
                           P_Tabname VARCHAR2) is
         select Column_Name
           from DBA_PART_KEY_COLUMNS
          where Owner = P_Owner
            and Name  = P_Tabname
          order by Column_Position;

   cursor SUBPART_COL_CURSOR (P_Owner    VARCHAR2,
                              P_Tabname VARCHAR2) is
         select Column_Name
           from DBA_SUBPART_KEY_COLUMNS
          where Owner = P_Owner
            and Name  = P_Tabname
          order by Column_Position;

   cursor TAB_PARTS_CURSOR (PT_Owner    VARCHAR2,
                            PT_Tabname VARCHAR2) is
         select Partition_Name,
                High_Value,
                Tablespace_Name,
                Pct_Free,
                Pct_Used,
                Ini_Trans,
                Max_Trans,
                Initial_Extent,
                Next_Extent,
```

```
            Min_Extent,
            Max_Extent,
            Pct_Increase,
            Freelists,
            Freelist_Groups,
            Buffer_Pool,
            Logging
      from DBA_TAB_PARTITIONS
     where Table_Owner = PT_Owner
       and Table_Name  = PT_Tabname
     order by Partition_Position;


   cursor TAB_SUBPARTS_CURSOR (PT_Owner    VARCHAR2,
                   PT_Tabname VARCHAR2,
                   PT_Partname VARCHAR2) is
      select Subpartition_Name,
             Tablespace_Name
        from DBA_TAB_SUBPARTITIONS
       where Table_Owner = PT_Owner
         and Table_Name  = PT_Tabname
         and Partition_Name = PT_Partname
       order by Subpartition_Position;


   cursor PART_TABS_CURSOR (TP_Owner    VARCHAR2,
                   TP_Tabname VARCHAR2) is
      select Partitioning_Type,
             Subpartitioning_Type
        from DBA_PART_TABLES
       where Owner = TP_Owner
         and Table_Name  = TP_Tabname;


   cursor CONS_CURSOR (Cons_Owner     VARCHAR2,
                   Cons_Tablename VARCHAR2) is
      select A.Owner,
             A.Constraint_Name,
             A.Constraint_Type,
             A.Table_Name,
             A.Search_Condition,
             B.Column_Name,
             B.Position
        from DBA_CONSTRAINTS  A,
             DBA_CONS_COLUMNS B
       where A.Owner = B.Owner
         and A.Constraint_Name = B.Constraint_Name
         and A.Table_Name      = B.Table_Name
         and A.Constraint_Type in ('C','P')
         and A.Owner           = Cons_Owner
         and A.Table_Name      = Cons_Tablename
       order by A.Constraint_Type,
```

```
                  A.Constraint_Name,
                  B.Position;

    cursor REF_CURSOR (R_Owner      VARCHAR2,
                       R_Tablename VARCHAR2) is
        select A.Owner,
               A.Table_Name,
               A.Constraint_Name,
               A.R_Constraint_Name,
               B.Column_Name,
               C.Owner,
               C.Table_Name,
               C.Column_Name,
               C.Position
          from DBA_CONSTRAINTS   A,
               DBA_CONS_COLUMNS B,
               DBA_CONS_COLUMNS C
         where A.Constraint_Name = B.Constraint_Name
           and A.Owner           = B.Owner
           and C.Constraint_name = A.R_Constraint_Name
           and B.Position        = C.Position
           and A.Owner           = R_Owner
           and A.Table_Name      = R_Tablename
         order by A.Constraint_Name,
                  A.Owner,
                  C.Position;

    cursor IOT_CURSOR (A_Owner VARCHAR2,
                       A_Table_Name VARCHAR2) is
        select I.Owner,
               I.Table_Name,
               I.Tablespace_Name,
               I.Pct_Free,
               I.Ini_Trans,
               I.Max_Trans,
               I.Initial_Extent,
               I.Next_Extent,
               I.Min_Extents,
               I.Max_Extents,
               I.Pct_Increase,
               I.Freelists,
               I.Freelist_Groups,
               I.Buffer_Pool,
               I.Pct_Threshold,
               I.Include_Column,
               C.Column_Name,
               I.Logging,
               I.Compression,
               I.Prefix_Length
```

```
        from DBA_INDEXES I, DBA_TABLES T, DBA_TAB_COLUMNS C
     where I.Owner = T.Owner
       and I.Table_Name = T.Table_Name
       and I.Index_Type = 'IOT - TOP'
       and T.Iot_Type = 'IOT'
       and C.Column_ID = I.Include_Column(+)
       and C.Owner = T.Owner
       and C.Table_Name = T.Table_Name
       and T.Owner = A_Owner
       and T.Table_Name = A_Table_Name;


  cursor IOT_OVER_CURSOR (Io_Owner VARCHAR2,
                          Io_Name VARCHAR2) is
     select IO.Tablespace_Name,
            IO.Ini_Trans,
            IO.Max_Trans,
            IO.Initial_Extent,
            IO.Next_Extent,
            IO.Min_Extents,
            IO.Max_Extents,
            IO.Pct_Increase,
            IO.Freelists,
            IO.Freelist_Groups,
            IO.Logging
       from DBA_TABLES IO
      where IO.Owner = Io_Owner
        and IO.Iot_Name = Io_Name
        and IO.Iot_Type = 'IOT_OVERFLOW';


Lv_Table_Owner          DBA_TABLES.Owner%TYPE;
Lv_Table_Name           DBA_TABLES.Table_Name%TYPE;
Lv_Tablespace_Name      DBA_TABLES.Tablespace_Name%TYPE;
Lv_Pct_Free             DBA_TABLES.Pct_Free%TYPE;
Lv_Pct_Used             DBA_TABLES.Pct_Used%TYPE;
Lv_Initial_Trans        DBA_TABLES.Ini_Trans%TYPE;
Lv_Max_Trans            DBA_TABLES.Max_Trans%TYPE;
Lv_Initial_Extent       DBA_TABLES.Initial_Extent%TYPE;
Lv_Next_Extent          DBA_TABLES.Next_Extent%TYPE;
Lv_Min_Extents          DBA_TABLES.Min_Extents%TYPE;
Lv_Max_Extents          DBA_TABLES.Max_Extents%TYPE;
Lv_Pct_Increase         DBA_TABLES.Pct_Increase%TYPE;
Lv_Freelists            DBA_TABLES.Freelists%TYPE;
Lv_Freelist_Groups      DBA_TABLES.Freelist_Groups%TYPE;
Lv_Degree               DBA_TABLES.Degree%TYPE;
Lv_Instances            DBA_TABLES.Instances%TYPE;
Lv_Cache                DBA_TABLES.Cache%TYPE;
Lv_Buffer_Pool          DBA_TABLES.Buffer_Pool%TYPE;
```

```
Lv_Partitioned              DBA_TABLES.Partitioned%TYPE;
Lv_Iot_Type                 DBA_TABLES.Iot_Type%TYPE;
Lv_Temporary                DBA_TABLES.Temporary%TYPE;
Lv_Duration                 DBA_TABLES.Duration%TYPE;
Lv_Logging                  DBA_TABLES.Logging%TYPE;
Lv_Row_Movement             DBA_TABLES.Row_Movement%TYPE;
Lv_Monitoring               DBA_TABLES.Monitoring%TYPE;

Lv_P_Column_Name            DBA_PART_KEY_COLUMNS.Column_Name%TYPE;

Lv_SP_Column_Name           DBA_SUBPART_KEY_COLUMNS.Column_Name%TYPE;

Lv_TP_Partition_Name        DBA_TAB_PARTITIONS.Partition_Name%TYPE;
Lv_TP_High_Value            DBA_TAB_PARTITIONS.High_Value%TYPE;
Lv_TP_Tablespace_Name       DBA_TAB_PARTITIONS.Tablespace_Name%TYPE;
Lv_TP_Pct_Free              DBA_TAB_PARTITIONS.Pct_Free%TYPE;
Lv_TP_Pct_Used              DBA_TAB_PARTITIONS.Pct_Used%TYPE;
Lv_TP_Ini_Trans             DBA_TAB_PARTITIONS.Ini_Trans%TYPE;
Lv_TP_Max_Trans             DBA_TAB_PARTITIONS.Max_Trans%TYPE;
Lv_TP_Initial_Extent        DBA_TAB_PARTITIONS.Initial_Extent%TYPE;
Lv_TP_Next_Extent           DBA_TAB_PARTITIONS.Next_Extent%TYPE;
Lv_TP_Min_Extents           DBA_TAB_PARTITIONS.Min_Extent%TYPE;
Lv_TP_Max_Extents           DBA_TAB_PARTITIONS.Max_Extent%TYPE;
Lv_TP_Pct_Increase          DBA_TAB_PARTITIONS.Pct_Increase%TYPE;
Lv_TP_Freelists             DBA_TAB_PARTITIONS.Freelists%TYPE;
Lv_TP_Freelist_Groups       DBA_TAB_PARTITIONS.Freelist_Groups%TYPE;
Lv_TP_Buffer_Pool           DBA_TAB_PARTITIONS.Buffer_Pool%TYPE;
Lv_TP_Logging               DBA_TAB_PARTITIONS.Logging%TYPE;

Lv_PT_Partitioning_Type     DBA_PART_TABLES.Partitioning_Type%TYPE;
Lv_PT_Subpartitioning_Type  DBA_PART_TABLES.Subpartitioning_Type%TYPE;

Lv_TSP_Subpartition_Name    DBA_TAB_SUBPARTITIONS.Subpartition_Name%TYPE;
Lv_TSP_Tablespace_Name      DBA_TAB_SUBPARTITIONS.Tablespace_Name%TYPE;

Lv_Column_Name              DBA_TAB_COLUMNS.Column_Name%TYPE;
Lv_Column_Data_Type         DBA_TAB_COLUMNS.Data_Type%TYPE;
Lv_Column_Data_Length       DBA_TAB_COLUMNS.Data_Length%TYPE;
Lv_Column_Data_Precision    DBA_TAB_COLUMNS.Data_Precision%TYPE;
Lv_Column_Data_Scale        DBA_TAB_COLUMNS.Data_Scale%TYPE;
Lv_Column_Nullable          DBA_TAB_COLUMNS.Nullable%TYPE;
Lv_Column_Default_Length    DBA_TAB_COLUMNS.Default_Length%TYPE;
Lv_Column_Data_Default      DBA_TAB_COLUMNS.Data_Default%TYPE;
Lv_Cons_Owner               DBA_CONSTRAINTS.Owner%TYPE;
Lv_Cons_Table_Name          DBA_CONSTRAINTS.Table_Name%TYPE;
Lv_Cons_Constraint_Name     DBA_CONSTRAINTS.Constraint_Name%TYPE;
Lv_Cons_Constraint_Type     DBA_CONSTRAINTS.Constraint_Type%TYPE;
Lv_Cons_Search_Cond         DBA_CONSTRAINTS.Search_Condition%TYPE;
Lv_Cons_Column_Name         DBA_CONS_COLUMNS.Column_Name%TYPE;
```

```
Lv_Cons_R_Constraint_Name    DBA_CONSTRAINTS.R_Constraint_Name%TYPE;
Lv_Cons_Ref_Owner            DBA_CONSTRAINTS.Owner%TYPE;
Lv_Cons_Ref_Table_Name       DBA_CONSTRAINTS.Table_Name%TYPE;
Lv_Cons_Ref_Column_Name      DBA_CONS_COLUMNS.Column_Name%TYPE;
Lv_Cons_Ref_Position         DBA_CONS_COLUMNS.Position%TYPE;
Lv_Cons_Exists               VARCHAR2(1);
Lv_String                    VARCHAR2(800);
Lv_String2                   VARCHAR2(800);
Lv_Lineno                    NUMBER;

Lv_Iot_Owner                 DBA_INDEXES.Owner%TYPE;
Lv_Iot_Table_Name            DBA_INDEXES.Table_Name%TYPE;
Lv_Iot_Tablespace_Name       DBA_INDEXES.Tablespace_Name%TYPE;
Lv_Iot_Pct_Free              DBA_INDEXES.Pct_Free%TYPE;
Lv_Iot_Initial_Trans         DBA_INDEXES.Ini_Trans%TYPE;
Lv_Iot_Max_Trans             DBA_INDEXES.Max_Trans%TYPE;
Lv_Iot_Initial_Extent        DBA_INDEXES.Initial_Extent%TYPE;
Lv_Iot_Next_Extent           DBA_INDEXES.Next_Extent%TYPE;
Lv_Iot_Min_Extents           DBA_INDEXES.Min_Extents%TYPE;
Lv_Iot_Max_Extents           DBA_INDEXES.Max_Extents%TYPE;
Lv_Iot_Pct_Increase          DBA_INDEXES.Pct_Increase%TYPE;
Lv_Iot_Freelists             DBA_INDEXES.Freelists%TYPE;
Lv_Iot_Freelist_Groups       DBA_INDEXES.Freelist_Groups%TYPE;
Lv_Iot_Buffer_Pool           DBA_INDEXES.Buffer_Pool%TYPE;
Lv_Iot_Pct_Threshold         DBA_INDEXES.Pct_Threshold%TYPE;
Lv_Iot_Include_Column        DBA_INDEXES.Include_Column%TYPE;
Lv_Iot_Column_Name           DBA_TAB_COLUMNS.Column_Name%TYPE;
Lv_Iot_Logging               DBA_INDEXES.Logging%TYPE;
Lv_Iot_Compression           DBA_INDEXES.Compression%TYPE;
Lv_Iot_Prefix_Length         DBA_INDEXES.Prefix_Length%TYPE;

Lv_Io_Tablespace_Name        DBA_TABLES.Tablespace_Name%TYPE;
Lv_Io_Initial_Trans          DBA_TABLES.Ini_Trans%TYPE;
Lv_Io_Max_Trans              DBA_TABLES.Max_Trans%TYPE;
Lv_Io_Initial_Extent         DBA_TABLES.Initial_Extent%TYPE;
Lv_Io_Next_Extent            DBA_TABLES.Next_Extent%TYPE;
Lv_Io_Min_Extents            DBA_TABLES.Min_Extents%TYPE;
Lv_Io_Max_Extents            DBA_TABLES.Max_Extents%TYPE;
Lv_Io_Pct_Increase           DBA_TABLES.Pct_Increase%TYPE;
Lv_Io_Freelists              DBA_TABLES.Freelists%TYPE;
Lv_Io_Freelist_Groups        DBA_TABLES.Freelist_Groups%TYPE;
Lv_Io_Logging                DBA_TABLES.Logging%TYPE;

procedure WRITE_OUT(P_Line INTEGER,   P_Owner VARCHAR2,
                    P_Name VARCHAR2, P_String VARCHAR2) is
begin
   insert into TAB_TEMP (Lineno, Id_Owner, Id_Name, Text)
         values (P_Line,P_Owner,P_Name,P_String);
 end;
```

```
procedure UPDATE_OUT(P_Line INTEGER,  P_Owner VARCHAR2,
                     P_Name VARCHAR2, P_String VARCHAR2) is
begin
   update TAB_TEMP
      set Text = P_String
    where Lineno = P_Line
      and Id_Owner = P_Owner
      and Id_Name  = P_Name;
end;

begin
   open TAB_CURSOR;
   loop
      fetch TAB_CURSOR into Lv_Table_Owner,
                            Lv_Table_Name,
                            Lv_Tablespace_Name,
                            Lv_Pct_Free,
                            Lv_Pct_Used,
                            Lv_Initial_Trans,
                            Lv_Max_Trans,
                            Lv_Initial_Extent,
                            Lv_Next_Extent,
                            Lv_Min_Extents,
                            Lv_Max_Extents,
                            Lv_Pct_Increase,
                            Lv_Freelists,
                            Lv_Freelist_Groups,
                            Lv_Degree,
                            Lv_Instances,
                            Lv_Cache,
                            Lv_Buffer_Pool,
                            Lv_Partitioned,
                            Lv_Iot_Type,
                            Lv_Temporary,
                            Lv_Duration,
                            Lv_Logging,
                            Lv_Row_Movement,
                            Lv_Monitoring;
      exit when TAB_CURSOR%NOTFOUND;

      Lv_Lineno := 1;

      if (Lv_Temporary = 'Y')
      then
          Lv_String:= ' GLOBAL TEMPORARY ';
      else
          Lv_String:=' ';
      end if;
```

```
Lv_String:= 'CREATE '||Lv_String||' TABLE '
                    || LOWER(Lv_Table_Owner)
                    || '.'
                    || LOWER(Lv_Table_Name);
WRITE_OUT(Lv_Lineno, Lv_Table_Owner, Lv_Table_Name, Lv_String);
Lv_Lineno := Lv_Lineno + 1;

Lv_string := '(';
WRITE_OUT(Lv_Lineno, Lv_Table_Owner, Lv_Table_Name, Lv_String);
Lv_Lineno := Lv_Lineno + 1;

open COL_CURSOR (Lv_Table_Owner,Lv_Table_Name);

loop
   fetch COL_CURSOR into Lv_Column_Name,
                         Lv_Column_Data_Type,
                         Lv_Column_Data_Length,
                         Lv_Column_Data_Precision,
                         Lv_Column_Data_Scale,
                         Lv_Column_Nullable,
                         Lv_Column_Default_Length,
                         Lv_Column_Data_Default;
   exit when COL_CURSOR%NOTFOUND;

   Lv_String := '     '                          ||
             RPAD(LOWER(Lv_Column_Name),35)  ||
             Lv_Column_Data_Type;

   if ( (Lv_Column_Data_Type = 'VARCHAR2' ) or
        (Lv_Column_Data_Type = 'RAW'      ) or
        (Lv_Column_Data_Type = 'CHAR'     ) )
   then
        Lv_String := Lv_String               ||
                    '('                       ||
                    Lv_Column_Data_Length ||
                    ')';
   elsif (Lv_Column_Data_Type = 'NUMBER')
   then
        if Lv_Column_Data_Precision IS NULL
        then
           Lv_Column_Data_Precision := 38;
           Lv_Column_Data_Scale     := 0;
        end if;
        Lv_String := Lv_String                  ||
                    '('                          ||
                    Lv_Column_Data_Precision ||
                    ','                          ||
```

```
                                Lv_Column_Data_Scale      ||
                                ')';
            end if;

            if (Lv_Column_Data_Default IS NOT NULL)
            then
                LV_String := Lv_String || ' DEFAULT '
                                       || SUBSTR(Lv_Column_Data_Default,
                                              1,Lv_Column_Default_Length);
            end if;
            if (Lv_Column_Nullable = 'N' )
            then
                Lv_String := Lv_String || '  NOT NULL';
            end if;

            Lv_String := Lv_String || ',';
            WRITE_OUT(Lv_Lineno, Lv_Table_Owner, Lv_Table_Name, Lv_String);
            Lv_Lineno := Lv_Lineno + 1;

    end loop;
    close COL_CURSOR;

    Lv_Cons_Exists := 'N';

    open CONS_CURSOR(Lv_Table_Owner, Lv_Table_Name);
    loop
        fetch CONS_CURSOR into Lv_Cons_Owner,
                               Lv_Cons_Constraint_Name,
                               Lv_Cons_Constraint_Type,
                               Lv_Cons_Table_Name,
                               Lv_Cons_Search_Cond,
                               Lv_Cons_Column_Name,
                               Lv_Cons_Ref_Position;
        exit when CONS_CURSOR%NOTFOUND;

        if (Lv_Cons_Constraint_Type = 'C') AND
           (INSTR(Lv_Cons_Search_Cond,'NOT NULL',1) = 0)
        then
            Lv_String := ' ';
            if  (INSTR(Lv_Cons_Constraint_Name,'SYS_C') = 0)
            then
                    Lv_String := Lv_String || 'CONSTRAINT ' ||
                                Lv_Cons_Constraint_Name || ' ';
            end if;
            Lv_String :=   Lv_String
                        || ' CHECK ('
                        || Lv_Cons_Search_Cond
                        || ')';
            WRITE_OUT(Lv_Lineno, Lv_Table_Owner, Lv_Table_Name,
```

```
                              Lv_String);
            Lv_Lineno := Lv_Lineno + 1;


            Lv_String := Lv_String || ',';
            WRITE_OUT(Lv_Lineno, Lv_Table_Owner, Lv_Table_Name, Lv_String);
            Lv_Lineno := Lv_Lineno + 1;

        end if;


        if (Lv_Cons_Constraint_Type = 'P')
        then
            Lv_Cons_Exists := 'Y';
            if (Lv_Cons_Ref_Position = 1)
            then

                Lv_String := ' ';
                if   (INSTR(Lv_Cons_Constraint_Name,'SYS_C') = 0)
                then
                    Lv_String := Lv_String || 'CONSTRAINT ' ||
                                 Lv_Cons_Constraint_Name || ' ';
                end if;

                Lv_String := Lv_String || 'PRIMARY KEY (' ||
                             Lv_Cons_Column_Name || ')';
            else
                Lv_String := REPLACE(Lv_String,')',',' ||
                             Lv_Cons_Column_Name|| ')' );
            end if;


        end if;
end loop;


if (Lv_Cons_Exists = 'Y')
then
  WRITE_OUT(Lv_Lineno, Lv_Table_Owner, Lv_Table_Name, Lv_String);
  Lv_Lineno := Lv_Lineno + 1;

  Lv_String := Lv_String || ',';
  WRITE_OUT(Lv_Lineno, Lv_Table_Owner, Lv_Table_Name, Lv_String);
  Lv_Lineno := Lv_Lineno + 1;
end if;


close CONS_CURSOR;

open  REF_CURSOR(Lv_Table_Owner, Lv_Table_Name);
loop
     fetch REF_CURSOR into Lv_Cons_Owner,
                           Lv_Cons_Table_Name,
```

```
                          Lv_Cons_Constraint_Name,
                          Lv_Cons_R_Constraint_Name,
                          Lv_Cons_Column_Name,
                          Lv_Cons_Ref_Owner,
                          Lv_Cons_Ref_Table_Name,
                          Lv_Cons_Ref_Column_Name,
                          Lv_Cons_Ref_Position;
     exit when REF_CURSOR%NOTFOUND;

     if (Lv_Cons_Ref_Position = 1)
     then

        Lv_String := ' ';
        if  (INSTR(Lv_Cons_Constraint_Name,'SYS_C',1) = 0)
        then
            Lv_String := Lv_String || 'CONSTRAINT '
                                   || Lv_Cons_Constraint_Name
                                   || ' ';
        end if;
        Lv_String  := Lv_String      || 'FOREIGN KEY ('
                                     || Lv_Cons_Column_Name
                                     || ')';
        WRITE_OUT(Lv_Lineno, Lv_Table_Owner, Lv_Table_Name,
                 Lv_String);
        Lv_Lineno := Lv_Lineno + 1;

        Lv_String2 := '   REFERENCES ' || Lv_Cons_Ref_Owner
                                       || '.'
                                       || Lv_Cons_Ref_Table_Name
                                       || '('
                                       || Lv_Cons_Ref_Column_Name
                                       || ')';
        WRITE_OUT(Lv_Lineno, Lv_Table_Owner, Lv_Table_Name,
                 Lv_String2);
        Lv_Lineno := Lv_Lineno + 1;


     else
        Lv_String  := REPLACE(Lv_String,  ')', ',' ||
                     Lv_Cons_Column_Name    || ')' );
        Lv_Lineno  := Lv_Lineno - 3;
        UPDATE_OUT(Lv_Lineno, Lv_Table_Owner, Lv_Table_Name,
                 Lv_String);
        Lv_Lineno  := Lv_Lineno + 1;

        Lv_String2 := REPLACE(Lv_String2, ')', ',' ||
                     Lv_Cons_Ref_Column_Name || ')' );
        UPDATE_OUT(Lv_Lineno, Lv_Table_Owner, Lv_Table_Name,
                 Lv_String2);
```

```
            Lv_Lineno   := Lv_Lineno + 2;
         end if;

         Lv_String := Lv_String || ',';
         WRITE_OUT(Lv_Lineno, Lv_Table_Owner, Lv_Table_Name, Lv_String);
         Lv_Lineno := Lv_Lineno + 1;


   end loop;
   close REF_CURSOR;

   Lv_Lineno   := Lv_Lineno - 1;
   Lv_String   := SUBSTR(Lv_String,1,(LENGTH(Lv_String) - 1));
   UPDATE_OUT(Lv_Lineno, Lv_Table_Owner, Lv_Table_Name,Lv_String);
   Lv_Lineno   := Lv_Lineno + 1;

   Lv_String   := ')';
   WRITE_OUT(Lv_Lineno, Lv_Table_Owner, Lv_Table_Name, Lv_String);
   Lv_Lineno := Lv_Lineno + 1;

if (Lv_Duration is NOT NULL)
then
    if (Lv_Duration = 'SYS$SESSION')
    then
        Lv_String:= ' ON COMMIT PRESERVE ROWS ';
    else
        Lv_String:= ' ON COMMIT DELETE ROWS ';
    end if;
end if;
WRITE_OUT(Lv_Lineno, Lv_Table_Owner, Lv_Table_Name, Lv_String);
Lv_Lineno := Lv_Lineno + 1;

if (Lv_Iot_Type is NOT NULL)
then

  Lv_String := ' ORGANIZATION INDEX ';
  WRITE_OUT(Lv_Lineno, Lv_Table_Owner, Lv_Table_Name, Lv_String);
  Lv_Lineno := Lv_Lineno + 1;

  open IOT_CURSOR(Lv_Table_Owner,Lv_Table_Name);
  loop
     fetch IOT_CURSOR into Lv_Iot_Owner,
                           Lv_Iot_Table_Name,
                           Lv_Iot_Tablespace_Name,
                           Lv_Iot_Pct_Free,
                           Lv_Iot_Initial_Trans,
                           Lv_Iot_Max_Trans,
                           Lv_Iot_Initial_Extent,
                           Lv_Iot_Next_Extent,
```

```
                              Lv_Iot_Min_Extents,
                              Lv_Iot_Max_Extents,
                              Lv_Iot_Pct_Increase,
                              Lv_Iot_Freelists,
                              Lv_Iot_Freelist_Groups,
                              Lv_Iot_Buffer_Pool,
                              Lv_Iot_Pct_Threshold,
                              Lv_Iot_Include_Column,
                              Lv_Iot_Column_Name,
                              Lv_Iot_Logging,
                              Lv_Iot_Compression,
                              Lv_Iot_Prefix_Length;
         exit when IOT_CURSOR%NOTFOUND;

         Lv_String := ' PCTTHRESHOLD '||Lv_Iot_Pct_Threshold;
         WRITE_OUT(Lv_Lineno, Lv_Table_Owner, Lv_Table_Name, Lv_String);
         Lv_Lineno := Lv_Lineno + 1;

         if (Lv_Iot_Compression = 'DISABLED')
         then
            Lv_String := ' NOCOMPRESS ';
         else
            Lv_String := ' COMPRESS '||Lv_Iot_Prefix_Length;
         end if;
         WRITE_OUT(Lv_Lineno, Lv_Table_Owner, Lv_Table_Name, Lv_String);
         Lv_Lineno := Lv_Lineno + 1;

         Lv_String  := 'TABLESPACE ' || Lv_Iot_Tablespace_Name ;
         WRITE_OUT(Lv_Lineno, Lv_Table_Owner, Lv_Table_Name, Lv_String);
         Lv_Lineno := Lv_Lineno + 1;

         if (Lv_Iot_Logging = 'YES')
         then
           Lv_String  := ' LOGGING ';
         else
           Lv_String  := ' NOLOGGING ';
         end if;
         WRITE_OUT(Lv_Lineno, Lv_Table_Owner, Lv_Table_Name, Lv_String);
         Lv_Lineno := Lv_Lineno + 1;

         Lv_String  := 'PCTFREE ' || Lv_Iot_Pct_Free ;
         WRITE_OUT(Lv_Lineno, Lv_Table_Owner, Lv_Table_Name, Lv_String);
         Lv_Lineno := Lv_Lineno + 1;

         Lv_String  := 'INITRANS ' || Lv_Iot_Initial_Trans ;
         WRITE_OUT(Lv_Lineno, Lv_Table_Owner, Lv_Table_Name, Lv_String);
         Lv_Lineno := Lv_Lineno + 1;

         Lv_String  := 'MAXTRANS ' || Lv_Iot_Max_Trans ;
```

```
WRITE_OUT(Lv_Lineno, Lv_Table_Owner, Lv_Table_Name, Lv_String);
Lv_Lineno := Lv_Lineno + 1;


Lv_String   := 'STORAGE';
WRITE_OUT(Lv_Lineno, Lv_Table_Owner, Lv_Table_Name, Lv_String);
Lv_Lineno := Lv_Lineno + 1;
Lv_String   := '(';
WRITE_OUT(Lv_Lineno, Lv_Table_Owner, Lv_Table_Name, Lv_String);
Lv_Lineno := Lv_Lineno + 1;

Lv_String   := '    INITIAL ' || Lv_Iot_Initial_Extent ;
WRITE_OUT(Lv_Lineno, Lv_Table_Owner, Lv_Table_Name, Lv_String);
Lv_Lineno := Lv_Lineno + 1;

Lv_String   := '    NEXT ' || Lv_Iot_Next_Extent ;
WRITE_OUT(Lv_Lineno, Lv_Table_Owner, Lv_Table_Name, Lv_String);
Lv_Lineno := Lv_Lineno + 1;

Lv_String   := '    MINEXTENTS ' || Lv_Iot_Min_Extents ;
WRITE_OUT(Lv_Lineno, Lv_Table_Owner, Lv_Table_Name, Lv_String);
Lv_Lineno := Lv_Lineno + 1;

Lv_String   := '    MAXEXTENTS ' || Lv_Iot_Max_Extents ;
WRITE_OUT(Lv_Lineno, Lv_Table_Owner, Lv_Table_Name, Lv_String);
Lv_Lineno := Lv_Lineno + 1;

Lv_String   := '    PCTINCREASE ' || Lv_Iot_Pct_Increase ;
WRITE_OUT(Lv_Lineno, Lv_Table_Owner, Lv_Table_Name, Lv_String);
Lv_Lineno := Lv_Lineno + 1;

Lv_String   := '    FREELISTS ' || Lv_Iot_Freelists ;
WRITE_OUT(Lv_Lineno, Lv_Table_Owner, Lv_Table_Name, Lv_String);
Lv_Lineno := Lv_Lineno + 1;

Lv_String   := '    FREELIST GROUPS ' || Lv_Iot_Freelist_Groups ;
WRITE_OUT(Lv_Lineno, Lv_Table_Owner, Lv_Table_Name, Lv_String);
Lv_Lineno := Lv_Lineno + 1;

Lv_String   := '    BUFFER_POOL ' || Lv_Iot_Buffer_Pool ;
WRITE_OUT(Lv_Lineno, Lv_Table_Owner, Lv_Table_Name, Lv_String);
Lv_Lineno := Lv_Lineno + 1;

Lv_String   := ')';
WRITE_OUT(Lv_Lineno, Lv_Table_Owner, Lv_Table_Name, Lv_String);
Lv_Lineno := Lv_Lineno + 1;

if (Lv_Iot_Include_Column is NOT NULL)
then
    Lv_String   := ' INCLUDING '|| Lv_Iot_Column_Name||' OVERFLOW ' ;
```

```
          WRITE_OUT(Lv_Lineno, Lv_Table_Owner, Lv_Table_Name, Lv_String);
          Lv_Lineno := Lv_Lineno + 1;
end if;

open IOT_OVER_CURSOR(Lv_Iot_Owner,Lv_Iot_Table_Name);
loop
   fetch IOT_OVER_CURSOR into Lv_Io_Tablespace_Name,
                              Lv_Io_Initial_Trans,
                              Lv_Io_Max_Trans,
                              Lv_Io_Initial_Extent,
                              Lv_Io_Next_Extent,
                              Lv_Io_Min_Extents,
                              Lv_Io_Max_Extents,
                              Lv_Io_Pct_Increase,
                              Lv_Io_Freelists,
                              Lv_Io_Freelist_Groups,
                              Lv_Io_Logging;
exit when IOT_OVER_CURSOR%NOTFOUND;


Lv_String  := 'TABLESPACE ' || Lv_Io_Tablespace_Name ;
WRITE_OUT(Lv_Lineno, Lv_Table_Owner, Lv_Table_Name, Lv_String);
Lv_Lineno := Lv_Lineno + 1;

if (Lv_Io_Logging = 'YES')
then
  Lv_String  := ' LOGGING ';
else
  Lv_String  := ' NOLOGGING ';
end if;
WRITE_OUT(Lv_Lineno, Lv_Table_Owner, Lv_Table_Name, Lv_String);
Lv_Lineno := Lv_Lineno + 1;

Lv_String  := 'INITRANS ' || Lv_Io_Initial_Trans ;
WRITE_OUT(Lv_Lineno, Lv_Table_Owner, Lv_Table_Name, Lv_String);
Lv_Lineno := Lv_Lineno + 1;

Lv_String  := 'MAXTRANS ' || Lv_Io_Max_Trans ;
WRITE_OUT(Lv_Lineno, Lv_Table_Owner, Lv_Table_Name, Lv_String);
Lv_Lineno := Lv_Lineno + 1;

Lv_String  := 'STORAGE';
WRITE_OUT(Lv_Lineno, Lv_Table_Owner, Lv_Table_Name, Lv_String);
Lv_Lineno := Lv_Lineno + 1;
Lv_String  := '(';
WRITE_OUT(Lv_Lineno, Lv_Table_Owner, Lv_Table_Name, Lv_String);
Lv_Lineno := Lv_Lineno + 1;
```

```
    Lv_String  := '    INITIAL ' || Lv_Io_Initial_Extent ;
    WRITE_OUT(Lv_Lineno, Lv_Table_Owner, Lv_Table_Name, Lv_String);
    Lv_Lineno := Lv_Lineno + 1;

    Lv_String  := '    NEXT ' || Lv_Io_Next_Extent ;
    WRITE_OUT(Lv_Lineno, Lv_Table_Owner, Lv_Table_Name, Lv_String);
    Lv_Lineno := Lv_Lineno + 1;

    Lv_String  := '    MINEXTENTS ' || Lv_Io_Min_Extents ;
    WRITE_OUT(Lv_Lineno, Lv_Table_Owner, Lv_Table_Name, Lv_String);
    Lv_Lineno := Lv_Lineno + 1;

    Lv_String  := '    MAXEXTENTS ' || Lv_Io_Max_Extents ;
    WRITE_OUT(Lv_Lineno, Lv_Table_Owner, Lv_Table_Name, Lv_String);
    Lv_Lineno := Lv_Lineno + 1;

    Lv_String  := '    PCTINCREASE ' || Lv_Io_Pct_Increase ;
    WRITE_OUT(Lv_Lineno, Lv_Table_Owner, Lv_Table_Name, Lv_String);
    Lv_Lineno := Lv_Lineno + 1;

    Lv_String  := '    FREELISTS ' || Lv_Io_Freelists ;
    WRITE_OUT(Lv_Lineno, Lv_Table_Owner, Lv_Table_Name, Lv_String);
    Lv_Lineno := Lv_Lineno + 1;

    Lv_String  := '    FREELIST GROUPS ' || Lv_Io_Freelist_Groups ;
    WRITE_OUT(Lv_Lineno, Lv_Table_Owner, Lv_Table_Name, Lv_String);
    Lv_Lineno := Lv_Lineno + 1;

    Lv_String  := ')';
    WRITE_OUT(Lv_Lineno, Lv_Table_Owner, Lv_Table_Name, Lv_String);
    Lv_Lineno := Lv_Lineno + 1;


    end loop;
    close IOT_OVER_CURSOR;

    end loop;
    close IOT_CURSOR;


else

if (Lv_Partitioned = 'NO')
then

  Lv_String  := 'TABLESPACE ' || Lv_Tablespace_Name ;
  WRITE_OUT(Lv_Lineno, Lv_Table_Owner, Lv_Table_Name, Lv_String);
  Lv_Lineno := Lv_Lineno + 1;
```

```
if (Lv_Logging = 'YES')
then
  Lv_String  := ' LOGGING ';
else
  Lv_String  := ' NOLOGGING ';
end if;
WRITE_OUT(Lv_Lineno, Lv_Table_Owner, Lv_Table_Name, Lv_String);
Lv_Lineno := Lv_Lineno + 1;

Lv_String  := 'PCTFREE ' || Lv_Pct_Free ;
WRITE_OUT(Lv_Lineno, Lv_Table_Owner, Lv_Table_Name, Lv_String);
Lv_Lineno := Lv_Lineno + 1;

Lv_String  := 'PCTUSED ' || Lv_Pct_Used ;
WRITE_OUT(Lv_Lineno, Lv_Table_Owner, Lv_Table_Name, Lv_String);
Lv_Lineno := Lv_Lineno + 1;

Lv_String  := 'INITRANS ' || Lv_Initial_Trans ;
WRITE_OUT(Lv_Lineno, Lv_Table_Owner, Lv_Table_Name, Lv_String);
Lv_Lineno := Lv_Lineno + 1;

Lv_String  := 'MAXTRANS ' || Lv_Max_Trans ;
WRITE_OUT(Lv_Lineno, Lv_Table_Owner, Lv_Table_Name, Lv_String);
Lv_Lineno := Lv_Lineno + 1;

Lv_String  := 'STORAGE';
WRITE_OUT(Lv_Lineno, Lv_Table_Owner, Lv_Table_Name, Lv_String);
Lv_Lineno := Lv_Lineno + 1;
Lv_String  := '(';
WRITE_OUT(Lv_Lineno, Lv_Table_Owner, Lv_Table_Name, Lv_String);
Lv_Lineno := Lv_Lineno + 1;

Lv_String  := '   INITIAL ' || Lv_Initial_Extent ;
WRITE_OUT(Lv_Lineno, Lv_Table_Owner, Lv_Table_Name, Lv_String);
Lv_Lineno := Lv_Lineno + 1;

Lv_String  := '   NEXT ' || Lv_Next_Extent ;
WRITE_OUT(Lv_Lineno, Lv_Table_Owner, Lv_Table_Name, Lv_String);
Lv_Lineno := Lv_Lineno + 1;

Lv_String  := '   MINEXTENTS ' || Lv_Min_Extents ;
WRITE_OUT(Lv_Lineno, Lv_Table_Owner, Lv_Table_Name, Lv_String);
Lv_Lineno := Lv_Lineno + 1;

Lv_String  := '   MAXEXTENTS ' || Lv_Max_Extents ;
WRITE_OUT(Lv_Lineno, Lv_Table_Owner, Lv_Table_Name, Lv_String);
Lv_Lineno := Lv_Lineno + 1;
```

```
   Lv_String   := '    PCTINCREASE ' || Lv_Pct_Increase ;
   WRITE_OUT(Lv_Lineno, Lv_Table_Owner, Lv_Table_Name, Lv_String);
   Lv_Lineno := Lv_Lineno + 1;

   Lv_String   := '    FREELISTS ' || Lv_Freelists ;
   WRITE_OUT(Lv_Lineno, Lv_Table_Owner, Lv_Table_Name, Lv_String);
   Lv_Lineno := Lv_Lineno + 1;

   Lv_String   := '    FREELIST GROUPS ' || Lv_Freelist_Groups ;
   WRITE_OUT(Lv_Lineno, Lv_Table_Owner, Lv_Table_Name, Lv_String);
   Lv_Lineno := Lv_Lineno + 1;

   Lv_String   := '    BUFFER_POOL ' || Lv_Buffer_Pool ;
   WRITE_OUT(Lv_Lineno, Lv_Table_Owner, Lv_Table_Name, Lv_String);
   Lv_Lineno := Lv_Lineno + 1;

   Lv_String   := ')';
   WRITE_OUT(Lv_Lineno, Lv_Table_Owner, Lv_Table_Name, Lv_String);
   Lv_Lineno := Lv_Lineno + 1;

 end if;
end if;

if (Lv_Partitioned = 'YES')
 then
   open PART_TABS_CURSOR (Lv_Table_Owner,Lv_Table_Name);
   loop
      fetch PART_TABS_CURSOR into Lv_PT_Partitioning_Type,
                                  Lv_PT_Subpartitioning_Type;
      exit when PART_TABS_CURSOR%NOTFOUND;

  if (Lv_PT_Partitioning_Type = 'RANGE' or Lv_PT_Partitioning_Type =
  'LIST') then

   Lv_String   := 'PARTITION BY '||Lv_PT_Partitioning_Type;
   WRITE_OUT(Lv_Lineno, Lv_Table_Owner, Lv_Table_Name, Lv_String);
   Lv_Lineno := Lv_Lineno + 1;
   Lv_String   := '(';
   WRITE_OUT(Lv_Lineno, Lv_Table_Owner, Lv_Table_Name, Lv_String);
   Lv_Lineno := Lv_Lineno + 1;

   open PART_COL_CURSOR (Lv_Table_Owner,Lv_Table_Name);

   loop
      fetch PART_COL_CURSOR into Lv_P_Column_Name;
      exit when PART_COL_CURSOR%NOTFOUND;
```

```
      Lv_String := Lv_P_Column_Name || ',';
      WRITE_OUT(Lv_Lineno, Lv_Table_Owner, Lv_Table_Name, Lv_String);
      Lv_Lineno := Lv_Lineno + 1;

   end loop;
   close PART_COL_CURSOR;
   Lv_Lineno  := Lv_Lineno - 1;
   Lv_String  := SUBSTR(Lv_String,1,(LENGTH(Lv_String) - 1));
   UPDATE_OUT(Lv_Lineno, Lv_Table_Owner, Lv_Table_Name,Lv_String);
   Lv_Lineno  := Lv_Lineno + 1;


   Lv_String  := ')';
   WRITE_OUT(Lv_Lineno, Lv_Table_Owner, Lv_Table_Name, Lv_String);
   Lv_Lineno := Lv_Lineno + 1;

if (Lv_PT_Subpartitioning_Type = 'HASH')
then

   Lv_String  := 'SUBPARTITION BY HASH';
   WRITE_OUT(Lv_Lineno, Lv_Table_Owner, Lv_Table_Name, Lv_String);
   Lv_Lineno := Lv_Lineno + 1;
   Lv_String  := '(';
   WRITE_OUT(Lv_Lineno, Lv_Table_Owner, Lv_Table_Name, Lv_String);
   Lv_Lineno := Lv_Lineno + 1;

   open SUBPART_COL_CURSOR (Lv_Table_Owner,Lv_Table_Name);

loop
      fetch SUBPART_COL_CURSOR into Lv_SP_Column_Name;
      exit when SUBPART_COL_CURSOR%NOTFOUND;


      Lv_String := Lv_SP_Column_Name || ',';
      WRITE_OUT(Lv_Lineno, Lv_Table_Owner, Lv_Table_Name, Lv_String);
      Lv_Lineno := Lv_Lineno + 1;

   end loop;
   close SUBPART_COL_CURSOR;
   Lv_Lineno  := Lv_Lineno - 1;
   Lv_String  := SUBSTR(Lv_String,1,(LENGTH(Lv_String) - 1));
   UPDATE_OUT(Lv_Lineno, Lv_Table_Owner, Lv_Table_Name,Lv_String);
   Lv_Lineno  := Lv_Lineno + 1;


   Lv_String  := ')';
   WRITE_OUT(Lv_Lineno, Lv_Table_Owner, Lv_Table_Name, Lv_String);
   Lv_Lineno := Lv_Lineno + 1;
```

```
end if;

  Lv_String  := '(';
  WRITE_OUT(Lv_Lineno, Lv_Table_Owner, Lv_Table_Name, Lv_String);
  Lv_Lineno := Lv_Lineno + 1;

  open TAB_PARTS_CURSOR (Lv_Table_Owner,Lv_Table_Name);

  loop
     fetch TAB_PARTS_CURSOR into  Lv_TP_Partition_Name,
                                  Lv_TP_High_Value,
                                  Lv_TP_Tablespace_Name,
                                  Lv_TP_Pct_Free,
                                  Lv_TP_Pct_Used,
                                  Lv_TP_Ini_Trans,
                                  Lv_TP_Max_Trans,
                                  Lv_TP_Initial_Extent,
                                  Lv_TP_Next_Extent,
                                  Lv_TP_Min_Extents,
                                  Lv_TP_Max_Extents,
                                  Lv_TP_Pct_Increase,
                                  Lv_TP_Freelists,
                                  Lv_TP_Freelist_Groups,
                                  Lv_TP_Buffer_Pool,
                                  Lv_TP_Logging;
    exit when TAB_PARTS_CURSOR%NOTFOUND;



  Lv_String := ' PARTITION '||Lv_TP_Partition_Name;
  WRITE_OUT(Lv_Lineno, Lv_Table_Owner, Lv_Table_Name, Lv_String);
  Lv_Lineno := Lv_Lineno + 1;

  Lv_String := ' VALUES LESS THAN ('||Lv_TP_High_Value||') ';
  WRITE_OUT(Lv_Lineno, Lv_Table_Owner, Lv_Table_Name, Lv_String);
  Lv_Lineno := Lv_Lineno + 1;

  Lv_String  := ' TABLESPACE ' || Lv_TP_Tablespace_Name ;
  WRITE_OUT(Lv_Lineno, Lv_Table_Owner, Lv_Table_Name, Lv_String);
  Lv_Lineno := Lv_Lineno + 1;

  if (Lv_TP_Logging = 'YES')
  then
    Lv_String  := ' LOGGING ';
  else
    Lv_String  := ' NOLOGGING ';
  end if;
```

```
   WRITE_OUT(Lv_Lineno, Lv_Table_Owner, Lv_Table_Name, Lv_String);
   Lv_Lineno := Lv_Lineno + 1;

   Lv_String  := ' PCTFREE ' || Lv_TP_Pct_Free ;
   WRITE_OUT(Lv_Lineno, Lv_Table_Owner, Lv_Table_Name, Lv_String);
   Lv_Lineno := Lv_Lineno + 1;

   Lv_String  := ' PCTUSED ' || Lv_TP_Pct_Used ;
   WRITE_OUT(Lv_Lineno, Lv_Table_Owner, Lv_Table_Name, Lv_String);
   Lv_Lineno := Lv_Lineno + 1;

   Lv_String  := ' INITRANS ' || Lv_TP_Ini_Trans ;
   WRITE_OUT(Lv_Lineno, Lv_Table_Owner, Lv_Table_Name, Lv_String);
   Lv_Lineno := Lv_Lineno + 1;

   Lv_String  := ' MAXTRANS ' || Lv_TP_Max_Trans ;
   WRITE_OUT(Lv_Lineno, Lv_Table_Owner, Lv_Table_Name, Lv_String);
   Lv_Lineno := Lv_Lineno + 1;

   if (Lv_TP_Initial_Extent is NOT NULL or
      Lv_TP_Next_Extent is NOT NULL or
      Lv_TP_Min_Extents is NOT NULL or
      Lv_TP_Max_Extents is NOT NULL or
      Lv_TP_Pct_Increase is NOT NULL or
      Lv_TP_Freelists is NOT NULL or
      Lv_TP_Freelist_Groups is NOT NULL or
      Lv_TP_Buffer_Pool is NOT NULL)
then

  Lv_String  := ' STORAGE';
  WRITE_OUT(Lv_Lineno, Lv_Table_Owner, Lv_Table_Name, Lv_String);
  Lv_Lineno := Lv_Lineno + 1;
  Lv_String  := '(';
  WRITE_OUT(Lv_Lineno, Lv_Table_Owner, Lv_Table_Name, Lv_String);
  Lv_Lineno := Lv_Lineno + 1;

  if (Lv_TP_Initial_Extent is NOT NULL)
  then
  Lv_String  := '   INITIAL ' || Lv_TP_Initial_Extent ;
  WRITE_OUT(Lv_Lineno, Lv_Table_Owner, Lv_Table_Name, Lv_String);
  Lv_Lineno := Lv_Lineno + 1;
  end if;

  if (Lv_TP_Next_Extent is NOT NULL)
  then
  Lv_String  := '   NEXT ' || Lv_TP_Next_Extent ;
  WRITE_OUT(Lv_Lineno, Lv_Table_Owner, Lv_Table_Name, Lv_String);
  Lv_Lineno := Lv_Lineno + 1;
  end if;
```

```
if (Lv_TP_Min_Extents is NOT NULL)
then
Lv_String  := '   MINEXTENTS ' || Lv_TP_Min_Extents ;
WRITE_OUT(Lv_Lineno, Lv_Table_Owner, Lv_Table_Name, Lv_String);
Lv_Lineno := Lv_Lineno + 1;
end if;

if (Lv_TP_Max_Extents is NOT NULL)
then
Lv_String  := '   MAXEXTENTS ' || Lv_TP_Max_Extents ;
WRITE_OUT(Lv_Lineno, Lv_Table_Owner, Lv_Table_Name, Lv_String);
Lv_Lineno := Lv_Lineno + 1;
end if;

if (Lv_TP_Pct_Increase is NOT NULL)
then
Lv_String  := '   PCTINCREASE ' || Lv_TP_Pct_Increase ;
WRITE_OUT(Lv_Lineno, Lv_Table_Owner, Lv_Table_Name, Lv_String);
Lv_Lineno := Lv_Lineno + 1;
end if;

if (Lv_TP_Freelists is NOT NULL)
then
Lv_String  := '   FREELISTS ' || Lv_TP_Freelists ;
WRITE_OUT(Lv_Lineno, Lv_Table_Owner, Lv_Table_Name, Lv_String);
Lv_Lineno := Lv_Lineno + 1;
end if;

if (Lv_TP_Freelist_Groups is NOT NULL)
then
Lv_String  := '   FREELIST GROUPS ' || Lv_TP_Freelist_Groups ;
WRITE_OUT(Lv_Lineno, Lv_Table_Owner, Lv_Table_Name, Lv_String);
Lv_Lineno := Lv_Lineno + 1;
end if;

if (Lv_TP_Buffer_Pool is NOT NULL)
then
Lv_String  := '   BUFFER_POOL ' || Lv_TP_Buffer_Pool ;
WRITE_OUT(Lv_Lineno, Lv_Table_Owner, Lv_Table_Name, Lv_String);
Lv_Lineno := Lv_Lineno + 1;
end if;

Lv_String  := ')';
WRITE_OUT(Lv_Lineno, Lv_Table_Owner, Lv_Table_Name, Lv_String);
Lv_Lineno := Lv_Lineno + 1;

end if;

if (Lv_PT_Subpartitioning_Type = 'HASH')
```

```
        then

        Lv_String  := '(';
        WRITE_OUT(Lv_Lineno, Lv_Table_Owner, Lv_Table_Name, Lv_String);
        Lv_Lineno := Lv_Lineno + 1;

open TAB_SUBPARTS_CURSOR (Lv_Table_Owner,Lv_Table_Name, Lv_TP_Partition_Name);
        loop
           fetch TAB_SUBPARTS_CURSOR into  Lv_TSP_Subpartition_Name,
                                           Lv_TSP_Tablespace_Name;
           exit when TAB_SUBPARTS_CURSOR%NOTFOUND;


           Lv_String := ' SUBPARTITION '||Lv_TSP_Subpartition_Name;
           WRITE_OUT(Lv_Lineno, Lv_Table_Owner, Lv_Table_Name, Lv_String);
           Lv_Lineno := Lv_Lineno + 1;


           Lv_String  := ' TABLESPACE ' || Lv_TSP_Tablespace_Name ;
           WRITE_OUT(Lv_Lineno, Lv_Table_Owner, Lv_Table_Name, Lv_String);
           Lv_Lineno := Lv_Lineno + 1;

           Lv_String := ',';
           WRITE_OUT(Lv_Lineno, Lv_Table_Owner, Lv_Table_Name, Lv_String);
           Lv_Lineno := Lv_Lineno + 1;

         end loop;
        close TAB_SUBPARTS_CURSOR;
        Lv_Lineno  := Lv_Lineno - 1;
        Lv_String  := SUBSTR(Lv_String,1,(LENGTH(Lv_String) - 1));
        UPDATE_OUT(Lv_Lineno, Lv_Table_Owner, Lv_Table_Name,Lv_String);
        Lv_Lineno  := Lv_Lineno + 1;

        Lv_String  := ')';
        WRITE_OUT(Lv_Lineno, Lv_Table_Owner, Lv_Table_Name, Lv_String);
        Lv_Lineno := Lv_Lineno + 1;

        end if;

        Lv_String := ',';
        WRITE_OUT(Lv_Lineno, Lv_Table_Owner, Lv_Table_Name, Lv_String);
        Lv_Lineno := Lv_Lineno + 1;

        end loop;
        close TAB_PARTS_CURSOR;
        Lv_Lineno  := Lv_Lineno - 1;
        Lv_String  := SUBSTR(Lv_String,1,(LENGTH(Lv_String) - 1));
        UPDATE_OUT(Lv_Lineno, Lv_Table_Owner, Lv_Table_Name,Lv_String);
        Lv_Lineno  := Lv_Lineno + 1;
```

```
  Lv_String  := ')';
  WRITE_OUT(Lv_Lineno, Lv_Table_Owner, Lv_Table_Name, Lv_String);
  Lv_Lineno := Lv_Lineno + 1;

else
 if (Lv_PT_Partitioning_Type = 'HASH')
 then

  Lv_String  := 'PARTITION BY HASH';
  WRITE_OUT(Lv_Lineno, Lv_Table_Owner, Lv_Table_Name, Lv_String);
  Lv_Lineno := Lv_Lineno + 1;
  Lv_String  := '(';
  WRITE_OUT(Lv_Lineno, Lv_Table_Owner, Lv_Table_Name, Lv_String);
  Lv_Lineno := Lv_Lineno + 1;

  open PART_COL_CURSOR (Lv_Table_Owner,Lv_Table_Name);

  loop
    fetch PART_COL_CURSOR into Lv_P_Column_Name;
    exit when PART_COL_CURSOR%NOTFOUND;


    Lv_String := Lv_P_Column_Name || ',';
    WRITE_OUT(Lv_Lineno, Lv_Table_Owner, Lv_Table_Name, Lv_String);
    Lv_Lineno := Lv_Lineno + 1;

  end loop;
  close PART_COL_CURSOR;
  Lv_Lineno  := Lv_Lineno - 1;
  Lv_String  := SUBSTR(Lv_String,1,(LENGTH(Lv_String) - 1));
  UPDATE_OUT(Lv_Lineno, Lv_Table_Owner, Lv_Table_Name,Lv_String);
  Lv_Lineno  := Lv_Lineno + 1;


  Lv_String  := ')';
  WRITE_OUT(Lv_Lineno, Lv_Table_Owner, Lv_Table_Name, Lv_String);
  Lv_Lineno := Lv_Lineno + 1;

  Lv_String  := '(';
  WRITE_OUT(Lv_Lineno, Lv_Table_Owner, Lv_Table_Name, Lv_String);
  Lv_Lineno := Lv_Lineno + 1;

  open TAB_PARTS_CURSOR (Lv_Table_Owner,Lv_Table_Name);

  loop
    fetch TAB_PARTS_CURSOR into  Lv_TP_Partition_Name,
                                 Lv_TP_High_Value,
                                 Lv_TP_Tablespace_Name,
                                 Lv_TP_Pct_Free,
```

```
                                            Lv_TP_Pct_Used,
                                            Lv_TP_Ini_Trans,
                                            Lv_TP_Max_Trans,
                                            Lv_TP_Initial_Extent,
                                            Lv_TP_Next_Extent,
                                            Lv_TP_Min_Extents,
                                            Lv_TP_Max_Extents,
                                            Lv_TP_Pct_Increase,
                                            Lv_TP_Freelists,
                                            Lv_TP_Freelist_Groups,
                                            Lv_TP_Buffer_Pool,
                                            Lv_TP_Logging;
            exit when TAB_PARTS_CURSOR%NOTFOUND;


        Lv_String := ' PARTITION '||Lv_TP_Partition_Name;
        WRITE_OUT(Lv_Lineno, Lv_Table_Owner, Lv_Table_Name, Lv_String);
        Lv_Lineno := Lv_Lineno + 1;


        Lv_String  := ' TABLESPACE ' || Lv_TP_Tablespace_Name ;
        WRITE_OUT(Lv_Lineno, Lv_Table_Owner, Lv_Table_Name, Lv_String);
        Lv_Lineno := Lv_Lineno + 1;

        Lv_String := ',';
        WRITE_OUT(Lv_Lineno, Lv_Table_Owner, Lv_Table_Name, Lv_String);
        Lv_Lineno := Lv_Lineno + 1;

        end loop;
        close TAB_PARTS_CURSOR;
        Lv_Lineno  := Lv_Lineno - 1;
        Lv_String  := SUBSTR(Lv_String,1,(LENGTH(Lv_String) - 1));
        UPDATE_OUT(Lv_Lineno, Lv_Table_Owner, Lv_Table_Name,Lv_String);
        Lv_Lineno  := Lv_Lineno + 1;

        Lv_String  := ')';
        WRITE_OUT(Lv_Lineno, Lv_Table_Owner, Lv_Table_Name, Lv_String);
        Lv_Lineno := Lv_Lineno + 1;

     end if;
    end if;
    end loop;
    close PART_TABS_CURSOR;

  end if;

      Lv_String  := 'PARALLEL ( DEGREE ' || Lv_Degree
                                         || ' INSTANCES '
```

```
                                      || Lv_Instances
                                      || ' )';
        WRITE_OUT(Lv_Lineno, Lv_Table_Owner, Lv_Table_Name, Lv_String);
        Lv_Lineno := Lv_Lineno + 1;

        if (Lv_Cache = 'Y')
        then
          Lv_String := ' CACHE ';
        else
          Lv_String := ' NOCACHE ';
        end if;
        WRITE_OUT(Lv_Lineno, Lv_Table_Owner, Lv_Table_Name, Lv_String);
        Lv_Lineno := Lv_Lineno + 1;

        if (Lv_Row_Movement = 'ENABLED')
        then
          Lv_String := ' ENABLE ROW MOVEMENT ';
          WRITE_OUT(Lv_Lineno, Lv_Table_Owner, Lv_Table_Name, Lv_String);
          Lv_Lineno := Lv_Lineno + 1;
        end if;

        if (Lv_Monitoring = 'YES')
        then
          Lv_String := ' MONITORING ';
          WRITE_OUT(Lv_Lineno, Lv_Table_Owner, Lv_Table_Name, Lv_String);
          Lv_Lineno := Lv_Lineno + 1;
        end if;

        Lv_String  := '/';
        WRITE_OUT(Lv_Lineno, Lv_Table_Owner, Lv_Table_Name, Lv_String);
        Lv_Lineno := Lv_Lineno + 1;


    end loop;
    close TAB_CURSOR;
end;
/
spool cre_tbl.sql
select Text
  from TAB_TEMP
 order by Id_Owner, Id_Name, Lineno
/
spool off
set newpage 1 verify on feedback 6 pagesize 24 linesize 80
heading on embedded off term on
undefine table_name
undefine table_owner
```

ANNOTATIONS

The script as written allows you to enter a wildcard value to select all tables for an owner. It can be easily modified to select all tables in the database. The script will generate a script to re-create the requested table(s) and any constraints on the table. The script uses a temporary table to hold individual lines of the **create table** statement, writing to the table rather than using DBMS_OUTPUT.PUT_LINE so that you can extract the information for an individual table from the temporary table. Using the temporary table greatly increases the script'sflexibility; using the DBMS_OUTPUT procedure would force you to save and edit the output file for the table you want.

For the sake of simplicity, all constraints will be re-created as table constraints rather than column constraints.

The first section of the script does the initial setup, prompting for the table name and table owner for later use via the **accept** command, which, unlike simply using the variable with the '&' or '&&' in a SQL statement, allows you to define your own prompt for the variable. You can enter the table name with wildcards (such as '%APP%') to generate a script for all tables with a similar name. You can enter '%' as the *table_name* variable value to generate a script for all tables for that table owner.

The SQL*Plus **set** command turns off headers (**pagesize 0**), row counts (**feedback off**), and displays of old and new values for the *table_name* and *tab_owner* variables (**verify off**).

```
set echo off term on verify off feedback off pagesize 0 heading off
select 'Creating table build script...' from DUAL;

accept table_name prompt "Enter the name of the Table: "
accept tab_owner prompt "Enter table owner: "
set term off
```

Next, a temporary table is created to hold each **create table** command and its owner. The Lineno column preserves the ordering of the lines of the **create table** command during later queries.

```
drop table TAB_TEMP;

create table TAB_TEMP (
        Lineno NUMBER,
        Id_Owner VARCHAR2(30),
        Id_Name VARCHAR2(30),
        Text VARCHAR2(2000))
/
```

In the next section of the script, the TAB_CURSOR cursor selects the storage definition information from DBA_TABLES, where the table name matches the input variable *table_name* and the table owner matches the input variable *table_owner*. Using **like** in the **where** clause allows for wildcards in the *table_name* variable.

In the next section of the script, the COL_CURSOR cursor selects the column definition information from DBA_TAB_COLUMNS, where the table name and owner match the table name and owner passed in from the TAB_CURSOR.

The next set of cursors, PART_COL_CURSOR, SUBPART_COL_CURSOR, TAB_PARTS_CURSOR, TAB_SUBPARTS_CURSOR, and PART_TABS_CURSOR, deal with the partitioning feature introduced as of Oracle8.x.

In the next section of the script, the CONS_CURSOR cursor, selects the constraint definition and column information from DBA_CONSTRAINTS and DBA_CONS_COLUMNS, where the table name and owner match the table name and owner passed in from the TAB_CURSOR and the constraint is either a Check constraint or the primary key (Constraint_Type in ['C','P']). The **order by** clause ensures that if the constraint is on multiple columns, it will be re-created in the proper column order.

The next section of the script extracts the foreign key relationships. Extracting the foreign key relationships from the data dictionary is slightly more complex than extracting the primary key. In addition to knowing the name of the foreign-key constraint and column(s) for the requested table, you must know the owner, table name, and column name(s) of the table being referenced. To retrieve the information, the DBA_CONS_COLUMNS view is joined twice into the REF_CURSOR cursor to extract the foreign key columns (C alias) and to extract the information on the primary key being referenced (B alias). The name of the primary-key constraint being referenced by the foreign key is contained in the R_Constraint_Name column of DBA_CONSTRAINTS.

The next section of the script defines the IOT_CURSOR and the IOT_OVER_CURSOR to deal with index-organized tables and their overflow storage clauses.

The procedure variables for the cursor are declared as TABLE_NAME.Column_Name%**TYPE**. This "anchoring" of datatypes takes the column definition from within the database itself. If the column definition changes in a different version of Oracle, the procedure will still work because the definition of the column has not been hard-coded. The *Lv_Cons_Exists* variable indicates whether a primary-key constraint exists on the requested table. The variable *Lv_Lineno* orders the lines of the **create** statement and is initialized to 0.

The next portion of the script defines two internal procedures: WRITE_OUT to do the **insert**s into the temporary table, and UPDATE_OUT to **update** rows in the table. You can use UPDATE_OUT to remove extra characters from lines once the command or section of the command has been written.

The TAB_CURSOR cursor forms an outer loop for each table. *Lv_Lineno* is used in conjunction with the table name to order the rows in the temporary table TAB_TEMP, so that if you prefer, you can extract the **create** statement for a single table at the end of the procedure.

The next section of the script inserts the beginning of the **create** statement into the temporary table. The SQL function **LOWER** is used to change the case of the table owner and table name to lowercase for readability.

To perform the **insert**, the WRITE_OUT procedure is executed, and line numbers are assigned to each inserted line.

Checking is also done to determine whether the table is a temporary table. GLOBAL TEMPORARY indicates that the table is temporary and its definition is visible to all sessions. Data in a temporary table is visible only to the session that inserts the data into the table.

```
if (Lv_Temporary = 'Y')
    then
        Lv_String:= ' GLOBAL TEMPORARY ';
    else
        Lv_String:=' ';
    end if;

Lv_String:= 'CREATE '||Lv_String||' TABLE '
                    || LOWER(Lv_Table_Owner)
                    || '.'
                    || LOWER(Lv_Table_Name);
WRITE_OUT(Lv_Lineno, Lv_Table_Owner, Lv_Table_Name, Lv_String);
Lv_Lineno := Lv_Lineno + 1;
```

The COL_CURSOR cursor forms the inner loop of the script, selecting all the column names in the table from DBA_TAB_COLUMNS. Each column'sdata definition will be processed and added to the temporary table before the next column is fetched. The inner cursor will be opened, fetched, and closed once for each table selected by the outer cursor.

The next section begins creating the string for the column definition with the column name. To make the line more readable, **RPAD** is used to pad the column name with blanks on the right before concatenating the datatype, so that the datatypes will line up.

```
Lv_String := '          '                          ||
                RPAD(LOWER(Lv_Column_Name),35)  ||
                Lv_Column_Data_Type;
```

VARCHAR2, RAW, and CHAR datatypes all have a data length associated with the column. If this column is one of these datatypes, the following section of the script appends the length enclosed in the required "( )".

```
if ( (Lv_Column_Data_Type = 'VARCHAR2' ) or
     (Lv_Column_Data_Type = 'RAW'       ) or
     (Lv_Column_Data_Type = 'CHAR'      ) )
    then
        Lv_String := Lv_String              ||
                     '('                     ||
                     Lv_Column_Data_Length  ||
                     ')';
```

If the column uses the NUMBER datatype, it can be defined with both a precision and scale. If the precision is NULL, the script sets the precision to 38 (the maximum definition for a numeric column) and the scale to 0 before adding them to the column definition. DATE and LONG datatypes do not need additional processing.

```
elsif (Lv_Column_Data_Type = 'NUMBER')
then
     if Lv_Column_Data_Precision IS NULL
     then
         Lv_Column_Data_Precision := 38;
         Lv_Column_Data_Scale     := 0;
     end if;
     Lv_String := Lv_String                  ||
                     '('                      ||
                     Lv_Column_Data_Precision ||
                     ','                       ||
                     Lv_Column_Data_Scale     ||
                     ')';
end if;
```

If you have defined a default value for the column, the default value needs to be added to the column definition. Since the Data_Default column in DBA_TAB_ COLUMNS is a LONG column, the script extracts the contents of the column by using the **SUBSTR** function. Defaults are used when you want to ensure that a particular value is inserted into a column if an **insert** command does not include a value for that column.

```
if (Lv_Column_Data_Default IS NOT NULL)
then
     Lv_String := Lv_String || ' DEFAULT '
                            || SUBSTR(Lv_Column_Data_Default,
                                 1, Lv_Column_Default_Length);
end if;
```

If the column is a required column, the *Lv_Column_Nullable* variable's value will be N and the phrase **NOT NULL** must be added to the string.

Add a comma to separate the columns, and write the column definition line to the temporary table. The inner loop will repeat for each column of the table.

```
if (Lv_Column_Nullable = 'N' )
then
     Lv_String := Lv_String || '  NOT NULL';
end if;

Lv_String := Lv_String || ',';
WRITE_OUT(Lv_Lineno, Lv_Table_Owner, Lv_Table_Name, Lv_String);
Lv_Lineno := Lv_Lineno + 1;

end loop;
```

The next section of the script determines whether there are any Check or primary-key constraints on the table; if they exist, the script generates the SQL statements to create them. The CONS_CURSOR cursor will fetch any constraints with a constraint type of 'C' or 'P'. The *Lv_Cons_Exists* variable determines whether or not you have extracted a primary-key constraint. Defining a column as NOT NULL adds a Check constraint to the data dictionary. Since we have already dealt with NOT NULL columns, we can ignore them here. Constraints can be named or unnamed. Unnamed constraints are named by Oracle and all these constraint names begin with *SYS_C*. If the constraint name does not begin with this string, you need to add the **constraint** *constraint_name* clause to the string before writing it to the temporary table.

The next section of the script will generate the statements to re-create the primary-key constraint on the table if one exists. Because the script builds the statement as a single string, you need to set a flag to determine whether a primary-key constraint exists, to write to the temporary table at the end of the cursor loop. The **order by** clause of the cursor definition, by placing Constraint_Type as the first column to sort on, puts the primary-key constraint, if it exists, as the last row fetched from the cursor.

The CONS_CURSOR and the REF_CURSOR cursors are used to add the constraints of the table at the table level. The CONS_CURSOR deals with the Check and primary-key constraints while the REF_CURSOR deals with the foreign-key constraints.

Because the procedure adds a comma to the end of every line of the column definition, an additional, unnecessary comma appears at the end of the last column. The variable *Lv_Lineno* is decremented to go back to that last line, and the procedure uses the **SUBSTR** command to extract all of the line except the comma. The line is then rewritten to the temporary table by the UPDATE_OUT procedure and the *Lv_Lineno* is incremented again.

```
close COL_CURSOR;
Lv_Lineno := Lv_Lineno - 1;
Lv_String := SUBSTR(Lv_String, 1,(LENGTH(Lv_String) - 1));
UPDATE_OUT(Lv_Lineno, Lv_Table_Owner, Lv_Table_Name,Lv_String);
Lv_Lineno := Lv_Lineno + 1;
```

Now that the column definitions have been completed, that part of the **create table** command is closed with a final closed parenthesis:

```
Lv_String := ')';
WRITE_OUT(Lv_Lineno, Lv_Table_Owner, Lv_Table_Name, Lv_String);
Lv_Lineno := Lv_Lineno + 1;
```

For temporary tables, you can specify whether the data is session- or transaction-specific by using the **ON COMMIT** keyword. The next section of code determines the persistency of the data in temporary tables.

```
if (Lv_Duration is NOT NULL)
then
    if (Lv_Duration = 'SYS$SESSION')
```

```
    then
        Lv_String:= ' ON COMMIT PRESERVE ROWS ';
    else
        Lv_String:= ' ON COMMIT DELETE ROWS ';
    end if;
  end if;
  WRITE_OUT(Lv_Lineno, Lv_Table_Owner, Lv_Table_Name, Lv_String);
  Lv_Lineno := Lv_Lineno + 1;
```

The next section determines whether the table is an index-organized table. If the table is an index-organized table, the IOT_CURSOR and the IOT_OVER_CURSOR cursors are used to generate the appropriate clauses.

```
if (Lv_Iot_Type is NOT NULL)
    then

    Lv_String := ' ORGANIZATION INDEX ';
    WRITE_OUT(Lv_Lineno, Lv_Table_Owner, Lv_Table_Name, Lv_String);
    Lv_Lineno := Lv_Lineno + 1;

    open IOT_CURSOR(Lv_Table_Owner,Lv_Table_Name);
    loop
       fetch IOT_CURSOR into Lv_Iot_Owner,
                             Lv_Iot_Table_Name,
                             Lv_Iot_Tablespace_Name,
                             Lv_Iot_Pct_Free,
                             Lv_Iot_Initial_Trans,
                             Lv_Iot_Max_Trans,
                             Lv_Iot_Initial_Extent,
                             Lv_Iot_Next_Extent,
                             Lv_Iot_Min_Extents,
                             Lv_Iot_Max_Extents,
                             Lv_Iot_Pct_Increase,
                             Lv_Iot_Freelists,
                             Lv_Iot_Freelist_Groups,
                             Lv_Iot_Buffer_Pool,
                             Lv_Iot_Pct_Threshold,
                             Lv_Iot_Include_Column,
                             Lv_Iot_Column_Name,
                             Lv_Iot_Logging,
                             Lv_Iot_Compression,
                             Lv_Iot_Prefix_Length;
       exit when IOT_CURSOR%NOTFOUND;

    Lv_String := ' PCTTHRESHOLD '||Lv_Iot_Pct_Threshold;
    WRITE_OUT(Lv_Lineno, Lv_Table_Owner, Lv_Table_Name, Lv_String);
    Lv_Lineno := Lv_Lineno + 1;
```

```
if (Lv_Iot_Compression = 'DISABLED')
then
   Lv_String := ' NOCOMPRESS ';
else
   Lv_String := ' COMPRESS '||Lv_Iot_Prefix_Length;
end if;
WRITE_OUT(Lv_Lineno, Lv_Table_Owner, Lv_Table_Name, Lv_String);
Lv_Lineno := Lv_Lineno + 1;

Lv_String  := 'TABLESPACE ' || Lv_Iot_Tablespace_Name ;
WRITE_OUT(Lv_Lineno, Lv_Table_Owner, Lv_Table_Name, Lv_String);
Lv_Lineno := Lv_Lineno + 1;

if (Lv_Iot_Logging = 'YES')
then
  Lv_String  := ' LOGGING ';
else
  Lv_String  := ' NOLOGGING ';
end if;
WRITE_OUT(Lv_Lineno, Lv_Table_Owner, Lv_Table_Name, Lv_String);
Lv_Lineno := Lv_Lineno + 1;

Lv_String  := 'PCTFREE ' || Lv_Iot_Pct_Free ;
WRITE_OUT(Lv_Lineno, Lv_Table_Owner, Lv_Table_Name, Lv_String);
Lv_Lineno := Lv_Lineno + 1;

Lv_String  := 'INITRANS ' || Lv_Iot_Initial_Trans ;
WRITE_OUT(Lv_Lineno, Lv_Table_Owner, Lv_Table_Name, Lv_String);
Lv_Lineno := Lv_Lineno + 1;

Lv_String  := 'MAXTRANS ' || Lv_Iot_Max_Trans ;
WRITE_OUT(Lv_Lineno, Lv_Table_Owner, Lv_Table_Name, Lv_String);
Lv_Lineno := Lv_Lineno + 1;

Lv_String  := 'STORAGE';
WRITE_OUT(Lv_Lineno, Lv_Table_Owner, Lv_Table_Name, Lv_String);
Lv_Lineno := Lv_Lineno + 1;
Lv_String  := '(';
WRITE_OUT(Lv_Lineno, Lv_Table_Owner, Lv_Table_Name, Lv_String);
Lv_Lineno := Lv_Lineno + 1;

Lv_String  := '   INITIAL ' || Lv_Iot_Initial_Extent ;
WRITE_OUT(Lv_Lineno, Lv_Table_Owner, Lv_Table_Name, Lv_String);
Lv_Lineno := Lv_Lineno + 1;

Lv_String  := '   NEXT ' || Lv_Iot_Next_Extent ;
WRITE_OUT(Lv_Lineno, Lv_Table_Owner, Lv_Table_Name, Lv_String);
Lv_Lineno := Lv_Lineno + 1;
```

```
Lv_String  := '   MINEXTENTS ' || Lv_Iot_Min_Extents ;
WRITE_OUT(Lv_Lineno, Lv_Table_Owner, Lv_Table_Name, Lv_String);
Lv_Lineno := Lv_Lineno + 1;


Lv_String  := '   MAXEXTENTS ' || Lv_Iot_Max_Extents ;
WRITE_OUT(Lv_Lineno, Lv_Table_Owner, Lv_Table_Name, Lv_String);
Lv_Lineno := Lv_Lineno + 1;


Lv_String  := '   PCTINCREASE ' || Lv_Iot_Pct_Increase ;
WRITE_OUT(Lv_Lineno, Lv_Table_Owner, Lv_Table_Name, Lv_String);
Lv_Lineno := Lv_Lineno + 1;


Lv_String  := '   FREELISTS ' || Lv_Iot_Freelists ;
WRITE_OUT(Lv_Lineno, Lv_Table_Owner, Lv_Table_Name, Lv_String);
Lv_Lineno := Lv_Lineno + 1;


Lv_String  := '   FREELIST GROUPS ' || Lv_Iot_Freelist_Groups ;
WRITE_OUT(Lv_Lineno, Lv_Table_Owner, Lv_Table_Name, Lv_String);
Lv_Lineno := Lv_Lineno + 1;


Lv_String  := '   BUFFER_POOL ' || Lv_Iot_Buffer_Pool ;
WRITE_OUT(Lv_Lineno, Lv_Table_Owner, Lv_Table_Name, Lv_String);
Lv_Lineno := Lv_Lineno + 1;


Lv_String  := ')';
WRITE_OUT(Lv_Lineno, Lv_Table_Owner, Lv_Table_Name, Lv_String);
Lv_Lineno := Lv_Lineno + 1;


if (Lv_Iot_Include_Column is NOT NULL)
then
    Lv_String  := ' INCLUDING '|| Lv_Iot_Column_Name||' OVERFLOW ' ;
    WRITE_OUT(Lv_Lineno, Lv_Table_Owner, Lv_Table_Name, Lv_String);
    Lv_Lineno := Lv_Lineno + 1;
end if;


open IOT_OVER_CURSOR(Lv_Iot_Owner,Lv_Iot_Table_Name);
loop
   fetch IOT_OVER_CURSOR into Lv_Io_Tablespace_Name,
                              Lv_Io_Initial_Trans,
                              Lv_Io_Max_Trans,
                              Lv_Io_Initial_Extent,
                              Lv_Io_Next_Extent,
                              Lv_Io_Min_Extents,
                              Lv_Io_Max_Extents,
                              Lv_Io_Pct_Increase,
                              Lv_Io_Freelists,
                              Lv_Io_Freelist_Groups,
                              Lv_Io_Logging;
exit when IOT_OVER_CURSOR%NOTFOUND;
```

```
Lv_String  := 'TABLESPACE ' || Lv_Io_Tablespace_Name ;
WRITE_OUT(Lv_Lineno, Lv_Table_Owner, Lv_Table_Name, Lv_String);
Lv_Lineno := Lv_Lineno + 1;

if (Lv_Io_Logging = 'YES')
then
  Lv_String  := ' LOGGING ';
else
  Lv_String  := ' NOLOGGING ';
end if;
WRITE_OUT(Lv_Lineno, Lv_Table_Owner, Lv_Table_Name, Lv_String);
Lv_Lineno := Lv_Lineno + 1;

Lv_String  := 'INITRANS ' || Lv_Io_Initial_Trans ;
WRITE_OUT(Lv_Lineno, Lv_Table_Owner, Lv_Table_Name, Lv_String);
Lv_Lineno := Lv_Lineno + 1;

Lv_String  := 'MAXTRANS ' || Lv_Io_Max_Trans ;
WRITE_OUT(Lv_Lineno, Lv_Table_Owner, Lv_Table_Name, Lv_String);
Lv_Lineno := Lv_Lineno + 1;

Lv_String  := 'STORAGE';
WRITE_OUT(Lv_Lineno, Lv_Table_Owner, Lv_Table_Name, Lv_String);
Lv_Lineno := Lv_Lineno + 1;
Lv_String  := '(';
WRITE_OUT(Lv_Lineno, Lv_Table_Owner, Lv_Table_Name, Lv_String);
Lv_Lineno := Lv_Lineno + 1;

Lv_String  := '   INITIAL ' || Lv_Io_Initial_Extent ;
WRITE_OUT(Lv_Lineno, Lv_Table_Owner, Lv_Table_Name, Lv_String);
Lv_Lineno := Lv_Lineno + 1;

Lv_String  := '   NEXT ' || Lv_Io_Next_Extent ;
WRITE_OUT(Lv_Lineno, Lv_Table_Owner, Lv_Table_Name, Lv_String);
Lv_Lineno := Lv_Lineno + 1;

Lv_String  := '   MINEXTENTS ' || Lv_Io_Min_Extents ;
WRITE_OUT(Lv_Lineno, Lv_Table_Owner, Lv_Table_Name, Lv_String);
Lv_Lineno := Lv_Lineno + 1;

Lv_String  := '   MAXEXTENTS ' || Lv_Io_Max_Extents ;
WRITE_OUT(Lv_Lineno, Lv_Table_Owner, Lv_Table_Name, Lv_String);
Lv_Lineno := Lv_Lineno + 1;

Lv_String  := '   PCTINCREASE ' || Lv_Io_Pct_Increase ;
WRITE_OUT(Lv_Lineno, Lv_Table_Owner, Lv_Table_Name, Lv_String);
Lv_Lineno := Lv_Lineno + 1;
```

```
Lv_String   := '    FREELISTS ' || Lv_Io_Freelists ;
WRITE_OUT(Lv_Lineno, Lv_Table_Owner, Lv_Table_Name, Lv_String);
Lv_Lineno := Lv_Lineno + 1;

Lv_String   := '    FREELIST GROUPS ' || Lv_Io_Freelist_Groups ;
WRITE_OUT(Lv_Lineno, Lv_Table_Owner, Lv_Table_Name, Lv_String);
Lv_Lineno := Lv_Lineno + 1;

Lv_String   := ')';
WRITE_OUT(Lv_Lineno, Lv_Table_Owner, Lv_Table_Name, Lv_String);
Lv_Lineno := Lv_Lineno + 1;


end loop;
close IOT_OVER_CURSOR;

end loop;
close IOT_CURSOR;
```

If the table is not an index-organized table, it is checked to see whether it is partitioned. If it is *not* partitioned, the appropriate clauses for its physical attributes and storage are generated.

```
else

  if (Lv_Partitioned = 'NO')
  then

    Lv_String   := 'TABLESPACE ' || Lv_Tablespace_Name ;
    WRITE_OUT(Lv_Lineno, Lv_Table_Owner, Lv_Table_Name, Lv_String);
    Lv_Lineno := Lv_Lineno + 1;

    if (Lv_Logging = 'YES')
    then
      Lv_String   := ' LOGGING ';
    else
      Lv_String   := ' NOLOGGING ';
    end if;
    WRITE_OUT(Lv_Lineno, Lv_Table_Owner, Lv_Table_Name, Lv_String);
    Lv_Lineno := Lv_Lineno + 1;

    Lv_String   := 'PCTFREE ' || Lv_Pct_Free ;
    WRITE_OUT(Lv_Lineno, Lv_Table_Owner, Lv_Table_Name, Lv_String);
    Lv_Lineno := Lv_Lineno + 1;

    Lv_String   := 'PCTUSED ' || Lv_Pct_Used ;
    WRITE_OUT(Lv_Lineno, Lv_Table_Owner, Lv_Table_Name, Lv_String);
    Lv_Lineno := Lv_Lineno + 1;
```

```
Lv_String  := 'INITRANS ' || Lv_Initial_Trans ;
WRITE_OUT(Lv_Lineno, Lv_Table_Owner, Lv_Table_Name, Lv_String);
Lv_Lineno := Lv_Lineno + 1;

Lv_String  := 'MAXTRANS ' || Lv_Max_Trans ;
WRITE_OUT(Lv_Lineno, Lv_Table_Owner, Lv_Table_Name, Lv_String);
Lv_Lineno := Lv_Lineno + 1;

Lv_String  := 'STORAGE';
WRITE_OUT(Lv_Lineno, Lv_Table_Owner, Lv_Table_Name, Lv_String);
Lv_Lineno := Lv_Lineno + 1;
Lv_String  := '(';
WRITE_OUT(Lv_Lineno, Lv_Table_Owner, Lv_Table_Name, Lv_String);
Lv_Lineno := Lv_Lineno + 1;

Lv_String  := '   INITIAL ' || Lv_Initial_Extent ;
WRITE_OUT(Lv_Lineno, Lv_Table_Owner, Lv_Table_Name, Lv_String);
Lv_Lineno := Lv_Lineno + 1;

Lv_String  := '   NEXT ' || Lv_Next_Extent ;
WRITE_OUT(Lv_Lineno, Lv_Table_Owner, Lv_Table_Name, Lv_String);
Lv_Lineno := Lv_Lineno + 1;

Lv_String  := '   MINEXTENTS ' || Lv_Min_Extents ;
WRITE_OUT(Lv_Lineno, Lv_Table_Owner, Lv_Table_Name, Lv_String);
Lv_Lineno := Lv_Lineno + 1;

Lv_String  := '   MAXEXTENTS ' || Lv_Max_Extents ;
WRITE_OUT(Lv_Lineno, Lv_Table_Owner, Lv_Table_Name, Lv_String);
Lv_Lineno := Lv_Lineno + 1;

Lv_String  := '   PCTINCREASE ' || Lv_Pct_Increase ;
WRITE_OUT(Lv_Lineno, Lv_Table_Owner, Lv_Table_Name, Lv_String);
Lv_Lineno := Lv_Lineno + 1;

Lv_String  := '   FREELISTS ' || Lv_Freelists ;
WRITE_OUT(Lv_Lineno, Lv_Table_Owner, Lv_Table_Name, Lv_String);
Lv_Lineno := Lv_Lineno + 1;

Lv_String  := '   FREELIST GROUPS ' || Lv_Freelist_Groups ;
WRITE_OUT(Lv_Lineno, Lv_Table_Owner, Lv_Table_Name, Lv_String);
Lv_Lineno := Lv_Lineno + 1;

Lv_String  := '   BUFFER_POOL ' || Lv_Buffer_Pool ;
WRITE_OUT(Lv_Lineno, Lv_Table_Owner, Lv_Table_Name, Lv_String);
Lv_Lineno := Lv_Lineno + 1;
```

```
      Lv_String  := ')';
      WRITE_OUT(Lv_Lineno, Lv_Table_Owner, Lv_Table_Name, Lv_String);
      Lv_Lineno := Lv_Lineno + 1;

  end if;
  end if;
```

If the table is partitioned, the partitioning type is determined and the appropriate clauses are generated.

```
if (Lv_Partitioned = 'YES')
   then
      open PART_TABS_CURSOR (Lv_Table_Owner,Lv_Table_Name);
      loop
         fetch PART_TABS_CURSOR into Lv_PT_Partitioning_Type,
                                     Lv_PT_Subpartitioning_Type;
         exit when PART_TABS_CURSOR%NOTFOUND;

      if (Lv_PT_Partitioning_Type = 'RANGE' or Lv_PT_Partitioning_Type =
      'LIST') then

      Lv_String  := 'PARTITION BY '||Lv_PT_Partitioning_Type;
      WRITE_OUT(Lv_Lineno, Lv_Table_Owner, Lv_Table_Name, Lv_String);
      Lv_Lineno := Lv_Lineno + 1;
      Lv_String  := '(';
      WRITE_OUT(Lv_Lineno, Lv_Table_Owner, Lv_Table_Name, Lv_String);
      Lv_Lineno := Lv_Lineno + 1;

      open PART_COL_CURSOR (Lv_Table_Owner,Lv_Table_Name);

      loop
         fetch PART_COL_CURSOR into Lv_P_Column_Name;
         exit when PART_COL_CURSOR%NOTFOUND;


         Lv_String := Lv_P_Column_Name || ',';
         WRITE_OUT(Lv_Lineno, Lv_Table_Owner, Lv_Table_Name, Lv_String);
         Lv_Lineno := Lv_Lineno + 1;

      end loop;
      close PART_COL_CURSOR;
      Lv_Lineno  := Lv_Lineno - 1;
      Lv_String  := SUBSTR(Lv_String,1,(LENGTH(Lv_String) - 1));
      UPDATE_OUT(Lv_Lineno, Lv_Table_Owner, Lv_Table_Name,Lv_String);
      Lv_Lineno  := Lv_Lineno + 1;
```

```
 Lv_String  := ')';
 WRITE_OUT(Lv_Lineno, Lv_Table_Owner, Lv_Table_Name, Lv_String);
 Lv_Lineno := Lv_Lineno + 1;

if (Lv_PT_Subpartitioning_Type = 'HASH')
then

 Lv_String  := 'SUBPARTITION BY HASH';
 WRITE_OUT(Lv_Lineno, Lv_Table_Owner, Lv_Table_Name, Lv_String);
 Lv_Lineno := Lv_Lineno + 1;
 Lv_String  := '(';
 WRITE_OUT(Lv_Lineno, Lv_Table_Owner, Lv_Table_Name, Lv_String);
 Lv_Lineno := Lv_Lineno + 1;

 open SUBPART_COL_CURSOR (Lv_Table_Owner,Lv_Table_Name);

 loop
    fetch SUBPART_COL_CURSOR into Lv_SP_Column_Name;
    exit when SUBPART_COL_CURSOR%NOTFOUND;


    Lv_String := Lv_SP_Column_Name || ',';
    WRITE_OUT(Lv_Lineno, Lv_Table_Owner, Lv_Table_Name, Lv_String);
    Lv_Lineno := Lv_Lineno + 1;

 end loop;
 close SUBPART_COL_CURSOR;
 Lv_Lineno  := Lv_Lineno - 1;
 Lv_String  := SUBSTR(Lv_String,1,(LENGTH(Lv_String) - 1));
 UPDATE_OUT(Lv_Lineno, Lv_Table_Owner, Lv_Table_Name,Lv_String);
 Lv_Lineno  := Lv_Lineno + 1;


 Lv_String  := ')';
 WRITE_OUT(Lv_Lineno, Lv_Table_Owner, Lv_Table_Name, Lv_String);
 Lv_Lineno := Lv_Lineno + 1;

end if;

 Lv_String  := '(';
 WRITE_OUT(Lv_Lineno, Lv_Table_Owner, Lv_Table_Name, Lv_String);
 Lv_Lineno := Lv_Lineno + 1;

 open TAB_PARTS_CURSOR (Lv_Table_Owner,Lv_Table_Name);

 loop
    fetch TAB_PARTS_CURSOR into  Lv_TP_Partition_Name,
                                 Lv_TP_High_Value,
                                 Lv_TP_Tablespace_Name,
```

```
                                Lv_TP_Pct_Free,
                                Lv_TP_Pct_Used,
                                Lv_TP_Ini_Trans,
                                Lv_TP_Max_Trans,
                                Lv_TP_Initial_Extent,
                                Lv_TP_Next_Extent,
                                Lv_TP_Min_Extents,
                                Lv_TP_Max_Extents,
                                Lv_TP_Pct_Increase,
                                Lv_TP_Freelists,
                                Lv_TP_Freelist_Groups,
                                Lv_TP_Buffer_Pool,
                                Lv_TP_Logging;
        exit when TAB_PARTS_CURSOR%NOTFOUND;



Lv_String := ' PARTITION '||Lv_TP_Partition_Name;
WRITE_OUT(Lv_Lineno, Lv_Table_Owner, Lv_Table_Name, Lv_String);
Lv_Lineno := Lv_Lineno + 1;


Lv_String := ' VALUES LESS THAN ('||Lv_TP_High_Value||') ';
WRITE_OUT(Lv_Lineno, Lv_Table_Owner, Lv_Table_Name, Lv_String);
Lv_Lineno := Lv_Lineno + 1;


Lv_String   := ' TABLESPACE ' || Lv_TP_Tablespace_Name ;
WRITE_OUT(Lv_Lineno, Lv_Table_Owner, Lv_Table_Name, Lv_String);
Lv_Lineno := Lv_Lineno + 1;


if (Lv_TP_Logging = 'YES')
then
  Lv_String  := ' LOGGING ';
else
  Lv_String  := ' NOLOGGING ';
end if;
WRITE_OUT(Lv_Lineno, Lv_Table_Owner, Lv_Table_Name, Lv_String);
Lv_Lineno := Lv_Lineno + 1;


Lv_String   := ' PCTFREE ' || Lv_TP_Pct_Free ;
WRITE_OUT(Lv_Lineno, Lv_Table_Owner, Lv_Table_Name, Lv_String);
Lv_Lineno := Lv_Lineno + 1;


Lv_String   := ' PCTUSED ' || Lv_TP_Pct_Used ;
WRITE_OUT(Lv_Lineno, Lv_Table_Owner, Lv_Table_Name, Lv_String);
Lv_Lineno := Lv_Lineno + 1;


Lv_String   := ' INITRANS ' || Lv_TP_Ini_Trans ;
WRITE_OUT(Lv_Lineno, Lv_Table_Owner, Lv_Table_Name, Lv_String);
Lv_Lineno := Lv_Lineno + 1;
```

```
         Lv_String  := ' MAXTRANS ' || Lv_TP_Max_Trans ;
         WRITE_OUT(Lv_Lineno, Lv_Table_Owner, Lv_Table_Name, Lv_String);
         Lv_Lineno := Lv_Lineno + 1;

         if (Lv_TP_Initial_Extent is NOT NULL or
             Lv_TP_Next_Extent is NOT NULL or
             Lv_TP_Min_Extents is NOT NULL or
             Lv_TP_Max_Extents is NOT NULL or
             Lv_TP_Pct_Increase is NOT NULL or
             Lv_TP_Freelists is NOT NULL or
             Lv_TP_Freelist_Groups is NOT NULL or
             Lv_TP_Buffer_Pool is NOT NULL)
      then

         Lv_String  := ' STORAGE';
         WRITE_OUT(Lv_Lineno, Lv_Table_Owner, Lv_Table_Name, Lv_String);
         Lv_Lineno := Lv_Lineno + 1;
         Lv_String  := '(';
         WRITE_OUT(Lv_Lineno, Lv_Table_Owner, Lv_Table_Name, Lv_String);
         Lv_Lineno := Lv_Lineno + 1;

         if (Lv_TP_Initial_Extent is NOT NULL)
         then
         Lv_String  := '   INITIAL ' || Lv_TP_Initial_Extent ;
         WRITE_OUT(Lv_Lineno, Lv_Table_Owner, Lv_Table_Name, Lv_String);
         Lv_Lineno := Lv_Lineno + 1;
         end if;

         if (Lv_TP_Next_Extent is NOT NULL)
         then
         Lv_String  := '   NEXT ' || Lv_TP_Next_Extent ;
         WRITE_OUT(Lv_Lineno, Lv_Table_Owner, Lv_Table_Name, Lv_String);
         Lv_Lineno := Lv_Lineno + 1;
         end if;

         if (Lv_TP_Min_Extents is NOT NULL)
         then
         Lv_String  := '   MINEXTENTS ' || Lv_TP_Min_Extents ;
         WRITE_OUT(Lv_Lineno, Lv_Table_Owner, Lv_Table_Name, Lv_String);
         Lv_Lineno := Lv_Lineno + 1;
         end if;

         if (Lv_TP_Max_Extents is NOT NULL)
         then
         Lv_String  := '   MAXEXTENTS ' || Lv_TP_Max_Extents ;
         WRITE_OUT(Lv_Lineno, Lv_Table_Owner, Lv_Table_Name, Lv_String);
         Lv_Lineno := Lv_Lineno + 1;
         end if;
```

```
      if (Lv_TP_Pct_Increase is NOT NULL)
      then
      Lv_String  := '   PCTINCREASE ' || Lv_TP_Pct_Increase ;
      WRITE_OUT(Lv_Lineno, Lv_Table_Owner, Lv_Table_Name, Lv_String);
      Lv_Lineno := Lv_Lineno + 1;
      end if;


      if (Lv_TP_Freelists is NOT NULL)
      then
      Lv_String  := '   FREELISTS ' || Lv_TP_Freelists ;
      WRITE_OUT(Lv_Lineno, Lv_Table_Owner, Lv_Table_Name, Lv_String);
      Lv_Lineno := Lv_Lineno + 1;
      end if;


      if (Lv_TP_Freelist_Groups is NOT NULL)
      then
      Lv_String  := '   FREELIST GROUPS ' || Lv_TP_Freelist_Groups ;
      WRITE_OUT(Lv_Lineno, Lv_Table_Owner, Lv_Table_Name, Lv_String);
      Lv_Lineno := Lv_Lineno + 1;
      end if;


      if (Lv_TP_Buffer_Pool is NOT NULL)
      then
      Lv_String  := '   BUFFER_POOL ' || Lv_TP_Buffer_Pool ;
      WRITE_OUT(Lv_Lineno, Lv_Table_Owner, Lv_Table_Name, Lv_String);
      Lv_Lineno := Lv_Lineno + 1;
      end if;


      Lv_String  := ')';
      WRITE_OUT(Lv_Lineno, Lv_Table_Owner, Lv_Table_Name, Lv_String);
      Lv_Lineno := Lv_Lineno + 1;

   end if;

      if (Lv_PT_Subpartitioning_Type = 'HASH')
      then

      Lv_String  := '(';
      WRITE_OUT(Lv_Lineno, Lv_Table_Owner, Lv_Table_Name, Lv_String);
      Lv_Lineno := Lv_Lineno + 1;

      open TAB_SUBPARTS_CURSOR (Lv_Table_Owner,Lv_Table_Name,
Lv_TP_Partition_Name);
      loop
         fetch TAB_SUBPARTS_CURSOR into  Lv_TSP_Subpartition_Name,
                                         Lv_TSP_Tablespace_Name;
        exit when TAB_SUBPARTS_CURSOR%NOTFOUND;
```

```
       Lv_String := ' SUBPARTITION '||Lv_TSP_Subpartition_Name;
       WRITE_OUT(Lv_Lineno, Lv_Table_Owner, Lv_Table_Name, Lv_String);
       Lv_Lineno := Lv_Lineno + 1;


       Lv_String  := ' TABLESPACE ' || Lv_TSP_Tablespace_Name ;
       WRITE_OUT(Lv_Lineno, Lv_Table_Owner, Lv_Table_Name, Lv_String);
       Lv_Lineno := Lv_Lineno + 1;

       Lv_String := ',';
       WRITE_OUT(Lv_Lineno, Lv_Table_Owner, Lv_Table_Name, Lv_String);
       Lv_Lineno := Lv_Lineno + 1;

      end loop;
     close TAB_SUBPARTS_CURSOR;
     Lv_Lineno  := Lv_Lineno - 1;
     Lv_String  := SUBSTR(Lv_String,1,(LENGTH(Lv_String) - 1));
     UPDATE_OUT(Lv_Lineno, Lv_Table_Owner, Lv_Table_Name,Lv_String);
     Lv_Lineno  := Lv_Lineno + 1;

     Lv_String  := ')';
     WRITE_OUT(Lv_Lineno, Lv_Table_Owner, Lv_Table_Name, Lv_String);
     Lv_Lineno := Lv_Lineno + 1;

    end if;

    Lv_String := ',';
    WRITE_OUT(Lv_Lineno, Lv_Table_Owner, Lv_Table_Name, Lv_String);
    Lv_Lineno := Lv_Lineno + 1;

    end loop;
    close TAB_PARTS_CURSOR;
    Lv_Lineno  := Lv_Lineno - 1;
    Lv_String  := SUBSTR(Lv_String,1,(LENGTH(Lv_String) - 1));
    UPDATE_OUT(Lv_Lineno, Lv_Table_Owner, Lv_Table_Name,Lv_String);
    Lv_Lineno  := Lv_Lineno + 1;

    Lv_String  := ')';
    WRITE_OUT(Lv_Lineno, Lv_Table_Owner, Lv_Table_Name, Lv_String);
    Lv_Lineno := Lv_Lineno + 1;

  else
   if (Lv_PT_Partitioning_Type = 'HASH')
   then

     Lv_String  := 'PARTITION BY HASH';
     WRITE_OUT(Lv_Lineno, Lv_Table_Owner, Lv_Table_Name, Lv_String);
     Lv_Lineno := Lv_Lineno + 1;
     Lv_String  := '(';
```

```
WRITE_OUT(Lv_Lineno, Lv_Table_Owner, Lv_Table_Name, Lv_String);
Lv_Lineno := Lv_Lineno + 1;

open PART_COL_CURSOR (Lv_Table_Owner,Lv_Table_Name);

loop
  fetch PART_COL_CURSOR into Lv_P_Column_Name;
  exit when PART_COL_CURSOR%NOTFOUND;


  Lv_String := Lv_P_Column_Name || ',';
  WRITE_OUT(Lv_Lineno, Lv_Table_Owner, Lv_Table_Name, Lv_String);
  Lv_Lineno := Lv_Lineno + 1;

end loop;
close PART_COL_CURSOR;
Lv_Lineno  := Lv_Lineno - 1;
Lv_String  := SUBSTR(Lv_String,1,(LENGTH(Lv_String) - 1));
UPDATE_OUT(Lv_Lineno, Lv_Table_Owner, Lv_Table_Name,Lv_String);
Lv_Lineno  := Lv_Lineno + 1;


Lv_String  := ')';
WRITE_OUT(Lv_Lineno, Lv_Table_Owner, Lv_Table_Name, Lv_String);
Lv_Lineno := Lv_Lineno + 1;

Lv_String  := '(';
WRITE_OUT(Lv_Lineno, Lv_Table_Owner, Lv_Table_Name, Lv_String);
Lv_Lineno := Lv_Lineno + 1;

open TAB_PARTS_CURSOR (Lv_Table_Owner,Lv_Table_Name);

loop
  fetch TAB_PARTS_CURSOR into  Lv_TP_Partition_Name,
                               Lv_TP_High_Value,
                               Lv_TP_Tablespace_Name,
                               Lv_TP_Pct_Free,
                               Lv_TP_Pct_Used,
                               Lv_TP_Ini_Trans,
                               Lv_TP_Max_Trans,
                               Lv_TP_Initial_Extent,
                               Lv_TP_Next_Extent,
                               Lv_TP_Min_Extents,
                               Lv_TP_Max_Extents,
                               Lv_TP_Pct_Increase,
                               Lv_TP_Freelists,
                               Lv_TP_Freelist_Groups,
                               Lv_TP_Buffer_Pool,
                               Lv_TP_Logging;
```

```
    exit when TAB_PARTS_CURSOR%NOTFOUND;


  Lv_String := ' PARTITION '||Lv_TP_Partition_Name;
  WRITE_OUT(Lv_Lineno, Lv_Table_Owner, Lv_Table_Name, Lv_String);
  Lv_Lineno := Lv_Lineno + 1;


  Lv_String := ' TABLESPACE ' || Lv_TP_Tablespace_Name ;
  WRITE_OUT(Lv_Lineno, Lv_Table_Owner, Lv_Table_Name, Lv_String);
  Lv_Lineno := Lv_Lineno + 1;

  Lv_String := ',';
  WRITE_OUT(Lv_Lineno, Lv_Table_Owner, Lv_Table_Name, Lv_String);
  Lv_Lineno := Lv_Lineno + 1;

  end loop;
  close TAB_PARTS_CURSOR;
  Lv_Lineno := Lv_Lineno - 1;
  Lv_String := SUBSTR(Lv_String,1,(LENGTH(Lv_String) - 1));
  UPDATE_OUT(Lv_Lineno, Lv_Table_Owner, Lv_Table_Name,Lv_String);
  Lv_Lineno := Lv_Lineno + 1;

  Lv_String := ')';
  WRITE_OUT(Lv_Lineno, Lv_Table_Owner, Lv_Table_Name, Lv_String);
  Lv_Lineno := Lv_Lineno + 1;

 end if;
end if;
end loop;
close PART_TABS_CURSOR;

end if;
```

The next section of the script deals with the **parallel** clause of the **create table** command, which determines the degree of parallelism for an operation on a single instance (the number of query servers used in the parallel operation) and is ignored by Oracle unless you have installed the Parallel Query Option. When you specify DEFAULT instead of an integer value, the number of query servers used is calculated from the number of CPUs and the number of devices storing the tables to be scanned in parallel. The **instances** clause within the **parallel** clause is ignored unless you are running Oracle Parallel Server, in which case it determines the number of parallel server instances to use in the operation.

```
  Lv_String := 'PARALLEL ( DEGREE ' || Lv_Degree
                                  || ' INSTANCES '
                                  || Lv_Instances
                                  || ' )';
```

```
        WRITE_OUT(Lv_Lineno, Lv_Table_Owner, Lv_Table_Name, Lv_String);
        Lv_Lineno := Lv_Lineno + 1;
```

Specifying **noparallel** when you create the table is the same as specifying **parallel (degree 1 instances 1)**.

The next section of the script deals with the CACHE and MONITORING attribute s of the table. Also, for partitioned tables, the ROW MOVEMENT clause specifies whether a row is allowed to be moved to a different partition or subpartition as a result of a change in one or more of its key value during an update operation.

```
if (Lv_Cache = 'Y')
      then
        Lv_String := ' CACHE ';
      else
        Lv_String := ' NOCACHE ';
      end if;
      WRITE_OUT(Lv_Lineno, Lv_Table_Owner, Lv_Table_Name, Lv_String);
      Lv_Lineno := Lv_Lineno + 1;

      if (Lv_Row_Movement = 'ENABLED')
      then
        Lv_String := ' ENABLE ROW MOVEMENT ';
        WRITE_OUT(Lv_Lineno, Lv_Table_Owner, Lv_Table_Name, Lv_String);
Lv_Lineno := Lv_Lineno + 1;
      end if;

      if (Lv_Monitoring = 'YES')
      then
        Lv_String := ' MONITORING ';
        WRITE_OUT(Lv_Lineno, Lv_Table_Owner, Lv_Table_Name, Lv_String);
Lv_Lineno := Lv_Lineno + 1;
      end if;
```

The final section of the script closes the cursor, spools the output to a file, and resets the environment to its original state:

```
end loop;
   close TAB_CURSOR;
end;
/
spool cre_tbl.sql
select Text
  from TAB_TEMP
 order by Id_Owner, Id_Name, Lineno
/
```

```
spool off
set newpage 1 verify on feedback 6 pagesize 24 linesize 80
heading on embedded off term on
undefine table_name
undefine table_owner
```

Display Data Distribution Across Table Partitions

As of Oracle8, you can use *partitions* to create physically separate sections of data within a table or an index. When you create a *range-based partitioned table*, you specify the maximum value for a *partition key* for each partition. When you store a row in the partitioned table, Oracle compares the partition key column's value to the ranges specified for the partitions. The row will be stored in one of the table's partitions, as determined by the value ranges defined for the partition key. By storing the data in partitions, you may simplify your database administration since the partitions will be smaller than a single table containing all of the partitions' data.

For example, if you have partitioned your table on time-based criteria, you may store all the records for the year 1999 in one partition and all the records for 2000 in a separate partition. Because the data is stored in two separate segments, you may find those segments easier to manage than if the data had been stored in a single segment. If you use partitions, you can also take advantage of the ability to perform DDL operations such as **truncate** and **alter index rebuild** on the partitions.

You must select your partition range values with care. You should monitor the distribution of data values across your table's partitions. If the table's data distribution does not match your expectations, you should consider altering the partition key ranges for the partitions. If the data values in your partitions are unevenly distributed, you may achieve only limited performance and administrative improvements from the use of partitions.

For this section, consider a table named WORKER. The **create table** command for the WORKER table is shown in the following listing:

```
create table WORKER (
Name            VARCHAR2(25),
Age             NUMBER,
Lodging         VARCHAR2(15),
constraint      WORKER_PK PRIMARY KEY(Name)
)
partition by range (Name)
  (partition PART1    values less than ('F'),
   partition PART2    values less than ('N'),
   partition PART3    values less than ('T'),
   partition PART4    values less than (MAXVALUE));
```

The WORKER table is partitioned based on the Name column. Names that begin with the letters *A* through *E* are stored in the partition called 'PART1'; names beginning *F* through *M* are stored in partition PART2; names beginning *N* through *S* are stored in partition PART3; and the rest of the names are stored in partition PART4. The Name column is the partition key, so its value determines where each row is physically stored.

For this example, sample records were inserted into each table. The WORKER table was then **analyze**d:

```
analyze table WORKER compute statistics;
```

PROGRAMMER'S NOTE   *You can **analyze** individual partitions. By default, all partitions of a table will be analyzed when you analyze a partitioned table.*

The part_dis.sql script, shown in the following listing, graphically displays the distribution of rows across partitions:

```
REM part_dis.sql
column Percent_of_Total format A60
column Partition_Name format A10
column High_Value format A8

select Partition_Name,
       High_Value,
       LPAD('o',100*DTP.Num_Rows/DBA_TABLES.Num_Rows-1,'o')
         Percent_of_Total
  from DBA_TAB_PARTITIONS DTP, DBA_TABLES
 where DBA_TABLES.Table_Name = '&table_name'
   and DBA_TABLES.Owner = '&owner'
   and DBA_TABLES.Table_Name = DTP.Table_Name
   and DBA_TABLES.Owner = DTP.Table_Owner
 order by Partition_Position;
clear columns
```

Sample output for the WORKER table is shown in the following listing:

```
PARTITION_ HIGH_VAL PERCENT_OF_TOTAL
---------- -------- ------------------------------------------------------
PART1      'F'      oooooooooooooooooooooooooooooooooooooooooooooooooooooo
PART2      'N'      oooooooooo
PART3      'T'      ooooooooooooooooooooooooooooooo
PART4      MAXVALUE oooo
```

The output graphically shows the distribution of rows across the partitions of the WORKER table. The PART1 partition, with a high value of 'F', contains the most rows, followed by PART3. The actual percentage values are not shown in this display, since the part_dis.sql script is intended to provide a quick visual report of the data distribution. In the "Annotations" section that follows, you will see additional ways to display the data.

Since the sample data is distributed unevenly, you may want to alter the partitioning rules used to create the table. You can use the partition-related clauses of the **alter table** command to modify partition ranges and add new partitions.

ANNOTATIONS

The part_dis.sql script uses the **LPAD** function to create a string of 'o' characters. In the part_dis.sql script, a partition's percentage of the total number of rows determines the number of 'o' characters displayed. If a partition accounts for 50 percent of the rows in a table, its record will contain 50 'o' characters.

The expression that generates the 'o' characters is shown here:

```
LPAD('o',100*DTP.Num_Rows/DBA_TABLES.Num_Rows-1,'o')
    Percent_of_Total
```

The number of rows in the partition (DTP.Num_Rows) divided by the number of rows in the table (DBA_TABLES.Num_Rows) is multiplied by 100 to determine the number of 'o' characters to print. Since one additional 'o' is always printed at the beginning, 1 is subtracted from the calculated percentage. If you add columns to the query, you will need to shorten the graphical part of the output. For example, you could cut the space required for the graphics in half by changing 100–50:

```
LPAD('o',50*DTP.Num_Rows/DBA_TABLES.Num_Rows-1,'o')
    Percent_of_Total
```

However, doing this will result in a graph that does not accurately show differences across partitions whose row volumes are very similar.

In addition to showing the row percentages graphically, you can select them by querying the Num_Rows values directly from the DBA_TAB_PARTITIONS data dictionary view. You can display the partitions across the page instead of down the page by creating a cross-tab report, as shown in the following listing. The cross-tab method requires you to know the names of the partitions; for this example the partition names for the WORKER table are used.

```
select SUM(DECODE(Partition_Name, 'PART1', Num_Rows, 0)) Part1,
       SUM(DECODE(Partition_Name, 'PART2', Num_Rows, 0)) Part2,
       SUM(DECODE(Partition_Name, 'PART3', Num_Rows, 0)) Part3,
       SUM(DECODE(Partition_Name, 'PART4', Num_Rows, 0)) Part4
  from DBA_TAB_PARTITIONS
 where Table_Name = '&table_name'
   and Table_Owner = '&table_owner';
```

Sample output is shown in this listing.

```
PART1       PART2       PART3       PART4
---------- ---------- ---------- ----------
    9216        2048        5120        1024
```

In the query, the Num_Rows values in DBA_TAB_PARTITIONS are summed. For the PART1 column of the query, any DBA_TAB_PARTITIONS row with a Partition_Name other than 'PART1' has its Num_Rows value replaced by 0:

```
select SUM(DECODE(Partition_Name, 'PART1', Num_Rows, 0)) Part1,
```

The same operation is performed on each partition name, resulting in the cross-tab report.

Generate Indexes

gen_indx_7.sql
gen_indx_80.sql
gen_indx_81n9.sql
part_idi.sql

Losing an index on a table can be a catastrophe in terms of performance. As you move a table from one database to another, or change the table within the database, it is difficult to save off and re-create indexes manually. The gen_indx_*.sql scripts can be used to generate a script to re-create all the indexes of a given table. The scripts gen_indx_7.sql and gen_indx_80.sql can be used for Oracle7.x and Oracle8.0.x, respectively, while gen_indx_81n9.sql can be used for Oracle8.1.x as well as Oracle9.x.

All the gen_indx_*.sql scripts are available on the CD-ROM included with the book; the following listing shows the script gen_indx_81n9.sql. Following the gen_indx_81n9.sql listing, you will see a sample set of generated index creation scripts.

```
REM
REM gen_indx_81n9.sql
REM This script can be used for Oracle8.1.x and above
REM
set echo off verify off term on feedback off pagesize 0
set heading off embedded off

select 'Creating index build script...' from DUAL;
accept table_name prompt "Enter the name of the Table: "
accept tab_owner prompt "Enter table owner: "
set term off

drop table I_TEMP;

create table I_TEMP (
        Lineno NUMBER,
        Id_Owner VARCHAR2(30),
        Id_Name VARCHAR2(30),
        Text VARCHAR2(800))
/

declare
    cursor IND_CURSOR is
            select Owner,
                    Index_Name,
                    Table_Owner,
                    Table_Name,
```

```
                    Uniqueness,
                    Tablespace_Name,
                    Ini_Trans,
                    Max_Trans,
                    Initial_Extent,
                    Next_Extent,
                    Min_Extents,
                    Max_Extents,
                    Pct_Increase,
                    Pct_Free,
                    Index_Type,
                    Degree,
                    Instances,
                    Logging,
                    Freelists,
                    Freelist_Groups,
                    Buffer_Pool,
                    Partitioned,
                    Compression,
                    Prefix_Length,
                    Funcidx_Status
            from DBA_INDEXES
        where Owner like UPPER('&&tab_owner')
          and Owner not in ('SYS','SYSTEM')
          and Table_Name like UPPER('&&table_name')
          and Index_Name not like 'SYS_%'
          and not exists (select 'x'
                            from DBA_CONSTRAINTS
                           where Constraint_Name = Index_Name
                             and Table_Name      = UPPER('&&tab_name'))
        order by Index_Name;
  cursor COL_CURSOR (I_Own VARCHAR2,
                     I_Ind VARCHAR2,
                     C_Own VARCHAR2,
                     C_Tab VARCHAR2) is
        select Column_Name
          from DBA_IND_COLUMNS
         where Index_Owner = I_Own
           and Index_Name  = I_Ind
           and Table_Owner = C_Own
           and Table_Name  = C_Tab
         order by Column_Position;

  cursor EXP_CURSOR (I_Own VARCHAR2,
                     I_Ind VARCHAR2,
                     C_Own VARCHAR2,
                     C_Tab VARCHAR2) is
        select Column_Expression
          from DBA_IND_EXPRESSIONS
```

```
        where Index_Owner = I_Own
          and Index_Name  = I_Ind
          and Table_Owner = C_Own
          and Table_Name  = C_Tab
        order by Column_Position;


cursor PART_IND_CURSOR (PI_Owner    VARCHAR2,
                        PI_Indname VARCHAR2) is
      select Locality,
             Partitioning_Type,
             Subpartitioning_Type
        from DBA_PART_INDEXES
       where Owner = PI_Owner
         and Index_Name  = PI_Indname;


cursor PART_COL_CURSOR (PI_Owner    VARCHAR2,
                        PI_Indname VARCHAR2) is
      select Column_Name
        from DBA_PART_KEY_COLUMNS
       where Owner = PI_Owner
         and Name  = PI_Indname
        order by Column_Position;


cursor IND_PARTS_CURSOR (PI_Owner    VARCHAR2,
                         PI_Tabname VARCHAR2) is
      select Partition_Name,
             High_Value,
             Tablespace_Name,
             Pct_Free,
             Ini_Trans,
             Max_Trans,
             Initial_Extent,
             Next_Extent,
             Min_Extent,
             Max_Extent,
             Pct_Increase,
             Freelists,
             Freelist_Groups,
             Buffer_Pool
        from DBA_IND_PARTITIONS
       where Index_Owner = PI_Owner
         and Index_Name  = PI_Tabname
        order by Partition_Position;


cursor IND_SUBPARTS_CURSOR (PI_Owner    VARCHAR2,
                            PI_Indname VARCHAR2,
                            PI_Partname VARCHAR2) is
      select Subpartition_Name,
             Tablespace_Name
```

```
        from DBA_IND_SUBPARTITIONS
       where Index_Owner = PI_Owner
         and Index_Name  = PI_Indname
         and Partition_Name = PI_Partname
       order by Subpartition_Position;



  Lv_Index_Owner          DBA_INDEXES.Owner%TYPE;
  Lv_Index_Name           DBA_INDEXES.Index_Name%TYPE;
  Lv_Table_Owner          DBA_INDEXES.Table_Owner%TYPE;
  Lv_Table_Name           DBA_INDEXES.Table_Name%TYPE;
  Lv_Uniqueness           DBA_INDEXES.Uniqueness%TYPE;
  Lv_Tablespace_Name      DBA_INDEXES.Tablespace_Name%TYPE;
  Lv_Ini_Trans            DBA_INDEXES.Ini_Trans%TYPE;
  Lv_Max_Trans            DBA_INDEXES.Max_Trans%TYPE;
  Lv_Initial_Extent       DBA_INDEXES.Initial_Extent%TYPE;
  Lv_Next_Extent          DBA_INDEXES.Next_Extent%TYPE;
  Lv_Min_Extents          DBA_INDEXES.Min_Extents%TYPE;
  Lv_Max_Extents          DBA_INDEXES.Max_Extents%TYPE;
  Lv_Pct_Increase         DBA_INDEXES.Pct_Increase%TYPE;
  Lv_Pct_Free             DBA_INDEXES.Pct_Free%TYPE;
  Lv_Index_Type           DBA_INDEXES.Index_Type%TYPE;
  Lv_Degree               DBA_INDEXES.Degree%TYPE;
  Lv_Instances            DBA_INDEXES.Instances%TYPE;
  Lv_Logging              DBA_INDEXES.Logging%TYPE;
  Lv_Freelists            DBA_INDEXES.Freelists%TYPE;
  Lv_Freelist_Groups      DBA_INDEXES.Freelist_Groups%TYPE;
  Lv_Buffer_Pool          DBA_INDEXES.Buffer_Pool%TYPE;
  Lv_Partitioned          DBA_INDEXES.Partitioned%TYPE;
  Lv_Compression          DBA_INDEXES.Compression%TYPE;
  Lv_Prefix_Length        DBA_INDEXES.Prefix_Length%TYPE;
  Lv_Funcidx_Status       DBA_INDEXES.Funcidx_Status%TYPE;


  Lv_Locality             DBA_PART_INDEXES.Locality%TYPE;
  Lv_Partitioning_Type    DBA_PART_INDEXES.Partitioning_Type%TYPE;
  Lv_Subpartitioning_Type DBA_PART_INDEXES.Subpartitioning_Type%TYPE;


  Lv_P_Column_Name    DBA_PART_KEY_COLUMNS.Column_Name%TYPE;

  Lv_IP_Partition_Name    DBA_IND_PARTITIONS.Partition_Name%TYPE;
  Lv_IP_High_Value        DBA_IND_PARTITIONS.High_Value%TYPE;
  Lv_IP_Tablespace_Name   DBA_IND_PARTITIONS.Tablespace_Name%TYPE;
  Lv_IP_Pct_Free          DBA_IND_PARTITIONS.Pct_Free%TYPE;
  Lv_IP_Ini_Trans         DBA_IND_PARTITIONS.Ini_Trans%TYPE;
  Lv_IP_Max_Trans         DBA_IND_PARTITIONS.Max_Trans%TYPE;
  Lv_IP_Initial_Extent    DBA_IND_PARTITIONS.Initial_Extent%TYPE;
```

```
    Lv_IP_Next_Extent              DBA_IND_PARTITIONS.Next_Extent%TYPE;
    Lv_IP_Min_Extents              DBA_IND_PARTITIONS.Min_Extent%TYPE;
    Lv_IP_Max_Extents              DBA_IND_PARTITIONS.Max_Extent%TYPE;
    Lv_IP_Pct_Increase             DBA_IND_PARTITIONS.Pct_Increase%TYPE;
    Lv_IP_Freelists                DBA_IND_PARTITIONS.Freelists%TYPE;
    Lv_IP_Freelist_Groups          DBA_IND_PARTITIONS.Freelist_Groups%TYPE;
    Lv_IP_Buffer_Pool              DBA_IND_PARTITIONS.Buffer_Pool%TYPE;

    Lv_ISP_Subpartition_Name DBA_IND_SUBPARTITIONS.Subpartition_
    Name%TYPE;
    Lv_ISP_Tablespace_Name   DBA_IND_SUBPARTITIONS.Tablespace_
    Name%TYPE;


    Lv_Column_Name                 DBA_IND_COLUMNS.Column_Name%TYPE;


    Lv_Column_Expression           DBA_IND_EXPRESSIONS.Column_Expression%TYPE;


    Lv_First_Rec         BOOLEAN;
    Lv_String            VARCHAR2(800);
    Lv_Lineno            NUMBER;
    Lv_Part_Type         VARCHAR2(10);

    procedure WRITE_OUT(P_Line INTEGER, P_Owner varchar2, P_Name
                        VARCHAR2, P_String VARCHAR2) is
    begin
       insert into I_TEMP (Lineno, Id_Owner, Id_Name, Text)
              values (P_Line,P_Owner,P_Name,P_String);
    end;


    procedure UPDATE_OUT(P_Line INTEGER,  P_Owner VARCHAR2,
                         P_Name VARCHAR2, P_String VARCHAR2) is
    begin
       update I_TEMP
          set Text = P_String
        where Lineno = P_Line
          and Id_Owner = P_Owner
          and Id_Name  = P_Name;
    end;


begin
    open IND_CURSOR;
    loop
       fetch IND_CURSOR into Lv_Index_Owner,
                             Lv_Index_Name,
                             Lv_Table_Owner,
                             Lv_Table_Name,
                             Lv_Uniqueness,
                             Lv_Tablespace_Name,
                             Lv_Ini_Trans,
```

```
                                Lv_Max_Trans,
                                Lv_Initial_Extent,
                                Lv_Next_Extent,
                                Lv_Min_Extents,
                                Lv_Max_Extents,
                                Lv_Pct_Increase,
                                Lv_Pct_Free,
                                Lv_Index_Type,
                                Lv_Degree,
                                Lv_Instances,
                                Lv_Logging,
                                Lv_Freelists,
                                Lv_Freelist_Groups,
                                Lv_Buffer_Pool,
                                Lv_Partitioned,
                                Lv_Compression,
                                Lv_Prefix_Length,
                                Lv_Funcidx_Status;
        exit when IND_CURSOR%NOTFOUND;
        Lv_Lineno := 1;
        Lv_First_Rec := TRUE;

        Lv_String:=' ';

        if (Lv_Uniqueness = 'UNIQUE')
        then
            Lv_String:=Lv_String||' UNIQUE ';
        end if;

        if (INSTR(Lv_Index_Type,'BITMAP',1) != 0)
        then
            Lv_String:=Lv_String||' BITMAP ';
        end if;

        Lv_String:= 'CREATE '||Lv_String||' INDEX '
                            ||LOWER(LV_INDEX_OWNER) || '.'
                            ||LOWER(Lv_Index_Name);
         WRITE_OUT(Lv_Lineno, Lv_Index_Owner, Lv_Index_Name, Lv_String);
         Lv_Lineno := Lv_Lineno + 1;


    if (Lv_Funcidx_Status IS NULL)
    then

      open COL_CURSOR(Lv_Index_Owner,Lv_Index_Name,Lv_Table_Owner,Lv_
      Table_Name);
      loop
         fetch COL_CURSOR into Lv_Column_Name;
         exit when COL_CURSOR%NOTFOUND;
```

```
    if (Lv_First_Rec)
    then
       Lv_String := '    ON '|| LOWER(Lv_Table_Owner) || '.' ||
                       LOWER(Lv_Table_Name)||' (';
       Lv_First_Rec := FALSE;
    else
       Lv_String := Lv_String || ',';
    end if;
    Lv_String := Lv_String || LOWER(Lv_Column_Name);
 end loop;
 close COL_CURSOR;
 Lv_String := Lv_String || ')';
 WRITE_OUT(Lv_Lineno, Lv_Index_Owner, Lv_Index_Name, Lv_String);
 Lv_Lineno := Lv_Lineno + 1;

else

 open EXP_CURSOR(Lv_Index_Owner,Lv_Index_Name,
Lv_Table_Owner,Lv_Table_Name);
 loop
    fetch EXP_CURSOR into Lv_Column_Expression;
    exit when EXP_CURSOR%NOTFOUND;
    if (Lv_First_Rec)
    then
       Lv_String := '    ON '|| LOWER(Lv_Table_Owner) || '.' ||
                       LOWER(Lv_Table_Name)||' (';
       Lv_First_Rec := FALSE;
    else
       Lv_String := Lv_String || ',';
    end if;
    Lv_String := Lv_String || LOWER(Lv_Column_Expression);
 end loop;
 close EXP_CURSOR;
 Lv_String := Lv_String || ')';
 WRITE_OUT(Lv_Lineno, Lv_Index_Owner, Lv_Index_Name, Lv_String);
 Lv_Lineno := Lv_Lineno + 1;

end if;


 if (Lv_Partitioned = 'YES')
 then
    open PART_IND_CURSOR(Lv_Index_Owner,Lv_Index_Name);
    loop
      fetch PART_IND_CURSOR into Lv_Locality,
                                 Lv_Partitioning_Type,
                                 Lv_Subpartitioning_Type;
      exit when PART_IND_CURSOR%NOTFOUND;
```

```
            if (Lv_Locality = 'GLOBAL')
            then

            Lv_String:=' GLOBAL PARTITION BY RANGE ';
            WRITE_OUT(Lv_Lineno, Lv_Index_Owner, Lv_Index_Name, Lv_String);
            Lv_Lineno := Lv_Lineno + 1;

            Lv_String   := '(';
            WRITE_OUT(Lv_Lineno, Lv_Index_Owner, Lv_Index_Name, Lv_String);
            Lv_Lineno := Lv_Lineno + 1;

                open PART_COL_CURSOR (Lv_Index_Owner,Lv_Index_Name);
                loop
                   fetch PART_COL_CURSOR into Lv_P_Column_Name;
                   exit when PART_COL_CURSOR%NOTFOUND;


                   Lv_String := Lv_P_Column_Name || ',';
                   WRITE_OUT(Lv_Lineno, Lv_Index_Owner,
Lv_Index_Name, Lv_String);
                   Lv_Lineno := Lv_Lineno + 1;

                end loop;
                close PART_COL_CURSOR;
                Lv_Lineno  := Lv_Lineno - 1;
                Lv_String  := SUBSTR(Lv_String,1,(LENGTH(Lv_String) - 1));
                UPDATE_OUT(Lv_Lineno, Lv_Index_Owner,
Lv_Index_Name,Lv_String);
                Lv_Lineno  := Lv_Lineno + 1;


                Lv_String  := ')';
                WRITE_OUT(Lv_Lineno, Lv_Index_Owner,
Lv_Index_Name, Lv_String);
                Lv_Lineno := Lv_Lineno + 1;

                Lv_String  := '(';
                WRITE_OUT(Lv_Lineno, Lv_Index_Owner,
Lv_Index_Name, Lv_String);
                Lv_Lineno := Lv_Lineno + 1;

                open IND_PARTS_CURSOR (Lv_Index_Owner,Lv_Index_Name);
                loop
                fetch IND_PARTS_CURSOR into  Lv_IP_Partition_Name,
                                             Lv_IP_High_Value,
                                             Lv_IP_Tablespace_Name,
                                             Lv_IP_Pct_Free,
                                             Lv_IP_Ini_Trans,
                                             Lv_IP_Max_Trans,
```

```
                        Lv_IP_Initial_Extent,
                        Lv_IP_Next_Extent,
                        Lv_IP_Min_Extents,
                        Lv_IP_Max_Extents,
                        Lv_IP_Pct_Increase,
                        Lv_IP_Freelists,
                        Lv_IP_Freelist_Groups,
                        Lv_IP_Buffer_Pool;
            exit when IND_PARTS_CURSOR%NOTFOUND;




            Lv_String := ' PARTITION '||Lv_IP_Partition_Name;
            WRITE_OUT(Lv_Lineno, Lv_Index_Owner,
Lv_Index_Name, Lv_String);
            Lv_Lineno := Lv_Lineno + 1;

            Lv_String :=' VALUES LESS THAN ('||Lv_IP_High_Value||') ';
            WRITE_OUT(Lv_Lineno, Lv_Index_Owner,
Lv_Index_Name, Lv_String);
            Lv_Lineno := Lv_Lineno + 1;

            Lv_String  := ' TABLESPACE ' || Lv_IP_Tablespace_Name ;
            WRITE_OUT(Lv_Lineno, Lv_Index_Owner,
Lv_Index_Name, Lv_String);
            Lv_Lineno := Lv_Lineno + 1;

            Lv_String  := ' PCTFREE ' || Lv_IP_Pct_Free ;
            WRITE_OUT(Lv_Lineno, Lv_Index_Owner,
Lv_Index_Name, Lv_String);
            Lv_Lineno := Lv_Lineno + 1;


            Lv_String  := ' INITRANS ' || Lv_IP_Ini_Trans ;
            WRITE_OUT(Lv_Lineno, Lv_Index_Owner,
Lv_Index_Name, Lv_String);
            Lv_Lineno := Lv_Lineno + 1;

            Lv_String  := ' MAXTRANS ' || Lv_IP_Max_Trans ;
            WRITE_OUT(Lv_Lineno, Lv_Index_Owner,
Lv_Index_Name, Lv_String);
            Lv_Lineno := Lv_Lineno + 1;

            Lv_String  := ' STORAGE';
            WRITE_OUT(Lv_Lineno, Lv_Index_Owner,
Lv_Index_Name, Lv_String);
            Lv_Lineno := Lv_Lineno + 1;
            Lv_String  := '(';
```

```
             WRITE_OUT(Lv_Lineno, Lv_Index_Owner,
Lv_Index_Name, Lv_String);
             Lv_Lineno := Lv_Lineno + 1;

             Lv_String  := '   INITIAL ' || Lv_IP_Initial_Extent ;
             WRITE_OUT(Lv_Lineno, Lv_Index_Owner,
Lv_Index_Name, Lv_String);
             Lv_Lineno := Lv_Lineno + 1;

             Lv_String  := '   NEXT ' || Lv_IP_Next_Extent ;
             WRITE_OUT(Lv_Lineno, Lv_Index_Owner,
Lv_Index_Name, Lv_String);
             Lv_Lineno := Lv_Lineno + 1;

             Lv_String  := '   MINEXTENTS ' || Lv_IP_Min_Extents ;
             WRITE_OUT(Lv_Lineno, Lv_Index_Owner,
Lv_Index_Name, Lv_String);
             Lv_Lineno := Lv_Lineno + 1;

             Lv_String  := '   MAXEXTENTS ' || Lv_IP_Max_Extents ;
             WRITE_OUT(Lv_Lineno, Lv_Index_Owner, Lv_Index_Name,
             Lv_String);
             Lv_Lineno := Lv_Lineno + 1;

             Lv_String  := '   PCTINCREASE ' || Lv_IP_Pct_Increase ;
             WRITE_OUT(Lv_Lineno, Lv_Index_Owner,
Lv_Index_Name, Lv_String);
             Lv_Lineno := Lv_Lineno + 1;

             Lv_String  := '   FREELISTS ' || Lv_IP_Freelists ;
             WRITE_OUT(Lv_Lineno, Lv_Index_Owner,
Lv_Index_Name, Lv_String);
             Lv_Lineno := Lv_Lineno + 1;

             Lv_String  := '   FREELIST GROUPS '
             || Lv_IP_Freelist_Groups ;
             WRITE_OUT(Lv_Lineno, Lv_Index_Owner,
Lv_Index_Name, Lv_String);
             Lv_Lineno := Lv_Lineno + 1;

             Lv_String  := '   BUFFER_POOL ' || Lv_IP_Buffer_Pool ;
             WRITE_OUT(Lv_Lineno, Lv_Index_Owner,
Lv_Index_Name, Lv_String);
             Lv_Lineno := Lv_Lineno + 1;

             Lv_String  := ')';
             WRITE_OUT(Lv_Lineno, Lv_Index_Owner,
Lv_Index_Name, Lv_String);
             Lv_Lineno := Lv_Lineno + 1;
```

```
                Lv_String := ',';
                WRITE_OUT(Lv_Lineno, Lv_Index_Owner,
    Lv_Index_Name, Lv_String);
                Lv_Lineno := Lv_Lineno + 1;

                end loop;
                close IND_PARTS_CURSOR;
                Lv_Lineno   := Lv_Lineno - 1;
                Lv_String   := SUBSTR(Lv_String,1,(LENGTH(Lv_String) - 1));
                UPDATE_OUT(Lv_Lineno, Lv_Index_Owner,
    Lv_Index_Name, Lv_String);
                Lv_Lineno   := Lv_Lineno + 1;

                Lv_String   := ')';
                WRITE_OUT(Lv_Lineno, Lv_Index_Owner,
    Lv_Index_Name, Lv_String);
                Lv_Lineno := Lv_Lineno + 1;



            else
                Lv_String:=' LOCAL ';
                WRITE_OUT(Lv_Lineno, Lv_Index_Owner,
    Lv_Index_Name, Lv_String);
                Lv_Lineno := Lv_Lineno + 1;

                Lv_Part_Type := null;

                if (Lv_Partitioning_Type = 'HASH')
                then
                    Lv_Part_Type:= 'HASH';
                else
                    if (Lv_Subpartitioning_Type IS NULL)
                    then
                        Lv_Part_Type:= 'RANGE';
                    else
                        Lv_Part_Type:='COMPOSITE';
                    end if;
                end if;

                Lv_String   := '(';
                WRITE_OUT(Lv_Lineno, Lv_Index_Owner,
    Lv_Index_Name, Lv_String);
                Lv_Lineno := Lv_Lineno + 1;

                open IND_PARTS_CURSOR (Lv_Index_Owner,Lv_Index_Name);
                loop
                fetch IND_PARTS_CURSOR into  Lv_IP_Partition_Name,
```

```
                                Lv_IP_High_Value,
                                Lv_IP_Tablespace_Name,
                                Lv_IP_Pct_Free,
                                Lv_IP_Ini_Trans,
                                Lv_IP_Max_Trans,
                                Lv_IP_Initial_Extent,
                                Lv_IP_Next_Extent,
                                Lv_IP_Min_Extents,
                                Lv_IP_Max_Extents,
                                Lv_IP_Pct_Increase,
                                Lv_IP_Freelists,
                                Lv_IP_Freelist_Groups,
                                Lv_IP_Buffer_Pool;
              exit when IND_PARTS_CURSOR%NOTFOUND;


              Lv_String := ' PARTITION '||Lv_IP_Partition_Name;
              WRITE_OUT(Lv_Lineno, Lv_Index_Owner,
Lv_Index_Name, Lv_String);
              Lv_Lineno := Lv_Lineno + 1;

              Lv_String   := ' TABLESPACE ' || Lv_IP_Tablespace_Name ;
              WRITE_OUT(Lv_Lineno, Lv_Index_Owner,
Lv_Index_Name, Lv_String);
              Lv_Lineno := Lv_Lineno + 1;

          if (Lv_Part_Type = 'RANGE' or Lv_Part_Type = 'COMPOSITE')
          then

              Lv_String   := ' PCTFREE ' || Lv_IP_Pct_Free ;
              WRITE_OUT(Lv_Lineno, Lv_Index_Owner,
Lv_Index_Name, Lv_String);
              Lv_Lineno := Lv_Lineno + 1;


              Lv_String   := ' INITRANS ' || Lv_IP_Ini_Trans ;
              WRITE_OUT(Lv_Lineno, Lv_Index_Owner,
Lv_Index_Name, Lv_String);
              Lv_Lineno := Lv_Lineno + 1;

              Lv_String   := ' MAXTRANS ' || Lv_IP_Max_Trans ;
              WRITE_OUT(Lv_Lineno, Lv_Index_Owner,
Lv_Index_Name, Lv_String);
              Lv_Lineno := Lv_Lineno + 1;

              Lv_String   := ' STORAGE';
              WRITE_OUT(Lv_Lineno, Lv_Index_Owner,
Lv_Index_Name, Lv_String);
              Lv_Lineno := Lv_Lineno + 1;
```

```
                    Lv_String  := '(';
                    WRITE_OUT(Lv_Lineno, Lv_Index_Owner,
Lv_Index_Name, Lv_String);
                    Lv_Lineno := Lv_Lineno + 1;

                    Lv_String  := '    INITIAL ' || Lv_IP_Initial_Extent ;
                    WRITE_OUT(Lv_Lineno, Lv_Index_Owner,
Lv_Index_Name, Lv_String);
                    Lv_Lineno := Lv_Lineno + 1;

                    Lv_String  := '    NEXT ' || Lv_IP_Next_Extent ;
                    WRITE_OUT(Lv_Lineno, Lv_Index_Owner,
Lv_Index_Name, Lv_String);
                    Lv_Lineno := Lv_Lineno + 1;

                    Lv_String  := '    MINEXTENTS ' || Lv_IP_Min_Extents ;
                    WRITE_OUT(Lv_Lineno, Lv_Index_Owner,
Lv_Index_Name, Lv_String);
                    Lv_Lineno := Lv_Lineno + 1;

                    Lv_String  := '    MAXEXTENTS ' || Lv_IP_Max_Extents ;
                    WRITE_OUT(Lv_Lineno, Lv_Index_Owner,
Lv_Index_Name, Lv_String);
                    Lv_Lineno := Lv_Lineno + 1;

                    Lv_String  := '    PCTINCREASE ' || Lv_IP_Pct_Increase ;
                    WRITE_OUT(Lv_Lineno, Lv_Index_Owner,
Lv_Index_Name, Lv_String);
                    Lv_Lineno := Lv_Lineno + 1;

                    Lv_String  := '    FREELISTS ' || Lv_IP_Freelists ;
                    WRITE_OUT(Lv_Lineno, Lv_Index_Owner,
Lv_Index_Name, Lv_String);
                    Lv_Lineno := Lv_Lineno + 1;

                    Lv_String  := '    FREELIST GROUPS '
                    || Lv_IP_Freelist_Groups ;
                    WRITE_OUT(Lv_Lineno, Lv_Index_Owner,
Lv_Index_Name, Lv_String);
                    Lv_Lineno := Lv_Lineno + 1;

                    Lv_String  := '    BUFFER_POOL ' || Lv_IP_Buffer_Pool ;
                    WRITE_OUT(Lv_Lineno, Lv_Index_Owner,
Lv_Index_Name, Lv_String);
                    Lv_Lineno := Lv_Lineno + 1;

                    Lv_String  := ')';
                    WRITE_OUT(Lv_Lineno, Lv_Index_Owner,
Lv_Index_Name, Lv_String);
```

```
            Lv_Lineno := Lv_Lineno + 1;

            if (Lv_Part_Type = 'COMPOSITE')
            then

                Lv_String  := '(';
                WRITE_OUT(Lv_Lineno, Lv_Index_Owner, Lv_Index_Name,
                        Lv_String);
                Lv_Lineno := Lv_Lineno + 1;
                open IND_SUBPARTS_CURSOR
(Lv_Index_Owner, Lv_Index_Name,Lv_IP_Partition_Name);
                loop
                fetch IND_SUBPARTS_CURSOR into
                            Lv_ISP_Subpartition_Name,
                            Lv_ISP_Tablespace_Name;
                exit when IND_SUBPARTS_CURSOR%NOTFOUND;


                Lv_String := ' SUBPARTITION '||
Lv_ISP_Subpartition_Name;
                WRITE_OUT(Lv_Lineno, Lv_Index_Owner, Lv_Index_Name,
                        Lv_String);
                Lv_Lineno := Lv_Lineno + 1;


                Lv_String  := ' TABLESPACE ' ||
Lv_ISP_Tablespace_Name ;
                WRITE_OUT(Lv_Lineno, Lv_Index_Owner, Lv_Index_Name,
                        Lv_String);
                Lv_Lineno := Lv_Lineno + 1;

                Lv_String := ',';
                WRITE_OUT(Lv_Lineno, Lv_Index_Owner, Lv_Index_Name,
                        Lv_String);
                Lv_Lineno := Lv_Lineno + 1;

                end loop;
                close IND_SUBPARTS_CURSOR;
                Lv_Lineno  := Lv_Lineno - 1;
                Lv_String  :=
                 SUBSTR(Lv_String,1,(LENGTH(Lv_String) - 1));
                UPDATE_OUT(Lv_Lineno, Lv_Index_Owner,
                        Lv_Index_Name,Lv_String);
                Lv_Lineno  := Lv_Lineno + 1;

                Lv_String := ')';
                WRITE_OUT(Lv_Lineno, Lv_Index_Owner, Lv_Index_Name,
                        Lv_String);
                Lv_Lineno := Lv_Lineno + 1;
```

```
              end if;


          end if;

            Lv_String := ',';
            WRITE_OUT(Lv_Lineno, Lv_Index_Owner,
Lv_Index_Name, Lv_String);
            Lv_Lineno := Lv_Lineno + 1;

            end loop;
            close IND_PARTS_CURSOR;
            Lv_Lineno  := Lv_Lineno - 1;
            Lv_String  := SUBSTR(Lv_String,1,(LENGTH(Lv_String) - 1));
            UPDATE_OUT(Lv_Lineno, Lv_Index_Owner,
Lv_Index_Name, Lv_String);
            Lv_Lineno  := Lv_Lineno + 1;

            Lv_String  := ')';
            WRITE_OUT(Lv_Lineno, Lv_Index_Owner,
Lv_Index_Name, Lv_String);
            Lv_Lineno := Lv_Lineno + 1;


        end if;

      end loop;
      close PART_IND_CURSOR;

    else

    Lv_String := null;
    Lv_String := 'PCTFREE ' || TO_CHAR(Lv_Pct_Free);
    WRITE_OUT(Lv_Lineno, Lv_Index_Owner, Lv_Index_Name, Lv_String);
    Lv_Lineno := Lv_Lineno + 1;
    Lv_String := 'INITRANS ' || TO_CHAR(Lv_Ini_Trans) ||
                ' MAXTRANS ' || TO_CHAR(Lv_Max_Trans);
    WRITE_OUT(Lv_Lineno, Lv_Index_Owner, Lv_Index_Name, Lv_String);
    Lv_Lineno := Lv_Lineno + 1;
    Lv_String := 'TABLESPACE ' || Lv_Tablespace_Name || ' STORAGE (';
    WRITE_OUT(Lv_Lineno, Lv_Index_Owner, Lv_Index_Name, Lv_String);
    Lv_Lineno := Lv_Lineno + 1;
    Lv_String := 'INITIAL ' || TO_CHAR(Lv_Initial_Extent) ||
                ' NEXT ' || TO_CHAR(Lv_Next_Extent);
    WRITE_OUT(Lv_Lineno, Lv_Index_Owner, Lv_Index_Name, Lv_String);
    Lv_Lineno := Lv_Lineno + 1;
    Lv_String :=  ' MINEXTENTS ' || TO_CHAR(Lv_Min_Extents) ||
                ' MAXEXTENTS ' || TO_CHAR(Lv_Max_Extents) ||
```

```
                                ' PCTINCREASE ' || TO_CHAR(Lv_Pct_Increase) ||
                                ' FREELISTS ' || Lv_Freelists ||
                                ' FREELIST GROUPS ' || Lv_Freelist_Groups ||
                                ' BUFFER_POOL ' || Lv_Buffer_Pool || ')';
        WRITE_OUT(Lv_Lineno, Lv_Index_Owner, Lv_Index_Name, Lv_String);
        Lv_Lineno := Lv_Lineno + 1;

      end if;

      if (Lv_Logging = 'YES')
      then
        Lv_String  := ' LOGGING ';
      else
        Lv_String  := ' NOLOGGING ';
      end if;
      WRITE_OUT(Lv_Lineno, Lv_Index_Owner, Lv_Index_Name, Lv_String);
      Lv_Lineno := Lv_Lineno + 1;

      Lv_String  := 'PARALLEL ( DEGREE ' || Lv_Degree
                                         || ' INSTANCES '
                                         || Lv_Instances
                                         || ' )';
      WRITE_OUT(Lv_Lineno, Lv_Index_Owner, Lv_Index_Name, Lv_String);
      Lv_Lineno := Lv_Lineno + 1;

      if (Lv_Compression = 'DISABLED')
      then
          Lv_String := ' NOCOMPRESS ';
      else
          Lv_String := ' COMPRESS '||Lv_Prefix_Length;
      end if;
      WRITE_OUT(Lv_Lineno, Lv_Index_Owner, Lv_Index_Name, Lv_String);
      Lv_Lineno := Lv_Lineno + 1;



      Lv_String := '/';
      WRITE_OUT(Lv_Lineno, Lv_Index_Owner, Lv_Index_Name, Lv_String);
      Lv_Lineno := Lv_Lineno + 1;
      Lv_Lineno := Lv_Lineno + 1;
      Lv_String:='                                                    ';
      WRITE_OUT(Lv_Lineno, Lv_Index_Owner, Lv_Index_Name, Lv_String);
    end loop;
    close IND_CURSOR;
end;
/

spool cre_indx.sql
set heading off
```

```
col Text format a80 word_wrap

select Text
  from I_TEMP
 order by Id_Owner, Id_Name, Lineno;
spool off
set newpage 1 verify on feedback 6 pagesize 24 linesize 80
set heading on embedded off recsep wrapped
undefine table_name
undefine table_owner
clear columns
```

Sample output for the gen_indx_81n9.sql script is shown in the following listing. The gen_indx_81n9.sql script will generate the following script to re-create all indexes on all the tables owned by the specified owner.

```
CREATE INDEX app.terminals_cpy_fk_I
ON app.app_terminals (cpy_abbr)
PCTFREE 0
INITRANS 2 MAXTRANS 255
TABLESPACE USER_INDEX STORAGE (
INITIAL 1048576 NEXT 516096
MINEXTENTS 1 MAXEXTENTS 300 PCTINCREASE 0)
/

CREATE INDEX app.terminals_epe_fk_i
ON app.app_terminals (epe_code)
PCTFREE 0
INITRANS 2 MAXTRANS 255
TABLESPACE USER_INDEX STORAGE (
INITIAL 1048576 NEXT 516096
MINEXTENTS 1 MAXEXTENTS 300 PCTINCREASE 0)
/

CREATE INDEX app.terminals_terminals_fk_i
ON app.app_terminals (terminals_terminal_no)
PCTFREE 0
INITRANS 2 MAXTRANS 255
TABLESPACE USER_INDEX STORAGE (
INITIAL 1048576 NEXT 516096
MINEXTENTS 1 MAXEXTENTS 300 PCTINCREASE 0)
/ CREATE    INDEX app.mind1
ON app.account (accountno,balance)
PCTFREE 10
INITRANS 2 MAXTRANS 255
TABLESPACE USERS STORAGE (
INITIAL 131072 NEXT 131072
MINEXTENTS 1 MAXEXTENTS 4096 PCTINCREASE 0 FREELISTS 1 FREELIST GROUPS 1
BUFFER_POOL DEFAULT)
```

```
LOGGING
PARALLEL ( DEGREE 1 INSTANCES 1 )
NOCOMPRESS
/

CREATE    INDEX app.mpart1i
ON app.mpart1 (c1)
GLOBAL PARTITION BY RANGE(C1)
(PARTITION PI1
VALUES LESS THAN (2)
TABLESPACE USERS PCTFREE 10
INITRANS 2 MAXTRANS 255
STORAGE
(INITIAL 131072 NEXT 131072
MINEXTENTS 1 MAXEXTENTS 4096
PCTINCREASE 0 FREELISTS 1
FREELIST GROUPS 1
BUFFER_POOL DEFAULT)
,
PARTITION PI2
VALUES LESS THAN (maxvalue)
TABLESPACE USERS PCTFREE 10
INITRANS 2 MAXTRANS 255
STORAGE
(INITIAL 131072 NEXT 131072
MINEXTENTS 1 MAXEXTENTS 4096
PCTINCREASE 0 FREELISTS 1
FREELIST GROUPS 1
BUFFER_POOL DEFAULT))
NOLOGGING
PARALLEL ( DEGREE 1 INSTANCES 1 )
NOCOMPRESS
/

CREATE    INDEX app.mpart1i_local
ON app.mpart1 (c2)
LOCAL
(PARTITION PI1L
TABLESPACE USERS PCTFREE 10
INITRANS 2 MAXTRANS 255
STORAGE
(INITIAL 131072 NEXT 131072
MINEXTENTS 1 MAXEXTENTS 4096
PCTINCREASE 0 FREELISTS 1
FREELIST GROUPS 1
BUFFER_POOL DEFAULT)
,
PARTITION PI2L
TABLESPACE USERS PCTFREE 10
```

```
INITRANS 2 MAXTRANS 255
STORAGE
(INITIAL 131072 NEXT 131072
MINEXTENTS 1 MAXEXTENTS 4096
PCTINCREASE 0 FREELISTS 1
FREELIST GROUPS 1
BUFFER_POOL DEFAULT))
NOLOGGING
PARALLEL ( DEGREE 1 INSTANCES 1 )
NOCOMPRESS
/


CREATE    INDEX app.mpart2i_local
ON app.mpart6 (c1)
LOCAL
(PARTITION PI100L
TABLESPACE TOOLS PCTFREE 10
INITRANS 2 MAXTRANS 255
STORAGE
(INITIAL 106496 NEXT 32768
MINEXTENTS 1 MAXEXTENTS 4096
PCTINCREASE 0 FREELISTS 1
FREELIST GROUPS 1
BUFFER_POOL DEFAULT)
,
PARTITION PI200L
TABLESPACE USERS PCTFREE 10
INITRANS 2 MAXTRANS 255
STORAGE
(INITIAL 106496 NEXT 131072
MINEXTENTS 1 MAXEXTENTS 4096
PCTINCREASE 0 FREELISTS 1
FREELIST GROUPS 1
BUFFER_POOL DEFAULT))
NOLOGGING
PARALLEL ( DEGREE 1 INSTANCES 1 )
NOCOMPRESS
/
```

ANNOTATIONS

The gen_indx_*.sql script generates all indexes created against all tables owned by a specified owner, excluding indexes named by Oracle (SYS_ #####) and named indexes created by a constraint declared on the table. Indexes are named by Oracle when a constraint is declared on the table or a column without naming the constraint. Re-creating these indexes manually can cause a conflict with a system-allocated name. Indexes created by a constraint are re-created when the constraint is re-created. SQL to re-create constraints is part of the gen_tbl_*.sql script in the preceding section of this chapter.

The script gen_indx_81n9.sql, shown previously, can be used for Oracle8.1.x and above; it uses a temporary table to hold individual lines of the **create index** statement, writing to the table rather than using DBMS_OUTPUT.PUT_LINE so that you can extract the information for an individual index or for all indexes on the table from the temporary table. Using the DBMS_OUTPUT procedure would force you to save and edit the output file for the index you want.

The first section of the script does the initial setup, prompting for the table name and table owner for later use via the **accept** command, which, unlike simply using the variable with the '&' or '&&' in a SQL statement, allows you to define your own prompt for the variable. You can enter **'%table_name%'** to generate a script for all indexes on tables with a similar name, or enter **'%'** to generate all indexes on all tables owned by *tab_owner*.

The SQL*Plus **set** command turns off headers (**pagesize 0**), row counts (**feedback off**), and displays of old and new values for the *table_name* and *tab_owner* variables (**verify off**).

```
set echo off verify off term on feedback off pagesize 0
set heading off embedded off

select 'Creating index build script...' from DUAL;
accept table_name prompt "Enter the name of the Table: "
accept tab_owner prompt "Enter table owner: "
set term off
```

The next section of the script creates a temporary table to hold each **create index** command and its owner. The Lineno column is used for ordering of the lines of the **create index** command by index name.

```
drop table I_TEMP;
create table I_TEMP (
        Lineno NUMBER,
        Id_Owner VARCHAR2(30),
        Id_Name VARCHAR2(30),
        Text VARCHAR2(800))
/
```

The IND_CURSOR cursor, defined in the next section of the script, selects the storage information from DBA_INDEXES, where the table name matches the input variable *table_name* and the table owner matches the input variable *tab_owner*. By selecting for Table_Name rather than Index_Name, all indexes on the table will be processed. Using **like** instead of = in the **where** clause allows for wildcards. The check for index names that are not like 'SYS_%' removes all indexes with Oracle-generated names from the rows returned. The **not exists** in the **where** clause of the **select** does not need an actual value returned; the check is just to see whether the index was created by a constraint. If the index was created by a constraint, the **not**

exists fails and the index will not be included in the generated SQL. Use the gen_tbl_*.sql script shown in the preceding section of this chapter to generate the SQL necessary to re-create those indexes.

```
declare
    cursor IND_CURSOR is
        select Owner,
                Index_Name,
                Table_Owner,
                Table_Name,
                Uniqueness,
                Tablespace_Name,
                Ini_Trans,
                Max_Trans,
                Initial_Extent,
                Next_Extent,
                Min_Extents,
                Max_Extents,
                Pct_Increase,
                Pct_Free,
                Index_Type,
                Degree,
                Instances,
                Logging,
                Freelists,
                Freelist_Groups,
                Buffer_Pool,
                Partitioned,
                Compression,
                Prefix_Length,
                Funcidx_Status
        from DBA_INDEXES
        where Owner like UPPER('&&tab_owner')
          and Table_Name like UPPER('&&table_name')
          and Index_Name not like 'SYS_%'
          and not exists (select 'x'
                            from DBA_CONSTRAINTS
                            where Constraint_Name = Index_Name
                              and Table_Name      = UPPER('&&tab_name'))
        order by Index_Name;
```

In the next section of the script, the COL_CURSOR cursor selects the column name from DBA_IND_COLUMNS for each index selected by the IND_CURSOR cursor. The results are ordered by Column_Position, so that indexes created on multiple columns will be re-created in the proper column order.

```
cursor COL_CURSOR (I_Own VARCHAR2,
                   I_Ind VARCHAR2,
                   C_Own VARCHAR2,
```

```
                    C_Tab VARCHAR2) is
    select Column_Name
      from DBA_IND_COLUMNS
     where Index_Owner = I_Own
       and Index_Name  = I_Ind
       and Table_Owner = C_Own
       and Table_Name  = C_Tab
     order by Column_Position;
```

In the next section of the script, the EXP_CURSOR cursor selects the column expressions from DBA_IND_EXPRESSIONS for each index selected by the IND_CURSOR cursor. The results are ordered by Column_Position, so that indexes created on multiple columns will be re-created in the proper column order. The EXP_CURSOR cursor allows for the handling of function-based indexes that are available as of Oracle8.1.x.

```
cursor EXP_CURSOR (I_Own VARCHAR2,
                   I_Ind VARCHAR2,
                   C_Own VARCHAR2,
                   C_Tab VARCHAR2) is
    select Column_Expression
      from DBA_IND_EXPRESSIONS
     where Index_Owner = I_Own
       and Index_Name  = I_Ind
       and Table_Owner = C_Own
       and Table_Name  = C_Tab
     order by Column_Position;
```

The next section of the script defines the cursors that are used with the partitioning feature available as of Oracle8.x. Range partitioned are allowed from Oracle8.0.x onward. Oracle8.1.x also allows hash and composite partitions. Further, Oracle9.x allows list partitions to be used. All types of partitions and subpartitions are covered by the script.

```
cursor PART_IND_CURSOR (PI_Owner   VARCHAR2,
                        PI_Indname VARCHAR2) is
    select Locality,
           Partitioning_Type,
           Subpartitioning_Type
      from DBA_PART_INDEXES
     where Owner = PI_Owner
       and Index_Name  = PI_Indname;

 cursor PART_COL_CURSOR (PI_Owner   VARCHAR2,
                         PI_Indname VARCHAR2) is
```

```
      select Column_Name
        from DBA_PART_KEY_COLUMNS
       where Owner = PI_Owner
         and Name  = PI_Indname
       order by Column_Position;

  cursor IND_PARTS_CURSOR (PI_Owner    VARCHAR2,
                    PI_Tabname VARCHAR2) is
      select Partition_Name,
             High_Value,
             Tablespace_Name,
             Pct_Free,
             Ini_Trans,
             Max_Trans,
             Initial_Extent,
             Next_Extent,
             Min_Extent,
             Max_Extent,
             Pct_Increase,
             Freelists,
             Freelist_Groups,
             Buffer_Pool
        from DBA_IND_PARTITIONS
       where Index_Owner = PI_Owner
         and Index_Name  = PI_Tabname
       order by Partition_Position;

  cursor IND_SUBPARTS_CURSOR (PI_Owner    VARCHAR2,
                    PI_Indname VARCHAR2,
                    PI_Partname VARCHAR2) is
      select Subpartition_Name,
             Tablespace_Name
        from DBA_IND_SUBPARTITIONS
       where Index_Owner = PI_Owner
         and Index_Name  = PI_Indname
         and Partition_Name = PI_Partname
       order by Subpartition_Position;
```

The procedure variables for the cursor are declared as TABLE_NAME.Column_
Name%**TYPE**. This anchoring of the datatypes takes the column definition from
within the database itself. If the column definition changes in a different version of
Oracle, the procedure will still work because the definition of the column has not
been hard coded. The variable *Lv_Lineno* orders the lines of the **create** statement.

```
Lv_Index_Owner          DBA_INDEXES.Owner%TYPE;
Lv_Index_Name           DBA_INDEXES.Index_Name%TYPE;
Lv_Table_Owner          DBA_INDEXES.Table_Owner%TYPE;
Lv_Table_Name           DBA_INDEXES.Table_Name%TYPE;
Lv_Uniqueness           DBA_INDEXES.Uniqueness%TYPE;
Lv_Tablespace_Name      DBA_INDEXES.Tablespace_Name%TYPE;
Lv_Ini_Trans            DBA_INDEXES.Ini_Trans%TYPE;
Lv_Max_Trans            DBA_INDEXES.Max_Trans%TYPE;
Lv_Initial_Extent       DBA_INDEXES.Initial_Extent%TYPE;
Lv_Next_Extent          DBA_INDEXES.Next_Extent%TYPE;
Lv_Min_Extents          DBA_INDEXES.Min_Extents%TYPE;
Lv_Max_Extents          DBA_INDEXES.Max_Extents%TYPE;
Lv_Pct_Increase         DBA_INDEXES.Pct_Increase%TYPE;
Lv_Pct_Free             DBA_INDEXES.Pct_Free%TYPE;
Lv_Index_Type           DBA_INDEXES.Index_Type%TYPE;
Lv_Degree               DBA_INDEXES.Degree%TYPE;
Lv_Instances            DBA_INDEXES.Instances%TYPE;
Lv_Logging              DBA_INDEXES.Logging%TYPE;
Lv_Freelists            DBA_INDEXES.Freelists%TYPE;
Lv_Freelist_Groups      DBA_INDEXES.Freelist_Groups%TYPE;
Lv_Buffer_Pool          DBA_INDEXES.Buffer_Pool%TYPE;
Lv_Partitioned          DBA_INDEXES.Partitioned%TYPE;
Lv_Compression          DBA_INDEXES.Compression%TYPE;
Lv_Prefix_Length        DBA_INDEXES.Prefix_Length%TYPE;
Lv_Funcidx_Status       DBA_INDEXES.Funcidx_Status%TYPE;


Lv_Locality                 DBA_PART_INDEXES.Locality%TYPE;
Lv_Partitioning_Type        DBA_PART_INDEXES.Partitioning_Type%TYPE;
Lv_Subpartitioning_Type     DBA_PART_INDEXES.Subpartitioning_Type%TYPE;


Lv_P_Column_Name        DBA_PART_KEY_COLUMNS.Column_Name%TYPE;

Lv_IP_Partition_Name        DBA_IND_PARTITIONS.Partition_Name%TYPE;
Lv_IP_High_Value            DBA_IND_PARTITIONS.High_Value%TYPE;
Lv_IP_Tablespace_Name       DBA_IND_PARTITIONS.Tablespace_Name%TYPE;
Lv_IP_Pct_Free              DBA_IND_PARTITIONS.Pct_Free%TYPE;
Lv_IP_Ini_Trans             DBA_IND_PARTITIONS.Ini_Trans%TYPE;
Lv_IP_Max_Trans             DBA_IND_PARTITIONS.Max_Trans%TYPE;
Lv_IP_Initial_Extent        DBA_IND_PARTITIONS.Initial_Extent%TYPE;
Lv_IP_Next_Extent           DBA_IND_PARTITIONS.Next_Extent%TYPE;
Lv_IP_Min_Extents           DBA_IND_PARTITIONS.Min_Extent%TYPE;
Lv_IP_Max_Extents           DBA_IND_PARTITIONS.Max_Extent%TYPE;
Lv_IP_Pct_Increase          DBA_IND_PARTITIONS.Pct_Increase%TYPE;
Lv_IP_Freelists             DBA_IND_PARTITIONS.Freelists%TYPE;
Lv_IP_Freelist_Groups       DBA_IND_PARTITIONS.Freelist_Groups%TYPE;
Lv_IP_Buffer_Pool           DBA_IND_PARTITIONS.Buffer_Pool%TYPE;
```

```
Lv_ISP_Subpartition_Name  DBA_IND_SUBPARTITIONS.Subpartition_Name%TYPE;
Lv_ISP_Tablespace_Name    DBA_IND_SUBPARTITIONS.Tablespace_Name%TYPE;

Lv_Column_Name            DBA_IND_COLUMNS.Column_Name%TYPE;

Lv_Column_Expression      DBA_IND_EXPRESSIONS.Column_Expression%TYPE;

Lv_First_Rec       BOOLEAN;
Lv_String          VARCHAR2(800);
Lv_Lineno          NUMBER;

Lv_Part_Type       VARCHAR2(10);
```

An internal procedure named WRITE_OUT will perform the **insert**s into the temporary table. The values inserted into the temporary table will later be queried to generate the **create index** command. Another procedure UPDATE_OUT is also used to update the temporary table.

```
procedure WRITE_OUT(P_Line INTEGER, P_Owner varchar2, P_Name
                    VARCHAR2, P_String VARCHAR2) is
begin
   insert into I_TEMP (Lineno, Id_Owner, Id_Name, Text)
          values (P_Line,P_Owner,P_Name,P_String);
end;

procedure UPDATE_OUT(P_Line INTEGER,  P_Owner VARCHAR2,
                     P_Name VARCHAR2, P_String VARCHAR2) is
begin
   update I_TEMP
      set Text = P_String
    where Lineno = P_Line
      and Id_Owner = P_Owner
      and Id_Name  = P_Name;
end;
```

In the first part of the executable commands section of the script, shown in the following listing, the IND_CURSOR cursor forms an outer loop for each index for the requested table. *Lv_Lineno* is used in conjunction with the index name to order the rows in the temporary table I_TEMP so you can extract the **create index** command for a single index at the end of the procedure if you want. *Lv_First_Rec* is a Boolean variable that distinguishes between the first column in the index, which is preceded by an open parenthesis, and the remaining columns in the index, which are preceded by a comma. *Lv_First_Rec* is initialized to TRUE to indicate that the procedure is beginning to process the index.

```
begin
   open IND_CURSOR;
   loop
      fetch IND_CURSOR into Lv_Index_Owner,
                            Lv_Index_Name,
                            Lv_Table_Owner,
                            Lv_Table_Name,
                            Lv_Uniqueness,
                            Lv_Tablespace_Name,
                            Lv_Ini_Trans,
                            Lv_Max_Trans,
                            Lv_Initial_Extent,
                            Lv_Next_Extent,
                            Lv_Min_Extents,
                            Lv_Max_Extents,
                            Lv_Pct_Increase,
                            Lv_Pct_Free,
                            Lv_Index_Type,
                            Lv_Degree,
                            Lv_Instances,
                            Lv_Logging,
                            Lv_Freelists,
                            Lv_Freelist_Groups,
                            Lv_Buffer_Pool,
                            Lv_Partitioned,
                            Lv_Compression,
                            Lv_Prefix_Length,
                            Lv_Funcidx_Status;
      exit when IND_CURSOR%NOTFOUND;
      Lv_Lineno := 1;
      Lv_First_Rec := TRUE;
```

Based on the value of the Uniqueness column and whether the index is a Bitmap index, the next portion of the gen_indx_81n9.sql script generates the proper **create** string and writes it to the temporary table. The **LOWER** function changes the text to all lowercase to make the output more readable.

```
Lv_String:=' ';

   if (Lv_Uniqueness = 'UNIQUE')
   then
       Lv_String:=Lv_String||' UNIQUE ';
   end if;

   if (INSTR(Lv_Index_Type,'BITMAP',1) != 0)
```

```
then
    Lv_String:=Lv_String||' BITMAP ';
end if;

Lv_String:= 'CREATE '||Lv_String||' INDEX '
                    ||LOWER(LV_INDEX_OWNER) || '.'
                    ||LOWER(Lv_Index_Name);
    WRITE_OUT(Lv_Lineno, Lv_Index_Owner, Lv_Index_Name, Lv_String);
    Lv_Lineno := Lv_Lineno + 1;
```

In the next section of the script, it is determined whether the index is a function-based index.

```
if (Lv_Funcidx_Status IS NULL)
```

If it is not a function-based index, the COL_CURSOR forms the inner loop, selecting all the column names in the index from DBA_IND_COLUMNS and concatenating them together to form the index key. The Boolean *Lv_First_Rec* is used here to determine whether to prefix the column name with the **on** *table_owner.table_name* clause for the first column in the index or with comma for all other columns in the index. Once all the column names have been selected and concatenated, the cursor is closed and the SQL statement is finished by appending a closing parenthesis before it is written to the temporary table.

The inner cursor will be opened, fetched, and closed once for each index selected by the outer cursor.

```
then

    open COL_CURSOR(Lv_Index_Owner,Lv_Index_Name,Lv_Table_Owner,Lv_
    Table_Name);
    loop
        fetch COL_CURSOR into Lv_Column_Name;
        exit when COL_CURSOR%NOTFOUND;
        if (Lv_First_Rec)
        then
            Lv_String := '    ON '|| LOWER(Lv_Table_Owner) || '.' ||
                        LOWER(Lv_Table_Name)||' (';
            Lv_First_Rec := FALSE;
        else
            Lv_String := Lv_String || ',';
        end if;
        Lv_String := Lv_String || LOWER(Lv_Column_Name);
    end loop;
    close COL_CURSOR;
    Lv_String := Lv_String || ')';
    WRITE_OUT(Lv_Lineno, Lv_Index_Owner, Lv_Index_Name, Lv_String);
    Lv_Lineno := Lv_Lineno + 1;
```

If, however, the index is a function-based index, the EXP_CURSOR is used.

```
else

    open EXP_CURSOR(Lv_Index_Owner,Lv_Index_Name,Lv_Table_Owner,Lv_
    Table_Name);
    loop
        fetch EXP_CURSOR into Lv_Column_Expression;
        exit when EXP_CURSOR%NOTFOUND;
        if (Lv_First_Rec)
        then
            Lv_String := '    ON '|| LOWER(Lv_Table_Owner) || '.' ||
                            LOWER(Lv_Table_Name)||' (';
            Lv_First_Rec := FALSE;
        else
            Lv_String := Lv_String || ',';
        end if;
        Lv_String := Lv_String || LOWER(Lv_Column_Expression);
    end loop;
    close EXP_CURSOR;
    Lv_String := Lv_String || ')';
    WRITE_OUT(Lv_Lineno, Lv_Index_Owner, Lv_Index_Name, Lv_String);
    Lv_Lineno := Lv_Lineno + 1;

    end if;
```

The next section of the script determines whether the index is a partitioned index or not. If it is a partitioned index,

```
if (Lv_Partitioned = 'YES')
    then
```

the necessary checking occurs to determine whether it is a global or a local partitioned index. The appropriate storage clauses are generated for the index.

```
open PART_IND_CURSOR(Lv_Index_Owner,Lv_Index_Name);
    loop
        fetch PART_IND_CURSOR into Lv_Locality,
                                    Lv_Partitioning_Type,
                                    Lv_Subpartitioning_Type;
        exit when PART_IND_CURSOR%NOTFOUND;

        if (Lv_Locality = 'GLOBAL')
        then

            Lv_String:=' GLOBAL PARTITION BY RANGE ';
            WRITE_OUT(Lv_Lineno, Lv_Index_Owner,
Lv_Index_Name, Lv_String);
            Lv_Lineno := Lv_Lineno + 1;

            Lv_String   := '(';
            WRITE_OUT(Lv_Lineno, Lv_Index_Owner,
```

```
Lv_Index_Name, Lv_String);
            Lv_Lineno := Lv_Lineno + 1;

            open PART_COL_CURSOR (Lv_Index_Owner,Lv_Index_Name);
            loop
               fetch PART_COL_CURSOR into Lv_P_Column_Name;
               exit when PART_COL_CURSOR%NOTFOUND;


               Lv_String := Lv_P_Column_Name || ',';
               WRITE_OUT(Lv_Lineno, Lv_Index_Owner,
Lv_Index_Name, Lv_String);
               Lv_Lineno := Lv_Lineno + 1;

            end loop;
            close PART_COL_CURSOR;
            Lv_Lineno  := Lv_Lineno - 1;
            Lv_String  := SUBSTR(Lv_String,1,(LENGTH(Lv_String) - 1));
            UPDATE_OUT(Lv_Lineno, Lv_Index_Owner,
Lv_Index_Name, Lv_String);
            Lv_Lineno  := Lv_Lineno + 1;


            Lv_String  := ')';
            WRITE_OUT(Lv_Lineno, Lv_Index_Owner,
Lv_Index_Name, Lv_String);
            Lv_Lineno := Lv_Lineno + 1;

            Lv_String  := '(';
            WRITE_OUT(Lv_Lineno, Lv_Index_Owner,
Lv_Index_Name, Lv_String);
            Lv_Lineno := Lv_Lineno + 1;

            open IND_PARTS_CURSOR (Lv_Index_Owner,Lv_Index_Name);
            loop
            fetch IND_PARTS_CURSOR into  Lv_IP_Partition_Name,
                                 Lv_IP_High_Value,
                                 Lv_IP_Tablespace_Name,
                                 Lv_IP_Pct_Free,
                                 Lv_IP_Ini_Trans,
                                 Lv_IP_Max_Trans,
                                 Lv_IP_Initial_Extent,
                                 Lv_IP_Next_Extent,
                                 Lv_IP_Min_Extents,
                                 Lv_IP_Max_Extents,
                                 Lv_IP_Pct_Increase,
                                 Lv_IP_Freelists,
                                 Lv_IP_Freelist_Groups,
                                 Lv_IP_Buffer_Pool;
```

```
            exit when IND_PARTS_CURSOR%NOTFOUND;



            Lv_String := ' PARTITION '||Lv_IP_Partition_Name;
            WRITE_OUT(Lv_Lineno, Lv_Index_Owner,
Lv_Index_Name, Lv_String);
            Lv_Lineno := Lv_Lineno + 1;

            Lv_String:= ' VALUES LESS THAN ('||Lv_IP_High_Value||') ';
            WRITE_OUT(Lv_Lineno, Lv_Index_Owner,
Lv_Index_Name, Lv_String);
            Lv_Lineno := Lv_Lineno + 1;

            Lv_String  := ' TABLESPACE ' || Lv_IP_Tablespace_Name ;
            WRITE_OUT(Lv_Lineno, Lv_Index_Owner,
Lv_Index_Name, Lv_String);
            Lv_Lineno := Lv_Lineno + 1;

            Lv_String  := ' PCTFREE ' || Lv_IP_Pct_Free ;
            WRITE_OUT(Lv_Lineno, Lv_Index_Owner,
Lv_Index_Name, Lv_String);
            Lv_Lineno := Lv_Lineno + 1;


            Lv_String  := ' INITRANS ' || Lv_IP_Ini_Trans ;
            WRITE_OUT(Lv_Lineno, Lv_Index_Owner,
Lv_Index_Name, Lv_String);
            Lv_Lineno := Lv_Lineno + 1;
            Lv_String  := ' MAXTRANS ' || Lv_IP_Max_Trans ;
            WRITE_OUT(Lv_Lineno, Lv_Index_Owner,
Lv_Index_Name, Lv_String);
            Lv_Lineno := Lv_Lineno + 1;

            Lv_String  := ' STORAGE';
            WRITE_OUT(Lv_Lineno, Lv_Index_Owner,
Lv_Index_Name, Lv_String);
            Lv_Lineno := Lv_Lineno + 1;
            Lv_String  := '(';
            WRITE_OUT(Lv_Lineno, Lv_Index_Owner,
Lv_Index_Name, Lv_String);
            Lv_Lineno := Lv_Lineno + 1;

            Lv_String  := '   INITIAL ' || Lv_IP_Initial_Extent ;
            WRITE_OUT(Lv_Lineno, Lv_Index_Owner,
Lv_Index_Name, Lv_String);
            Lv_Lineno := Lv_Lineno + 1;
```

```
            Lv_String  := '    NEXT ' || Lv_IP_Next_Extent ;
            WRITE_OUT(Lv_Lineno, Lv_Index_Owner,
Lv_Index_Name, Lv_String);
            Lv_Lineno := Lv_Lineno + 1;


            Lv_String  := '    MINEXTENTS ' || Lv_IP_Min_Extents ;
            WRITE_OUT(Lv_Lineno, Lv_Index_Owner,
Lv_Index_Name, Lv_String);
            Lv_Lineno := Lv_Lineno + 1;


            Lv_String  := '    MAXEXTENTS ' || Lv_IP_Max_Extents ;
            WRITE_OUT(Lv_Lineno, Lv_Index_Owner,
Lv_Index_Name, Lv_String);
            Lv_Lineno := Lv_Lineno + 1;


            Lv_String  := '    PCTINCREASE ' || Lv_IP_Pct_Increase ;
            WRITE_OUT(Lv_Lineno, Lv_Index_Owner,
Lv_Index_Name, Lv_String);
            Lv_Lineno := Lv_Lineno + 1;


            Lv_String  := '    FREELISTS ' || Lv_IP_Freelists ;
            WRITE_OUT(Lv_Lineno, Lv_Index_Owner,
Lv_Index_Name, Lv_String);
            Lv_Lineno := Lv_Lineno + 1;


            Lv_String  := '    FREELIST GROUPS ' ||
            Lv_IP_Freelist_Groups ;
            WRITE_OUT(Lv_Lineno, Lv_Index_Owner,
Lv_Index_Name, Lv_String);
            Lv_Lineno := Lv_Lineno + 1;


            Lv_String  := '    BUFFER_POOL ' || Lv_IP_Buffer_Pool ;
            WRITE_OUT(Lv_Lineno, Lv_Index_Owner,
Lv_Index_Name, Lv_String);
            Lv_Lineno := Lv_Lineno + 1;


            Lv_String  := ')';
            WRITE_OUT(Lv_Lineno, Lv_Index_Owner,
Lv_Index_Name, Lv_String);
            Lv_Lineno := Lv_Lineno + 1;


            Lv_String := ',';
            WRITE_OUT(Lv_Lineno, Lv_Index_Owner,
Lv_Index_Name, Lv_String);
            Lv_Lineno := Lv_Lineno + 1;

            end loop;
            close IND_PARTS_CURSOR;
            Lv_Lineno  := Lv_Lineno - 1;
```

```
                Lv_String  := SUBSTR(Lv_String,1,(LENGTH(Lv_String) - 1));
                UPDATE_OUT(Lv_Lineno, Lv_Index_Owner,
Lv_Index_Name, Lv_String);
                Lv_Lineno  := Lv_Lineno + 1;

                Lv_String  := ')';
                WRITE_OUT(Lv_Lineno, Lv_Index_Owner,
Lv_Index_Name, Lv_String);
                Lv_Lineno := Lv_Lineno + 1;



        else
                Lv_String:=' LOCAL ';
                WRITE_OUT(Lv_Lineno, Lv_Index_Owner,
Lv_Index_Name, Lv_String);
                Lv_Lineno := Lv_Lineno + 1;

                Lv_Part_Type := null;

                if (Lv_Partitioning_Type = 'HASH')
                then
                    Lv_Part_Type:= 'HASH';
                else
                    if (Lv_Subpartitioning_Type IS NULL)
                    then
                        Lv_Part_Type:= 'RANGE';
                    else
                        Lv_Part_Type:='COMPOSITE';
                    end if;
                end if;

                Lv_String  := '(';
                WRITE_OUT(Lv_Lineno, Lv_Index_Owner,
Lv_Index_Name, Lv_String);
                Lv_Lineno := Lv_Lineno + 1;

                open IND_PARTS_CURSOR (Lv_Index_Owner,Lv_Index_Name);
                loop
                fetch IND_PARTS_CURSOR into  Lv_IP_Partition_Name,
                                    Lv_IP_High_Value,
                                    Lv_IP_Tablespace_Name,
                                    Lv_IP_Pct_Free,
                                    Lv_IP_Ini_Trans,
                                    Lv_IP_Max_Trans,
                                    Lv_IP_Initial_Extent,
                                    Lv_IP_Next_Extent,
                                    Lv_IP_Min_Extents,
                                    Lv_IP_Max_Extents,
```

```
                        Lv_IP_Pct_Increase,
                        Lv_IP_Freelists,
                        Lv_IP_Freelist_Groups,
                        Lv_IP_Buffer_Pool;
            exit when IND_PARTS_CURSOR%NOTFOUND;


            Lv_String := ' PARTITION '||Lv_IP_Partition_Name;
            WRITE_OUT(Lv_Lineno, Lv_Index_Owner,
Lv_Index_Name, Lv_String);
            Lv_Lineno := Lv_Lineno + 1;

            Lv_String  := ' TABLESPACE ' || Lv_IP_Tablespace_Name ;
            WRITE_OUT(Lv_Lineno, Lv_Index_Owner,
Lv_Index_Name, Lv_String);
            Lv_Lineno := Lv_Lineno + 1;

        if (Lv_Part_Type = 'RANGE' or Lv_Part_Type = 'COMPOSITE')
        then

            Lv_String  := ' PCTFREE ' || Lv_IP_Pct_Free ;
            WRITE_OUT(Lv_Lineno, Lv_Index_Owner,
Lv_Index_Name, Lv_String);
            Lv_Lineno := Lv_Lineno + 1;


            Lv_String  := ' INITRANS ' || Lv_IP_Ini_Trans ;
            WRITE_OUT(Lv_Lineno, Lv_Index_Owner,
Lv_Index_Name, Lv_String);
            Lv_Lineno := Lv_Lineno + 1;

            Lv_String  := ' MAXTRANS ' || Lv_IP_Max_Trans ;
            WRITE_OUT(Lv_Lineno, Lv_Index_Owner,
Lv_Index_Name, Lv_String);
            Lv_Lineno := Lv_Lineno + 1;

            Lv_String  := ' STORAGE';
            WRITE_OUT(Lv_Lineno, Lv_Index_Owner,
Lv_Index_Name, Lv_String);
            Lv_Lineno := Lv_Lineno + 1;
            Lv_String  := '(';
            WRITE_OUT(Lv_Lineno, Lv_Index_Owner,
Lv_Index_Name, Lv_String);
            Lv_Lineno := Lv_Lineno + 1;

            Lv_String  := '   INITIAL ' || Lv_IP_Initial_Extent ;
            WRITE_OUT(Lv_Lineno, Lv_Index_Owner,
Lv_Index_Name, Lv_String);
            Lv_Lineno := Lv_Lineno + 1;
```

```
                Lv_String  := '    NEXT ' || Lv_IP_Next_Extent ;
                WRITE_OUT(Lv_Lineno, Lv_Index_Owner,
Lv_Index_Name, Lv_String);
                Lv_Lineno := Lv_Lineno + 1;

                Lv_String  := '    MINEXTENTS ' || Lv_IP_Min_Extents ;
                WRITE_OUT(Lv_Lineno, Lv_Index_Owner,
Lv_Index_Name, Lv_String);
                Lv_Lineno := Lv_Lineno + 1;

                Lv_String  := '    MAXEXTENTS ' || Lv_IP_Max_Extents ;
                WRITE_OUT(Lv_Lineno, Lv_Index_Owner,
Lv_Index_Name, Lv_String);
                Lv_Lineno := Lv_Lineno + 1;

                Lv_String  := '    PCTINCREASE ' || Lv_IP_Pct_Increase ;
                WRITE_OUT(Lv_Lineno, Lv_Index_Owner,
Lv_Index_Name, Lv_String);
                Lv_Lineno := Lv_Lineno + 1;

                Lv_String  := '    FREELISTS ' || Lv_IP_Freelists ;
                WRITE_OUT(Lv_Lineno, Lv_Index_Owner,
Lv_Index_Name, Lv_String);
                Lv_Lineno := Lv_Lineno + 1;

                Lv_String  := '    FREELIST GROUPS ' ||
                Lv_IP_Freelist_Groups ;
                WRITE_OUT(Lv_Lineno, Lv_Index_Owner,
Lv_Index_Name, Lv_String);
                Lv_Lineno := Lv_Lineno + 1;

                Lv_String  := '    BUFFER_POOL ' || Lv_IP_Buffer_Pool ;
                WRITE_OUT(Lv_Lineno, Lv_Index_Owner,
Lv_Index_Name, Lv_String);
                Lv_Lineno := Lv_Lineno + 1;

                Lv_String  := ')';
                WRITE_OUT(Lv_Lineno, Lv_Index_Owner,
Lv_Index_Name, Lv_String);
                Lv_Lineno := Lv_Lineno + 1;

                if (Lv_Part_Type = 'COMPOSITE')
                then

                    Lv_String  := '(';
                    WRITE_OUT(Lv_Lineno, Lv_Index_Owner,
Lv_Index_Name, Lv_String);
                    Lv_Lineno := Lv_Lineno + 1;
```

```
                        open IND_SUBPARTS_CURSOR (Lv_Index_Owner,
Lv_Index_Name, Lv_IP_Partition_Name);
                        loop
                        fetch IND_SUBPARTS_CURSOR into
Lv_ISP_Subpartition_Name, Lv_ISP_Tablespace_Name;
                        exit when IND_SUBPARTS_CURSOR%NOTFOUND;


                        Lv_String := ' SUBPARTITION '||
                        Lv_ISP_Subpartition_Name;
                        WRITE_OUT(Lv_Lineno, Lv_Index_Owner,
Lv_Index_Name, Lv_String);
                        Lv_Lineno := Lv_Lineno + 1;


                        Lv_String  := ' TABLESPACE ' ||
Lv_ISP_Tablespace_Name ;
                        WRITE_OUT(Lv_Lineno, Lv_Index_Owner,
Lv_Index_Name, Lv_String);
                        Lv_Lineno := Lv_Lineno + 1;

                        Lv_String := ',';
                        WRITE_OUT(Lv_Lineno, Lv_Index_Owner,
Lv_Index_Name, Lv_String);
                        Lv_Lineno := Lv_Lineno + 1;

                        end loop;
                        close IND_SUBPARTS_CURSOR;
                        Lv_Lineno  := Lv_Lineno - 1;
                        Lv_String :=
                          SUBSTR(Lv_String,1,(LENGTH(Lv_String) - 1));
                        UPDATE_OUT(Lv_Lineno, Lv_Index_Owner,
Lv_Index_Name,Lv_String);
                        Lv_Lineno  := Lv_Lineno + 1;

                        Lv_String := ')';
                        WRITE_OUT(Lv_Lineno, Lv_Index_Owner,
Lv_Index_Name, Lv_String);
                        Lv_Lineno := Lv_Lineno + 1;

                    end if;


                end if;

              Lv_String := ',';
              WRITE_OUT(Lv_Lineno, Lv_Index_Owner,
```

```
Lv_Index_Name, Lv_String);
                Lv_Lineno := Lv_Lineno + 1;

          end loop;
          close IND_PARTS_CURSOR;
          Lv_Lineno  := Lv_Lineno - 1;
          Lv_String  := SUBSTR(Lv_String,1,(LENGTH(Lv_String) - 1));
          UPDATE_OUT(Lv_Lineno, Lv_Index_Owner,
          Lv_Index_Name,Lv_String);
          Lv_Lineno  := Lv_Lineno + 1;

          Lv_String  := ')';
          WRITE_OUT(Lv_Lineno, Lv_Index_Owner,
Lv_Index_Name, Lv_String);
                Lv_Lineno := Lv_Lineno + 1;


      end if;

    end loop;
    close PART_IND_CURSOR;
```

If, on the other hand, the index is not a partitioned index, the storage clauses are generated by the **else** part of the script.

```
else

     Lv_String := null;
     Lv_String := 'PCTFREE ' || TO_CHAR(Lv_Pct_Free);
     WRITE_OUT(Lv_Lineno, Lv_Index_Owner, Lv_Index_Name, Lv_String);
     Lv_Lineno := Lv_Lineno + 1;
     Lv_String := 'INITRANS ' || TO_CHAR(Lv_Ini_Trans) ||
                  ' MAXTRANS ' || TO_CHAR(Lv_Max_Trans);
     WRITE_OUT(Lv_Lineno, Lv_Index_Owner, Lv_Index_Name, Lv_String);
     Lv_Lineno := Lv_Lineno + 1;
     Lv_String := 'TABLESPACE ' || Lv_Tablespace_Name || ' STORAGE (';
     WRITE_OUT(Lv_Lineno, Lv_Index_Owner, Lv_Index_Name, Lv_String);
     Lv_Lineno := Lv_Lineno + 1;
     Lv_String := 'INITIAL ' || TO_CHAR(Lv_Initial_Extent) ||
                  ' NEXT ' || TO_CHAR(Lv_Next_Extent);
     WRITE_OUT(Lv_Lineno, Lv_Index_Owner, Lv_Index_Name, Lv_String);
     Lv_Lineno := Lv_Lineno + 1;
     Lv_String :=  ' MINEXTENTS ' || TO_CHAR(Lv_Min_Extents) ||
                   ' MAXEXTENTS ' || TO_CHAR(Lv_Max_Extents) ||
                   ' PCTINCREASE ' || TO_CHAR(Lv_Pct_Increase) ||
                   ' FREELISTS ' || Lv_Freelists ||
                   ' FREELIST GROUPS ' || Lv_Freelist_Groups ||
                   ' BUFFER_POOL ' || Lv_Buffer_Pool || ')';
     WRITE_OUT(Lv_Lineno, Lv_Index_Owner, Lv_Index_Name, Lv_String);
```

```
        Lv_Lineno := Lv_Lineno + 1;

    end if;
```

The next section deals with the logging, compression, and parallel attributes of the index.

```
if (Lv_Logging = 'YES')
    then
       Lv_String  := ' LOGGING ';
    else
       Lv_String  := ' NOLOGGING ';
    end if;
    WRITE_OUT(Lv_Lineno, Lv_Index_Owner, Lv_Index_Name, Lv_String);
    Lv_Lineno := Lv_Lineno + 1;

    Lv_String  := 'PARALLEL ( DEGREE ' || Lv_Degree
                                        || ' INSTANCES '
                                        || Lv_Instances
                                        || ' )';
    WRITE_OUT(Lv_Lineno, Lv_Index_Owner, Lv_Index_Name, Lv_String);
    Lv_Lineno := Lv_Lineno + 1;

    if (Lv_Compression = 'DISABLED')
    then
       Lv_String := ' NOCOMPRESS ';
    else
       Lv_String := ' COMPRESS '||Lv_Prefix_Length;
    end if;
    WRITE_OUT(Lv_Lineno, Lv_Index_Owner, Lv_Index_Name, Lv_String);
    Lv_Lineno := Lv_Lineno + 1;
```

A final line of blanks is written to make the output file generated at the end of the procedure more readable. The outer cursor loop ends and the procedure will loop back through the IND_CURSOR until all indexes have been generated. Then the outer cursor is closed and the procedure exits.

```
    Lv_String := '/';
    WRITE_OUT(Lv_Lineno, Lv_Index_Owner, Lv_Index_Name, Lv_String);
    Lv_Lineno := Lv_Lineno + 1;         Lv_Lineno := Lv_Lineno + 1;
    Lv_String:='
                                                          ';
    WRITE_OUT(Lv_Lineno, Lv_Index_Owner, Lv_Index_Name, Lv_String);
    end loop;
    close IND_CURSOR;
end;
/
```

Once the **create** statements for all the indexes have been generated, they are spooled to a file for later execution.

```
spool cre_indx.sql
set heading off col Text format a80 word_wrap

select Text
  from I_TEMP
 order by Id_Owner, Id_Name, Lineno;
spool off
```

As an alternative, you can use this script to document all the indexes on all tables for a particular owner. To document all the indexes for a user, remove the **accept** *table_name* statement at the beginning of the script and change the **where** clause for the IND_CURSOR cursor to use a '%' for table_name:

```
where Owner = UPPER('&&tab_owner')
        and Index_Name not like 'SYS_%'
        and not exists (select 'x'
                           from DBA_CONSTRAINTS
                          where Constraint_Name = Index_Name
                          and Table_Owner = UPPER('&&tab_owner'))
```

If you want to document all indexes in your database that are not owned by SYS, remove the two **accept** statements from the beginning of the script and change the **where** clause for the IND_CURSOR cursor to this:

```
where Owner != 'SYS'
        and Index_Name not like 'SYS_%'
        and not exists (select 'x'
                           from DBA_CONSTRAINTS
                          where Constraint_Name = Index_Name
                            and Table_Owner = Owner)
```

You can easily modify the gen_indx_*.sql script to focus on only the specified table by changing this clause

```
and Table_Name like UPPER('&&table_name')
```

to this:

```
and Table_Name = UPPER('&&table_name')
```

in the cursor IND_CURSOR.

part_idi.sql

Display Data Distribution Across Index Partitions

Oracle supports two types of indexes on partitioned tables: local and global. A *local* index has a one-to-one relationship to a partition. For the example WORKER table, a local index would have four partitions, each matching one of the table's partitions. The data distribution among the local indexes would match the data distribution among the table partitions.

A *global* index spans the entire partitioned table. For example, an index on the Lodging column of the WORKER table could contain values from all four partitions. To complicate matters further, you can partition a global index. You can create the index on the Lodging column with multiple index partitions, in which case the distribution of data values in the index's partitions would not match the distribution of values in the table's partitions.

For example, the following command creates an index on the Lodging column of the WORKER table created in the previous section. The index has two partitions: one for values less than 'N' and a second for all other values.

```
create index WORKER_LODGING
    on WORKER(Lodging)
global partition by range (Lodging)
(partition IPART1 values less than ('N'),
 partition IPART2 values less than (MAXVALUE));
```

The next query selects the index partitioning data from DBA_IND_PARTITIONS and statistical data from DBA_INDEXES. Like the query of the table partition ranges, this query generates a graphical display of the distribution of values across your index partitions.

PROGRAMMER'S NOTE *Prior to running this script, you must **analyze** the global index to populate the statistics columns queried by the script.*

```
REM part_idi.sql
column Percent_of_Total format A60
column Partition_Name format A10
column High_Value format A8

select Partition_Name,
       High_Value,
       LPAD('o',50*DIP.Num_Rows/DBA_INDEXES.Num_Rows-1,'o')
         Percent_of_Total
  from DBA_IND_PARTITIONS DIP, DBA_INDEXES
 where DBA_INDEXES.Index_Name = '&index_name'
   and DBA_INDEXES.Owner = '&owner'
   and DBA_INDEXES.Index_Name = DIP.Index_Name
   and DBA_INDEXES.Owner = DIP.Index_Owner
 order by Partition_Position;
```

Sample output is shown in the following listing:

```
PARTITION_ HIGH_VAL PERCENT_OF_TOTAL
---------- -------- -------------------------------------------------------
IPART1     'N'
IPART2     MAXVALUE ooooooooooooooooooooooooooooooooooooooooooooooooooooo
```

As this output shows, the IPART2 partition contains all the Lodging values. Given this distribution, partitioning the index has not helped you from either a performance or an administrative standpoint.

ANNOTATIONS

Since partition ranges are set when tables and indexes are created, the ranges are based on estimates of the data distribution. You should therefore periodically evaluate the actual distribution of values to make sure the estimates used at creation time accurately reflect the actual data distribution.

Like the part_dis.sql script in the previous section, the part_idi.sql script relies on the statistics generated by executing the **analyze** command. You may **analyze** an index without analyzing the table it indexes. If the index is partitioned, you can **analyze** all partitions or only specific partitions of the index. You can create a partitioned global index on a nonpartitioned table.

The part_idi.sql script, shown in the following listing, retrieves statistics about the index partition from DBA_IND_PARTITIONS and compares them to statistics from DBA_INDEXES.

```
column Percent_of_Total format A60
column Partition_Name format A10
column High_Value format A8

select Partition_Name,
       High_Value,
       LPAD('o',50*DIP.Num_Rows/DBA_INDEXES.Num_Rows-1,'o')
          Percent_of_Total
  from DBA_IND_PARTITIONS DIP, DBA_INDEXES
 where DBA_INDEXES.Index_Name = '&index_name'
   and DBA_INDEXES.Owner = '&owner'
   and DBA_INDEXES.Index_Name = DIP.Index_Name
   and DBA_INDEXES.Owner = DIP.Index_Owner
 order by Partition_Position;
```

The LPAD expression, shown in the following listing, generates the line of 'o' characters representing the percentage of the index's rows found in the index partition.

```
       LPAD('o',50*DIP.Num_Rows/DBA_INDEXES.Num_Rows-1,'o')
          Percent_of_Total
```

In this example, a multiplier of 50 is used instead of 100 to reduce the space requirements of the output; every 2 percent is represented by one 'o' character in the output.

You can use the output of the part_dis.sql and part_idi.sql scripts to determine whether your actual space usage and data distribution mirror your expected values. In Chapter 6, you will see additional scripts related to the evaluation of current space usage and future space needs.

Generate Triggers

gen_trig_7n80.sql
gen_trig_81n9.sql

Tables can have many types of triggers defined on them, including **before row**, **after row**, **before statement**, and **after statement** for **delete**, **insert**, and **update**. In addition, as of Oracle8.1.x, you can define triggers for DML events (such as DELETE, INSERT, or UPDATE of columns) or DDL events or database events (by specifying one or more particular states of the database that cause the trigger to fire). Further, in Oracle8.1.x onward, the trigger can be defined at the SCHEMA or DATABASE level in addition to object level. Also, beginning with Oracle8.x, INSTEAD OF triggers can be used to cause Oracle to fire the trigger instead of executing the triggering event.

Managing all possible types and ensuring that they are documented is complex. As you move a table from one database to another, or change the table itself within the database, it is difficult to save off and re-create triggers manually. The gen_trig_*.sql script will generate a script to re-create all the triggers of a given table. The gen_trig_7n80.sql works for Oracle7.x and Oracle8.0.x, while the script gen_trig_81n9.sql can be used for Oracle8.1.x and later. Both the scripts are available on the CD-ROM with the book. The script gen_trig_81n9.sql is shown next. An annotated walk-through of the gen_trig_81n9.sql script follows the script listing and sample output.

```
REM
REM gen_trig_81n9.sql
REM This script can be used for Oracle8.1.x and above.
REM
set echo off term on verify off feedback off long 30000
set pagesize 0 heading off
select 'Creating trigger build script...' from DUAL;

accept table_name  prompt "Enter the name of the Table: "
accept tab_owner prompt "Enter table owner: "
set term off

drop table TRIG_TEMP;

create table TRIG_TEMP (
        Lineno   NUMBER,
        Id_Owner VARCHAR2(30),
        Id_Name  VARCHAR2(30),
        Text     LONG)
/
```

```
declare
   cursor TRIG_CURSOR is
        select Owner,
                Trigger_Name,
                Trigger_Type,
                Triggering_Event,
                Table_Owner,
                Table_Name,
                Referencing_Names,
                When_Clause,
                Status,
                Description,
                Trigger_Body,
                Column_Name,
                Action_Type,
                Base_Object_Type
          from DBA_TRIGGERS
         where Table_Owner  = UPPER('&&tab_owner')
           and Table_Name like UPPER('&&table_name')
         order by Trigger_Name;

   cursor TRIG_COL_CURSOR (A_Trigger_Owner VARCHAR2,
                           A_Trigger_Name  VARCHAR2) is
        select Table_Owner,
                Table_Name,
                Column_Name
          from DBA_TRIGGER_COLS
         where Trigger_Owner = A_Trigger_Owner
           and Trigger_Name  = A_Trigger_Name
           and Column_List   = 'YES';

   Lv_Trig_Owner              DBA_TRIGGERS.Owner%TYPE;
   Lv_Trig_Name               DBA_TRIGGERS.Trigger_Name%TYPE;
   Lv_Trig_Type               DBA_TRIGGERS.Trigger_Type%TYPE;
   Lv_Trig_Event              DBA_TRIGGERS.Triggering_Event%TYPE;
   Lv_Trig_Table_Owner        DBA_TRIGGERS.Table_Owner%TYPE;
   Lv_Trig_Table_Name         DBA_TRIGGERS.Table_Name%TYPE;
   Lv_Trig_Referencing_Names  DBA_TRIGGERS.Referencing_Names%TYPE;
   Lv_Trig_When_Clause        DBA_TRIGGERS.When_Clause%TYPE;
   Lv_Trig_Status             DBA_TRIGGERS.Status%TYPE;
   Lv_Description             DBA_TRIGGERS.Description%TYPE;
   Lv_Trig_Body               DBA_TRIGGERS.Trigger_Body%TYPE;
   Lv_Column_Name             DBA_TRIGGERS.Column_Name%TYPE;
   Lv_Action_Type             DBA_TRIGGERS.Action_Type%TYPE;
   Lv_Base_Object_Type        DBA_TRIGGERS.Base_Object_Type%TYPE;
   Lv_Col_Tab_Owner           DBA_TRIGGER_COLS.Trigger_Owner%TYPE;
   Lv_Col_Tab_Name            DBA_TRIGGER_COLS.Table_Name%TYPE;
   Lv_Col_Tab_Col_Name        DBA_TRIGGER_COLS.Column_Name%TYPE;
```

```
        Lv_String                       VARCHAR2(800);
        Lv_String2                      VARCHAR2(80);
        Lv_String3                      VARCHAR2(80);
        Lv_Of_Count                     INTEGER;
        Lv_Lineno                       NUMBER;
        procedure WRITE_OUT(P_Line INTEGER,  P_Owner VARCHAR2,
                        P_Name VARCHAR2, P_String VARCHAR2) is
    begin
        insert into TRIG_TEMP (Lineno, Id_Owner, Id_Name, Text)
                values (P_Line,P_Owner,P_Name,P_String);
      end;

begin
    open TRIG_CURSOR;
    loop
        fetch TRIG_CURSOR into Lv_Trig_Owner,
                                Lv_Trig_Name,
                                Lv_Trig_Type,
                                Lv_Trig_Event,
                                Lv_Trig_Table_Owner,
                                Lv_Trig_Table_Name,
                                Lv_Trig_Referencing_Names,
                                Lv_Trig_When_Clause,
                                Lv_Trig_Status,
                                Lv_Description,
                                Lv_Trig_Body,
                                Lv_Column_Name,
                                Lv_Action_Type,
                                Lv_Base_Object_Type;
        exit when TRIG_CURSOR%NOTFOUND;

        Lv_Lineno := 1;

        Lv_String:= 'CREATE OR REPLACE TRIGGER ' || LOWER(Lv_Trig_Owner)
                                    || '.'
                                    || LOWER(Lv_Trig_Name);
        WRITE_OUT(Lv_Lineno, Lv_Trig_Owner, Lv_Trig_Name, Lv_String);
        Lv_Lineno := Lv_Lineno + 1;

        Lv_String2:= SUBSTR(Lv_Trig_Type,1,INSTR(Lv_Trig_Type,' '));
        if (Lv_String2 = 'INSTEAD ')
        then
            LV_String2 := Lv_String2 || 'OF ';
        end if;

        Lv_string := Lv_String2 || Lv_Trig_Event;
        WRITE_OUT(Lv_Lineno, Lv_Trig_Owner, Lv_Trig_Name, Lv_String);
        Lv_Lineno := Lv_Lineno + 1;
```

```
Lv_Of_Count := 0;
open TRIG_COL_CURSOR (Lv_Trig_Owner,Lv_Trig_Name);
loop
    fetch TRIG_COL_CURSOR into      Lv_Col_Tab_Owner,
                                    Lv_Col_Tab_Name,
                                    Lv_Col_Tab_Col_Name;
    exit when TRIG_COL_CURSOR%NOTFOUND;
    Lv_Of_Count := Lv_Of_Count + 1;

    If ( Lv_Of_Count = 1 )
    then
            Lv_String  := '  OF ' || LOWER(Lv_Col_Tab_Col_Name);
    else
            Lv_String  := '    ,' ||LOWER(Lv_Col_Tab_Col_Name);
    end if;
    WRITE_OUT(Lv_Lineno, Lv_Trig_Owner, Lv_Trig_Name, Lv_String);
    Lv_Lineno := Lv_Lineno + 1;
end loop;
close TRIG_COL_CURSOR;

Lv_String := 'ON ';

if (Lv_Base_Object_Type in ('TABLE','VIEW'))
then

        Lv_String3 := ' ';

        if (Lv_Column_Name IS NOT NULL)
        then

            Lv_String3:=' NESTED TABLE '        ||
                        Lv_Column_Name          ||
                        ' OF ';
        end if;

        Lv_String:= Lv_String                       ||
                    Lv_String3                      ||
                    LOWER(Lv_Trig_Table_Owner)  ||
                    '.'                             ||
                    LOWER(Lv_Trig_Table_Name);


    elsif (Lv_Base_Object_Type = 'DATABASE')
        then

            Lv_String:= Lv_String                   ||
                        ' DATABASE ';
```

```
        else

            Lv_String:= Lv_String                ||
                        Lv_Trig_Table_Owner      ||
                        '.SCHEMA';

    end if;

    WRITE_OUT(Lv_Lineno, Lv_Trig_Owner, Lv_Trig_Name, Lv_String);
    Lv_Lineno := Lv_Lineno + 1;


    WRITE_OUT(Lv_Lineno, Lv_Trig_Owner, Lv_Trig_Name,
              Lv_Trig_Referencing_Names);
    Lv_Lineno := Lv_Lineno + 1;

    if (INSTR(Lv_Trig_Type,'EACH ROW') > 0)
    then
        Lv_String := 'FOR EACH ROW';
        WRITE_OUT(Lv_Lineno, Lv_Trig_Owner, Lv_Trig_Name, Lv_String);
        Lv_Lineno := Lv_Lineno + 1;

    elsif (INSTR(Lv_Trig_Type,'STATEMENT') > 0)
    then
        Lv_String := 'FOR EACH STATEMENT';
        WRITE_OUT(Lv_Lineno, Lv_Trig_Owner, Lv_Trig_Name, Lv_String);
        Lv_Lineno := Lv_Lineno + 1;
    end if;
    if (Lv_Trig_When_Clause IS NOT NULL)
    then
        Lv_String := 'WHEN (' || Lv_Trig_When_Clause || ')';
        WRITE_OUT(Lv_Lineno, Lv_Trig_Owner, Lv_Trig_Name, Lv_String);
        Lv_Lineno := Lv_Lineno + 1;
    end if;

    if (Lv_Action_Type = 'CALL')
    then
        Lv_String := ' CALL ';
        WRITE_OUT(Lv_Lineno, Lv_Trig_Owner, Lv_Trig_Name, Lv_String);
        Lv_Lineno := Lv_Lineno + 1;
    end if;

    WRITE_OUT(Lv_Lineno, Lv_Trig_Owner, Lv_Trig_Name, Lv_Trig_Body);
    Lv_Lineno := Lv_Lineno + 1;

    WRITE_OUT(Lv_Lineno, Lv_Trig_Owner, Lv_Trig_Name, '/');
    Lv_Lineno := Lv_Lineno + 1;

end loop;
```

```
    close TRIG_CURSOR;
end;
/
spool cre_trig.sql
select Text
  from TRIG_TEMP
 order by Id_Owner, Id_Name, Lineno
/
spool off
set newpage 1 verify on feedback 6 pagesize 24 linesize 80
set heading on embedded off term on long 80
undefine table_name
undefine tab_owner
```

The gen_trig_81n9.sql script generates a script to re-create all triggers for the given table and owner. Sample output for the gen_trig_81n9.sql script is shown in the following listing:

```
CREATE OR REPLACE TRIGGER app.ref_pre_upd_dbt
BEFORE UPDATE
ON app.app_referrals
REFERENCING NEW AS NEW OLD AS OLD
FOR EACH ROW
DECLARE
begin
BEGIN
set_audit_proc('U', :new.usr_crtd, :new.dt_crtd,
        :new.usr_mdfd, :new.dt_mdfd);
   END;
END;


/
CREATE OR REPLACE TRIGGER app.ref_pre_ins_dbt
BEFORE INSERT
ON app.app_referrals
REFERENCING NEW AS NEW OLD AS OLD
FOR EACH ROW
DECLARE
BEGIN
begin
set_audit_proc('I', :new.usr_crtd, :new.dt_crtd,
        :new.usr_mdfd, :new.dt_mdfd);
   END;
END;

/
```

The generated script provides the commands necessary to re-create the two triggers on the APP_REFERRALS table.

ANNOTATIONS

The gen_trig_81n9.sql script generates the code for all triggers created against a given table. Triggers can be used to enforce business rules that cannot be enforced with check or referential integrity constraints or to generate more detailed auditing information than Oracle auditing provides. Triggers can enforce referential integrity across the different nodes of a distributed database. Triggers can be defined on both a row and statement level, to be executed before or after the DML operation executes, and they can be defined on one or more of the DML operations. As of Oracle8, triggers can be configured to execute instead of the SQL operation that causes the trigger to fire.

The gen_trig_81n9.sql script uses a temporary table to hold individual lines of the **create trigger** statement, writing to the table rather than using DBMS_OUTPUT. PUT_LINE so that you can extract the information for an individual trigger or for all triggers on the table. Using the DBMS_OUTPUT procedure would force you to save and edit the output file for the trigger you want.

The first section of the script does the initial setup, prompting for the table name and table owner for later use via the **accept** command. You can enter '%*table_name*%' to generate a script for all triggers on tables with a similar name, or enter '%' at the table name prompt to generate a script for all triggers on all tables for that owner.

The SQL*Plus **set** command turns off headers (**pagesize 0**), row counts (**feedback off**), and displays of old and new values for the *table_name* and *tab_owner* variables (**verify off**).

```
set echo off term on verify off feedback off long 30000
set pagesize 0 heading off
select 'Creating trigger build script...' from DUAL;

accept table_name  prompt "Enter the name of the Table: "
accept tab_owner prompt "Enter table owner: "
set term off
```

In the next part of the script, a temporary table is created to hold each **create trigger** command and its owner. The Lineno column provides ordering for the lines of the **create trigger** command by trigger name.

```
drop table TRIG_TEMP;

create table TRIG_TEMP (
        Lineno   NUMBER,
        Id_Owner VARCHAR2(30),
        Id_Name  VARCHAR2(30),
        Text     LONG)
/
```

The next section of the script creates the main cursor for the script, TRIG_CURSOR, which selects the information from DBA_TRIGGERS where the table name matches the input variable *table_name* and the table owner matches the input variable *tab_owner*. By selecting for Table_Name rather than Trigger_Name, all triggers on the table will be processed. Using **like** in the **where** clause instead of = allows for wildcards.

```
declare
    cursor TRIG_CURSOR is
        select Owner,
                Trigger_Name,
                Trigger_Type,
                Triggering_Event,
                Table_Owner,
                Table_Name,
                Referencing_Names,
                When_Clause,
                Status,
                Description,
                Trigger_Body,
                Column_Name,
                Action_Type,
                Base_Object_Type
          from DBA_TRIGGERS
         where Table_Owner  = UPPER('&&tab_owner')
           and Table_Name like UPPER('&&table_name')
         order by Trigger_Name;
```

The cursor TRIG_COL_CURSOR, in the following listing, selects the name of any column listed in an **update** trigger. Update triggers have a slightly different syntax than **insert** and **delete** triggers, including the name of the column or columns that cause the trigger to fire. If Column_List in the DBA_TRIGGER_COLS table is 'YES', that column is part of an **update** trigger.

```
    cursor TRIG_COL_CURSOR (A_Trigger_Owner VARCHAR2,
                            A_Trigger_Name  VARCHAR2) is
        select Table_Owner,
                Table_Name,
                Column_Name
          from DBA_TRIGGER_COLS
         where Trigger_Owner = A_Trigger_Owner
           and Trigger_Name  = A_Trigger_Name
           and Column_List   = 'YES';
```

In the next section of the script, the procedure variables for the cursor are declared as TABLE_NAME.Column_Name%**TYPE**. This anchoring of datatypes takes the column definition from within the database itself. If the column definition changes in a different version of Oracle, the procedure will still work because the definition of the column has not been hard coded. *Lv_Of_Count* counts the columns in the **of** clause of an **update** trigger statement to include or remove commas from that clause of the statement. The variable *Lv_Lineno* orders the lines of the **create** statement and is initialized to 0.

```
Lv_Trig_Owner                  DBA_TRIGGERS.Owner%TYPE;
Lv_Trig_Name                   DBA_TRIGGERS.Trigger_Name%TYPE;
Lv_Trig_Type                   DBA_TRIGGERS.Trigger_Type%TYPE;
Lv_Trig_Event                  DBA_TRIGGERS.Triggering_Event%TYPE;
Lv_Trig_Table_Owner            DBA_TRIGGERS.Table_Owner%TYPE;
Lv_Trig_Table_Name             DBA_TRIGGERS.Table_Name%TYPE;
Lv_Trig_Referencing_Names      DBA_TRIGGERS.Referencing_Names%TYPE;
Lv_Trig_When_Clause            DBA_TRIGGERS.When_Clause%TYPE;
Lv_Trig_Status                 DBA_TRIGGERS.Status%TYPE;
Lv_Description                 DBA_TRIGGERS.Description%TYPE;
Lv_Trig_Body                   DBA_TRIGGERS.Trigger_Body%TYPE;
Lv_Column_Name                 DBA_TRIGGERS.Column_Name%TYPE;
Lv_Action_Type                 DBA_TRIGGERS.Action_Type%TYPE;
Lv_Base_Object_Type            DBA_TRIGGERS.Base_Object_Type%TYPE;
Lv_Col_Tab_Owner               DBA_TRIGGER_COLS.Trigger_Owner%TYPE;
Lv_Col_Tab_Name                DBA_TRIGGER_COLS.Table_Name%TYPE;
Lv_Col_Tab_Col_Name            DBA_TRIGGER_COLS.Column_Name%TYPE;

Lv_String                      VARCHAR2(800);
Lv_String2                     VARCHAR2(80);
Lv_String3                     VARCHAR2(80);
Lv_Of_Count                    INTEGER;
Lv_Lineno                      NUMBER := 0;
```

The internal procedure WRITE_OUT is defined to do the **insert** into the temporary table. WRITE_OUT will be called later in the script to help build the **create table** script.

```
procedure WRITE_OUT(P_Line INTEGER,  P_Owner VARCHAR2,
                    P_Name VARCHAR2, P_String VARCHAR2) is
begin
   insert into TRIG_TEMP (Lineno, Id_Owner, Id_Name, Text)
          values (P_Line,P_Owner,P_Name,P_String);
   end;
```

The next section of the script begins the executable commands. TRIG_CURSOR forms an outer loop for each trigger for the requested table. The *Lv_Lineno* variable, in conjunction with the trigger name, orders the rows in the temporary table TRIG_TEMP so that if you prefer, you can extract the **create trigger** statement for a single trigger at the end of the procedure.

```
begin
   open TRIG_CURSOR;
   loop
```

```
fetch TRIG_CURSOR into Lv_Trig_Owner,
                       Lv_Trig_Name,
                       Lv_Trig_Type,
                       Lv_Trig_Event,
                       Lv_Trig_Table_Owner,
                       Lv_Trig_Table_Name,
                       Lv_Trig_Referencing_Names,
                       Lv_Trig_When_Clause,
                       Lv_Trig_Status,
                       Lv_Description,
                       Lv_Trig_Body,
                       Lv_Column_Name,
                       Lv_Action_Type,
                       Lv_Base_Object_Type;
exit when TRIG_CURSOR%NOTFOUND;
```

The script generates the proper **create** string and writes it to the temporary table. Using the **create or replace** syntax ensures that if the trigger exists, no error will be generated when the script is run. The **LOWER** function changes the text to all lowercase to make the output more readable.

```
Lv_String:= 'CREATE OR REPLACE TRIGGER ' || LOWER(Lv_Trig_Owner)
                                          || '.'
                                          || LOWER(Lv_Trig_Name);
WRITE_OUT(Lv_Lineno, Lv_Trig_Owner, Lv_Trig_Name, Lv_String);
Lv_Lineno := Lv_Lineno + 1;
```

The *Lv_Trig_Type* variable value contains the type of trigger. The syntax of a **create trigger** statement needs only the word **before** or **after** at this point, not the full type of the trigger. The portion of the script in the next listing will extract the required word, keeping the blank after it so that a blank does not need to be concatenated in, and then concatenate it with the triggering event—the DML operation—before writing it to the temporary table.

The **SUBSTR** function trims the *Lv_Trig_Type* value based on the location of the first space in the value. The **INSTR** function determines the location of the first space in the *Lv_Trig_Type* variable's value, and **SUBSTR** uses that location when determining the number of characters to select. A new trigger type, **INSTEAD OF**, was introduced in Oracle8. This trigger is used to **delete**, **update**, or **insert** into views that are not inherently modifiable. These views are created by the following:

◆ set operators

◆ group functions

◆ **group by**, **connect by**, or **start with** clauses

◆ the DISTINCT operator

◆ joins (a subset of join views are updatable)

Because the script extracts the trigger type only up to the first space, it will miss the full syntax of the new trigger type. It will check for the new trigger type and add the **OF** back into the string.

```
Lv_String2:= SUBSTR(Lv_Trig_Type,1,INSTR(Lv_Trig_Type,' '));
if (Lv_String2 = 'INSTEAD ')
then
    LV_String2 := Lv_String2 || 'OF ';
end if;


Lv_string := Lv_String2 || Lv_Trig_Event;
WRITE_OUT(Lv_Lineno, Lv_Trig_Owner, Lv_Trig_Name, Lv_String);
Lv_Lineno := Lv_Lineno + 1;
```

If the trigger is an **update** trigger, the columns that cause it to fire are stored in the DBA_TRIGGERING_COLS table, referenced by the TRIG_COL_CURSOR. As shown in the following listing, the columns are retrieved by the cursor, and, depending on whether or not the column is the first one, they are prefixed by either **OF** or a comma. Each column is written to the temporary table. The **LOWER** function makes the output more readable.

```
Lv_Of_Count := 0;
open TRIG_COL_CURSOR (Lv_Trig_Owner,Lv_Trig_Name);
loop
    fetch TRIG_COL_CURSOR into      Lv_Col_Tab_Owner,
                                    Lv_Col_Tab_Name,
                                    Lv_Col_Tab_Col_Name;
    exit when TRIG_COL_CURSOR%NOTFOUND;
    Lv_Of_Count := Lv_Of_Count + 1;

    If ( Lv_Of_Count = 1 )
    then
            Lv_String   := '  OF ' || LOWER(Lv_Col_Tab_Col_Name);
    else
            Lv_String   := '     ,' ||LOWER(Lv_Col_Tab_Col_Name);
    end if;
    WRITE_OUT(Lv_Lineno, Lv_Trig_Owner, Lv_Trig_Name, Lv_String);
    Lv_Lineno := Lv_Lineno + 1;
end loop;
close TRIG_COL_CURSOR;
```

The next section of the script adds the lines defining the table owner and table and the correlation names to the temporary table. We also determine whether the trigger is defined at the database, schema, or object level. Further, this script also deals with triggers placed on nested tables. The correlation names allow you to refer to both the old and new values of a column in the trigger.

```
Lv_String := 'ON ';

    if (Lv_Base_Object_Type in ('TABLE','VIEW'))
    then

        Lv_String3 := ' ';

        if (Lv_Column_Name IS NOT NULL)
        then

            Lv_String3:=' NESTED TABLE '        ||
                        Lv_Column_Name          ||
                        ' OF ';
        end if;

        Lv_String:= Lv_String                   ||
                    Lv_String3                  ||
                    LOWER(Lv_Trig_Table_Owner)  ||
                    '.'                         ||
                    LOWER(Lv_Trig_Table_Name);


    elsif
        (Lv_Base_Object_Type = 'DATABASE')
        then

            Lv_String:= Lv_String               ||
                        ' DATABASE ';

        else

            Lv_String:= Lv_String               ||
                        Lv_Trig_Table_Owner     ||
                        '.SCHEMA';


    end if;

    WRITE_OUT(Lv_Lineno, Lv_Trig_Owner, Lv_Trig_Name, Lv_String);
    Lv_Lineno := Lv_Lineno + 1;


    WRITE_OUT(Lv_Lineno, Lv_Trig_Owner, Lv_Trig_Name,
```

```
                     Lv_Trig_Referencing_Names);
      Lv_Lineno := Lv_Lineno + 1;
```

At this point in the script, the type of trigger (row or statement) needs to be added to the **create trigger** command in the temporary table. By default, triggers are created as statement triggers, and nothing needs to be added to the temporary table. Statement triggers fire once for the DML statement, regardless of the number of rows affected. Row-level triggers fire for each row affected by the DML operation.

```
if (INSTR(Lv_Trig_Type,'EACH ROW') > 0)
then
    Lv_String := 'FOR EACH ROW';
    WRITE_OUT(Lv_Lineno, Lv_Trig_Owner, Lv_Trig_Name, Lv_String);
    Lv_Lineno := Lv_Lineno + 1;
elsif (INSTR(Lv_Trig_Type,'STATEMENT') > 0)
then
    Lv_String := 'FOR EACH STATEMENT';
    WRITE_OUT(Lv_Lineno, Lv_Trig_Owner, Lv_Trig_Name, Lv_String);
    Lv_Lineno := Lv_Lineno + 1;
end if;
```

The next portion of the script determines whether any **when** clauses affect the trigger's execution. You can limit when a trigger will fire based on a SQL condition. You can specify this restriction only on row-level triggers.

```
if (Lv_Trig_When_Clause IS NOT NULL)
then
    Lv_String := 'WHEN (' || Lv_Trig_When_Clause || ')';
    WRITE_OUT(Lv_Lineno, Lv_Trig_Owner, Lv_Trig_Name, Lv_String);
    Lv_Lineno := Lv_Lineno + 1;
end if;
```

The next section determines whether an inline PL/SQL code block is executed or an external procedure called.

```
if (Lv_Action_Type = 'CALL')
then
    Lv_String := ' CALL ';
    WRITE_OUT(Lv_Lineno, Lv_Trig_Owner, Lv_Trig_Name, Lv_String);
    Lv_Lineno := Lv_Lineno + 1;
end if;
```

The final section of the script re-creates the actual PL/SQL block that will execute if the trigger fires. The trigger body is written to the temporary table, and the **create trigger** statement is ended with a slash (/) so that it will execute when you run the generated script. The cursor loop will repeat for each trigger on the requested table.

Once the final entry has been inserted into the temporary table, the script selects the command syntax from the temporary table.

```
        WRITE_OUT(Lv_Lineno, Lv_Trig_Owner, Lv_Trig_Name, Lv_Trig_Body);
        Lv_Lineno := Lv_Lineno + 1;

        WRITE_OUT(Lv_Lineno, Lv_Trig_Owner, Lv_Trig_Name, '/');
        Lv_Lineno := Lv_Lineno + 1;

   end loop;
   close TRIG_CURSOR;
end;
/

spool cre_trig.sql
select Text
  from TRIG_TEMP
 order by Id_Owner, Id_Name, Lineno
/
spool off
```

Once the **create trigger** commands for all the triggers have been generated, they are spooled to a file for later execution.

A sample-generated **create trigger** script is shown in the following listing.

```
CREATE OR REPLACE TRIGGER app.ref_pre_upd_dbt
BEFORE UPDATE
ON app.app_referrals
REFERENCING NEW AS NEW OLD AS OLD
FOR EACH ROW
DECLARE
begin
BEGIN
set_audit_proc('U', :new.usr_crtd, :new.dt_crtd,
        :new.usr_mdfd, :new.dt_mdfd);
   END;
END;


/
CREATE OR REPLACE TRIGGER app.ref_pre_ins_dbt
BEFORE INSERT
ON app.app_referrals
REFERENCING NEW AS NEW OLD AS OLD
FOR EACH ROW
DECLARE
BEGIN
begin
set_audit_proc('I', :new.usr_crtd, :new.dt_crtd,
        :new.usr_mdfd, :new.dt_mdfd);
```

```
    END;
END;

/
```

The sample table has two triggers, a **before update** and a **before insert** on each row. The **referencing new as new old as old** clause allows the PL/SQL block in the trigger to refer to the new column values and the old column values in the same procedure by prefixing the column names with **:new** or **:old**.

As an alternative, if you want to use this script to document all the triggers on all tables for a particular owner, remove the **accept** *table_name* statement at the beginning of the script and change the **where** clause for the TRIG_CURSOR cursor like so:

```
where Table_Owner  = UPPER('&&tab_owner')
```

If you want to document all triggers in your database that are not owned by SYS, remove the two **accept** statements from the beginning of the script and change the **where** clause for the TRIG_CURSOR cursor like so:

```
where Table_Owner != 'SYS'
```

Generate Views

gen_view_7.sql
gen_view_8.sql
gen_view_9.sql

Views present a tailored picture of the data in the database. You can create views that are exact replicas of the underlying table, to allow for table modifications without creating problems in application code, or that show selected columns and rows of one or more tables. You can use views to rename columns and to restrict access to certain columns or the data they contain. The script gen_view_*.sql will generate a script to re-create a view. The scripts gen_view_7.sql, gen_view_8.sql, and gen_view_9.sql can be used with Oracle7.x, Oracle8.x, and Oracle9.x, respectively. All the gen_view_*.sql scripts are available on the CD-ROM with this book.

The script gen_view_9.sql is listed here:

```
REM
REM gen_view_9.sql
REM This script can be used for Oracle9.x only.
REM
set echo off verify off term on feedback off pagesize 0 long 32760
set heading off
select 'Creating view build script...' from DUAL;

accept view_name prompt "Enter the name of the View: "
accept view_owner prompt "Enter view owner: "
set term off

drop    table VIEW_TEMP
/
```

```
create table VIEW_TEMP (
        Lineno NUMBER,
        Id_Owner VARCHAR2(30),
        Id_Name VARCHAR2(30),
        Text LONG)
/

declare
   cursor VIEW_CURSOR is
        select Owner,
                View_Name,
                Text_Length,
                Text,
                Oid_Text,
                View_Type_Owner,
                View_Type,
                Superview_Name
          from DBA_VIEWS
         where Owner like UPPER('&&view_owner')
           and Owner not in ('SYS','SYSTEM')
           and View_Name like UPPER('&&view_name')
         order by Owner, View_Name;

    Cursor VIEW_COLS_CURSOR (V_Name VARCHAR2, V_Owner VARCHAR2) is
         select Column_Name
           from DBA_TAB_COLUMNS
          where Table_Name = V_Name
            and Owner = V_Owner
          order by Column_ID;

    Lv_Owner            DBA_VIEWS.Owner%TYPE;
    Lv_View_Name        DBA_VIEWS.View_Name%TYPE;
    Lv_Text_Length      DBA_VIEWS.Text_Length%TYPE;
    Lv_Text             DBA_VIEWS.Text%TYPE;
    Lv_Oid_Text         DBA_VIEWS.Oid_Text%TYPE;
    Lv_View_Type_owner  DBA_VIEWS.View_Type_Owner%TYPE;
    Lv_View_Type        DBA_VIEWS.View_Type%TYPE;
    Lv_Superview_Name   DBA_VIEWS.Superview_Name%TYPE;
    Lv_Column_Name      DBA_TAB_COLUMNS.Column_Name%TYPE;
    Lv_Separator        VARCHAR2(1);
    Lv_Substr_Start     NUMBER;
    Lv_Substr_Len       NUMBER;
    Lv_String           VARCHAR2(32760);
    Lv_Lineno           NUMBER;

    procedure WRITE_OUT(P_Line INTEGER, P_Owner varchar2, P_Name VARCHAR2,
                        P_String VARCHAR2) is
    begin
       insert into VIEW_TEMP (Lineno, Id_Owner, Id_Name, Text)
```

```
             values (P_Line,P_Owner,P_Name,P_String);
        end;

begin
   open VIEW_CURSOR;
   loop
      fetch VIEW_CURSOR into Lv_Owner,
                             Lv_View_Name,
                             Lv_Text_Length,
                             Lv_Text,
                             Lv_Oid_Text,
                             Lv_View_Type_Owner,
                             Lv_View_Type,
                             Lv_Superview_Name;
      exit when VIEW_CURSOR%NOTFOUND;

      Lv_Lineno := 1;

      Lv_String:= 'CREATE OR REPLACE VIEW ' || LOWER(Lv_Owner)
                                            || '.'
                                            || LOWER(Lv_View_Name);
      WRITE_OUT(Lv_Lineno, Lv_Owner, Lv_View_Name, Lv_String);
      Lv_Lineno := Lv_Lineno + 1;

      if (Lv_View_Type_Owner is not null)
      then
          Lv_String:= ' OF '|| LOWER(Lv_View_Type_Owner)
                            || '.'
                            || LOWER(Lv_View_Type);
          if (Lv_Superview_Name is null)
          then
              Lv_String:= Lv_String||' WITH OBJECT IDENTIFIER
('||Lv_Oid_Text||')';
          else
              Lv_String:= Lv_String||' UNDER '||Lv_Owner||'.'||
Lv_Superview_Name;
          end if;

          WRITE_OUT(Lv_Lineno, Lv_Owner, Lv_View_Name, Lv_String);
          Lv_Lineno := Lv_Lineno + 1;

      else

          Lv_String := '';
          Lv_Separator := '(';
          open VIEW_COLS_CURSOR (Lv_View_Name, Lv_Owner);

          loop
            fetch VIEW_COLS_CURSOR into Lv_Column_Name;
```

```
       exit when VIEW_COLS_CURSOR%NOTFOUND;

       Lv_String := Lv_Separator
                     || Lv_Column_Name;
       Lv_Separator := ',';
       WRITE_OUT(Lv_Lineno, Lv_Owner, Lv_View_Name, Lv_String);
       Lv_Lineno := Lv_Lineno + 1;

     end loop;

     Lv_String := ')';
     WRITE_OUT(Lv_Lineno, Lv_Owner, Lv_View_Name, Lv_String);
     Lv_Lineno := Lv_Lineno + 1;
     close VIEW_COLS_CURSOR;

   end if;

   Lv_string := 'AS';
   WRITE_OUT(Lv_Lineno, Lv_Owner, Lv_View_Name, Lv_String);
   Lv_Lineno := Lv_Lineno + 1;

   Lv_Substr_Start := 1;
   Lv_Substr_Len   := Lv_Text_Length;
   if Lv_Substr_Len > 32760
   then
       Lv_Substr_Len := 32760;
   end if;

   loop
       Lv_String := SUBSTR(Lv_Text,Lv_Substr_Start, Lv_Substr_Len);
       WRITE_OUT(Lv_Lineno, Lv_Owner, Lv_View_Name, Lv_String);
       Lv_Lineno := Lv_Lineno + 1;

       Lv_Substr_Start := Lv_Substr_Start + Lv_Substr_Len;
       if (Lv_Substr_Start + Lv_Substr_Len) > Lv_Text_Length
       then
           Lv_Substr_Len := Lv_Text_Length -
                             (Lv_Substr_Start + Lv_Substr_Len);
       end if;
       exit when Lv_Substr_Start > Lv_Text_Length;
   end loop;

   Lv_String   := '/';
   WRITE_OUT(Lv_Lineno, Lv_Owner, Lv_View_Name, Lv_String);
   Lv_Lineno := Lv_Lineno + 1;

 end loop;
 close VIEW_CURSOR;
end;
```

```
/
spool cre_view.sql
select Text
  from VIEW_TEMP
 order by Id_Owner, Id_Name, Lineno
/
spool off
set newpage 1 verify on feedback 6 pagesize 24 linesize 80
set heading on embedded off term on long 80
undefine view_name
undefine view_owner
```

Sample output for the gen_view_9.sql script is shown here:

```
CREATE OR REPLACE VIEW demo.sales
(SALESPERSON_ID
,CUSTOMER_ID
,CUSTOMER
,PRODUCT_ID
,PRODUCT
,AMOUNT
)
AS
SELECT SALESPERSON_ID, SALES_ORDER.CUSTOMER_ID, CUSTOMER.NAME CUSTOMER,
       PRODUCT.PRODUCT_ID, DESCRIPTION PRODUCT, SUM(ITEM.TOTAL) AMOUNT
FROM SALES_ORDER, ITEM, CUSTOMER, PRODUCT
WHERE SALES_ORDER.ORDER_ID = ITEM.ORDER_ID
AND SALES_ORDER.CUSTOMER_ID = CUSTOMER.CUSTOMER_ID
AND ITEM.PRODUCT_ID = PRODUCT.PRODUCT_ID
GROUP BY SALESPERSON_ID, SALES_ORDER.CUSTOMER_ID, CUSTOMER.NAME,
         PRODUCT.PRODUCT_ID, DESCRIPTION

/
```

The generated script is automatically saved to a file that you can edit and execute.

ANNOTATIONS

Although all information about a view is stored in a single row of the DBA_VIEWS view, the script uses a cursor to allow you to enter a wildcard value or to modify the script to select all views for an owner or all views in the database. The gen_view.sql script uses a temporary table to hold individual lines of the **create view** statement, writing to the table rather than using DBMS_OUTPUT.PUT_LINE so that you can extract the information for an individual view or for all views. Using the DBMS_OUTPUT procedure would force you to save and edit the output file for the view you want.

The first section of the script does the initial setup, prompting for the view name and view owner for later use via the **accept** command. You can enter the view name with the '%' wildcard to generate a script for all views with a similar name. Also, you can enter the view owner with a '%' wildcard to generate a script for all views within the database.

The SQL*Plus **set** command turns off headers (**pagesize 0**), row counts (**feedback off**), and displays of old and new values for the *view_name* and *view_owner* variables (**verify off**).

```
set echo off verify off term on feedback off pagesize 0 long 32760
set heading off
select 'Creating view build script...' from DUAL;
accept view_name prompt "Enter the name of the View: "
accept view_owner prompt "Enter view owner: "
set term off
```

The next section of the script, shown in the following listing, creates a temporary table to hold each **create view** command and its owner. The Lineno column orders the lines of the **create view** command. Since the Text column of DBA_VIEWS is defined with a LONG datatype, the Text column of the temporary table is also defined LONG, to allow the sections of the view definition to be stored.

```
drop    table VIEW_TEMP
/

create table VIEW_TEMP (
        Lineno NUMBER,
        Id_Owner VARCHAR2(30),
        Id_Name VARCHAR2(30),
        Text LONG)
/
```

The next section of the script defines the VIEW_CURSOR cursor, which selects the storage information from DBA_VIEWS, where the view name matches the input variable *view_name* and the table owner matches the input variable *view_owner*. While a cursor is not needed if you are running the script for a single view, using the cursor with **like** in the **where** clause allows you to enter a wildcard value ('%*view_name*%' or '%') to match more than one view name.

```
declare
   cursor VIEW_CURSOR is
        select Owner,
               View_Name,
               Text_Length,
               Text,
               Oid_Text,
               View_Type_Owner,
               View_Type
          from DBA_VIEWS
        where Owner like UPPER('&&view_owner')
          and Owner not in ('SYS','SYSTEM')
```

```
        and View_Name like UPPER('&&view_name')
    order by Owner, View_Name;
```

The next section of the script defines the VIEW_COLS_CURSOR. You can create views with column names that do not match those of the underlying tables. One use for this is a view that takes a column with the same name from two different tables. Since you can't create duplicate column names in a table or view, you have to rename one or both of the columns. Column names for views are stored in the DBA_TAB_COLUMNS data dictionary view. This cursor will extract all column names for each view selected. No distinction is made between renamed columns and those whose names match the underlying table columns.

```
Cursor VIEW_COLS_CURSOR (V_Name VARCHAR2, V_Owner VARCHAR2) is
        select Column_Name
          from DBA_TAB_COLUMNS
        where Table_Name = V_Name
          and Owner = V_Owner
        order by Column_ID;
```

The procedure variables for the cursor are declared as TABLE_NAME.Column_Name%**TYPE**. The anchoring of datatypes takes the column definition from within the database itself. If the column definition changes in a different version of Oracle, the procedure will still work because the definition of the column has not been hard coded.

Since the Text column in DBA_VIEWS is a LONG datatype, containing the entire view definition, the script needs to allow for long values. You cannot define a PL/SQL variable as a LONG, so the insert string variable *Lv_String* is defined as VARCHAR2(32760), and *Lv_Substr_Start* and *Lv_Substr_Len* will help break the Text column into several lines that can be handled by the PL/SQL variable *Lv_String*. The variable *Lv_Lineno* is used to order the lines of the **create view** statement and is initialized to 0.

```
Lv_Owner              DBA_VIEWS.Owner%TYPE;
Lv_View_Name          DBA_VIEWS.View_Name%TYPE;
Lv_Text_Length        DBA_VIEWS.Text_Length%TYPE;
Lv_Text               DBA_VIEWS.Text%TYPE;
Lv_Oid_Text           DBA_VIEWS.Oid_Text%TYPE;
Lv_View_Type_owner    DBA_VIEWS.View_Type_Owner%TYPE;
Lv_View_Type          DBA_VIEWS.View_Type%TYPE;
Lv_Column_Name        DBA_TAB_COLUMNS.Column_Name%TYPE;
Lv_Separator          VARCHAR2(1);
Lv_Substr_Start       NUMBER;
Lv_Substr_Len         NUMBER;
Lv_String             VARCHAR2(32760);
Lv_Lineno             NUMBER;
```

The next section of the script creates WRITE_OUT, an internal procedure that performs the **insert** into the temporary table.

```
procedure WRITE_OUT(P_Line INTEGER, P_Owner VARCHAR2, P_Name VARCHAR2,
                    P_String VARCHAR2) is
begin
   insert into VIEW_TEMP (Lineno, Id_Owner, Id_Name, Text)
           values (P_Line,P_Owner,P_Name,P_String);
   end;
```

In the next section of the gen_view_8.sql script, shown in the following listing, the VIEW_CURSOR is executed. A cursor is used in this section of the script to allow for wildcards in the entered *view_name* and to allow for changes to the script to select all views for a given user or all views in the database.

```
begin
   open VIEW_CURSOR;
   loop
      fetch VIEW_CURSOR into Lv_Owner,
                             Lv_View_Name,
                             Lv_Text_Length,
                             Lv_Text,
                             Lv_Oid_Text,
                             Lv_View_Type_Owner,
                             Lv_View_Type;
      exit when VIEW_CURSOR%NOTFOUND;
```

The next section of the script begins the generation of the **create view** command script. The **create or replace** clause retains all grants on a view that is being replaced. If you were to drop the view and then create it, all grants would be lost.

```
      Lv_Lineno := 1;

      Lv_String:= 'CREATE OR REPLACE VIEW ' || LOWER(Lv_Owner)
                                            || '.'
                                            || LOWER(Lv_View_Name);
      WRITE_OUT(Lv_Lineno, Lv_Owner, Lv_View_Name, Lv_String);
      Lv_Lineno := Lv_Lineno + 1;
```

The next section of the script processes the column names for the view. No distinction is made between view columns whose names match those of the underlying table columns and those who have been renamed. View columns, like table columns, are listed in the DBA_TAB_COLUMNS data dictionary view. The column names are fetched by the VIEW_COLS_CURSOR inserted into the temporary table one by one. As of Oracle8.x, you can create object views, and the following code section also determines whether the view is an object view and generates the appropriate clause.

```
if (Lv_View_Type_Owner is not null)
    then
        Lv_String:= ' OF '|| LOWER(Lv_View_Type_Owner)
                          || '.'
                          || LOWER(Lv_View_Type);
        Lv_String:= Lv_String||' WITH OBJECT OID ('||Lv_Oid_Text||')';

        WRITE_OUT(Lv_Lineno, Lv_Owner, Lv_View_Name, Lv_String);
        Lv_Lineno := Lv_Lineno + 1;

    else

        Lv_String := '';
        Lv_Separator := '(';
        open VIEW_COLS_CURSOR (Lv_View_Name, Lv_Owner);

        loop
          fetch VIEW_COLS_CURSOR into Lv_Column_Name;
          exit when VIEW_COLS_CURSOR%NOTFOUND;

          Lv_String := Lv_Separator
                        || Lv_Column_Name;
          Lv_Separator := ',';
          WRITE_OUT(Lv_Lineno, Lv_Owner, Lv_View_Name, Lv_String);
          Lv_Lineno := Lv_Lineno + 1;

        end loop;

        Lv_String := ')';
        WRITE_OUT(Lv_Lineno, Lv_Owner, Lv_View_Name, Lv_String);
        Lv_Lineno := Lv_Lineno + 1;
        close VIEW_COLS_CURSOR;

    end if;
```

The next portion of the script, shown in the next listing, selects the view's base query from the data dictionary. Because that column in the data dictionary is defined with a LONG datatype, you need to modify the manner in which you select the data.

PL/SQL variables can be defined to a maximum length of 32,767, but LONG columns can contain text up to 2GB. To capture the entire view definition if it is longer than 32,767 bytes, a loop is used and the text is **SUBSTR**ed out in chunks of 32,760 bytes and written to the temporary table before the next chunk is extracted. The **SUBSTR** start variable, *Lv_Substr_Start*, is incremented by the length of the previous substring, *Lv_Substr_Len*, and if the next chunk will go past the end of the Text column, the **SUBSTR** length variable is reset to the number of bytes remaining. The loop ends when the start point is greater than the total length of the view text.

Unfortunately, it isn't possible to guarantee that the text will break on a space. If your views tend to be extremely long, review the generated script for valid line breaks before running it.

```
Lv_string := 'AS';
WRITE_OUT(Lv_Lineno, Lv_Owner, Lv_View_Name, Lv_String);
Lv_Lineno := Lv_Lineno + 1;

Lv_Substr_Start := 1;
Lv_Substr_Len   := Lv_Text_Length;
if Lv_Substr_Len > 32760
then
    Lv_Substr_Len := 32760;
end if;

loop
    Lv_String := SUBSTR(Lv_Text,Lv_Substr_Start, Lv_Substr_Len);
    WRITE_OUT(Lv_Lineno, Lv_Owner, Lv_View_Name, Lv_String);
    Lv_Lineno := Lv_Lineno + 1;

    Lv_Substr_Start := Lv_Substr_Start + Lv_Substr_Len;
    if (Lv_Substr_Start + Lv_Substr_Len) > Lv_Text_Length
    then
        Lv_Substr_Len := Lv_Text_Length -
                         (Lv_Substr_Start + Lv_Substr_Len);
    end if;
    exit when Lv_Substr_Start > Lv_Text_Length;
end loop;
```

In the final portion of the script, the cursor loop ends and the procedure will loop back through the VIEW_CURSOR until all views have been generated. Then the cursor closes and the procedure exits.

```
Lv_String  := '/';
WRITE_OUT(Lv_Lineno, Lv_Owner, Lv_View_Name, Lv_String);
Lv_Lineno := Lv_Lineno + 1;

end loop;
close VIEW_CURSOR;
end;
/

spool cre_view.sql
select   Text
  from   VIEW_TEMP
order by Id_Owner, Id_Name, Lineno
/
```

```
spool off
set newpage 1 verify on feedback 6 pagesize 24 linesize 80
set heading on embedded off term on long 80
undefine view_name
undefine view_owner
```

Once the **create** statements for all the views have been generated, they are spooled to a file called cre_view.sql for later execution. The following listing shows a sample cre_view.sql file:

```
CREATE OR REPLACE VIEW demo.sales
 (SALESPERSON_ID
,CUSTOMER_ID
,CUSTOMER
,PRODUCT_ID
,PRODUCT
,AMOUNT
)
AS
SELECT SALESPERSON_ID, SALES_ORDER.CUSTOMER_ID, CUSTOMER.NAME CUSTOMER,
       PRODUCT.PRODUCT_ID, DESCRIPTION PRODUCT, SUM(ITEM.TOTAL) AMOUNT
FROM SALES_ORDER, ITEM, CUSTOMER, PRODUCT
WHERE SALES_ORDER.ORDER_ID = ITEM.ORDER_ID
AND SALES_ORDER.CUSTOMER_ID = CUSTOMER.CUSTOMER_ID
AND ITEM.PRODUCT_ID = PRODUCT.PRODUCT_ID
GROUP BY SALESPERSON_ID, SALES_ORDER.CUSTOMER_ID, CUSTOMER.NAME,
         PRODUCT.PRODUCT_ID, DESCRIPTION
/
```

The gen_view.sql script will generate a script for a single view. As an alternative, if you want to use this script to document all the views for a particular owner, remove the **accept** *view_name* statement at the beginning of the script and change the **where** clause for the VIEW_CURSOR cursor like so:

```
where Owner = UPPER('&&view_owner')
```

or you can use '%' for the wildcard.

If you want to document all views in your database that are not owned by SYS, remove the two **accept** statements from the beginning of the script and change the **where** clause for the VIEW_CURSOR cursor to this:

```
where Owner != 'SYS'
```

Oracle9i allows you to create a view as a subview based on an object superview. The script gen_view_9.sql extends the script gen_view_8.sql by allowing the creation of views based on superviews.

Generate Synonyms

Synonyms mask the real name and owner of an object. Synonyms simplify SQL statements and simplify public access to an object. You can use synonyms to hide the location and ownership of an object and to move an object without forcing re-coding of the application.

You can create both public and private synonyms in your database. Public synonyms are accessible to all users, but you will still need to grant object privileges to the users before they can execute the procedure or view the data in the table. If you use roles in your database, you should create public synonyms for the objects that will be accessed, since roles cannot own synonyms. You can grant the object privileges to the role. If you have the CREATE PUBLIC SYNONYM privilege or the DBA role, you can create synonyms for other users.

When evaluating the name and permissions to an object, Oracle first checks to see whether the user owns an object of that name; it then checks to see whether the user owns a private synonym with that name. Finally, Oracle checks to see whether a public synonym with that name exists. You should keep track of both private and public synonyms so that you don't have duplicates for the same object.

The script in this section, gen_syn.sql, generates the SQL commands needed to re-create all synonyms, public or private, for a specified object. Synonyms can be created for tables, views, sequences, database links, packages, procedures, and functions. The following listing shows the full gen_syn.sql script:

```
REM
REM gen_syn.sql
REM This script can be used for Oracle7.x and above
REM
set echo off term on verify off feedback off pagesize 0 heading off
select 'Creating synonym build script...' from DUAL;

accept syn_object prompt "Enter the synonym object: "
accept syn_owner prompt "Enter the object owner: "
set term off

drop    table SYN_TEMP
/

create table SYN_TEMP (
        Lineno NUMBER,
        Id_Owner VARCHAR2(30),
        Id_Name VARCHAR2(30),
        Text VARCHAR2(350))
/

declare
   cursor SYN_CURSOR is
```

```
           select Owner,
                  Synonym_Name,
                  Table_Owner,
                  Table_Name,
                  Db_Link
             from DBA_SYNONYMS
            where Table_Owner like UPPER('&&syn_owner')
              and Table_Owner not in ('SYS','SYSTEM','PUBLIC')
              and Table_Name like UPPER('&&syn_object')
            order by Owner, Table_Owner, Table_Name;


   Lv_Owner              DBA_SYNONYMS.Owner%TYPE;
   Lv_Synonym_Name       DBA_SYNONYMS.Synonym_Name%TYPE;
   Lv_Table_Owner        DBA_SYNONYMS.Table_Owner%TYPE;
   Lv_Table_Name         DBA_SYNONYMS.Table_Name%TYPE;
   Lv_DBLink             DBA_SYNONYMS.DB_Link%TYPE;
   Lv_String             VARCHAR2(350);
   Lv_Lineno             NUMBER;

   procedure WRITE_OUT(P_Line INTEGER, P_Owner VARCHAR2, P_Name VARCHAR2,
                   P_String VARCHAR2) is
   begin
      insert into SYN_TEMP (Lineno, Id_Owner, Id_Name, Text)
             values (P_Line,P_Owner,P_Name,P_String);
    end;

begin
   open SYN_CURSOR;
   Lv_Lineno  := 1;
   loop
      fetch SYN_CURSOR into    Lv_Owner,
                               Lv_Synonym_Name,
                               Lv_Table_Owner,
                               Lv_Table_Name,
                               Lv_DBLink;
      exit when SYN_CURSOR%NOTFOUND;

      if ( Lv_Owner = 'PUBLIC' )
      then
         Lv_String  := 'CREATE PUBLIC SYNONYM ' || Lv_Synonym_Name
                                                || ' FOR '
                                                || Lv_Table_Owner
                                                || '.'
                                                || Lv_Table_Name;       else
         Lv_String  := 'CREATE SYNONYM '        || Lv_Owner
                                                || '.'
                                                || Lv_Synonym_Name
                                                || ' FOR '
```

```
                                                  || Lv_Table_Owner
                                                  || '.'
                                                  || Lv_Table_Name;
        end if;

        if (Lv_DBLink is NOT NULL)
        then
            Lv_String := Lv_String || '@' || Lv_DBLink;
        end if;

        WRITE_OUT(Lv_Lineno, Lv_Owner, Lv_Table_Name, Lv_String);
        Lv_Lineno := Lv_Lineno + 1;
        WRITE_OUT(Lv_Lineno, Lv_Owner, Lv_Table_Name, '/');
        Lv_Lineno := Lv_Lineno + 1;
    end loop;

    close SYN_CURSOR;
end;
/
spool cre_syn.sql
select Text
  from SYN_TEMP
 order by Id_Owner, Id_Name, Lineno
/
spool off
set newpage 1 verify on feedback 6 pagesize 24 linesize 80
set heading on embedded off term on
undefine syn_object
undefine syn_owner
```

Sample generated output for this script is shown in the following listing.

```
CREATE PUBLIC SYNONYM EMP_ADDRESSES FOR APP.EMP_ADDRESSES
/
CREATE SYNONYM QCUSER1.EMP_ADDRESSES FOR APP.EMP_ADDRESSES
/
```

Oracle will write the script's output to a file named cre_syn.sql, which you can edit
and execute.

ANNOTATIONS

Because multiple synonyms can exist for the same object, the script uses a cursor both to
extract the synonym information and to allow you to enter a wildcard value for the table
name. The script uses a temporary table to hold individual lines of the **create synonym**
statement, writing to the table rather than using DBMS_OUTPUT.PUT_LINE so that
you can extract the information for an individual synonym on the object. Using the
DBMS_OUTPUT procedure would force you to save and edit the output file for the
synonym you want.

The first section of the script does the initial setup, prompting for the object name and object owner for later use via the **accept** command, which, unlike simply using the variable with the '&' or '&&' in a SQL statement, allows you to define your own prompt for the variable. You can enter the object name with '%' to generate a script for all synonyms for all objects with a similar name. Also you can use '%' for object owner.

The SQL*Plus **set** command turns off headers (**pagesize 0**), row counts (**feedback off**), and displays of old and new values for the *object_name* and *object_owner* variables (**verify off**).

```
set echo off term on verify off feedback off pagesize 0 heading off
select 'Creating synonym build script...' from DUAL;

accept syn_object prompt "Enter the synonym object: "
accept syn_owner prompt "Enter the object owner: "
set term off
```

The next section of the script, shown in the following listing, creates a temporary table to hold each **create synonym** command and its owner. The Lineno column orders the lines of the **create synonym** command.

```
drop    table SYN_TEMP
/

create table SYN_TEMP (
        Lineno NUMBER,
        Id_Owner VARCHAR2(30),
        Id_Name VARCHAR2(30),
        Text VARCHAR2(350))
/
```

The SYN_CURSOR cursor, shown in the following listing, selects the information from DBA_SYNONYMS, where the table name matches the input variable *object_name* and the table owner matches the input variable *object_owner*. The column names in DBA_SYNONYMS are misleading because synonyms can be created on objects other than tables. Using **like** in the **where** clause instead of = allows for wildcards.

```
declare
   cursor SYN_CURSOR is
        select Owner,
               Synonym_Name,
               Table_Owner,
               Table_Name,
               Db_Link
          from DBA_SYNONYMS
         where Table_Owner like UPPER('&&syn_owner')
```

```
      and Table_Name like UPPER('&&syn_object')
      order by Owner, Table_Owner, Table_Name;
```

In the next section of the script, the procedure variables for the cursor are declared as TABLE_NAME.Column_Name%TYPE. Anchoring the variable definitions in this manner takes the column definition from within the database itself. If the column definition changes in a different version of Oracle, the procedure will still work because the definition of the column has not been hard coded. The variable *Lv_Lineno*, which orders the lines of the **create synonym** command, is initialized to 0.

```
   Lv_Owner                DBA_SYNONYMS.Owner%TYPE;
   Lv_Synonym_Name         DBA_SYNONYMS.Synonym_Name%TYPE;
   Lv_Table_Owner          DBA_SYNONYMS.Table_Owner%TYPE;
   Lv_Table_Name           DBA_SYNONYMS.Table_Name%TYPE;
   Lv_DBLink               DBA_SYNONYMS.DB_Link%TYPE;
   Lv_String               VARCHAR2(350);
   Lv_Lineno               NUMBER;
```

The next section of the script creates an internal procedure named WRITE_OUT to **insert** rows into the temporary table the script uses.

```
procedure WRITE_OUT(P_Line INTEGER, P_Owner VARCHAR2, P_Name VARCHAR2,
                    P_String VARCHAR2) is
begin
   insert into SYN_TEMP (Lineno, Id_Owner, Id_Name, Text)
         values (P_Line,P_Owner,P_Name,P_String);
end;
```

You can create multiple synonyms for a single database object. The cursor SYN_CURSOR, shown in the following listing, extracts all the synonyms, public and private. *Lv_Lineno* is used in conjunction with the object name to order the rows in the temporary table SYN_TEMP so that if you prefer, you can extract the **create synonym** statement for a single synonym at the end of the procedure.

```
begin
   open SYN_CURSOR;
   Lv_Lineno  := 1;
   loop
      fetch SYN_CURSOR into      Lv_Owner,
                                 Lv_Synonym_Name,
                                 Lv_Table_Owner,
                                 Lv_Table_Name,
                                 Lv_DBLink;
      exit when SYN_CURSOR%NOTFOUND;
```

There is a slight variation in the syntax for creating public and private synonyms. Because there is no real user named PUBLIC in the database, any synonym owned by PUBLIC is accessible to all. The section of the script shown in the following listing creates the proper syntax for public synonyms.

```
if ( Lv_Owner = 'PUBLIC' )
then
    Lv_String  := 'CREATE PUBLIC SYNONYM ' || Lv_Synonym_Name
                                           || ' FOR '
                                           || Lv_Table_Owner
                                           || '.'
                                           || Lv_Table_Name;
else
    Lv_String  := 'CREATE SYNONYM '        || Lv_Owner
                                           || '.'
                                           || Lv_Synonym_Name
                                           || ' FOR '
                                           || Lv_Table_Owner
                                           || '.'
                                           || Lv_Table_Name;
end if;
```

In addition to being able to create a synonym for a database link, you can create synonyms for objects that exist on remote databases, using a database link to define the object. If the object does not exist in the local database, the link information is added to the **create synonym** string by the following section of the script.

```
if (Lv_DBLink is NOT NULL)
then
    Lv_String := Lv_String || ' ' || Lv_DBLink;
end if;
```

The generated **create synonym** string is written to the temporary table, and the loop repeats until all synonyms have been processed. Once all synonyms have been processed, the cursor closes and the procedure exits.

```
    WRITE_OUT(Lv_Lineno, Lv_Owner, Lv_Table_Name, Lv_String);
    Lv_Lineno := Lv_Lineno + 1;
    WRITE_OUT(Lv_Lineno, Lv_Owner, Lv_Table_Name, '/');
    Lv_Lineno := Lv_Lineno + 1;
  end loop;
  close SYN_CURSOR;
end;
/
spool cre_syn.sql
select Text
  from SYN_TEMP
 order by Id_Owner, Id_Name, Lineno
/
spool off
```

Once the **create** statements for all the synonyms have been generated, they are spooled to a file named cre_syn.sql for later execution. The environment is finally reset to its original value.

```
set newpage 1 verify on feedback 6 pagesize 24 linesize 80
set heading on embedded off term on
undefine syn_object
undefine syn_owner
```

A sample cre_syn.sql output file is shown here:

```
CREATE PUBLIC SYNONYM EMP_ADDRESSES FOR APP.EMP_ADDRESSES
/
CREATE SYNONYM QCUSER1.EMP_ADDRESSES FOR APP.EMP_ADDRESSES
/
```

One public synonym appears in this listing, making the underlying object accessible to all users. One user has his own synonym with the same name as that of the public one. You should avoid creating multiple synonyms for the same object (such as is the case in this example). Using multiple synonyms for the same object makes managing the database objects and users more difficult.

If you want to use this script to document all the synonyms for all the objects for a particular owner, remove the **accept** *object_name* statement at the beginning of the script and change the **where** clause for the SYN_CURSOR cursor like so:

```
where Owner  = UPPER('&&object_owner')
```

or you can use '%' when prompted for object.

If you want to document all synonyms in your database that are not owned by SYS, remove the two **accept** statements from the beginning of the script and change the **where** clause for the SYN_CURSOR cursor to this:

```
where Owner != 'SYS'
```

or use '%' when prompted for the user.

gen_proc.sql

Generate Procedures

When you use stored procedures, you keep compiled PL/SQL code within the database, avoiding performance degradation from runtime compilation. Unlike anonymous PL/SQL blocks, stored procedures can also be pinned in the SGA, again improving performance. The following script, gen_proc.sql, generates a script to re-create a stored procedure.

```
REM
REM gen_proc.sql
REM This script can be used for Oracle7.x and above
```

```
REM
set echo off verify off term on feedback off pagesize 0 heading off
set long 2000
select 'Creating procedure build script...' from DUAL;

accept procedure_name prompt "Enter the name of the procedure: "
accept procedure_owner prompt "Enter procedure owner: "
set term off

drop    table PROC_TEMP
/

create table PROC_TEMP (
        Lineno NUMBER,
        Id_Owner VARCHAR2(30),
        Id_Name VARCHAR2(30),
        Text VARCHAR2(2000))
/

declare
    cursor PROC_CURSOR is
         select Owner,
                Name,
                Type,
                Line,
                Text
           from DBA_SOURCE
          where Type  = 'PROCEDURE'
            and Owner like UPPER('&&procedure_owner')
            and Owner not in ('SYS','SYSTEM')
            and Name  like UPPER('&&procedure_name')
          order by Owner, Name, Type, Line;

    Lv_Owner              DBA_SOURCE.Owner%TYPE;
    Lv_Name               DBA_SOURCE.Name%TYPE;
    Lv_Type               DBA_SOURCE.Type%TYPE;
    Lv_Text               DBA_SOURCE.Text%TYPE;
    Lv_Line               DBA_SOURCE.Line%TYPE;

    Lv_String             VARCHAR2(2000);
    Lv_Lineno             NUMBER;

    procedure WRITE_OUT(P_Line INTEGER, P_Owner VARCHAR2, P_Name VARCHAR2,
                        P_String VARCHAR2) is
    begin
       insert into PROC_TEMP (Lineno, Id_Owner, Id_Name, Text)
              values (P_Line,P_Owner,P_Name,P_String);
     end;
```

```
begin
   open PROC_CURSOR;
   Lv_Lineno  := 1;
   loop
      fetch PROC_CURSOR into Lv_Owner,
                             Lv_Name,
                             Lv_Type,
                             Lv_Line,
                             Lv_Text;
      exit when PROC_CURSOR%NOTFOUND;

      if (Lv_Line = 1)
      then
          Lv_String  := 'CREATE OR REPLACE PROCEDURE ';
          WRITE_OUT(Lv_Lineno, Lv_Owner, Lv_Name, Lv_String);
          Lv_Lineno  := Lv_Lineno + 1;

          Lv_String  := SUBSTR(Lv_Text,LENGTH(Lv_Type)+1,
                           (LENGTH(Lv_Text) - LENGTH(Lv_Type)));
          Lv_String  := Lv_Owner || '.' || LTRIM(Lv_String);
          WRITE_OUT(Lv_Lineno, Lv_Owner, Lv_Name, Lv_String);
          Lv_Lineno  := Lv_Lineno + 1;
      else
          WRITE_OUT(Lv_Lineno, Lv_Owner, Lv_Name, Lv_Text);
          Lv_Lineno := Lv_Lineno + 1;
      end if;
   end loop;
   WRITE_OUT(Lv_Lineno, Lv_Owner, Lv_Name, '/');
   close PROC_CURSOR;
end;
/
spool cre_proc.sql
select Text
  from PROC_TEMP
 order by Id_Owner, Id_Name, Lineno
/
spool off
set newpage 1 verify on feedback 6 pagesize 24 linesize 80
set heading on embedded off term on long 80
undefine procedure_name
undefine procedure_owner
```

The following listing shows a sample output file (named cre_proc.sql) generated by the gen_proc.sql script.

```
CREATE OR REPLACE PROCEDURE
APP.remove_customer(
  p_temp_cust_id IN number )
IS
BEGIN
```

```
        delete from app_account_payments where cust_id = p_temp_cust_id;
        delete from app_customer_mailers where cust_id = p_temp_cust_id;
        delete from app_customer_points where cust_id = p_temp_cust_id;
        delete from app_gift_certificates where cust_id = p_temp_cust_id;
        delete from app_orders where cust_id = p_temp_cust_id;
        delete from app_unfound_orders where cust_id = p_temp_cust_id;
        delete from app_credit_cards where cust_id = p_temp_cust_id;
        delete from app_telephones where cust_id = p_temp_cust_id;
        delete from app_addresses where cust_id = p_temp_cust_id;
        delete from app_customers where id = p_temp_cust_id;
        commit;
END remove_customer;
/
```

The generated script is written to the cre_proc.sql file. You can edit the cre_proc.sql file prior to executing it.

ANNOTATIONS

Because each line of a procedure is stored as a separate row in DBA_SOURCE, the script uses a cursor both to extract the procedure information and to allow you to enter a wildcard value or to modify the script to select all procedures for an owner or all procedures in the database. The script generates an output file containing the commands necessary to re-create the requested stored procedure. The gen_proc.sql script uses a temporary table to hold individual lines of the **create procedure** statement, writing to the table rather than using DBMS_OUTPUT.PUT_LINE so that you can extract the information for an individual procedure from the temporary table. Using the DBMS_OUTPUT procedure would force you to save and edit the output file for the procedure you want.

The first section of the script, shown in the following listing, does the initial setup, prompting for the procedure name and procedure owner for later use via the **accept** command, which, unlike simply using the variable with '&' or '&&' in a SQL statement, allows you to define your own prompt for the variable. You can enter the procedure name with '%' to generate a script for all procedures with a similar name.

The SQL*Plus **set** command turns off headers (**pagesize 0**), row counts (**feedback off**), and displays of old and new values for the *procedure_name* and *procedure_owner* variables (**verify off**).

```
set echo off verify off term on feedback off pagesize 0 heading off
set long 2000
select 'Creating procedure build script...' from DUAL;

accept procedure_name prompt "Enter the name of the procedure: "
accept procedure_owner prompt "Enter procedure owner: "
set term off
```

The next section of the script, shown in the following listing, creates a temporary table to hold each **create procedure** command and its owner. The Lineno column orders the lines of the **create procedure** command.

```
drop    table PROC_TEMP
/

create table PROC_TEMP (
        Lineno NUMBER,
        Id_Owner VARCHAR2(30),
        Id_Name VARCHAR2(30),
        Text VARCHAR2(2000))
/
```

The PROC_CURSOR cursor, shown in the following listing, selects the information from DBA_SOURCE where the procedure name matches the input variable *procedure_name* and the procedure owner matches the input variable *procedure_owner*. Using **like** in the **where** clause instead of = allows for wildcards.

```
declare
    cursor PROC_CURSOR is
        select Owner,
               Name,
               Type,
               Line,
               Text
          from DBA_SOURCE
         where Type  = 'PROCEDURE'
           and Owner like UPPER('&&procedure_owner')
           and owner not in ('SYS','SYSTEM')
           and Name like UPPER('&&procedure_name')
        order by Owner, Name, Type, Line;
```

In the next portion of the script, the procedure variables for the cursor are declared as TABLE_NAME.Column_Name%**TYPE**. Anchoring the variables via the %**TYPE** operator takes the column definition from within the database itself. If the column definition changes in a different version of Oracle, the procedure will still work because the definition of the column has not been hard coded. The variable *Lv_Lineno* orders the lines of the **create procedure** statement and is initialized to 0.

```
Lv_Owner              DBA_SOURCE.Owner%TYPE;
Lv_Name               DBA_SOURCE.Name%TYPE;
Lv_Type               DBA_SOURCE.Type%TYPE;
Lv_Text               DBA_SOURCE.Text%TYPE;
Lv_Line               DBA_SOURCE.Line%TYPE;
```

```
Lv_String              VARCHAR2(2000);
Lv_Lineno              NUMBER;
```

The next section of the script creates an internal procedure to perform the **insert** into the temporary table used by the gen_proc.sql script.

```
procedure WRITE_OUT(P_Line INTEGER, P_Owner VARCHAR2, P_Name VARCHAR2,
                    P_String VARCHAR2) is
 begin
    insert into PROC_TEMP (Lineno, Id_Owner, Id_Name, Text)
          values (P_Line,P_Owner,P_Name,P_String);
  end;
```

Unlike triggers and views, the lines of a stored procedure are stored as separate lines in the data dictionary. The cursor PROC_CURSOR extracts all the lines of the stored procedure. *Lv_Lineno* is used in conjunction with the procedure name to order the rows in the temporary table PROC_TEMP so that if you prefer, you can extract the **create procedure** statement for a single procedure at the end of the script.

```
begin
   open PROC_CURSOR;
   Lv_Lineno   := 1;
   loop
      fetch PROC_CURSOR into Lv_Owner,
                             Lv_Name,
                             Lv_Type,
                             Lv_Line,
                             Lv_Text;
      exit when PROC_CURSOR%NOTFOUND;
```

The **create or replace** clause, used in the next section of gen_proc.sql, retains all grants on a procedure that is being replaced. If you drop a procedure and then create it, all grants are lost.

```
      if (Lv_Line = 1)
      then
         Lv_String   := 'CREATE OR REPLACE PROCEDURE ';
         WRITE_OUT(Lv_Lineno, Lv_Owner, Lv_Name, Lv_String);
         Lv_Lineno   := Lv_Lineno + 1;
```

Oracle stores the first line of a procedure as **PROCEDURE** *procedure_name*. Because the script concatenates the owner's name to the name of the stored procedure in the generated script, the word PROCEDURE has to be removed from the first line of the stored source code. The **SUBSTR** function, along with the **LENGTH** of the variable *Lv_Type* (which contains the type of source code), extracts the rest of the line and places it in the string variable *Lv_String* to be written to the temporary table. The **LTRIM** function removes any leading spaces before concatenating the string with the owner's name.

```
        Lv_String   := SUBSTR(Lv_Text,LENGTH(Lv_Type)+1,
                       (LENGTH(Lv_Text) - LENGTH(Lv_Type)));
        Lv_String   := Lv_Owner || '.' || LTRIM(Lv_String);
        WRITE_OUT(Lv_Lineno, Lv_Owner, Lv_Name, Lv_String);
        Lv_Lineno   := Lv_Lineno + 1;
```

If this is not the first line of the stored procedure in DBA_SOURCE, the text as read from the database is inserted into the temporary table. The cursor loop ends and the procedure will loop back through the PROC_CURSOR until all procedures have been generated. Then the cursor closes and the procedure exits.

```
    else
        WRITE_OUT(Lv_Lineno, Lv_Owner, Lv_Name, Lv_Text);
        Lv_Lineno := Lv_Lineno + 1;
    end if;
  end loop;
  WRITE_OUT(Lv_Lineno, Lv_Owner, Lv_Name, '/');
  close PROC_CURSOR;
end;
/
spool cre_proc.sql
select Text
  from PROC_TEMP
 order by Id_Owner, Id_Name, Lineno
/
spool off
```

Once the **create** statements for all the procedures have been generated, they are spooled to a file name cre_proc.sql for later execution. The environment is finally reset to its original state.

```
set newpage 1 verify on feedback 6 pagesize 24 linesize 80
set heading on embedded off term on
undefine procedure_name
undefine procedure_owner
```

A sample cre_proc.sql file is shown in the following listing:

```
CREATE OR REPLACE PROCEDURE
APP.remove_customer(
  p_temp_cust_id IN number )
IS
BEGIN

    delete from app_account_payments where cust_id = p_temp_cust_id;
    delete from app_customer_mailers where cust_id = p_temp_cust_id;
    delete from app_customer_points where cust_id = p_temp_cust_id;
```

```
      delete from app_gift_certificates where cust_id = p_temp_cust_id;
      delete from app_orders where cust_id = p_temp_cust_id;
      delete from app_unfound_orders where cust_id = p_temp_cust_id;
      delete from app_credit_cards where cust_id = p_temp_cust_id;
      delete from app_telephones where cust_id = p_temp_cust_id;
      delete from app_addresses where cust_id = p_temp_cust_id;
      delete from app_customers where id = p_temp_cust_id;
      commit;
END remove_customer;
/
```

To use this script to document all the stored procedures for a particular owner, remove the **accept** *procedure_name* command at the beginning of the script and change the **where** clause for the PROC_CURSOR cursor to this:

```
where Owner  like  UPPER('&&procedure_owner')
```

Or you can use '%' for a wildcard for the object as well as the owner.

gen_func.sql

Generate Functions

When you use functions, you keep compiled PL/SQL code within the database, avoiding performance degradation from runtime compilation. A function is identical to a procedure except that functions always return a single value while procedures return nothing. The following script, gen_func.sql, generates a script to re-create a function.

```
REM
REM gen_func.sql
REM This script can be used for Oracle7.x and above
REM
set echo off verify off term on feedback off pagesize 0 heading off
select 'Creating function build script...' from DUAL;

accept function_name prompt "Enter the name of the function: "
accept function_owner prompt "Enter function owner: "
set term off

drop   table FUNC_TEMP
/

create table FUNC_TEMP (
       Lineno NUMBER,
       Id_Owner VARCHAR2(30),
       Id_Name VARCHAR2(30),
       Text VARCHAR2(2000))
/

declare
   cursor FUNC_CURSOR is
```

```
        select Owner,
               Name,
               Type,
               Line,
               Text
          from DBA_SOURCE
         where Type  = 'FUNCTION'
           and Owner like UPPER('&&function_owner')
           and Owner not in ('SYS','SYSTEM')
           and Name  like UPPER('&&function_name')
         order by Owner, Name, Type, Line;

   Lv_Owner             DBA_SOURCE.Owner%TYPE;
   Lv_Name              DBA_SOURCE.Name%TYPE;
   Lv_Type              DBA_SOURCE.Type%TYPE;
   Lv_Text              DBA_SOURCE.Text%TYPE;
   Lv_Line              DBA_SOURCE.Line%TYPE;

   Lv_String            VARCHAR2(2000);
   Lv_Lineno            NUMBER;

   procedure WRITE_OUT(P_Line INTEGER, P_Owner VARCHAR2, P_Name VARCHAR2,
                       P_String VARCHAR2) is
   begin
      insert into FUNC_TEMP (Lineno, Id_Owner, Id_Name, Text)
             values (P_Line,P_Owner,P_Name,P_String);
    end;

begin
   open FUNC_CURSOR;
   Lv_Lineno  := 1;

   loop
      fetch FUNC_CURSOR into Lv_Owner,
                             Lv_Name,
                             Lv_Type,
                             Lv_Line,
                             Lv_Text;
      exit when FUNC_CURSOR%NOTFOUND;

      if (Lv_Line = 1)
      then
          Lv_String  := 'CREATE OR REPLACE FUNCTION ';
          WRITE_OUT(Lv_Lineno, Lv_Owner, Lv_Name, Lv_String);
          Lv_Lineno  := Lv_Lineno + 1;

          Lv_String  := SUBSTR(Lv_Text,LENGTH(Lv_Type)+1,
                        (LENGTH(Lv_Text) - LENGTH(Lv_Type)));
          Lv_String  := Lv_Owner || '.' || LTRIM(Lv_String);
```

```
        WRITE_OUT(Lv_Lineno, Lv_Owner, Lv_Name, Lv_String);
        Lv_Lineno   := Lv_Lineno + 1;
    else
        WRITE_OUT(Lv_Lineno, Lv_Owner, Lv_Name, Lv_Text);
        Lv_Lineno := Lv_Lineno + 1;
    end if;
  end loop;
  WRITE_OUT(Lv_Lineno, Lv_Owner, Lv_Name, '/');
  close FUNC_CURSOR;
end;
/

spool cre_func.sql
select Text
  from FUNC_TEMP
 order by Id_Owner, Id_Name, Lineno
/
spool off
set newpage 1 verify on feedback 6 pagesize 24 linesize 80
set heading on embedded off term on
undefine function_name
undefine function_owner
```

Sample output for the script is shown in this listing:

```
CREATE OR REPLACE FUNCTION
APP.f_date(
t_date IN varchar2 )
RETURN date IS
BEGIN
  BEGIN
    DECLARE
    tmp_dt date;
    BEGIN
    IF lower(t_date) in ('sun', 'mon', 'tue',
                        'wed', 'thu', 'fri', 'sat')
    THEN
       tmp_dt:= next_day(sysdate, t_date);
    ELSE
       IF substr(t_date,5,2) BETWEEN 0 AND 49 THEN
         tmp_dt := to_date(substr(t_date, 1, 2)||'/'||
                           substr(t_date, 3, 2)||'/'||
                           '20'||substr(t_date, 5, 2), 'mm/dd/yyyy');
       ELSE
          tmp_dt := to_date(substr(t_date, 1, 2)||'/'||
                           substr(t_date, 3, 2)||'/'||
                           '19'||substr(t_date, 5, 2), 'mm/dd/yyyy');
       END IF;
    END IF;
     return(tmp_dt);
```

```
    END;
  END f_date;
END f_date;
/
```

The output is written to a file called cre_func.sql. You can edit or execute the cre_func.sql file.

ANNOTATIONS

Because each line of a function is stored as a separate row in DBA_SOURCE, the gen_func.sql script uses a cursor to extract the function information and to allow you to enter a wildcard value. You can also modify the script to select all functions for an owner or all functions in the database or you can use '%' for the wildcards. The gen_func.sql script generates an output file containing a script to re-create the requested function. The gen_func.sql script uses a temporary table to hold individual lines of the **create function** statement, writing to the table rather than using DBMS_OUTPUT.PUT_LINE so that you can extract the information for an individual function from the table. Using the DBMS_OUTPUT procedure would force you to save and edit the output file for the function you want.

The first section of the script, shown in the following listing, does the initial setup, prompting for the function name and function owner for later use via the **accept** command. Unlike simply using the variable with the '&' or '&&' in a SQL statement, **accept** allows you to define your own prompt for the variable. You can enter the function name with '%' to generate a script for all functions with a similar name.

The SQL*Plus **set** command turns off headers (**pagesize 0**), row counts (**feedback off**), and displays of old and new values for the *function_name* and *function_owner* variables (**verify off**).

```
set echo off verify off term on feedback off pagesize 0
select 'Creating function build script...' from DUAL;

accept function_name prompt "Enter the name of the function: "
accept function_owner prompt "Enter function owner: "
set term off
```

The next portion of the script creates a temporary table to hold each **create function** command and its owner. The Lineno column orders the lines of the **create function** command.

```
drop    table FUNC_TEMP
/

create table FUNC_TEMP (
        Lineno NUMBER,
        Id_Owner VARCHAR2(30),
```

```
      Id_Name VARCHAR2(30),
      Text VARCHAR2(2000))
/
```

The next portion of the script creates the FUNC_CURSOR cursor. The FUNC_CURSOR cursor selects the information from DBA_SOURCE where the function name matches the input variable *function_name* and the function owner matches the input variable *function_owner*. Using **like** in the **where** clause instead of = allows for wildcards.

```
declare
   cursor FUNC_CURSOR is
          select Owner,
                 Name,
                 Type,
                 Line,
                 Text
            from DBA_SOURCE
           where Type   = 'FUNCTION'
             and Owner like  UPPER('&&function_owner')
             and Owner not in ('SYS','SYSTEM')
             and Name   like UPPER('&&function_name')
        order by Owner, Name, Type, Line;
```

The procedure variables for the cursor are declared as TABLE_NAME.Column_Name%**TYPE**. Anchoring the datatypes in this manner takes the column definition from within the database itself. If the column definition changes in a different version of Oracle, the procedure will still work because the definition of the column has not been hard coded. The variable *Lv_Lineno* orders the lines of the **create function** statement and is initialized to 0.

```
   Lv_Owner               DBA_SOURCE.Owner%TYPE;
   Lv_Name                DBA_SOURCE.Name%TYPE;
   Lv_Type                DBA_SOURCE.Type%TYPE;
   Lv_Text                DBA_SOURCE.Text%TYPE;
   Lv_Line                DBA_SOURCE.Line%TYPE;
   Lv_String              VARCHAR2(2000);
   Lv_Lineno              NUMBER;
```

The next section of the script creates WRITE_OUT, an internal procedure to **insert** rows into the temporary table used by the gen_func.sql script.

```
procedure WRITE_OUT(P_Line INTEGER, P_Owner VARCHAR2, P_Name VARCHAR2,
                    P_String VARCHAR2) is
begin
   insert into FUNC_TEMP (Lineno, Id_Owner, Id_Name, Text)
        values (P_Line,P_Owner,P_Name,P_String);
 end;
```

As with stored procedures, the lines of a function are stored as separate lines in the data dictionary. The cursor FUNC_CURSOR extracts all the lines of the function. *Lv_Lineno*, in conjunction with the function name, orders the rows in the temporary table FUNC_TEMP so you can extract the **create function** statement for a single function at the end of the procedure.

```
begin
    open FUNC_CURSOR;
    Lv_Lineno  := 1;
    loop
        fetch FUNC_CURSOR into Lv_Owner,
                               Lv_Name,
                               Lv_Type,
                               Lv_Line,
                               Lv_Text;
        exit when FUNC_CURSOR%NOTFOUND;
```

The **create or replace** clause retains all grants on a function that is being replaced. If you drop the function and then create it, all grants are lost.

```
        if (Lv_Line = 1)
        then
            Lv_String  := 'CREATE OR REPLACE FUNCTION ';
            WRITE_OUT(Lv_Lineno, Lv_Owner, Lv_Name, Lv_String);
            Lv_Lineno  := Lv_Lineno + 1;
```

Oracle stores the first line of a function as **FUNCTION** *function_name*. Because the script concatenates the owner's name to the name of the function in the generated script, it has to remove the word **FUNCTION** from the first line of the stored source code. In the following section of the script, the **SUBSTR** function, along with the **LENGTH** of the variable *Lv_Type*, extracts the rest of the line and places it in the string variable *Lv_String* to be written to the temporary table. The **LTRIM** function removes any leading spaces before concatenating the string with the owner's name.

```
            Lv_String  := SUBSTR(Lv_Text,LENGTH(Lv_Type)+1,
                            (LENGTH(Lv_Text) - LENGTH(Lv_Type)));
            Lv_String  := Lv_Owner || '.' || LTRIM(Lv_String);
            WRITE_OUT(Lv_Lineno, Lv_Owner, Lv_Name, Lv_String);
            Lv_Lineno  := Lv_Lineno + 1;
```

The final section of the script completes the entries into the temporary table. If this is not the first line of the function in DBA_SOURCE, the text as read from the database is inserted into the temporary table. The cursor loop ends and the procedure will loop back through the FUNC_CURSOR until all functions have been generated, at which point the cursor closes and the procedure exits.

Once the **create function** statements for all the functions have been generated, they are spooled to a file for later execution.

```
    else
        WRITE_OUT(Lv_Lineno, Lv_Owner, Lv_Name, Lv_Text);
        Lv_Lineno := Lv_Lineno + 1;
    end if;
  end loop;
  WRITE_OUT(Lv_Lineno, Lv_Owner, Lv_Name, '/');
  close FUNC_CURSOR;
end;
/

spool cre_func.sql
select Text
  from FUNC_TEMP
 order by Id_Owner, Id_Name, Lineno
/
spool off
```

The environment is finally reset to its original state.

```
set newpage 1 verify on feedback 6 pagesize 24 linesize 80
set heading on embedded off term on
undefine function_name
undefine function_owner
```

The following listing shows a sample cre_func.sql file for a function called F_DATE:

```
CREATE OR REPLACE FUNCTION
APP.f_date(
t_date IN varchar2 )
RETURN date IS
BEGIN
  BEGIN
    DECLARE
    tmp_dt date;
    BEGIN
    IF lower(t_date) in ('sun', 'mon', 'tue',
                          'wed', 'thu', 'fri', 'sat')
    THEN
      tmp_dt:= next_day(sysdate, t_date);
    ELSE
      IF substr(t_date,5,2) BETWEEN 0 AND 49 THEN
        tmp_dt := to_date(substr(t_date, 1, 2)||'/'||
                          substr(t_date, 3, 2)||'/'||
                          '20'||substr(t_date, 5, 2), 'mm/dd/yyyy');
      ELSE
```

```
            tmp_dt := to_date(substr(t_date, 1, 2)||'/'||
                              substr(t_date, 3, 2)||'/'||
                              '19'||substr(t_date, 5, 2), 'mm/dd/yyyy');
        END IF;
      END IF;
       return(tmp_dt);
      END;
  END f_date;
END f_date;
/
```

gen_pkg.sql

Generate Packages

Packages provide a means of grouping together related functions and procedures and storing them as a unit in the database. Like procedures and functions, they are stored as compiled code, and the procedures and functions in a package are loaded into memory once, improving performance. Like procedures, they can be pinned in memory. Unlike procedures and functions, packages are stored as two objects in the database—the package specification and the package body. The following script, gen_pkg.sql, generates a script to re-create both the package specification and package body.

```
REM
REM gen_pkg.sql
REM This script can be used for Oracle7.x and above.
REM
set echo off verify off feedback off pagesize 0 heading off
set term on
select 'Creating package build script...' from DUAL;

accept package_name prompt "Enter the name of the package: "
accept package_owner prompt "Enter package owner: "
set term off

drop    table PACK_TEMP
/

create table PACK_TEMP (
        Lineno NUMBER,
        Id_Owner VARCHAR2(30),
        Id_Name VARCHAR2(30),
        text VARCHAR2(2000))
/

declare
    cursor PACK_CURSOR is
        select Owner,
               Name,
```

```
               Type,
               Line,
               Text
          from DBA_SOURCE
         where Type in ('PACKAGE','PACKAGE BODY')
           and Owner like UPPER('&&package_owner')
            and Owner not in ('SYS','SYSTEM')
            and Name like UPPER('&&package_name')
         order by Owner, Name, Type, Line;

     Lv_Owner            DBA_SOURCE.Owner%TYPE;
     Lv_Name             DBA_SOURCE.Name%TYPE;
     Lv_Type             DBA_SOURCE.Type%TYPE;
     Lv_Text             DBA_SOURCE.Text%TYPE;
     Lv_Line             DBA_SOURCE.Line%TYPE;
     Lv_String           VARCHAR2(2000);
     Lv_Lineno           NUMBER;

     procedure WRITE_OUT(P_Line INTEGER, P_Owner VARCHAR2, P_Name VARCHAR2,
                     P_String VARCHAR2) is
     begin
        insert into PACK_TEMP (Lineno, Id_Owner, Id_Name, Text)
             values (P_Line,P_Owner,P_Name,P_String);
      end;

begin
   open PACK_CURSOR;
   Lv_Lineno  := 1;
   loop
      fetch PACK_CURSOR into Lv_Owner,
                             Lv_Name,
                             Lv_Type,
                             Lv_Line,
                             Lv_Text;
      exit when PACK_CURSOR%NOTFOUND;

      if (Lv_Line = 1)
      then
          if (Lv_Type = 'PACKAGE BODY')
          then
              WRITE_OUT(Lv_Lineno, Lv_Owner, Lv_Name, '/');
              Lv_Lineno  := Lv_Lineno + 1;
          end if;

          Lv_String  := 'CREATE OR REPLACE ' || UPPER(Lv_Type)  || ' ';
          WRITE_OUT(Lv_Lineno, Lv_Owner, Lv_Name, Lv_String);
          Lv_Lineno  := Lv_Lineno + 1;

          Lv_String  := SUBSTR(Lv_Text,LENGTH(Lv_Type)+1,
```

```
                         (LENGTH(Lv_Text) - LENGTH(Lv_Type)));
          Lv_String   := Lv_Owner || '.' || LTRIM(Lv_String);
          WRITE_OUT(Lv_Lineno, Lv_Owner, Lv_Name, Lv_String);
          Lv_Lineno   := Lv_Lineno + 1;
      else
          WRITE_OUT(Lv_Lineno, Lv_Owner, Lv_Name, Lv_Text);
          Lv_Lineno := Lv_Lineno + 1;
      end if;
    end loop;

    WRITE_OUT(Lv_Lineno, Lv_Owner, Lv_Name, '/');
    close PACK_CURSOR;
end;
/
spool cre_pkg.sql
select Text
  from PACK_TEMP
 order by Id_Owner, Id_Name, Lineno
/
spool off
set newpage 1 verify on feedback 6 pagesize 24 linesize 80
set heading on embedded off term on
undefine package_name
undefine package_owner
```

Sample output for the gen_pkg.sql script is shown in the following listing:

```
CREATE OR REPLACE PACKAGE
APP.APP_EMPLOYEE_PKG IS
  PROCEDURE APP_EMP_SWITCH_UPDATE(
  EMP_ID IN VARCHAR2 )
;
PROCEDURE APP_EMPL_ACT_DETAILS_PROC(
  EMP_ID IN CHAR ,
  ACT_DESC IN CHAR ,
  START_TIME IN DATE ,
  PROJ IN CHAR ,
  DUR IN NUMBER )
;

END APP_EMPLOYEE_PKG;
/
CREATE OR REPLACE PACKAGE BODY
APP.APP_EMPLOYEE_PKG IS
 /* If an employee goes on a project then the necessary info is recorded
 in the app_employee_activity_details table for use by the supervisor
 */

  PROCEDURE APP_EMP_SWITCH_UPDATE(
  EMP_ID IN VARCHAR2 )
```

```
    IS
    BEGIN
     update app_employee_time_records_1
       set status='I',clock_out=sysdate
         where epe_code=emp_id AND STATUS='A' AND PAYTIMTYPE_CODE='T';
           commit;
      IF SQL%NOTFOUND THEN
        NULL;
        END IF;
    END;

    PROCEDURE APP_EMPL_ACT_DETAILS_PROC(
    EMP_ID IN CHAR ,
    ACT_DESC IN CHAR ,
    START_TIME IN DATE ,
    PROJ IN CHAR ,
    DUR IN NUMBER )
    IS
        M_ID        NUMBER(10);
        ACT_CODE    APP_EMPLOYEE_ACTIVITY_DETAILS.ACTIVITY%TYPE;
        M_END_TIME  DATE;
    BEGIN
        /* Sequence no is generated */
        SELECT APP_ID_SEQ.NEXTVAL INTO M_ID FROM DUAL;
 /* Using duration and start_date/time the end_date/time is evaluated*/
        M_END_TIME :=START_TIME +(DUR/24/60);
        INSERT INTO
APP_EMPLOYEE_ACTIVITY_DETAILS(EPE_CODE,ACTIVITY,START_DATE,ID,
        ACTIVITY_CODE,END_DATE,SPECIAL)
        VALUES(EMP_ID,PROJ,START_TIME,M_ID,'PROJ',M_END_TIME,ACT_DESC);
        COMMIT;
    END;
END APP_EMPLOYEE_PKG;
/
```

The gen_pkg.sql script writes its output to a file called cre_pkg.sql. You can edit or execute the cre_pkg.sql file.

ANNOTATIONS

Oracle enforces certain restrictions on functions and procedures that can be called from SQL statements. For functions and procedures stored as standalones, Oracle can enforce the restrictions by checking the function or procedure body directly. In packages, however, only the specification of the function or procedure is visible. Therefore, for functions and procedures that will be called outside the package itself, you must use the *pragma* (compiler directive) RESTRICT_REFERENCES to enforce the rules. The pragma tells the PL/SQL compiler to deny the packaged function read/ write access to database tables, packaged variables, or both. If you try to compile a function body that violates the pragma, you get a compilation error. For details on how to code the pragma, see Appendix A.

Because each line of a package is stored as a separate row in DBA_SOURCE, the script uses a cursor to extract the package information and to allow you to enter a wildcard value for the package name (*%package_name%*) or to modify the script to select all packages for an owner or all packages in the database. The gen_pkg.sql script generates a script to re-create the requested package. The gen_pkg.sql script uses a temporary table to hold individual lines of the **create package** and **create package body** statements, writing to the table rather than using DBMS_OUTPUT.PUT_LINE so that you can extract the information for an individual package from the table. Using the DBMS_OUTPUT procedure would force you to save and edit the output file for the package you want.

The first section of the script, shown in the following listing, does the initial setup, prompting for the package name and package owner for later use via the **accept** command, which, unlike simply using the variable with the '&' or '&&' in a SQL statement, allows you to define your own prompt for the variable. You can enter a value for the package name with '%' to generate a script for all packages with a similar name.

The SQL*Plus **set** command turns off headers (**pagesize 0**), row counts (**feedback off**), and displays of old and new values for the *package_name* and *package_owner* variables (**verify off**).

```
set echo off verify off feedback off pagesize 0
set term on
select 'Creating package build script...' from DUAL;

accept package_name prompt "Enter the name of the package: "
accept package_owner prompt "Enter package owner: "
set term off
```

The next section of the script creates a temporary table to hold each **create package** and associated **create package body** command and owner. The Lineno column orders the lines of the **create package** and **create package body** command.

```
drop    table PACK_TEMP
/

create table PACK_TEMP (
        Lineno NUMBER,
        Id_Owner VARCHAR2(30),
        Id_Name VARCHAR2(30),
        text VARCHAR2(2000))
/
```

The next section of the script, shown in the following listing, creates the PACK_CURSOR cursor. The PACK_CURSOR cursor selects the information from DBA_SOURCE, where the package name matches the input variable *package_name* and the package owner matches the input variable *package_owner*. Using **like** in the **where** clause instead of = allows for wildcards. Selecting for **Type in ('PACKAGE','PACKAGE BODY')** selects all the lines for both the package specification and the package body. The **order by** clause orders by Type before Line, so all lines of the package specification will be returned before any line of the package body.

```
declare
    cursor PACK_CURSOR is
        select Owner,
               Name,
               Type,
               Line,
               Text
          from DBA_SOURCE
         where Type in ('PACKAGE','PACKAGE BODY')
           and Owner like UPPER('&&package_owner')
           and Owner is not in ('SYS','SYSTEM')
           and Name like UPPER('&&package_name')
         order by Owner, Name, Type, Line;
```

The procedure variables for the cursor are declared as TABLE_NAME.Column_Name%**TYPE**. Anchoring the variable declarations to columns takes the column definition from within the database itself. If the column definition changes in a different version of Oracle, the procedure will still work because the definition of the column has not been hard coded. The variable *Lv_Lineno* orders the lines of the **create package** statement.

```
Lv_Owner                DBA_SOURCE.Owner%TYPE;
Lv_Name                 DBA_SOURCE.Name%TYPE;
Lv_Type                 DBA_SOURCE.Type%TYPE;
Lv_Text                 DBA_SOURCE.Text%TYPE;
Lv_Line                 DBA_SOURCE.Line%TYPE;
Lv_String               VARCHAR2(2000);
Lv_Lineno               NUMBER;
```

The next section of the script creates WRITE_OUT, an internal procedure to perform the **insert**s into the temporary table.

```
procedure WRITE_OUT(P_Line INTEGER, P_Owner VARCHAR2, P_Name VARCHAR2,
                    P_String VARCHAR2) is
begin
```

```
    insert into PACK_TEMP (Lineno, Id_Owner, Id_Name, Text)
          values (P_Line,P_Owner,P_Name,P_String);
  end;
```

The lines of a package specification or package body are stored as separate lines in the data dictionary. The cursor PACK_CURSOR extracts all the lines of both the package specification and the package body. *Lv_Lineno*, in conjunction with the package name, orders the rows in the temporary table PACK_TEMP so you can extract the **create package** command for a single package at the end of the procedure.

```
begin
  open PACK_CURSOR;
  Lv_Lineno  := 1;
  loop
     fetch PACK_CURSOR into Lv_Owner,
                            Lv_Name,
                            Lv_Type,
                            Lv_Line,
                            Lv_Text;
     exit when PACK_CURSOR%NOTFOUND;
```

The **order by** clause of **PACK_CURSOR** ensures that all the lines of the package specification are returned before the lines of the package body. Because the script is creating two SQL statements, a '/' is inserted before the second statement (for the package body) is created.

```
     if (Lv_Line = 1)
     then
         if (Lv_Type = 'PACKAGE BODY')
         then
             WRITE_OUT(Lv_Lineno, Lv_Owner, Lv_Name, '/');
             Lv_Lineno  := Lv_Lineno + 1;
         end if;
```

The **create or replace** clause retains all grants on a package that is being replaced. If you drop the package and then create it, all grants are lost.

```
     Lv_String  := 'CREATE OR REPLACE ' || UPPER(Lv_Type)  || ' ';
     WRITE_OUT(Lv_Lineno, Lv_Owner, Lv_Name, Lv_String);
     Lv_Lineno  := Lv_Lineno + 1;
```

Oracle stores the first line of each part of a package as **PACKAGE [BODY]** *package_name*. Because the script concatenates the owner's name to the name of the package in the generated script, it has to remove the term **"PACKAGE"** or **"PACKAGE BODY"** from the first line of the stored source code. The **SUBSTR** function, along with the variable *Lv_Type*, extracts the rest of the line and places it in the string variable *Lv_String* to be written to the temporary table. The **LTRIM** function removes extra blanks from the beginning of the string.

```
Lv_String    := SUBSTR(Lv_Text,LENGTH(Lv_Type)+1,
                    (LENGTH(Lv_Text) - LENGTH(Lv_Type)));
Lv_String    := Lv_Owner || '.' || LTRIM(Lv_String);
WRITE_OUT(Lv_Lineno, Lv_Owner, Lv_Name, Lv_String);
Lv_Lineno    := Lv_Lineno + 1;
```

If this is not the first line of the package or package body in DBA_SOURCE, the text as read from the database is inserted into the temporary table. The cursor loop ends and the procedure will loop back through the PACK_CURSOR until all packages have been generated. The cursor then closes and the procedure exits. Once the **create** statements for all the packages and package bodies have been generated, they are spooled to a file for later execution.

```
    else
        WRITE_OUT(Lv_Lineno, Lv_Owner, Lv_Name, Lv_Text);
        Lv_Lineno := Lv_Lineno + 1;
    end if;
  end loop;
  WRITE_OUT(Lv_Lineno, Lv_Owner, Lv_Name, '/');
  close PACK_CURSOR;
end;
/

spool cre_pkg.sql
select Text
  from PACK_TEMP
 order by Id_Owner, Id_Name, Lineno
/
spool off
```

The environment is finally reset to its original state:

```
set newpage 1 verify on feedback 6 pagesize 24 linesize 80
set heading on embedded off term on
undefine package_name
undefine package_owner
```

The following listing shows a sample cre_pkg.sql file generated by the gen_pkg.sql script:

```
CREATE OR REPLACE PACKAGE
APP.APP_EMPLOYEE_PKG IS
```

```
    PROCEDURE APP_EMP_SWITCH_UPDATE(
    EMP_ID IN VARCHAR2 )
;
PROCEDURE APP_EMPL_ACT_DETAILS_PROC(
    EMP_ID IN CHAR ,
    ACT_DESC IN CHAR ,
    START_TIME IN DATE ,
    PROJ IN CHAR ,
    DUR IN NUMBER )
;

END APP_EMPLOYEE_PKG;
/
CREATE OR REPLACE PACKAGE BODY
APP.APP_EMPLOYEE_PKG IS
 /* If an employee goes on a project then the necessary info is recorded
 in the app_employee_activity_details table for use by the supervisor
 */

  PROCEDURE APP_EMP_SWITCH_UPDATE(
  EMP_ID IN VARCHAR2 )
  IS
  BEGIN
   update app_employee_time_records_1
     set status='I',clock_out=sysdate
      where epe_code=emp_id AND STATUS='A' AND PAYTIMTYPE_CODE='T';
        commit;
    IF SQL%NOTFOUND THEN
     NULL;
     END IF;
  END;

  PROCEDURE APP_EMPL_ACT_DETAILS_PROC(
  EMP_ID IN CHAR ,
  ACT_DESC IN CHAR ,
  START_TIME IN DATE ,
  PROJ IN CHAR ,
  DUR IN NUMBER )
  IS
      M_ID         NUMBER(10);
      ACT_CODE     APP_EMPLOYEE_ACTIVITY_DETAILS.ACTIVITY%TYPE;
      M_END_TIME   DATE;
  BEGIN
      /* Sequence no is generated */
      SELECT APP_ID_SEQ.NEXTVAL INTO M_ID FROM DUAL;
   /* Using duration and start_date/time the end_date/time is evaluated*/
      M_END_TIME :=START_TIME +(DUR/24/60);
      INSERT INTO
APP_EMPLOYEE_ACTIVITY_DETAILS(EPE_CODE,ACTIVITY,START_DATE,ID,
```

```
      ACTIVITY_CODE,END_DATE,SPECIAL)
      VALUES(EMP_ID,PROJ,START_TIME,M_ID,'PROJ',M_END_TIME,ACT_DESC);
      COMMIT;
   END;
END APP_EMPLOYEE_PKG;
/
```

Alternatively, you can change/combine the Gen_XXX.sql for functions, procedures, and packages to generate whatever type of object is desired by using the cursor shown here:

```
accept object_name prompt "Enter the name of the Object: "
accept object_owner prompt "Enter object owners name: "
accept object_type prompt "Enter object type: (Function, Procedure, ...) "

set term off

drop    table OBJ_TEMP
/

create table OBJ_TEMP (
        Lineno NUMBER,
        Id_Owner VARCHAR2(30),
        Id_Name VARCHAR2(30),
        Text VARCHAR2(2000))
/

declare
   cursor OBJ_CURSOR is
        select Owner,
               Name,
               Type,
               Line,
               Text
          from DBA_SOURCE
         where Type  = UPPER('&&object_type')
           and Owner like UPPER('&&object_owner')
           and Owner not in ('SYS','SYSTEM')
           and Name  like UPPER('&&object_name')
         order by Owner, Name, Type, Line;
```

gen_lib.sql

Generate Libraries

Beginning with Oracle8.x, on platforms that support shared libraries and dynamic linking, the CREATE LIBRARY statement can be used to create a schema object associated with an operating system shared library. The name of this schema object can then be used in the call specification of CREATE FUNCTION or CREATE PROCEDURE statements, or when declaring a function or procedure in a package or type. Using libraries, SQL or PL/SQL can make calls to third-generation (3GL) functions and procedures. The following listing gen_lib.sql can be used to generate a script to create the library objects in your database.

```
REM
REM gen_lib.sql
REM This script can be used for Oracle8.x and above
REM
set echo off term on verify off feedback off pagesize 0 heading off
select 'Creating library build script...' from DUAL;

accept lib_object prompt "Enter the library object: "
accept lib_owner prompt "Enter the object owner: "
set term off

drop    table LIB_TEMP
/

create table LIB_TEMP (
        Lineno NUMBER,
        Id_Owner VARCHAR2(30),
        Id_Name VARCHAR2(30),
        Text VARCHAR2(350))
/

declare
    cursor LIB_CURSOR is
        select Owner,
               Library_Name,
               File_Spec
          from DBA_LIBRARIES
         where Owner like UPPER('&&lib_owner')
           and Library_Name like UPPER('&&lib_object')
           and Owner not in ('SYS','SYSTEM')
         order by Owner, Library_Name;

    Lv_Owner            DBA_LIBRARIES.Owner%TYPE;
    Lv_Library_Name     DBA_LIBRARIES.Library_Name%TYPE;
    Lv_File_Spec        DBA_LIBRARIES.File_Spec%TYPE;

    Lv_String           VARCHAR2(350);
    Lv_Lineno           NUMBER;

    procedure WRITE_OUT(P_Line INTEGER, P_Owner VARCHAR2, P_Name VARCHAR2,
                        P_String VARCHAR2) is
    begin
        insert into LIB_TEMP (Lineno, Id_Owner, Id_Name, Text)
               values (P_Line,P_Owner,P_Name,P_String);
    end;
```

```
begin
   open LIB_CURSOR;
   Lv_Lineno  := 1;
   loop
      fetch LIB_CURSOR into      Lv_Owner,
                                 Lv_Library_Name,
                                 Lv_File_Spec;
      exit when LIB_CURSOR%NOTFOUND;
      if LENGTH(Lv_File_Spec) > 1
      then
         Lv_String  := 'CREATE OR REPLACE LIBRARY '  || Lv_Owner
                                                      || '.'
                                                      || Lv_Library_Name
                                                      || ' IS '
                                                      || ''''
                                                      || Lv_File_Spec
                                                      || '''';


         WRITE_OUT(Lv_Lineno, Lv_Owner, Lv_Library_Name, Lv_String);
         Lv_Lineno := Lv_Lineno + 1;
         WRITE_OUT(Lv_Lineno, Lv_Owner, Lv_Library_Name, '/');
         Lv_Lineno := Lv_Lineno + 1;
         Lv_File_Spec := Null;
      end if;
   end loop;

   close LIB_CURSOR;
end;
/
set long 350
spool cre_lib.sql
select Text
  from LIB_TEMP
 order by Id_Owner, Id_Name, Lineno
/
spool off
set newpage 1 verify on feedback 6 pagesize 24 linesize 80
set heading on embedded off term on long 80
undefine lib_owner
undefine lib_object
```

Sample output of running the script gen_lib.sql is shown here:

```
CREATE OR REPLACE LIBRARY MEGH.AQ_LIB IS '/u1/mylib/aq.so'
/
CREATE OR REPLACE LIBRARY MEGH.DEFER_ENQ_UTL_LIB IS '/u1/mylib/denq.so'
/
CREATE OR REPLACE LIBRARY MEGH.PICKLER_LIB IS '/u1/mylib/pi.so'
```

```
/
CREATE OR REPLACE LIBRARY MEGH.REPAPI_LIB IS '/u1/mylib/rep.so'
/
CREATE OR REPLACE LIBRARY MEGH.UTL_REF_LIB IS '/u1/mylib/utl.so'
/
```

gen_seq.sql

Generate Sequences

A *sequence* is a database object often used to generate unique integers. You can use sequences to generate primary key values automatically or as part of a timestamp. Sequences can have groups of values cached in the SGA for faster retrieval, although any values stored in the cache will be lost if the database is shut down or if the shared pool is flushed. If you need consecutive numbers with no gaps, do not cache sequence values. If uniqueness is not required, the sequence can be configured to cycle through a set of numbers. The following listing shows the full gen_seq.sql script:

```
REM
REM gen_seq.sql
REM This script can be used for Oracle7.x and above
REM
set echo off term on verify off feedback off pagesize 0
select 'Creating sequences build script...' from DUAL;

accept sequence_name  prompt "Enter the name of the sequence: "
accept sequence_owner prompt "Enter sequence owner: "
set term off long 300 linsize 300

drop    table SEQ_TEMP
/

create table SEQ_TEMP (
        Lineno NUMBER,
        Id_Owner VARCHAR2(30),
        Id_Name VARCHAR2(30),
        Text VARCHAR2(300))
/
declare
    cursor SEQ_CURSOR is
            select Sequence_Owner,
                    Sequence_Name,
                    Min_Value,
                    Max_Value,
                    Increment_By,
                    Cycle_Flag,
                    Order_Flag,
                    Cache_Size,
                    Last_Number
                from DBA_SEQUENCES
```

```
        where Sequence_Owner like UPPER('&&sequence_owner')
          and Sequence_Owner not in ('SYS','SYSTEM')
          and Sequence_Name like UPPER('&&sequence_name')
        order by Sequence_Owner, Sequence_Name;

    Lv_Seq_Owner           DBA_SEQUENCES.Sequence_Owner%TYPE;
    Lv_Seq_Name            DBA_SEQUENCES.Sequence_Name%TYPE;
    Lv_Seq_Min_Value       DBA_SEQUENCES.Min_Value%TYPE;
    Lv_Seq_Max_Value       DBA_SEQUENCES.Max_Value%TYPE;
    Lv_Seq_Increment_By    DBA_SEQUENCES.Increment_By%TYPE;
    Lv_Seq_Cycle_Flag      DBA_SEQUENCES.Cycle_Flag%TYPE;
    Lv_Seq_Order_Flag      DBA_SEQUENCES.Order_Flag%TYPE;
    Lv_Seq_Cache_Size      DBA_SEQUENCES.Cache_Size%TYPE;
    Lv_Seq_Last_Number     DBA_SEQUENCES.Last_Number%TYPE;
    Lv_String              VARCHAR2(300);
    Lv_Lineno              NUMBER;
    Lv_Start_No            INTEGER;

    procedure WRITE_OUT(P_Line INTEGER, P_Owner VARCHAR2, P_Name VARCHAR2,
                        P_String VARCHAR2) is
    begin
       insert into SEQ_TEMP (Lineno, Id_Owner, Id_Name, Text)
             values (P_Line,P_Owner,P_Name,P_String);
     end;

begin
    open SEQ_CURSOR;
    Lv_Lineno  := 1;
    loop
       fetch SEQ_CURSOR into Lv_Seq_Owner,
                             Lv_Seq_Name,
                             Lv_Seq_Min_Value,
                             Lv_Seq_Max_Value,
                             Lv_Seq_Increment_By,
                             Lv_Seq_Cycle_Flag,
                             Lv_Seq_Order_Flag,
                             Lv_Seq_Cache_Size,
                             Lv_Seq_Last_Number;

       exit when SEQ_CURSOR%NOTFOUND;

      Lv_Start_No := Lv_Seq_Last_Number + Lv_Seq_Increment_By;
      Lv_String  := 'CREATE SEQUENCE ' || LOWER(Lv_Seq_Owner)
                                       || '.'
                                       || LOWER(Lv_Seq_Name)
                                       || ' START WITH '
                                       || Lv_Start_No;
      WRITE_OUT(Lv_Lineno, Lv_Seq_Owner, Lv_Seq_Name, Lv_String);
      Lv_Lineno  := Lv_Lineno + 1;
```

```
        Lv_String := 'MAXVALUE '|| Lv_Seq_Max_Value ;
        Lv_String := Lv_String  || ' MINVALUE '       || Lv_Seq_Min_Value;
        Lv_String := Lv_String  || ' INCREMENT BY '   || Lv_Seq_Increment_By;

        if ( Lv_Seq_Cycle_Flag = 'Y' )
        then
            Lv_String := Lv_String || ' CYCLE ';
        else
            Lv_String := Lv_String || ' NOCYCLE ';
        end if;

        if ( Lv_Seq_Order_Flag = 'Y' )
        then
            Lv_String := Lv_String || ' ORDER ';
        else
            Lv_String := Lv_String || ' NOORDER ';
        end if;

        if ( Lv_Seq_Cache_Size = 0 )
        then
            Lv_String := Lv_String || ' NOCACHE ';
        else
            Lv_String := Lv_String || ' CACHE ' || Lv_Seq_Cache_Size;
        end if;
        WRITE_OUT(Lv_Lineno, Lv_Seq_Owner, Lv_Seq_Name, Lv_String);
        Lv_Lineno   := Lv_Lineno + 1;

        WRITE_OUT(Lv_Lineno, Lv_Seq_Owner, Lv_Seq_Name, '/');
        Lv_Lineno   := Lv_Lineno + 1;

    end loop;
    close SEQ_CURSOR;
end;
/
spool cre_seq.sql
select Text
  from SEQ_TEMP
 order by Id_Owner, Id_Name, Lineno
/
spool off
set newpage 1 verify on feedback 6 pagesize 24 linesize 80
set heading on embedded off term on long 80
undefine sequence_owner
undefine sequence_name
```

Sample output for the gen_seq.sql script is shown in the following listing:

```
CREATE SEQUENCE scott.chess_saveid START WITH 2
MAXVALUE 9999999999999999999999999999 MINVALUE 1
```

```
INCREMENT BY 1 NOCYCLE   NOORDER CACHE 20
/
```

By default, the gen_seq.sql script writes its output to a file named cre_seq.sql.

ANNOTATIONS

Although the script as written will return information for a single sequence, it uses a cursor to allow you to enter a wildcard value or to modify the script to select all sequences for an owner or all sequences in the database. The gen_seq.sql script generates a script to re-create the requested sequence, and it uses a temporary table to hold individual lines of the **create sequence** statement, writing to the table rather than using DBMS_OUTPUT.PUT_LINE so that you can extract the information for an individual sequence from the table. Using the DBMS_OUTPUT procedure would force you to save and edit the output file for the sequence you want.

The first section of the script, shown in the next listing, does the initial setup, prompting for the sequence name and sequence owner for later use via the **accept** command, which, unlike simply using the variable with the '&' or '&&' in a SQL statement, allows you to define your own prompt for the variable. You can enter a value for the sequence name with '%' to generate a script for all sequences with a similar name.

The SQL*Plus **set** command turns off headers (**pagesize 0**), row counts (**feedback off**), and displays of old and new values for the *sequence_name* and *sequence_owner* variables (**verify off**).

```
set echo off term on verify off feedback off pagesize 0
select 'Creating sequences build script...' from DUAL;

accept sequence_name prompt "Enter the name of the sequence: "
accept sequence_owner prompt "Enter sequence owner: "
set term off long 300 linsize 300
```

The next section of the script, shown in the following listing, creates a temporary table to hold each **create sequence** command and its owner. The Lineno column orders the lines of the **create sequence** command.

```
drop    table SEQ_TEMP
/

create table SEQ_TEMP (
        Lineno NUMBER,
        Id_Owner VARCHAR2(30),
        Id_Name VARCHAR2(30),
        Text VARCHAR2(300))
/
```

The SEQ_CURSOR cursor selects the information from DBA_SEQUENCES, where the sequence name matches the input variable *sequence_name* and the sequence owner matches the input variable *sequence_owner*. Using **like** in the **where** clause instead of = allows for wildcards in the sequence name as well as the sequence owner.

```
declare
  cursor SEQ_CURSOR is
        select Sequence_Owner,
               Sequence_Name,
               Min_Value,
               Max_Value,
               Increment_By,
               Cycle_Flag,
               Order_Flag,
               Cache_Size,
               Last_Number
          from DBA_SEQUENCES
         where Sequence_Owner like UPPER('&&sequence_owner')
           and Sequence_Owner not in ('SYS','SYSTEM')
           and Sequence_Name like UPPER('&&sequence_name')
         order by Sequence_Owner, Sequence_Name;
```

The procedure variables for the cursor are declared as TABLE_NAME.Column_Name%TYPE. Anchoring the variables' datatypes takes the column definition from within the database itself. If the column definition changes in a different version of Oracle, the procedure will still work because the definition of the column has not been hard coded. The variable *Lv_Lineno* orders the lines of the **create sequence** statement and is initialized to 0. The variable *Lv_Start_No* holds what will be the next value of the sequence so that you will not overwrite a value already used.

```
Lv_Seq_Owner          DBA_SEQUENCES.Sequence_Owner%TYPE;
Lv_Seq_Name           DBA_SEQUENCES.Sequence_Name%TYPE;
Lv_Seq_Min_Value      DBA_SEQUENCES.Min_Value%TYPE;
Lv_Seq_Max_Value      DBA_SEQUENCES.Max_Value%TYPE;
Lv_Seq_Increment_By   DBA_SEQUENCES.Increment_By%TYPE;
Lv_Seq_Cycle_Flag     DBA_SEQUENCES.Cycle_Flag%TYPE;
Lv_Seq_Order_Flag     DBA_SEQUENCES.Order_Flag%TYPE;
Lv_Seq_Cache_Size     DBA_SEQUENCES.Cache_Size%TYPE;
Lv_Seq_Last_Number    DBA_SEQUENCES.Last_Number%TYPE;
Lv_String             VARCHAR2(300);
Lv_Lineno             NUMBER;
Lv_Start_No           INTEGER;
```

The next portion of the script creates an internal procedure to do the **insert** into the temporary table.

```
procedure WRITE_OUT(P_Line INTEGER, P_Owner VARCHAR2, P_Name VARCHAR2,
                    P_String VARCHAR2) is
begin
   insert into SEQ_TEMP (Lineno, Id_Owner, Id_Name, Text)
         values (P_Line,P_Owner,P_Name,P_String);
 end;
```

The cursor SEQ_CURSOR extracts all the information about the sequences. *Lv_Lineno*, in conjunction with the sequence name, orders the rows in the temporary table SEQ_TEMP so that if you prefer, you can extract the **create sequence** statement for a single sequence at the end of the procedure.

```
begin
   open SEQ_CURSOR;
   Lv_Lineno   := 1;
   loop
      fetch SEQ_CURSOR into Lv_Seq_Owner,
                            Lv_Seq_Name,
                            Lv_Seq_Min_Value,
                            Lv_Seq_Max_Value,
                            Lv_Seq_Increment_By,
                            Lv_Seq_Cycle_Flag,
                            Lv_Seq_Order_Flag,
                            Lv_Seq_Cache_Size,
                            Lv_Seq_Last_Number;
      exit when SEQ_CURSOR%NOTFOUND;
```

The *Lv_Seq_Last_Number* variable contains the last sequence number written to disk. If a sequence uses caching, this number is the last number placed in the sequence cache in the SGA and is likely to be greater than the last sequence number that was really used. Because it is possible for this number to equal the last sequence value actually used, the start number for the **create sequence** statement is generated by incrementing this number by the sequence increment value. If you are using the sequence to generate consecutive numbers, and cannot have any missing values, you should not cache the sequence.

```
      Lv_Start_No := Lv_Seq_Last_Number + Lv_Seq_Increment_By;
```

The next section of the script, shown in the following listing, inserts the beginning of the **create** statement into the temporary table. The **LOWER** function converts the text to lowercase to improve its readability. The generated start number is added to the string and written to the temporary table.

```
      Lv_String   := 'CREATE SEQUENCE '  || LOWER(Lv_Seq_Owner
                                         || '.'
                                         || LOWER(Lv_Seq_Name)
```

```
                                    || ' START WITH '
                                    || Lv_Start_No;
        WRITE_OUT(Lv_Lineno, Lv_Seq_Owner, Lv_Seq_Name, Lv_String);
        Lv_Lineno  := Lv_Lineno + 1;
```

If you create a sequence with **nomaxvalue**, Oracle will specify a maximum value of 10^{27} for an ascending sequence and –1 for a descending sequence. Since the script cannot distinguish between a specified value of 10^{27} using the keyword **maxvalue** and the keyword **nomaxvalue**, the keyword **maxvalue** is always used. The keyword **minvalue** specifies the lowest allowable value for a sequence and has no use unless the sequence has been generated to wrap back to the beginning number once the **maxvalue** has been reached. If the sequence is generated to wrap back, **minvalue** specifies the minimum value the sequence can have. The **increment by** result can be positive or negative, but it cannot be 0. If it is negative, the sequence will generate descending numbers; if it is positive, the sequence will generate ascending numbers.

```
        Lv_String := 'MAXVALUE '|| Lv_Seq_Max_Value ;
        Lv_String := Lv_String   || ' MINVALUE '    || Lv_Seq_Min_Value;
        Lv_String := Lv_String   || ' INCREMENT BY '  || Lv_Seq_Increment_By;
```

The next section of the script examines the **cycle** setting for the sequence. If **nocycle** is specified, the sequence will stop generating numbers once the maximum value (for ascending sequences) or minimum value (for descending sequences) has been reached. If you create a sequence with **cycle**, the sequence will wrap back to its beginning value once the maximum or minimum value has been reached.

```
        if ( Lv_Seq_Cycle_Flag = 'Y' )
        then
            Lv_String := Lv_String || ' CYCLE ';
        else
            Lv_String := Lv_String || ' NOCYCLE ';
        end if;
```

The **order** clause guarantees that sequence numbers will be generated in the order that they are requested and is not essential for primary keys, where only a unique value is needed. If you are using the sequence to generate consecutive numbers, like invoice or check numbers, you should specify **order** for the sequence.

```
        if ( Lv_Seq_Order_Flag = 'Y' )
        then
            Lv_String := Lv_String || ' ORDER ';
        else
            Lv_String := Lv_String || ' NOORDER ';
        end if;
```

The **cache** clause specifies how many values Oracle will pre-generate and keep in memory for the sequence. Caching sequence values improves performance, but values that are cached are lost when the database is shut down and when the shared pool is flushed. The minimum number of values you can cache is two. The section of the gen_seq.sql script shown in the following listing generates the proper **nocache** or **cache** setting for the sequence.

```
    if ( Lv_Seq_Cache_Size = 0 )
    then
        Lv_String := Lv_String || ' NOCACHE ';
    else
        Lv_String := Lv_String || ' CACHE ' || Lv_Seq_Cache_Size;
    end if;
```

The final portion of the script writes the generated commands to the temporary table. The cursor loop ends and the procedure will loop back through the SEQ_CURSOR until all sequences have been generated. Once the **create** statements for all the sequences have been generated, they are spooled to a file named cre_seq.sql for later execution.

```
    WRITE_OUT(Lv_Lineno, Lv_Seq_Owner, Lv_Seq_Name, Lv_String);
    Lv_Lineno   := Lv_Lineno + 1;

    WRITE_OUT(Lv_Lineno, Lv_Seq_Owner, Lv_Seq_Name, '/');
    Lv_Lineno   := Lv_Lineno + 1;
  end loop;
  close SEQ_CURSOR;
end;
/
spool cre_seq.sql
select Text
  from SEQ_TEMP
 order by Id_Owner, Id_Name, Lineno
/
spool off
```

The environment is finally reset to its original state:

```
set newpage 1 verify on feedback 6 pagesize 24 linesize 80
set heading on embedded off term on long 80
undefine sequence_owner
undefine sequence_name
```

A sample cre_seq.sql script is shown here:

```
CREATE SEQUENCE scott.chess_saveid START WITH 2
MAXVALUE 999999999999999999999999999 MINVALUE 1
INCREMENT BY 1 NOCYCLE  NOORDER CACHE 20
/
```

As an alternative, if you want to use this script to document all the sequences for a particular owner, remove the **accept** *sequence_name* statement at the beginning of the script and change the **where** clause for the SEQ_CURSOR cursor as follows:

```
where Owner  = UPPER('&&sequence_owner')
```

or you can use the wildcard '%'.

PROGRAMMER'S NOTE   *Due to the dynamic nature of sequences the last number changes frequently and should be checked before regenerating the sequences.*

Generate Database Links

gen_dblnk_7.sql
gen_dblnk_8n9.sql

Database links are used to connect to another database and access data contained within the remote database. You can use database links to separate data while maintaining location transparency when accessing data. The gen_dblnk_*.sql script generates a script to document the existing database links in your database. With some minor editing, the generated script can be run to re-create these links. The gen_dblnk_7.sql script works with Oracle7.x, while the gen_dblnk_8n9.sql script works for Oracle8.x onward. Both scripts are available on the CD-ROM included with this book.

The following listing shows the gen_dblnk_8n9.sql script:

```
REM
REM gen_dblnk_8n9.sql
REM This script can be used for Oracle8.x and above.
REM
set term on echo off feedback off verify off heading off pagesize 0
select 'Creating database link build script...' from DUAL;
set term off
drop table DL_TEMP;

create table DL_TEMP (Grantor_Owner VARCHAR2(30),
                      Text VARCHAR2(800));
declare
   cursor LINK_CURSOR is
          select U.Name,
                 L.Name,
                 L.Userid,
                 L.Password,
                 L.Host,
                 L.Flag,
                 L.Authusr,
                 L.Authpwd
            from SYS.LINK$ L,
                 SYS.USER$ U
           where L.Owner# = U.User#
           order by L.Name;
```

```
    Lv_Owner      SYS.USER$.Name%TYPE;
    Lv_Db_Link    SYS.LINK$.Name%TYPE;
    Lv_Username   SYS.LINK$.Userid%TYPE;
    Lv_Password   SYS.LINK$.Password%TYPE;
    Lv_Host       SYS.LINK$.Host%TYPE;
    Lv_Flag       SYS.LINK$.Flag%TYPE;
    Lv_Authusr    SYS.LINK$.Authusr%TYPE;
    Lv_Authpwd    SYS.LINK$.Authpwd%TYPE;
    Lv_String     VARCHAR2(800);
    Lv_String1    VARCHAR2(10) := NULL;
    Lv_String2    VARCHAR2(10) := NULL;
    Lv_User       VARCHAR2(255);
    Lv_Auth       VARCHAR2(255);
    Lv_Connect    VARCHAR2(255);
    Lv_Text       VARCHAR2(800);

  procedure WRITE_OUT(P_Owner VARCHAR2, P_String VARCHAR2) is
  begin
      insert into DL_TEMP (Grantor_Owner, Text)
                values (P_Owner,P_String);
  end;
begin
  open LINK_CURSOR;
  loop
      fetch LINK_CURSOR into Lv_Owner,
                             Lv_Db_Link,
                             Lv_Username,
                             Lv_Password,
                             Lv_Host,
                             Lv_Flag,
                             Lv_Authusr,
                             Lv_Authpwd;
      exit when LINK_CURSOR%NOTFOUND;

      if (Lv_Flag = 1)
      then
         Lv_String1 := 'SHARED';
      end if;

      if (Lv_Owner = 'PUBLIC')
      then
         Lv_String2 := 'PUBLIC';
      end if;

      Lv_String := ('CREATE '||Lv_String1||' '||Lv_String2||' '||
                    'DATABASE LINK '||LOWER(Lv_Db_Link));

      if (Lv_Username is not null)
      then
```

```
        if (Lv_Username = 'CURRENT_USER')
        then
         Lv_User := ('CONNECT TO CURRENT_USER');
        else
         Lv_User := ('CONNECT TO '||LOWER(Lv_Username)||
                   ' IDENTIFIED BY '||LOWER(Lv_Password));
        end if;
      end if;

      if (Lv_Authusr is not null)
      then
        Lv_Auth := ('AUTHENTICATED BY '||LOWER(Lv_Authusr)||
                   ' IDENTIFIED BY '||LOWER(Lv_Authpwd));
      end if;

      if (Lv_Host is not null)
      then
         Lv_Connect := ('USING '''||Lv_Host||''''||';');
      end if;

    Lv_Text := Lv_String || ' ' || Lv_User ||
' ' || Lv_Auth || ' ' || Lv_Connect || ';';
    WRITE_OUT(Lv_Owner, Lv_Text);
    Lv_User := ' ';
    Lv_Connect := ' ';

    Lv_String := ' ';

    Lv_String1 := ' ';

    Lv_String2 := ' ';

    Lv_Auth := ' ';

    Lv_Text := ' ';
  end loop;
  close link_cursor;
end;
/
define cr=chr(10)
spool cre_dblnk.sql
break on Downer skip 1
col Text format a60 word_wrap
select 'connect ' || DECODE (Grantor_Owner, 'PUBLIC', 'SYS',
        Grantor_Owner)|| '/' Downer,
        &cr||Text
  from DL_TEMP
 order by Downer
 /
```

```
spool off
 set newpage 1 verify on feedback 6 pagesize 24 linesize 80
set heading on embedded off term on
clear columns
clear breaks
undefine cr
```

Sample output for the gen_dblnk_8n9.sql script is shown here:

```
connect APP/

CREATE DATABASE LINK myprod.world
CONNECT TO app IDENTIFIED BY appowner USING 'PROD';

CREATE DATABASE LINK mytest.world
CONNECT TO app IDENTIFIED BY appowner USING 'TEST';

connect SYS/

CREATE DATABASE LINK deve.world
CONNECT TO app IDENTIFIED BY appowner USING 'DEVE';

CREATE DATABASE LINK test.world
CONNECT TO app IDENTIFIED BY appowner USING 'TEST';

CREATE DATABASE LINK prod.world
CONNECT TO app IDENTIFIED BY appowner USING 'PROD';

connect SYSTEM/

CREATE DATABASE LINK sdeve.world
CONNECT TO system IDENTIFIED BY manager USING 'DEVE';
```

The generated file contains incomplete commands—the **connect** commands do not specify the passwords for the accounts. You will need to modify the created file (called credblnk.sql) to re-create the database links.

ANNOTATIONS

Because a DBA cannot create a private database link on behalf of a user, the output script will contain **connect** commands before each **create database link** command. For the database links to be created under the correct schema, you must add each user's password to the **connect** command.

PUBLIC database links require you to **connect** as 'SYS' or any user with the DBA role or with the CREATE PUBLIC DATABASE LINK system privilege.

The first portion of the gen_dblnk_8n9.sql script, shown in the following listing, sets up the environment for the gen_dblnk_8n9.sql script. The gen_dblnk_8n9.sql script does not prompt the user for any variables. After the environment is configured, the script creates a temporary table to hold each **create database link** command and its owner. The Grantor_Owner column generates the **connect** command before each **create** command.

```
set term on echo off feedback off verify off heading off pagesize 0
select 'Creating database link build script...' from DUAL;
set term off
create table DL_TEMP (Lineno NUMBER, Grantor_Owner VARCHAR2(20),
                      Text VARCHAR2(800));
```

The LINK_CURSOR cursor, shown in the following listing, uses the SYS.LINK$ table rather than the data dictionary view DBA_DB_LINKS because the password for the user you are connecting to in the link is not stored in clear text in the view, but is in the SYS.LINK$ table. The password is needed for the **connect to** clause of the **create database link** statement. The SYS.LINK$ table is joined to the SYS.USER$ table to extract the name of the owner of the database link.

```
declare
    cursor LINK_CURSOR is
          select U.Name,
                 L.Name,
                 L.Userid,
                 L.Password,
                 L.Host,
                 L.Flag,
                 L.Authusr,
                 L.Authpwd
            from SYS.LINK$ L,
                 SYS.USER$ U
           where L.Owner# = U.User#
           order by L.Name;
```

In the following listing, the procedure variables for the cursor are declared as TABLE_NAME.Column_Name%**TYPE**. Anchoring the variable definitions takes the column definition from within the database itself. If the column definition changes in a different version of Oracle, the procedure will still work because the definition of the column has not been hard coded.

```
Lv_Owner     SYS.USER$.Name%TYPE;
Lv_Db_Link   SYS.LINK$.Name%TYPE;
Lv_Username  SYS.LINK$.Userid%TYPE;
Lv_Password  SYS.LINK$.Password%TYPE;
Lv_Host      SYS.LINK$.Host%TYPE;
```

```
Lv_Flag      SYS.LINK$.Flag%TYPE;
Lv_Authusr   SYS.LINK$.Authusr%TYPE;
Lv_Authpwd   SYS.LINK$.Authpwd%TYPE;
Lv_String    VARCHAR2(800);
Lv_String1   VARCHAR2(10)  := NULL;
Lv_String2   VARCHAR2(10)  := NULL;
Lv_User      VARCHAR2(255);
Lv_Auth      VARCHAR2(255);
Lv_Connect   VARCHAR2(255);
Lv_Text      VARCHAR2(800);
```

The next portion of the gen_dblnk_8n9.sql script creates WRITE_OUT, an internal procedure to do the **insert** into the temporary table:

```
procedure WRITE_OUT(P_Owner VARCHAR2, P_String VARCHAR2) is
begin
   insert into DL_TEMP (Grantor_Owner, Text)
            values (P_Owner,P_String);
end;
```

Public database links are owned by a pseudo-user named PUBLIC. The syntax for the **create database link** command differs depending on whether the link is public or private. The portion of the gendblnk.sql script shown in the following listing generates the proper **create** syntax. The SQL function **LOWER** is used to change the database link name to lowercase for readability. As of Oracle8.x, you can create SHARED public database links. Shared public database links allow you to use a single network connection to create a public database link that can be shared between multiple users. Shared database links are available only with the multithreaded server configuration.

```
begin
  open LINK_CURSOR;
  loop
    fetch LINK_CURSOR into Lv_Owner,
                           Lv_Db_Link,
                           Lv_Username,
                           Lv_Password,
                           Lv_Host,
                           Lv_Flag,
                           Lv_Authusr,
                           Lv_Authpwd;
    exit when LINK_CURSOR%NOTFOUND;

    if (Lv_Flag = 1)
    then
      Lv_String1 := 'SHARED';
```

```
end if;

if (Lv_Owner = 'PUBLIC')
then
   Lv_String2 := 'PUBLIC';
end if;

Lv_String := ('CREATE '||Lv_String1||' '||Lv_String2||' '||
              'DATABASE LINK '||LOWER(Lv_Db_Link));
```

The next section of the gen_dblnk_8n9.sql script determines whether the database link is a current user database link. This clause is available as of Oracle8.x. The current user must be a global user with a valid account on the remote database. If the database links is used directly and not from within a stored object, the current user is the same as the connected user. However, if a stored object invokes the database link, the current user is the owner of the stored object and not the user that called the stored object.

```
if (Lv_Username is not null)
then
  if (Lv_Username = 'CURRENT_USER')
  then
   Lv_User := ('CONNECT TO CURRENT_USER');
  else
   Lv_User := ('CONNECT TO '||LOWER(Lv_Username)||
               ' IDENTIFIED BY '||LOWER(Lv_Password));
  end if;
end if;
```

The next section determines whether the authenticated clause is used. This clause is available as of Oracle8.x.

```
if (Lv_Authusr is not null)
then
   Lv_Auth := ('AUTHENTICATED BY '||LOWER(Lv_Authusr)||
               ' IDENTIFIED BY '||LOWER(Lv_Authpwd));
end if;
```

The final portion of the gendblnk.sql script, shown in the following listing, generates the **using** clause for the link. The *Lv_Host* value is the database specification for the remote database.

Following the **using** clause generation, the script inserts the information on this database link into the temporary table and initializes the variables for the next link to be processed.

```
if (Lv_Host is not null)
   then
```

```
        Lv_Connect := ('USING '''||Lv_Host||''''||';');
      end if;

      Lv_Text := Lv_String || ' ' || Lv_User ||
 ' ' || Lv_Auth || ' ' || Lv_Connect || ';';
      WRITE_OUT(Lv_Owner, Lv_Text);
      Lv_User := ' ';
      Lv_Connect := ' ';
      Lv_String := ' ';

      Lv_String1 := ' ';

      Lv_String2 := ' ';

      Lv_Auth := ' ';

      Lv_Text := ' ';
   end loop;
   close link_cursor;
end;
/
define cr=chr(10)
```

The SQL*Plus command **define** allows you to assign a value to an internal variable
and use it later with the '&' or '&&' feature to substitute the value into a command.
In this section of the gendblnk.sql script, the variable *cr* is assigned the ASCII value
of 10, or carriage return.

Now that all the links have been read and processed, the script extracts the information
into a file to document the database links. Public database links are owned by SYS so
the **DECODE** function is used to replace the owner PUBLIC with SYS in the **connect**
command. If you prefer, you can substitute the name of any user ID with either the
DBA role or CREATE PUBLIC DATABASE LINK privilege for SYS.

The **break** on the Downer column in the following listing suppresses the display
of repeated values for the column. If multiple database links are owned by this user,
the **connect** command will be generated only once. The **skip 1** of the **break** command
forces a new line after the '/'. Concatenating the *cr* variable with the text string forces
a new line for every database link displayed.

```
spool credblnk.sql
break on Downer skip 1
col Text format a60 word_wrap
select    'connect ' || DECODE (Grantor_Owner, 'PUBLIC', 'SYS',
                          Grantor_Owner)|| '/' Downer,
        &cr||Text
```

```
from      DL_TEMP
order by Downer
/
spool off
```

The following listing shows a sample cre_dblnk.sql file:

```
connect APP/

CREATE DATABASE LINK myprod.world
CONNECT TO app IDENTIFIED BY appowner USING 'PROD';

CREATE DATABASE LINK mytest.world
CONNECT TO app IDENTIFIED BY appowner USING 'TEST';

connect SYS/

CREATE DATABASE LINK deve.world
CONNECT TO app IDENTIFIED BY appowner USING 'DEVE';

CREATE DATABASE LINK test.world
CONNECT TO app IDENTIFIED BY appowner USING 'TEST';

CREATE DATABASE LINK prod.world
CONNECT TO app IDENTIFIED BY appowner USING 'PROD';

connect SYSTEM/

CREATE DATABASE LINK sdeve.world
CONNECT TO system IDENTIFIED BY manager USING 'DEVE';
```

The output cannot be run without minor editing. Because you cannot create a database link for someone else, there must be a **connect** for each database link owner in the credblnk.sql file. You must edit the output file to include the passwords before running credblnk.sql. There is only one **connect** statement per database link owner because of the **break** command.

Each of the database link names has the default domain, .WORLD, included as part of the name. You can create a database link name without specifying the default domain, and Oracle will append it to your database link name. You should not specify the default domain name in the **using** clause.

Generate Snapshots/Materialized Views

To improve the performance of applications using distributed data, you may make local copies of remote tables. Snapshots/materialized views are provided by Oracle as a means of managing local copies of remote tables. Using snapshots/materialized views, you can replicate all or part of a single table or replicate the result of a query against multiple tables. It should be noted that as of Oracle8.1.x, materialized views are synonymous with snapshots. To use snapshots/materialized views, you should have installed the distributed option within your Oracle database.

The gen_snap_7.sql and gen_snap_80.sql scripts can be used to generate a script to create snapshots in Oracle7.x and Oracle8.0.x databases, respectively, while the script gen_mview_81n9.sql can be used to generate a script to create materialized views in Oracle8.1.x onward. All the scripts (gen_snap_7.sql, gen_snap_80.sql, and gen_mview_81n9.sql) are available on the CD-ROM in this book.

The script gen_mview_81n9.sql is shown in the following listing:

```
REM
REM gen_mview_81n9.sql
REM This script can be used for Oracle8.1.x and above
REM
set echo off term on verify off feedback off pagesize 0 heading off
select 'Creating materialized view build script...' from DUAL;

accept mview_master prompt "Enter the materialized view master object: "
accept mview_owner prompt "Enter the object owner: "
set term off

drop    table MVIEW_TEMP
/

create table MVIEW_TEMP (
        Lineno NUMBER,
        Id_Owner VARCHAR2(30),
        Id_Name VARCHAR2(30),
        Text VARCHAR2(350))
/

declare
   cursor MVIEW_CURSOR is
        select S.Owner,
               S.Name,
               S.Type,
```

```
                  S.Start_With,
                  S.Next,
                  S.Refresh_Method,
                  S.Master_Rollback_Seg,
                  R.Rollback_Seg,
                  S.Updatable,
                  S.Query,
                  S.Prebuilt,
                  M.Rewrite_Enabled,
                  M.Refresh_Mode,
                  M.Refresh_Method,
                  M.Build_Mode,
                  M.Last_Refresh_Type
             from DBA_SNAPSHOTS S, DBA_REFRESH R, DBA_MVIEWS M
            where S.Owner like UPPER('&&mview_owner')
              and S.Owner not in ('SYS','SYSTEM')
              and S.Name = ('&&mview_master')
              and R.Refgroup (+) = S.Refresh_Group
              and M.Owner = S.Owner
              and M.Mview_Name = S.Name
            order by S.Owner, S.Name;


    cursor TAB_CURSOR (C_Owner VARCHAR2,
                       C_Tabname VARCHAR2) is
         select Owner,
                Table_Name,
                Tablespace_Name,
                Pct_Free,
                Pct_Used,
                Ini_Trans,
                Max_Trans,
                Initial_Extent,
                Next_Extent,
                Min_Extents,
                Max_Extents,
                Pct_Increase,
                Degree,
                Instances,
                Logging,
                Cache
           from DBA_TABLES
          where Owner = C_Owner
            and Table_Name = C_Tabname
          order by Table_Name;

    cursor IND_CURSOR (C_Tabowner VARCHAR2,
                       C_Tabname VARCHAR2) is
         select Owner,
```

```
          Index_Name,
          Tablespace_Name,
          Pct_Free,
          Ini_Trans,
          Max_Trans,
          Initial_Extent,
          Next_Extent,
          Min_Extents,
          Max_Extents,
          Pct_Increase
     from DBA_Indexes
    where Owner = C_Tabowner
      and Table_Name = C_Tabname
    order by Table_Name;


Lv_Mview_Owner              DBA_SNAPSHOTS.Owner%TYPE;
Lv_Mview_Name               DBA_SNAPSHOTS.Name%TYPE;
Lv_Type                     DBA_SNAPSHOTS.Type%TYPE;
Lv_Start_With               DBA_SNAPSHOTS.Start_With%TYPE;
Lv_Next                     DBA_SNAPSHOTS.Next%TYPE;
Lv_Refresh_Method           DBA_SNAPSHOTS.Refresh_Method%TYPE;
Lv_Updatable                DBA_SNAPSHOTS.Updatable%TYPE;
Lv_Query                    DBA_SNAPSHOTS.Query%TYPE;
Lv_Prebuilt                 DBA_SNAPSHOTS.Prebuilt%TYPE;
Lv_Master_Rollback_Segment  DBA_SNAPSHOTS.Master_Rollback_Seg%TYPE;
Lv_Local_Rollback_Segment   DBA_REFRESH.Rollback_Seg%TYPE;

Lv_Rewrite_Enabled          DBA_MVIEWS.Rewrite_Enabled%TYPE;
Lv_Refresh_Mode             DBA_MVIEWS.Refresh_Mode%TYPE;
Lv_M_Refresh_Method         DBA_MVIEWS.Refresh_Method%TYPE;
Lv_Build_Mode               DBA_MVIEWS.Build_Mode%TYPE;
Lv_Last_Refresh_Type        DBA_MVIEWS.Last_Refresh_Type%TYPE;


Lv_Table_Owner              DBA_TABLES.Owner%TYPE;
Lv_Table_Name               DBA_TABLES.Table_Name%TYPE;
Lv_Tablespace_Name          DBA_TABLES.Tablespace_Name%TYPE;
Lv_Pct_Free                 DBA_TABLES.Pct_Free%TYPE;
Lv_Pct_Used                 DBA_TABLES.Pct_Used%TYPE;
Lv_Initial_Trans            DBA_TABLES.Ini_Trans%TYPE;
Lv_Max_Trans                DBA_TABLES.Max_Trans%TYPE;
Lv_Initial_Extent           DBA_TABLES.Initial_Extent%TYPE;
Lv_Next_Extent              DBA_TABLES.Next_Extent%TYPE;
Lv_Min_Extents              DBA_TABLES.Min_Extents%TYPE;
Lv_Max_Extents              DBA_TABLES.Max_Extents%TYPE;
Lv_Pct_Increase             DBA_TABLES.Pct_Increase%TYPE;
Lv_Degree                   DBA_TABLES.Degree%TYPE;
```

```
    Lv_Instances                    DBA_TABLES.Instances%TYPE;
    Lv_Logging                      DBA_TABLES.Logging%TYPE;
    Lv_Cache                        DBA_TABLES.Cache%TYPE;

    Lv_Index_Owner                     DBA_INDEXES.Owner%TYPE;
    Lv_Index_Name                      DBA_INDEXES.Index_Name%TYPE;
    Lv_Ind_Tablespace_Name             DBA_INDEXES.Tablespace_Name%TYPE;
    Lv_Ind_Pct_Free                    DBA_INDEXES.Pct_Free%TYPE;
    Lv_Ind_Initial_Trans               DBA_INDEXES.Ini_Trans%TYPE;
    Lv_Ind_Max_Trans                   DBA_INDEXES.Max_Trans%TYPE;
    Lv_Ind_Initial_Extent              DBA_INDEXES.Initial_Extent%TYPE;
    Lv_Ind_Next_Extent                 DBA_INDEXES.Next_Extent%TYPE;
    Lv_Ind_Min_Extents                 DBA_INDEXES.Min_Extents%TYPE;
    Lv_Ind_Max_Extents                 DBA_INDEXES.Max_Extents%TYPE;
    Lv_Ind_Pct_Increase                DBA_INDEXES.Pct_Increase%TYPE;


    Lv_String            VARCHAR2(350);
    Lv_Lineno            NUMBER;

    procedure WRITE_OUT(P_Line INTEGER, P_Owner VARCHAR2, P_Name VARCHAR2,
                    P_String VARCHAR2) is
    begin
       insert into MVIEW_TEMP (Lineno, Id_Owner, Id_Name, Text)
             values (P_Line,P_Owner,P_Name,P_String);
      end;

begin
    open MVIEW_CURSOR;
    loop
       fetch MVIEW_CURSOR into Lv_Mview_Owner,
                              Lv_Mview_Name,
                              Lv_Type,
                              Lv_Start_With,
                              Lv_Next,
                              Lv_Refresh_Method,
                              Lv_Master_Rollback_Segment,
                              Lv_Local_Rollback_Segment,
                              Lv_Updatable,
                              Lv_Query,
                              Lv_Prebuilt,
                              Lv_Rewrite_Enabled,
                              Lv_Refresh_Mode,
                              Lv_M_Refresh_Method,
                              Lv_Build_Mode,
                              Lv_Last_Refresh_Type;
        exit when MVIEW_CURSOR%NOTFOUND;
```

```
    Lv_Lineno := 1;

    Lv_String:= 'CREATE MATERIALIZED VIEW ' || LOWER(Lv_Mview_Owner)
                                            || '.'
                                            || LOWER(Lv_Mview_Name);
    WRITE_OUT(Lv_Lineno, Lv_Mview_Owner, Lv_Mview_Name, Lv_String);
    Lv_Lineno := Lv_Lineno + 1;

    if (Lv_Prebuilt = 'YES')
    then

     Lv_String:= ' ON PREBUILT TABLE ';
     WRITE_OUT(Lv_Lineno, Lv_Mview_Owner, Lv_Mview_Name, Lv_String);
     Lv_Lineno := Lv_Lineno + 1;

    else

     open TAB_CURSOR (Lv_Mview_Owner, Lv_Mview_Name);
     loop
      fetch TAB_CURSOR into Lv_Table_Owner,
                            Lv_Table_Name,
                            Lv_Tablespace_Name,
                            Lv_Pct_Free,
                            Lv_Pct_Used,
                            Lv_Initial_Trans,
                            Lv_Max_Trans,
                            Lv_Initial_Extent,
                            Lv_Next_Extent,
                            Lv_Min_Extents,
                            Lv_Max_Extents,
                            Lv_Pct_Increase,
                            Lv_Degree,
                            Lv_Instances,
                            Lv_Logging,
                            Lv_Cache;
       exit when TAB_CURSOR%NOTFOUND;


     Lv_String   := 'TABLESPACE ' || Lv_Tablespace_Name ;
     WRITE_OUT(Lv_Lineno, Lv_Mview_Owner, Lv_Mview_Name, Lv_String);
     Lv_Lineno := Lv_Lineno + 1;

     Lv_String   := 'PCTFREE ' || Lv_Pct_Free ;
     WRITE_OUT(Lv_Lineno, Lv_Mview_Owner, Lv_Mview_Name, Lv_String);
     Lv_Lineno := Lv_Lineno + 1;
```

```
Lv_String   := 'PCTUSED ' || Lv_Pct_Used ;
WRITE_OUT(Lv_Lineno, Lv_Mview_Owner, Lv_Mview_Name, Lv_String);
Lv_Lineno := Lv_Lineno + 1;

Lv_String   := 'INITRANS ' || Lv_Initial_Trans ;
WRITE_OUT(Lv_Lineno, Lv_Mview_Owner, Lv_Mview_Name, Lv_String);
Lv_Lineno := Lv_Lineno + 1;

Lv_String   := 'MAXTRANS ' || Lv_Max_Trans ;
WRITE_OUT(Lv_Lineno, Lv_Mview_Owner, Lv_Mview_Name, Lv_String);
Lv_Lineno := Lv_Lineno + 1;

if (Lv_Logging = 'YES')
then
    Lv_String  := ' LOGGING ';
else
    Lv_String  := ' NOLOGGING ';
end if;

WRITE_OUT(Lv_Lineno, Lv_Mview_Owner, Lv_Mview_Name, Lv_String);
Lv_Lineno := Lv_Lineno + 1;

if (Lv_Cache = 'Y')
then
    Lv_String  := ' CACHE ';
else
    Lv_String  := ' NOCACHE ';
end if;

WRITE_OUT(Lv_Lineno, Lv_Mview_Owner, Lv_Mview_Name, Lv_String);
Lv_Lineno := Lv_Lineno + 1;

Lv_String   := 'PARALLEL ( DEGREE ' || Lv_Degree
                                     || ' INSTANCES '
                                     || Lv_Instances
                                     || ' )';
WRITE_OUT(Lv_Lineno, Lv_Mview_Owner, Lv_Mview_Name, Lv_String);
Lv_Lineno := Lv_Lineno + 1;

if (Lv_Build_Mode = 'DEFERRED')
then
 Lv_String  := ' BUILD DEFERRED ';
else
 Lv_String  := ' BUILD IMMEDIATE ';
end if;

WRITE_OUT(Lv_Lineno, Lv_Mview_Owner, Lv_Mview_Name, Lv_String);
Lv_Lineno := Lv_Lineno + 1;
```

```
    Lv_String   := 'STORAGE';
    WRITE_OUT(Lv_Lineno, Lv_Mview_Owner, Lv_Mview_Name, Lv_String);
    Lv_Lineno := Lv_Lineno + 1;

    Lv_String   := '(';
    WRITE_OUT(Lv_Lineno, Lv_Mview_Owner, Lv_Mview_Name, Lv_String);
    Lv_Lineno := Lv_Lineno + 1;

    Lv_String   := '   INITIAL ' || Lv_Initial_Extent ;
    WRITE_OUT(Lv_Lineno, Lv_Mview_Owner, Lv_Mview_Name, Lv_String);
    Lv_Lineno := Lv_Lineno + 1;

    Lv_String   := '   NEXT ' || Lv_Next_Extent ;
    WRITE_OUT(Lv_Lineno, Lv_Mview_Owner, Lv_Mview_Name, Lv_String);
    Lv_Lineno := Lv_Lineno + 1;

    Lv_String   := '   MINEXTENTS ' || Lv_Min_Extents ;
    WRITE_OUT(Lv_Lineno, Lv_Mview_Owner, Lv_Mview_Name, Lv_String);
    Lv_Lineno := Lv_Lineno + 1;

    Lv_String   := '   MAXEXTENTS ' || Lv_Max_Extents ;
    WRITE_OUT(Lv_Lineno, Lv_Mview_Owner, Lv_Mview_Name, Lv_String);
    Lv_Lineno := Lv_Lineno + 1;

    Lv_String   := '   PCTINCREASE ' || Lv_Pct_Increase ;
    WRITE_OUT(Lv_Lineno, Lv_Mview_Owner, Lv_Mview_Name, Lv_String);
    Lv_Lineno := Lv_Lineno + 1;

    Lv_String   := ')';
    WRITE_OUT(Lv_Lineno, Lv_Mview_Owner, Lv_Mview_Name, Lv_String);
    Lv_Lineno := Lv_Lineno + 1;

  end loop;
  close TAB_CURSOR;

end if;

open IND_CURSOR (Lv_Mview_Owner, Lv_Mview_Name);
loop
    fetch IND_CURSOR into Lv_Index_Owner,
                         Lv_Index_Name,
                         Lv_Ind_Tablespace_Name,
                         Lv_Ind_Pct_Free,
                         Lv_Ind_Initial_Trans,
                         Lv_Ind_Max_Trans,
                         Lv_Ind_Initial_Extent,
                         Lv_Ind_Next_Extent,
                         Lv_Ind_Min_Extents,
```

```
                        Lv_Ind_Max_Extents,
                        Lv_Ind_Pct_Increase;
   exit when IND_CURSOR%NOTFOUND;


if (Lv_Index_Name is NOT NULL)
then
  Lv_String  := ' USING INDEX ' ;
  WRITE_OUT(Lv_Lineno, Lv_Mview_Owner, Lv_Mview_Name, Lv_String);
  Lv_Lineno := Lv_Lineno + 1;

  Lv_String  := 'TABLESPACE ' || Lv_Ind_Tablespace_Name ;
  WRITE_OUT(Lv_Lineno, Lv_Mview_Owner, Lv_Mview_Name, Lv_String);
  Lv_Lineno := Lv_Lineno + 1;

  Lv_String  := 'PCTFREE ' || Lv_Ind_Pct_Free ;
  WRITE_OUT(Lv_Lineno, Lv_Mview_Owner, Lv_Mview_Name, Lv_String);
  Lv_Lineno := Lv_Lineno + 1;

  Lv_String  := 'INITRANS ' || Lv_Ind_Initial_Trans ;
  WRITE_OUT(Lv_Lineno, Lv_Mview_Owner, Lv_Mview_Name, Lv_String);
  Lv_Lineno := Lv_Lineno + 1;

  Lv_String  := 'MAXTRANS ' || Lv_Ind_Max_Trans ;
  WRITE_OUT(Lv_Lineno, Lv_Mview_Owner, Lv_Mview_Name, Lv_String);
  Lv_Lineno := Lv_Lineno + 1;

  Lv_String  := 'STORAGE';
  WRITE_OUT(Lv_Lineno, Lv_Mview_Owner, Lv_Mview_Name, Lv_String);
  Lv_Lineno := Lv_Lineno + 1;

  Lv_String  := '(';
  WRITE_OUT(Lv_Lineno, Lv_Mview_Owner, Lv_Mview_Name, Lv_String);
  Lv_Lineno := Lv_Lineno + 1;

  Lv_String  := '   INITIAL ' || Lv_Ind_Initial_Extent ;
  WRITE_OUT(Lv_Lineno, Lv_Mview_Owner, Lv_Mview_Name, Lv_String);
  Lv_Lineno := Lv_Lineno + 1;

  Lv_String  := '   NEXT ' || Lv_Ind_Next_Extent ;
  WRITE_OUT(Lv_Lineno, Lv_Mview_Owner, Lv_Mview_Name, Lv_String);
  Lv_Lineno := Lv_Lineno + 1;

  Lv_String  := '   MINEXTENTS ' || Lv_Ind_Min_Extents ;
  WRITE_OUT(Lv_Lineno, Lv_Mview_Owner, Lv_Mview_Name, Lv_String);
  Lv_Lineno := Lv_Lineno + 1;
```

```
        Lv_String  := '   MAXEXTENTS ' || Lv_Ind_Max_Extents ;
        WRITE_OUT(Lv_Lineno, Lv_Mview_Owner, Lv_Mview_Name, Lv_String);
        Lv_Lineno := Lv_Lineno + 1;

        Lv_String  := '   PCTINCREASE ' || Lv_Ind_Pct_Increase ;
        WRITE_OUT(Lv_Lineno, Lv_Mview_Owner, Lv_Mview_Name, Lv_String);
        Lv_Lineno := Lv_Lineno + 1;

        Lv_String  := ')';
        WRITE_OUT(Lv_Lineno, Lv_Mview_Owner, Lv_Mview_Name, Lv_String);
        Lv_Lineno := Lv_Lineno + 1;
      end if;


  end loop;
  close IND_CURSOR;



  if (Lv_M_Refresh_Method = 'NEVER')
  then
     Lv_String := ' NEVER REFRESH ';
  else

     Lv_String  := ' REFRESH '||Lv_M_Refresh_Method||' ON '||Lv_Refresh_Mode;
     WRITE_OUT(Lv_Lineno, Lv_Mview_Owner, Lv_Mview_Name, Lv_String);
     Lv_Lineno := Lv_Lineno + 1;


     if (Lv_Start_With is NOT NULL)
     then
       Lv_String  := ' START WITH to_date('''||Lv_Start_With||''',
''DD-MON-YYYY HH24:MI:SS'')';
       WRITE_OUT(Lv_Lineno, Lv_Mview_Owner, Lv_Mview_Name, Lv_String);
       Lv_Lineno := Lv_Lineno + 1;
     end if;

     if (Lv_Next is NOT NULL)
     then
       Lv_String  := ' NEXT '||Lv_Next;
       WRITE_OUT(Lv_Lineno, Lv_Mview_Owner, Lv_Mview_Name, Lv_String);
       Lv_Lineno := Lv_Lineno + 1;
     end if;

     Lv_String  := ' WITH '||Lv_Refresh_Method;
     WRITE_OUT(Lv_Lineno, Lv_Mview_Owner, Lv_Mview_Name, Lv_String);
     Lv_Lineno := Lv_Lineno + 1;
```

```
        Lv_String  := ' ';
        if (Lv_Master_Rollback_Segment is NULL)
        then
         if (Lv_Local_Rollback_Segment is NOT NULL)
         then
           Lv_String:=Lv_String||' USING LOCAL ROLLBACK SEGMENT
'||Lv_Local_Rollback_Segment;
          end if;
        else
         Lv_String:=Lv_String||' USING MASTER ROLLBACK SEGMENT
'||Lv_Master_Rollback_Segment;
        end if;

        WRITE_OUT(Lv_Lineno, Lv_Mview_Owner, Lv_Mview_Name, Lv_String);
        Lv_Lineno := Lv_Lineno + 1;

      end if;

      if (Lv_Updatable = 'YES')
      then
          Lv_String  := ' FOR UPDATE ';
          WRITE_OUT(Lv_Lineno, Lv_Mview_Owner, Lv_Mview_Name, Lv_String);
          Lv_Lineno := Lv_Lineno + 1;
      end if;

      if (Lv_Rewrite_Enabled = 'Y')
      then
        Lv_String := ' ENABLE QUERY REWRITE ';
      else
        Lv_String := 'DISABLE QUERY REWRITE ';
      end if;
      WRITE_OUT(Lv_Lineno, Lv_Mview_Owner, Lv_Mview_Name, Lv_String);
      Lv_Lineno := Lv_Lineno + 1;


        Lv_String  := ' AS '||Lv_Query;
        WRITE_OUT(Lv_Lineno, Lv_Mview_Owner, Lv_Mview_Name, Lv_String);
        Lv_Lineno := Lv_Lineno + 1;

        Lv_String  := '/';
        WRITE_OUT(Lv_Lineno, Lv_Mview_Owner, Lv_Mview_Name, Lv_String);
        Lv_Lineno := Lv_Lineno + 1;

   end loop;
   close MVIEW_CURSOR;
end;
/
spool cre_mview.sql
select Text
```

```
   from MVIEW_TEMP
 order by Id_Owner, Id_Name, Lineno
/
spool off
set newpage 1 verify on feedback 6 pagesize 24 linesize 80
set heading on embedded off term on
undefine mview_master
undefine mview_owner
```

Sample output of running the script gen_mview_81n9.sql against an Oracle9.x database is shown here:

```
CREATE MATERIALIZED VIEW app.msnap1
 ON PREBUILT TABLE
 REFRESH FORCE ON DEMAND
 WITH PRIMARY KEY
DISABLE QUERY REWRITE
 AS SELECT "EMP"."EMPNO" "EMPNO","EMP"."ENAME" "ENAME",
"EMP"."JOB" "JOB","EMP"."MGR" "MGR",
"EMP"."HIREDATE" "HIREDATE",
"EMP"."SAL" "SAL","EMP"."COMM" "COMM","EMP"."DEPTNO" "DEPTNO"
FROM "SCOTT"."EMP" "EMP"
/
CREATE MATERIALIZED VIEW app.msnap2
 ON PREBUILT TABLE
 REFRESH FORCE ON DEMAND
 WITH PRIMARY KEY
DISABLE QUERY REWRITE
 AS SELECT "EMP"."EMPNO" "EMPNO","EMP"."ENAME" "ENAME",
"EMP"."JOB" "JOB","EMP"."
MGR" "MGR","EMP"."HIREDATE" "HIREDATE",
"EMP"."SAL" "SAL","EMP"."COMM" "COMM","EMP"."DEPTNO" "DEPTNO"
FROM "SCOTT"."EMP" "EMP"
/
CREATE MATERIALIZED VIEW system.msnap5
TABLESPACE TOOLS PCTFREE 10
PCTUSED 40 INITRANS 1
MAXTRANS 255
 LOGGING
 NOCACHE
PARALLEL ( DEGREE             1 INSTANCES            1 )
 BUILD IMMEDIATE
STORAGE
(  INITIAL 32768    NEXT 32768
   MINEXTENTS 1     MAXEXTENTS 4096
```

```
     PCTINCREASE 0 )
  USING INDEX
TABLESPACE TOOLS PCTFREE 10
INITRANS 2 MAXTRANS 255
STORAGE
(   INITIAL 32768    NEXT 32768
    MINEXTENTS 1     MAXEXTENTS 4096
    PCTINCREASE 0 )
  REFRESH FORCE ON DEMAND
  START WITH to_date('17-JUL-01','DD-MON-YYYY HH24:MI:SS')
  NEXT sysdate+1
  WITH PRIMARY KEY
DISABLE QUERY REWRITE
  AS SELECT "EMP"."EMPNO" "EMPNO","EMP"."ENAME" "ENAME",
"EMP"."JOB" "JOB","EMP"."
MGR" "MGR","EMP"."HIREDATE" "HIREDATE",
"EMP"."SAL" "SAL","EMP"."COMM" "COMM","EMP"."DEPTNO" "DEPTNO"
FROM "SCOTT"."EMP" "EMP"
/
CREATE MATERIALIZED VIEW system.msnap6
TABLESPACE TOOLS PCTFREE 10
PCTUSED 40 INITRANS 1
MAXTRANS 255
  LOGGING
  NOCACHE
PARALLEL ( DEGREE          1 INSTANCES          1 )
  BUILD IMMEDIATE
STORAGE
(   INITIAL 32768    NEXT 32768
    MINEXTENTS 1     MAXEXTENTS 4096
    PCTINCREASE 0 )
  USING INDEX
TABLESPACE TOOLS
PCTFREE 10 INITRANS 2
MAXTRANS 255
STORAGE
(   INITIAL 32768    NEXT 32768
    MINEXTENTS 1     MAXEXTENTS 4096
    PCTINCREASE 0 )
  REFRESH FORCE ON DEMAND
  START WITH to_date('17-JUL-01','DD-MON-YYYY HH24:MI:SS')
  NEXT sysdate+1
  WITH ROWID
DISABLE QUERY REWRITE
```

```
   AS SELECT "EMP"."EMPNO" "EMPNO","EMP"."ENAME" "ENAME",
"EMP"."JOB" "JOB","EMP"."
MGR" "MGR","EMP"."HIREDATE" "HIREDATE",
"EMP"."SAL" "SAL","EMP"."COMM" "COMM","EMP"."DEPTNO" "DEPTNO"
FROM "SCOTT"."EMP" "EMP"
/
```

Generate Snapshots Logs/Materialized Views Logs

gen_snap_log_7.sql
n_snap_log_80.sql
_mview_log_81.sql
n_mview_log_9.sql

When simple snapshots are used, each record in the snapshot is based on a single row in a single master table. With simple snapshots, you can use snapshot logs as well. Created on a master table, a snapshot log is a table that records the date on which every changed row within the master table was last replicated. Information in the snapshot logs allows efficient refresh of snapshots by sending out to snapshots only those rows that have changed in the master table. It is possible for multiple simple snapshots based on the same table to use the same snapshot log.

Note that as of Oracle8.1.x, materialized view logs are synonymous with snapshot logs. To use snapshots/materialized views, you should have installed the distributed option within your Oracle database. The gen_snap_log_7.sql, gen_snap_log_80.sql, gen_mview_log_81.sql, and gen_mview_log_9.sql scripts can be used to generate a script to create snapshot logs/materialized view logs in Oracle7.x, Oracle8.0.x, Oracle8.1.x, and Oracle9.x databases, respectively. All the scripts (gen_snap_log_7.sql, gen_snap_log_80.sql, gen_mview_log_81.sql, and gen_mview_log_9.sql) are available on the CD-ROM with this book.

The script gen_mview_log_9.sql is shown in this listing:

```
REM
REM gen_mview_log_9.sql
REM This script can be used for Oracle9.x only
REM
set echo off term on verify off feedback off pagesize 0 heading off
select 'Creating materialized view log build script...' from DUAL;

accept mview_log_master prompt
"Enter the materialized view log master object: "
accept mview_log_owner prompt "Enter the object owner: "
set term off

drop    table MVIEW_LOG_TEMP
/

create table MVIEW_LOG_TEMP (
        Lineno NUMBER,
        Id_Owner VARCHAR2(30),
        Id_Name VARCHAR2(30),
```

```
        Text VARCHAR2(350))
/

declare
   cursor MVIEW_LOG_CURSOR is
        select Log_Owner,
                Log_Table,
                Master,
                Rowids,
                Primary_Key,
                Filter_Columns,
                Object_Id,
                Sequence,
                Include_New_Values
           from DBA_SNAPSHOT_LOGS
          where Log_Owner like UPPER('&&mview_log_owner')
            and Master like UPPER('&&mview_log_master')
            and Log_Owner not in ('SYS','SYSTEM')
          order by Log_Owner, Master;

   cursor TAB_CURSOR (C_Owner VARCHAR2,
                      C_Tabname VARCHAR2) is
        select Owner,
                Table_Name,
                Tablespace_Name,
                Pct_Free,
                Pct_Used,
                Ini_Trans,
                Max_Trans,
                Initial_Extent,
                Next_Extent,
                Min_Extents,
                Max_Extents,
                Pct_Increase,
                Degree,
                Instances,
                Logging,
                Cache,
                Freelists,
                Freelist_Groups
           from DBA_TABLES
          where Owner = C_Owner
            and Table_Name = C_Tabname
          order by Table_Name;

   cursor FIL_COLS_CURSOR (C_Owner   VARCHAR2,
                           C_Tabname VARCHAR2) is
        select Column_Name
           from DBA_SNAPSHOT_LOG_FILTER_COLS
```

```
          where Owner        = C_Owner
            and Name  = C_Tabname
          order by rowid;


   Lv_Log_Owner              DBA_SNAPSHOT_LOGS.Log_Owner%TYPE;
   Lv_Log_Table              DBA_SNAPSHOT_LOGS.Log_Table%TYPE;
   Lv_Master                 DBA_SNAPSHOT_LOGS.Master%TYPE;
   Lv_Rowids                 DBA_SNAPSHOT_LOGS.Rowids%TYPE;
   Lv_Primary_Key            DBA_SNAPSHOT_LOGS.Primary_Key%TYPE;
   Lv_Filter_Columns         DBA_SNAPSHOT_LOGS.Filter_Columns%TYPE;
   Lv_Object_id              DBA_SNAPSHOT_LOGS.Object_id%TYPE;
   Lv_Sequence               DBA_SNAPSHOT_LOGS.Sequence%TYPE;
   Lv_Include_New_Values     DBA_SNAPSHOT_LOGS.Include_New_Values%TYPE;


   Lv_Table_Owner             DBA_TABLES.Owner%TYPE;
   Lv_Table_Name              DBA_TABLES.Table_Name%TYPE;
   Lv_Tablespace_Name         DBA_TABLES.Tablespace_Name%TYPE;
   Lv_Pct_Free                DBA_TABLES.Pct_Free%TYPE;
   Lv_Pct_Used                DBA_TABLES.Pct_Used%TYPE;
   Lv_Initial_Trans           DBA_TABLES.Ini_Trans%TYPE;
   Lv_Max_Trans               DBA_TABLES.Max_Trans%TYPE;
   Lv_Initial_Extent          DBA_TABLES.Initial_Extent%TYPE;
   Lv_Next_Extent             DBA_TABLES.Next_Extent%TYPE;
   Lv_Min_Extents             DBA_TABLES.Min_Extents%TYPE;
   Lv_Max_Extents             DBA_TABLES.Max_Extents%TYPE;
   Lv_Pct_Increase            DBA_TABLES.Pct_Increase%TYPE;
   Lv_Degree                  DBA_TABLES.Degree%TYPE;
   Lv_Instances               DBA_TABLES.Instances%TYPE;
   Lv_Logging                 DBA_TABLES.Logging%TYPE;
   Lv_Cache                   DBA_TABLES.Cache%TYPE;
   Lv_Freelists               DBA_TABLES.Freelists%TYPE;
   Lv_Freelist_Groups         DBA_TABLES.Freelist_Groups%TYPE;

   Lv_Column_Name            DBA_SNAPSHOT_LOG_FILTER_COLS.COLUMN_NAME%TYPE;

   Lv_String         VARCHAR2(350);
   Lv_Lineno         NUMBER;

procedure WRITE_OUT(P_Line INTEGER, P_Owner VARCHAR2, P_Name VARCHAR2,
                P_String VARCHAR2) is
begin
   insert into MVIEW_LOG_TEMP (Lineno, Id_Owner, Id_Name, Text)
         values (P_Line,P_Owner,P_Name,P_String);
 end;


 procedure UPDATE_OUT(P_Line INTEGER,   P_Owner VARCHAR2,
                  P_Name VARCHAR2, P_String VARCHAR2) is
 begin
```

```
        update MVIEW_LOG_TEMP
           set Text = P_String
        where Lineno = P_Line
          and Id_Owner = P_Owner
          and Id_Name  = P_Name;
      end;

begin
   open MVIEW_LOG_CURSOR;
   loop
      fetch MVIEW_LOG_CURSOR into Lv_Log_Owner,
                                 Lv_Log_Table,
                                 Lv_Master,
                                 Lv_Rowids,
                                 Lv_Primary_Key,
                                 Lv_Filter_Columns,
                                 Lv_Object_Id,
                                 Lv_Sequence,
                                 Lv_Include_New_Values;
      exit when MVIEW_LOG_CURSOR%NOTFOUND;


      Lv_Lineno := 1;

      Lv_String:= 'CREATE MATERIALIZED VIEW LOG ON '
                      || LOWER(Lv_Log_Owner)
                      || '.'
                      || LOWER(Lv_Master);
      WRITE_OUT(Lv_Lineno, Lv_Log_Owner, Lv_Master, Lv_String);
      Lv_Lineno := Lv_Lineno + 1;


     open TAB_CURSOR (Lv_Log_Owner, Lv_Log_Table);
     loop
        fetch TAB_CURSOR into Lv_Table_Owner,
                             Lv_Table_Name,
                             Lv_Tablespace_Name,
                             Lv_Pct_Free,
                             Lv_Pct_Used,
                             Lv_Initial_Trans,
                             Lv_Max_Trans,
                             Lv_Initial_Extent,
                             Lv_Next_Extent,
                             Lv_Min_Extents,
                             Lv_Max_Extents,
                             Lv_Pct_Increase,
                             Lv_Degree,
                             Lv_Instances,
                             Lv_Logging,
                             Lv_Cache,
```

```
                  Lv_Freelists,
                  Lv_Freelist_Groups;
  exit when TAB_CURSOR%NOTFOUND;



Lv_String  := 'TABLESPACE ' || Lv_Tablespace_Name ;
WRITE_OUT(Lv_Lineno, Lv_Log_Owner, Lv_Master, Lv_String);
Lv_Lineno := Lv_Lineno + 1;


Lv_String  := 'PCTFREE ' || Lv_Pct_Free ;
WRITE_OUT(Lv_Lineno, Lv_Log_Owner, Lv_Master, Lv_String);
Lv_Lineno := Lv_Lineno + 1;

Lv_String  := 'PCTUSED ' || Lv_Pct_Used ;
WRITE_OUT(Lv_Lineno, Lv_Log_Owner, Lv_Master, Lv_String);
Lv_Lineno := Lv_Lineno + 1;

Lv_String  := 'INITRANS ' || Lv_Initial_Trans ;
WRITE_OUT(Lv_Lineno, Lv_Log_Owner, Lv_Master, Lv_String);
Lv_Lineno := Lv_Lineno + 1;

Lv_String  := 'MAXTRANS ' || Lv_Max_Trans ;
WRITE_OUT(Lv_Lineno, Lv_Log_Owner, Lv_Master, Lv_String);
Lv_Lineno := Lv_Lineno + 1;

if (Lv_Logging = 'YES')
then
     Lv_String  := ' LOGGING ';
else
     Lv_String  := ' NOLOGGING ';
end if;

WRITE_OUT(Lv_Lineno, Lv_Log_Owner, Lv_Master, Lv_String);
Lv_Lineno := Lv_Lineno + 1;

if (Lv_Cache = 'Y')
then
     Lv_String  := ' CACHE ';
else
     Lv_String  := ' NOCACHE ';
end if;

WRITE_OUT(Lv_Lineno, Lv_Log_Owner, Lv_Master, Lv_String);
Lv_Lineno := Lv_Lineno + 1;

Lv_String  := 'PARALLEL ( DEGREE ' || Lv_Degree
                                    || ' INSTANCES '
```

```
                                                      || Lv_Instances
                                                      || ' )';
            WRITE_OUT(Lv_Lineno, Lv_Log_Owner, Lv_Master, Lv_String);
            Lv_Lineno := Lv_Lineno + 1;


            Lv_String  := 'STORAGE';
            WRITE_OUT(Lv_Lineno, Lv_Log_Owner, Lv_Master, Lv_String);
            Lv_Lineno := Lv_Lineno + 1;
            Lv_String  := '(';
            WRITE_OUT(Lv_Lineno, Lv_Log_Owner, Lv_Master, Lv_String);
            Lv_Lineno := Lv_Lineno + 1;

            Lv_String  := '   INITIAL ' || Lv_Initial_Extent ;
            WRITE_OUT(Lv_Lineno, Lv_Log_Owner, Lv_Master, Lv_String);
            Lv_Lineno := Lv_Lineno + 1;

            Lv_String  := '   NEXT ' || Lv_Next_Extent ;
            WRITE_OUT(Lv_Lineno, Lv_Log_Owner, Lv_Master, Lv_String);
            Lv_Lineno := Lv_Lineno + 1;

            Lv_String  := '   MINEXTENTS ' || Lv_Min_Extents ;
            WRITE_OUT(Lv_Lineno, Lv_Log_Owner, Lv_Master, Lv_String);
            Lv_Lineno := Lv_Lineno + 1;

            Lv_String  := '   MAXEXTENTS ' || Lv_Max_Extents ;
            WRITE_OUT(Lv_Lineno, Lv_Log_Owner, Lv_Master, Lv_String);
            Lv_Lineno := Lv_Lineno + 1;

            Lv_String  := '   PCTINCREASE ' || Lv_Pct_Increase ;
            WRITE_OUT(Lv_Lineno, Lv_Log_Owner, Lv_Master, Lv_String);
            Lv_Lineno := Lv_Lineno + 1;

            Lv_String  := '   FREELISTS ' || Lv_Freelists ;
            WRITE_OUT(Lv_Lineno, Lv_Log_Owner, Lv_Master, Lv_String);
            Lv_Lineno := Lv_Lineno + 1;

            Lv_String  := '   FREELIST GROUPS ' || Lv_Freelist_Groups ;
            WRITE_OUT(Lv_Lineno, Lv_Log_Owner, Lv_Master, Lv_String);
            Lv_Lineno := Lv_Lineno + 1;

            Lv_String  := ')';
            WRITE_OUT(Lv_Lineno, Lv_Log_Owner, Lv_Master, Lv_String);
            Lv_Lineno := Lv_Lineno + 1;

    end loop;
    close TAB_CURSOR;

        Lv_String := NULL;
```

```
if (Lv_Rowids = 'YES')
then
    Lv_String := ' ROWID ';
end if;

if (Lv_Primary_Key = 'YES')
then
    if (Lv_String is NULL)
    then
        Lv_String := ' PRIMARY KEY ';
    else
        Lv_String := Lv_String||', PRIMARY KEY ';
    end if;
end if;

if (Lv_Object_Id = 'YES')
then
    if (Lv_String is NULL)
    then
        Lv_String := ' OBJECT ID ';
    else
        Lv_String := Lv_String||', OBJECT ID ';
    end if;
end if;

if (Lv_Sequence = 'YES')
then
    if (Lv_String is NULL)
    then
        Lv_String := ' SEQUENCE ';
    else
        Lv_String := Lv_String||', SEQUENCE ';
    end if;
end if;


Lv_String:=' WITH '||Lv_String;
WRITE_OUT(Lv_Lineno, Lv_Log_Owner, Lv_Master, Lv_String);
Lv_Lineno := Lv_Lineno + 1;

if (Lv_Filter_Columns = 'YES')
then
    Lv_string := '(';
    WRITE_OUT(Lv_Lineno, Lv_Log_Owner, Lv_Master, Lv_String);
    Lv_Lineno := Lv_Lineno + 1;

    open FIL_COLS_CURSOR(Lv_Log_Owner, Lv_Master);
```

```
        loop
            fetch FIL_COLS_CURSOR into Lv_Column_Name;
            exit when FIL_COLS_CURSOR%NOTFOUND;

            Lv_String := Lv_Column_Name||' ,';
            WRITE_OUT(Lv_Lineno, Lv_Log_Owner, Lv_Master, Lv_String);
            Lv_Lineno := Lv_Lineno + 1;

        end loop;

          Lv_Lineno  := Lv_Lineno - 1;
          Lv_String  := SUBSTR(Lv_String,1,(LENGTH(Lv_String) - 1));
          UPDATE_OUT(Lv_Lineno, Lv_Log_Owner, Lv_Master,Lv_String);
          Lv_Lineno  := Lv_Lineno + 1;


          Lv_String  := ')';
          WRITE_OUT(Lv_Lineno, Lv_Log_Owner, Lv_Master, Lv_String);
          Lv_Lineno := Lv_Lineno + 1;


      end if;

      if (Lv_Include_New_Values = 'YES')
      then

          Lv_String := ' INCLUDING NEW VALUES ';
          WRITE_OUT(Lv_Lineno, Lv_Log_Owner, Lv_Master, Lv_String);
          Lv_Lineno := Lv_Lineno + 1;

      end if;

      Lv_String  := '/';
      WRITE_OUT(Lv_Lineno, Lv_Log_Owner, Lv_Master, Lv_String);
      Lv_Lineno := Lv_Lineno + 1;

    end loop;
    close MVIEW_LOG_CURSOR;
end;
/
spool cre_mview_log.sql
select Text
  from MVIEW_LOG_TEMP
 order by Id_Owner, Id_Name, Lineno
/
spool off
set newpage 1 verify on feedback 6 pagesize 24 linesize 80
set heading on embedded off term on
```

```
undefine mview_log_master
undefine mview_log_owner
```

Sample output of running the script gen_mview_log_9.sql against an Oracle9.x database is shown here:

```
CREATE MATERIALIZED VIEW LOG ON app.apt1
TABLESPACE TOOLS
PCTFREE 60
PCTUSED 30
INITRANS 1
MAXTRANS 255
 LOGGING
 NOCACHE
PARALLEL ( DEGREE           1 INSTANCES          1 )
STORAGE
(
   INITIAL 16384   NEXT 16384
   MINEXTENTS 1    MAXEXTENTS 505
   PCTINCREASE 50  FREELISTS 1
   FREELIST GROUPS 1
)
 WITH  PRIMARY KEY
(mc2 , mc1)
 INCLUDING NEW VALUES
/
CREATE MATERIALIZED VIEW LOG ON app.apt2
TABLESPACE TOOLS
PCTFREE 60
PCTUSED 30
INITRANS 1
MAXTRANS 255
 LOGGING
 NOCACHE
PARALLEL ( DEGREE             1 INSTANCES          1 )
STORAGE
(
   INITIAL 16384   NEXT 16384
   MINEXTENTS 1    MAXEXTENTS 505
   PCTINCREASE 50  FREELISTS 1
   FREELIST GROUPS 1
)
 WITH  ROWID
/
```

Generate Abstract Datatypes

As of Oracle8, you can create *abstract datatypes* and use them as if they were Oracle-provided datatypes such as NUMBER and VARCHAR2. By using abstract datatypes, you can standardize the representation of complex data (such as address information). Because they are abstract datatypes, you can create methods for the datatypes you create. *Methods* are user-defined functions that you can use to act on and access data stored using your abstract datatypes.

In this section, you will learn how to regenerate the commands used to create abstract datatypes and their methods. All types of abstract datatypes, including nested tables, varying arrays, and incomplete types, are covered by this script.

The gen_type.sql script regenerates **create type** commands. For example, consider a simple abstract datatype. The script in the following listing creates an abstract datatype named ANIMAL_TY.

```
create or replace type ANIMAL_TY as object
(Breed      VARCHAR2(25),
 Name       VARCHAR2(25),
 BirthDate  DATE,
member function AGE (BirthDate IN DATE) return NUMBER,
PRAGMA RESTRICT_REFERENCES(AGE, WNDS));
```

In this example, the ANIMAL_TY datatype has three attributes: Breed, Name, and BirthDate. You can use the ANIMAL_TY datatype as a datatype in your tables:

```
create table ZOO_INVENTORY
(Section    VARCHAR2(25),
 Animal     ANIMAL_TY);
```

Because the Animal column of the ZOO_INVENTORY table is defined via the ANIMAL_TY datatype, you can specify Breed, Name, and Birthdate for the Animal column's values. You can use any methods defined on the ANIMAL_TY datatype on the data in the ZOO_INVENTORY table's Animal column. A full explanation of the usage of abstract datatypes is beyond the scope of this book; see *Oracle8: The Complete Reference*, by George Koch and Kevin Loney (Osborne/McGraw-Hill, 1998; ISBN: 0-07-882396-X), for detailed examples of the creation and usage of abstract datatypes and methods.

The ANIMAL_TY datatype's **create type** command includes a specification for a method called AGE:

```
member function AGE (BirthDate IN DATE) return NUMBER,
PRAGMA RESTRICT_REFERENCES(AGE, WNDS));
```

You must use the **create type body** command to create the AGE method:

```
create or replace type body ANIMAL_TY as
member function Age (BirthDate DATE) return NUMBER is
begin
  RETURN ROUND(SysDate - BirthDate);
end;
end;
/
```

The AGE method, when provided with the animal's birthdate, will return the current age of the animal. Because the ANIMAL_TY method is dependent on the ANIMAL_TY datatype, you must create the datatype before you create the method.

You can also create a nested table using ANIMAL_TY. The command in the following listing creates a nested table called ANIMAL_NT:

```
create type ANIMAL_NT as table of ANIMAL_TY;
```

Once the ANIMAL_NT datatype has been created, you can use it as a datatype in tables, the same way ANIMAL_TY was used in the previous example. Because ANIMAL_NT is a nested table, a single record in a table can contain multiple sets of values in a column defined via ANIMAL_NT.

To limit the number of possible entries in a nested table, you should use a varying array in place of the nested table. You can use a varying array as a datatype in tables. A single record in a table can contain multiple values for the varying array column, up to the limit defined for the varying array. Varying arrays are created via the **create type** command, as shown in the following example,

```
create type ANIMAL_VA as varying array (10) of ANIMAL_TY;
```

In this example, the **create type** command creates a varying array named ANIMAL_VA, using the ANIMAL_TY datatype as its base structure. You can use the ANIMAL_VA datatype as the datatype for a column in a table. The ANIMAL_VA varying array has a limit of 10 entries per record.

If two datatypes depend on each other, you must design a way to create one of the two types first. For example, if the ANIMAL_TY datatype used the MAMMAL_TY datatype for one of its attributes, and MAMMAL_TY used ANIMAL_TY for one of its datatypes, you need to be able to create one of those two types first. You can use the **create type** command to create *incomplete types*, which resolves the interdependency problem. As shown in the following listing, an incomplete type does not have attributes. After creating the incomplete type, you can create additional types that use the incomplete type; you can later use the **create or replace type** command to specify the attributes for the incomplete type.

```
create or replace type incomp_type as object;
```

When you create an incomplete type, you will receive an error:

Warning: Type created with compilation errors.

Despite the error message, the incomplete type will be created.

Because there are four different types of abstract datatypes (abstract datatypes, nested tables, varying arrays, and incomplete types), the script that re-creates abstract datatypes must re-create each type correctly. The script must also re-create the type bodies containing the code for methods associated with abstract datatypes. The gen_type.sql script, shown in the following listing, will create a SQL script that contains the **create type** commands needed to re-create all existing types. The output will be written to a file called cre_type.sql. Sample input is shown following the code, and an annotated walk-through of the gen_type.sql script follows the sample output.

```
REM
REM gen_type.sql
REM This script can be used for Oracle8.x and above.
REM
set echo off verify off feedback off pagesize 0 term on heading off
select 'Creating abstract datatype build script...' from DUAL;

accept datatype_name prompt "Enter the name of the datatype: "
accept datatype_owner prompt "Enter datatype owner: "
set term off

drop    table TYPE_TEMP
/

create table TYPE_TEMP (
        Lineno NUMBER,
        Id_Owner VARCHAR2(30),
        Id_Name VARCHAR2(30),
        Text VARCHAR2(2000))
/

declare
   cursor TYPE_CURSOR is
        select Owner,
               Name,
               Type,
               Line,
               Text
          from DBA_SOURCE
         where Type in ('TYPE','TYPE BODY')
           and Owner like UPPER('&&datatype_owner')
           and Owner not in ('SYS','SYSTEM')
           and Name like UPPER('&&datatype_name')
         order by Owner, Name, Type, Line;
```

```
    Lv_Owner                DBA_SOURCE.Owner%TYPE;
    Lv_Name                 DBA_SOURCE.Name%TYPE;
    Lv_Type                 DBA_SOURCE.Type%TYPE;
    Lv_Text                 DBA_SOURCE.Text%TYPE;
    Lv_Line                 DBA_SOURCE.Line%TYPE;
    Lv_String               VARCHAR2(2000);
    Lv_Lineno               NUMBER;

    procedure WRITE_OUT(P_Line INTEGER, P_Owner VARCHAR2, P_Name VARCHAR2,
                        P_String VARCHAR2) is
    begin
       insert into TYPE_TEMP (Lineno, Id_Owner, Id_Name, Text)
              values (P_Line,P_Owner,P_Name,P_String);
     end;

begin
   open TYPE_CURSOR;
   Lv_Lineno   := 1;
   loop
      fetch TYPE_CURSOR into Lv_Owner,
                             Lv_Name,
                             Lv_Type,
                             Lv_Line,
                             Lv_Text;
      exit when TYPE_CURSOR%NOTFOUND;

      if (Lv_Line = 1)
      then
          WRITE_OUT(Lv_Lineno, Lv_Owner, Lv_Name, '/');
          Lv_String   := 'CREATE OR REPLACE ' || UPPER(Lv_Type)  || ' ';
          WRITE_OUT(Lv_Lineno, Lv_Owner, Lv_Name, Lv_String);
          Lv_Lineno   := Lv_Lineno + 1;

          Lv_String   := SUBSTR(Lv_Text,LENGTH(Lv_Type)+1,
                          (LENGTH(Lv_Text) - LENGTH(Lv_Type)));
          Lv_String   := Lv_Owner || '.' || LTRIM(Lv_String);
          WRITE_OUT(Lv_Lineno, Lv_Owner, Lv_Name, Lv_String);
          Lv_Lineno   := Lv_Lineno + 1;
      else
          WRITE_OUT(Lv_Lineno, Lv_Owner, Lv_Name, Lv_Text);
          Lv_Lineno := Lv_Lineno + 1;
      end if;
   end loop;

   WRITE_OUT(Lv_Lineno, Lv_Owner, Lv_Name, '/');
   close TYPE_CURSOR;
   delete from TYPE_TEMP where LineNo=1 and Text='/';
end;
/
```

```
spool cre_type.sql
select Text
  from TYPE_TEMP
 order by Id_Owner, Id_Name, Lineno
/
spool off
set newpage 1 verify on feedback 6 pagesize 24 linesize 80
set heading on embedded off term on
undefine datatype_name
undefine datatype_owner
```

Sample results for the gen_type.sql script are shown in this listing:

```
CREATE OR REPLACE TYPE
DORA.ANIMAL_NT as table of ANIMAL_TY;
/
CREATE OR REPLACE TYPE
DORA.ANIMAL_TY as object
(Breed        VARCHAR2(25),
 Name         VARCHAR2(25),
 BirthDate   DATE,
member function AGE (BirthDate IN DATE) return NUMBER,
PRAGMA RESTRICT_REFERENCES(AGE, WNDS));
/
CREATE OR REPLACE TYPE BODY
DORA.ANIMAL_TY as
member function Age (BirthDate DATE) return NUMBER is
begin
   RETURN ROUND(SysDate - BirthDate);
end;
end;
/
CREATE OR REPLACE TYPE
DORA.ANIMAL_VA as varying array (10) of ANIMAL_TY;
/
CREATE OR REPLACE TYPE
DORA.INCOMP_TYPE as object
/
```

PROGRAMMER'S NOTE *The **create type** commands generated by gen_type.sql may not appear in the proper order. The datatypes are listed in alphabetical order.*

As shown by this output, you may need to edit the cre_type.sql file prior to running it. In this example, the first type creates the ANIMAL_NT datatype:

```
CREATE OR REPLACE TYPE
DORA.ANIMAL_NT as table of ANIMAL_TY;
/
```

However, the ANIMAL_TY datatype is not created until the next step in the script, so attempting to create ANIMAL_NT before ANIMAL_TY will fail.

ANNOTATIONS

As noted in the previous section, the output of the gen_type.sql script attempts to create datatypes in alphabetical order. Although the script may be modified to account for some dependencies, other dependencies cannot be accounted for. For example, if you create an incomplete type and later modify the type to create its attributes, the data dictionary no longer records the earlier (incomplete) structure of the type. Suppose you create an incomplete type called INCOMP_TYPE:

```
create type INCOMP_TYPE as object;
```

You can then create another datatype that uses INCOMP_TYPE as a datatype. You may then modify the INCOMP_TYPE datatype, like so:

```
create or replace type INCOMP_TYPE
(Some_Attribute  VARCHAR2(30));
```

When you issue the **create or replace type** command, the earlier definition of the INCOMP_TYPE datatype is overwritten. If INCOMP_TYPE and the second type you created are both dependent on each other, gen_type.sql will not generate the proper **create type** commands because the information it needs about the incomplete type is no longer in the data dictionary. To create the proper sequence of commands, you will need to manually edit the cre_type.sql file generated.

The code needed to re-create datatypes is stored in the DBA_SOURCE data dictionary view. Because each line of code for a datatype is stored as a separate row in DBA_SOURCE, the gen_type.sql script uses a cursor to extract the datatype information and to allow you to enter a wildcard value for the datatype name (*%datatype_name%*) or to modify the script to select all datatypes for an owner or all datatypes in the database. The gen_type.sql script generates a script (called cre_type.sql) to re-create the requested datatype. The gen_type.sql script uses a temporary table to hold individual lines of the **create type** and **create type body** commands, writing to the table rather than using the DBMS_OUTPUT.PUT_LINE procedure. By writing the data to a temporary table, you can extract the information for an individual datatype from the table. Using the DBMS_OUTPUT procedure would force you to save and edit the output file for the datatype you want.

PROGRAMMER'S NOTE   *Abstract datatypes have owners. If you create an abstract datatype via the* **create type** *command, you can* **grant** *other users EXECUTE privilege on the datatype. See the section "Generate Object Grants," later in this chapter, for a script to re-create* **grant** *commands.*

The first section of the gen_type.sql script, shown in the next listing, does the initial setup, prompting for the datatype name and owner for later use via the **accept** command.

Using the **accept** command allows you to define your own prompt for the variable. You can enter a value for the datatype name with '%' to generate a script for all datatypes with a similar name, or you can use the wildcard for the owner as well to generate all type definitions.

The SQL*Plus **set** command turns off headers (**pagesize 0**), row counts (**feedback off**), and displays of old and new values for the *datatype_name* and *datatype_owner* variables (**verify off**).

```
set echo off verify off feedback off pagesize 0
set term on
select 'Creating abstract datatype build script...' from DUAL;


accept datatype_name prompt "Enter the name of the datatype: "
accept datatype_owner prompt "Enter datatype owner: "
set term off
```

The next section of the script creates a temporary table to hold each **create type** and associated **create type body** command and owner. The Lineno column orders the lines of the **create type** and **create type body** commands.

```
drop    table TYPE_TEMP
/

create table TYPE_TEMP (
        Lineno NUMBER,
        Id_Owner VARCHAR2(30),
        Id_Name VARCHAR2(30),
        Text VARCHAR2(2000))
/
```

The next section of the script, shown in the following listing, creates the TYPE_ CURSOR cursor. The TYPE_CURSOR cursor selects the information from DBA_SOURCE, where the datatype name matches the input variable *datatype_name* and the datatype owner matches the input variable *datatype_owner*. Using **like** in the **where** clause instead of = allows for wildcards. Selecting for **Type in ('TYPE', 'TYPE BODY')** selects all the lines for both the datatype specification and the datatype body. The **order by** clause orders by Type before Line, so all lines of the datatype specification will be returned before any line of the type body.

```
declare
   cursor TYPE_CURSOR is
           select Owner,
                  Name,
                  Type,
                  Line,
                  Text
```

```
        from DBA_SOURCE
      where Type in ('TYPE','TYPE BODY')
        and Owner like UPPER('&&datatype_owner')
        and Owner is not in ('SYS','SYSTEM')
        and Name like UPPER('&&datatype_name')
      order by Owner, Name, Type, Line;
```

The procedure variables for the cursor are declared as TABLE_NAME.Column_Name%TYPE. Anchoring the variable declarations to columns via the **%TYPE** operator takes the column definition from within the database itself. If the column definition changes in a different version of Oracle, the procedure will still work because the definition of the column has not been hard coded. The variable *Lv_Lineno* orders the lines of the **create type** statement and is initialized to 0.

```
    Lv_Owner            DBA_SOURCE.Owner%TYPE;
    Lv_Name             DBA_SOURCE.Name%TYPE;
    Lv_Type             DBA_SOURCE.Type%TYPE;
    Lv_Text             DBA_SOURCE.Text%TYPE;
    Lv_Line             DBA_SOURCE.Line%TYPE;
    Lv_String           VARCHAR2(2000);
    Lv_Lineno           NUMBER;
```

The next section of the script creates WRITE_OUT, an internal procedure to perform the **insert**s into the temporary table.

```
Please make following small code      procedure WRITE_OUT(P_Line
INTEGER, P_Owner VARCHAR2, P_Name VARCHAR2,
                         P_String VARCHAR2) is
    begin
        insert into TYPE_TEMP (Lineno, Id_Owner, Id_Name, Text)
               values (P_Line,P_Owner,P_Name,P_String);
    end;
```

The lines of a datatype specification or type body are stored as separate lines in the data dictionary. The cursor TYPE_CURSOR extracts all the lines of both the datatype specification and the type body. *Lv_Lineno*, in conjunction with the datatype name, orders the rows in the temporary table TYPE_TEMP so you can extract the **create type** command for a single datatype at the end of the procedure. In the next section of the gen_type.sql script, shown in the following listing, the TYPE_CURSOR cursor is opened and a value is fetched into the script variables.

```
begin
    open TYPE_CURSOR;
    Lv_Lineno   := 1;
    loop
        fetch TYPE_CURSOR into Lv_Owner,
```

```
                    Lv_Name,
                    Lv_Type,
                    Lv_Line,
                    Lv_Text;
         exit when TYPE_CURSOR%NOTFOUND;
```

The **order by** clause of the cursor ensures that all the lines of a datatype specification are returned before the lines of the type body. Oracle does not store the final '/' used to execute each **create type** or **create type body** command. Because the script is creating multiple SQL statements, a '/' is inserted into the temporary table before each command is generated. The next section of the script, shown in the following listing, inserts the '/' line and then generates the **create or replace** command. The **or replace** clause prevents the loss of **grant**s you would experience if you dropped and re-created the datatype.

```
if (Lv_Line = 1)
then
    WRITE_OUT(Lv_Lineno, Lv_Owner, Lv_Name, '/');
    Lv_String  := 'CREATE OR REPLACE ' || UPPER(Lv_Type)  || ' ';
    WRITE_OUT(Lv_Lineno, Lv_Owner, Lv_Name, Lv_String);
    Lv_Lineno  := Lv_Lineno + 1;
```

Oracle stores the first line of each part of a datatype as **TYPE [BODY]** *datatype_name*. Because the script concatenates the owner's name to the name of the datatype in the generated script, the next section of the gen_type.sql script has to remove the word **TYPE** or **TYPE BODY** from the first line of the stored source code. The **SUBSTR** function, along with the variable *Lv_Type*, extracts the rest of the line and places it in the string variable *Lv_String* to be written to the temporary table. The **LTRIM** function removes extra blanks from the beginning of the string.

```
    Lv_String  := SUBSTR(Lv_Text,LENGTH(Lv_Type)+1,
                        (LENGTH(Lv_Text) - LENGTH(Lv_Type)));
    Lv_String  := Lv_Owner || '.' || LTRIM(Lv_String);
    WRITE_OUT(Lv_Lineno, Lv_Owner, Lv_Name, Lv_String);
    Lv_Lineno  := Lv_Lineno + 1;
```

If this is not the first line of the datatype or type body in DBA_SOURCE, the text as read from the database is inserted into the temporary table. The cursor loop ends and the procedure will loop back through the TYPE_CURSOR until all datatypes have been generated. The cursor then closes and the procedure exits. Once the **create** statements for all the types and type bodies have been generated, they are spooled to a file for later execution. A final **delete** command deletes the extra '/' generated prior to the first **create** command in the output file.

```
else
    WRITE_OUT(Lv_Lineno, Lv_Owner, Lv_Name, Lv_Text);
    Lv_Lineno := Lv_Lineno + 1;
end if;
```

```
    end loop;

    WRITE_OUT(Lv_Lineno, Lv_Owner, Lv_Name, '/');
    close TYPE_CURSOR;
    delete from TYPE_TEMP where Lineno=1 and Text='/';
end;
/
spool cre_type.sql
select Text
  from TYPE_TEMP
 order by Id_Owner, Id_Name, Lineno
/
spool off
```

The environment is finally reset to its original state:

```
set newpage 1 verify on feedback 6 pagesize 24 linesize 80
set heading on embedded off term on
undefine datatype_name
undefine datatype_owner
```

Sample contents of the cre_type.sql script are shown in the following listing. Note that the types are listed in alphabetical order, and all of the types are created before their associated type bodies. The sample listing shows that the gen_type.sql script generates the source code for abstract datatypes, nested tables, varying arrays, and incomplete types.

```
CREATE OR REPLACE TYPE
DORA.ANIMAL_NT as table of ANIMAL_TY;
/
CREATE OR REPLACE TYPE
DORA.ANIMAL_TY as object
(Breed        VARCHAR2(25),
 Name         VARCHAR2(25),
 BirthDate  DATE,
member function AGE (BirthDate IN DATE) return NUMBER,
PRAGMA RESTRICT_REFERENCES(AGE, WNDS));
/
CREATE OR REPLACE TYPE BODY
DORA.ANIMAL_TY as
member function Age (BirthDate DATE) return NUMBER is
begin
  RETURN ROUND(SysDate - BirthDate);
end;
end;
```

```
/
CREATE OR REPLACE TYPE
DORA.ANIMAL_VA as varying array (10) of ANIMAL_TY;
/
CREATE OR REPLACE TYPE
DORA.INCOMP_TYPE as object
/
```

If you want to use this script to document all the datatypes for a particular owner, remove the **accept** *datatype_name* statement at the beginning of the script and change the **where** clause for the TYPE_CURSOR cursor to this:

```
where Owner  = UPPER('&&datatype_owner')
```

or you can use the wildcard '%' when prompted.

You can determine which of your datatypes are nested tables or varying arrays by querying the DBA_COLL_TYPES data dictionary view (USER_COLL_TYPES is also available). The Coll_Type column of DBA_COLL_TYPES will have a value of 'TABLE' for nested tables and 'VARYING ARRAY' for varying arrays. For varying arrays, the Upper_Bound column of DBA_COLL_TYPES shows the maximum number of entries in the array. As shown in the following listing, the Elem_Type_Name column of USER_COLL_TYPES lists the datatype on which the nested table or varying array is based.

```
select * from USER_COLL_TYPES;
```

TYPE_NAME	COLL_TYPE	UPPER_BOUND
----------------------------	------------------------------	-----------
ELEM_TY ELEM_TYPE_OWNER	ELEM_TYPE_NAME	LENGTH
------- ----------------------	------------------------------	----------
PRECISION SCALE CHARACTER_SET_NAME		
---------- ---------- ---		
ANIMAL_NT	TABLE	
DORA	ANIMAL_TY	
ANIMAL_VA	VARYING ARRAY	10
DORA	ANIMAL_TY	

You can use this information to further customize the gen_type.sql script. To retrieve only nested tables and varying arrays, modify the TYPE_CURSOR cursor's query to retrieve only types listed in DBA_COLL_TYPES:

```
cursor TYPE_CURSOR is
    select Owner,
           Name,
           Type,
           Line,
```

```
        Text
  from DBA_SOURCE
 where Type in ('TYPE','TYPE BODY')
   and Owner = UPPER('&&datatype_owner')
   and Name like UPPER('&&datatype_name')
   and exists
       (select 'x' from DBA_COLL_TYPES
          where DBA_COLL_TYPES.Owner=DBA_SOURCE.Owner
            and DBA_COLL_TYPES.Type_Name=DBA_SOURCE.Name)
 order by Owner, Name, Type, Line;
```

This condition was added:

```
   and exists
       (select 'x' from DBA_COLL_TYPES
          where DBA_COLL_TYPES.Owner=DBA_SOURCE.Owner
            and DBA_COLL_TYPES.Type_Name=DBA_SOURCE.Name)
```

This condition performs an existence check; if the type is listed in both DBA_SOURCE and DBA_COLL_TYPES, it is either a nested table or a varying array. You could also query the DBA_TYPES data dictionary view; if the TypeCode column of DBA_TYPES has a value of 'COLLECTION', the datatype is either a nested table or a varying array.

To determine which datatypes are incomplete, you can query the DBA_TYPES data dictionary view. If a type is incomplete, the Incomplete column of DBA_TYPES will be set to a value of 'YES'. If the type is complete, the Incomplete column of DBA_TYPES will have a value of 'NO.'

Generate Object Grants

gen_grnt_7n8.sql
gen_grnt_9.sql

For someone to use an object that you own, you must grant that person the privilege to use it. You can grant access to tables, views, sequences, synonyms, and snapshots. You can also grant the right to execute packages, procedures, and functions. In addition, you can grant another user the right to grant access to your object with the **with grant option** clause. Unless you have been granted access **with grant option**, you cannot grant access to another user's objects, even if you have been given the DBA role. Be cautious about using **with grant option**; if you revoke the privilege from the user who has the grant option, the revoke cascades and the privilege is revoked from any user that he or she has granted the privilege to as well.

Grants can be made to PUBLIC, which allows all users in the database to access the object. However, before another user can write a package, procedure, or function that accesses an object you own, you must specifically grant him or her access to the object. Privileges inherited through a role, even the PUBLIC role, are not sufficient.

The object privileges you can grant are listed here.

◆ **ALTER** This privilege is applicable on tables and sequences, and it allows you to alter the definition of the object.

- **SELECT** This privilege is applicable on tables, views, sequences, and snapshots/materialized views, and it allows you to query the object.

- **INSERT** This privilege is applicable on tables, views, and updatable snapshots/updatable materialized views, and it allows you to insert into the object.

- **UPDATE** This privilege is applicable on tables, views, and updatable snapshots/updatable materialized views, and it allows you to update the object.

- **DELETE** This privilege is applicable on tables, views, and updatable snapshots/updatable materialized views, and it allows you to delete from the object.

- **INDEX** This privilege is applicable only on tables and allows you to create an index on the table.

- **REFERENCES** This privilege is applicable on tables and views only, and it allows you to create a constraint that references the table or view. This privilege cannot be granted to a role.

- **EXECUTE** This privilege is applicable on procedures, functions, and packages. As of Oracle8.1.x, it can also be granted on libraries, operators, user-defined types, and index types. This privilege allows you to compile a procedure or function or execute it directly, or access any program object defined in the specification of a package. This privilege is not needed to execute a procedure, function, or package indirectly.

- **ON COMMIT REFRESH** As of Oracle8.1.x, this privilege is applicable on tables and allows you to create a refresh-on-commit materialized view on the specified table.

- **QUERY REWRITE** As of Oracle8.1.x, this privilege is applicable on tables and allows you to create a materialized view for query rewrite using the specified table.

- **UNDER** As of Oracle8.x, this privilege is applicable on tables, views, and user-defined types, and it allows you to create a subobject under this object—for example, you can create a subtable under the specified table. You can grant this privilege only if you have the appropriate UNDER ANY TABLE/VIEW/TYPE privilege WITH GRANT OPTION on the immediate supertable/superview/supertype of this table/view/type respectively.

- **READ** As of Oracle8.x, the READ privilege allows you to access operating system directories.

In addition to granting privileges on entire objects, you can specify the table or view columns on which privileges are to be granted. Columns can be specified in this manner only when granting INSERT, UPDATE, or REFERENCES privileges. If columns are not specified, the grantee has the specified privilege on all the columns of the table or view.

The script gen_grnt_7n8.sql generates a script to document the grants on an object in an Oracle7.x or Oracle8.x database while the script gen_grnt_9.sql generates a similar script for Oracle9.x. Both the scripts are available on the CD-ROM in this book.

The next script, gen_grnt_7n8.sql, generates a script to document the grants on a table. With some minor editing of the output file to include the appropriate password, the script can be run to re-create the grants.

NOTE

The following script only creates grant statements of objects, it does not handle any system priveleges that have been granted.

```
REM
REM gen_grnt_7n8.sql
REM This script can be used for Oracle7.x and Oracle8.x only
REM This script can be used to generate SQL to grant object privileges
REM
set echo off term off verify off feedback off  pagesize 0 heading off
set term on
select 'Creating grants build script...' from DUAL;
accept table_name  prompt "Enter the name of the table: "
accept tab_owner   prompt "Enter table owner        : "
set term off

drop    table GRANT_TEMP
/

create table GRANT_TEMP
    (
        Lineno        NUMBER,
        Table_Owner VARCHAR2(30),
        Table_Name  VARCHAR2(30),
        Text          VARCHAR2(800)
    )
/
declare
   cursor GRANT_TAB_CURSOR is
        select Grantee,
               Grantor,
               Owner,
               Table_Name,
               Privilege,
               Grantable
          from DBA_TAB_PRIVS
         where Owner      like UPPER('&&tab_owner')
           and Owner not in ('SYS','SYSTEM')
```

```
            and Table_Name like UPPER('&&table_name')
        order by Owner,Table_Name,Grantor,Grantee,Privilege,Grantable;

    cursor GRANT_JAVA_CURSOR is
        select DTP.Grantee,
               DTP.Grantor,
               DTP.Owner,
               DTP.Table_Name,
               DTP.Privilege,
               DOB.Object_Type,
               DTP.Grantable
          from DBA_TAB_PRIVS DTP, DBA_OBJECTS DOB
         where DTP.Owner      like UPPER('&&tab_owner')
           and DTP.Owner      not in ('SYS','SYSTEM')
           and DTP.Table_Name like UPPER('&&table_name')
           and DTP.Owner = DOB.Owner
           and DTP.Table_Name = DOB.Object_Name
           and DOB.Object_Type in ('JAVA SOURCE', 'JAVA RESOURCE')
        order by DTP.Owner,DTP.Table_Name,DTP.Grantor,DTP.Grantee,
DTP.Privilege,DTP.Grantable;

    cursor GRANT_COL_CURSOR is
        select Grantee,
               Grantor,
               Owner,
               Table_Name,
               Column_Name,
               Privilege,
               Grantable
          from DBA_COL_PRIVS
         where Owner      like UPPER('&&tab_owner')
           and Owner not in ('SYS','SYSTEM')
           and Table_Name like UPPER('&&table_name')
        order by
Owner,Table_Name,Grantor,Grantee,Privilege,Column_Name,Grantable;


    Lv_TP_Grantee        SYS.DBA_TAB_PRIVS.Grantee%TYPE;
    Lv_TP_Grantor        SYS.DBA_TAB_PRIVS.Grantor%TYPE;
    Lv_TP_Owner          SYS.DBA_TAB_PRIVS.Owner%TYPE;
    Lv_TP_Table_Name     SYS.DBA_TAB_PRIVS.Table_Name%TYPE;
    Lv_TP_Privilege      SYS.DBA_TAB_PRIVS.Privilege%TYPE;
    Lv_TP_Grantable      SYS.DBA_TAB_PRIVS.Grantable%TYPE;
    Prior_Grantor        SYS.DBA_TAB_PRIVS.Grantor%TYPE;
    Lv_CP_Column_Name    SYS.DBA_COL_PRIVS.Column_Name%TYPE;
    Lv_JV_Object_Type    SYS.DBA_OBJECTS.Object_Type%TYPE;
    Lv_String            VARCHAR2(800);
    Lv_Lineno            NUMBER;
```

```
      procedure WRITE_OUT(P_Line INTEGER, P_Owner varchar2, P_Name VARCHAR2,
                          P_String VARCHAR2) is
   begin
      insert into GRANT_TEMP (Lineno, Table_Owner, Table_Name, Text)
             values (P_Line,P_Owner,P_Name,P_String);
      end;

begin
   Prior_Grantor := ' ';
   Lv_Lineno := 1;
   open GRANT_TAB_CURSOR;

   loop
      fetch GRANT_TAB_CURSOR into        Lv_TP_Grantee,
                                         Lv_TP_Grantor,
                                         Lv_TP_Owner,
                                         Lv_TP_Table_Name,
                                         Lv_TP_Privilege,
                                         Lv_TP_Grantable;
      exit when GRANT_TAB_CURSOR%NOTFOUND;

      if (Prior_Grantor != Lv_TP_Grantor)
      then
          Prior_Grantor := Lv_TP_Grantor;
          Lv_String  := 'CONNECT ' || Lv_TP_Grantor || '/PASSWORD';
          WRITE_OUT(Lv_Lineno, Lv_TP_Grantor,
Lv_TP_Table_Name, Lv_String);
          Lv_Lineno  := Lv_Lineno + 1;
      end if;

      if (Lv_TP_Privilege = 'READ')
      then
          Lv_String := 'GRANT '          ||
                       Lv_TP_Privilege   ||
                       ' ON DIRECTORY '  ||
                       Lv_TP_Table_Name  ||
                       ' TO '            ||
                       Lv_TP_Grantee;
      else

          Lv_String := 'GRANT '          ||
                       Lv_TP_Privilege   ||
                       ' ON '            ||
                       Lv_TP_Owner       ||
                       '.'               ||
                       Lv_TP_Table_Name  ||
                       ' TO '            ||
                       Lv_TP_Grantee;
```

```
        end if;

        if (Lv_TP_Grantable = 'YES' )
        then
            Lv_String := Lv_String      || ' WITH GRANT OPTION';
        end if;

        WRITE_OUT(Lv_Lineno, Lv_TP_Owner, Lv_TP_Table_Name, Lv_String);
        Lv_Lineno    := Lv_Lineno + 1;
        WRITE_OUT(Lv_Lineno, Lv_TP_Owner, Lv_TP_Table_Name, '/');
        Lv_Lineno     := Lv_Lineno + 1;

    end loop;

    close GRANT_TAB_CURSOR;

    Prior_Grantor := ' ';
    open GRANT_JAVA_CURSOR;

    loop
        fetch GRANT_JAVA_CURSOR into     Lv_TP_Grantee,
                                         Lv_TP_Grantor,
                                         Lv_TP_Owner,
                                         Lv_TP_Table_Name,
                                         Lv_TP_Privilege,
                                         Lv_JV_Object_Type,
                                         Lv_TP_Grantable;
        exit when GRANT_JAVA_CURSOR%NOTFOUND;

        if (Prior_Grantor != Lv_TP_Grantor)
        then
            Prior_Grantor := Lv_TP_Grantor;
            Lv_String  := 'CONNECT ' || Lv_TP_Grantor || '/PASSWORD';
            WRITE_OUT(Lv_Lineno, Lv_TP_Grantor,
Lv_TP_Table_Name, Lv_String);
            Lv_Lineno  := Lv_Lineno + 1;
        end if;
            Lv_String := 'GRANT '          ||
                        Lv_TP_Privilege    ||

                        ' ON '             ||
                        Lv_JV_Object_Type  ||
                        ' '                ||
                        Lv_TP_Owner        ||
                        '.'                ||
                        Lv_TP_Table_Name   ||
                        ' TO '             ||
                        Lv_TP_Grantee;
```

```
        if (Lv_TP_Grantable = 'YES' )
        then
            Lv_String := Lv_String    || ' WITH GRANT OPTION';
        end if;

        WRITE_OUT(Lv_Lineno, Lv_TP_Owner, Lv_TP_Table_Name, Lv_String);
        Lv_Lineno    := Lv_Lineno + 1;
        WRITE_OUT(Lv_Lineno, Lv_TP_Owner, Lv_TP_Table_Name, '/');
        Lv_Lineno    := Lv_Lineno + 1;


    end loop;

    close GRANT_JAVA_CURSOR;


    Prior_Grantor := ' ';
    open GRANT_COL_CURSOR;

    loop
        fetch GRANT_COL_CURSOR into     Lv_TP_Grantee,
                                        Lv_TP_Grantor,
                                        Lv_TP_Owner,
                                        Lv_TP_Table_Name,
                                        Lv_CP_Column_Name,
                                        Lv_TP_Privilege,
                                        Lv_TP_Grantable;
        exit when GRANT_COL_CURSOR%NOTFOUND;

        if (Prior_Grantor != Lv_TP_Grantor)
        then
            Prior_Grantor := Lv_TP_Grantor;
            Lv_String  := 'CONNECT ' || Lv_TP_Grantor || '/PASSWORD';
            WRITE_OUT(Lv_Lineno, Lv_TP_Grantor,
Lv_TP_Table_Name, Lv_String);
            Lv_Lineno   := Lv_Lineno + 1;
        end if;

        Lv_String := 'GRANT '        ||
                     Lv_TP_Privilege ||
                     '('             ||
                     Lv_CP_Column_Name||
                     ')'             ||
                     ' ON '          ||
                     Lv_TP_Owner     ||
                     '.'             ||
                     Lv_TP_Table_Name ||
                     ' TO '          ||
                     Lv_TP_Grantee;
```

```
        if (Lv_TP_Grantable = 'YES' )
        then
            Lv_String := Lv_String      || ' WITH GRANT OPTION';
        end if;

        WRITE_OUT(Lv_Lineno, Lv_TP_Owner, Lv_TP_Table_Name, Lv_String);
        Lv_Lineno      := Lv_Lineno + 1;
        WRITE_OUT(Lv_Lineno, Lv_TP_Owner, Lv_TP_Table_Name, '/');
        Lv_Lineno      := Lv_Lineno + 1;

    end loop;

    close GRANT_COL_CURSOR;

end;
/

spool cre_grnt.sql
select Text
  from GRANT_TEMP
 order by Lineno
/
spool off
set newpage 1 verify on feedback 6 pagesize 24 linesize 80
set heading on embedded off term on
undefine table_name
undefine tab_owner
```

Sample output for the gen_grnt_7n8.sql script is shown in the following listing:

```
CONNECT DEMO/PASSWORD
GRANT SELECT ON DEMO.JOB TO PUBLIC
/
GRANT SELECT ON DEMO.JOB TO QC_USER
/
GRANT SELECT ON DEMO.JOB TO SCOTT WITH GRANT OPTION
/
CONNECT SCOTT/PASSWORD
GRANT SELECT ON DEMO.JOB TO QC_USER
/
```

Prior to running the cre_grnt.sql script, you must provide the passwords for each of the accounts used.

ANNOTATIONS

Since a DBA cannot create a grant on behalf of a user unless specifically granted the privilege **with grant option**, the output script will contain **connect** clauses before the

grant statement(s) if the grantor changes. For the privileges to be granted, you must replace the word "PASSWORD" with the correct user'spassword in the **connect** clause.

Although the script as written will return grants for a single object, it uses a cursor because there can be multiple grants on an object. In addition, using a cursor also allows you to enter a wildcard value or to modify the script to select all objects for an owner or all objects in the database. The script will generate a script to re-create the grants on the requested object. It uses a temporary table to hold individual lines of the **connect** and **grant** statements, writing to the table rather than using DBMS_OUTPUT.PUT_LINE so that you can extract the information for an individual grant on the table. Using the DBMS_OUTPUT procedure would force you to save and edit the output file for the grant you want.

The first section of the script, shown in the following listing, does the initial setup, prompting for the table name and table owner for later use via the **accept** command. The **accept** command, unlike the '&' or '&&' operators, allows you to define your own prompt for the variable. You can enter the table name with the '%' wildcard to generate a script for all grants on objects with a similar name.

Although the prompt asks for the table name and owner, the word *table* is misleading and is used merely to be consistent with Oracle's terminology in the DBA_TAB_PRIVS data dictionary view. You can issue grants on tables, views, sequences, synonyms, snapshots/materialized views, packages, procedures, and functions; as of Oracle8, directories; and as of Oracle8i, java source and java resource.

The SQL*Plus **set** command turns off headers (**pagesize 0**), row counts (**feedback off**), and displays of old and new values for the *table_name* and *table_owner* variables (**verify off**).

```
set echo off term off verify off feedback off pagesize 0 heading off

set term on
select 'Creating grants build script...' from DUAL;

accept table_name  prompt "Enter the name of the table: "
accept tab_owner   prompt "Enter table owner          : "
set term off
```

The next section of the gen_grnt_7n8.sql script, shown in the following listing, creates a temporary table to hold each **connect** and **grant** command and its owner. The Lineno column orders the lines of the **connect** and **grant** commands.

```
drop    table GRANT_TEMP
/

create table GRANT_TEMP
    (
        Lineno      NUMBER,
        Table_Owner VARCHAR2(30),
        Table_Name  VARCHAR2(30),
```

```
        Text            VARCHAR2(800)
    )
/
```

The next section of the script defines the necessary cursors. The GRANT_CURSOR cursor selects the information from DBA_TAB_PRIVS, where the table name matches the input variable *table_name* and the table owner matches the input variable *tab_owner*. Using **like** in the **where** clause instead of = allows for wildcards. Both the owner and the grantor are selected from the view. In most cases, the grantor and the owner will be the same. The grantor can be a user other than the owner if a user has been granted the privilege **with grant option**.

```
declare
    cursor GRANT_TAB_CURSOR is
        select Grantee,
               Grantor,
               Owner,
               Table_Name,
               Privilege,
               Grantable
          from DBA_TAB_PRIVS
         where Owner        like UPPER('&&tab_owner')
           amd Owner            not in ('SYS','SYSTEM')
           and Table_Name like UPPER('&&table_name')
         order by Owner,Table_Name,Grantor,Grantee,Privilege,Grantable;
```

The GRANT_JAVA_CURSOR cursor selects all the JAVA objects by querying the DBA_OBJECTS dictionary view for object types of 'JAVA SOURCE' or 'JAVA RESOURCE':

```
small code    cursor GRANT_JAVA_CURSOR is
        select DTP.Grantee,
               DTP.Grantor,
               DTP.Owner,
               DTP.Table_Name,
               DTP.Privilege,
               DOB.Object_Type,
               DTP.Grantable
          from DBA_TAB_PRIVS DTP, DBA_OBJECTS DOB
         where DTP.Owner        like UPPER('&&tab_owner')
           and DTP.Owner            not in ('SYS','SYSTEM')
           and DTP.Table_Name like UPPER('&&table_name')
           and DTP.Owner = DOB.Owner
           and DTP.Table_Name = DOB.Object_Name
           and DOB.Object_Type in ('JAVA SOURCE', 'JAVA RESOURCE')
         order by DTP.Owner,DTP.Table_Name,DTP.Grantor,DTP.Grantee,
               DTP.Privilege,DTP.Grantable;
```

The GRANT_COL_CURSOR cursor selects all privileges that have been granted at the column level (not on the entire object):

```
cursor GRANT_COL_CURSOR is
     select Grantee,
            Grantor,
            Owner,
            Table_Name,
            Column_Name,
            Privilege,
            Grantable
       from DBA_COL_PRIVS
      where Owner      like UPPER('&&tab_owner')
        and Owner          not in ('SYS','SYSTEM')
        and Table_Name like UPPER('&&table_name')
      order by Owner,Table_Name,Grantor,Grantee,
               Privilege,Column_Name,Grantable;
```

The procedure variables for the cursor are declared as TABLE_NAME.Column_Name%**TYPE**. Anchoring the variables' definitions takes the column definition from within the database itself. If the column definition changes in a different version of Oracle, the procedure will still work because the definition of the column has not been hard coded. The variable *Prior_Grantor* determines when a new **connect** statement is required. The variable *Lv_Lineno* orders the lines of the **connect** and **grant** statements and is initialized to 0.

```
Lv_TP_Grantee          SYS.DBA_TAB_PRIVS.Grantee%TYPE;
Lv_TP_Grantor          SYS.DBA_TAB_PRIVS.Grantor%TYPE;
Lv_TP_Owner            SYS.DBA_TAB_PRIVS.Owner%TYPE;
Lv_TP_Table_Name       SYS.DBA_TAB_PRIVS.Table_Name%TYPE;
Lv_TP_Privilege        SYS.DBA_TAB_PRIVS.Privilege%TYPE;
Lv_TP_Grantable        SYS.DBA_TAB_PRIVS.Grantable%TYPE;
Prior_Grantor          SYS.DBA_TAB_PRIVS.Grantor%TYPE;
Lv_CP_Column_Name      SYS.DBA_COL_PRIVS.Column_Name%TYPE;
Lv_JV_Object_Type      SYS.DBA_OBJECTS.Object_Type%TYPE;
Lv_String          VARCHAR2(800);
Lv_Lineno          NUMBER;
```

The next section of the script creates WRITE_OUT, an internal procedure to **insert** the generated text into the temporary table:

```
small code  procedure WRITE_OUT(P_Line INTEGER, P_Owner VARCHAR2,
P_Name VARCHAR2,
                  P_String VARCHAR2) is
  begin
    insert into GRANT_TEMP (Lineno, Table_Owner, Table_Name, Text)
```

```
              values (P_Line,P_Owner,P_Name,P_String);
   end;
```

Granted privileges are stored as separate rows in the DBA_TAB_PRIVS view. Even if you **grant all** to a user, Oracle converts that to the individual privileges and stores them separately. Additionally, you can **grant** privileges on an object to more than one user. Because of this, the cursor GRANT_CURSOR is used to extract all the granted privileges on the object. *Lv_Lineno* is used to order the rows in the temporary table GRANT_TEMP so that if you prefer, you can extract the **connect** and **grant** statements for a single grantee at the end of the procedure.

```
begin
   Prior_Grantor := ' ';
   Lv_Lineno := 1;
   open GRANT_CURSOR;

   loop
      fetch GRANT_CURSOR into      Lv_TP_Grantee,
                                   Lv_TP_Grantor,
                                   Lv_TP_Owner,
                                   Lv_TP_Table_Name,
                                   Lv_TP_Privilege,
                                   Lv_TP_Grantable;
      exit when GRANT_CURSOR%NOTFOUND;
```

Each time the grantor changes, a new **connect** statement is necessary. The variable *Prior_Grantor* tracks when the grantor changes. The following section of the gen_grnt_7n8.sql script generates the proper **connect** command:

```
      if (Prior_Grantor != Lv_TP_Grantor)
      then
         Prior_Grantor := Lv_TP_Grantor;
         Lv_String  := 'CONNECT ' || Lv_TP_Grantor || '/PASSWORD';
         WRITE_OUT(Lv_Lineno, Lv_TP_Grantor,
Lv_TP_Table_Name, Lv_String);
         Lv_Lineno  := Lv_Lineno + 1;
      end if;
```

The next section of the script determines whether the privilege is READ and hence applicable on directories only; otherwise, it is applicable to non-directory objects.

```
if (Lv_TP_Privilege = 'READ')
    then
         Lv_String := 'GRANT '          ||
                      Lv_TP_Privilege   ||
                      ' ON DIRECTORY '  ||
```

```
                    Lv_TP_Table_Name ||
                    ' TO '           ||
                    Lv_TP_Grantee;
    else

        Lv_String := 'GRANT '        ||
                    Lv_TP_Privilege  ||
                    ' ON '           ||
                    Lv_TP_Owner      ||
                    '.'              ||
                    Lv_TP_Table_Name ||
                    ' TO '           ||
                    Lv_TP_Grantee;
    end if;
```

The next section of the script determines whether the privilege has been granted **with grant option**; that information is added to the statement before it is written to the table. There will be one **grant** command for each privilege.

```
    if (Lv_TP_Grantable = 'YES' )
    then
        Lv_String := Lv_String    || ' WITH GRANT OPTION';
    end if;
```

In the next section of the script, the statement is written to the file and a '/' is added to complete the SQL command.

The cursor loop ends and the procedure will loop back through the GRANT_CURSOR until **grant** statements for all privileges on the object have been generated. The cursor then closes.

```
    WRITE_OUT(Lv_Lineno, Lv_TP_Owner, Lv_TP_Table_Name, Lv_String);
    Lv_Lineno    := Lv_Lineno + 1;
    WRITE_OUT(Lv_Lineno, Lv_TP_Owner, Lv_TP_Table_Name, '/');
    Lv_Lineno    := Lv_Lineno + 1;
end loop;

    close GRANT_CURSOR;
```

The next section of the script generates the equivalent grant statements for JAVA SOURCE and JAVA RESOURCE objects by using the GRANT_JAVA_CURSOR:

```
Prior_Grantor := ' ';
    open GRANT_JAVA_CURSOR;

    loop
        fetch GRANT_JAVA_CURSOR into    Lv_TP_Grantee,
                                        Lv_TP_Grantor,
```

```
                                 Lv_TP_Owner,
                                 Lv_TP_Table_Name,
                                 Lv_TP_Privilege,
                                 Lv_JV_Object_Type,
                                 Lv_TP_Grantable;
        exit when GRANT_JAVA_CURSOR%NOTFOUND;

        if (Prior_Grantor != Lv_TP_Grantor)
        then
            Prior_Grantor := Lv_TP_Grantor;
            Lv_String  := 'CONNECT ' || Lv_TP_Grantor || '/PASSWORD';
            WRITE_OUT(Lv_Lineno, Lv_TP_Grantor,
Lv_TP_Table_Name, Lv_String);
            Lv_Lineno  := Lv_Lineno + 1;
        end if;

        Lv_String := 'GRANT '         ||
                     Lv_TP_Privilege  ||
                     ' ON '           ||
                     Lv_JV_Object_Type ||
                     ' '              ||
                     Lv_TP_Owner      ||
                     '.'              ||
                     Lv_TP_Table_Name ||
                     ' TO '           ||
                     Lv_TP_Grantee;

        if (Lv_TP_Grantable = 'YES' )
        then
            Lv_String := Lv_String     || ' WITH GRANT OPTION';
        end if;

        WRITE_OUT(Lv_Lineno, Lv_TP_Owner, Lv_TP_Table_Name, Lv_String);
        Lv_Lineno    := Lv_Lineno + 1;
        WRITE_OUT(Lv_Lineno, Lv_TP_Owner, Lv_TP_Table_Name, '/');
        Lv_Lineno    := Lv_Lineno + 1;

    end loop;

    close GRANT_JAVA_CURSOR;
```

The next section uses the GRANT_COL_CURSOR to determine grants at the column level:

```
Prior_Grantor := ' ';
    open GRANT_COL_CURSOR;

    loop
```

```
        fetch GRANT_COL_CURSOR into       Lv_TP_Grantee,
                                          Lv_TP_Grantor,
                                          Lv_TP_Owner,
                                          Lv_TP_Table_Name,
                                          Lv_CP_Column_Name,
                                          Lv_TP_Privilege,
                                          Lv_TP_Grantable;
        exit when GRANT_COL_CURSOR%NOTFOUND;

        if (Prior_Grantor != Lv_TP_Grantor)
        then
            Prior_Grantor := Lv_TP_Grantor;
            Lv_String  := 'CONNECT ' || Lv_TP_Grantor || '/PASSWORD';
            WRITE_OUT(Lv_Lineno, Lv_TP_Grantor,
Lv_TP_Table_Name, Lv_String);
            Lv_Lineno  := Lv_Lineno + 1;
        end if;

        Lv_String := 'GRANT '          ||
                     Lv_TP_Privilege   ||
                     '('               ||
                     Lv_CP_Column_Name ||
                     ')'               ||
                     ' ON '            ||
                     Lv_TP_Owner       ||
                     '.'               ||
                     Lv_TP_Table_Name  ||
                     ' TO '            ||
                     Lv_TP_Grantee;

        if (Lv_TP_Grantable = 'YES' )
        then
            Lv_String := Lv_String     || ' WITH GRANT OPTION';
        end if;

        WRITE_OUT(Lv_Lineno, Lv_TP_Owner, Lv_TP_Table_Name, Lv_String);
        Lv_Lineno      := Lv_Lineno + 1;
        WRITE_OUT(Lv_Lineno, Lv_TP_Owner, Lv_TP_Table_Name, '/');
        Lv_Lineno      := Lv_Lineno + 1;

    end loop;

    close GRANT_COL_CURSOR;

end;
/
```

After the **connect** and **grant** statements for all the privileges have been generated, they are spooled to a file for later execution. By default, the output file is named cre_grnt.sql. A sample cre_grnt.sql file is shown in the following listing:

```
CONNECT DEMO/PASSWORD
GRANT SELECT ON DEMO.JOB TO PUBLIC
/
GRANT SELECT ON DEMO.JOB TO QC_USER
/
GRANT SELECT ON DEMO.JOB TO SCOTT WITH GRANT OPTION
/
CONNECT SCOTT/PASSWORD
GRANT SELECT ON DEMO.JOB TO QC_USER
/
```

In this sample output, the **SELECT** privilege has been **grant**ed directly to PUBLIC, QC_USER and to SCOTT **with grant option**. In addition, SCOTT has in turn **grant**ed the **SELECT** privilege directly to QC_USER. Should the DEMO user **revoke** the **SELECT** privilege from SCOTT, the QC_USER will also lose that privilege from SCOTT but will keep it from DEMO. Because of this cascading **revoke**, you should be careful when using **with grant option**.

As an alternative, if you want to use this script to document all the privileges on all objects for a particular owner, remove the **accept** *table_name* statement at the beginning of the script and change the **where** clause for the GRANT_CURSOR cursor as shown here:

```
where Owner  = UPPER('&&table_owner')
```

or you can use the wildcard '%'.

The gen_grnt_9.sql script, available on the CD-ROM in this book, extends the gen_grnt_7n8.sql script for an Oracle9.x database by supporting the WITH HIERARCHY OPTION of Oracle9i. The WITH HIEARCHY OPTION in Oracle9i allows you to grant the specified object privilege on all subobjects of the object.

Space Management

To manage the space used by your data, you need to understand how data is stored, where it is stored, and how new space is acquired. In this chapter, you will see scripts that simplify the management of the space available to your objects. For example, you can use the diagnostic scripts in this chapter to determine how the current space is allocated, and you can use the utility scripts to estimate the space requirements for new objects.

PROGRAMMER'S NOTE *All the scripts in this chapter assume that the database block size is consistent across tablespaces. Beginning with Oracle9.x, you can change the database block size at the tablespace level. Refer to Chapter 1 for an example of how to deal with variable block size in Oracle9.x and above.*

The major scripts presented in this chapter are shown in Table 6-1.

Script	Description
free_ext.sql	List available space within each datafile and tablespace
fragment.sql	List contiguous extents within each datafile of a tablespace
file_ext.sql	List the tablespace datafiles and extension information
free_spc.sql	Report on free space percentages within each tablespace
usr_quot.sql	List by user and by tablespace the resources used and the quota allocated
issystem_def_temp_tblspc.sql	List the users who are using the SYSTEM tablespace as their default and/or temporary tablespace
schema_obj_count.sql	Determine the type and count of objects by user
user_dbspc_usage.sql	Report the database space used by each user
def_stor.sql	List the default storage values for objects created within tablespaces
tab_part_storage.sql	Determine the default storage parameters for a partitioned table as well as the current storage settings for its partitions
seg_spac.sql	List the space used and the next extent for all segments owned by a user
obj_size_7.sql	Report on the size of stored objects (Oracle7.x only)
obj_size_8.sql	Report on the size of stored objects (Oracle8.x and above)
seg_info.sql	List the default storage for a segment and all the extents allocated to this segment
temp_seg.sql	List the size and number of extents of all temporary segments in the database
max_exts.sql	List the segments that do not have maxextents set to unlimited
large_tables.sql	Report objects with a large number of extents

TABLE 6-1. Major Scripts in This Chapter

Script	Description
segments_in_datafile.sql	List the segments in the specified datafile
db_block_map.sql	Display the block map of the entire database
coalesce.sql	Force a tablespace to be coalesced
len_long.sql	Measure the length of a LONG value
len_lob.sql	Measure the length of a LOB value
len_row.sql	Measure the average row length for a table
size_tab.sql	Estimate the storage requirements for a table
size_ind.sql	Estimate the storage requirements for an index

TABLE 6-1. Major Scripts in This Chapter *(continued)*

Diagnostics

You can use the scripts in this section to determine how the space in your database is allocated. The diagnostic scripts include reports of space used by objects (such as tables and temporary segments) as well as free space.

free_ext.sql

Space Available in the Database

How large is your database? How many tablespaces do you have, and how many datafiles are located within the tablespaces? How much space within each of the tablespaces is still available? Rather than learning this information only after users are getting errors, it is important for you to monitor the available space within the tablespaces as well as the database as a whole. This allows you to allocate additional datafiles or to defragment existing datafiles before users begin to have problems.

The following script will tell you the total space allocated and the total space remaining by datafile within the tablespace for every datafile and tablespace in the database.

```
REM free_ext.sql
set feedback off term off echo off pagesize 60
set linesize 80 newpage 0
spool free_space.log
ttitle center 'DATABASE REMAINING SPACE BY TABLESPACE '
col Tablespace_Name heading 'TABLESPACE|NAME' format a15
col File_Name heading 'FILE' format a30
col Remaining heading 'BLOCKS|REMAINING' format 9,999,999
col Total_Space heading 'TOTAL|SPACE' format 9,999,999
```

```
break on report on Tablespace_Name
           skip 1 on File_Name on Total_Space
compute sum of Remaining on Tablespace_Name
compute sum of Remaining on report
compute sum of Total_Space on Tablespace_Name
compute sum of Total_Space on report

select FS.Tablespace_Name,
       DF.File_Name,
       SUM(FS.Blocks) Remaining,
       DF.Blocks Total_Space
  from DBA_FREE_SPACE FS, DBA_DATA_FILES DF
 where FS.File_Id = DF.File_Id
 group by FS.Tablespace_Name,
       DF.File_Name, DF.Blocks
order by FS.Tablespace_Name, DF.File_Name
/spool off
clear computes
clear breaks
ttitle off
set feedback 6 term on pagesize 24 newpage 1
```

Sample output for the preceding script is shown here:

```
              DATABASE REMAINING SPACE BY TABLESPACE

TABLESPACE                                    BLOCKS       TOTAL
NAME             FILE                       REMAINING      SPACE
--------------   --------------------------  ----------  ----------
IDX1             /home01/oracle/indx_1_test   426,218     511,744
                 /home01/oracle/indx_2_test   146,228     511,744
**************   **************************  ----------  ----------
sum                                           572,446   1,023,488


RBS              /home01/oracle/rbs_test      508,543     511,744
**************   **************************  ----------  ----------
sum                                           508,543     511,744


SYSTEM           /home01/oracle/sys_test        5,427      25,344
**************   **************************  ----------  ----------
sum                                             5,427      25,344


TEMP             /home01/oracle/temp2_test    511,743     511,744
                 /home01/oracle/temp_test      25,343      25,344
```

```
***************    *****************************  ----------  ----------
sum                                                  537,086     537,088

TEMP_TABLES        /home01/oracle/temptbl.dbf          1,279       1,280
***************    *****************************  ----------  ----------
sum                                                    1,279       1,280

USR1               /home01/oracle/user_1_test         13,446     511,744
                   /home01/oracle/user_2_test         15,893     511,744
***************    *****************************  ----------  ----------
sum                                                   29,339   1,023,488


                                                 ----------  ----------
sum                                                1,654,120   3,122,432
```

The output lists not only the space available within the tablespace but also space within each datafile in the tablespace. A tablespace can have a large amount of remaining free space and still not have enough room for the next extent requested. This would be caused by a large number of datafiles with only a small amount of space available in each one—the USR1 tablespace is an example of this.

The TEMP tablespace shows almost the entire allocated space as free space. This indicates that the report was run when there was little activity in the database. If the report was run during a period of high activity, temporary segments would be in use and the tablespace would not be totally available.

NOTE

Even if no space has been allocated within a datafile, one block will always be in use for the datafile header block.

ANNOTATIONS

The free_ext.sql script uses the SQL*Plus reporting capabilities to format the output for readability. The **break on** command suppresses the display of duplicate values in a column. If you omit an action with the **break on** command, it also marks the place in the report that SQL*Plus will perform the computation you specify in a corresponding **compute** command.

```
set feedback off term off echo off pagesize 60
set linesize 80 newpage 0
spool free_space.log
ttitle center 'DATABASE REMAINING SPACE BY TABLESPACE '
col Tablespace_Name heading 'TABLESPACE|NAME' format a15
col File_Name heading 'FILE' format a30
col Remaining heading 'BLOCKS|REMAINING' format 9,999,999
```

```
col Total_Space heading 'TOTAL|SPACE' format 9,999,999
break on report on Tablespace_Name
                skip 1 on File_Name on Total_Space
```

If multiple **on** clauses are used in a **break** command, the breaks are processed from left to right (outermost to innermost break) with a break at the outermost level superceding the break on an inner level.

This section of the script instructs SQL*Plus to compute the values of all columns in a **compute** command at the end of the script (on report); to skip a line each time the tablespace name changes (on Tablespace_Name skip 1); to compute the values of all columns in a **compute** command each time the tablespace name changes and to suppress the printing of the tablespace name if more than one data file is associated with it (on Tablespace_Name); and to suppress the printing of the total space used by the tablespace each time the filename changes, by having that clause (on Total_Space) follow the File_Name break.

```
compute sum of Remaining on Tablespace_Name
compute sum of Remaining on report
compute sum of Total_Space on Tablespace_Name
compute sum of Total_Space on report
```

This section of the script will compute subtotals and totals of the remaining and total space each time the tablespace name or report breaks. For the **compute** command to be processed, the column it references in the **on** clause must be part of the **select** command and also part of the most recent **break** command.

```
select FS.Tablespace_Name,
       File_Name,
       SUM(FS.Blocks) Remaining,
       DF.Blocks Total_Space
  from DBA_FREE_SPACE FS, DBA_DATA_FILES DF
 where FS.File_Id = DF.File_Id
 group by FS.Tablespace_Name,
       File_Name, DF.Blocks
order by FS.Tablespace_Name,File_Name
/
spool off
clear computes
clear breaks
ttitle off
set feedback 6 term on pagesize 24 newpage 1
```

The DBA_FREE_SPACE view contains a row for every free extent in the database. It is neither practical nor useful to list every free extent available. To display a summary row of data per datafile, the **group by** clause of the **select** command is used. The selected columns in a **select** statement with the **group by** clause must either be a group function (such as **SUM**) or be listed in the **group by** clause itself.

```
               DATABASE REMAINING SPACE BY TABLESPACE
```

TABLESPACE NAME	FILE	BLOCKS REMAINING	TOTAL SPACE
---------------	--------------------------------	----------	----------
IDX1	/home01/oracle/indx_1_test	426,218	511,744
	/home01/oracle/indx_2_test	146,228	511,744
***************	****************************	----------	----------
sum		572,446	1,023,488
RBS	/home01/oracle/rbs_test	508,543	511,744
***************	****************************	----------	----------
sum		508,543	511,744
SYSTEM	/home01/oracle/sys_test	5,427	25,344
***************	****************************	----------	----------
sum		5,427	25,344
TEMP	/home01/oracle/temp2_test	511,743	511,744
	/home01/oracle/temp_test	25,343	25,344
***************	****************************	----------	----------
sum		537,086	537,088
TEMP_TABLES	/home01/oracle/temptbl.dbf	1,279	1,280
***************	****************************	----------	----------
sum		1,279	1,280
USR1	/home01/oracle/user_1_test	13,446	511,744
	/home01/oracle/user_2_test	15,893	511,744
***************	****************************	----------	----------
sum		29,339	1,023,488
		----------	----------
sum		1,654,120	3,122,432

You can use this report to track how space usage is growing within your database. By comparing reports over time, you can see how quickly tablespaces are filling and add datafiles before space allocation errors start plaguing your applications.

The space allocated and used is stated in database blocks and is relative to the database block size of your database (set by the DB_BLOCK_SIZE init.ora parameter during database creation). In the preceding example, the initial datafile in the SYSTEM tablespace has 5427 database blocks remaining, an indication that it is time to add another datafile to SYSTEM, especially if a large number of stored procedures are being developed for this application. Stored procedure source code is stored in SYS.SOURCE$ and other data dictionary tables. You cannot move those data dictionary tables out of the SYSTEM tablespace, so you must maintain adequate free space in the SYSTEM tablespace.

PROGRAMMER'S NOTE   *The script free_ext.sql doesn't consider temporary files. Information about temporary files is available in DBA_TEMP_FILES and can't be obtained by querying DBA_DATA_FILES or V$DATAFILE.*

fragment.sql

Tablespace Fragmentation

While the script in the previous section shows you the total amount of space available within each datafile and tablespace, it does not tell you how fragmented that space is. Even if a large amount of space is available, you can get space allocation errors if your tablespace is very fragmented. The PL/SQL script that follows will display the extents available within your tablespace and the size of each extent.

To run the PL/SQL script, you must first create a table to hold the intermediate results:

```
create table FREESP (
Fname   VARCHAR2(513),
Tspace VARCHAR2(30),
First  NUMBER(10),
Blocks NUMBER(10),
Last   NUMBER(10))
/
```

Rather than create this table each time the PL/SQL script is run (and further fragment the tablespace), FREESP is created once and **truncate**d before each use in the fragment.sql script:

```
REM fragment.sql
set feedback off term off verify off pagesize 60
set newpage 0 linesize 66
truncate table FREESP;
declare
  Fileid     NUMBER(9);
  Filename   VARCHAR2(513);
```

```
   Tsname      VARCHAR2(30);
   Cursor Tablespaces is
      select File_Name, File_ID, Tablespace_Name
        from DBA_DATA_FILES
        where Tablespace_Name = upper('&1');
begin
open tablespaces;
loop
  fetch Tablespaces into Filename, Fileid, Tsname;
  exit when Tablespaces%NOTFOUND;
declare
  First   NUMBER(10);
  Blocks  NUMBER(10);
  Last    NUMBER(10);
  Tfirst  NUMBER(10);
  Tblocks NUMBER(10);
  Tlast   NUMBER(10);
  Cursor Free is
    select Block_ID a, Blocks b, Block_ID+Blocks c
      from DBA_FREE_SPACE
     where File_ID = Fileid
     order by Block_ID;
begin
  open Free;
  fetch Free into First, Blocks, Last;
  if Free%NOTFOUND
   then
       goto close_free;
  end if;
  loop
    fetch Free into Tfirst, Tblocks, Tlast;
    exit when Free%NOTFOUND;
    if Tfirst = Last
      then
        Blocks := Blocks + Tblocks;
        Last := Tlast;
      else
        insert into FREESP
          values (Filename, Tsname, First, Blocks, Last-1);
        commit;
        First := Tfirst;
        Blocks := Tblocks;
        Last := Tlast;
    end if;
```

```
    end loop;
        insert into FREESP
            values (Filename, Tsname, First, Blocks, Last-1);
    commit;
<<close_free>>
  close Free;
end;
end loop;
commit;
close Tablespaces;
end;
/
```

Alternatively, you can write this code block without using the goto statement. Use of goto statements should generally be avoided unless there is no other way to handle the problem.

The following block of code demonstrates an alternative way of doing the same task, but it uses while loop instead of the goto statement.

```
declare
  Fileid      NUMBER(9);
  Filename  VARCHAR2(513);
  Tsname      VARCHAR2(30);
  Cursor Tablespaces is
    select File_Name, File_ID, Tablespace_Name
    from DBA_DATA_FILES
    where Tablespace_Name = upper('&1');
begin
  open tablespaces;
  fetch Tablespaces into Filename, Fileid, Tsname;
  while Tablespaces%FOUND loop
    declare
      First    NUMBER(10);
      Blocks  NUMBER(10);
      Last     NUMBER(10);
      Tfirst  NUMBER(10);
      Tblocks NUMBER(10);
      Tlast    NUMBER(10);
      Cursor Free is
        select Block_ID a, Blocks b, Block_ID+Blocks c
        from DBA_FREE_SPACE
        where File_ID = Fileid
        order by Block_ID;
    begin
```

```
      open Free;
      fetch Free into First, Blocks, Last;
      while Free%FOUND loop
        fetch Free into Tfirst, Tblocks, Tlast;
        exit when Free%NOTFOUND;
        if Tfirst = Last then
          Blocks := Blocks + Tblocks;
          Last := Tlast;
        else
          insert into FREESP
            values (Filename, Tsname, First, Blocks, Last-1);
          commit;
          First := Tfirst;
          Blocks := Tblocks;
          Last := Tlast;
        end if;
      end loop;
      insert into FREESP
        values (Filename, Tsname, First, Blocks, Last-1);
      commit;
      close Free;
    end;
    fetch Tablespaces into Filename, Fileid, Tsname;
  end loop;
  commit;
  close Tablespaces;
end;
/
```

Once this code block is run, the table FREESP is populated with the
fragmentation information about all the tablespaces.

```
col Db_Name new_value Instance
select 'INSTANCE NAME' Description, value Db_name from V$PARAMETER
   where UPPER(Name) = 'DB_NAME'
/
ttitle center Instance ' TABLESPACE FRAGMENTATION REPORT'
col Tspace heading 'TABLESPACE|NAME' format a10 trunc
col Fname heading 'FILE' format A30 trunc
col First heading 'START|BLOCK' format 999,999
col Blocks heading 'BLOCKS|REMAINING' format 99,999,999
break on report on Tspace skip 1 on Fname skip 1
compute sum of Blocks on Fname
compute sum of Blocks on report
```

```
spool fragmentation.rpt
select Tspace, Fname, First, Blocks
  from FREESP
 order by Tspace,Fname,First;

spool off
ttitle off
clear computes
clear breaks
set feedback 6 pagesize 24 newpage 1 linesize 80
```

The script runs for a single tablespace and expects the tablespace name as input. The output of the script is shown here:

```
                 test TABLESPACE FRAGMENTATION REPORT
```

TABLESPACE NAME	FILE	START BLOCK	BLOCKS REMAINING
USR1	/home01/oracle/user_1_test	3,215	3
		4,065	40
		5,586	75
		8,475	145
		10,080	110
		10,545	100
		21,832	3,215
		50,563	85
		61,054	111
		85,045	1,420
		95,996	7
		108,526	70
		121,503	121
		125,689	275
		127,250	450
		131,418	58
		151,903	895
		159,394	50
		171,876	325
		270,022	665
		292,477	18
		328,862	50
		328,922	85
		334,617	110
		344,614	285

359,493	670
360,328	675
365,297	125
366,197	325
366,567	435
369,117	33
371,945	13
372,033	220
372,833	155
375,651	150
423,382	195
425,657	100
431,110	72
434,692	1,905
481,830	40

```
******************************                        -----------
sum                                                        13,881

/home01/oracle/user_2_test         4,812            125
                                  10,849             50
                                  10,924             40
                                  26,151            102
                                  28,888            360
                                  29,758            455
                                  31,909            355
                                  51,235            105
                                 135,832            145
                                 136,197            325
                                 166,270             18
                                 186,381            590
                                 202,906          2,503
```

```
             test TABLESPACE FRAGMENTATION REPORT
```

TABLESPACE NAME	FILE	START BLOCK	BLOCKS REMAINING
USR1	/home01/oracle/user_2_test	258,757	2,910
		346,192	50
		401,162	1,705
		442,167	40
		468,537	1,090
		476,277	1,205

478,717	50
481,342	110
481,477	1,450
483,367	235
487,142	915
502,107	345

```
******************************                    ----------
sum                                                 15,278


**********                                        ----------
sum                                                 29,159
```

This tablespace is badly fragmented, and while it might seem that plenty of space is available, most of the extents are less than 500 blocks. Unless this tablespace is read-only or contains tables that are updated infrequently, another datafile should be added.

ANNOTATIONS

The fragment.sql script will read the DBA_FREE_SPACE data dictionary view; sum up contiguous extents if necessary; store the results in a temporary table; and report, by datafile, on the fragmentation in your tablespace. Unless you have set the **pctincrease** for the tablespace to non-zero, Oracle will not automatically coalesce this space until you either coalesce it manually (via the **coalesce** option of the **alter tablespace** command) or force Oracle to coalesce extents dynamically by requesting an extent that is larger than any of those that are available.

Oracle does not merge contiguous free extents unless there is no alternative; thus the tablespace becomes more and more fragmented as Oracle first allocates space from the largest free extent it encounters in the tablespace before reusing and coalescing the smaller free extents created as objects are dropped. Figure 6-1 illustrates available extents within a tablespace before and after a request for an extent has been allocated.

Used	Free 5 Bits	Free 20 Bits	Used	Free 30 Bits	Used

Used	Free 5 Bits	Free 20 Bits	Used	Alloc 25 bits	Free 5 Bits	Used

FIGURE 6-1.   Extents available in a tablespace before and after a request for an extent

To run the fragment.sql script, you must first build a table called FREESP, which is used to store information about the datafiles and extents. If your tablespace has a non-zero **pctincrease**, the data in this table will be the same as that in DBA_FREE_SPACE, since SMON periodically coalesces the free space in tablespaces with non-zero **pctincrease** settings.

To create the FREESP table, execute the following script:

```
create table FREESP (
Fname   VARCHAR2(513),
Tspace VARCHAR2(30),
First   NUMBER(10),
Blocks NUMBER(10),
Last    NUMBER(10))
/
```

The first section of the fragment.sql script will read through the DBA_DATA_FILES view for the datafiles associated with the requested tablespace. For each datafile found, the script loops through DBA_FREE_SPACE to extract the extent information.

```
set feedback off term off verify off pagesize 60
set newpage 0 linesize 66
truncate table FREESP;
declare
  Fileid      NUMBER(9);
  Filename   VARCHAR2(513);
  Tsname      VARCHAR2(30);
  Cursor Tablespaces is
     select File_Name, File_ID, Tablespace_Name
       from DBA_DATA_FILES
      where Tablespace_Name = upper('&1');
begin
  open tablespaces;
  fetch Tablespaces into Filename, Fileid, Tsname;
  while Tablespaces%FOUND loop
```

For every datafile found, the script will open a cursor named "free" and read through DBA_FREE_SPACE, summing up the contiguous extents as it goes. Separate extents are contiguous if the Block_ID value plus the number of blocks minus 1 equals the next Block_ID found. If the extents are contiguous, the number of blocks is added to a holding variable and the next Block_ID is read. If the extents are not contiguous, the holding information is inserted into the FREESP table and the holding variables are reset. Once all the extents for a datafile have been processed, the inner cursor is closed and the next datafile information is obtained. Once all

datafiles have been processed, the outer cursor is closed and the data in the
intermediate table FREESP is reported.

```
declare
  Fileid    NUMBER(9);
  Filename  VARCHAR2(513);
  Tsname    VARCHAR2(30);
  Cursor Tablespaces is
    select File_Name, File_ID, Tablespace_Name
    from DBA_DATA_FILES
    where Tablespace_Name = upper('&1');
begin
  open tablespaces;
  fetch Tablespaces into Filename, Fileid, Tsname;
  while Tablespaces%FOUND loop
    declare
      First   NUMBER(10);
      Blocks  NUMBER(10);
      Last    NUMBER(10);
      Tfirst  NUMBER(10);
      Tblocks NUMBER(10);
      Tlast   NUMBER(10);
      Cursor Free is
        select Block_ID a, Blocks b, Block_ID+Blocks c
        from DBA_FREE_SPACE
        where File_ID = Fileid
        order by Block_ID;
    begin
      open Free;
      fetch Free into First, Blocks, Last;
      while Free%FOUND loop
        fetch Free into Tfirst, Tblocks, Tlast;
        exit when Free%NOTFOUND;
        if Tfirst = Last then
          Blocks := Blocks + Tblocks;
          Last := Tlast;
        else
          insert into FREESP
            values (Filename, Tsname, First, Blocks, Last-1);
          commit;
          First := Tfirst;
          Blocks := Tblocks;
          Last := Tlast;
        end if;
```

```
      end loop;
      insert into FREESP
        values (Filename, Tsname, First, Blocks, Last-1);
      commit;
      close Free;
    end;
    fetch Tablespaces into Filename, Fileid, Tsname;
  end loop;
  commit;
  close Tablespaces;
end;
/
```

After all the datafiles have been checked, the information gathered in the FREESP table is displayed via SQL*Plus reporting commands. Using the **value** parameter, the instance name is captured for display in all page headers. The **break** and **compute** commands are used to create subtotal, total, and grand total values.

```
col Db_Name new_value Instance
select 'INSTANCE NAME' Description, value Db_name
from V$PARAMETER
where UPPER(Name) = 'DB_NAME'
/
ttitle center Instance ' TABLESPACE FRAGMENTATION REPORT'
col Tspace heading 'TABLESPACE|NAME' format a10 trunc
col Fname heading 'FILE' format A30 trunc
col First heading 'START|BLOCK' format 999,999
col Blocks heading 'BLOCKS|REMAINING' format 99,999,999
break on report on Tspace skip 1 on Fname skip 1
compute sum of Blocks on Fname
compute sum of Blocks on report

spool fragmentation.rpt
select Tspace, Fname, First, Blocks
  from FREESP
 order by Tspace,Fname,First;

spool off
ttitle off
clear computes
clear breaks
set feedback 6 pagesize 24 newpage 1 linesize 80
```

The output in the following listing shows that the tablespace USR1 in the TEST database is extremely fragmented. Although 29,159 blocks are available in the USR1 tablespace, the largest single extent that can be allocated is 3215 blocks, with most of the extents much smaller. This tablespace may appear to have a good deal of space available, based on the total blocks available, but closer examination indicates possible problems. Monitoring the changes in this report over several days or weeks will show when additional datafiles will be needed.

```
            test TABLESPACE FRAGMENTATION REPORT


TABLESPACE                              START    BLOCKS
NAME         FILE                       BLOCK    REMAINING
----------   ---------------------      --------  -----------
USR1         /home01/oracle/user_1_test   3,215        3
                                          4,065       40
                                          5,586       75
                                          8,475      145
                                         10,080      110
                                         10,545      100
                                         21,832    3,215
                                         50,563       85
                                         61,054      111
                                         85,045    1,420
                                         95,996        7
                                        108,526       70
                                        121,503      121
                                        125,689      275
                                        127,250      450
                                        131,418       58
                                        151,903      895
                                        159,394       50
                                        171,876      325
                                        270,022      665
                                        292,477       18
                                        328,862       50
                                        328,922       85
                                        334,617      110
                                        344,614      285
                                        359,493      670
                                        360,328      675
                                        365,297      125
                                        366,197      325
                                        366,567      435
                                        369,117       33
                                        371,945       13
                                        372,033      220
```

```
                                       372,833          155
                                       375,651          150
                                       423,382          195
                                       425,657          100
                                       431,110           72
                                       434,692        1,905
                                       481,830           40
         *****************************              -----------
         sum                                          13,881

         /home01/oracle/user_2_test      4,812          125
                                        10,849           50
                                        10,924           40
                                        26,151          102
                                        28,888          360
                                        29,758          455
                                        31,909          355
                                        51,235          105
                                       135,832          145
                                       136,197          325
                                       166,270           18
                                       186,381          590
                                       202,906        2,503
```

            test TABLESPACE FRAGMENTATION REPORT

TABLESPACE NAME	FILE	START BLOCK	BLOCKS REMAINING
USR1	/home01/oracle/user_2_test	258,757	2,910
		346,192	50
		401,162	1,705
		442,167	40
		468,537	1,090
		476,277	1,205
		478,717	50
		481,342	110
		481,477	1,450
		483,367	235
		487,142	915
		502,107	345

```
         *****************************              -----------
         sum                                          15,278
```

```
*********                                         - - - - - - - - - - -
sum                                                        29,159
```

If you periodically coalesce your tablespaces, or you have set the **pctincrease** to a non-zero value, you can run the fragment.sql script that follows without creating a permanent FREESP table to store the intermediate information on fragmentation. The script reads through the DBA_FREE_SPACE view and reports the same information as the fragment.sql script. Because tablespaces with a non-zero **pctincrease** will not be coalesced, they are excluded from the report for readability. In general, it is not a good idea for the temporary tablespace to have a non-zero **pctincrease**. The following script will generate the same output as the original script, as long as the requested tablespace has a non-zero **pctincrease**.

```
col Db_Name new_value Instance
select 'INSTANCE NAME' Description, value Db_name
from V$PARAMETER
where UPPER(Name) = 'DB_NAME'
/
ttitle center instance ' TABLESPACE FRAGMENTATION REPORT'
col Tablespace_Name heading 'TABLESPACE|NAME' format a10 trunc
col File_Name heading 'FILE' format a30 trunc
col Block_ID heading 'START|BLOCK' format 999,999
col Blocks heading 'BLOCKS|REMAINING' format 99,999,999
break on report on Tablespace_Name skip 1 on File_Name skip 1
compute sum of blocks on File_Name
compute sum of blocks on report
spool fragment.rpt

select A.Tablespace_Name, A.File_Name, B.Block_ID, B.Blocks
  from DBA_DATA_FILES A, DBA_FREE_SPACE B, DBA_TABLESPACES C
 where C.Pct_Increase > 0
   and A.Tablespace_Name=C.Tablespace_Name
   and A.File_ID=B.File_ID
   and A.Tablespace_Name = upper('&1')
 order by A.Tablespace_Name, A.File_ID, B.Block_ID;

spool off
```

The output of this script, shown next, is identical to the output of the previous script. However, if the tablespace selected does not have a non-zero **pctincrease**, this script will return an empty report while the previous one will return data.

```
            test TABLESPACE FRAGMENTATION REPORT
```

TABLESPACE NAME	FILE	START BLOCK	BLOCKS REMAINING
USR1	/home01/oracle/user_1_test	3,215	3
		4,065	40
		5,586	75
		8,475	145
		10,080	110
		10,545	100
		21,832	3,215
		50,563	85
		61,054	111
		85,045	1,420
		95,996	7
		108,526	70
		121,503	121
		125,689	275
		127,250	450
		131,418	58
		151,903	895
		159,394	50
		171,876	325
		270,022	665
		292,477	18
		328,862	50
		328,922	85
		334,617	110
		344,614	285
		359,493	670
		360,328	675
		365,297	125
		366,197	325
		366,567	435
		369,117	33
		371,945	13
		372,033	220
		372,833	155
		375,651	150
		423,382	195
		425,657	100
		431,110	72

```
                                        434,692          1,905
                                        481,830             40
            ****************************              -----------
            sum                                        13,881


            /home01/oracle/user_2_test    4,812            125
                                         10,849             50
                                         10,924             40
                                         26,151            102
                                         28,888            360
                                         29,758            455
                                         31,909            355
                                         51,235            105
                                        135,832            145
                                        136,197            325
                                        166,270             18
                                        186,381            590
                                        202,906          2,503
```

test TABLESPACE FRAGMENTATION REPORT

TABLESPACE NAME	FILE	START BLOCK	BLOCKS REMAINING
USR1	/home01/oracle/user_2_test	258,757	2,910
		346,192	50
		401,162	1,705
		442,167	40
		468,537	1,090
		476,277	1,205
		478,717	50
		481,342	110
		481,477	1,450
		483,367	235
		487,142	915
		502,107	345

```
            ****************************              -----------
            sum                                        15,278



            **********                                 -----------
            sum                                        29,159
```

file_ext.sql

Which Files Can Extend

As of Oracle7.2, you can set datafiles within a tablespace to extend automatically when they run out of space. Although implementing this option will ensure that users never run out of space (unless you run out of space on the disk that stores the datafile), you should use automatic extensions cautiously and monitor your space usage closely. Datafile extension is an indication that the objects within the database are not sized correctly and can mask a more serious problem within the application.

The **autoextend** clause can be implemented at the time you create the datafile via the **alter tablespace** or **create tablespace** command, or it can be added to an existing datafile via the **alter database datafile** command.

To **autoextend on**, use the clause

```
autoextend on [next [K/M] maxsize [UNLIMITED/integer [K/M]]]
```

PROGRAMMER'S NOTE *It is highly recommended that temporary and rollback tablespaces never be set to* *autoextend as this can crash the database if a query uses excessive sorts or the transaction is on a* *large table.*

The **autoextend** clause specifies the maximum size to which the datafile can expand and the size of each incremental extension. If you leave off the **next** and **maxsize** parameters, the default for **maxsize** is UNLIMITED and the default for **next** is one data block. Turning **autoextend off** sets **maxsize** and **next** to zero, and they must be reset if **autoextend** is turned back on. **Autoextend** cannot be used when using raw partitions. There are no flags within the database to indicate when a datafile has **autoextended**.

The next script lists which datafiles can extend and the extension sizes.

```
REM file_ext.sql

set term off echo off verify off feedback off
set linesize 80 pagesize 60
col Value new_value blksz noprint
col Maxext format 999999999999 heading 'MAXIMUM|EXTENDED SIZE'
col Incr format 999999999 heading 'EXTENSION|INCREMENT'
col Tablespace_Name format a15 heading 'TABLESPACE'
col File_Name format a30 heading 'FILE NAME'

select Value
  from V$PARAMETER
 where Name = 'db_block_size';

set term on
```

```
select Tablespace_Name,
       File_Name,
       Maxextend*&&blksz Maxext,
       Inc*&&blksz Incr
  from DBA_DATA_FILES, SYS.FILEXT$
 where File_Id=File#(+)
 order by Tablespace_Name, File_Name
/
set verify on feedback 6  pagesize 24
```

PROGRAMMER'S NOTE   *If no tablespace has ever had **autoextend** turned on, the SYS.FILEXT$ table will not have been created and the script will fail.*

Sample output for the preceding query is shown in the following listing.

TABLESPACE	FILE NAME	MAXIMUM EXTENDED SIZE	EXTENSION INCREMENT
ROLLBACK_DATA	D:ORCL.ORA		
SYSTEM	D:ORCL.ORA	209715200	10485760
TEMPORARY_DATA	D:ORCL.ORA	157286400	5242880
USER_DATA	D:ORCL.ORA	157286400	5242880

A NULL value for the maximum size and increment indicates that the datafile does not have **autoextend** turned on.

ANNOTATIONS

The **column** command for the Value column will store the value of Value in the *blksz* variable for later use in the script. The **noprint** clause keeps the result of the query from displaying.

```
set term off verify off echo off feedback off
set linesize 80 pagesize 60
col Value new_value blksz noprint
col Maxext format 999999999999 heading 'MAXIMUM|EXTENDED SIZE'
col Incr format 999999999 heading 'EXTENSION|INCREMENT'
col Tablespace_Name format a15 heading 'TABLESPACE'
col File_Name format a30 heading 'FILE NAME'

select Value
  from V$PARAMETER
 where Name = 'db_block_size';

set term on
```

Maximum extension size and extent increments are stored in the database in a number of database blocks. To convert these to meaningful numbers, they are multiplied by the value of the database block size, stored in the variable *blksz*, and extracted in the prior **select** statement. For a database with a 4KB blocksize, setting **maxsize** to UNLIMITED translates to 17,179,860,992 (17GB).

This query displays all datafiles, whether or not they are **autoextend**able. Datafiles that are not in the SYS.FILEXT$ table and that are therefore not extendable are included in the output by the use of the outer join **(+)** clause. If you want to display only datafiles that can extend, remove the outer join clause from the query.

```
select Tablespace_Name,
       File_Name,
       Maxextend*&&blksz Maxext,
       Inc*&&blksz Incr
  from DBA_DATA_FILES, SYS.FILEXT$
 where File_Id=File#(+)
 order by Tablespace_Name, File_Name
/
set verify on feedback 6  pagesize 24
```

If no datafile has been created with **autoextend** on, the SYS.FILEXT$ table will not exist. This table does not get dropped once created, even if all datafiles have **autoextend** turned off.

```
               MAXIMUM  EXTENSION
TABLESPACE          FILE NAME             EXTENDED SIZE  INCREMENT
---------------     -------------------   -------------  ----------
ROLLBACK_DATA       D:ORCL.ORA
SYSTEM              D:ORCL.ORA               209715200    10485760
TEMPORARY_DATA      D:ORCL.ORA               157286400     5242880
USER_DATA           D:ORCL.ORA               157286400     5242880
```

The output listing shows that the SYSTEM, TEMPORARY_DATA, and USER_DATA tablespaces have **autoextend** set to on. The USER_DATA tablespace can grow to a maximum of 150MB, in 5MB increments.

Beginning with Oracle8, the data dictionary view DBA_DATA_FILES has been modified to contain the **autoextend** information. The following query will return the same results as the prior query, but accesses only one view.

The Autoextensible column has a possible value of YES or NO. If Autoextensible is NO, the MaxBytes, MaxBlocks, and Increment_By columns will contain zeros.

```
set term off verify off echo off feedback off
set linesize 80 pagesize 60
col Value new_value blksz noprint
col Maxext format a15 heading 'MAXIMUM|EXTENDED SIZE'
```

```
col Incr format a10 heading 'EXTENSION|INCREMENT'
col Tablespace_Name format a15 heading 'TABLESPACE'
col File_Name format a30 heading 'FILE NAME'

select Value
  from V$PARAMETER
 where Name = 'db_block_size';

set term on

select Tablespace_Name,
    File_Name,
    LPAD(DECODE(Maxblocks,0,' ',Maxblocks*&&blksz),15) Maxext,
    LPAD(DECODE(Increment_By,0,' ',Increment_By*&&blksz),10) Incr
  from DBA_DATA_FILES
 order by Tablespace_Name, File_Name
/
```

Sample output for the preceding query is shown here:

TABLESPACE	FILE NAME	MAXIMUM EXTENDED SIZE	EXTENSION INCREMENT
ROLLBACK_DATA	D:ORCL.ORA		
SYSTEM	D:ORCL.ORA	209715200	10485760
TEMPORARY_DATA	D:ORCL.ORA	157286400	5242880
USER_DATA	D:ORCL.ORA	157286400	5242880

ANNOTATIONS

The difference in the two code sections described above is shown in the following section of the **select** statement:

```
LPAD(DECODE(Maxblocks,0,' ',Maxblocks*&&blksz),15) Maxext,
LPAD(DECODE(Increment_By,0,' ',Increment_By*&&blksz),10) Incr
  from DBA_DATA_FILES
```

In this script, the **DECODE** function replaces the zero value in the nonextendable rows with a NULL to make the output more readable. The **LPAD** function inserts leading blanks to right-justify the numeric values.

If you allow Oracle8 to create the database for you (via the Oracle installer), the SYSTEM and temporary tablespaces will be created with **autoextend** on.

free_spc.sql

Free Space Within the Database

The queries in the preceding sections revealed the total amount of space allocated to the database and the greatest possible extension of each datafile. In this section, you will see queries that report on the free space within the database. Free space within datafiles has not yet been allocated by any extents in that datafile.

The following free space query uses the **from** clause subquery feature to group two queries separately and then join the result sets on the Tablespace_Name value. The query output will show the largest free extent in the tablespace, the number of free extents in the tablespace, the total free space in the tablespace, and the percentage of the tablespace's available space that is free.

```
REM free_spc.sql
column Tablespace_Name format A20
column Pct_Free format 999.99

select A.Tablespace_Name,
       B.Max_Blocks,
       B.Count_Blocks,
       B.Sum_Free_Blocks,
       100*B.Sum_Free_Blocks/A.Sum_Alloc_Blocks AS Pct_Free
  from (select Tablespace_Name, SUM(Blocks) Sum_Alloc_Blocks
          from DBA_DATA_FILES
         group by Tablespace_Name) A,
       (select Tablespace_Name FS_TS_NAME,
               MAX(Blocks) AS Max_Blocks,
               COUNT(Blocks) AS Count_Blocks,
               SUM(Blocks) AS Sum_Free_Blocks
          from DBA_FREE_SPACE
         group by Tablespace_Name) B
 where A.Tablespace_Name = FS_TS_NAME;
```

Sample output for the preceding query is shown here:

TABLESPACE_NAME	MAX_BLOCKS	COUNT_BLOCKS	SUM_FREE_BLOCKS	PCT_FREE
IDX1	487198	29	965726	94.36
RBS	452943	243	501343	97.97
SYSTEM	2763	4	3195	12.61
TEMP	460943	283	537086	100.00
TEMP_TABLES	634	1	634	49.53
USR1	293683	145	501372	48.99

The output shows the structure of the free space within each tablespace. In the USR1 tablespace, for example, there are 501,372 free database blocks (the Sum_Free_Blocks column). Those 501,372 blocks of free space are in 145 separate sections (the Count_ Blocks column). The largest single free extent is 293,683 blocks in length (the Max_ Blocks column). The free space within the USR1 tablespace accounts for 48.99 percent of the space in that tablespace (the Pct_Free column).

ANNOTATIONS

The query selects the tablespace name within each of the **from** clause subqueries. In the first **from** clause subquery, the Tablespace_Name column is selected from the DBA_DATA_FILES data dictionary view. An alias of Sum_Alloc_Blocks is given to the summation of the Blocks column in the DBA_DATA_FILES view. The Sum_ Alloc_Blocks column's value will reflect the total number of allocated blocks in the database.

```
from (select Tablespace_Name, SUM(Blocks) Sum_Alloc_Blocks
        from DBA_DATA_FILES
        group by Tablespace_Name) A,
```

The second query in the **from** clause selects free space statistics from the DBA_ FREE_SPACE view. In this query, the Tablespace_Name column is given the alias Fs_Ts_Name to avoid ambiguity with the Tablespace_Name column previously selected from the DBA_DATA_FILES data dictionary view. The maximum free extent size, number of free extents, and total free space statistics are selected and given aliases.

```
(select Tablespace_Name FS_TS_NAME,
        MAX(Blocks) AS Max_Blocks,
        COUNT(Blocks) AS Count_Blocks,
        SUM(Blocks) AS Sum_Free_Blocks
    from DBA_FREE_SPACE
  group by Tablespace_Name) B
```

The Sum_Free_Blocks column from the second **from** clause subquery, divided by the Sum_Alloc_Blocks from the first **from** clause subquery, generates the value for the Pct_Free for each tablespace:

```
100*B.Sum_Free_Blocks/A.Sum_Alloc_Blocks AS Pct_Free
```

The two Tablespace_Name values are joined; the Fs_Ts_Name alias assigned in the second **from** clause subquery provides the join value for the DBA_FREE_SPACE portion of the join.

```
where A.Tablespace_Name = FS_TS_NAME;
```

The Max_Blocks column lists the largest available extent in the tablespace. The Count_Blocks column value is the number of free extents in the tablespace. Sum_Free_Blocks is the total amount of space available in the tablespace. The Pct_Free column shows how close you are to needing to add another datafile to the tablespace. In the output in the following listing, the SYSTEM tablespace is dangerously low on space.

```
TABLESPACE_NAME   MAX_BLOCKS  COUNT_BLOCKS  SUM_FREE_BLOCKS  PCT_FREE
---------------   ----------  ------------  ---------------  --------
IDX1                  487198            29           965726     94.36
RBS                   452943           243           501343     97.97
SYSTEM                  2763             4             3195     12.61
TEMP                  460943           283           537086    100.00
TEMP_TABLES              634             1              634     49.53
USR1                  293683           145           501372     48.99
```

Rollback and temporary tablespaces will tend to have a high Pct_Free as the extents are released when not immediately needed for sorts and rollback segments.

Space Usage Within the Database by User

usr_quot.sql
issystem_def_temp_tblspc.sql
schema_obj_count.sql
user_dbspc_usage.sql

You can use the DBA_TS_QUOTAS view to display the allocated space, by user, in each tablespace, along with the space quota for each user. If a user has an unlimited quota in a tablespace, the quota will be displayed as a negative value. Querying DBA_TS_QUOTAS is a quick way to see which users own objects in which tablespaces and how close users are to their quotas. The following script queries the space quota and usage data from DBA_TS_QUOTAS:

```
REM usr_quot.sql

set heading on linesize 66
set pagesize 60 term off echo off feedback off
col Username format a20 heading 'USER'
col Tablespace_Name format a20 heading 'RESOURCE|TBS'
col Blocks format 999,999,999 heading 'USED|BLOCKS'
col Max_Blocks format 999,999,999 heading 'QUOTA|BLOCKS'
break on Username skip 1
ttitle center 'USER QUOTAS BY TABLESPACE'
btitle left 'QUOTA OF -1 SIGNIFIES UNLIMITED QUOTA'

select Username, Tablespace_Name, Blocks, Max_Blocks
  from DBA_TS_QUOTAS
 order by Username, Tablespace_Name
```

```
/
set linesize 24 pagesize 24 term on feedback 6
```

Sample output for the preceding query is shown here:

```
                        USER QUOTAS BY TABLESPACE
                  RESOURCE              USED        QUOTA
USER              TBS                 BLOCKS       BLOCKS
----------------- ----------------- ----------  -----------

DEMO              USR1               10,345          -1

QC_USER           IDX1               10,240          -1
                  USR1               23,855          -1

QUOTA OF -1 SIGNIFIES UNLIMITED QUOTA
```

The output shows, by user, the tablespaces in which resource quotas have been allocated or used. The quotas are expressed in database blocks. Because all the quotas in this example are –1, the users have unlimited resources available in the tablespaces.

In addition to determining the user quota in the various tablespaces, it is also useful to identify inappropriate use of tablespaces such as the SYSTEM tablespace. The following script issystem_def_temp_tblspc.sql can be used to determine the users that are currently using the SYSTEM tablespace as their default or temporary tablespace.

```
REM issystem_def_temp_tblspc.sql
REM This script can be used for Oracle7.x and above
REM This script can be used to determine users who have
REM     the SYSTEM tablespaces as their default
REM     and/or temporary tablespace.

ttitle center 'Users that have SYSTEM tablespace
               as DEFAULT and/or TEMPORARY'
col username heading "USER"
col usage heading "USES SYSTEM TABLESPACE AS" format a25
col ordercol noprint

select
  username,
  decode(default_tablespace,'SYSTEM',
   decode(temporary_tablespace,'SYSTEM', 'DEFAULT AND TEMPORARY',
                                          'DEFAULT'),
                        'TEMPORARY')  usage,
  decode(default_tablespace,'SYSTEM',
```

```
      decode(temporary_tablespace,'SYSTEM', 3, 1), 2)  ordercol
from  sys.dba_users
where
  default_tablespace = 'SYSTEM' or
  temporary_tablespace = 'SYSTEM'
order by ordercol
/
ttitle off
```

Sample output of running the preceding script is shown here.

```
    Users that have SYSTEM tablespace as DEFAULT and/or TEMPORARY
USER                           USES SYSTEM TABLESPACE AS
------------------------------ -------------------------
SYS                            DEFAULT
JIM                            TEMPORARY
HLB                            TEMPORARY
MSJ                            TEMPORARY
DBSNMP                         DEFAULT AND TEMPORARY
MEGH                           DEFAULT AND TEMPORARY
JKDEA                          DEFAULT AND TEMPORARY
MEGH1                          DEFAULT AND TEMPORARY
JKDEA2                         DEFAULT AND TEMPORARY
RRPETER                        DEFAULT AND TEMPORARY
```

ANNOTATIONS

The DBA_USERS data dictionary view contains information about the users in the
database and their default and temporary tablespaces.

```
ttitle center 'Users that have SYSTEM tablespace
                    as DEFAULT and/or TEMPORARY'
col username heading "USER"
col usage heading "USES SYSTEM TABLESPACE AS" format a25
col ordercol noprint

select
  username,
  decode(default_tablespace,'SYSTEM',
   decode(temporary_tablespace,'SYSTEM', 'DEFAULT AND TEMPORARY',
                                        'DEFAULT'),
                        'TEMPORARY')  usage,
  decode(default_tablespace,'SYSTEM',
```

```
    decode(temporary_tablespace,'SYSTEM', 3, 1), 2)   ordercol
from   sys.dba_users
```

The query issystem_def_temp_tblspc.sql selects the username, default_ tablespace, and temporary_tablespace from the DBA_USERS view. An additional "ordercol": column is defined, and **noprint** specifies that this column should not to be displayed. We use the ordercol column for sorting the results in a particular order. The **decode** function is used to determine whether the default and/or temporary tablespace for a user is SYSTEM.

```
decode(default_tablespace,'SYSTEM',
  decode(temporary_tablespace,'SYSTEM', 'DEFAULT AND TEMPORARY',
                                             'DEFAULT'),
                        'TEMPORARY')  usage,
```

The **decode** function is also used to specify the order of the result display. Here, results will be displayed in the following order: users using the SYSTEM tablespace as DEFAULT, followed by those using the SYSTEM tablespace as temporary, and finally those users who make use of SYSTEM tablespace as both DEFAULT and TEMPORARY.

```
decode(default_tablespace,'SYSTEM',
 decode(temporary_tablespace,'SYSTEM', 3, 1), 2)   ordercol
```

The **where** clause is used to focus on the SYSTEM tablepace only,

```
where
  default_tablespace = 'SYSTEM' or
  temporary_tablespace = 'SYSTEM'
```

and the results are ordered by the ordercol:

```
order by ordercol
```

The following script can be used to determine the type and count of the various objects that are owned by the user in the current database:

```
REM schema_obj_count.sql
REM This script can be used for Oracle7.x and above
REM This script can be used to determine the type and
REM      count of objects by user
REM

ttitle center 'Object type and count by user'

column owner format a18 trunc heading "SCHEMA"
column clu format 9999 heading "CLUSTERS"
column tab format 9999 heading "TABLES"
```

```
column idx format 9999 heading "INDEXES"
column seq format 9999 heading "SEQUENCES"
column trg format 9999 heading "TRIGGERS"
column fnc format 9999 heading "FUNCTIONS"
column pro format 9999 heading "PROCEDURES"
column pac format 9999 heading "PACKAGES"
column pab format 9999 heading "PACKAGE|BODIES"
column dbl format 9999 heading "DATABASE|LINKS"
column viw format 9999 heading "VIEWS"
column syn format 999999 heading "SYNONYMS"
column oth format 999999 heading "OTHER"
break on report
compute sum of clu tab idx seq trg fnc pro pac viw syn oth
          on report

set feedback off heading on pagesize 50

select owner,
       sum(decode(object_type,'CLUSTER',1,0)) clu,
       sum(decode(object_type,'TABLE',1,0)) tab,
       sum(decode(object_type,'INDEX',1,0)) idx,
       sum(decode(object_type,'SEQUENCE',1,0)) seq,
       sum(decode(object_type,'TRIGGER',1,0)) trg,
       sum(decode(object_type,'FUNCTION',1,0)) fnc,
       sum(decode(object_type,'PROCEDURE',1,0)) pro,
       sum(decode(object_type,'PACKAGE',1,0)) pac,
       sum(decode(object_type,'PACKAGE BODY',1,0)) pab,
       sum(decode(object_type,'DATABASE LINK',1,0)) dbl,
       sum(decode(object_type,'VIEW',1,0)) viw,
       sum(decode(object_type,'SYNONYM',1,0)) syn,
       sum(decode(object_type,'CLUSTER',0,
                             'TABLE',0,
                             'INDEX',0,
                             'SEQUENCE',0,
                             'TRIGGER',0,
                             'FUNCTION',0,
                             'PROCEDURE',0,
                             'PACKAGE',0,
                             'PACKAGE BODY',0,
                             'DATABASE LINK',0,
                             'VIEW',0,
                             'SYNONYM',0,
                             1)) oth
```

```
from dba_objects
group by owner
order by
    decode(owner, 'SYS', 1, 'SYSTEM', 2, 'PUBLIC', 3, 4),
    owner
/
ttitle off
clear breaks
clear computes
```

This script retrieves the object_type of each object from the DBA_OBJECTS view, and the **decode** function is applied on the object_type to determine its type: for example,

```
decode(object_type,'TABLE',1,0)
```

After the object type is determined, the objects are grouped by owner and are counted.

```
sum(decode(object_type,'CLUSTER',1,0)) clu,
    sum(decode(object_type,'TABLE',1,0)) tab,
    sum(decode(object_type,'INDEX',1,0)) idx,
    sum(decode(object_type,'SEQUENCE',1,0)) seq,
    sum(decode(object_type,'TRIGGER',1,0)) trg,
    sum(decode(object_type,'FUNCTION',1,0)) fnc,
    sum(decode(object_type,'PROCEDURE',1,0)) pro,
    sum(decode(object_type,'PACKAGE',1,0)) pac,
    sum(decode(object_type,'PACKAGE BODY',1,0)) pab,
    sum(decode(object_type,'DATABASE LINK',1,0)) dbl,
    sum(decode(object_type,'VIEW',1,0)) viw,
    sum(decode(object_type,'SYNONYM',1,0)) syn,
    sum(decode(object_type,'CLUSTER',0,
                          'TABLE',0,
                          'INDEX',0,
                          'SEQUENCE',0,
                          'TRIGGER',0,
                          'FUNCTION',0,
                          'PROCEDURE',0,
                          'PACKAGE',0,
                          'PACKAGE BODY',0,
                          'DATABASE LINK',0,
                          'VIEW',0,
                          'SYNONYM',0,
                          1)) oth
```

```
from dba_objects
group by owner
```

The results are ordered by the owner in a specific order: SYS, SYSTEM, PUBLIC, and then alphabetically in ascending order.

```
order by
    decode(owner, 'SYS', 1, 'SYSTEM', 2, 'PUBLIC', 3, 4),
    owner
```

Sample output of running the script schema_obj_count.sql on an Oracle9i database is shown here:

Object type and count by user

SCHEMA	CLUSTERS	TABLES	INDEXES	SEQUENCES	TRIGGERS	FUNCTIONS	PROCEDURES	PACKAGES	PACKAGE BODIES	DATABASE LINKS	VIEWS	SYNONYMS	OTHER
SYS	10	290	279	38	3	29	20	269	262	0	1816	6	396
SYSTEM	0	125	145	20	2	2	4	1	1	2	12	8	61
PUBLIC	0	0	0	0	0	0	0	0	0	0	0	1658	0
MT	1	1	1	0	0	0	1	0	0	0	0	0	0
DBSNMP	0	0	0	0	0	0	0	0	0	0	0	4	0
XT	0	7	19	3	2	0	2	0	0	0	1	0	0
S123456	0	5	0	0	0	0	1	1	1	0	22	0	0
S202018	0	5	0	0	0	0	1	1	1	0	23	0	0

```
S1234                    0         5         0            0         0         0
              1         1         1         0        23         0         0

S92783                   0         5         0            0         0         0
              1         1         1         0        22         0         0

MTMON                    0         5         0            0         0         0
              1         1         1         0        17         0         0

OUTLN                    0         3         3            0         0         0
              1         0         0         0         0         0         0

Q12345DEV                0         7         5            2         1         4
              0         0         0         1         2         0         0

Q12345PROD               0         4         4            2         1         4
              0         0         0         2         2         0         0

R1028                    0        19         8            1         0         4
              7         2         2         0         2         0         0

S29301                   0       194       186           19         0         2
              0        25        25         0         9         0         0

SCOTT                    0         5         0            0         0         0
              0         0         0         0         0         0         0

SH                       0         3         3            0         0         0
              0         0         0         0         0         0         3

SOO                      0         5         0            0         0         0
              1         1         1         0        22         0         0

S89201                   0         0         0            0         0         0
              0         0         0         0         0         1         0

AUSIM                    0        14         2            0         0         0
              1         1         1         0         0         0        90


sum                     11       702       655           85         9        45
             42       304                      1973      1677       550
```

Frequently, you may want to determine the amount of space used by various users in the entire database. This script will also allow you to determine the data distribution for a particular user in the various tablespaces.

```
REM user_dbspc_usage.sql
REM This script can be used for Oracle7.x and above
REM This script reports the database space used by each user
REM

ttitle center "Database Space Usage"
break on un skip 2

col un format a20 heading "User Name"
col tb format a30 heading "Tablespace Name"
col ks format 999,999,999 heading "Size (in KBytes)"
set pagesize 50



select
        u.name un,
        t.name tb,
        sum(s.blocks*t.blocksize)/1024 ks
from
        sys.user$ u,
        sys.ts$ t,
        sys.seg$ s
where
        s.user# = u.user# and
        t.ts# = s.ts#
 group by u.name, t.name
 order by
    decode(u.name, 'SYS', 1, 'SYSTEM', 2, 'PUBLIC', 3, 4),
    u.name;
ttitle off
clear breaks
```

Sample output of running the script on an Oracle9i database is shown here:

```
                        Database Space Usage
User Name             Tablespace Name               Size (in KBytes)
-------------------   --------------------------    ----------------
SYS                   SYSTEM                               136,384
                      UNDOTBS                                  640
```

SYSTEM	SYSTEM	3,764
	USERS	64
MT	BB	192
H1	EXAMPLE	25,600
	USERS	300,000
	UZERS	50,000
H12345	USERS	320
H23456	USERS	320

The output shows that user H1 uses a large amount of space in the database in three tablespaces: EXAMPLE, USERS, and UZERS. (If you experience a lot of I/O contention, you might want to move some objects from the USERS tablespace to other tablespaces.) The preceding result is sorted by username and that, too, appears in a particular order: SYS, SYSTEM, PUBLIC, and the others.

```
order by
  decode(u.name, 'SYS', 1, 'SYSTEM', 2, 'PUBLIC', 3, 4),
  u.name;
```

Default Storage for Objects

def_stor.sql
tab_part_storage.sqlzz

Unless you include the **storage** clause when executing a **create** statement, an object will be created with the default storage parameters of the tablespace in which it is created. To see the default storage by tablespace, run the following SQL statement:

```
REM def_stor.sql

col Tablespace_Name format a20
col Pct_Increase format 999 heading 'PCT|INCR'
select Tablespace_Name,
       Initial_Extent,
       Next_Extent,
       Min_Extents,
       Max_Extents,
```

```
        Pct_Increase
  from DBA_TABLESPACES;
```

Sample output for the preceding query is shown in the following listing:

					PCT
TABLESPACE	INITIAL_EXTENT	NEXT_EXTENT	MIN_EXTENTS	MAX_EXTENTS	INCR
SYSTEM	12288	12288	1	249	50
RBS	819200	819200	20	249	0
TEMP	819200	8192000	1	249	0
USR1	20480	20480	1	2147483645	50
TEMP_TABLES	20480	20480	1	249	50
IDX1	20480	20480	1	249	50

The output shows the default storage parameters (such as the initial extent size) for any new segment created. The storage parameters specified during object creation override the tablespaces' default values. Changing the default parameters does not affect the storage parameters of previously created objects.

ANNOTATIONS

If a tablespace is created without the **default storage** clause, the **initial** and **next** extent sizes default to 5 blocks and the **pctincrease** defaults to 50 percent. As of Oracle7, it is possible to set the rollback segment maximum extents to UNLIMITED, although in practice this defaults to 2,147,483,645.

Beginning with Oracle7.3. you can designate a tablespace as either PERMANENT or TEMPORARY. All tablespaces are created as PERMANENT by default. A tablespace whose contents are designated as TEMPORARY can contain only temporary segments. Dedicating a tablespace to temporary segments can improve sorting performance if your application frequently uses temporary segments for sorting, as the temporary segments do not disappear once the sort is done. Tablespaces designated as TEMPORARY should also have **initial** and **next** extent sizes that are equal, as well as a **pctincrease** of 0. This will result in identically sized segments and will ensure reusability of the extents after the temporary segment is dropped.

To check the status and contents of a tablespace, run the following query:

```
select Tablespace_Name,
       Status,
       Contents
  from DBA_TABLESPACES;
```

The output is shown here:

```
TABLESPACE_NAME STATUS    CONTENTS
--------------- --------- ---------
SYSTEM          ONLINE    PERMANENT
RBS             ONLINE    PERMANENT
TEMP            ONLINE    TEMPORARY
USR1            ONLINE    PERMANENT
TEMP_TABLES     ONLINE    PERMANENT
IDX1            ONLINE    PERMANENT
```

As with the DBA_DATA_FILES view, the DBA_TABLESPACES view has been modified for Oracle8 to provide more information.

Several of the additional columns that were introduced with Oracle8. are as follows:

- **MIN_EXTLEN** Ensures that every used and/or free extent size in the tablespace is at least as large as and is a multiple of this value. This parameter is used to control free space fragmentation.

- **LOGGING** Defines whether or not certain DML (Data Manipulation Language) and DDL (Data Definition Language) operations are logged. Operations that can support **nologging** are

  - **DML** direct-load INSERT and Direct path SQL*Loader
  - **DDL** create table ... as select; create index; alter index ... rebuild; alter index ... rebuild partition; alter index ... split partition; alter table ... split partition; and alter table ... move partition

In general, operations that are simpler and faster to re-create from the beginning are ideal candidates for **nologging**. The **logging** attribute of a tablespace can be overridden for tables, indexes, and partitions, just as the **storage** parameters can be. Changing the **logging** attribute of a tablespace does not affect the **logging** attributes of existing objects within the tablespace.

To view the new columns, modify the previous query to read as follows:

```
select Tablespace_Name,
       Contents,
       Logging
from DBA_TABLESPACES;
```

The output of the modified query is shown here:

```
TABLESPACE_NAME  CONTENTS   LOGGING
---------------  ---------  ---------
SYSTEM           PERMANENT  LOGGING
USER_DATA        PERMANENT  LOGGING
ROLLBACK_DATA    PERMANENT  LOGGING
TEMPORARY_DATA   TEMPORARY  NOLOGGING
```

As the name indicates, the tablespace TEMPORARY_DATA can contain only temporary segments, and, because temporary segments do not contain data needed for recovery, the tablespace has been set to **nologging**.

As of Oracle8.x, you can partition tables and indexes. Partitioning provides a number of advantages such as ease of management, backups and recovery, and performance improvement. The storage parameters (initial, next, minextents, maxextents, pctincrease, freelists, and freelist groups) for partitions, first default to the corresponding default parameters for the table. If default storage parameters do not exist for the table (values are DEFAULT), the parameters default to the storage parameters of the tablespace hosting the partition. For a partitioned table, the default storage parameters can be found in the DBA_PART_TABLES data dictionary view (the columns DEF_INITIAL_EXTENT, DEF_NEXT_EXTENT, DEF_MIN_EXTENTS, DEF_MAX_EXTENTS, DEF_PCT_INCREASE, DEF_FREELISTS, and DEF_FREELIST_GROUPS). The default storage parameters for a partitioned indexes can be obtained by querying the corresponding columns of DBA_PART_INDEXES.

The CREATE TABLE statement can be used to set the default storage parameters for all parameters referenced. These default storage parameters can be changed using the **MODIFY DEFAULT ATTRIBUTES** clause of the ALTER TABLE statement. All storage parameters that have not been explicitly defined in the CREATE TABLE statement will have default values of DEFAULT after table creation. It should be noted that the default storage parameters for a partitioned table impact only new partitions (partitions added after the default value was established). The following script, tab_part_storage.sql, can be used to determine the default storage parameters as well as the current storage parameters for all the partitions of the specified partitioned table:

```
REM tab_part_storage.sql
REM This script can be used in Oracle8.1.x and above
REM For Oracle8.0.x, the script can be modified by
REM      removing the references to sub-partitioning.
REM This script can be used to determine the default
REM      storage parameters for a partitioned table as well
REM      as the current        storage settings for
REM         its partitions
REM
```

```
set linesize 100 pagesize 50
ttitle off


col partitioning_type heading "part_type" trunc format a8
col subpartitioning_type heading "subpart_type" trunc format a8
REM For 8.0.x remove the preceding line
col def_tablespace_name heading "d_tblspc" trunc format a10
col def_pct_used heading "d_pctused" trunc format 999
col def_pct_free heading "d_pctfree" trunc format 999
col def_initial_extent heading "d_iniext" trunc format 999999
col def_next_extent heading "d_nxtext" trunc format 999999
col def_pct_increase heading "d_pctincr" trunc format 9999
col def_min_extents heading "d_minexts" trunc format 9999
col def_max_extents heading "d_maxexts" trunc format 999999999999
col def_freelists heading "d_freelsts" trunc format 9999
col def_freelist_groups heading "d_freelgrps" trunc format 9999


col partition_name heading "part_name" trunc format a12
col tablespace_name heading "tspace_name" trunc format a10
col pct_used heading "pctused" trunc format 999
col pct_free heading "pctfree" trunc format 999
col initial_extent heading "iniext" trunc format 999999
col next_extent heading "nxtext" trunc format 999999
col pct_increase heading "pctincr" trunc format 9999
col min_extent heading "minexts" trunc format 9999
col max_extent heading "maxexts" trunc format 999999999999
col freelists heading "freelsts" trunc format 9999
col freelist_groups heading "freelgrps" trunc format 9999
col blocks heading "blks" trunc format 999999999
col empty_blocks heading "emp_blks" trunc format 999999999
col avg_space heading "avg_spc" trunc format 999999999


set verify off term on feedback off echo off

accept own prompt 'Enter Owner: '
accept tabname prompt 'Enter Table Name: '

prompt **************************
prompt Default storage information
prompt **************************
```

```
select partitioning_type,
       subpartitioning_type,
REM For 8.0.x remove the preceding line
       def_tablespace_name,
       def_pct_used,
       def_pct_free,
       def_initial_extent,
       def_next_extent,
       def_pct_increase,
       def_min_extents,
       def_max_extents,
       def_freelists,
       def_freelist_groups
from dba_part_tables
where owner = UPPER('&&own') and
       table_name = UPPER('&&tabname');

 prompt **************
 prompt Partion storage
 prompt **************

 select partition_name,
        tablespace_name,
        pct_used,
        pct_free,
        initial_extent,
        next_extent,
        pct_increase,
        min_extent,
        max_extent,
        freelists,
        freelist_groups,
        blocks,
        empty_blocks,
        avg_space
   from dba_tab_partitions
   where table_owner = UPPER('&&own') and
         table_name = UPPER('&&tabname');
undefine own
undefine tabname
set verify on term off feedback 6 linesize 80
```

The query asks for the owner and the name of the partitioned table. These inputs are used to query DBA_PART_TABLES to obtain the default storage parameters, and then the DBA_TAB_PARTITIONS view is queried to determine the current storage settings of all the partitions of the particular partitioned table.

Sample output of the above script is shown here:

```
Enter Owner: system
Enter Table Name: mtest_part
***************************
Default storage information
***************************

part_typ subpart_ d_tblspc   d_pctused d_pctfree d_iniext
-------- -------- ---------- --------- --------- --------------

d_nxtext                                d_pctincr
--------------------------------------- ----------------------

d_minexts                               d_maxexts
 d_freelsts
--------------------------------------- ----------------------

d_freelgrps
-----------
RANGE    NONE    SYSTEM              40        10 DEFAULT
2                                       DEFAULT
DEFAULT                                 DEFAULT
  0
          0


*****************
Partition storage
*****************

part_name    tspace_nam pctused pctfree iniext  nxtext  pctincr
 minexts        maxexts freelsts
------------ ---------- ------- ------- ------- ------- -------
------- ------------- --------
freelgrps       blks    emp_blks        avg_spc

--------- ----------   --------- ----------

P1             USERS01       40      10   65536
       1  2147483645       1
          1
P2             USERS02       20      20   65536
       1  2147483645       1
          1
```

The output shows that the table mtest_part uses RANGE-based partition. The default storage settings for the table are different from the current storage settings of partitions P1 and P2.

Segment Space Usage

seg_spac.sql
obj_size_7.sql
obj_size_8.sql

In addition to knowing how much space a tablespace and its associated datafiles are using, you should monitor and track the individual segment sizes within the database. The following query will display, by selected user, the segment name, tablespace it resides in, type of segment, allocated size of the segment in both bytes and blocks, number of extents allocated to the segment, and size of the next extent to be allocated when needed.

```
REM seg_spac.sql

col Segment_Name format a20
col Segment_Type format a5 heading 'TYPE'
col Tablespace_Name format a10 heading 'TABLESPACE'
col Bytes format 999,999,999
col Blocks format 9,999,999
col Extents format 999,999
col Next_Extent format 999,999,999
set linesize 100 pagesize 60

select Segment_Name,
       Segment_Type,
       Tablespace_Name,
       Bytes,
       Blocks,
       Extents,
       Next_Extent
  from DBA_SEGMENTS
 where Owner = UPPER('&owner')
 order by Segment_Name;
set linesize 80 pagesize 24
```

Sample output for the preceding query is shown next:

```
SEGMENT_NAME          TYPE  TABLESPACE          BYTES       BLOCKS
    EXTENTS   NEXT_EXTENT
------------------- ----- ---------- ------------- -----------
-------- ------------
```

			Bytes	Blocks
BRANCH	TABLE	USR1	20,480	5
1	20,480			
CARDHOLDER	TABLE	USR1	1,761,280	430
10	860,160			
CH_IDX	INDEX	USR1	348,160	85
6	167,936			
CK_LOG	TABLE	USR1	20,480	5
1	20,480			
DEPTREE_TEMPTAB	TABLE	USR1	20,480	5
1	20,480			
HOLIDAY	TABLE	USR1	20,480	5
1	20,480			
PK_CH_ACCT	INDEX	USR1	348,160	85
6	167,936			
PK_TRANSACTION	INDEX	USR1	20,480	5
1	20,480			
PK_TRANS_ID	INDEX	USR1	348,160	85
6	167,936			
RANDOMNESS	TABLE	USR1	1,269,760	310
60	20,480			
TEMPOPRIV	TABLE	USR1	2,621,440	640
11	1,290,240			
TEMPSPRIV	TABLE	USR1	20,480	5
1	20,480			
TRANSACTION	TABLE	USR1	20,480	5
1	20,480			

Segments are objects that take up physical space within the database. The Bytes column lists the number of bytes the segment is currently allocated within the tablespace. The Blocks column lists the number of database blocks allocated. The Extents column contains the number of extents allocated to the segment. In general, it is more efficient to keep the number of extents small. The Next_Extent column lists the number of contiguous bytes that will be needed the next time the segment needs more space. In the preceding example, the TEMPOPRIV table will need an extent of 1,290,240 bytes, and the request may fail, depending on how fragmented the tablespace is.

ANNOTATIONS

On running the seg_spac.sql query, the user will be prompted for the name of the segment owner to populate the &*owner* variable. To run this query for all users in the database, remove the **where** clause

```
where Owner = UPPER('&owner')
```

and change the **order by** to

```
order by Owner, Segment_Name
```

If you run the report for multiple owners, you should add the following **break** for readability:

```
break on Owner
```

You can list segments within a tablespace in descending order of size to determine whether enough space exists in the tablespace for growth and to determine whether an object should be moved to another tablespace. To list the segments in descending order of size, change the **order by** clause to

```
order by Next_Extent desc, Segment_Name
```

PROGRAMMER'S NOTE   *If you are planning to run the report script for multiple owners, you might want to add the 'OWNER' column to the select list, else you won't know who owns the segment.*

If you are running the report for multiple owners, you must add the 'OWNER' column to the **order by** clause, as shown in the following listing. This report may become extremely lengthy, depending on the number of owners and the number of segments each owner has.

```
order by Owner, Next_Extent desc, Segment_Name
```

The initial output, re-run with the **order by** Next_Extent desc, Segment_Name clause is shown in the following listing:

```
SEGMENT_NAME          TYPE  TABLESPACE        BYTES      BLOCKS
  EXTENTS   NEXT_EXTENT
------------------- ----- ---------- ------------ -----------
-------- ------------
TEMPOPRIV             TABLE USR1            2,621,440        640
```

11	1,290,240			
CARDHOLDER		TABLE USR1	1,761,280	430
10	860,160			
CH_IDX		INDEX USR1	348,160	85
6	167,936			
PK_CH_ACCT		INDEX USR1	348,160	85
6	167,936			
PK_TRANS_ID		INDEX USR1	348,160	85
6	167,936			
BRANCH		TABLE USR1	20,480	5
1	20,480			
CK_LOG		TABLE USR1	20,480	5
1	20,480			
DEPTREE_TEMPTAB		TABLE USR1	20,480	5
1	20,480			
HOLIDAY		TABLE USR1	20,480	5
1	20,480			
PK_TRANSACTION		INDEX USR1	20,480	5
1	20,480			
RANDOMNESS		TABLE USR1	1,269,760	310
60	20,480			
TEMPSPRIV		TABLE USR1	20,480	5
1	20,480			
TRANSACTION		TABLE USR1	20,480	5
1	20,480			

In general, you should keep all the data in a table within one extent. The more extents a segment has, the more work is involved in retrieving data and administering it. A table can be resized via the Export/Import utilities using the COMPRESS=Y flag. Compressing a table via Export/Import will result in a table with a single extent equal to the allocated size of the original table. If there are no free extents in the tablespace that can support the compressed size of the segment, the Import command will fail when it attempts to create the table. In such cases, you will not be able to compress the extents unless you create a large enough free extent by adding a new datafile, extending an existing datafile, or reorganizing the entire tablespace to compress free extents.

The following script can be used to report the size of all the stored objects in your database:

```
REM obj_size_7.sql
REM This script can be used for Oracle7.x only
REM Report on the size of stored objects
REM
```

```
set verify off heading on feedback off
col ow format a18 heading 'Owner' noprint
col ty format a10 heading 'Type'
col na format a30 heading 'Name'
col ks format 999,999,999 heading 'Size (in KBytes)'
compute sum of ks on ow

define code_tables = "('ARGUMENT$','DEPENDENCY$','SOURCE$',
    'IDL_SB4$','IDL_UB4$','IDL_UB2$','IDL_CHAR$',
    'IDL_UB1$','PSTUBTBL')"

spool obj_size.lst

 prompt ********************
 prompt Table and Index size
 prompt ********************


select  us.name ow, 'Table' ty, obj.name na,
        seg.blocks*db.value/1024 ks
from    sys.user$ us,
        sys.obj$ obj,
        sys.seg$ seg,
        sys.tab$ tab,
        (select value
         from v$parameter
         where name = 'db_block_size') db
where   us.user# = seg.user#
and     obj.obj# = tab.obj#
and     tab.file# = seg.file#
and     tab.block# = seg.block#
and     tab.clu# is null
and     obj.name in &code_tables
union
select  us.name ow, '  Index' ty, tab.name||'/'||obj.name na1,
        seg.blocks*db.value/1024 ks
from    sys.user$ us,
        sys.obj$ obj,
        sys.obj$ tab,
        sys.seg$ seg,
        sys.ind$ ind,
        (select value
         from v$parameter
```

```
          where name = 'db_block_size') db
where    us.user#  = seg.user#
and      obj.obj#  = ind.obj#
and      ind.bo#   = tab.obj#
and      ind.file# = seg.file#
and      ind.block# = seg.block#
and      tab.name in &code_tables
order by 1,3
/

 prompt ***************************
 prompt Size of other stored objects
 prompt ***************************

select count(name) num_instances,
       type,
       sum(source_size)+sum(parsed_size)
           +sum(code_size)+sum(error_size) total_size
from dba_object_size
group by type
order by 2
/
spool off
undefine code_tables
clear computes
set verify on feedback 6
```

This script can be used only for Oracle7.x. An equivalent script that can be used for Oracle8.x and above is shown here:

```
REM obj_size_8.sql
REM This script can be used for Oracle8.x and above
REM Report on the size of stored objects
REM

set verify off heading on feedback off
col ow format a18 heading 'Owner' noprint
col ty format a10 heading 'Type'
col na format a30 heading 'Name'
col ks format 999,999,999 heading 'Size (in KBytes)'
compute sum of ks on ow

define code_tables = "('ARGUMENT$','DEPENDENCY$','SOURCE$',
    'IDL_SB4$','IDL_UB4$','IDL_UB2$','IDL_CHAR$',
```

```
      'IDL_UB1$','PSTUBTBL')"

spool obj_size.lst

 prompt *******************
 prompt Table and Index size
 prompt *******************


select  us.name ow, 'Table' ty, obj.name na,
        seg.blocks*db.value/1024 ks
from    sys.user$ us,
        sys.obj$ obj,
        sys.seg$ seg,
        sys.tab$ tab,
        (select value
          from v$parameter
          where name = 'db_block_size') db
where   us.user# = seg.user#
and     obj.obj# = tab.obj#
and     tab.file# = seg.file#
and     tab.block# = seg.block#
and     obj.name in &code_tables
union
select  us.name ow, '   Index' ty, tab.name||'/'||obj.name na1,
        seg.blocks*db.value/1024 ks
from    sys.user$ us,
        sys.obj$ obj,
        sys.obj$ tab,
        sys.seg$ seg,
        sys.ind$ ind,
        (select value
          from v$parameter
          where name = 'db_block_size') db
where   us.user# = seg.user#
and     obj.obj# = ind.obj#
and     ind.bo#  = tab.obj#
and     ind.file# = seg.file#
and     ind.block# = seg.block#
and     tab.name in &code_tables
order by 1,3
/
```

```
prompt ****************************
prompt Size of other stored objects
prompt ****************************

select count(name) num_instances,
       type,
       sum(source_size)+sum(parsed_size)
       +sum(code_size)+sum(error_size) total_size
from dba_object_size
group by type
order by 2
/
spool off
undefine code_tables
clear computes
set verify on feedback 6
```

PROGRAMMER'S NOTE   *The Oracle8 scripts obj_size_7.sql and obj_size_8.sql assume that the database block size is consistent across tablespaces. In Oracle9.x and later, you can change the database block size at the tablespace level. Refer to Chapter 1 for an example of how to deal with variable block size in Oracle9.x and above.*

Sample output of running the previous script against an Oracle8.x database is shown next:

```
********************
Table and Index size
********************
```

Type	Name	Size (in KBytes)
Table	ARGUMENT$	3,910
Index	ARGUMENT$/I_ARGUMENT1	4,010
Table	DEPENDENCY$	1,710
Index	DEPENDENCY$/I_DEPENDENCY1	1,510
Index	DEPENDENCY$/I_DEPENDENCY2	1,510
Table	IDL_CHAR$	2,510
Index	IDL_CHAR$/I_IDL_CHAR1	376
Table	IDL_SB4$	4,710
Index	IDL_SB4$/I_IDL_SB41	856
Table	IDL_UB1$	43,510
Index	IDL_UB1$/I_IDL_UB11	848

```
Type          Name                                Size (in KBytes)
----------    -------------------------------     ----------------
Table         IDL_UB2$                                     24,112
   Index      IDL_UB2$/I_IDL_UB21                             848
Table         PSTUBTBL                                        10
Table         SOURCE$                                     119,010
   Index      SOURCE$/I_SOURCE1                            37,810


****************************
Size of other stored objects
****************************

NUM_INSTANCES TYPE            TOTAL_SIZE
------------- -------------   ----------
          567 FUNCTION           4683745
          797 PACKAGE            7931112
          775 PACKAGE BODY      94459322
          411 PROCEDURE          6508420
          259 SEQUENCE             68659
          101 SYNONYM              16752
         3375 TABLE             4248364
            7 TYPE                  3945
          315 VIEW               221422
```

ANNOTATIONS

The script obj_size_8.sql (as well as obj_size_7.sql) query the v$parameter view to determine the database block size.

```
(select value
        from v$parameter
        where name = 'db_block_size') db
```

The sys.user$, sys.obj$, sys.seg$, and sys.tab$ tables are queried to determine the object sizes. The **code_tables** variable is used to specify the list of tables and indexes whose sizes need to be determined. You can change the list to indicate other objects as well.

```
select  us.name ow, 'Table' ty, obj.name na,
        seg.blocks*db.value/1024 ks
from    sys.user$ us,
```

```
            sys.obj$ obj,
            sys.seg$ seg,
            sys.tab$ tab,
            (select value
             from sys.v_$parameter
             where name = 'db_block_size') db
where       us.user# = seg.user#
and         obj.obj# = tab.obj#
and         tab.file# = seg.file#
and         tab.block# = seg.block#
and         obj.name in &code_tables
union
select      us.name ow, '  Index' ty, tab.name||'/'||obj.name na1,
            seg.blocks*db.value/1024 ks
from        sys.user$ us,
            sys.obj$ obj,
            sys.obj$ tab,
            sys.seg$ seg,
            sys.ind$ ind,
            (select value
             from sys.v_$parameter
             where name = 'db_block_size') db
where       us.user# = seg.user#
and         obj.obj# = ind.obj#
and         ind.bo#  = tab.obj#
and         ind.file# = seg.file#
and         ind.block# = seg.block#
and         tab.name in &code_tables
```

The DB_OBJECT_SIZE view is queried to determine the size of other stored objects, such as functions, packages, and so on, and the result is grouped by the type of object.

```
select count(name) num_instances,
       type,
       sum(source_size)+sum(parsed_size)
       +sum(code_size)+sum(error_size) total_size
from dba_object_size
group by type
order by 2
```

In these queries, the database block size is used to convert the blocks to object size (in KB).

```
seg.blocks*db.value/1024 ks
```

seg_info.sql

Extents Showing Increasing Extent Size and Location

In addition to monitoring the overall space usage of a segment, you can monitor how the extents are allocated and the size of each extent. The following queries list the default storage for a segment and all the extents allocated to this segment. When you execute these queries, you will be prompted for values for the *owner* and *segment_name* variables.

```
REM seg_info.sql

undefine owner
undefine segment_name
set verify off
select Segment_Name,
       Initial_Extent,
       Next_Extent,
       Pct_Increase
  from DBA_SEGMENTS
 where Segment_Name = UPPER('&&segment_name')
   and Owner=UPPER('&&owner');

select Tablespace_Name,
       File_ID,
       Block_ID,
       Blocks
  from DBA_EXTENTS
 where Owner = UPPER('&&owner')
   and Segment_Name = UPPER('&&segment_name')
 order by File_ID, Block_ID;

undefine owner
undefine segment_name
```

Sample output for the script is shown here:

SEGMENT_NAME	INITIAL_EXTENT	NEXT_EXTENT	PCT_INCREASE
RANDOMNESS	20480	860,160	50

TABLESPACE_NAME	FILE_ID	BLOCK_ID	BLOCKS
USR1	4	53123	45

USR1	4	53168	65
USR1	4	53233	95
USR1	4	132321	5
USR1	5	37995	5
USR1	5	38000	15
USR1	5	38015	20
USR1	5	38035	35
USR1	5	64164	140

This output shows the results for the query when run for a database user who owns a segment named RANDOMNESS. The result of the first query in the script shows that the segment's extent size increases by 50 percent with each extension. The initial extent size is 20,480 bytes—20 KB. The database block size for this example is 4KB, so the initial extent is 5 blocks in size. The 5KB entry in the second query's output is the first extent of the segment.

The segment's **next** extent value must have initially been set at 20KB (5 blocks). The segment's second extent is 5 blocks in size. The segment's third extent should be 50 percent greater than 5 blocks—7.5 blocks. However, Oracle will never allocate fractions of blocks, and usually rounds up block sizes to the nearest multiple of five (to improve the chances for reusing dropped extents). Therefore, the third extent should be 10 blocks in size. However, in this case, Oracle has found a free extent of 15 blocks available. Instead of taking 10 of those blocks and leaving only 5, Oracle allocates all 15 blocks.

Because the table's **pctincrease** value is non-zero, the segment's extent sizes increase in a geometric fashion after the second extent has been allocated. The initial extent size is only 20,480 bytes. The next extent to be allocated (and the tenth overall for the segment) will be 860,160 bytes!

ANNOTATIONS

The first query is run to show the initial extent size, next extent size, and percent increase for the segment. If this query is not run, the implications of the second query's output are difficult to interpret. Without knowing the **pctincrease** set for the segment, you cannot estimate the growth pattern of that segment.

Before the first query is executed, any previous settings for the *owner* and *segment_name* variables are undefined. The **set verify off** command eliminates the writing of "old" and "new" values to the output every time a value is substituted for a variable. The variables are defined with double ampersands (&&) so the user will not be prompted for the same values multiple times. The **undefine** commands are repeated at the end of the script so that any values assigned to the variables will be undefined for the rest of the user's session.

```
undefine owner
undefine segment_name
```

```
set verify off

select Segment_Name,
       Initial_Extent,
       Next_Extent,
       Pct_Increase
  from DBA_SEGMENTS
 where Segment_Name = UPPER('&&segment_name')
   and Owner=UPPER('&&owner');
```

The second query extracts the locations and sizes of the extents in the segment.

```
select Tablespace_Name,
       File_ID,
       Block_ID,
       Blocks
  from DBA_EXTENTS
 where Owner = UPPER('&&owner')
   and Segment_Name = UPPER('&&segment_name')
 order by File_ID, Block_ID;
```

The output from the second query shows that the segment's extents are stored in two separate files: four extents in file 4 and five extents in file 5.

SEGMENT_NAME	INITIAL_EXTENT	NEXT_EXTENT	PCT_INCREASE
RANDOMNESS	20480	860,160	50

TABLESPACE_NAME	FILE_ID	BLOCK_ID	BLOCKS
USR1	4	53123	45
USR1	4	53168	65
USR1	4	53233	95
USR1	4	132321	5
USR1	5	37995	5
USR1	5	38000	15
USR1	5	38015	20
USR1	5	38035	35
USR1	5	64164	140

Looking at the listing, there is no way to determine which file will be used to store the next extent of the table. You can tell how large the next extent will be (via the Next_Extent value in the first query's output), but there is no discernible pattern to the file assignments for the extent allocations. By allowing the table to extend, and by using a non-zero value for **pctincrease**, the table owner has given up the ability to predictably manage space allocation for the table.

Temporary Segments Size

temp_seg.sql

During operations that involve sorts (such as index creations or **order by** operations), Oracle allocates space in memory to perform the sort. The memory area used to perform the sort is called the *sort area*. If the sort area is not large enough to store all of the data used for the sort, the sort data is written to a disk area called a *temporary segment*. The temporary segment is dropped when the sort is completed unless you have designated the tablespace as a TEMPORARY tablespace. If you designate a tablespace as a TEMPORARY tablespace, the temporary segment is not dropped after the sort operation has completed.

While a sort is underway, you can view information about its temporary segment by querying the DBA_SEGMENTS data dictionary view. The following query will list the current size and number of extents for each of the temporary segments currently in use in your database.

```
REM temp_seg.sql

col Segment_Name format a20
col Tablespace_Name format a10 heading 'TABLESPACE'
col Bytes format 999,999,999
col Blocks format 9,999,999
col Extents format 999,999
col Next_Extent format 999,999,999
set linesize 100 pagesize 60
select Owner,
       Segment_Name,
       Tablespace_Name,
       Bytes,
       Blocks,
       Extents,
       Next_Extent
  from DBA_SEGMENTS
 where Segment_Type = 'TEMPORARY'
 order by Owner, Segment_Name;
set linesize 80 pagesize 24
```

If there are no sort operations currently underway in your database, the preceding query will return no records.

max_exts.sql
large_objects.sql

Segments Not Set to maxextents UNLIMITED

Setting the **maxextents** parameter for a segment to UNLIMITED means you will never have to worry that the segment will run out of extents. While it is tempting to set **maxextents** UNLIMITED on all segments, it is not a good idea. Temporary segment tablespaces and rollback segments should not have UNLIMITED extents since runaway transactions that continue for a long time will continue to extend the rollback segment or temporary segment until the disk is full.

The query shown in the following listing will generate a list of all the segments owned by a specific user for which the **maxextents** value has not been set to UNLIMITED.

```
REM max_exts.sql

col Segment_Name format a20
col Segment_Type format a5 heading 'TYPE'
col Tablespace_Name format a10 heading 'TABLESPACE'
col Bytes format 999,999,999
col Blocks format 9,999,999
col Extents format 999,999
col Next_Extent format 999,999,999
set linesize 100 pagesize 60

select Segment_Name,
       Segment_Type,
       Tablespace_Name,
       Bytes,
       Blocks,
       Extents,
       Next_Extent
  from DBA_SEGMENTS
 where Owner = UPPER('&owner')
   and Max_Extents < 2147483645
 order by Segment_Name;
set linesize 80 pagesize 24
```

The **where** clause limits the rows returned based on the value of the Max_Extents column of the DBA_SEGMENTS data dictionary view. If you set a segment's **maxextents** value to UNLIMITED, Oracle assigns a **maxextents** value of 2147483645 to the segment. Any value less than this satisfies the **where** clause and the row is returned. If a segment has a **maxextents** value other than UNLIMITED, it may potentially reach its maximum number of extents.

The output of the query is shown next.

```
SEGMENT_NAME         TYPE  TABLESPACE        BYTES      BLOCKS
  EXTENTS   NEXT_EXTENT
------------------ ----- ---------- ------------- -----------
-------- ------------
BRANCH               TABLE USR1            20,480          5
     1        20,480
CARDHOLDER           TABLE USR1         1,761,280        430
    10       860,160
CH_IDX               INDEX USR1           348,160         85
     6       167,936
CK_LOG               TABLE USR1            20,480          5
     1        20,480
DEPTREE_TEMPTAB      TABLE USR1            20,480          5
     1        20,480
HOLIDAY              TABLE USR1            20,480          5
     1        20,480
PK_CH_ACCT           INDEX USR1           348,160         85
     6       167,936
PK_TRANSACTION       INDEX USR1            20,480          5
     1        20,480
PK_TRANS_ID          INDEX USR1           348,160         85
     6       167,936
RANDOMNESS           TABLE USR1         1,269,760        310
    60        20,480
TEMPOPRIV            TABLE USR1         2,621,440        640
    11     1,290,240
TEMPSPRIV            TABLE USR1            20,480          5
     1        20,480
TRANSACTION          TABLE USR1            20,480          5
     1        20,480
```

The following query, large_objects.sql, can be used to report the tables that have a large number of extents (as specified by an input parameter) as well as mark a flag (*) for those tables that are nearing their **maxextents** (as specified by an input threshold value).

```
REM large_objects.sql
REM Report objects with a large number of extents
REM
```

```
set newpage 0 verify off feedback off
ttitle center 'Objects with a large number of extents'
col ow format a18 heading 'Owner'
col ty format a10 heading 'Type'
col na format a30 heading 'Name'
col exts format 9,999 heading 'Extents'
col max_e format 999,999,999,999 heading 'Max'
col flag format a1 heading ' '
col nline newline
accept min_e prompt 'Enter minimum no of Extents to
                     include in report[default=5] '
accept threshold prompt 'An * will be displayed for
    objects nearing maxextents. Enter threshold [default=5] '

set pagesize 54 linesize 78 heading off embedded on feedback 6

spool large_tables.lst

select 'Minimum number of Extents = '||
       to_char(decode('&&min_e',null,5,to_number('&&min_E')))
from sys.dual
/
select 'An * will be displayed when Max_Extents - Extents <= '||
   to_char(decode('&&threshold',null,5,to_number('&&threshold'))),
       null nline
from sys.dual
/
set heading on

prompt **********Begin Report**********

select  us.name              ow,
        obj.name             na,
            'Table'          ty,
        seg.extents          exts,
        seg.maxexts          max_e,
        decode(sign(seg.maxexts-seg.extents-
        decode('&&threshold',null,5,to_number('&&threshold')))
            ,-1,'*',' ') flag
from    sys.user$  us,
        sys.obj$   obj,
        sys.seg$   seg,
```

```
        sys.tab$    tab
where   seg.extents >= decode('&&min_e',null,5,to_number('&&min_e'))
and     us.user# = seg.user#
and     obj.obj# = tab.obj#
and     tab.file# = seg.file#
and     tab.block# = seg.block#
union
select  us.name              ow,
        obj.name             na,
            'Index'              ty,
        seg.extents          exts,
        seg.maxexts          max_e,
        decode(sign(seg.maxexts-seg.extents-
        decode('&&threshold',null,5,to_number('&&threshold')))
            ,-1,'*',' ') flag
from    sys.user$  us,
        sys.obj$   obj,
        sys.seg$   seg,
        sys.ind$   ind
where   seg.extents >= decode('&&min_e',null,5,to_number('&&min_e'))
and     us.user# = seg.user#
and     obj.obj# = ind.obj#
and     ind.file# = seg.file#
and     ind.block# = seg.block#
union
select  us.name              ow,
        obj.name             na,
            'Cluster'            ty,
        seg.extents          exts,
        seg.maxexts          max_e,
        decode(sign(seg.maxexts-seg.extents-
        decode('&&threshold',null,5,to_number('&&threshold')))
            ,-1,'*',' ') flag
from    sys.user$  us,
        sys.obj$   obj,
        sys.seg$   seg,
        sys.clu$   clu
where   seg.extents >= decode('&&min_e',null,5,to_number('&&min_e'))
and      us.user# = seg.user#
and     obj.obj# = clu.obj#
and     clu.file# = seg.file#
and     clu.block# = seg.block#
```

```
union
select  us.name            ow,
        undo.name          na,
            'Rollback'      ty,
        seg.extents         exts,
        seg.maxexts         max_e,
        decode(sign(seg.maxexts-seg.extents-
        decode('&&threshold',null,5,to_number('&&threshold')))
            ,-1,'*',' ') flag
from   sys.user$   us,
       sys.seg$    seg,
       sys.undo$   undo
where seg.extents >= decode('&&min_e',null,5,to_number('&&min_e'))
and    us.user# = undo.user#
and    seg.file# = undo.file#
and    seg.block# = undo.block#
order by 1,2
/
prompt **********End of Report**********
spool off
set newpage 1 verify on feedback 6 pagesize 24
set linesize 80 heading on embedded on
undefine min_e
undefine threshold
```

Sample output of running large_objects.sql is shown here:

```
                    Objects with a large number of extents
Minimum number of Extents = 8

An * will be displayed when Max_Extents - Extents <= 20



**********Begin Report**********
Owner               Name                    Type        Extents
----------------    ----------------------- ----------  -------
         . Max
----------------  -
REP01               JOB_AUDITS              Table            12
            121

REP01               JOB_ERRORS              Table            10
            121
```

```
REP01              *  IB_HTML                 Table          1990
            2,000

REP01                 IB_HTML_PK              Index             8
            2,000

REP02                 GL_ACCOUNT              Table             9
       2,147,483,645
```

This output shows that the table REP01.IB_HTML is nearing its **maxextents** value. The query determines information about the various objects by querying a number of sys-owned tables:

◆ For tables: sys.user$, sys.obj$, sys.seg$, and sys.tab$

◆ For indexes: sys.user$, sys.obj$, sys.seg$, and sys.ind$

◆ For clusters: sys.user$, sys.obj$, sys.seg$, and sys.clu$

◆ For rollback segments: sys.user$, sys.seg$, and sys.undo$

A flag (*) is displayed if the number of extents for an object is nearing its **maxextents** value:

```
decode('&&threshold',null,5,to_number('&&threshold')))
           ,-1,'*',' ') flag
```

Also, the result set is filtered to show only those objects that have a minimum number of extents as specified by an input parameter:

```
where seg.extents >= decode('&&min_e',null,5,to_number('&&min_e'))
```

Database Block Map

segments_in_datafile.sql
db_block_map.sql

When I/O contention exists, you may be able to isolate the datafiles that are experiencing contention. After the datafile(s) are identified, you may want to identify the segments in the datafile to determine the best manner in which to rearrange the datafiles and the physical structure of the database to minimize I/O contention. The following script, segments_in_datafile.sql, can be used to list the segments in a specified datafile:

```
REM segments_in_datafile.sql
REM This script can be used for Oracle7.x and higher
REM This script can be used to obtain a list of the segments
```

```
REM in the specified datafile
REM

set verify off

prompt This database contains the following datafiles:

select file_name
from dba_data_files
/

accept fname prompt 'Specify a datafile whose contents
                     are to be determined: '

ttitle center 'Database Segments in File &fname'  skip 2

col stype format a15 justify c heading 'Segment Type'
col sown format a15 justify c heading 'Segment Owner'
col sname format a40 justify c heading 'Segment Name'

break on stype skip 1 on sown skip 1

select
  e.segment_type         stype,
  e.owner                 sown,
  e.segment_name         sname
from
  dba_extents            e,
  dba_data_files         f
where
  f.file_name = '&fname'
 and
  e.file_id = f.file_id
order by
  e.segment_type,
  e.owner,
  e.segment_name
/
ttitle off
clear breaks
undefine fname
```

ANNOTATIONS

The query segments_in_datafile.sql first displays the datafiles available in the current database:

```
prompt This database contains the following datafiles:

select file_name
from dba_data_files
/
```

The user is then prompted to specify a datafile whose contents are to be determined:

```
accept fname prompt 'Specify a datafile whose
              contents are to be determined: '
```

The datafile name supplied by the user is used to query the DBA_EXTENTS and the DBA_DATA_FILES views to determine the segments in that datafile. The result is ordered by segment type, owner, and segment name.

```
select
  e.segment_type         stype,
  e.owner                 sown,
  e.segment_name          sname
from
  dba_extents             e,
  dba_data_files          f
where
  f.file_name = '&fname'
 and
  e.file_id = f.file_id
order by
  e.segment_type,
  e.owner,
  e.segment_name
/
```

The **break on** setting of SQL*Plus is used to break the report when the segment type changes as well as when the owner changes:

```
break on stype skip 1 on sown skip 1
```

Sample output of running the query against an Oracle9.x database is shown here:

```
This database contains the following datafiles:
Database Segments in
          File /u1/ora900/app/oracle/product/900/oradata/mt900/

FILE_NAME
----------------------------------------------------------------
/u1/ora900/app/oracle/product/900/oradata/mt900/system01.dbf
/u1/ora900/app/oracle/product/900/oradata/mt900/newtemp1.dbf
/u1/ora900/app/oracle/product/900/dbs/db3.dbf
/u1/ora900/app/oracle/product/900/oradata/mt900/undotbs01.dbf
/u1/ora900/app/oracle/product/900/oradata/mt900/example01.dbf
/u1/ora900/app/oracle/product/900/oradata/mt900/indx01.dbf
/u1/ora900/app/oracle/product/900/oradata/mt900/tools01.dbf
/u1/ora900/app/oracle/product/900/oradata/mt900/users01.dbf
/u1/ora900/app/oracle/product/900/oradata/mt900/users02.dbf
/u1/ora900/app/oracle/product/900/oradata/mt900/BB.dbf
/u1/ora900/app/oracle/product/900/oradata/mt900/QCO.dbf
/u1/ora900/app/oracle/product/900/dbs/db1.dbf
/u1/ora900/app/oracle/product/900/dbs/db2.dbf

13 rows selected.

Specify a datafile whose contents are to be determined:
/u1/ora900/app/oracle/product/900/oradata/mt900/example01.dbf
 Segment Type    Segment Owner
--------------- ---------------
                      Segment Name
----------------------------------------------------------------
INDEX           HR
COUNTRY_C_ID_PK


DEPT_ID_PK



DEPT_LOCATION_IX


EMP_DEPARTMENT_IX


EMP_EMAIL_UK
```

```
EMP_EMP_ID_PK

EMP_JOB_IX

EMP_MANAGER_IX

EMP_NAME_IX

JHIST_DEPARTMENT_IX
```

In addition to determining the segments in a particular datafile, it can be useful to determine the block map of the entire database.

PROGRAMMER'S NOTE *Determining the block map of the entire database can take a long time if the database has a large number of extents; therefore, you should be careful.*

The fragmentation as well as the tablespace usage in the entire database can be determined by looking at the block map of the database. The query db_block_map.sql shown next can be used to obtain the database block map. It queries the DBA_EXTENTS and the DBA_FREE_SPACE views to determine the block distribution of the various segments in the database.

```
REM db_block_map.sql
REM This script can be used for Oracle7.x and above
REM This script can be used to display the block map of
REM the entire database
REM CAUTION: This script may take a long time to execute
REM


set verify off term on heading off

select 'Block Map of database: '||name
from sys.v_$database;

set heading on

ttitle off
```

```
prompt ********************
prompt    BEGIN REPORT
prompt ********************

col tablespace format    a15 justify c trunc heading 'Tablespace'
col file_id     format         990 justify c      heading 'File'
col block_id    format   9,999,990 justify c      heading 'Block Id'
col blocks      format     999,990 justify c      heading 'Size'
col segment     format         a38 justify c trunc heading 'Segment'

break on tablespace skip page

select
  tablespace_name              tablespace,
  file_id,
  block_id,
  blocks,
  owner||'.'||segment_name     segment
from
  dba_extents
union
select
  tablespace_name  tablespace,
  file_id,
  block_id,
  blocks,
  '<free>'
from
  dba_free_space
order by
  1,2,3
/
prompt *******************
prompt    END REPORT
prompt *******************
set verify on term on heading on
clear breaks
```

Sample output of running the query is shown here:

```
Block Map of database: MT900

*******************
```

```
BEGIN REPORT
********************
  Tablespace      File  Block Id    Size
--------------- ---- ---------- ---------
                Segment
----------------------------------------
MT                9          17     16
MT.MT

                  9          33     16
MT.MT_CLUSTER

                  9          49     16
<free>

                  9          65     16
MT.MT_INDEX

                  9          81   5,040
<free>

  Tablespace      File  Block Id    Size
--------------- ---- ---------- --------
                Segment
----------------------------------------
EXAMPLE           3          17    256
KO.REGIONS

                  3         273    256
KO.REG_ID_PK

                  3         529    256
KO.COUNTRY_C_ID_PK

                  3         785    256
KO.LOCATIONS

                  3       1,041    256
```

KO.LOC_ID_PK

3	1,297	256

KO.DEPARTMENTS

3	1,553	256

KO.DEPT_ID_PK

3	1,809	256

KO.JOBS

3	2,065	256

KO.JOB_ID_PK

3	2,321	256

KO.EMPLOYEES

3	2,577	256

KO.EMP_EMAIL_UK

3	2,833	256

KO.EMP_EMP_ID_PK

3	3,089	256

KO.JOB_HISTORY

3	3,345	256

KO.JHIST_EMP_ID_ST_DATE_PK

3	3,601	256

KO.EMP_DEPARTMENT_IX

3	3,857	256

KO.EMP_JOB_IX

3	4,113	256

KO.EMP_MANAGER_IX

Utilities

In the following sections, you'll see scripts that you can use to alter the manner in which data is stored in your database. The scripts in this section provide a means of coalescing free space and estimating space usage of new objects.

Forcing a Coalesce of Free Space in a Tablespace

coalesce.sql

The extents of a segment are marked as free extents when the segment is dropped. If the extents areadjacent, they can be coalesced into a single free extent. The coalesced extent will be larger than either of the two separate free extents, and thus will be more likely to be reused.

Figure 6-2 illustrates the extent allocations before and after a tablespace coalesce is performed.

The SMON background process periodically coalesces neighboring free extents into larger free extents. However, there is a potential problem with the SMON-based free space coalesce implementation.

The SMON background process only coalesces free extents in tablespaces whose default **pctincrease** storage parameter is non-zero. Since temporary and rollback segment tablespaces typically use a **pctincrease** of 0, the free space in their tablespaces will not be coalesced. If you have set the default **pctincrease** to 0 for a data tablespace, you may experience free space fragmentation in the tablespace. You may think that SMON is coalescing the tablespace's free space, while in fact it is skipping the tablespace.

Several solutions are available to resolve the free space coalescing problem. First, you can size your extents properly so that the reuse of free extents will be maximized and the impact of noncoalesced free extents will be minimized. Second, you can set the default **pctincrease** value for your data and index tablespaces to a non-zero value. You could, for example, set the default **pctincrease** for each tablespace to a value of 1, and then override the default setting when creating objects within the tablespace. Third, as of Oracle7.3, you can manually coalesce the free space in a tablespace. Other users of the tablespace will not be affected by the free space coalesce.

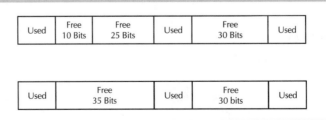

FIGURE 6-2. Extents available in a tablespace before and after a coalesce

To determine whether a tablespace needs to be coalesced, you can use a new data dictionary view, DBA_FREE_SPACE_COALESCED.

Ideally, the Percent_Blocks_Coalesced column of DBA_FREE_SPACE_ COALESCED should be 100 percent. You can display the free space coalescence percentage for the tablespaces using the following query:

```
REM coalesce.sql

select Tablespace_Name,
       Percent_Blocks_Coalesced
  from DBA_FREE_SPACE_COALESCED
 order by Percent_Blocks_Coalesced
/
```

Sample output for the query is shown in the following listing.

TABLESPACE_NAME	PERCENT_BLOCKS_COALESCED
TEMP	.074475968
RBS	.629248657
SYSTEM	100
USR1	100
TEMP_TABLES	100
IDX1	100

The output shows the percentage of each tablespace's free extents that are coalesced. A value of 100 means that all of the tablespace's free extents are coalesced—that is, there are no adjacent free extents.

ANNOTATIONS

The tablespace with the lowest percentage of free extents coalesced will be displayed first due to the **order by** clause specified.

```
REM coalesce.sql

select Tablespace_Name,
       Percent_Blocks_Coalesced
  from DBA_FREE_SPACE_COALESCED
 order by Percent_Blocks_Coalesced
/
```

Use the **alter tablespace** command shown in the following listing to coalesce the free extents in a tablespace. If a tablespace frequently has uncoalesced free extents, you should check the default **pctincrease** value for the tablespace and the extent sizes for the segments stored in the tablespace.

```
alter tablespace TEMP coalesce;
```

Executing the query in the test database yields the following results after the TEMP tablespace has been coalesced:

TABLESPACE_NAME	PERCENT_BLOCKS_COALESCED
RBS	.629248657
SYSTEM	100
TEMP	100
USR1	100
TEMP_TABLES	100
IDX1	100

The tablespace TEMP now has all the free extents coalesced into a single extent, with no fragmentation in the tablespace at all.

SMON can take a long time to clean up temporary segments and/or coalesce the free extents in a tablespace. In such cases, SMON appears to be spinning and consuming a large amounts of CPU time. This situation is seen particularly in Oracle8.x and seems to appear even if you issue the command **alter tablespace <tablespace_ name > coalesce**. A normal shutdown would force SMON to complete the cleanup, but it is not always possible or practical to issue a shutdown of the database for purposes of routine maintenance such as cleanup of stray temporary segments. As of Oracle8.0.x, you can set an event that forces the cleanup of temporary segments. When this event is set, all the temporary segments in a tablespace that are not currently locked are identified and dropped.

The following steps can be used to remove the stray temporary segments:

1. Determine the ts# of the tablespace in question by querying sys.ts$.

    ```
    Select name, ts# from sys.ts$;
    ```

2. Set the event to specify that the stray temporary segments in the tablespace are to be dropped immediately.

    ```
    Alter session set events 'immediate trace name DROP_SEGMENTS
    level TS#+1';
    ```

As seen previously, the parameters to pass in are TS# + 1 for the level. TS# is the tablespace number. If the value is 2147483547, the temporary segments of *all* the tablespaces are dropped; otherwise, only the segments in a tablespace whose number is equal to the 'level' specification are dropped.

len_long.sql

How Long Is a LONG?

If you use Oracle's LONG datatype for one of your columns, you are restricted in the ways in which you can use the column. For example, consider a table with two columns, one of which uses a LONG datatype:

```
create table TOY
(Toy_ID        NUMBER,
Description    LONG);
```

In the TOY table, the Description column uses the LONG datatype. If you try to use any function on the Description column, your query will fail:

```
select LENGTH(Description)
  from TOY;

select LENGTH(Description)
              *
ERROR at line 1:
ORA-00932: inconsistent datatypes
```

The "inconsistent datatypes" error is raised because you are attempting to perform a function on a column (Description) defined by a LONG datatype. If you had used a VARCHAR2 datatype instead, the query would have succeeded—but the text storage would have been limited by the VARCHAR2 datatype. In Oracle7, VARCHAR2 can store only 2,000 characters; in Oracle8, is can store 4,000 characters. Thus, if you want to store more than 4,000 characters of text per column, you can't use a VARCHAR2 for your text searches.

As of Oracle8, you can use the LOB datatypes (described in the next section) for storing long data. The LONG datatype is supported in Oracle7, Oracle8, and Oracle8i, and the inability to perform functions on LONG columns makes managing LONG columns difficult. In this section, you will see how to use PL/SQL variables to perform functions on LONG data.

The following script, len_long.sql, evaluates the length of the LONG column in the TOY table via an anonymous PL/SQL block. The output of the block is displayed via the execution of the DBMS_OUTPUT package.

For this example, a single record was inserted into TOY, with a description 21 characters in length. The script shown in the following listing was then executed.

```
REM len_long.sql
```

```
set serveroutput on

declare
  length_var    NUMBER;
  cursor TOY_CURSOR is
      select * from TOY;
  toy_val TOY_CURSOR%ROWTYPE;
begin
  open TOY_CURSOR;
  fetch TOY_CURSOR into toy_val;
    length_var := LENGTH(toy_val.Description);
    DBMS_OUTPUT.PUT_LINE('Length of Description: '||length_var);
  close TOY_CURSOR;
end;
/
```

The output for the sample data is shown here:

```
Length of Description: 21

PL/SQL procedure successfully completed.
```

Because the script uses the DBMS_OUTPUT package, it includes the **set serveroutput on** command to enable the writing of output from within the PL/SQL block.

```
set serveroutput on
```

The TOY_CURSOR cursor defines the query against the TOY table—in this case, since only one record is in the table, no **where** clause is necessary. The **declare** portion of the PL/SQL block also contains a variable named *length_var* to hold the length value prior to displaying the value.

```
declare
  length_var    NUMBER;
  cursor TOY_CURSOR is
      select * from TOY;
  toy_val TOY_CURSOR%ROWTYPE;
```

Within the PL/SQL block's executable section, the cursor is opened and the record is fetched into the *toy_val* variable. The *toy_val* variable's definition is anchored to the *toy_cursor* results via the %ROWTYPE flag. The next step of the script executes the **LENGTH** function on the Description column of the *toy_val* variable and returns that value via the DBMS_OUTPUT execution.

```
begin
  open TOY_CURSOR;
```

```
    fetch TOY_CURSOR into toy_val;
      length_var := LENGTH(toy_val.Description);
      DBMS_OUTPUT.PUT_LINE('Length of Description: '||length_var);
    close TOY_CURSOR;
end;
/
```

PROGRAMMER'S NOTE   *When you select the values into PL/SQL variables, the Description column's value is selected into a PL/SQL string variable. Because VARCHAR2 datatypes in PL/SQL cannot exceed 32,767 characters in length, this script will work only if the Description column's value fits within that length.*

You can expand this script to report the lengths of multiple LONG values by using a loop within your PL/SQL block. You will see the use of a cursor FOR loop within your PL/SQL block in the "Annotations" section that follows. In addition to this modification, you could make the query a variable as well, via the use of dynamic SQL. See the DELETE_COMMIT procedure in Chapter 4 for an example of dynamic SQL.

ANNOTATIONS

The len_long.sql script acts on only one record. You can modify the script to use a cursor FOR loop so multiple records can be evaluated. Because multiple length values will be returned by the script, the modified script selects the Toy_ID values as well as the lengths of the Description fields.

In a cursor FOR loop, the results of a query are used dynamically to determine the number of times the loop is executed. In a cursor FOR loop, the opening, fetching, and closing of cursors are performed implicitly; you do not need to command these actions explicitly.

The following listing shows a cursor FOR loop that queries the Toy_ID and Description values from the TOY table. For each row returned, the DBMS_OUTPUT package is called to display the results.

```
set serveroutput on

declare
  length_var    NUMBER;
  cursor TOY_CURSOR is
      select * from TOY;
  toy_val TOY_CURSOR%ROWTYPE;
begin
  for toy_val in TOY_CURSOR
    loop
      length_var := LENGTH(toy_val.Description);
```

```
      DBMS_OUTPUT.PUT_LINE('ID: '||toy_val.Toy_ID);
      DBMS_OUTPUT.PUT_LINE('Length of Description: '||length_var);
   end loop;
end;
/
```

Sample output for the cursor FOR loop is shown in the following listing.

```
ID: 1
Length of Description: 21
ID: 2
Length of Description: 27
```

```
PL/SQL procedure successfully completed.
```

In a cursor FOR loop, there is no **open** or **fetch** command. The command

```
for toy_val in TOY_CURSOR
```

implicitly opens the TOY_CURSOR cursor and fetches a value into the *toy_val* variable. When there are no more records in the cursor, the loop is exited and the cursor is closed. In a cursor FOR loop, there is no need for a **close** command.

The loop is controlled by the existence of a fetchable record in the TOY_CURSOR cursor. There is no need to check the cursor's %NOTFOUND attribute—that is automated via the cursor FOR loop. Within the loop, the *length_var* variable is defined and the DBMS_OUTPUT package is executed to display the results. Both executions of the DBMS_OUTPUT package use the PUT_LINE procedure, so each value is displayed on a new line.

```
length_var := LENGTH(toy_val.Description);
DBMS_OUTPUT.PUT_LINE('ID: '||toy_val.Toy_ID);
DBMS_OUTPUT.PUT_LINE('Length of Description: '||length_var);
```

len_lob.sql

How Long Is a LOB?

As of Oracle8, you can use LOB (large object) datatypes. LOB datatypes include BLOB (binary large objects), CLOB (character string large objects), and BFILE (binary files stored external to the database). LOB datatype columns are much more easily managed than LONG datatype columns. For example, you are limited to a single LONG datatype column per table, but you can have multiple LOB columns. You cannot perform functions on LONG columns; Oracle provides functions that you can execute on columns that use LOB datatypes. In this section, you will see an example of the use of the **GETLENGTH** function of the DBMS_LOB package.

For the examples in this section, the TOY table will be created using a CLOB datatype for the Description column. A CLOB datatype column can be up to 4GB in length; the data is stored within the database.

```
create table TOY
(Toy_ID       NUMBER,
Description    CLOB);
```

The data for LOB columns, whether stored inside or outside the database, is not always physically stored with the table. Within the TOY table, Oracle stores locator values that point to data locations. For BFILE datatypes, the locator points to an external file; for BLOB and CLOB datatypes, the locator points to a separate data location that the database creates to hold the LOB data. Thus, the LOB data is not necessarily stored directly with the rest of the data in the TOY table.

When you execute functions on the LOB data, you must select the locator value for the LOB and pass that value as a parameter to the function. In this example, the goal is to determine the length of the LOB value, so the script will execute the **GETLENGTH** function of the DBMS_LOB package. You cannot use the **LENGTH** function on LOB values.

The **GETLENGTH** function of the DBMS_LOB package has only one input parameter: the locator value for the LOB. In the following listing, variables are declared to hold the locator value and the output value. The **GETLENGTH** function is then executed, and the result is reported via the PUT_LINE procedure.

```
REM len_lob.sql

declare
   locator_var    CLOB;
   length_var     INTEGER;
begin
  select Description into locator_var
    from TOY
   where Toy_ID = 1;
  length_var := DBMS_LOB.GETLENGTH(locator_var);
  DBMS_OUTPUT.PUT_LINE('Length of LOB: '|| length_var);
end;
/
```

The output for this script is shown here:

```
Length of LOB: 21

PL/SQL procedure successfully completed.
```

If the LOB value is NULL, the **GETLENGTH** function will return a value of NULL.

ANNOTATIONS

The first section of the PL/SQL block defines two variables. The script uses the first variable, *locator_var*, to store the locator value for the Description column value. The *locator_var* variable has the same datatype (CLOB) as the Description column. The second variable, *length_var*, is an integer value that will store the length of the Description value.

```
declare
   locator_var    CLOB;
   length_var     INTEGER;
```

Once those two variables have been defined, the Description column's value is selected into the *locator_var* variable for a particular record.

```
begin
   select Description into locator_var
     from TOY
   where Toy_ID = 1;
```

The **GETLENGTH** function of the DBMS_LOB procedure is executed next, using the *locator_var* variable as its only input. The output of the **GETLENGTH** function is then displayed via the PUT_LINE procedure of the DBMS_OUTPUT package.

```
   length_var := DBMS_LOB.GETLENGTH(locator_var);
   DBMS_OUTPUT.PUT_LINE('Length of LOB: '|| length_var);
end;
/
```

In addition to the **GETLENGTH** function, the DBMS_LOB package contains the **INSTR** function and the **SUBSTR** function. You cannot use the SQL **INSTR** function on LOB columns; the **INSTR** function of the DBMS_LOB package provides this capability. The **SUBSTR** function of the DBMS_LOB package performs **SUBSTR** operations on LOB columns.

len_row.sql

Measuring Row Length

When performing calculations of the actual and estimated space used by data, you will often need to know the length of each row. In this section, you will see how to generate scripts that report the average space used for each row and each column of a table.

The examples in this section evaluate the space usage of rows in the STUDENT table. The **create table** command for the STUDENT table is shown in the following listing.

```
create table STUDENT
(Student_ID    NUMBER,
 First_Name    VARCHAR2(25),
 Middle_Init   CHAR(1),
 Last_Name     VARCHAR2(25),
 Birth_Date    DATE);
```

The STUDENT table contains columns using the NUMBER, VARCHAR2, CHAR, and DATE datatypes.

PROGRAMMER'S NOTE *The row length queries in this section will not work for columns defined with LONG or LOB datatypes. See the preceding sections of this chapter for ways to calculate the actual length of LONG and LOB columns.*

The script in the following listing, len_row.sql, generates a SQL command. The only parameter for the script is the name of the table.

```
REM len_row.sql
set pagesize 0
set verify off
set feedback off
undefine tablename
column ordercol noprint

select 1 OrderCol, 'select  ' from dual
union
select 2 OrderCol, 'AVG(VSIZE(' || Column_name || ')),'
from USER_TAB_COLUMNS
where column_id < (select max(column_id)
                   from USER_TAB_COLUMNS
                   where table_name = UPPER('&&table_name')) and
      table_name = UPPER('&&table_name')
union
select 3 OrderCol, 'AVG(VSIZE(' || Column_name || ')),'
from USER_TAB_COLUMNS
where column_id = (select max(column_id)
                   from USER_TAB_COLUMNS
                   where table_name = UPPER('&&table_name')) and
      table_name = UPPER('&&table_name')
```

```
union
select 4 OrderCol,'from ' || '&&table_name' || ';'
from USER_TABLES
where table_name = upper('&&table_name')
order by 1
/
set pagesize 24
set verify on
set feedback 6
```

Sample output for the preceding script is shown in the following listing. In the listing, the STUDENT table is supplied as input when the script prompts the user for a value for the *tablename* variable.

```
Enter value for tablename: STUDENT
select
 AVG(VSIZE(FIRST_NAME)),
 AVG(VSIZE(LAST_NAME)),
 AVG(VSIZE(MIDDLE_INIT)),
 AVG(VSIZE(STUDENT_ID)),
 AVG(VSIZE(BIRTH_DATE))
 from STUDENT;
```

The output shown in the preceding listing contains the following SQL statement:

```
select
 AVG(VSIZE(FIRST_NAME)),
 AVG(VSIZE(LAST_NAME)),
 AVG(VSIZE(MIDDLE_INIT)),
 AVG(VSIZE(STUDENT_ID)),
 AVG(VSIZE(BIRTH_DATE))
from STUDENT;
```

The generated SQL statement selects the average space used (the **VSIZE** function) for each column in the table. The **spool** commands create a file called vsizes.sql to store the generated SQL script.

You can now execute the vsizes.sql script. The following listing shows the execution of the vsizes.sql script along with sample output for data in the STUDENT table.

```
@@vsizes

AVG(VSIZE(FIRST_NAME)) AVG(VSIZE(LAST_NAME))AVG(VSIZE(MIDDLE_INIT))
---------------------- -----------------------------------------------
AVG(VSIZE(STUDENT_ID)) AVG(VSIZE(BIRTH_DATE))
---------------------- ----------------------
```

5.85714286	7.14285714	1
2	7	

The query output shows the average length of each column in the STUDENT table. The **VSIZE** function returns the actual space used, not the maximum space used. If you have used only 3 characters of a 25-character VARCHAR2 column, **VSIZE** returns a 3, not 25.

PROGRAMMER'S NOTE *Because the vsizes.sql script has no input parameters, you can alter the len_row.sql script to execute the vsizes.sql script automatically as soon as len_row.sql completes.*

The output shown in the preceding listing illustrates several important space usage facts:

- **CHAR columns use their maximum width** If you define a column with a CHAR datatype, a **VSIZE** of that column will return the maximum width as the actual width.

- **VARCHAR2 columns use their exact size** If you define a column with a VARCHAR2 datatype, a **VSIZE** of that column will return the number of used characters, not the defined length.

- **DATE columns use 7 bytes** Regardless of the date value, DATE datatypes in Oracle always use 7 bytes (one each for century, year, month, day, hour, minute, and second). If you write out a date in the standard DD-MON-YY format, you use nine characters; Oracle's internal storage of DATEs is independent of the format used for displaying the values.

- **NUMBER datatypes are stored efficiently** Internally, Oracle uses a method called "exponent in excess of 64 notation" that allows it to store numbers in few bytes. In the sample data used for the STUDENT table, some of the numbers were greater than 1,000. In the sample data, on average, Oracle used just 2 bytes to store each numeric value. However, in reality the number of bytes required for storage is based on the number of significant digits in the number. The storage space increases linearly; for 1 significant digit, 2 bytes; for 10 digits, 6 bytes; for 20 digits, 11 bytes; for 38 digits, 20 bytes; and so on.

ANNOTATIONS

The len_row.sql script builds the vsizes.sql script based on data retrieved from data dictionary views. To construct the SQL statement properly, the len_row.sql script uses a hidden column. A column named OrderCol is defined as hidden via the **noprint** clause of the **column** command, as shown in the following listing:

```
column OrderCol noprint
```

Each section of the script specifies a value for the OrderCol column. For example, the first part of the script uses an OrderCol value of 1:

```
select 1 ord, 'select  ' from dual
```

Because the display of the OrderCol column is suppressed via the **noprint** clause, the output of this query will be the word *select*. The next section of the script retrieves the column names for all but the last column in the table. Each column name has a comma appended to it; if you appended a comma to the last column, the SQL would be improperly formatted.

```
union
select 2 OrderCol, 'AVG(VSIZE(' || Column_name || ')),'
from USER_TAB_COLUMNS
where column_id < (select max(column_id)
                   from USER_TAB_COLUMNS
                   where table_name = UPPER('&&table_name')) and
      table_name = UPPER('&&table_name')
```

Since the queries are **union**ed, you must obey the formatting rules for **union**s. In each query, the columns must be of the same datatype. The datatypes and column names for the **union** query are determined by the datatypes of the first query in the **union**. You don't need to specify column names for the columns in any but the first query of the **union**.

The third section of the len_row.sql script retrieves the column name of the last column in the table; no comma is appended to it. The fourth section of the len_row .sql script generates the **from** clause for the generated query. At the end of the query, the rows returned are ordered by their OrderCol values (even though that column's value is not displayed).

```
order by 1, 2
```

This **order by** clause uses the column's ordinal positions. Prior to Oracle7.1, you had to use ordinal positions in your **order by** clauses if you used an expression (such as in this script, because the script selects text strings instead of column values). As of Oracle7.1, you can use the **as** clause to name a selected expression, and you can use that name in your **order by** clauses. Therefore, you do not need to use ordinal values in your **order by** clauses—unless you are using a **union**. If you use a **union** clause in your queries, you should use the ordinal positions of the columns in your **order by** clause. The use of ordinal positions in **order by** clauses for **union** queries is advisable because you may select different columns in each part of the query; as long as they have the same datatype, the query will succeed.

PROGRAMMER'S NOTE   *The results of the **VSIZE** function may be inconsistent for columns defined via abstract datatypes.*

At the beginning of the script, **verify** and **feedback** are turned **off**, suppressing the variable value display (for the *tablename* variable) and the display of the number of records returned. The **pagesize** control is set to 0, disabling the display of page and column headings. At the end of the len_row.sql script, **pagesize** is set to 20, re-enabling the column headings for the vsizes.sql report output.

The len_row.sql script shows the average length of each column value individually. Instead of adding the column lengths manually, you can alter the query to force Oracle to add them for you. Instead of appending commas to the end of each generated column value, append a plus sign (+), as shown in the following listing:

```
set pagesize 0
set verify off
set feedback off
column TotalSize format 999,999.99 heading "TotalSize"
undefine tablename
column ordercol noprint

select '1' ordercol,
       'select ' textcol
  from USER_TABLES
 where Table_Name = UPPER('&&tablename')
union
select '2',
       ' AVG(VSIZE('||Column_Name||'))+ '
  from USER_TAB_COLUMNS
 where Table_Name = UPPER('&&tablename')
union
select '3',
       '0 totalsize from '||'&&tablename'||'; '
       from USER_TABLES
 where Table_Name = UPPER('&&tablename')

spool vsizes.sql
/
spool off
undefine tablename
set pagesize 20
set verify on
set feedback 6
```

This query has three sections instead of four. Each column (including the last column) has a plus sign (+) appended to its generated value. The text generated in the last section of the **union** query starts with a 0, so the column's total average length will have 0 added to it. The total average column length will be unaffected by the addition, allowing the script to be simplified.

Sample output for the preceding script is shown in the following listing. The output is generated for the STUDENT table.

```
Enter value for tablename: STUDENT
select
 AVG(VSIZE(BIRTH_DATE))+
 AVG(VSIZE(FIRST_NAME))+
 AVG(VSIZE(LAST_NAME))+
 AVG(VSIZE(MIDDLE_INIT))+
 AVG(VSIZE(STUDENT_ID))+
0 totalsize from STUDENT;
```

As with the len_row.sql script's output, this output is written to a file named vsizes.sql. A sample execution of the preceding vsizes.sql script is shown in the following listing:

```
unknown command beginning "Enter valu..." - rest of line ignored.


  TotalSize
-----------
      23.00
```

The error shown at the start of the output listing is generated by the presence of this

```
Enter value for tablename: STUDENT
```

line in the vsizes.sql file. The output shows that the total average length of a row in the STUDENT table is 23 bytes.

You can modify the script again, generating both the individual column lengths and the total length in a single SQL script. The following script expands len_row.sql in this manner.

```
set pagesize 0
set verify off
set feedback off
column TotalSize format 999,999.99 heading "TotalSize"
undefine tablename
column ordercol noprint

select '1' ordercol,
       'select ' textcol
  from USER_TABLES
 where Table_Name = UPPER('&&tablename')
```

```
union
select '2',
        ' AVG(VSIZE('||Column_Name||')), '
  from USER_TAB_COLUMNS
 where Table_Name = UPPER('&&tablename')
union
select '3',
        ' AVG(VSIZE('||Column_Name||'))+ '
  from USER_TAB_COLUMNS
 where Table_Name = UPPER('&&tablename')
union
select '4',
        '0 totalsize from '||'&&tablename'||'; '
  from USER_TABLES
 where Table_Name = UPPER('&&tablename')

spool vsizes.sql
/
spool off
undefine tablename
set pagesize 24
set verify on
set feedback 6
```

The first section, which generates the **select** command, is left unchanged.

```
select '1' ordercol,
        'select ' textcol
  from USER_TABLES
 where Table_Name = UPPER('&&tablename')
```

The second part of the original len_row.sql script is modified to include all columns of the table by removing the limiting condition on the Column_ID value.

```
select '2',
        ' AVG(VSIZE('||Column_Name||')), '
  from USER_TAB_COLUMNS
 where Table_Name = UPPER('&&tablename')
```

The third part of the new query generates the addition section, totalling the average sizes of the columns.

```
select '3',
        ' AVG(VSIZE('||Column_Name||'))+ '
  from USER_TAB_COLUMNS
 where Table_Name = UPPER('&&tablename')
```

As with the previous addition query, a 0 is added to the output prior to the **from** clause generation.

```
select '4',
       '0 totalsize from '||'&&tablename'||'; '
  from USER_TABLES
 where Table_Name = UPPER('&&tablename')
```

The modified query generates a vsizes.sql script that will, when executed, calculate the average size of each column and the total average size of a row in the table. Sample output for the modified query is shown here:

```
Enter value for tablename: STUDENT
select
 AVG(VSIZE(BIRTH_DATE)),
 AVG(VSIZE(FIRST_NAME)),
 AVG(VSIZE(LAST_NAME)),
 AVG(VSIZE(MIDDLE_INIT)),
 AVG(VSIZE(STUDENT_ID)),
 AVG(VSIZE(BIRTH_DATE))+
 AVG(VSIZE(FIRST_NAME))+
 AVG(VSIZE(LAST_NAME))+
 AVG(VSIZE(MIDDLE_INIT))+
 AVG(VSIZE(STUDENT_ID))+
0 totalsize from STUDENT;
```

When you run this version of vsizes.sql, your output will show the average size of each column as well as the average size of each row.

SIZE ISSUES FOR OIDS AND REFS

As of Oracle8, the system generates a unique identifier called an *OID* (object ID) for each row in an object table. The OID generator is a network function that generates a globally unique identifier, RAW(16), based on network address, current time, and so on. An OID is referenced via a *REF*. In this section, you will see how to estimate the size of the automatically generated data for OIDs and their associated REFs.

Object tables have a hidden column, SYS_NC_OID$, that stores the system-generated OID and is always 16 bytes long. Beginning with Oracle8, you can define object views over relational tables; object views will not have this system-generated OID. In object views, the OID is synthesized based on a primary key that the view definer specifies. These primary key–based OIDs (called *PKOIDs*) can be as long as the primary key value itself. In Oracle8, PKOIDs are never stored.

Object tables maintain relationships via REF datatypes and do not directly retrieve and manipulate OID values. The REF value contains the OID and other items, such as the identifier of the object table or view in which the row object with the OID may be found.

OIDs are assigned to row objects and to metadata objects such as object tables and abstract datatypes. These identifiers assigned to the object table and type enable identifying and sharing object tables and types across databases.

As stated, system-generated OID is 16 bytes long, and a PKOID can be as long as the primary-key values. Correspondingly, REF values stored in the database can be of varying sizes. REFs contain 2 length bytes + 2 bytes of flags + 16 bytes for the object table OID + 16 bytes OID (or length of PKOID) + optionally, 10 bytes RowID. When a REF value is stored in a column, if the column is not declared to be scoped nor declared to store the RowID, the REF that is stored is stripped of its RowID. If the REF column is declared as scoped, in Oracle8, only the OID of the referenced row object is stored—that is, the REF is completely stripped of its overhead bytes and the object table's OID. If the REF column is unscoped and declared to store the RowID, the entire REF is stored in the column. Note that in Oracle8, the primary key–based REF is not allowed to be stored.

size_tab.sql

Sizing a Table

The more accurately you size your tables and indexes, the less administrative work you will have to perform as the tables and indexes grow. In this section, you will see scripts related to the calculation of space requirements for tables. In the next section, you will see scripts related to the space requirements of indexes. Each of these sections requires that you be able to calculate the average length of the rows and columns involved; see the previous sections in this chapter for scripts related to row-length calculations.

The following script, when executed, will prompt you for five variables. Those five variables, combined with database block size information from the database, determine the space required for your table's data.

```
REM size_tab.sql

set verify off
undefine pctfree
undefine avg_row_length
undefine number_of_columns
undefine number_of_cols_over_250_bytes
undefine number_of_rows

select &&number_of_rows/
   (((100-&&pctfree)*(Value-90))
      /(100*(&&avg_row_length + 3 + &&number_of_columns
            + &&number_of_cols_over_250_bytes))) Blocks_Required
   from V$PARAMETER
```

```
 where Name = 'db_block_size';
set verify on
undefine pctfree
undefine avg_row_length
undefine number_of_columns
undefine number_of_cols_over_250_bytes
undefine number_of_rows
```

PROGRAMMER'S NOTE   *The script size_tab.sql script assumes that the database block size is consistent across tablespaces. In Oracle9.x and later, you can change the database block size at the tablespace level. Refer to Chapter 1 for an example of how to deal with variable block size in Oracle9.x and later.*

When you execute the script, you will be prompted for values for the five variables, as shown in the following listing. The query will use those variable values, along with the database block size, to calculate the table's storage requirements.

```
Enter value for number_of_rows: 100000
Enter value for pctfree: 10
Enter value for avg_row_length: 23
Enter value for number_of_columns: 5
Enter value for number_of_cols_over_250_bytes: 0


BLOCKS_REQUIRED
---------------
      859.821379
```

The output shows that for the given table parameters, Oracle will require about 860 blocks to store the table's data.

PROGRAMMER'S NOTE   *The storage calculations are estimates. You should develop a set of standard extent sizes (such as 1MB, 2MB, 4MB, 8MB, etc.) and round up the storage requirements so they make the best use of your standard extent sizes.*

When you execute the size_tab.sql script, you are prompted for five variables:

◆ **number_of_rows**   Enter the number of rows you expect to store in this table. For this example, 100,000 rows are used.

◆ **pctfree**   Enter the **pctfree** setting for the table. The space set aside via **pctfree** is used during **update**s of rows already stored in the block.

◆ **avg_row_length**   Enter the average row length of the table. For this example, the STUDENT table's statistics are used—the average row length for rows in STUDENT is 23. See the section on average row length earlier in this chapter for details on calculating average row length.

◆ **number_of_columns**   Enter the number of columns in the table. For this example, the STUDENT table is used; it has five columns.

◆ **number_of_cols_over_250_bytes**   Enter the number of columns whose average length exceeds 250. If a column length exceeds 250 bytes, Oracle will need an additional length byte for row overhead.

Your settings for these five parameters are re-initialized each time you execute the size_tab.sql script, so you can execute the script repeatedly to determine the impact of different variable settings on your table's space requirements.

ANNOTATIONS

The completed size_tab.sql script contains many variables; if you wish to see only specific information about your database blocks, you can run portions of the script, as shown in the following listings.

Before executing the individual scripts, you should first re-initialize the variables, as shown here:

```
set verify off
undefine pctfree
undefine avg_row_length
undefine number_of_columns
undefine number_of_cols_over_250_bytes
undefine number_of_rows
```

To see the space available for a table in a database block, execute the following query. This query uses an estimate of 90 bytes for the block header within a database block. The resulting number is given the alias Space_in_Block.

```
select Value-90    Space_in_Block
  from V$PARAMETER
 where Name = 'db_block_size';
```

Sample output for the preceding query is shown in the following listing. In this example, the database block size is 4KB:

```
SPACE_IN_BLOCK
--------------
          4006
```

Of the 4,096 bytes in the database block, 4,006 are available for use.

Next, you need to take into account the **pctfree** setting. The **pctfree** setting determines the percentage of the space in the block (not including the 90 bytes for the block header) that is not used during **insert**s of new rows. The free space is used when previously **insert**ed rows in the block are **update**d. The more you **update** your rows, the more free space you need to maintain in your blocks. The query shown in the following listing returns the space that is available for **inserts**:

```
REM Available space - take pctfree into account

select ((100-&&pctfree)*(Value-90))/100    Available_Space
  from V$PARAMETER
where Name = 'db_block_size';
```

Sample output from the query is shown in the following listing. For this example, the database block size is 4KB. During the execution of this query, you will be prompted for a value for the *pctfree* variable. The *pctfree* variable here is set to 10.

```
Enter value for pctfree: 10


AVAILABLE_SPACE
---------------
        3605.4
```

As shown by the output, 90 percent of the available space in the block (4096-90)*0.90 is available for **inserts** of new rows. For consistency, the *pctfree* variable setting will not be altered for the remaining queries shown in this section.

Next, you can calculate the number of rows that will fit into the available space. A row's space requirements come from several sources:

◆ 3 bytes for row overhead

◆ Total average number of bytes used for each row

◆ Number of columns in the table (1 byte is needed for each to indicate the length of the value)

◆ Number of columns in the table whose data exceeds 250 bytes in length (and thus require an additional byte to store the length information)

In the following query, these four factors are combined to determine the number of bytes required per row. The calculation from the previous query provides the total number of bytes available per block. By dividing the available bytes by the bytes per row, you can determine the number of rows that can be stored in each block.

```
REM  Calculate rows per block

select ((100-&&pctfree)*(Value-90))/
        (100*(&&avg_row_length + 3 + &&number_of_columns
          + &&number_of_cols_over_250_bytes)) Rows_Per_Block
```

```
   from V$PARAMETER
 where Name = 'db_block_size';
```

Sample output from the preceding query is shown in the following listing. When you execute the query, you will be prompted for values for the *avg_row_length*, *number_of_columns*, and *number_of_cols_over_250_bytes* variables. The *pctfree* variable will use the value (10) set in the earlier example.

```
Enter value for avg_row_length: 23
Enter value for number_of_columns: 5
Enter value for number_of_cols_over_250_bytes: 0


ROWS_PER_BLOCK
--------------
    116.303226
```

The output shows that 116 rows can be stored in each block. Oracle does not store partial rows per block for **insert**s unless a row is larger than the database block size (4KB)—a condition called a *spanned row*.

For this example, the sizing information for the STUDENT table is used: the average row length is 23 bytes, there are five columns, and none of the columns has an average row length exceeding 250 bytes. The better you can estimate your average row length, the more accurately you can forecast your table's space requirements.

You can now combine the previous queries into the size_tab.sql script, as shown in the following listing. The combined script divides the number of rows you expect for the table by the average number of rows per block.

```
set verify off
select &&number_of_rows/
  (((100-&&pctfree)*(Value-90))
    /(100*(&&avg_row_length + 3 + &&number_of_columns
           + &&number_of_cols_over_250_bytes))) Blocks_Required
  from V$PARAMETER
 where Name = 'db_block_size';
```

When you execute the query in this sequence, the only undefined parameter is the *number_of_rows* parameter. In the sample output shown next, the space requirement is calculated based on an estimate of 100,000 rows for the table.

```
Enter value for number_of_rows: 100000


BLOCKS_REQUIRED
---------------
    859.821379
```

Although Oracle calculates the number of blocks required to multiple increments after the decimal, partial blocks are never allocated for tables. Round the result up to a value that makes sense for your environment and sizing standards. Oracle may dynamically change your space requirements when you create the table, based on the size of the available free extents in your tablespace.

size_ind.sql

Estimating Index Size

The more accurately you size your tables and indexes, the less administrative work you will have to perform as the tables and indexes grow. In this section, you will see scripts related to the calculation of space requirements for indexes. These scripts require that you be able to calculate the average length of the columns involved; see the earlier sections in this chapter for scripts related to column- and row-length calculations.

The following script, when executed, will prompt you for five variables. Those five variables, combined with database block size information from the database, determine the space required for your index's data.

```
REM size_ind.sql

set verify off
undefine pctfree
undefine avg_length_of_indexed_cols
undefine number_of_indexed_cols
undefine num_of_ind_cols_over_127_bytes
undefine number_of_rows

select &&number_of_rows/(((100-&&pctfree)*(Value-161))
  /(100*(&&avg_length_of_indexed_cols+8+&&number_of_indexed_cols
  + &&num_of_ind_cols_over_127_bytes))) Blocks_Required
  from V$PARAMETER
 where Name = 'db_block_size';
set verify on
undefine pctfree
undefine avg_length_of_indexed_cols
undefine number_of_indexed_cols
undefine num_of_ind_cols_over_127_bytes
undefine number_of_rows
```

PROGRAMMER'S NOTE   *The script size_ind.sql assumes that the database block size is consistent across tablespaces. In Oracle9.x and later, you can change the database block size at the tablespace level. Refer to Chapter 1.*

When you execute the script, you will be prompted for values for the five variables, as shown in the following listing. The query will use those variable values, along with the database block size, to calculate the index's storage requirements.

```
Enter value for number_of_rows: 100000
Enter value for pctfree: 2
Enter value for avg_length_of_indexed_cols: 15
Enter value for number_of_indexed_cols: 2
Enter value for num_of_ind_cols_over_127_bytes: 0


BLOCKS_REQUIRED
---------------
     648.289811
```

The output shows that for the given parameters, Oracle will require about 650 blocks to store the index data.

PROGRAMMER'S NOTE   *The storage calculations are estimates. Develop a set of standard extent sizes (such as 1MB, 2MB, 4MB, 8MB, etc.) and round up the storage requirements so they make the best use of your standard extent sizes.*

When you execute the size_ind.sql script, you are prompted for five variables:

- **number_of_rows**   Enter the number of rows you expect to store in this table for which the index will have a value. For this example, 100,000 rows were used.

- **pctfree**   Enter the **pctfree** setting for the index. The space set aside via **pctfree** is used during **update**s of rows already stored in the block. Because Oracle does not **update** index entries in place (instead, a **delete** and **insert** is performed), you should set **pctfree** to a low value (such as 1 or 2) for your indexes.

- **avg_length_of_indexed_cols**   Enter the total average row length of the columns to be indexed. For this example, a two-column index will be used as the basis for calculations. The two columns' average length, added together, will be assumed to be 15 bytes. See the section on average row length earlier in this chapter for details on calculating average column length.

- **number_of_indexed_cols**   Enter the number of columns in the index. For this example, the index is a concatenated index of two columns.

- **num_of_ind_cols_over_127_bytes**   Enter the number of columns in the index whose average length exceeds 127 bytes. If a column length exceeds 127 bytes, Oracle will need an additional length byte for index entry overhead.

Your settings for these five parameters are re-initialized each time you execute the size_ind.sql script, so you can execute the script repeatedly to determine the impact of different variable settings on your index's space requirements.

ANNOTATIONS

The completed size_ind.sql script contains many variables; if you wish to see only specific information about your database blocks, you can run portions of the script, as shown in the following listings.

Before executing the individual scripts, you should first re-initialize the variables, as shown here:

```
set verify off
undefine pctfree
undefine avg_length_of_indexed_cols
undefine number_of_indexed_cols
undefine num_of_ind_cols_over_127_bytes
undefine number_of_rows
```

To see the space available for an index in a database block, execute the following query. This query uses an estimate of 161 bytes for the index block header within a database block. The resulting number is given the alias Space_in_Block.

```
select Value-161 Space_in_Block
  from V$PARAMETER
 where Name = 'db_block_size';
```

Sample output for the query is shown in the following listing. In this example, the database block size is 4KB. For the sake of simplicity, the index's *initrans* parameter is assumed to be the default value of 1.

```
SPACE_IN_BLOCK
--------------
          3935
```

Of the 4,096 bytes in the database block, 3,935 are available for use.

Next, you need to take into account the **pctfree** setting. The **pctfree** setting determines the percentage of the space in the block (not including the 161 bytes for the block header) that is not used during **insert**s of new index entries. Since Oracle does not **update** index entries in place, you need little space reserved via **pctfree**. The query shown inext returns the space that is available for **insert**s of new index entries.

```
REM  Available space in the block

select ((100-&&pctfree)*(Value-161))/100  Available_Space
```

```
   from V$PARAMETER
 where Name = 'db_block_size';
```

Sample output from the query is shown in the following listing. For this example, the database block size is 4KB. During the execution of this query, you will be prompted for a value for the *pctfree* variable. The *pctfree* variable here is set to 2.

```
Enter value for pctfree: 2

AVAILABLE_SPACE
---------------
         3856.3
```

As shown by the output, 98 percent of the available space in the block (4096-161)* 0.98 is available for **insert**s of new rows. For consistency, the *pctfree* variable setting will not be altered for the remaining queries shown in this section.

Next, you can calculate the number of index entries that will fit into the available space. An index entry's space requirements come from several sources:

◆ 8 bytes for entry overhead

◆ Total average number of bytes used for each entry

◆ Number of columns in the index (1 byte is needed for each column to indicate the length of the value)

◆ Number of columns in the table whose data exceeds 127 bytes in length (and thus require an additional byte to store the length information)

In the following query, these four factors are combined to determine the number of bytes required per index entry. The calculation from the previous query provides the total number of bytes available per block. By dividing the available bytes by the bytes per row, you can determine the number of rows that can be stored in each block.

```
REM   Calculate Entries per Block

select ((100-&&pctfree)*(value-161))/
  (100*(&&avg_length_of_indexed_cols+8+&&number_of_indexed_cols
        + &&num_of_ind_cols_over_127_bytes)) Entries_Per_Block
  from V$PARAMETER
 where Name = 'db_block_size';
```

Sample output from the preceding query is shown in the following listing. When you execute the query, you will be prompted for values for the *avg_length_of_ indexed_cols*, *number_of_indexed_cols*, and *number_of_cols_over_127_bytes* variables. The *pctfree* variable will use the value (2) set in the earlier example.

```
Enter value for avg_length_of_indexed_cols: 15
Enter value for number_of_indexed_cols: 2
Enter value for num_of_ind_cols_over_127_bytes: 0


ENTRIES_PER_BLOCK
-----------------
         154.252
```

The output shows that 154 index entries can be stored in each block. Oracle does not store partial index entries in a block.

You can now combine the previous queries into the size_ind.sql script, as shown in the following listing. The combined script divides the number of rows you expect for the table by the average number of index entries per block.

```
select &&number_of_rows/(((100-&&pctfree)*(Value-161))/
   (100*(&&avg_length_of_indexed_cols+8+&&number_of_indexed_cols
        + &&num_of_ind_cols_over_127_bytes))) Blocks_Required
  from V$PARAMETER
 where Name = 'db_block_size';
```

When you execute the query in this sequence, the only undefined parameter is the *number_of_rows* parameter. In the sample output shown in the following listing, the space requirement is calculated based on an estimate of 100,000 rows for the table.

```
Enter value for number_of_rows: 100000


BLOCKS_REQUIRED
---------------
      648.289811
```

As shown by the query output, you can store 100,000 of the index entries in approximately 650 blocks. Although Oracle calculates the number of blocks required to multiple places after the decimal, partial blocks are never allocated for indexes. Round up the result to a value that makes sense for your environment and sizing standards. Oracle may dynamically change your space requirements based on the size of the available free extents in your tablespace.

User Management

user_obj.sql	copyuser.sql
obj_typs.sql	gen_grnts.sql
usr_sprv.sql	gen_role.sql
usr_oprv.sql	chngtblspc.sql
usr_sesn.sql	unlockall8.sql
usr_quot.sql	locknondba8.sql

Every database user account has characteristics that define and limit it. In this chapter, you will see scripts used for managing your database users. You can use the scripts to re-create user accounts, list each user's privileges, and determine the activity of current users. You will also see scripts that you can use to re-create roles. Privileges that are directly granted to a user are always active, but privileges granted via a role are active only during the user's session while the role is enabled for the user. The scripts in this chapter complement the capabilities already provided via tools such as Oracle Enterprise Manager.

The major scripts presented in this chapter are shown in Table 7-1. In the first section of this chapter, you will see diagnostic scripts you can use to identify the characteristics of the users in your database. In the second part, you will see utilities you can use when re-creating users, privileges, and roles.

Diagnostic Scripts

In the following sections, you will see scripts that report on the users already created in the database. This set of scripts relies on queries of the data dictionary tables for displaying commonly needed diagnostic information about your users. The scripts in this section will help you in determining a variety of things about your database users, such as, their resource quotas, system and object privileges allocated to them, the objects (if any) they own and so on.

Script	Description
user_obj.sql	Users who own objects
obj_typs.sql	Types of objects owned
usr_sprv.sql	User system and role privileges
usr_oprv.sql	User object privileges
usr_sesn.sql	User session information
usr_quot.sql	User resource quotas
copyuser.sql	Re-create user
gen_grnts.sql	Generate grant commands
gen_role.sql	Generate commands to create roles
chngtblspc.sql	Change the default and temporary tablespaces of database users
unlockall8.sql	Unlock all locked accounts
locknondba8.sql	Lock all database user accounts that don't have the DBA role

TABLE 7-1. Major Scripts in This Chapter

user_obj.sql

Users Who Own Objects

The DBA_USERS data dictionary view lists all the users in the database, along with their assigned default tablespaces and temporary tablespaces; you can also see the encrypted version of each user's password. If you are encountering a database for the first time, you will need to know which of these users own objects. The more you know about the object ownership within a database application, the better you will be able to support the application.

The first script selects from the data dictionary all object owners other than SYS. The SYS owner is not selected for several reasons: First, the objects owned by SYS should be the same across instances. Second, the SYS owner owns many objects (such as tables, views, and synonyms) that are not part of your application; listing them with the rest of the output will not add to your knowledge of the application.

The script shown in the following listing queries DBA_OBJECTS for all types of objects owned by any user other than SYS. The objects shown in the output will include tables, indexes, views, synonyms, and sequences.

```
REM user_obj.sql

select distinct Owner
  from DBA_OBJECTS
 where Owner <> 'SYS'
 order by Owner asc;
```

Sample output from the query is shown in the following listing.

```
OWNER
------------------------------
DBSNMP
PUBLIC
SCOTT
SYSTEM
```

obj_typs.sql

Types of Objects Owned

In addition to listing the users who own objects, you can list the objects themselves. Before generating a full listing of the objects, you should generate a summary that shows the number and type of objects owned.

The following query displays the number of objects owned, by owner and object type.

```
REM obj_typs.sql

select Owner,
       Object_Type,
```

```
     COUNT(*)
  from DBA_OBJECTS
 where Owner <> 'SYS'
 group by Owner, Object_Type;
```

Sample output from the preceding query is shown here:

OWNER	OBJECT_TYPE	COUNT(*)
DBSNMP	SYNONYM	4
PUBLIC	SYNONYM	586
SCOTT	TABLE	5
SYSTEM	INDEX	15
SYSTEM	SEQUENCE	1
SYSTEM	SYNONYM	8
SYSTEM	TABLE	14
SYSTEM	LOB	9
SYSTEM	VIEW	3

ANNOTATIONS

In the query output in the preceding listing, an Object_Type value LOB was displayed for nine objects owned by the SYSTEM user. The LOB object type was introduced in Oracle8; it refers to LOB segments. When you create a table that uses an internal LOB datatype (such as BLOB or CLOB), the LOB data is not usually stored with the base data. Instead, the base table contains a *LOB locator* value that points to a separate storage area that contains the LOB data. When you create a table using a BLOB or CLOB datatype, Oracle dynamically creates and manages a separate storage area for the LOB data.

The preceding query tells you how many objects of each type are owned by each non-SYS user. You can select further information about the objects. DBA_OBJECTS is the only data dictionary view that shows the date on which an object was created (the Created column) or last modified (the Last_DDL_Time column). For example, the following query will return the creation date for each table owned by the user named SCOTT:

```
select Object_Name,
       Created
  from DBA_OBJECTS
 where Owner = 'SCOTT'
   and Object_Type = 'TABLE';
```

PROGRAMMER'S NOTE   *The Last_DDL_Time column will also reflect changes to privileges granted on the object, as well as the creation of constraints if the object is a table. To see the time when the structure of the object was last changed, query the Timestamp column.*

Users' System and Role Privileges

What system privileges and roles do your users have? And which of your users' roles inherit privileges from other roles? Since there can be a hierarchical relationship among roles, you will need to use the **connect by** operator during your query. Due to the various types of available privileges and the restrictions on the way in which the **connect by** is used, a temporary work table will be created for use by the script in this section.

The following script should be saved as a single file (called usr_sprv.sql). When executed, it will prompt you for the name of the user account to examine. The script annotations follow the sample output provided.

```
REM usr_sprv.sql
set verify off head off  feedback off pagesize 20
undefine usernm
accept usernm char prompt 'Enter username for system privileges report: '

set termout off echo off
drop table TEMPSPRIV;
create table TEMPSPRIV
(Grantee,Granted_Role,PrivType)
tablespace TEMP_TABLES
as
select Grantee,Granted_Role,'R'
  from DBA_ROLE_PRIVS;

insert into TEMPSPRIV
select distinct Grantee,
       DECODE(Grantee, 'DBA', 'DBA-role (+- 80 privs)',
               'IMP_FULL_DATABASE','Role of 35 privs',
               'EXP_FULL_DATABASE','Role of 2 privs',
               privilege),
       'P'
from DBA_SYS_PRIVS;

set termout on heading on
col Title format a30 heading "UserID/Role" trunc
col Privtype format a40 heading "System Privilege"
prompt SYSTEM PRIVILEGES
break on title

select LPAD(Grantee,LENGTH(Grantee)+Level*3) title,
       DECODE (PrivType,'R',NULL,'P',Granted_Role) Privtype
```

```
    from TEMPSPRIV
connect by Grantee = prior Granted_Role
  start with Grantee = UPPER('&usernm');

undefine usernm

set verify on heading on  feedback 6 pagesize 24 termout on
  clear breaks
```

When the script is executed, you will be prompted for the username to show, and the output will then be displayed. The following is a sample output of running the script against an Oracle8.1.6 database:

```
SQL>> @usr_sprv
Enter username to show SYSTEM privileges of: DBSNMP
SYSTEM PRIVILEGES

UserID/Role                      System Privilege
-----------------------------    ----------------------------------
DBSNMP
        CONNECT                  ALTER SESSION
                                 CREATE CLUSTER
                                 CREATE DATABASE LINK
                                 CREATE SEQUENCE
                                 CREATE SESSION
                                 CREATE SYNONYM
                                 CREATE TABLE
                                 CREATE VIEW
DBSNMP
        RESOURCE                 CREATE CLUSTER
                                 CREATE INDEXTYPE
                                 CREATE OPERATOR
                                 CREATE PROCEDURE
                                 CREATE SEQUENCE
                                 CREATE TABLE
                                 CREATE TRIGGER
                                 CREATE TYPE
DBSNMP
        SNMPAGENT                ANALYZE ANY
DBSNMP                           CREATE PUBLIC SYNONYM
DBSNMP                           UNLIMITED TABLESPACE
```

The output shows several related columns presented as a single column of data. The far-left data is the username—in this example, DBSNMP. If the privileges are obtained via a role, the role name will be shown indented under the username. In this example, the DBSNMP user has been granted three roles: CONNECT, RESOURCE, and SNMPAGENT.

For each role, the privileges associated with it are shown on the far-right column of data in the output. For example, the RESOURCE role gives the DBSNMP user the following system privileges: CREATE CLUSTER, CREATE INDEXTYPE, CREATE OPERATOR, CREATE PROCEDURE, CREATE SEQUENCE, CREATE TABLE, CREATE TRIGGER, and CREATE TYPE.

PROGRAMMER'S NOTE *The CREATE TYPE system privilege was introduced with Oracle8; you will not see that privilege if you run this script under Oracle7.*

If a system-level privilege has been granted directly to the user, that privilege is shown without an associated role. For example, in the preceding output listing, the CREATE PUBLIC SYNONYM privilege has been granted directly to the DBSNMP user; that privilege allows the DBSNMP user to create a public synonym without requiring the DBA role. The second privilege directly granted to the user is the UNLIMITED TABLESPACE privilege; that privilege cannot be granted via a role.

ANNOTATIONS

The script has three separate parts. In the first part of the script, shown in the following listing, the temporary work table that will hold the role privileges data is created and populated with role-related data.

```
set verify off head off   feedback off pagesize 20
undefine usernm
accept usernm char prompt 'Enter username for system privileges report: '

set termout off echo off
drop table TEMPSPRIV;
create table TEMPSPRIV
(Grantee,Granted_Role,PrivType)
tablespace TEMP_TABLES
as
select Grantee,Granted_Role,'R'
  from DBA_ROLE_PRIVS;
```

As a consequence of running this script, the user executing the script will see a table named TEMPSPRIV in his or her schema. The script does not first attempt to determine whether the TEMPSPRIV table already exists. If the TEMPSPRIV table does not already exist, the **drop table** command will fail, but the failure will not be reported as an error to the user because of the **set termout off** setting that precedes it. Because repeatedly running this script will cause the table to be dropped and re-created multiple times, you should create a tablespace to store the table apart from your SYSTEM tablespace.

When the data from DBA_ROLE_PRIVS is inserted into the TEMPSPRIV table, its PrivType value is set to 'R' to indicate that those records are associated with roles. The PrivType designations are used as part of the query that generates the final report output.

The second part of the script, shown in the following listing, generates the entries for directly granted privileges. Roles are directly granted to users, so the script uses the **DECODE** function to add entries and avoid listing all privileges for those three roles.

```
insert into TEMPSPRIV
select distinct Grantee,
       DECODE(Grantee, 'DBA', 'DBA-role (+- 80 privs)',
               'IMP_FULL_DATABASE','Role of 35 privs',
               'EXP_FULL_DATABASE','Role of 2 privs',
               privilege),
       'P'
  from DBA_SYS_PRIVS;
```

After this **insert** completes, the TEMPSPRIV table contains roles granted directly to the user, privileges granted directly to the user, and privileges granted directly to roles. You can now select the data from the TEMPSPRIV table and use the **connect by** clause to show the relationship between the roles and privileges.

```
set termout on heading on
col Title format a30 heading "UserID/Role" trunc
col Privtype format a40 heading "System Privilege"
prompt SYSTEM PRIVILEGES
break on title

select LPAD(Grantee,LENGTH(Grantee)+Level*3) title,
       DECODE (PrivType,'R',NULL,'P',Granted_Role)
  from TEMPSPRIV
connect by Grantee = prior Granted_Role
 start with Grantee = UPPER('&usernm');


undefine usernm
```

Using the **insert**s, *all* the roles and *all* the system privileges in the database are inserted into TEMPSPRIV. The final query is the only point at which the username is used as a limiting condition on the output. After the query completes, the *usernm* variable is undefined. Thus, you could run the final query again, using a different value for the *usernm* variable. When you enter a slash (/) on the SQL*Plus command line, the last SQL command in the buffer will be executed. Since the last SQL command is the query from TEMPSPRIV, the query will be re-executed. Since the *usernm* variable has been undefined, you will be prompted for a new *usernm* value.

Users' Object Privileges

What table privileges do your users have, and which of your users' table privileges are granted via roles? In this section, you will see a script that generates a listing of a user's table privileges—both those that are directly granted and those that are granted via roles. Since there can be a hierarchical relationship among roles, you will need to use the **connect by** operator during your query. Because of the different types of privileges you can have and the restrictions on the way in which the **connect by** is used, a temporary work table will be created for use by the script in this section.

Since table privileges may be granted via roles, you need to query DBA_ROLE_PRIVS, just as was done in the previous section. When displaying table privileges, you will need to query DBA_TAB_PRIVS for the information. However, you need to know more about table privileges than you do about system privileges. For example, you need to know what type of table privilege has been granted to a user, and whether or not the user was granted the privilege **with grant option**. Thus, the temporary work table used by the queries in this section will contain columns that were not a part of the temporary work table used in the preceding section.

The following script should be saved as a single file (called usr_oprv.sql). When executed, it will prompt you for the name of the user account to examine. The script annotations follow the sample output provided.

```
REM usr_oprv.sql
set verify off head off  feedback off pagesize 20
undefine usernm
accept usernm char prompt 'Enter username for obj privileges report: '

set termout off echo off
drop table TEMPOPRIV;
create table TEMPOPRIV
(Grantee,Granted_Role,PrivType,TableName,Grantable)
tablespace TEMP_TABLES
as
select Role,
       Privilege,
       'P',
       Table_Name,
       Grantable
  from ROLE_TAB_PRIVS;

insert into TEMPOPRIV
select Grantee,
       Granted_Role,
       'R',
       'NULL',
       NULL
  from DBA_ROLE_PRIVS;
```

```
insert into TEMPOPRIV
select distinct Grantee,
       Privilege,
       'P',
       Table_Name,
       Grantable
  from DBA_TAB_PRIVS;

set termout on heading on
col Title format a30 heading "UserID/Role" trunc
col Privtype format a10 heading "Object Privilege"
col Grantable format a10
prompt OBJECT PRIVILEGES
break on title

select LPAD(Grantee,LENGTH(Grantee)+Level*3) title,
       TableName,
       DECODE (PrivType,'R',NULL,'P',Granted_Role) Privtype,
       Grantable
  from TEMPOPRIV
connect by Grantee = prior Granted_Role
 start with Grantee = UPPER('&usernm');
set verify on feedback 6 pagesize 24
 clear breaks
```

This script is similar to the usr_sprv.sql script in the previous section. The primary differences are the data dictionary views queried, the columns in the temporary work table, and the number of **insert** statements. In this script, three sets of records are inserted into the TEMPOPRIV table: the role grants, the table privileges granted to the roles, and the table privileges granted directly to users.

ANNOTATIONS

In the first part of the usr_tprv.sql script, the temporary work table TEMPOPRIV is created:

```
drop table TEMPOPRIV;
create table TEMPOPRIV
(Grantee,Granted_Role,PrivType,TableName,Grantable)
tablespace TEMP_TABLES
as
select Role,
       Privilege,
       'P',
       Table_Name,
       Grantable
  from ROLE_TAB_PRIVS;
```

The code does not check to determine whether a TEMPOPRIV table already exists prior to executing the **drop table** command. If a table with that name already exists in your schema, it will be dropped when you run the script. When the script completes, the TEMPOPRIV table is not dropped. The TEMPOPRIV table, which contains all the role and table privilege information for your database, remains in your schema, and all its data remains in the database. As with the script in the prior section, the table that stores the data is stored in the TEMP_TABLES tablespace to avoid fragmenting the SYSTEM tablespace.

During the TEMPOPRIV data load process, you may **insert** many records into the table; the number of records depends on the number of user accounts and objects maintained in your database, and on the extent to which you use roles to manage table privileges. Since these **insert**s are transactions, Oracle will maintain rollback segment entries for the transactions. If the rollback segment entry sizes exceed the available space in your rollback segments, you have two options: you could add a **commit** command following each **insert** command in the script, or you could use the **nologging** option when the table is created. (This option is available as of Oracle8; it is an enhanced version of the **unrecoverable** option introduced in Oracle7.2.)

You may wish to run both reports together, which would allow you to see a user's system privileges and table privileges. In that case, you could simply create a single SQL script that calls the other two:

```
start usr_sprv
start usr_oprv
```

You'll be prompted for the *usernm* variable value twice (once by each script) unless you remove the **undefine** command from the end of the usr_sprv.sql script and the beginning of the usr_oprv.sql script. For a SQL*Plus variable to maintain its value, you need to change the single ampersand values (&) to double ampersands (&&). Change the *&usernm* variable reference to *&&usernm* in both scripts and the variable will maintain its value throughout your session (until an **undefine** command is executed).

You can also grant privileges at the column level. For example, you can grant a user UPDATE privilege on only certain columns of a table. Since the column privilege data dictionary views' structure closely parallels the structure of the table privilege data dictionary views, you can easily modify the usr_tprv.sql script shown in this section to support the display of column-level privileges. For example, DBA_COL_PRIVS contains the same columns as DBA_TAB_PRIVS, with the addition of a Column_Name column.

If you do not have DBA privileges, you can execute modified versions of the privilege scripts shown in this section and the preceding section. If you replace DBA_ROLE_PRIVS with USER_ROLE_PRIVS, you will see the role privilege information for all roles that have been granted to you. If you replace DBA_TAB_PRIVS with ALL_TAB_PRIVS, you will see the table privileges for all tables that you own or to which you have been granted access.

Active Roles and Privileges

How can you tell which privileges and roles are currently active for a user? Privileges that are directly granted to a user are always active, but privileges granted via a role are active only during the user's session while the role is enabled for the user. Roles are enabled for users via the **set role** command; a user may also have default roles that are enabled on login.

Two views, each with a single column, list the privileges and roles currently enabled for the current session, as shown in this table:

SESSION_PRIVS	The Privilege column lists all system privileges available to the session, whether granted directly or via roles.
SESSION_ROLES	The Role column lists all roles that are currently enabled for the session.

You do not have to be a DBA to access these views; SESSION_PRIVS and SESSION_ROLES are available to all users.

How Many Users Have Logged In?

To determine how many users have logged in to your database, you could use Oracle's auditing features. However, the auditing features do not provide data that easily shows you the number of concurrent users who were active. To see that information, you should query the V$LICENSE dynamic view.

The following listing shows a query of the V$LICENSE view, along with sample output.

```
select *
  from V$LICENSE;


SESSIONS_MAX SESSIONS_WARNING SESSIONS_CURRENT SESSIONS_HIGHWATER  USERS_MAX
------------ ---------------- ---------------- ------------------ ----------
           0                0               12                 55          0
```

Currently, 12 sessions are accessing the database. The highest number of concurrent sessions (as displayed in the Sessions_Highwater column) was 55. The Sessions_Max, Sessions_Warning, and Users_Max columns reflect the settings of parameters in the database's init.ora file.

To limit the number of named users in a database, set a value for the LICENSE_MAX_USERS parameter in the database's init.ora file. The setting in the following example sets the maximum number of named users to 100:

```
LICENSE_MAX_USERS = 100
```

If you have already created more than 100 users in your database, starting Oracle with a LICENSE_MAX_USERS setting of 100 will cause a warning to be displayed (a warning will also be written to the alert log for the database). To avoid the error, set the LICENSE_MAX_USERS parameter value to a value that properly reflects your usage and database usage licensing.

To change the maximum named users limit while a database is open, use the **alter system** command with the **license_max_users** clause. The following example changes the maximum number of named users to 200:

```
alter system set LICENSE_MAX_USERS = 200;
```

To set the maximum number of concurrent sessions for an instance, set a value for the LICENSE_MAX_SESSIONS init.ora parameter, as shown in the following listing:

```
LICENSE_MAX_SESSIONS = 80
```

You can also set a warning limit for the number of concurrent sessions; if the warning limit is exceeded, a warning message will be written to the database's alert log. To set a warning limit, set a value for the LICENSE_SESSIONS_WARNING init.ora parameter, as shown here:

```
LICENSE_SESSIONS_WARNING = 70
```

You can change both the LICENSE_MAX_SESSIONS parameter value and the LICENSE_SESSIONS_WARNING parameter value while the database is open. The **alter system** command contains clauses that manipulate these settings, as shown in the following listing.

```
alter system set LICENSE_MAX_SESSIONS = 64;
alter system set LICENSE_SESSIONS_WARNING = 54;
```

To change either of these parameter values permanently, change the value of the parameter in the init.ora file.

When you query from the V$LICENSE view, the output shows both the system usage and the current parameter settings, as shown here:

```
select *
  from V$LICENSE;
```

SESSIONS_MAX	SESSIONS_WARNING	SESSIONS_CURRENT	SESSIONS_HIGHWATER	USERS_MAX
0	0	12	55	0

The Sessions_Max column value is the value of the LICENSE_MAX_SESSIONS parameter; none has been specified, so Oracle reports a value of 0. The value is not really 0, though, because such a setting would prevent Oracle from starting. Oracle will report a value of 0 for a license parameter for which a value has not been set. The Sessions_Warning column corresponds to the LICENSE_SESSIONS_WARNING parameter setting. The Users_Max column corresponds to the LICENSE_MAX_ USERS setting.

User Session Information

usr_sesn.sql

You can query V$SESSION to see information about current active sessions in the database. In this section, you will see a script that retrieves and formats the data from V$SESSION in an easy-to-use manner.

The following script, usr_sesn.sql, queries V$SESSION and embeds character strings in the output. To make the output more readable, the script places carriage returns in the output by concatenating an ASCII character—via the **CHR**(10) function—at the proper places in the output.

```
REM usr_sesn.sql

col "Session Info" form a80

select ' Sid, Serial#, Aud sid : '|| S.sid||
    ' , '||S.Serial#||' , '|| S.audsid||CHR(10)||
    'DB User / OS User : '||S.Username||
    '    /    '||S.OSuser||CHR(10)||
    '    Machine - Terminal : '|| S.Machine||
    ' - '|| S.Terminal||CHR(10)||
    '        OS Process Ids : '|| S.Process||
    ' (Client) '||P.Spid||' (Server)'|| CHR(10)||
    '    Client Program Name : '||S.Program "Session Info"
  from V$PROCESS P, V$SESSION S
 where P.Addr = S.Paddr
   and S.Audsid = USERENV('SESSIONID');
```

Sample output is shown in the following listing:

```
Session Info
----------------------------------------------------------
 Sid, Serial#, Aud sid : 8 , 251 , 1044
    DB User / OS User : BONNIE    /    appadmin
   Machine - Terminal : myhost1  -  ttyp4
        OS Process Ids : 12100 (Client)  12103 (Server)
   Client Program Name : sqlplus@myhost1 (TNS V1-V3)
```

User Resource Quotas

usr_quot.sql

You can query the DBA_TS_QUOTAS data dictionary view to see the current and maximum space allocation per tablespace. In the following listing, all the columns are selected from DBA_TS_QUOTAS, ordered by tablespace name and username.

```
REM usr_quot.sql

select * from DBA_TS_QUOTAS
order by Tablespace_Name, Username;
```

Sample output is shown in the following listing. Because of the length of the lines of output, it is wrapped across two lines per row returned.

```
TABLESPACE_NAME                 USERNAME                          BYTES
------------------------------  ------------------------------  ----------
   MAX_BYTES     BLOCKS MAX_BLOCKS
  ----------  ---------- ----------
APP_D1                          APPLOADER                    1.1889E+10
        -1    1451241          -1
APP_D2                          APPLOADER                             0
  52428800          0        6400
APP_I1                          APPLOADER                    7503986688
        -1     916014          -1
APP_I2                          APPLOADER                    7474888704
        -1     912462          -1
```

The output shows the tablespace quotas and usage for a single user over four tablespaces. The APPLOADER user has no maximum space quota on three of the tablespaces (those for which the Max_Bytes column displays a value of –1). For the APP_D2 tablespace, a quota of 52,428,800 bytes (50MB) has been established. The database block size is 8KB, as you can tell by dividing one of the Bytes values by its matching Blocks value.

The Bytes and Blocks values reflect the current allocated space within each tablespace for each user. Thus, in the APP_I1 tablespace, the APPLOADER user has allocated 916,014 database blocks. There is no space quota for the APPLOADER user in the APP_I1 tablespace, so the user's space allocation in that tablespace is limited only by the size of the tablespace's datafiles.

PROGRAMMER'S NOTE *You can alter a user's quota on a tablespace at any time via the **alter user** command. If you change the quota to a value below the user's current space allocation, the user will not be able to create new tables or indexes and will encounter an error when attempting to acquire more space for an existing object. Objects already created and extents already obtained will not be dropped to reduce the user's allocated space.*

ANNOTATIONS

You can allow your datafiles to extend. When you configure the extension parameters for your datafiles, you specify an extent size to acquire and the maximum size to which the file can extend. You cannot specify the maximum number of extents your file will acquire.

If any of the datafiles in your database can extend, records will appear in the table SYS.FILEXT$. If your datafiles cannot extend, this table will not exist in your database.

You can determine which users own objects in which tablespaces (and datafiles) by querying the data dictionary views. To see scripts that map objects to tablespaces, see Chapter 6.

Utilities

In the first section of this chapter, you saw scripts that report on the current status of the users in the database. In this section, the scripts provided will modify the users in the database or will generate code tol help you manage your users.

copyuser.sql

Re-creating Users

You can use the information in the data dictionary to generate a **create user** command that will reflect the current settings for each user. For example, if you have changed a user's default tablespace since the user was created, this script will capture the current setting of that parameter. The script will even capture the user's password (via an undocumented option of the **create user** command).

The script is in three parts. The first part generates the **create user** command. The second part generates the **alter user** commands that will assign resource quotas for the user. The third part uses a PL/SQL loop to generate the **alter user** command that will set the proper default roles for the user. The annotations of the script follow the sample output.

```
REM copyuser.sql

set heading off verify off feedback off echo off term on
column X format a40 word_wrapped
undefine usernm

select 'create user '||Username||
        ' identified '||
            DECODE(Password,NULL, 'EXTERNALLY',
            ' by values '||''''||Password||'''')||
        ' default tablespace '||Default_Tablespace||
        ' temporary tablespace '||Temporary_Tablespace||
        ' profile '||Profile||'; ' X
  from DBA_USERS
 where Username = UPPER('&&usernm');

select 'alter user '||Username||
        ' quota '||DECODE(Max_Bytes,-1,'UNLIMITED',Max_Bytes)||
        ' on '||Tablespace_Name||'; '
  from DBA_TS_QUOTAS
 where Username = UPPER('&&usernm');


set serveroutput on
declare
```

```
    usernam      VARCHAR2(32) := '&&usernm';
    roles_list VARCHAR2(32767) := 'NONE';
    cursor roles_cursor is
        select *
          from DBA_ROLE_PRIVS
        where (Grantee = UPPER(usernam) or Grantee = 'PUBLIC')
          and Default_Role = 'YES';
    role_val roles_cursor%ROWTYPE;
begin
open roles_cursor;
  loop
    fetch roles_cursor into role_val;
    exit when roles_cursor%NOTFOUND;
      roles_list := roles_list||','||role_val.Granted_Role;
  end loop;
if LENGTH(roles_list)>5 THEN
  roles_list:=SUBSTR(roles_list,6);
end if;
DBMS_OUTPUT.PUT_LINE('alter user '||usernam||
        ' default role ' ||roles_list||';');
end;
/
set heading on verify on feedback 6 term on
 undefine usernm
```

When you execute the copyuser.sql script, you should save the output to a file via the **spool** command. Sample generated output is shown here:

```
SQL>> @copyuser
Enter value for usernm: BONNIE

create user BONNIE identified by
values '8808AD4E97AAAF0E' default
tablespace SOURCE_D1 temporary
tablespace LOAD_TEMP profile DEFAULT;


alter user BONNIE quota UNLIMITED on APP_IP1;
alter user BONNIE quota UNLIMITED on APP_DA1;
alter user BONNIE quota UNLIMITED on APP_D1;
alter user BONNIE quota UNLIMITED on APP_I1;


alter user BONNIE default role
```

```
ATLOADER_SEL_ROLE,CONNECT,DIMLOADER_SEL_ROLE,DPCLOADER_SEL_ROLE;

PL/SQL procedure successfully completed.
```

The output contains three separate sets of SQL commands. The first SQL command in the output is the **create user** command that specifies the default and temporary tablespace for the user. The user's encrypted password is also captured; the password encryption setting is described in the "Annotations" section that follows. The second set of SQL commands alters the user by applying the space quotas the user has been granted. There is one **alter user** command for each tablespace for which the user has a space quota. The third part of the output shows the command that will specify the user's default roles (since not all roles may be assigned as default roles).

ANNOTATIONS

The copyuser.sql script uses a number of tricks and techniques. First, it makes use of the way in which the Import utility assigns passwords to users when it creates users. When a user is created in a database via Import, the Import utility uses the **identified by values** clause of the **create user** command to specify the encrypted version of the user's password. The copyuser.sql script uses this same technique—if the user has a password, the encrypted version of the password is selected as part of the **create user** command generation:

```
set heading off verify off feedback off echo off term on
column X format a40 word_wrapped
undefine usernm

select 'create user '||Username||
       ' identified '||
           DECODE(Password,NULL, 'EXTERNALLY',
           ' by values '||''''||Password||'''')||
       ' default tablespace '||Default_Tablespace||
       ' temporary tablespace '||Temporary_Tablespace||
       ' profile '||Profile||'; ' X
  from DBA_USERS
 where Username = UPPER('&&usernm');
```

In the first part of the script, four output settings are turned off: heading, feedback, echo, and verify. The **set heading off** command will suppress the display of the column headings in output. The **set feedback off** command will suppress the display of messages such as "4 rows selected." The **set verify off** command will suppress the display of "old" and "new" values for a variable when a variable has a value assigned to it. The **set echo off** command will suppress the display of the SQL statements being processed. The **set term on** command ensures that the results of the SQL statements are displayed.

The first part of the script surrounds the encrypted password value with single quotes by concatenating strings of four single quotes before and after the password value. A string of four single quotes is interpreted as a single quote: the outer two quotes signal that the string is a character string, and the inner two quotes are transformed into a single quote.

The second part of the script is the simplest of the three parts: one row is generated for each tablespace for which the user has been granted a space quota:

```
select 'alter user '||Username||
       ' quota '||DECODE(Max_Bytes,-1,'UNLIMITED',Max_Bytes)||
       ' on '||Tablespace_Name||'; '
  from DBA_TS_QUOTAS
 where Username = UPPER('&&usernm');
```

There is no requirement that all of the space quota commands be specified in a single command, so this section of the script generates a separate **alter user** command for each tablespace. When you select multiple rows from a table, Oracle normally tells you how many rows were retrieved; this display is suppressed via the **set feedback off** command at the beginning of the script.

The third part of the script generates a single command that specifies the default roles for your user. All of the default roles for a user must be specified in a single **alter user** command, so this part of the script must generate a single command based on the output of multiple rows in the DBA_ROLE_PRIVS data dictionary view. To create a single command from multiple rows, a PL/SQL loop is used.

First, the **set serveroutput on** command is executed to enable display of the values generated within the PL/SQL block. Next, four variables are declared. The variables are the username, whose value is inherited from the *usernm* variable used earlier in the script; the list of default roles; a cursor that selects data from DBA_ROLE_PRIVS; and a variable that has the same structure as the cursor.

```
set serveroutput on
declare
  usernam    VARCHAR2(32) := '&&usernm';
  roles_list VARCHAR2(32767) := 'NONE';
  cursor roles_cursor is
      select *
        from DBA_ROLE_PRIVS
       where (Grantee = UPPER(usernam) or Grantee = 'PUBLIC')
         and Default_Role = 'YES';
  role_val roles_cursor%ROWTYPE;
```

By default, the *roles_list* parameter is set to NONE. If a user has no default roles, the command **alter user** *username* **default role NONE;** will be generated by this script. The *usernm* variable in the PL/SQL block will have as its default value the value of the *usernm* variable used in the first two parts of the script.

In the next section of the PL/SQL block, a simple loop is created. The cursor that queries DBA_ROLE_PRIVS is opened. For each record that is retrieved, the value of the Granted_Role column is appended to the *roles_list* variable's value. When no more rows are returned by the cursor, the loop is exited.

```
begin
open roles_cursor;
  loop
    fetch roles_cursor into role_val;
    exit when roles_cursor%NOTFOUND;
      roles_list := roles_list||','||role_val.Granted_Role;
  end loop;
```

If any rows have been returned by the cursor, the value of the *roles_list* variable will begin with NONE, followed by the default roles. To remove the NONE part of the command, check the length of the *roles_list* variable, as shown in the following listing. If the length is greater than five characters, the user has at least one default role and the NONE section at the start of the variable's value is stripped. To strip out the first five characters of the *roles_list* variable value, use the **SUBSTR**(roles_list,6) function. The "6" in that function tells Oracle to begin the **SUBSTR** function at the sixth character of the string. Since no length parameter is specified for the **SUBSTR** function, the entire rest of the string will be selected.

```
if LENGTH(roles_list)>5 THEN
  roles_list:=SUBSTR(roles_list,6);
end if;
```

You can now output the list of default roles via the **PUT_LINE** function of the DBMS_OUTPUT package, as shown here:

```
DBMS_OUTPUT.PUT_LINE('alter user '||usernam||
                    ' default role ' ||roles_list||';');
end;
/
```

When the script has completed, the *usernm* variable still has a value assigned to it. The *usernm* variable will retain its value until you undefine it (via the **undefine** command) or until you run the copyuser.sql script again (since it contains an **undefine** command in its first section).

gen_grnts.sql

Generate Grant Commands

You can use the information in the data dictionary views to generate the commands necessary to re-create system and object privileges. In most cases, you should use the Export and Import utilities to re-create grants. However, you can generate the SQL scripts needed to re-create the grants you need.

To use the Export/Import method, perform a full Export of the database while using the ROWS=N and GRANTS=Y parameters. All of the object definitions will be exported along with all of the **grant** commands that apply to those objects. When you re-create the object elsewhere, you can use the Export dump file to retrieve all of the object grants. Since **grant**s on a table can be made by multiple users, the Export/Import method allows you to re-create all **grant**s no matter who made them. However, you may wish to generate the privilege creation scripts yourself.

As long as the privilege structure is not tiered, you can easily re-create the **grant** commands by querying the data dictionary. That is, if you have not granted privileges on an object via an account other than the object owner account, you can generate the proper **grant** commands by querying the necessary data from DBA_TAB_PRIVS, DBA_COL_PRIVS, and DBA_ROLE_PRIVS. See the user diagnostics section in the first section of this chapter for examples of privilege diagnostics queries.

You can generate the system privilege commands as well. For example, the following script generates the **grant** commands for system privileges. The basic system-level roles such as CONNECT and RESOURCE are not displayed in the output; only user-created roles and individual users will be shown. As with the script in the prior section, you should save the script output to a file via the **spool** command.

```
REM gen_grnts.sql

set verify off feedback off termout on echo off pagesize 0

select 'grant ' || RPAD(Privilege,30) || ' to ' || Grantee ||
       DECODE(Admin_Option,'YES',' with admin option;',';')
  from DBA_SYS_PRIVS
 where Grantee not in ('CONNECT','RESOURCE','DBA',
            'EXP_FULL_DATABASE','IMP_FULL_DATABASE')
 order by Grantee;
```

Sample output is shown here:

```
grant CREATE SESSION                to BOB;
grant CREATE SESSION                to BONNIE;
grant CREATE SYNONYM                to CAROLYN;
grant CREATE PUBLIC SYNONYM         to DBSNMP;
grant UNLIMITED TABLESPACE          to DBSNMP;
```

As you can see from the preceding listing, one **grant** command is generated for each distinct privilege for each user.

Generate Roles

In addition to re-creating users and **grant** commands, you can re-create the **create role** commands. The script provided in this section will generate the commands

gen_role.sql

necessary for creating all the roles in the database. This script will not generate the **create role** commands for the basic Oracle roles such as CONNECT, RESOURCE, and DBA.

```
REM gen_role.sql

REM  For Oracle7, the column name in USER$ is    Type
REM  For Oracle8, the column name in USER$ is    Type#
set echo off verify off feedback off pagesize 0

select 'create role ' || Role || ' not identified;'
  from DBA_ROLES
 where Role not in ('CONNECT','RESOURCE','DBA', 'EXP_FULL_DATABASE',
                    'IMP_FULL_DATABASE')
   and Password_Required='NO' ;

select 'create role ' || Role || ' identified by values ' ||
       '''' || Password || '''' || ';'
  from DBA_ROLES, sys.USER$
 where Role not in ('CONNECT','RESOURCE','DBA', 'EXP_FULL_DATABASE',
                    'IMP_FULL_DATABASE')
   and Password_Required='YES'
   and DBA_ROLES.Role=USER$.Name
   and USER$.Type#=0 ;

select 'grant ' || Granted_Role || ' to ' || Grantee ||
       ' with admin option;'
  from DBA_ROLE_PRIVS
 where Admin_Option='YES'
   and Granted_Role not in ('CONNECT','RESOURCE','DBA',
                            'EXP_FULL_DATABASE', 'IMP_FULL_DATABASE')
   order by Grantee ;
```

Sample output from the preceding script is shown in the following listing.

```
create role APP_USER_ROLE not identified;
create role LOADER_ROLE not identified;
create role APP_ADMIN_ROLE not identified;
create role SNMPAGENT not identified;
grant APP_USER_ROLE to BONNIE with admin option;
grant LOADER_ROLE to BONNIE with admin option;
grant APP_ADMIN_ROLE to BONNIE with admin option;
grant SNMPAGENT to SYS with admin option;
```

ANNOTATIONS

The output shows the **create role** commands for four roles. Because each of the roles has been created without an associated password, they are created with the **not**

identified clause. The commands for roles with no passwords are created via the first part of the script:

```
select 'create role ' || Role || ' not identified;'
  from DBA_ROLES
 where Role not in ('CONNECT','RESOURCE','DBA', 'EXP_FULL_DATABASE',
                    'IMP_FULL_DATABASE')
   and Password_Required='NO' ;
```

The second part of the script queries the data dictionary for information on roles that have passwords associated with them. The passwords for roles are stored in the SYS.USER$ table. Each role has an entry in SYS.USER$; its password is stored encrypted, and the USER$.Type# (USER$.Type in Oracle7) column has a value of 0 for each role.

```
select 'create role ' || Role || ' identified by values ' ||
       '''' || Password || '''' || ';'
  from DBA_ROLES, SYS.USER$
 where Role not in ('CONNECT','RESOURCE','DBA', 'EXP_FULL_DATABASE',
                    'IMP_FULL_DATABASE')
   and Password_Required='YES'
   and DBA_ROLES.Role=USER$.Name
   and USER$.Type=0 ;
```

The query of SYS.USER$ uses the same technique shown in the preceding section on re-creating users to capture a user's password. In this case, it is the role's password.

The third section of the script captures any roles that have been granted **with admin option**:

```
select 'grant ' || Granted_Role || ' to ' || Grantee ||
       ' with admin option;'
  from DBA_ROLE_PRIVS
 where Admin_Option='YES'
   and Granted_Role not in ('CONNECT','RESOURCE','DBA',
                            'EXP_FULL_DATABASE', 'IMP_FULL_DATABASE')
 order by Grantee ;
```

The **with admin option** clause gives the recipient the ability to grant the role to other users. In general, you can simplify your role maintenance by always creating roles under the SYSTEM user and always granting access to them via a single DBA-privileged user. In this example, the user BONNIE has been granted **with admin option** on each of her roles. As a result, she can grant those roles to other users. However, if she grants those roles to other users, re-creating the role and privilege structure in your database becomes much more difficult. The simpler you keep the privilege structure in your database, the simpler it will be to re-create your users and their privilege structure.

Change the Default and Temporary Tablespaces

As part of ongoing maintenance or to resolve some disk I/O–related performance problems, a DBA may want to create new default and/or temporary tablespaces or allow existing users to start using new tablespaces as their default and temporary tablespaces. The script chngtblspc.sql can be used to generate SQL statements that can change the default tablespace and the temporary tablespace for all database users that are affected by the change in disk structure or tablespace utilization policies of the company.

```
REM chngtblspc.sql
REM This script can be used to generate SQL to change
REM      the DEFAULT and TEMPORARY tablespace for database users

set heading off echo off verify off feedback off pagesize 0 termout on
column X format a200 word_wrapped

undefine old_default_tblspc
undefine old_temp_tblspc
undefine new_default_tblspc
undefine new_temp_tblspc

spool change_def_n_temp_tblspc.sql

SELECT 'ALTER USER '||username||
            ' DEFAULT TABLESPACE &&new_default_tblspc TEMPORARY TABLESPACE
&&new_temp_tblspc;' X
FROM dba_users
WHERE default_tablespace=UPPER('&&old_default_tblspc')
  AND temporary_tablespace = UPPER('&&old_temp_tblspc')
  AND username NOT IN ('SYSTEM', 'SYS', 'PUBLIC', '_NEXT_USER');

spool off
set heading on verify on feedback 6 pagesize 24 termout on
 undefine old_default_tblspc
undefine old_temp_tblspc
undefine new_default_tblspc
undefine new_temp_tblspc
```

When this script is run, it generates the required SQL statements and places them in the file change_def_n_temp_tblspc.sql. Sample output from the script is shown here:

```
Enter value for new_default_tblspc: new_default
Enter value for new_temp_tblspc: new_temp
Enter value for old_default_tblspc: users
Enter value for old_temp_tblspc: temp
ALTER USER USER1 DEFAULT TABLESPACE new_default
```

```
                        TEMPORARY TABLESPACE new_temp;
ALTER USER USER2 DEFAULT TABLESPACE new_default
                        TEMPORARY TABLESPACE new_temp;
ALTER USER USER3 DEFAULT TABLESPACE new_default
                        TEMPORARY TABLESPACE new_temp;
ALTER USER USER4 DEFAULT TABLESPACE new_default
                        TEMPORARY TABLESPACE new_temp;
```

ANNOTATIONS

When run, the query chngtblspc.sql asks for four input values:

- The new default tablespace name
- The new temporary tablespace name
- The old default tablespace name
- The old temporary tablespace name

SQL statements are then generated by querying the DBA_USERS data dictionary view and identifying all database users that have the following conditions satisfied:

- Current default tablespace name for the user matches the input value for old_default_tblspc
- Current temporary tablespace name for the user matches the input value for old_temp_tblspc
- The user is neither SYSTEM, SYS, PUBLIC, nor _NEXT_USER

It is generally not recommended to change the default and/or temporary tablespaces for the SYSTEM, SYS, PUBLIC, and _NEXT_USER users, and therefore they are filtered out from the output of the query.

The output of the query generates ALTER USER statements that can be used to change the default tablespace and temporary tablespace to new_default_tblspc and new_temp_tblspc, respectively, for all database users that currently have their default and temporary tablespaces set to old_default_tblspc and old_temp_tblspc, respectively.

unlockall8.sql
locknondba8.sql

Lock and Unlock Database User Accounts

Starting with Oracle8, an Oracle DBA can lock and unlock database user accounts just like a system administrator can lock and unlock operating system accounts. Both of these tasks can be achieved by using the ALTER USER command. As of Oracle8, you can use profiles to manage the expiration, reuse, and complexity of passwords. For example, you can limit the lifetime of a password and lock an account whose password is too old. You can also force a password to be at least moderately complex and lock any account that has repeated failed login attempts. Oracle provides a script file called utlpwdmg.sql (usually found in the /rdbms/ admin directory under the Oracle software home directory) that provides a good basis for enforcing password complexity.

You may have set up account lockup characteristics as mentioned previously, and if users frequently forget their passwords and lock their accounts, it would be helpful for you to scan the available user accounts periodically and unlock the accounts (after verifying that they are not *supposed* to be locked out due to security issues).

The script unlockall8.sql can be used in Oracle8.x and later to generate ALTER USER statements that can be used to unlock all accounts that are currently locked:

```
REM unlockall8.sql
REM This script can be used to unlock all locked database user accounts
REM
REM This script is valid only for Oracle8.x onwards
REM

set heading off echo off verify off feedback off pagesize 0 termout on
column X format a200 word_wrapped

spool unlockall8sql.sql

SELECT 'ALTER USER '||username||
            ' ACCOUNT UNLOCK;' X
FROM dba_users
WHERE account_status = 'LOCKED';

spool off
set heading on verify on feedback 6 pagesize 24
```

When this query is run, it queries the DBA_USERS data dictionary view to determine all the database users who currently have their accounts locked and generates the necessary ALTER USER statements to unlock those users' accounts. The generated SQL statements are placed in the file unlockall8sql.sql.

Sample output from executing the query unlockall8.sql is shown here:

```
ALTER USER MLOCK1 ACCOUNT UNLOCK;
ALTER USER MLOCK ACCOUNT UNLOCK;
```

Occasionally, due to maintenance reasons, an Oracle DBA may want to allow only those database users who have been given a specific role to access the database. The query locknondba8.sql shows how SQL statements can be generated to lock all database users accounts that don't have the DBA role assigned.

```
REM locknondba8.sql
REM This script can be used to lock all database user accounts that
REM          have not been assigned the DBA role.
REM
REM This script is valid only for Oracle8.x onwards
```

```
REM

set heading off echo off verify off feedback off
set pagesize 0 termout on
column X format a200 word_wrapped

spool locknondba8sql.sql

SELECT 'ALTER USER '||username||
            ' ACCOUNT LOCK;' X
FROM dba_users
WHERE account_status = 'OPEN'
  AND username not in (SELECT grantee
                       FROM DBA_ROLE_PRIVS
                       WHERE granted_role='DBA');

spool off
set heading on verify on feedback 6 pagesize 24
```

This query looks at the DBA_ROLE_PRIVS data dictionary view to determine all user accounts that have been granted the DBA role.

```
(SELECT grantee
   FROM DBA_ROLE_PRIVS
  WHERE granted_role='DBA');
```

Once the users with DBA roles are identified, they are eliminated from the result set by using the NOT IN operator:

```
AND username not in (SELECT grantee
                     FROM DBA_ROLE_PRIVS
                     WHERE granted_role='DBA');
```

In addition, the DBA_USERS data dictionary view is examined to determine all currently unlocked accounts (for those users that don't have the DBA role), and the necessary ALTER USER statements to lock these accounts are generated and placed in the file locknondba8sql.sql file.

Sample output from the execution of the query locknondba8.sql is shown here:

```
ALTER USER SCOTT ACCOUNT LOCK;
ALTER USER DBSNMP ACCOUNT LOCK;
ALTER USER TRACESVR ACCOUNT LOCK;
ALTER USER USER1 ACCOUNT LOCK;
ALTER USER USER2 ACCOUNT LOCK;
ALTER USER USER3 ACCOUNT LOCK;
ALTER USER USER4 ACCOUNT LOCK;
ALTER USER USER5 ACCOUNT LOCK;
ALTER USER USER6 ACCOUNT LOCK;
```

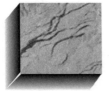

Index

Symbols

% (percent) wildcard
 using with cre_type.sql
  script, 432
 using with gen_proc.sql
  script, 365
 using with gen_view.sql
  script, 345
 using with table
  names, 264
&& (double ampersands)
 purpose in generating
  list of users' table
  privileges, 557
 purpose in monitoring
  allocation of
  extents, 504
'/'
 in gen_type.sql
  script, 430
 in grnt_7n8.sql
  script, 445
' (single quote), placing in
 output, 129-130, 565
(+) (outer join clause),
 purpose in extending
 files, 473
) (final parenthesis), purpose
 in gen_tbl_9.sql script, 268

* flag for tables nearing
 maxextents, 508-512
+ (plus sign), purpose in
 len_row.sql script, 534
, (comma) in columns if
 gen_tbl_9.sql script,
 267-268
-- (two dashes), using with
 comments, 66
/ (slash) after **create trigger**
 statement, 339-340
; (semicolon)
 advisory when using
  DELETE_COMMIT
  procedure, 174
 using with SQL
  statements, 103
_ (underscore), preceding
 parameters with, 96-97
| (pipe) symbol, using in
 heading definition of
 list_sub.sql script, 215

A

Absolute file numbers, 170
Abstract datatypes
 determining array
  status of, 432

determining nested-table
 status of, 432
generating, 422-433
incomplete type of,
 423-424, 427
owners for, 427
types of, 424
accept command
 purpose in providing
  full descriptions of
  tables, 203
 using with abstract
  datatypes, 427-428
AGE method, specifying for
 ANIMAL_TY abstract
 datatype, 422-423
Alert logs, using with redo
 locks and log switches,
 144-145
ALTER commands, using
 with plsql_compiler_flags
 initialization parameter, 9
ALTER object privilege, 433
alter rollback segment
 command, 116-118
alter session and **alter
 system** commands, using
 with parameter settings,
 92-93

INTERNATIONAL CONTACT INFORMATION

AUSTRALIA
McGraw-Hill Book Company Australia Pty. Ltd.
TEL +61-2-9417-9899
FAX +61-2-9417-5687
http://www.mcgraw-hill.com.au
books-it_sydney@mcgraw-hill.com

CANADA
McGraw-Hill Ryerson Ltd.
TEL +905-430-5000
FAX +905-430-5020
http://www.mcgrawhill.ca

GREECE, MIDDLE EAST,
NORTHERN AFRICA
McGraw-Hill Hellas
TEL +30-1-656-0990-3-4
FAX +30-1-654-5525

MEXICO (Also serving Latin America)
McGraw-Hill Interamericana Editores S.A. de C.V.
TEL +525-117-1583
FAX +525-117-1589
http://www.mcgraw-hill.com.mx
fernando_castellanos@mcgraw-hill.com

SINGAPORE (Serving Asia)
McGraw-Hill Book Company
TEL +65-863-1580
FAX +65-862-3354
http://www.mcgraw-hill.com.sg
mghasia@mcgraw-hill.com

SOUTH AFRICA
McGraw-Hill South Africa
TEL +27-11-622-7512
FAX +27-11-622-9045
robyn_swanepoel@mcgraw-hill.com

UNITED KINGDOM & EUROPE
(Excluding Southern Europe)
McGraw-Hill Education Europe
TEL +44-1-628-502500
FAX +44-1-628-770224
http://www.mcgraw-hill.co.uk
computing_neurope@mcgraw-hill.com

ALL OTHER INQUIRIES Contact:
Osborne/McGraw-Hill
TEL +1-510-549-6600
FAX +1-510-883-7600
http://www.osborne.com
omg_international@mcgraw-hill.com

Get Your FREE Subscription to *Oracle Magazine*

Oracle Magazine is essential gear for today's information technology professionals. Stay informed and increase your productivity with every issue of *Oracle Magazine*. Inside each **FREE,** bimonthly issue you'll get:

- Up-to-date information on Oracle Database Server, Oracle Applications, Internet Computing, and tools
- Third-party news and announcements
- Technical articles on Oracle products and operating environments
- Development and administration tips
- Real-world customer stories

Three easy ways to subscribe:

1. Web
**Visit our Web site at www.oracle.com/oramag/.
You'll find a subscription form there, plus much more!**

2. Fax
Complete the questionnaire on the back of this card and fax the questionnaire side only to **+1.847.647.9735.**

3. Mail
Complete the questionnaire on the back of this card and mail it to P.O. Box 1263, Skokie, IL 60076-8263.

If there are other Oracle users at your location who would like to receive their own subscription to *Oracle Magazine*, please photocopy this form and pass it along.

☐ YES! Please send me a FREE subscription to *Oracle Magazine*.   ☐ NO

To receive a free bimonthly subscription to *Oracle Magazine*, you must fill out the entire card, sign it, and date it (incomplete cards cannot be processed or acknowledged). You can also fax your application to **+1.847.647.9735. Or subscribe at our Web site at www.oracle.com/oramag/**

SIGNATURE (REQUIRED)	X	DATE	

NAME	TITLE
COMPANY	TELEPHONE
ADDRESS	FAX NUMBER
CITY	STATE	POSTAL CODE/ZIP CODE
COUNTRY	E-MAIL ADDRESS

☐ From time to time, Oracle Publishing allows our partners exclusive access to our e-mail addresses for special promotions and announcements. To be included in this program, please check this box.

You must answer all eight questions below.

1 What is the primary business activity of your firm at this location? *(check only one)*
- ☐ 03 Communications
- ☐ 04 Consulting, Training
- ☐ 06 Data Processing
- ☐ 07 Education
- ☐ 08 Engineering
- ☐ 09 Financial Services
- ☐ 10 Government—Federal, Local, State, Other
- ☐ 11 Government—Military
- ☐ 12 Health Care
- ☐ 13 Manufacturing—Aerospace, Defense
- ☐ 14 Manufacturing—Computer Hardware
- ☐ 15 Manufacturing—Noncomputer Products
- ☐ 17 Research & Development
- ☐ 19 Retailing, Wholesaling, Distribution
- ☐ 20 Software Development
- ☐ 21 Systems Integration, VAR, VAD, OEM
- ☐ 22 Transportation
- ☐ 23 Utilities (Electric, Gas, Sanitation)
- ☐ 98 Other Business and Services
  _____

2 Which of the following best describes your job function? *(check only one)*

CORPORATE MANAGEMENT/STAFF
- ☐ 01 Executive Management (President, Chair, CEO, CFO, Owner, Partner, Principal)
- ☐ 02 Finance/Administrative Management (VP/Director/ Manager/Controller, Purchasing, Administration)
- ☐ 03 Sales/Marketing Management (VP/Director/Manager)
- ☐ 04 Computer Systems/Operations Management (CIO/VP/Director/ Manager MIS, Operations)

IS/IT STAFF
- ☐ 07 Systems Development/ Programming Management
- ☐ 08 Systems Development/ Programming Staff
- ☐ 09 Consulting
- ☐ 10 DBA/Systems Administrator
- ☐ 11 Education/Training
- ☐ 14 Technical Support Director/ Manager
- ☐ 16 Other Technical Management/Staff
- ☐ 98 Other _____

3 What is your current primary operating platform? *(check all that apply)*
- ☐ 01 DEC UNIX
- ☐ 02 DEC VAX VMS
- ☐ 03 Java
- ☐ 04 HP UNIX
- ☐ 05 IBM AIX
- ☐ 06 IBM UNIX
- ☐ 07 Macintosh
- ☐ 09 MS-DOS
- ☐ 10 MVS
- ☐ 11 NetWare
- ☐ 12 Network Computing
- ☐ 13 OpenVMS
- ☐ 14 SCO UNIX
- ☐ 24 Sequent DYNIX/ptx
- ☐ 15 Sun Solaris/SunOS
- ☐ 16 SVR4
- ☐ 18 UnixWare
- ☐ 20 Windows
- ☐ 21 Windows NT
- ☐ 23 Other UNIX _____
- ☐ 98 Other _____
- 99 ☐ **None of the above**

4 Do you evaluate, specify, recommend, or authorize the purchase of any of the following? *(check all that apply)*
- ☐ 01 Hardware
- ☐ 02 Software
- ☐ 03 Application Development Tools
- ☐ 04 Database Products
- ☐ 05 Internet or Intranet Products
- 99 ☐ **None of the above**

5 In your job, do you use or plan to purchase any of the following products or services? *(check all that apply)*

SOFTWARE
- ☐ 01 Business Graphics
- ☐ 02 CAD/CAE/CAM
- ☐ 03 CASE
- ☐ 05 Communications
- ☐ 06 Database Management
- ☐ 07 File Management
- ☐ 08 Finance
- ☐ 09 Java
- ☐ 10 Materials Resource Planning
- ☐ 11 Multimedia Authoring
- ☐ 12 Networking
- ☐ 13 Office Automation
- ☐ 14 Order Entry/Inventory Control
- ☐ 15 Programming
- ☐ 16 Project Management
- ☐ 17 Scientific and Engineering
- ☐ 18 Spreadsheets
- ☐ 19 Systems Management
- ☐ 20 Workflow

HARDWARE
- ☐ 21 Macintosh
- ☐ 22 Mainframe
- ☐ 23 Massively Parallel Processing
- ☐ 24 Minicomputer
- ☐ 25 PC
- ☐ 26 Network Computer
- ☐ 28 Symmetric Multiprocessing
- ☐ 29 Workstation

PERIPHERALS
- ☐ 30 Bridges/Routers/Hubs/Gateways
- ☐ 31 CD-ROM Drives
- ☐ 32 Disk Drives/Subsystems
- ☐ 33 Modems
- ☐ 34 Tape Drives/Subsystems
- ☐ 35 Video Boards/Multimedia

SERVICES
- ☐ 37 Consulting
- ☐ 38 Education/Training
- ☐ 39 Maintenance
- ☐ 40 Online Database Services
- ☐ 41 Support
- ☐ 36 Technology-Based Training
- ☐ 98 Other _____
- 99 ☐ **None of the above**

6 What Oracle products are in use at your site? *(check all that apply)*

SERVER/SOFTWARE
- ☐ 01 Oracle8
- ☐ 30 Oracle8*i*
- ☐ 31 Oracle8*i* Lite
- ☐ 02 Oracle7
- ☐ 03 Oracle Application Server
- ☐ 04 Oracle Data Mart Suites
- ☐ 05 Oracle Internet Commerce Server
- ☐ 32 Oracle *inter*Media
- ☐ 33 Oracle JServer
- ☐ 07 Oracle Lite
- ☐ 08 Oracle Payment Server
- ☐ 11 Oracle Video Server

TOOLS
- ☐ 13 Oracle Designer
- ☐ 14 Oracle Developer
- ☐ 54 Oracle Discoverer
- ☐ 53 Oracle Express
- ☐ 51 Oracle JDeveloper
- ☐ 52 Oracle Reports
- ☐ 50 Oracle WebDB
- ☐ 55 Oracle Workflow

ORACLE APPLICATIONS
- ☐ 17 Oracle Automotive
- ☐ 35 Oracle Business Intelligence System
- ☐ 19 Oracle Consumer Packaged Goods
- ☐ 39 Oracle E-Commerce
- ☐ 18 Oracle Energy
- ☐ 20 Oracle Financials
- ☐ 28 Oracle Front Office
- ☐ 21 Oracle Human Resources
- ☐ 37 Oracle Internet Procurement
- ☐ 22 Oracle Manufacturing
- ☐ 40 Oracle Process Manufacturing
- ☐ 23 Oracle Projects
- ☐ 34 Oracle Retail
- ☐ 29 Oracle Self-Service Web Applications
- ☐ 38 Oracle Strategic Enterprise Management
- ☐ 25 Oracle Supply Chain Management
- ☐ 36 Oracle Tutor
- ☐ 41 Oracle Travel Management

ORACLE SERVICES
- ☐ 61 Oracle Consulting
- ☐ 62 Oracle Education
- ☐ 60 Oracle Support
- ☐ 98 Other _____
- 99 ☐ **None of the above**

7 What other database products are in use at your site? *(check all that apply)*
- ☐ 01 Access
- ☐ 02 Baan
- ☐ 03 dbase
- ☐ 04 Gupta
- ☐ 05 IBM DB2
- ☐ 06 Informix
- ☐ 07 Ingres
- ☐ 08 Microsoft Access
- ☐ 09 Microsoft SQL Server
- ☐ 10 PeopleSoft
- ☐ 11 Progress
- ☐ 12 SAP
- ☐ 13 Sybase
- ☐ 14 VSAM
- ☐ 98 Other _____
- 99 ☐ **None of the above**

8 During the next 12 months, how much do you anticipate your organization will spend on computer hardware, software, peripherals, and services for your location? *(check only one)*
- ☐ 01 Less than $10,000
- ☐ 02 $10,000 to $49,999
- ☐ 03 $50,000 to $99,999
- ☐ 04 $100,000 to $499,999
- ☐ 05 $500,000 to $999,999
- ☐ 06 $1,000,000 and over

If there are other Oracle users at your location who would like to receive a free subscription to *Oracle Magazine*, please photocopy this form and pass it along, or contact Customer Service at +1.847.647.9630

Form 5

OPRESS

Knowledge is power. To which we say,

crank up the power.

Are you ready for a power surge?

Accelerate your career—become an **Oracle Certified Professional (OCP)**. With Oracle's cutting-edge *Instructor-Led Training*, *Technology-Based Training*, and this *guide*, you can prepare for certification faster than ever. Set your own trajectory by logging your personal training plan with us. Go to **http://education.oracle.com/tpb**, where we'll help you pick a training path, select your courses, and track your progress. We'll even send you an email when your courses are offered in your area. If you don't have access to the Web, call us at 1-800-441-3541 (Outside the U.S. call +1-310-335-2403).
Power learning has never been easier.

University

About the CD-ROM

The CD-ROM that comes with this book includes the electronic versions of two chapters and an appendix and the major scripts featured in this book. The first time you access the CD-ROM, the End User License Agreement (EULA) will automatically appear onscreen, and after you agree to the terms listed in the EULA, you will not see it again.

The chapters that you will find on this CD-ROM as follows:

◆ **Chapter 8: Database Management** This chapter shows you scripts that can be used to regenerate tablespaces and databases.

◆ **Chapter 9: Managing Java in the Database** This chapter shows you scripts that can be used to manage Java classes, sources, resources as well as the Java Virtual Machine of Oracle.

◆ **Appendix A: PL/SQL, Dynamic PL/SQL, and Procedures** This appendix contains descriptions of PL/SQL, stored procedures, dynamic PL/SQL as well as the new native PL/SQL compilation feature of Oracle9i.

Because of space constraints, these chapters are not in printed form and can be found only on the CD-ROM. The chapters are in Adobe Acrobat PDF format. If you do not have the Acrobat Reader installed, you will find a copy available for installation (on Windows systems) on the CD-ROM. To start the installation program, double-click the rs405eng.exe file.

Scripts

The scripts are available individually and as part of "zipped" files on a chapter-by-chapter basis. For details on the use of the scripts and interpretation of the output, see the appropriate chapter of this book. The script file names on the CD match the script file names shown in each chapter. The script directories on the CD-ROM are listed in this table:

Directory	Description
ZIPS	Contains the "zipped" files for all of the chapters. The other directories contain the individual files extracted from their "zipped" files. The directories are named after the type of script rather than the chapter number.
ORACLE9i	Contains the Oracle9i-specific scripts from Chapter 1
PERFORM	Contains the performance management scripts from Chapter 2

Directory	Description
TRANSACT	Contains the transaction management scripts from Chapter 3
DATAMGMT	Contains the data management scripts from Chapter 4
OBJECTS	Contains the object management scripts from Chapter 5
SPACE	Contains the space management scripts from Chapter 6
USERS	Contains the user management scripts from Chapter 7
DBMGMT	Contains the database management scripts from Chapter 8
MNGJAVA	Contains the scripts for managing Java in the database from Chapter 9

LICENSE AGREEMENT

THIS PRODUCT (THE "PRODUCT") CONTAINS PROPRIETARY SOFTWARE, DATA AND INFORMATION (INCLUDING DOCUMENTATION) OWNED BY THE McGRAW-HILL COMPANIES, INC. ("McGRAW-HILL") AND ITS LICENSORS. YOUR RIGHT TO USE THE PRODUCT IS GOVERNED BY THE TERMS AND CONDITIONS OF THIS AGREEMENT.

LICENSE: Throughout this License Agreement, "you" shall mean either the individual or the entity whose agent opens this package. You are granted a non-exclusive and non-transferable license to use the Product subject to the following terms:
(i) If you have licensed a single user version of the Product, the Product may only be used on a single computer (i.e., a single CPU). If you licensed and paid the fee applicable to a local area network or wide area network version of the Product, you are subject to the terms of the following subparagraph (ii).
(ii) If you have licensed a local area network version, you may use the Product on unlimited workstations located in one single building selected by you that is served by such local area network. If you have licensed a wide area network version, you may use the Product on unlimited workstations located in multiple buildings on the same site selected by you that is served by such wide area network; provided, however, that any building will not be considered located in the same site if it is more than five (5) miles away from any building included in such site. In addition, you may only use a local area or wide area network version of the Product on one single server. If you wish to use the Product on more than one server, you must obtain written authorization from McGraw-Hill and pay additional fees.
(iii) You may make one copy of the Product for back-up purposes only and you must maintain an accurate record as to the location of the back-up at all times.

COPYRIGHT; RESTRICTIONS ON USE AND TRANSFER: All rights (including copyright) in and to the Product are owned by McGraw-Hill and its licensors. You are the owner of the enclosed disc on which the Product is recorded. You may not use, copy, decompile, disassemble, reverse engineer, modify, reproduce, create derivative works, transmit, distribute, sublicense, store in a database or retrieval system of any kind, rent or transfer the Product, or any portion thereof, in any form or by any means (including electronically or otherwise) except as expressly provided for in this License Agreement. You must reproduce the copyright notices, trademark notices, legends and logos of McGraw-Hill and its licensors that appear on the Product on the back-up copy of the Product which you are permitted to make hereunder. All rights in the Product not expressly granted herein are reserved by McGraw-Hill and its licensors.

TERM: This License Agreement is effective until terminated. It will terminate if you fail to comply with any term or condition of this License Agreement. Upon termination, you are obligated to return to McGraw-Hill the Product together with all copies thereof and to purge all copies of the Product included in any and all servers and computer facilities.

DISCLAIMER OF WARRANTY: THE PRODUCT AND THE BACK-UP COPY ARE LICENSED "AS IS." McGRAW-HILL, ITS LICENSORS AND THE AUTHORS MAKE NO WARRANTIES, EXPRESS OR IMPLIED, AS TO THE RESULTS TO BE OBTAINED BY ANY PERSON OR ENTITY FROM USE OF THE PRODUCT, ANY INFORMATION OR DATA INCLUDED THEREIN AND/OR ANY TECHNICAL SUPPORT SERVICES PROVIDED HEREUNDER, IF ANY ("TECHNICAL SUPPORT SERVICES"). McGRAW-HILL, ITS LICENSORS AND THE AUTHORS MAKE NO EXPRESS OR IMPLIED WARRANTIES OF MERCHANTABILITY OR FITNESS FOR A PARTICULAR PURPOSE OR USE WITH RESPECT TO THE PRODUCT. McGRAW-HILL, ITS LICENSORS, AND THE AUTHORS MAKE NO GUARANTEE THAT YOU WILL PASS ANY CERTIFICATION EXAM WHATSOEVER BY USING THIS PRODUCT. NEITHER McGRAW-HILL, ANY OF ITS LICENSORS NOR THE AUTHORS WARRANT THAT THE FUNCTIONS CONTAINED IN THE PRODUCT WILL MEET YOUR REQUIREMENTS OR THAT THE OPERATION OF THE PRODUCT WILL BE UNINTERRUPTED OR ERROR FREE. YOU ASSUME THE ENTIRE RISK WITH RESPECT TO THE QUALITY AND PERFORMANCE OF THE PRODUCT.

LIMITED WARRANTY FOR DISC: To the original licensee only, McGraw-Hill warrants that the enclosed disc on which the Product is recorded is free from defects in materials and workmanship under normal use and service for a period of ninety (90) days from the date of purchase. In the event of a defect in the disc covered by the foregoing warranty, McGraw-Hill will replace the disc.

LIMITATION OF LIABILITY: NEITHER McGRAW-HILL, ITS LICENSORS NOR THE AUTHORS SHALL BE LIABLE FOR ANY INDIRECT, SPECIAL OR CONSEQUENTIAL DAMAGES, SUCH AS BUT NOT LIMITED TO, LOSS OF ANTICIPATED PROFITS OR BENEFITS, RESULTING FROM THE USE OR INABILITY TO USE THE PRODUCT EVEN IF ANY OF THEM HAS BEEN ADVISED OF THE POSSIBILITY OF SUCH DAMAGES. THIS LIMITATION OF LIABILITY SHALL APPLY TO ANY CLAIM OR CAUSE WHATSOEVER WHETHER SUCH CLAIM OR CAUSE ARISES IN CONTRACT, TORT, OR OTHERWISE. Some states do not allow the exclusion or limitation of indirect, special or consequential damages, so the above limitation may not apply to you.

U.S. GOVERNMENT RESTRICTED RIGHTS: Any software included in the Product is provided with restricted rights subject to subparagraphs (c), (1) and (2) of the Commercial Computer Software-Restricted Rights clause at 48 C.F.R. 52.227-19. The terms of this Agreement applicable to the use of the data in the Product are those under which the data are generally made available to the general public by McGraw-Hill. Except as provided herein, no reproduction, use, or disclosure rights are granted with respect to the data included in the Product and no right to modify or create derivative works from any such data is hereby granted.

GENERAL: This License Agreement constitutes the entire agreement between the parties relating to the Product. The terms of any Purchase Order shall have no effect on the terms of this License Agreement. Failure of McGraw-Hill to insist at any time on strict compliance with this License Agreement shall not constitute a waiver of any rights under this License Agreement. This License Agreement shall be construed and governed in accordance with the laws of the State of New York. If any provision of this License Agreement is held to be contrary to law, that provision will be enforced to the maximum extent permissible and the remaining provisions will remain in full force and effect.